Lakeville, Massachusetts Gravestone Inscriptions, 1711 to 2003

A complete compilation of epitaphs from the thirty-one
known cemeteries in the Town of Lakeville

Jean A. Douillette

To Deb,
Best Wishes.
Jean A. Douillette

Urn and Willow Publishing
Lakeville, Massachusetts

Published by:
Urn and Willow Publishing
P. O. Box 922
Lakeville, Massachusetts 02347-0922

10 9 8 7 6 5 4 3 2 1

Library of Congress Control Number: 2007930372

ISBN-13: 978-0-9796644-0-3
ISBN-10:   0-9796644-0-3

First Edition, September 2007
Printed in the United States of America.

This book may be purchased through the website: www.jadoui.com.

This book is dedicated to the memory of my grandmother, "George"
who first stimulated my interest in our ancestors with her stories,
and my father, who encouraged me to research my genealogy.

Acknowledgements

I would especially like to thank Marilyn Mansfield, Lakeville Veteran's Agent, whose encouragement and support helped get this project started. I would also like to thank her son, Chris, for his 1985 Eagle Scout Project, *Veterans in Lakeville Cemeteries*, which formed the starting point for this book.

Special thanks must go to the late Sandy Horton, Lakeville Town Clerk, whose help was invaluable. She patiently helped me access the Vital Records of the Town of Lakeville, and shared her suggestions and knowledge of the town. She became my friend, and was a continual source of encouragement to me.

Thank you to:
Donna Tibbetts, Director, Lakeville Library, who allowed special access to the Middleboro Vital Records books.
Brian Reynolds, Lakeville Historical Commission, who identified the property references for several unconfirmed cemeteries.
William Aman, Stephen Avila, Roan Barber, and Robert Ranahan, property owners, who me allowed access to the cemeteries located on or through their land, and who took the time to discuss the cemeteries located on their property with me.
Denise Haskins, who loaned me her GPS unit, and showed me the location of Haskins # 2/3 Cemetery.
Kevin St. George, who showed me the location of Indian Shore Cemetery.
Lois Atwood, former Cemetery Commissioner, who explained that Haskins 2 and Haskins 3 was actually the same cemetery.
The late Merrill S. Norton, Sampson Cemetery Trustee, who gave me initial permission to work within Sampson Cemetery, and Robert Darling, Jr., Sampson Cemetery Trustee for his cooperation and information regarding Sampson Cemetery.
Gerel Crosby, Mullein Hill Cemetery Commission, for her information on the older section of that cemetery.
Jackie Barnicoat of Barnicoat Monuments, for her help in identifying the surnames of the deceased whose stones contained only given names.
Glenna Protami, Lakeville Assessor's Office, for her help in finding the owner of record for the cemeteries as well as locating old town landmarks.
Lillian Drane, Chairwoman, who allowed me access to some of the Cemetery Commission files for information to aid in this project.
The Sampson Cemetery Trustees, Mullein Hill Cemetery Committee members, and Lakeville Cemetery Trustees who granted me permission to publish photographs of individual stones within the cemeteries.

A special thank you goes to my husband, Alan, for providing the technical tools to accomplish this book and for putting up with my obsession to complete it. I also want to thank my daughter, Laura, for her valued help, and my son, Steven, for his expert technical assistance.

Lakeville Cemetery Locations

See Table of Contents for key to labeled map locations.

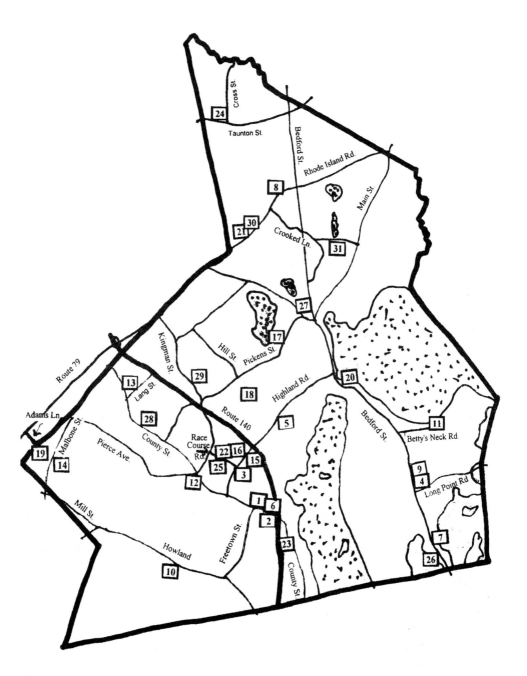

Table of Contents

Preface

Many amateur genealogists throughout the United States and Canada have helped me in researching my ancestors by taking the time to do lookups and visiting cemeteries to check gravestones for me. I decided to record the inscriptions on the gravestones within my hometown as a way of giving back to the genealogical community. I wanted to preserve the information on the stones before time and weather obliterated the inscriptions or destroyed the stones. When I started this project in 1999, I naively thought it would take 18 months. It has taken over seven years. I soon found that reading the inscriptions was not so simple. Lichen can cover up the inscription on slate stones while rain weathers marble leaving little depth to the inscription. I have learned a lot over the years and have developed a bag of tricks to read these inscriptions.

My approach to this project was from a genealogical viewpoint. Included with the basic information from the stones, i.e., name, age, and dates, are the poems and carvings that give additional details about the deceased. Added comments about the condition of many of the stones provide a record of present conditions and a baseline for comparison in the future. All stones present in the town through the year 2003, the 150th anniversary of Lakeville, were transcribed. Each chapter contains a photograph of the cemetery. An additional 138 photographs demonstrate the variety of stones in Lakeville and provide close-ups of detailed features such as carvings, unique lettering, sculptor signatures, and even the sculptor's fee carved in the stone.

Cemeteries are continually changing. Since I started working on this book, stones have been added and others have been removed. Fencing has been replaced, and fallen trees have damaged some stones. Some footstones, organizational markers, and flags were found to be repositioned from one visit to the next. In the past, gravestones have been moved or rearranged to facilitate cleanup of a cemetery or for other reasons (See Lang and the Booth Cemeteries). Were they put back in the right place? Several people have stones in more than one cemetery. Where were they actually buried? I researched the answer to these questions and many others. I found many people from Middleborough buried in Lakeville cemeteries. I expected this since Lakeville comprised the southwestern portion of Middleborough prior to its incorporation as a separate town in 1853. However, I was surprised to find that people who lived in the neighboring communities of East Taunton, Freetown, and Rochester were also buried in Lakeville cemeteries.

Introduction

When I started this project to locate and document the cemeteries in Lakeville, Massachusetts, I consulted Christopher Mansfield's 1985 Eagle Scout Project, *Veteran's in Lakeville Cemeteries*. His list of cemetery names corresponded with the names I found painted on the signs identifying the cemeteries in 1999. I chose to use those same names for this book, each cemetery having its own chapter, arranged alphabetically.

Additionally, I consulted Gladys Vigers' 1952 book, *History of the Town of Lakeville Massachusetts*, and Charles M. Thatcher's work transcribing stones in the late 1880s, which lists basic information from the stones for people with death dates prior to 1851. The names they used for the cemeteries sometimes differed from the painted signs. I have included those names in the chapter's introductory paragraph. Assuming that the stones were in better shape when Thatcher saw them in the 1880s than they are now, I used his original work for reference when older stones could not be read due to weathering or breakage. Any difference between his records and what I found on the stones was noted. Stones that Thatcher transcribed that could not be located were listed in the Additional Notes section at the end of the transcriptions. Information taken from the cemetery cards at the Lakeville Town Hall was also included in this section. Girl scouts compiled these cards in 1965 under the direction of Lois Atwood, Cemetery Commissioner.

When conflicting or lack of information existed, vital and other historical records were consulted. Additional information of genealogical value has been included. Within each chapter, the names from the gravestones are listed alphabetically as they were spelled on the gravestones. Discrepancies and spelling mistakes in the inscriptions were recorded as is and noted.

Maps were created for all cemeteries except Indian Shore and Smallpox Cemeteries. The stones in these cemeteries were not permanently set in the ground. These maps were made to show stones in relation to each other and were not scaled. The alphabetical index and the location index can be used to find a specific grave as well as the names of those buried nearby.

I have added five appendices. Appendix A contains information about cemeteries referenced by Vigers and Thatcher that I could not access or find. Appendix B lists other gravestone-like markers that were found throughout the town. Appendix C lists cemetery locations by assessor's plot number and by Global Positioning System coordinates. Appendix D lists the addresses of the monument companies obtained from the metal tags on the more recent monuments. Appendix E lists older gravestones that were signed by their sculptor.

Chapter 1
Booth #1 Cemetery

Booth #1 Cemetery is set back from the road, and must be accessed through private property located at 167 County Street. Tall stone posts, whose metal rails are long gone, surround the cemetery on three sides. A stone wall forms the fourth, rear border. There is no sign for this cemetery. The only inscribed stones currently present are two footstones that face east and are dated 1784 & 1802. The Lakeville Assessor's Office lists this as a private cemetery, 36 by 24 feet. The owners of record are Abiel and Susanna Booth, who died in the early 1800s. Entries were recorded March 24, 2000.

Booth, John   *"Mr. / John / Booth / died / 1802"* is inscribed on this slate footstone. A veteran's marker and flag are present at this gravesite. There is a slate headstone for John Booth in Booth #2 Cemetery. There is also a veteran's marker for this same John Booth in Race Course Cemetery. (See entries under Booth #2 Cemetery and Race Course Cemetery.)

Booth, Lydia   *"Mrs. / Lydia / Booth / 1784"* is inscribed on this slate footstone. There is a slate headstone for Lydia Booth in Booth #2 Cemetery. (See entry under Booth #2 Cemetery.)

Additional Notes:

The current owner of the abutting property stated that an upright fieldstone near the family plot marked the gravesite of an unnamed indentured servant of the Booth family. He also stated that he was informed that Abiel and Susanna Booth were buried in this cemetery, but their stones were moved across County Road into Booth #2 Cemetery for easier access for visitors. (See Booth #2 Cemetery for their gravestone inscriptions and also that of Emeline A. Bennett, listed below.)

According to Mansfield (1985), gravestones but not remains, were moved from this cemetery to Booth #2 Cemetery in the late 1960s or early 1970s. He reports that in 1972 legal action was taken, and a court order was received that stated the stones couldn't be moved back to their original locations.

To determine who is actually buried in Booth #1 Cemetery, we look to Thatcher who, in the late 1800s, transcribed all stones prior to 1851. He lists only the following three people as being buried in this cemetery:
"Bennett: Emeline A., dau. of Holden & Hannah, Aug. 20, 1847, 20 yrs., 3 mos."
"Booth: Abiel, died Sept. 29th, 1836, 71 yrs., 6 mos., 22 days."
"Booth: Susanna, wife of Abiel & dau. of Capt. Henry Pierce, died Sept. 16th, 1823, in her 54th year."
He lists John and Lydia Booth as buried in Race Course Cemetery.

Vigers (1952) reports: "This cemetery, which is enclosed by a fence, has only five graves."

Mansfield (1985) quotes Town Counsel Maddigan's 1978 opinion that Mary A. Jordan, the former owner of the entire property, was buried in Lakeville, "...probably in her cemetery." Her death certificate, on file in Brockton, documents her death on August 19, 1910, and her burial in Lakeville (no cemetery listed). Middleborough Vital Records indicate that she was the granddaughter of Abiel P. and Betsy Booth and the daughter of Elijah Barrows who were buried in Booth #2 Cemetery. The possible identity of the fifth gravesite that Vigers mentions is unknown.

Booth Cemetery #1 Index and Map

1 – Booth, John (~1729-1802)   2 – Booth, Lydia (~1733-1784)

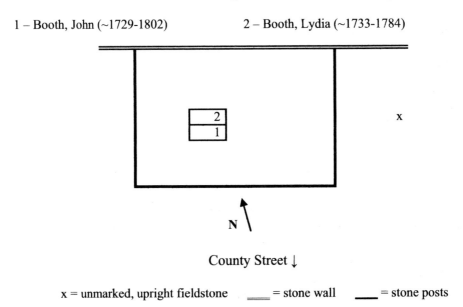

County Street ↓

x = unmarked, upright fieldstone   ▭ = stone wall   ▬ = stone posts

Chapter 2
Booth Cemetery #2

Booth #2 Cemetery is located close to the road, east of 174 County Street. It is bordered on the east with a stone wall, on the south by a decaying, split rail fence, and on the west by a stone post and metal rail fence. The north side, which faces the street, is open. A weathered sign is present on this side. In 2000, after the initial visit, the split rail fence was removed, and the sign was repainted. At that time, the name on the sign was changed to Booth #1. The gate to the cemetery appears to have been originally on the west side, and the stones face that direction. Fieldstones mark several additional graves. Stones currently present in this cemetery date from 1784 to 1887. The Lakeville Assessor's Office lists this cemetery as town owned, about 3600 square feet in area. Thatcher refers to this as "Cemetery in Winslow Neighborhood on County Road, known as Brooman Square." Entries were recorded March 24, 2000.

Barrows, Elijah W.   *"FATHER"* is inscribed on the top horizontal surface of this gravestone. *"REV. / ELIJAH W. BARROWS / BORN / JUNE 20, 1805 / DIED / MAY 25, 1887. / BLESSED ARE THE DEAD / WHO DIE IN THE LORD."* is inscribed on the front of this stone.

Bennett, Emeline A.   *"In memory of / EMELINE A. / Daughter of Holden & / Hannah Bennett. / who died / Aug. 20, 1847, aged / 20 Yrs. & 3 Mos. /*
Sweet is thy memory, Emeline:
Thy person, voice and love.
Thy body now lies silent here,
But thou shall rise above."
This stone had been broken through the first line of the poem, but was successfully repaired. Thatcher lists her as being buried in Booth #1 Cemetery.

Booth, Abiel   *"IN MEMORY OF / Mr. ABIEL BOOTH. / who died / Sept. 29, AD. 1836. / Æt. 71 yrs. 6 mo's, & / 22 days. /*

> *Reader, behold as you pass by,*
> *As you are now so once was I!*
> *As I am now so you must be,*
> *Prepare for death and follow me."*

This stone is lying on its back. There is a carving of a willow at the top. The stone is weathered, making it very hard to read. A veteran's marker and flag are present. Thatcher lists him as being buried in Booth # 1 Cemetery.

Booth, Abiel P., Esq. *"ABIEL P. BOOTH, ESQ. / died Oct. 31, 1850. / Aged 59 years / 8 months / & 28 ds. / Farewell dear suffering Father, /*
> *All thy pains and toils are o'er;*
> *Thou hast gained a home with Jesus,*
> *On that peaceful happy shore."*

The first line is carved in relief.

Booth, Betsey B. *"BETSEY B. / Wife of / ABIEL P. BOOTH, / Died July 6th 1861: / Aged 71 Years 3 Mo's. / & 5 days. / We'll meet again when life is o'er."* is inscribed on this textured stone.

Booth, Henry B. *"HENRY B. BOOTH, / Born Oct. 8, 1819, / Died Feb. 2, 1880."*

Booth, Henry P. *"HENRY P. BOOTH, / Died / in East Freetown, / Aug. 13, 1869: / Aged 68 yrs. 5 m's."*

Booth, John *"_n MEMORY of Mr. John / Booth who died Nov. 30th / ÆD 1802. in the 74 Year of / his Age. /*
> *Depart my sying friends*
> *And wipe your weeping eyes*
> *Here I must lie 'till Christ desends*
> *And bids my body rise."*

There is a frond carving at the top of this slate stone. The poem on this stone is difficult to read due to weathering. Notice the spelling of *sying* and *desends*. Thatcher lists him as being buried in Race Course Cemetery. His veteran's stone is located there. A footstone for John Booth is present in Booth #1 Cemetery.

Booth, Lydia

> *"In memory of*
> *Mrs. Lydia wife of*
> *Mr. John Booth*
> *who died March ye*
> *28th, 1784. in ye 52d*
> *Year of her age."*

There is a frond carving at the top of this slate stone. Thatcher lists her as being buried in Race Course Cemetery.

Booth, Susanna *"In / memory of / MRS. SUSANNA / wife of / Mr. ABIEL BOOTH / dau. of / Capt. Henry Peirce / who died Sept. 16, 1823 in her 54 year /*
> *Her joys be mine each reader cries*
> *When the last hour arrives*

They shall be thine, my verse replies
If such have been your lives."

There is an urn and willow carved at the top of this stone. It is broken through the third line of the poem, and is lying face down on the ground. Thatcher lists her as being buried in Booth #1 Cemetery.

H., E. *"E. H."* is inscribed on this fieldstone. Thatcher indicates that this is "supposed to be Ebenezer Hafford, born June 20, 1707, died ____."

Robinson, Sarah B. *"SARAH B. / wife of / A.J. Robinson, / Born May 1, 1832, / Died May 11, 1881."*

Thompson, Jacob, Capt. *"CAPT. / JACOB THOMPSON / died June 27, 1848. / Aged 38 years / 10 months / & 28 ds. /*
> *Friends nor physicians could not save*
> *His mortal body from the grave:*
> *Nor can the grave confine him here*
> *When Christ doth call him to appear."*

The first two lines are carved in relief. *Town of Middleboro Vital Records Index: 1649 - 1945* online lists his marriage to Ariadna V. Booth, daughter of Abiel P. and Betsy Booth, on August 19, 1845.

Washburn, Eliza

> *"ELIZA D.*
> *daughter of*
> *Milton & Abby*
> *Washburn.*
> *died Aug. 6,*
> *1845.*
> *Aged 3 years*
> *5 Mo's & 11 D's."*

The first line is carved in shallow relief.
Thatcher lists her age in days as 18.
"E. D. W." is inscribed on the footstone.

Washburn, Lysander *"LYSANDER / Son of Milton & / Abigail Washburn, / died Sept. 29, 1829. Æt. 10 Mos. /*
> *This lovely bud so young & fair*
> *Call'd home by early doom*
> *Just came to show how sweet a flower*
> *In paradise would bloom."*

The first line is carved in shallow relief.

Additional Notes:

Thatcher also lists:
"J. __, supposed to be John Haford, born Jan. 7, 1712, died ___."
"Also about 6 or 8 other graves supposed to be Haffords, with rough stones for

markers."

The cemetery cards at the Lakeville Town Hall also list the following, but no stones were found for them:

"Hannah P. Booth Bennett, no dates, probably b. about 1800. h. Holden P. Bennett."

"Holden P. Bennett, no dates, probably b. about 1800, wife – Hannah P. Booth"

Booth #2 Cemetery Index and Map

Alphabetical:

Barrows, Elijah, Rev. (1805-1887) – 8
Bennett, Emeline (1827-1847) – 10
Booth, Abiel (1765-1836) – 2
Booth, Abiel P., Esq. (1791-1850) – 4
Booth, Betsey B. (1790-1861) – 5
Booth, Henry B. (1819-1880) – 3
Booth, Henry P. (1801-1869) – 9
Booth, John (~1729-1802) – 12
Booth, Lydia (~1733-1784) – 11
Booth, Susanna (~1770-1823) – 1
Hafford, Ebenezer (1707-___) – 13
Robinson, Sarah B. (1832-1881) – 6
Thompson, Jacob, Capt. (1809-1848) – 7
Washburn, Eliza D. (1842-1845) – 15
Washburn, Lysander (1828-1829) – 14

By Location:

1 – Booth, Susanna (~1770-1823)
2 – Booth, Abiel (1765-1836)
3 – Booth, Henry B. (1819-1880)
4 – Booth, Abiel P., Esq. (1791-1850)
5 – Booth, Betsey B. (1790-1861)
6 – Robinson, Sarah B. (1832-1881)
7 – Thompson, Jacob, Capt. (1809-1848)
8 – Barrows, Elijah, Rev. (1805-1887)
9 – Booth, Henry P. (1801-1869)
10 – Bennett, Emeline (1827-1847)
11 – Booth, Lydia (~1733-1784)
12 – Booth, John (~1729-1802)
13 – Hafford, Ebenezer (1707-___)
14 – Washburn, Lysander (1828-1829)
15 – Washburn, Eliza D. (1842-1845)

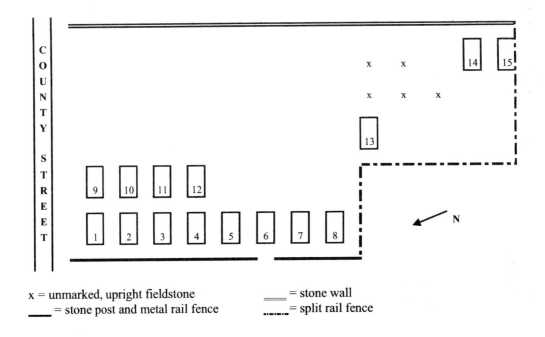

x = unmarked, upright fieldstone   ___ = stone wall
___ = stone post and metal rail fence   ......= split rail fence

Chapter 3
Canedy Cemetery

Canedy Cemetery is located between 97 Highland Road and a cranberry bog. A stone post and metal rail fence originally surrounded the cemetery. It was replaced with a white vinyl fence in January 2000. The rear boundary was extended at this time to include the gravestone for Jose Fialho. The sign is in good repair. Gravestones face west, and date from 1836 to 1957. The Lakeville Assessor's Office lists this as a town owned cemetery, 5940 square feet in area. This includes the land extending 20 feet around the sides and back of the cemetery along its original fence line. This extra land was acquired in 1972. Thatcher refers to this as a "Cemetery at head of "Race–course" road, near Canedy's Corner." Entries were recorded November 2, 1999.

Canedy, Alexander *"ALEXANDER CANEDY / DIED / July 20, 1854, / Æ. 64 y'rs."* The first line is carved along an arch.

Canedy, Alexander *"ALEXANDER CANEDY / died August 23, 1893, / Aged 62 years."* The first line is carved in relief along an arch.

Canedy, Benjamin B. *"BENJAMIN / B. CANEDY / Son of / Alexander / & Sarah V. / CANEDY, / Died at / Carrolton, / Louisiana / May 10, 1855, / Æ. 28 y'rs."* The first line is carved along an arch.

Canedy, Charity L. *"CHARITY L. CANEDY / died / April 17, 1899. / Aged 74 Y'rs 2 Mo's / 12 Days."* The first line is carved in relief along an arch.

Canedy, infant girl *"A Daughter of / Zebulon L. & / Olive Canedy / died / July 27, 1836. / aged 14 days."* This small headstone is weathered. There is no given name entered in the Lakeville Vital Records.

Canedy, Lucy W. See Zebulon L. Canedy Monument entry.
"L. W. C." is inscribed on the footstone.

Canedy, Mary G. *"SACRED / to the memory of / MARY G. / wife of / William*

Canedy E^{sq} / who died / March 21, 1836, / aged 71 years." The first line is carved along an arch.

Canedy, Olive   "*OLIVE CANEDY / 1799 – 1886*" "*MOTHER*" is inscribed on the vertical surface of the upper base. This grave and that of Zebulon Canedy share a second base. A separate stone post and metal rail fence surrounds these two graves.

Canedy, Sarah O.   "*SARAH O. / Dau. of / Alexander & Sarah V. / CANEDY, / Died Apr. 5th, 1861: / Aged 19 Years 1 Mo'. / & 24 days.*"

Canady, Sarah V.   "*SARAH V. / Widow of / ALEXANDER CANADY, / Died Oct. 30th, 1860; / Aged 61 years 10 mo's, / & 8 days.*" This gravestone is lying face up on the ground, behind its base. Lakeville Vital Records list Sarah's last name as "Canedy."

Canedy, Susan S.   "*SUSAN S. / Dau. of / Alexander & Sarah V, / CANEDY, / Died Jan. 26th, 1860: / Aged 25 Years 1 Mo. / & 24 days.*" This gravestone is lying on the ground face up behind its base.

Canedy, William, Esq.   "*SACRED / to the memory of / WILLIAM / CANEDY Esq. / who died / Nov. 21. 1836. / aged 79 years.*" This gravestone is lying face up on the ground behind its base. The first line is carved along an arch.

Canedy, Wm. B.   "*Wm. B. CANEDY, / Died Apr. 6, 1855 / Æ. 70 y'rs.*" Above the inscription, a circular depression is carved in the stone. An All-Seeing Eye and an open book with a Mason's symbol on it are carved in relief within this circle.

Canedy, Zebulon L. Monument   "*CANEDY*" is carved in relief on the front of the monument. "*ZEBULON L. CANEDY / 1864 – 1936 / LUCY W. CANEDY / 1869 – 1940*" is inscribed on the back.
"*Z. L. C.*" is inscribed on the footstone.

Canedy, Zebulon L.   "*ZEBULON L. CANEDY / 1793 – 1840*" "*FATHER*" is inscribed on the vertical surface of the upper base. His gravestone shares a second base with his wife. A separate stone post and metal rail fence surrounds their graves.

Fialho, Jose Silveira   "*FIAHLO / JOSE SILVEIRA / 1862 – 1957*" This gravestone was located behind Canedy Cemetery, outside of the fenced area. When the stone post and metal rail fence was replaced in January 2000, the rear fence line was extended to include this gravestone within the cemetery.

Canedy Cemetery Index and Map

Alphabetical:

Canedy, Alexander (~1790-1854) – 1
Canedy, Alexander (~1831-1893) – 10
Canedy, Benjamin B. (~1827-1855) – 13
Canedy, Charity L. (1825-1899) – 11
Canedy, (infant girl) (1836-1836) – 12
Canedy, Lucy W. (1869-1940) – 15, 16
Canedy, Mary G. (~1765-1836) – 6
Canedy, Olive (1799-1886) – 8
Canedy, Sarah O. (1842-1861) – 4
Canady (sic), Sarah V. (1798-1860) – 2
Canedy, Susan S. (1834-1860) – 3
Canedy, William, Esq. (~1757-1836) – 5
Canedy, Wm. B. (~1785-1855) – 9
Canedy, Zebulon L. (1793-1840) – 7
Canedy, Zebulon L. (1864-1936) – 14, 16
Fialho, Jose Silveira (1862-1957) – 17

By Location:

1 – Canedy, Alexander (~1790-1854)
2 – Canady (sic), Sarah V. (1798-1860)
3 – Canedy, Susan S. (1834-1860)
4 – Canedy, Sarah O. (1842-1861)
5 – Canedy, William, Esq. (~1757-1836)
6 – Canedy, Mary G. (~1765-1836)
7 – Canedy, Zebulon L. (1793-1840)
8 – Canedy, Olive (1799-1886)
9 – Canedy, Wm. B. (~1785-1855)
10 – Canedy, Alexander (~1831-1893)
11 – Canedy, Charity L. (1825-1899)
12 – Canedy, (infant girl) (1836-1836)
13 – Canedy, Benjamin B. (~1827-1855)
14 – Canedy, Zebulon L. (1864-1936)
15 – Canedy, Lucy W. (1869-1940)
16 – Canedy, Zebulon L. (1864-1936)
    Canedy, Lucy W. (1869-1940)
17 – Fialho, Jose Silveira (1862-1957)

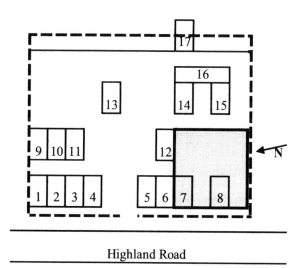

Highland Road

New and old rear fence lines are indicated on map above.

_____ = stone post and metal rail fence

_ _ _ _ = new vinyl fence

_____ = rear location of old stone post and metal rail
         fence before its removal

Chapter 4
Clark Cemetery

Clark Cemetery is located between 457 and 459 Bedford Street (Route 105), just north of Long Point Road. It is adjacent and immediately south of Horr Cemetery. The only separation between the two cemeteries is a short dirt road. There is no fence present, and the sign needs repainting. Since the initial visit, the sign was repainted, and a sign for Horr Cemetery was added below it. Gravestones face west, and date from 1820 to 1995. The Lakeville Assessor's Office lists Clark and Horr Cemetery as one plot, town owned, about 27,000 square feet in area. Thatcher refers to this as a "Cemetery on New Bedford Road, near Long Point Road." Entries were recorded May 25, 2000.

Briggs, Betsey   See Joseph Briggs Monument entry.

Briggs, Joseph H. Monument   *"JOSEPH H. BRIGGS / DIED JAN. 18, 1907, / AGED 85 YRS. 9 MOS. 5 DAYS. / BETSEY, HIS WIFE / DIED MARCH 3, 1901, / AGED 78 YRS. 5 MOS. 4 DAYS."* "BRIGGS" is carved in relief on the base of this monument.

Clark, Anner   *"ANNER, / relict of / NOAH CLARK ESQ. / died Jan. 18, / 1839. / aged 86 years."* There is an urn and willow carving at the top of this stone.

Clark, Elizabeth E.   *"Sacred / to the memory of / MISS. ELIZABETH E. / dau of Mr. Noah & / Mrs. Elizabeth E. Clark. / she died Jan. 1, 1832, / aged 21 years, / 6 mo's & 18 days. /*
Beauty shed her graces o'er her
Youth spread her blooming sweets before her
Love threw her soft enchantment round
And joy her chosen notary crown'd
But death insidious, aimed his dart,
And pierc'd his victim to the heart.
Now love is cold and joy is fled

> *Youth decay'd and beauty dead.*
> *Is all then gone, all perish'd: no!*
> *Virtue survives death's fatal blow.*
> *And strews upon her favourite's tomb*
> *Flowers of never fading bloom."*

There is an urn and willow carving at the top of this stone. The third line is carved in outline. Thatcher lists her age in days as 21. A footstone is present, but it is partially buried underground. No inscription was found on it.

Clark, Elizabeth E.   *"Elizabeth E. / daughter of / John & Hannah W. / Clark, died / Oct. 21 1846. / Æ. 5 m's 4 d's."*

Clark, Elizabeth E.   *"ELIZABETH E. CLARK, / wife of / Noah Clark, / died Nov. 21, 1849, / Æ. 63 years."* The first line is carved along an arch.
"E. E. C." is inscribed on the footstone which is partially buried underground. It faces the headstone.

Clark, Hannah A.   *"Hannah A. / daughter of / John & Hannah W. / Clark, died / Oct. 11, 1849. / Æ. 3 years 4 ms. / & 24 d's."* This small stone is weathered.

Clark, Hannah W.   *"HANNAH W. / wife of / JOHN CLARK / Died Oct. 5, 1895, / Aged 80 yrs, 8 m's."* The first line is carved in relief along an arch. This stone is loose upon its base.

Clark, John   *"JOHN CLARK / Died / Nov 13, 1878; / Aged 66 yrs. 4 m's / & 11 d's. / Safe in the arms of Jesus."* The first line is carved in relief along an arch. There is a 10" crack in the center bottom of this stone.

Clark, John T.   *"JOHN T. / son of John & Hannah W. T. / Clark; / died Sept. 23 1838, / aged 6 m. & 23 / days."*

Clark, Lucy   *"LUCY, / daughter of the late / NOAH CLARK ESQ. / died July 9, 1848. / in the 60 th year / of her age."* The first line is carved in relief along an arch. A partially buried footstone is present, but no inscription was found.

Clark, Noah   *"NOAH CLARK, / died July 24, / 1841, / in the 60th year / of his age."* The first line is carved in outline. *"Warren, Taunton."* is inscribed in the lower right corner of this stone.
"N. C." is inscribed on the footstone that is partially buried underground. The inscription faces the headstone.

Clark, Noah, Esq.   *"ERECTED / to the memory of / NOAH CLARK, ESQ. / who died / Oct. 25, 1830. / in the 81. year / of his age."* There is an urn and willow carving at the top of this stone. The first line is carved along an arch. The third line is carved in outline. A *"SAR 1775"* marker and a flag are present.

Clark, William, Rev.   *"REV. / WILLIAM C. CLARK / BORN / SEPT. 13, 1817, / DIED SEPT. 6, 1875. / Eternal Hope."* The second line is carved along an arch. Flower and leaf designs are carved at the top of this stone.

Cudworth, Abbie C.   See Elisha G. Cudworth Monument entry.

Cudworth, Abigail S.   *"Heaven our home / ABIGAIL S. / wife of James D. T. /*

Cudworth, / died Sept. 4, 1851, / Aged 30 yrs. & 14 d's." A left hand with the index finger pointed up is carved between *Heaven* and *our home*. The second line is carved in relief.

Cudworth, Abigail S. *"ABIGAIL S. / Dau. of James D. T. / & Abigail S. / Cudworth, died / Sept. 21, 1851, / Æ. 7 weeks 1 day."* There is a relief carving of a broken bud at the top of this stone. Her death year is inscribed inside a carved out rectangular area.

Cudworth, Alton K. Monument *"CUDWORTH"* is inscribed on the front of the monument. Floral designs are carved in the upper corners. *"1903 ALTON K. CUDWORTH 1981 / HIS WIFE / 1906 DOROTHY L. DOUGLASS 1980 / 1941 EVELYN E. CUDWORTH 1941 / 1877 JOHN H. DOUGLASS 1945"* is inscribed on the back. A Barnicoat Monuments metal tag is present.

Cudworth, Benjamin *"BENJAMIN F. CUDWORTH / DIED / JUNE 29, 1902 / AGED 72 YRS. 6 MOS / 15 DAYS."* The first line is carved along an arch.

Cudworth, Chloe F. *"Chloe F. / dau. of James D. T. & / Martha Y. Cudworth, / died Dec 22, 1878, / Aged 6 yrs. 4 m's, / & 4 d's. / Of such is the kingdom of / Heaven."*

Cudworth, Dorothy See Alton K. Cudworth Monument entry.

Cudworth, Elisha A. *"CUDWORTH / 1868 ELISHA A. 1938"* Floral designs are carved at the top of this monument. The first line is carved in relief.

Cudworth, Elisha G. Monument *"C"* monogram is carved in shallow relief at the top of this monument. *"ELISHA G. CUDWORTH / JULY 19, 1826 – FEB. 7, 1909 / ABBIE C. NYE / HIS WIFE / MAR. 28, 1844 – APRIL 27, 1931"* *"CUDWORTH"* is carved in relief on the base.

Cudworth, Elisha G. *"ELISHA G. / youngest son of / James D. T. & / Martha Y. / Cudworth, / died Mar. 7, 1863, / Æ. 1 y'r 5 m. 1 d'y."* There is a sculptured carving of a lamb above the inscription on this small stone.

Cudworth, Evelyn See Alton K. Cudworth Monument entry.
"BABY / EVELYN E." is inscribed on a separate stone to the right of the Alton K. Cudworth Monument. A child and a lamb are carved on the lower left corner of this

flat, ground level stone. It is beginning to be buried underground.

Cudworth, James A. *"JAMES A. CUDWORTH / 1858 - 1943 / N.E. LOWELL / LEAGUE 1887"* A carving of two crossed baseball bats with four baseballs is in the middle of the third and fourth lines on this flat, ground level stone. He was a professional baseball player. See "The Baseball Biography Project" website <http://bioproj.sabr.org> for more information about his career.

Cudworth, James D. *"JAMES D. T. CUDWORTH / DEC. 10, 1831, / DEC. 15, 1910"* The first line is carved along an arch.

Cudworth, Lizzie J. *"LIZZIE J. / Dau. of / ELISHA G. & ABBIE C. / CUDWORTH. / Died Sept. 23, 1893. / Aged 20 yrs. 8 mos. / 20 days."* A carving of her overlapped initials is at the top of this stone. The first line is carved in relief along an arch. *"GONE BEFORE*

Dear Lizzie, we miss thee,
But we know thou art blest;
Our Father has tenderly called thee to rest,
Tho' bright the path which in life thou trod.
Thy feet are now stayed by the throne of God.
Where tempest and danger can reach thee
no more.
Thou hast passed the dark waters and
gained the bright shore.
Now out of the reach of sorrow and care,
Glad in the robes that the glorified wear,
Nevermore wilt thou heed the discord of life;
Thou art done with its weariness, done with
its strife.
Thy tears wiped away, thy burdens laid down,
The cross has been borne, thou art wearing
the crown.
Rest sweetly, beloved one; our lonely hearts yearn
For thy presence and love, but ye may not return
Yet we know, by passionate longing and pain,
Our parting is brief, we shall meet thee again."

is inscribed on the back of the stone. The first line is carved along an arch.

Cudworth, Lucy B. *"LUCY B. Dau. of / Elisha A. & Delia F. / Cudworth / May 24, 1892 / Aug. 2, 1893."*

Cudworth, Lulia A. *"LULIA A. / dau. of Elisha G. / & Abbie C. / Cudworth, / died Apr. 14, 1869; / Aged 3 yrs. 6 m. / & 27 d's.*
Rest little weary one
Thy sufferings now are o'er:
We loved thee Oh! how well
But Jesus loved thee more."

Cudworth, Martha Y. *"MARTHA Y. L. / wife of James D. T. / Cudworth. / died June 20, 1882 / Aged 47 yrs. 2 m's / "Tender and true and faithful / unto death.""*

"M. Y. L. C." is inscribed on the footstone that is partially buried underground.

Cudworth, Mary A.   *"MARY A. CUDWORTH"* is inscribed on the front of this monument. There are floral designs in the upper corners of this stone. *"1863 – 1956 / DAU. OF ELISHA G. AND ABBIE C. CUDWORTH"* is inscribed on the back.

Dandrow, Louise D.   See Randall M. Douglass Monument entry.

Douglass, Helen   See Randall M. Douglass Monument entry.

Douglass, John H.   See Alton K. Cudworth Monument entry.
"FATHER / JOHN H. DOUGLASS" is inscribed on a separate flat stone to the right of the monument. It is beginning to be buried.

Douglass, Randall M. Monument   *"DOUGLASS"* is inscribed on the front of this monument. Floral designs are carved in the upper corners. *"1904 RANDALL M. 1989 / HIS WIFE / 1909 HELEN M. 1988 / HIS MOTHER / 1882 LOUISE DANDROW 1969."* is inscribed on the back. A Barnicoat Monuments metal tag is present.

Emerson, Grace   See Henry Emerson Monument entry.
Fairhaven Vital Records show she was born Grace B. Tallman on July 29, 1882. Her obituary in *The Middleborough Gazette* 12/10/1959:12 reports her death on December 3, 1959, at 77 years old.

Emerson, Henry   *"EMERSON / HENRY   GRACE B. / EVERLASTING PEACE"* A rose and leaves are carved in the top left corner of this monument. There are no dates on this stone. A Barnicoat Monuments metal tag is present. Middleborough Vital Records list his marriage to Grace B. Tallman on October 17, 1900, at 24 years old, making his birth year about 1876. His obituary in *The Middleborough Gazette* 09/20/1951:8 reports his death on September 17, 1951, at 74 years old.

Emerson, Infant son   *"The Infant Son of / J. L. & M. E. / Emerson, / died Apr. 28, 1856 / Æ. 9 days."*

Emerson, John L.   *"J. L. EMERSON / CO. D, / 18TH MASS. INF."* is carved in relief within a recessed shield shaped area. *"DIED APR. 1, 1885 / AGED 52."* is inscribed below the shield. There is a *"GAR 8 110"* marker and a flag at this site.

His wife's stone tells us his first name was John. (See Mary Emerson entry.) *Massachusetts Civil War Soldiers & Sailors, 1861-1865*, Vol. II, p. 370 shows that he enlisted in 1861 at age 28. Lakeville Vital Records list his death on April 1, 1885, at 52 years, 9 mos. and 5 days old.

Emerson, Mary E. *"MARY E. / WIFE OF / JOHN L. EMERSON / DIED JAN. 15, 1899. / AGED 64 YRS. 7 MOS."* The first line is carved in relief.

H., S. A. *"S. A. H."* is inscribed on this footstone. No headstone is present.

Harvey, Francis A. *"FRANCIS A. HARVEY / CO A / 3 MASS CAV"* is carved in relief within a recessed shield shaped area. There are no dates on this stone. Lakeville Vital Records indicate that Francis Alexander Harvey was born on March 8, 1833, and died April 28, 1920.

Nye, Loren B. *"LOREN B. NYE / died / MAR 18, 1888 / Aged 85 years / & 6 d's."* The first line is carved along an arch. There are two small cracks running through the bottom of this stone.

Nye, Mary *"MARY / Wife of / Loren B. Nye. / died July 9, 1883; / Aged 76 yrs. 8 m's / 3 d's. / Blessed are the dead which die in / the Lord."* The first line is carved in relief. There is a crack through the bottom of this stone. It extends from the base to the letter "L" in the last line.

Nye, William C. *"WM. C. NYE / U.S. NAVY"* is inscribed within a recessed shield shaped area. A *"GAR 8 111"* marker and flag are present at this gravesite. There are no dates on this stone. Lakeville Vital Records list his death on April 19, 1889, at 52 years, 3 mos., and 15 days old. Lakeville Vital Records show his wife, Sarah (Sampson), died April 24, 1891, and was buried in Middleborough.

Pace, George M. Monument *"PACE"* is inscribed at the top of this monument. There is a carving of a rose and leaves in the upper left corner. *"GEORGE M / 1919 – 1963"* is inscribed on the lower left. *"VIOLA M. / 1923 – ____ "* is inscribed on the lower right. There is a Barnicoat Monuments metal tag present. *"✝ / GEORGE M PACE / MASSACHUSETTS / SKI USNR / WORLD WAR II / FEB 18 1919 MARCH 19 1963"* is inscribed on this flat marker. It is located behind the Pace Monument, on the left. It is slightly below ground level. A veteran's flag is present. An azalea, growing to the right of this grave, is partially covering it up.

Pace, Viola See George Pace Monument entry.

Putnam, Lucy *"LUCY C. PUTNAM / DAU. OF / LORING B. & MARY NYE / DIED AUG 13, 1868 / AGED 26 YRS. 5 MOS. / THERE IS REST IN HEAVEN"* Lakeville Vital Records indicate that she was the wife of Dan F. Putnam.

Sturtevant, Abigail *"In / memory of / MRS. ABIGAIL wife of / Mr. Otis Sturtevant / & dau. of / Noah Clark Esq. & / Mrs. Anner his wife who / died Dec. 22. 1820 / in her 41 year."* An urn and willow are carved in relief at the top of this stone. The first line is inscribed on the raised base of the urn. The rest of the inscription is inscribed on a raised circle below this.

Sturtevant, Sophronia *"In / memory of / SOPHRONIA ANN / dau. Of Mr. Otis &*

/ Mrs. Abigail Sturtevant / & granddau. of / Noah Clark Esq. & / Mrs. Anner his wife who / died Feb. 24, 182 / aged 16 years" An urn and willow are carved in relief at the top of this stone. The first line is inscribed on the raised base of the urn. The rest of the inscription is inscribed on a raised circle below this. A partially buried footstone is present, but no inscription was found on it.

Vickery, Baby   *"BABY VICKER / FEBRUARY 1, 1948"* is inscribed on this flat, ground level marker.

White, Lewis A.   *"WHITE"* is inscribed between two floral carvings at the top of this black monument. *"LEWIS A. / SEPT. 28, 1907 / AUG. 1, 1995"* is inscribed on the lower left. *"NORMA C. / OCT. 30, 1911 / NOV. 2, 1981"* is inscribed on the lower right. A REX Memorials metal tag is present.

White, Norma C.   See Lewis A. White Monument entry.

Wilbur, Jean   *"JEAN MARILYN / WILBUR / JUNE 28*29, 1937 / DAU. OF LLOYD & EDITH"* A child praying is carved on the right side of this flat six-inch high stone.

Additional Notes:

The cemetery cards at the Lakeville Town Hall also list the following: "Augusta A. Harvey, died Sept. 23, 1918." No marker was found, but Lakeville Vital Records show Augusta Harvey was buried in Clark Cemetery. She was born February 16, 1827, and died September 23, 1918.

Clark Cemetery Map Index

Alphabetical:

Emerson, Grace B. (1882-1959) – 15
Emerson, Henry (~1876-1951) – 15
Emerson, Infant son (1856) – 42
Emerson, John L. (1832-1885) – 13
Emerson, Mary E. (1834-1899) – 14
H., S. A. (no dates) – 48
Harvey, Francis A. (1833-1920) – 45
Nye, Loren B. (1803-1888) – 10
Nye, Mary (1806-1883) – 11
Nye, William C. (1837-1889) – 17

Pace, George M. (1919-1963) – 16, 34
Pace, Viola M. (1923-____) – 16
Putnam, Lucy C. (1842-1868) – 9
Sturtevant, Abigail (~1780-1820) – 25
Sturtevant, Sophronia A. (~1809-1825) – 24
Vickery, Baby (1948) – 47
White, Lewis A. (1907-1995) – 43
White, Norma C. (1911-1981) – 43
Wilbur, Jean Marilyn (1937) – 4

By Location:

1 – Clark, Noah, Esq. (~1750-1830)
2 – Clark, Anner (~1753-1839)
3 – Clark, Noah (~1782-1841)
4 – Clark, Elizabeth E. (~1786-1849)
5 – Clark, William C., Rev. (1817-1875)
6 – Clark, Lucy (~1789-1848)
7 – Clark, John (1812-1878)
8 – Clark, Hannah W. (1815-1895)
9 – Putnam, Lucy C. (1842-1868)
10 – Nye, Loren B. (1803-1888)
11 – Nye, Mary (1806-1883)
12 – Douglass, Randall M. (1904-1989)
   Douglass, Helen M. (1909-1988)
   Dandrow, Louise (1882-1969)
13 – Emerson, John L. (1832-1885)
14 – Emerson, Mary E. (1834-1899)
15 – Emerson, Henry (~1876-1951)
   Emerson, Grace B. (1882-1959)
16 – Pace, George M. (1919-1963)
   Pace, Viola M. (1923-____)
17 – Nye, William C. (1837-1889)
18 – Cudworth, Elisha G. (1826-1909)
   Cudworth, Abbie C. (1844-1931)
19 – Cudworth, Lulia A. (1865-1869)
20 – Cudworth, Lizzie J. (1873-1893)
21 – Cudworth, Mary A. (1863-1956)
22 – Cudworth, Elisha A. (1868-1938)
23 – Cudworth, Lucy B. (1892-1893)
24 – Sturtevant, Sophronia A. (~1809-1825)

25 – Sturtevant, Abigail (~1780-1820)
26 – Clark, Elizabeth E. (1810-1832)
27 – Cudworth, Abigail S. (1821-1851)
28 – Cudworth, Abigail S. (1851)
29 – Cudworth, Elisha C. (1861-1863)
30 – Cudworth, Chloe F. (1872-1878)
31 – Cudworth, Martha Y. L. (1835-1882)
32 – Cudworth, James D. T. (1831-1910)
33 – Cudworth, James A. (1858-1943)
34 – Pace, George M. (1919-1963)
35 – Cudworth, Benjamin F. (1829-1902)
36 – Cudworth, Alton K. (1903-1981)
   Cudworth, Dorothy L. (1906-1980)
   Cudworth, Evelyn E. (1941)
   Douglass, John H. (1877-1945)
37 – Cudworth, Evelyn E. (1941)
38 – Douglass, John H. (1877-1945)
39 – Clark, John T. (1837-1838)
40 – Clark, Elizabeth E. (1846)
41 – Clark, Hannah A. (1846-1849)
42 – Emerson, Infant son (1856)
43 – White, Lewis A. (1907-1995)
   White, Norma C. (1911-1981)
44 – Briggs, Joseph H. (1821-1907)
   Briggs, Betsey (1822-1901)
45 – Harvey, Francis A. (1833-1920)
46 – Wilbur, Jean Marilyn (1937-1937)
47 – Vickery, Baby (1948)
48 – H., S. A. (no dates)

Clark Cemetery Map

N

ROUTE 105

BEDFORD STREET

HORR
CEM.

Chapter 5
Douglas Cemetery

Douglas Cemetery is located on private property between 49 Highland Road and Clark Road, in woods behind a field. Mansfield states that it sits back about 550 feet from the road. A stone wall starts at Highland Avenue, continues east past the cemetery area and comes close to the southern border. The sign for this cemetery has fallen down, and is leaning against the sign poles. It needs repainting. Many flat, upright fieldstones are present, and one chiseled fieldstone is present. With fallen trees, overgrown brush, and uneven ground, it is impossible to determine how many people are buried here. Graves face west, and those with inscriptions date from 1793 to 1798. The current property owner stated that the cemetery is 40 feet by 45 feet on his plot map. Thatcher refers to this as the "Douglass Yard." Entries were recorded April 14, 2000.

Douglas, Jotham   *"In MEMORY of / M^r. Jotham Douglas / who died July 12th / 1795. in y̆^{e} 26th. / Year of his age."* The tympanum is broken off of this slate stone, but remnants of a rising sun can be seen carved on what remains.

Douglas, Prudence   *"In MEMORY of M^{rs}, / Pruden_e widow of M^r, / George Douglas she died March / 14th. 1798 in y^e 64th. Year of her / Age. /*
My Sun is set, my glass is run,
The holy will of God is done."
The carver ran out of room on the fourth line, and carved the word *Age* underneath *her*. This lichen encrusted slate stone is difficult to read. Thatcher lists her day of death as March 4th.

Douglas, George   *"di__ 1793"* This slate stone is broken into many pieces. The inscription above is all that was found on the pieces of slate present. Thatcher lists: "Douglass, George, died April 13th, 1793, in his 63rd year."

Additional Notes:

Thatcher also lists:
"Haskins, Miriam, wife of John, Nov. 23rd, 1795, in her 53rd year." This stone was present in 1985 when Mansfield did his survey, but was not found in 2000.
"… about half a dozen graves unmarked …"

No cemetery cards were found for Douglas Cemetery at the Lakeville Town Hall.

Douglas Cemetery Index and Map

Alphabetical:
Douglas, Jotham (~1770-1795) – 3
Douglas, Prudence (~1735-1798) – 2
Douglas, George (~1731-1793) – 1

By Location:
1 – Douglas, George (~1731-1793)
2 – Douglas, Prudence (~1735-1798)
3 – Douglas, Jotham (~1770-1795)

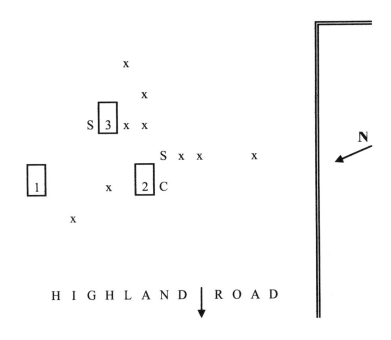

x = upright, unmarked fieldstone
C = chiseled, unmarked fieldstone
S = unmarked slate stone, lying flat on the ground
___ = stone wall

Chapter 6
Hafford Cemetery

Hafford Cemetery sits back from the road roughly across the street from Booth #2 Cemetery. It is located behind and to the left of the house at 177 County Street. A stone post and metal rail fence surrounds it. The entrance and sign are on the southwest side of the cemetery. On the initial visit, the sign was in need of painting. It was repainted in 2000 with the erroneous name "Booth 2". The gravestones face northwest and date from 1799 to 1905. The Lakeville Assessor's Office lists this as a town owned cemetery, 1250 square feet in area. Entries were recorded March 24, 2000.

Hafford, Abigail   "ABIGAIL, / wife of / EBENEZER HAFFORD, / died July 5, 1839, / Aged 80 yrs. 3 ms. / & 25 d's." is inscribed on this slate stone.

Haford, Allis   "In Memory of Miss. / ALLIS, Du^{tr} of Mr. EBENEZER / HAFORD she died Oct^t, 6th, 1806. / Aged 24 Years & 3 days. /
> Physicians skill is vain,
> When God commissians death;
> Youth & beauties avrry train
> Must yield to him their breath.
> $5-50"

Note the spelling of *commissians* and *avrry*. This stone is leaning to the right. An urn and willow are carved at the top of this slate stone. Note the price of the stone is carved at the bottom. The dollar sign is carved backwards.

Hafford, Ebenezer   "In memory of / MR. EBENEZER HAFFORD / who died Sept. 22, 1839, / Æ. 88 Yrs. 3 Ms. / & 4 Da's." There is a branching design carved at the top of this slate stone. A "SAR 1775" marker and flag are present.

Hafford, Ebenezer Monument   "EBENEZER / HAFFORD / died at / Cloverdale, / Cal. / Dec. 24, 1863; / Aged 34 yrs. / 2 m's & 19 d's." is inscribed on the front of this obelisk. The first line is carved along an arch. *"HAFFORD."* is inscribed on the front base. *"REUBEN F. / HAFFORD / died at / Bakersfield / Cal. / Dec. 21, 1900. / Aged 66 yrs. / 7 m's & 4 d's."* is inscribed on the right side. There are no inscriptions on the left side or the back. A *"SAR 1775"* marker and flag are present.

Hafford, Hannah   *"MRS. / HANNAH HAFFORD, / born Feb. 2, 1715, / died Feb. 1, 1799."* is inscribed on this slate stone.
"H. H." is inscribed on the footstone that faces the headstone. It is leaning against the back fence.

Hafford, Lucy   *"LUCY, / wife of / ___ben Hafford, / died Feb. 18, 1891, / Aged 87 yrs. 7 m's / & 8 d's."* The first line is carved in relief along an arch. This stone was broken in half diagonally through the third, fourth, and fifth lines. A repair was attempted, but failed. The repair cement covers the first three letters of the third line. The top half is loosely set in place in its approximate position. There is a 6 inch crack at the bottom of the stone. Lucy was the wife of Reuben Hafford.

Hafford, Lucy T.   *"LUCY T. / Dau. of / Thomas F. & Mary / HAFFORD, / Nov. 29, 1858, / Mar. 11, 1898."*

Hafford, Mary   *"MARY, / Wife of / THOMAS F. HAFFORD / Dec. 17, 1828. / Sept. 13, 1899."*

Haford, Prissilla   *"In memory of Mrs. Prissilla / wife of Mr. Eben ', HAFORD / she died July 31ˢᵗ, Ð. 1806. / Aged 51 Years, 2 m, and 3 days. /*
> *Rejoice in glorious hope,*
> *Jesus the judge will come;*
> *And th take his servants up,*
> *To their eternal home."*

An ornate urn and simple willow are carved at the top of this slate stone. Note the spelling of *Prissilla* and *Haford*. The letters *th* are inscribed between the words *And* and *take* on the third line of the poem. It appears that they were inscribed in error, and an attempt to grind down these letters was made.

Hafford, Reuben   *"REUBEN HAFFORD / died / Jan. 27, 1879, / Aged 81 yrs, 8 m's / & 10 d's."* The first line is carved in relief along an arch.

Hafford, Reuben F.   See Ebenezer Hafford Monument entry.

Hafford, Samuel
"MR.
SAMUEL HAFFORD,
born May 15, 1717.
died July 10, 1801."

is inscribed on this slate stone. Thatcher lists his birth day as May 5ᵗʰ.

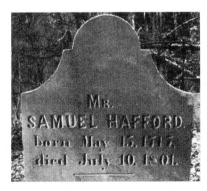

Hafford, Sarah   *"In memory of / MISS SARAH, / daughter of Ebenezer & /*

Priscilla Hafford, / who died May 30, 1838, / Æ. 52 Yrs. 6 Ms. / & 22 Da's." A branching design is carved at the top of this slate stone.

Hafford, Sylvia *"MISS. / SYLVIA HAFFORD / died / Mar. 2, 1873; / Aged 93 yrs. 1 mo. / & 3 d's."* The second line is carved along an arch. The stone is loose on its base, and a board is propping it up. A seven-inch crack runs through the base.

Hafford, Thomas F. *"THOMAS F. / HAFFORD / Mar. 17, 1827, / Oct. 15, 1905."*

Hafford, William A. *"In Memorium. / WILLIAM A. HAFFORD / Died / Sept. 30, 1869: / Aged 37 yrs. 7 mos. / & 10 d's. / Dear Husband, we'll meet again in / Heaven."* The first and second lines are carved along an arch. A Mason's symbol is carved between the first and second lines. A 6-inch crack radiates from the center bottom.

Hafford, William F. *"WILLIAM F. / HAFFORD, / Died / June 21, 1876, / Aged 77 yrs. 2 m's / & 13 d's."* A 12 inch crack runs through the stone at the center bottom.

Peirce, Abraham *"ABRAHAM PEIRCE / Born July 8, 1779; / Died Nov. 14, 1850:"*
"A. P." is inscribed on the footstone. It faces the headstone.

Peirce, Mary *"MARY / wife of / Abraham Peirce. / Born Feb. 13, 1779; / Died April 18, 1848;"*

Hafford Cemetery Map Index

Hafford Cemetery Map

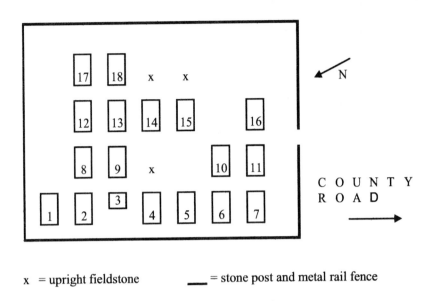

x = upright fieldstone   ___ = stone post and metal rail fence

The price carved at the bottom of Allis Haford's headstone.

Chapter 7
Haskell Cemetery

Haskell Cemetery is located on the east side of Bedford Street, 0.6 miles north of the Freetown line. It is set back a little bit from the road, in the woods. The sign is up but needs repainting. There is no fence around the cemetery, but there is a stone post and metal rail fence around the graves of Silas and Mercy Haskell and their children. It is in good repair. There are two unmarked fieldstones inside this fenced area, on the left side. They are in line with the head and footstones of the rest of the family. A sunken area behind the grave of Mercy Ann Haskell may indicate a second unidentified grave. Stones face north, and date from 1785 to 1883. The cemetery is on land owned by the City of New Bedford. According to Mansfield, this cemetery is about 1467 square feet. Thatcher refers to this as a "Cemetery on New Bedford Road, near Quittacus Pond." Entries were recorded May 25, 2000.

Haskell, Abiah   *"Memento mortis. / In Memory of / M^{rs}. Abiah Haskell Relict of / Elder Mark Haskell who died / Decr. 2^d 1791. Aged 84. Years 7. / Months & _. Days. /*
When into vision faith shall turn
Oh how will love increase and burn!
Then walk awhile in faith and love
And soon you'll join with sai^{n}ts above."

A winged angel is carved between the first and second line. A chip of slate is missing where the number of days would have been. Thatcher does not list her age in days. *The Nelson Family of Plymouth, Middleboro, and Lakeville, Massachusetts* p. 46 lists her as being the widow of John Nelson (~1702-1732), who married Mark Haskell in 1740. A piece of slate stone is located in the footstone area, but it is broken and no inscription was found.

Haskell, Abigail   *"In memory of / Mrs. ABIGAIL HASKELL / wife of / Mr. ZEBULON HASKELL / who died July 26, 1811 / aged 53 years 8 mont_ / _ hs & 18 days /*
Tis God who lifts our comforts high,

Or sinks them in the grave,
He takes and blessed be his name
He takes but what he gave."

A willow and an urn are carved at the top of this slate stone. A curved design is carved down the sides, and a scalloped chain is carved above the inscription. The hyphen for *months* is in the lowered position, and is found at both the end of the line and at the beginning of the next.

"Mrs. Abigail Haskell" is inscribed on the slate footstone. It is broken off at the ground level and is lying face up on the ground.

Haskell, Anna   *"ANNA / wife of / ELISHA HASKELL / born / Nov. 26. 1746 / died / Dec. 2. 1831 / Æ. 85."*
"A. H." is inscribed on the footstone.

Haskell, Elisha   *"ELISHA HASKELL / died Feb. 24, 1829. / aged 84 years / 11 mo, 22 ds. / Respected in life / and lamented in death."*
"E. H." is inscribed on the footstone.

Haskell, Elmira   *"ELMIRA / Dau. of / Silas & Mercy / Haskell, died / Aug. 31, 1883, aged / 80 years 2 m's. / At rest."* This stone is broken in three places above the inscribed area. The three pieces are loosely set in place.
"E. H." is inscribed on the footstone.

Haskel, Judith   *"Mrs. Judith Hask___ / wife of / Mr. Roger Haskel / died March 23 1806 / 62 Years & 7 Day_ /*
In virtuous ways while here she___
We trust she now is with_____
*Joi'd with the Heavenl_*
... __g of endless love."

This slate stone is broken below the first line, and diagonally through the poem. What is left of the tympanum contains an urn carving. It is located behind the bottom piece. The middle piece is in front of the bottom piece. Notice the spelling of Haskel.
"_rs. / Judith Haskel" This slate footstone is exfoliating at the top.

Haskell, Mark, Elder   The slate headstone is broken, and the top piece is missing. All that remains is a poem on the bottom portion of the stone:
"Let it be fix'd upon your minds;
That the straight way to God above,
Is faith that works by purest love."
"This was the first person laid here." is inscribed below this. Both *The Nelson Family of Plymouth, Middleboro, and Lakeville, Massachusetts*, p. 46 and Thatcher lists his death on August 25, 1785, at 76 years, and 4 months old.
"Elder / Mark Haskell" is inscribed on the slate footstone.

Haskell, Mercy   *"MERCY. / wife of / Silas Haskell. / died May 2, 1856. / Æ. 83 Yrs. & 3 m's. /*
Domestic love made bright her lingering years
And still remaining this memento rears."
This stone is broken in half through the fifth line. The top piece is in front of the bottom piece. They are leaning against each other, holding each other up.

"*M. H.*" is inscribed on the footstone.

Haskell, Mercy A.   "*MERCY ANN. / Dau. of Silas & / Mercy Haskell. / died July 31. 1851. / Aged 15 years. /*

> *In her each human being found a friend*
> *Her life was lovely hopeful was her end*"

This stone is broken below the inscription and the top piece is in front of the bottom piece, leaning against it.

"*M. A. H.*" is inscribed on the footstone.

Haskell, Silas   "*Mr. / Silas Haskell. / Died / May 31, 1852 / in his 84ᵗʰ year /*

> *Affection marks where rests a parents dust*
> *His soul to Jesus' faithful care we trust*"

This stone is broken into three pieces. The top two pieces are lying in front of and against the upright bottom portion.

"*S. H.*" is inscribed on the footstone.

Haskell, Silas Jr.   "*SILAS HASKELL J^R. / died Dec 9. 1870; / Aged 70 yrs, 6 m's, / & 16 d's. /*

> *Farewell, Brother, tears are falling,*
> *That thou from our paths must go:*
> *But our God in love is calling*
> *Would we bid thee stay? Oh no.*"

"*S. H.*" is inscribed on the footstone.

Haskel, Thomas   "*Erected in memory of / Mr. THOMAS HASKEL, / who was drowned / Feb. 1ˢᵗ, 1795: / in the 27ᵗʰ year / of his age. /*

> *Death snatch'd the victim's precious soul away*
> *Eternity's vast regions to survey*
> *But oh! Our cheeks are stain'd with pity's tear*
> *And each sad bosom heaves the sigh sincere.*"

"*This Monument's given by a / friend to the deceased T. H. / B₊ Adams*" is inscribed at the bottom. There is an urn and willow carved in relief at the top of this thick, slate stone. Columns are carved on the sides. This stone is broken diagonally from the tympanum to the fourth line, and diagonally below the poem. Two of the pieces are lying on the ground, in front of the bottom piece. Notice the spelling of *Haskel*.

"*Mr. / Thomas Haskel.*" is inscribed on the slate footstone. There is a leaf design carved at the top.

Our life contains a thousand springs,
And dies if one be gone;
Strange! that a harp of thousand strings
Should keep in tune so long;

Haskell, Zebulon   *"In / memory of / MR. ZEBULON HASKELL / who died / Oct 28. 1820 / Æ. 73 years / Our life contains a thousand springs.*
And dies if one be gone;
Strange! That a harp of thousand strings
Should keep in tune so long."
An urn and willow carving is at the top of this slate stone. Scroll like designs are carved on either side of the inscription and small crescents are carved opposite the poem. A veteran's marker and flag are present.

Taber, Eliza   *"In m... / Mrs. Eliza___h / wid⁰ of / Mr. Thomas Taber / who died / April 15 1818⁹ / ___d 84 years"* This partial stone is leaning against the gravestone of Elisha Haskell. It appears that the last number in her death year is an 8 with a 9 carved on top of it. Thatcher lists her death year as 1818. The thickness of the slate and the border carving on it matches the bottom stone remnant that is in position 8 on the map below.

Additional Notes:

Thatcher also lists:
"Decost, John, son of Capt. Nash & Batsey, Apr. 1, 1806, 2 mos. 9 days." No stone was found for this baby.

The cemetery cards at the Lakeville Town Hall list:
"Lucy Leach, died Dec. 19, 1798, aged 53 years, relict of Abill Leach." Thatcher has no listing for a Lucy Leach, and no stone was found for her.

Haskell Cemetery Map Index

Haskell Cemetery Map

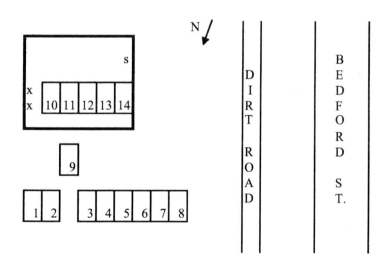

x = fieldstone   s = sunken area   ___ = stone post and metal rail fence

Chapter 8
Haskins Cemetery

Haskins Cemetery is located 0.2 miles west of Southworth Street. A stone post and metal rail fence surrounds it. A second, low stone post and metal rail fence separates the Reed burial plot from the rest of the cemetery. The sign is in good repair. Gravestones face southeast and date from 1842 to 1992. The Lakeville Assessor's Office lists this cemetery as town owned, about 0.15 acres in area. Mansfield records that a small plot was added to this cemetery for Thomas Orrall in 1938 on the left side. At the time of his research, this plot was outside of the fenced area. Since then the fence has been extended to include this plot. Thatcher refers to this as a "Cemetery near Haskins Neighborhood." Entries were recorded November 16, 1999.

Bernhardt, Serena S.   See James A. Suttie Monument entry.

Bernhardt, Wesley   See James A. Suttie Monument entry.

Coombs, Betsey H.   See Levi H. Coombs Monument entry.

Coombs, Herbert M.   *"HERBERT M. COOMBS / 1859 – 1901"* is inscribed on this slanted monument.

Coombs, Joseph C.   *"JOSEPH C. COOMBS / Nov. 28, 1831 / May 27, 1896."* A Mason's symbol is carved on the top slanted surface of this monument. The carving and the first line are carved in shallow relief.

Coombs, Levi H. Monument   *"LEVI H. COOMBS / 1825 – 1903"* is inscribed on the left side of this slanted monument, and *"BETSEY H. COOMBS / 1834 – 1913"* is inscribed on the right side. On the vertical section below this, *"FATHER"* is inscribed on the left side and *"MOTHER"* is inscribed on the right side with a *"C"* monogram in the middle. This monument is covered with lichen.

Coombs, Sarah   *"SARAH, / wife of / Simeon Coombs / Died ... / Aged 87 yrs. 5* *mos, / 13 days. / The children arise up and / call her blessed.*" This stone has broken off at its base, and is lying face up behind it. It was also broken along the fourth line, rendering most of that line unreadable. Repairs to these breaks have failed. Lakeville Vital Records list her death date as Dec. 28, 1881.

Coombs, Simeon "*SIMEON COOMBS, / Died / June 24, 1871. / Aged / 75 years. 8 months. / 26 day.*" "*BURT & KING, Taunton.*" is inscribed in the lower right corner, above the base.

Coombs, Walter H. "*WALTER H.*" is carved in relief on the top slanted surface of this stone. "*son of Levi H. & / Betsey H. Coombs, / died Oct. 20. 1862. / Aged 1 year 8 mo. / & 27 d's. / Not lost but gone before.*" is inscribed on the front vertical surface. The footstone has no inscription.

Dean, Helen Amelia "*HELEN AMELIA, / Dau. of / JOHN & ZILPHA L. H. / DEAN. / Died Dec. 29, 1873 / Aged 24 yrs. 1 mo. / 27 days. /*
She sleeps beneath her native earth
And near the spot that gave her birth
We mourn her loss it's hard to bear
But she's in heaven we'll meet her there"
"*H.A.D.*" is inscribed on the footstone.

Haskins, Albert M. See Myrick Haskins Monument entry.
A "*GAR 8 105*" marker, and a veteran's marker and flag are present near the monument in memory of Albert M. Haskins. *Massachusetts Civil War Soldiers and Sailors, 1861-1865,* Vol. I, p. 496 shows him enlisting in 1861. He served in the 7th Infantry, Co. F.
"*A. M. H.*" This footstone is located slightly in front of the monument, on the left.

Haskins, Arlina M. See Cephas Haskins Monument entry.
"*A M H*" This footstone is located to the right of the monument.

Haskins, Betsey M. See Cephas Haskins Monument entry.
"*B. M. H.*" This footstone is located directly in front of the monument.

  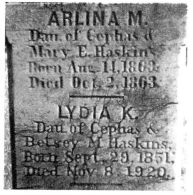

Haskins, Cephas Obelisk "*CEPHAS HASKINS / Born / July 25, 1825. / Died Jan. 19, 1896. / BETSEY M. / His Wife / Born Feb. 21, 1832; / Died Nov. 30, 1858. / MARY E. / His Wife / Born Dec. 30, 1834; / Died Aug. 14, 1908.*" is inscribed on the

front of this obelisk. The first line is carved along an arch. Their names are carved in relief. *"ARLINA M. / Dau. of Cephas & / Mary E. Haskins, / Born Aug. 14, 1863: / Died Oct. 2, 1863. / LYDIA K. / Dau. of Cephas & / Betsey M. Haskins, / Born Sept. 29, 1851, / Died Nov. 8, 1920."* is inscribed on the left side. *"GEORGE S. / SON OF / CEPHAS & BETSEY M. / HASKINS, / JAN. 27, 1856, / MAR. 13. 1910. / MARY A. HASKINS / 1853 – 1932"* is inscribed on the back. There is no inscription on the right side.
"C. H." This footstone is located in front of the monument, on the right.

Haskins, Charles W.   See Myrick Haskins Monument entry.

Haskins, Cornelia A.   See Myrick Haskins Monument entry.
"C. A. H." This footstone is located in front of the monument, on the far left.

Haskins, Edmund   *"EDMUND, / Son of / CAPT. ENOCH AND / PHŒBE HASKINS, / Died / Mar. 12, 1889. / Aged / 71 Yrs. 4 Mos. 20 Days. / Out of the darkness, / Into the light."* Notice the overlap of the *O* and *E* in *PHŒBE*.

Haskins, Eliza R.   *"ELIZA R. / Wife of / FRANKLIN HASKINS. / Died July 24. 1892. / Aged 75 yrs. 5 mos. / 6 days. / The ransomed of the Lord shall / return, and come to Zion with songs / and everlasting joy upon their heads."*

Haskins, Enoch, Capt.   *"In memory of / CAPT. / ENOCH HASKINS, / who died / May 21, 1863; / Aged 84 yrs. 6 m. / & 15 d's. /*
Friends and Physicians could not save
His mortal body from the grave;
Nor can the grave confine him here,
When Christ shall bid him to appear."

Haskins, Franklin   *"FRANKLIN HASKINS / Died / March 12, 1902. / Aged 85 yrs. 10 mos. / 8 days. / Eighty-six years I lived on earth.*
No remnant now remains.
I lived till Jesus thought it best;
To take me to his promised rest."

Haskins, Galen   *"GALEN HASKINS / died Dec.16, 1866; / Aged 58 yrs. 8 m. / & 23 d's. /*
Yet again we hope to meet thee,
When the day of life is fled;
Then in heaven with joy to greet thee,
Where no farewell tear is shed."

Haskins, George S.   See Cephas Haskins Monument entry.
"G. S. H." This footstone is located behind of the monument, on the right.

Haskins, Hannah Hall   *"HANNAH HALL, / Wife of / EDMUND HASKINS, / And daughter of / ALONZO & LYDIA DEAN, / of Easton, / Born Jan. 3, 1826. / Passed to the Higher Life, / Jan. 15, 1874. / To die is gain."* *"BURT, Taunton."* is inscribed on the lower right

corner of the upper base.
"H. H. H." is inscribed on the footstone.

Haskins, Harriet L.   *"HARRIET L. / WIFE OF / BARTLETT HASKINS, / BORN APR. 29, 1829 / DIED FEB. 1, 1889. /*

> *A precious one from us has gone,*
> *A voice we loved is stilled;*
> *A place is vacant in our home,*
> *Which never can be filled.*
> *God in his wisdom has recalled,*
> *The boon His love had given.*
> *And though the body slumbers here,*
> *The soul is safe in Heaven."*

"H. L. H." is inscribed on the footstone.

Haskins, Leonard A.   *"LEONARD A. / son of / Bartlett & Harriet L. / Haskins, / died Dec. 10, 1867; / Aged 18 yrs. 3 m's / & 14 d's. /*

> *He is not dea(d), (b)ut living,*
> *Not lost, (b)ut gone (be)fore;*
> *He's living lov(i)ng (j)ust the same,*
> *On a brig(h)ter, (h)appier shore."*

The first line is carved in relief along an arch. There is a sculptured carving of a flower at the top. This stone was broken on the bottom right side. This break has been successfully repaired along with several other cracks in the area. The repairs obliterate some of the letters in the poem. These letters have been added in parenthesis above by the author.
"L. A. H." is inscribed on the footstone.

Haskins, Lydia K.   See Cephas Haskins Monument entry.
"L. K. H." This footstone is located behind the monument, on the left.

Haskins, Mary A.   See Cephas Haskins Monument entry.
"M. A. H." is inscribed on the footstone which is located behind the monument.

Haskins, Mary E.   See Cephas Haskins Monument entry.
"M. E. H." This footstone is located in front of the monument, on the left.

Haskins, Myrick Monument   *"MYRICK / BORN JULY 5, 1814, / DIED JUNE 7, 1887. / CORNELIA A. / BORN OCT. 24, 1819. / DIED SEPT. 12. 1842. / NANCY J. C. / BORN MAY 18, 1817. / DIED JAN. 17. 1886."* is inscribed on the front of this monument. *"HASKINS"* is carved in relief on the base. *"CHARLES W. / SON OF / MYRICK & NANCY J. C. / HASKINS, / BORN DEC. 14, 1849. / DIED MAY 25, 1850. / ALBERT M. / SON OF / MYRICK & CORNELIA A. / HASKINS, / BORN JULY 30, 1842. / DIED APR. 24, 1881."* is inscribed on the right side. *"FRED A. JOHNSON / 1865 – 1931 / HIS WIFE / ANNA MASON JOHNSON / 1867 – 1936"* is inscribed on the back. There is no inscription on the left side. An urn sculpture is carved on top of this monument.
"M. H." This footstone is located directly in front of the monument.

Haskins, Nancy J. C.   See Myrick Haskins Monument entry.

"N. J. C. H." This footstone is located in front of the monument, on the left.

Haskins, Phebe *"In memory of / PHEBE, / wife of / CAPT. ENOCH HASKINS: / who died Sept. 21, 1853, / aged 64 years. /*
> *My flesh shall slumber in the ground,*
> *'Till the last trumpets joyfully sound;*
> *Then burst the chains with glad surprise,*
> *And in my Saviours image rise."*

The second line is carved in shadow.

Haskins, Sarah C. *"SARAH C / Wife of / GALEN HASKINS, / died May 8, 1880, / Aged 67 yrs. 3 m. / Faithful unto death."*

Haskins, Serena R. *"SERENA R. / dau. of / Galen & Sarah C. / HASKINS /..."* The first line is carved in relief along an arch. The bottom of the gravestone is buried in the cement base up to the middle of the fourth line. *Middleborough, Massachusetts Vital Records,* Vol. 1, p. 427, lists her birth on April 23, 1833. Her Vital Records index card at the Middleborough Town Clerk's Office lists her death on June 13, 1858, at 25 years, 1 month and 21 days old.

Johnson, Anna M. See Myrick Haskins Monument entry.
"ANNA / 1936" This footstone is located behind the monument.

Johnson, Fred A. See Myrick Haskins Monument entry.
"FRED / 1931" This footstone is located behind the monument, on the left.

Orrall, Barbara V. Monument *"ORRALL"* is inscribed at the top of the monument within a cloud. A scene of grazing cows on a farm is carved below this. *"BARBARA V. / 1906 – 1992"* is inscribed on the bottom left and *"THOMAS E. / 1904 – 1974"* is inscribed on the bottom right. A Barnicoat Monuments metal tag is present.

Orrall, Thomas E. See Barbara Orrall Monument entry.

Reed, Clarinda See Levi Reed Monument entry.
"CLARINDA" is carved in relief on the top slanted surface of this stone. It is

located to the far left of the monument.

"Come you my friends look down and view
The hollow gaping tomb;
This gloomy prison and for you
Whene'er the summons come"

is inscribed on the front of this small stone. Thatcher lists her death year as 1847.

Reed, Levi Monument   *"LEVI REED"* is carved in relief on the front vertical surface of this table like monument. *"Hathaway"* is inscribed on the bottom left side. Floral carvings are on either side. *"CLARINDA REED / died Dec. 17, 18__. / aged 22 Yrs. 2 Ms. / & 13 Das. / LEVI REED JR. / died Feb. 8. 1855, / aged 34 Yrs. 11 Ds."* is inscribed on the left side of the horizontal surface of this monument. *"LEVI REED. / died Apr. 21, 1877. / aged 77 Yrs. 3 Mos. / 21 Ds. / His wife / SOPHIA. / Born May 20, 1799, / died May 27, 1886."* is inscribed on the right side. The inscriptions on the top are very weathered.
"LEVI" is carved in relief on the top slanted surface of this small stone that is located in front of the monument, on the left. A poem is carved on the front, but is too weathered to read.

Reed, Levi, Jr. Monument   This monument is carved to look like two headstones placed together. *"FATHER. / LEVI REED JR. / JAN. 28, 1821. / FEB. 8, 1855."* is inscribed on the left side and *"MOTHER. / MAHALA C. REED / JULY 9, 1820 / JAN 6, 1909"* is inscribed on the right side. It is located behind the Levi Reed Monument, on the right.
See also the Levi Reed Monument entry.

Reed, Mahala C.   See Levi Reed, Jr. Monument entry.

Reed, Sophia   See Levi Reed Monument entry.
"SOPHIA" is carved in relief on the top slanted surface of a small stone. It is located in front of the monument, on the far left.

Suttie, James A. Monument   *"SUTTIE / JAMES A. SUTTIE / 1863 – 1920 / SERENA S. BERNHARDT / 1862 – 1956 / WESLEY BERNHARDT / 1856 – 1932"* Geometric designs are carved on the sides.

Vail, Adoniram W.   *"ADONIRAM W. / 1831 – 1898"* is inscribed on this flat, ground level stone. It is located behind the Washburn Monument, on the right.

Vail, Mary A. *"MARY A. / 1842 – 1904"* is inscribed on this flat, ground level stone. It is located directly behind the Washburn Monument, on the right side.

Washburn-Vail Monument *"WASHBURN"* is inscribed on the front of this monument, and *"VAIL"* is inscribed on the back of this monument. Floral designs are carved in the upper corners. No other inscriptions are present.

Washburn, Alberta F. *"ALBERTA F. 1865 – 1955"* is inscribed on this flat ground level stone. It is located directly in front of the Washburn Monument, on the right side.

Washburn, Clarice E. *"CLARICE E. WASHBURN / DIED AUG. 17, 1892. / AGED 5 MOS."* is inscribed on this slanted stone. Ivy is carved at the top. It is located directly in front of the Washburn Monument, on the left side.

Washburn, Maurice W. *"MAURICE W. 1900 – 1971"* This flat, ground level stone is located in front of the Washburn Monument, on the far right.

Washburn, Nathan F. *"NATHAN F. 1863 – 1946"* This flat, ground level stone is located in front of the Washburn Monument, on the right side.

Additional Notes:

The cemetery cards at the Lakeville Town Hall also show that "Orrall, (baby)" was buried in Haskins Cemetery. Lakeville Vital Records list this child of Thomas and Barbara (Washburn) Orrall as stillborn on May 9, 1938. No gravestone was found for this baby.

Haskins Cemetery Map Index

Alphabetical:

Haskins, Sarah C. (1813-1880) – 19
Haskins, Serena R. (1833-1858) – 17
Johnson, Anna M. (1867-1936) – 24, 39
Johnson, Fred A. (1865-1931) – 24, 38
Orrall, Barbara V. (1906-1992) – 1
Orrall, Thomas E. (1904-1974) – 1
Reed, Clarinda (1825-1847) – 45, 46
Reed, Levi (1799-1877) – 44, 46
Reed, Levi, Jr. (1821-1855) – 46, 47
Reed, Mahala C. (1820-1909) – 47

Reed, Sophia (1799-1886) – 43, 46
Suttie, James A. (1863-1920) – 31
Vail, Adoniram W. (1831-1898) – 37
Vail, Mary A. (1842-1904) – 36
Washburn / Vail Monument – 22
Washburn, Alberta F. (1865-1955) – 3
Washburn, Clarice E. (1892-1892) –2
Washburn, Maurice (1900-1971) – 5
Washburn, Nathan F. (1863-1946) – 4

By Location:

1 – Orrall, Barbara V. (1906-1992)
   Orrall, Thomas E. (1904-1974)
2 – Washburn, Clarice E. (1892-1892)
3 – Washburn, Alberta F. (1865-1955)
4 – Washburn, Nathan F. (1863-1946)
5 – Washburn, Maurice (1900-1971)
6 – Haskins, Cornelia A. (1819-1842)
7 – Haskins, Nancy J. C. (1817-1886)
8 – Haskins, Myrick (1814-1887)
9 – Haskins, Mary E. (1834-1908)
10 – Haskins, Betsey M. (1832-1858)
11 – Haskins, Cephas (1825-1896)
12 – Haskins, Harriet L. (1829-1889)
13 – Coombs, Sarah (1794-1881)
14 – Coombs, Simeon (1795-1871)
15 – Coombs, Joseph C. (1831-1896)
16 – Coombs, Levi H. (1825-1903)
   Coombs, Betsey H. (1834-1913)
17 – Haskins, Serena R. (1833-1858)
18 – Haskins, Galen (1808-1866)
19 – Haskins, Sarah C. (1813-1880)
20 – Haskins, Enoch, Capt. (1778-1863)
21 – Haskins, Phebe (~1789-1853)
22 – Washburn / Vail Monument
23 – Haskins, Albert M. (1842-1881)
24 – Haskins, Myrick (1814-1887)
   Haskins, Cornelia A. (1819-1842)
   Haskins, Nancy J. C. (1817-1886)
   Haskins, Charles W. (1849-1850)
   Haskins, Albert M. (1842-1881)
   Johnson, Fred A. (1865-1931)
   Johnson, Anna M. (1867-1936)
25 – Haskins, Cephas (1825-1896)
   Haskins, Betsey M. (1832-1858)

25 – Haskins, Mary E. (1834-1908)
   Haskins, Arlina M. (1863)
   Haskins, Lydia K. (1851-1920)
   Haskins, George S. (1856-1910)
   Haskins, Mary A. (1853-1932)
26 – Haskins, Arlina M. (1863)
27 – Haskins, Leonard A. (1849-1867)
28 – Dean, Helen Amelia (1849-1873)
29 – Coombs, Herbert M. (1859-1901)
30 – Coombs, Walter H. (1861-1862)
31 – Suttie, James A. (1863-1920)
   Bernhardt, Serena S. (1862-1956)
   Bernhardt, Wesley (1856-1932)
32 – Haskins, Franklin (1816-1902)
33 – Haskins, Eliza R. (1817-1892)
34 – Haskins, Edmund (1817-1889)
35 – Haskins, Hannah H. (1826-1874)
36 – Vail, Mary A. (1842-1904)
37 – Vail, Adoniram W. (1831-1898)
38 – Johnson, Fred A. (1865-1931)
39 – Johnson, Anna M. (1867-1936)
40 – Haskins, Lydia K. (1851-1920)
41 – Haskins, Mary A. (1853-1932)
42 – Haskins, George S. (1856-1910)
43 – Reed, Sophia (1799-1886)
44 – Reed, Levi (1799-1877)
45 – Reed, Clarinda (1825-1847)
46 – Reed, Clarinda (1825-1847)
   Reed, Levi, Jr. (1821-1855)
   Reed, Levi (1799-1877)
   Reed, Sophia (1799-1886)
47 – Reed, Levi, Jr. (1821-1855)
   Reed, Mahala C. (1820-1909

Haskins Cemetery Map

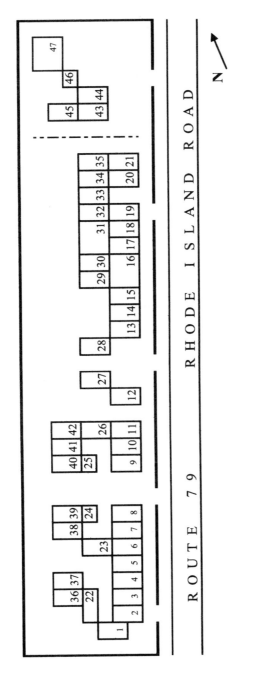

= stone post and metal rail fence   ------ = low stone post and metal rail fence

_____ = stone post and metal rail fence

Chapter 9
Horr Cemetery

Horr Cemetery is located north of Long Point Road, between 457 and 459 Bedford Street (Route 105). It is next to Clark Cemetery and separated from it by a short dirt road. There is no fence present. A sign has been added since the initial visit. Gravestones face west and date from 1858 to 2001. Vigers states the cemetery was originally part of the Benjamin E. Horr farm. The Lakeville Assessor's Office lists Horr and Clark Cemetery as one plot, town owned, about 27,000 square feet in area. Entries were recorded May 25, 2000, and later updated.

Cobb, Marilyn   *"COBB"* is inscribed on the front of this monument. A scene of a windmill on a farm, wooden shoes, tulips and a floral design are carved on the front. *"MOTHER / MARILYN MANTON COBB / NOV. 17, 1926 – NOV. 24, 1973"* is inscribed on the back.

DeMaranville, Alton   *"OUR BOY"* is carved in relief on the top curved surface of this stone. *"ALTON / Son of / Joseph & Chloe A. / DEMARANVILLE, / Died Dec. 26, 1901 / Aged 16 yrs. 7 mos. / 29 days"* is carved on the front. The first line is carved in relief.

DeMaranville, Chloe A.   See Joseph DeMaranville Monument entry.

DeMaranville, Clarence   *"OUR BOY"* is carved on the top curved surface of this monument. *"CLARENCE DEMARANVILLE / JAN. 14, 1896 / SEPT. 19, 1917."* is inscribed on the front.

DeMaranville, Fred   *"OUR BOY"* is carved in relief on the top curved surface of this stone. *"FRED / Son of / Joseph & Chloe A. / DEMARANVILLE. / Died Sept. 21, 1897 / Aged 15 yrs. 4 mos. / 17 days."* is inscribed on the front. The first line is carved in relief. There are two cracks radiating from the bottom.

DeMaranville, Joseph Monument   *"DEMARANVILLE   /   JOSEPH*

DEMARANVILLE / 1848 – 1923 / HIS WIFE / CHLOE ANN HORR / 1856 – 1917" is inscribed on the front of this monument. The first line is carved in relief. *"MAUDE DEMARANVILLE / 1887 – 1978"* is inscribed on the back.

DeMaranville, Katie G. *"KATIE G. / WIFE OF / WILLIAM / DEMARANVILLE / MAY 13, 1869 / SEPT. 25, 1926"* The first line is carved in relief along an arch. There is a "WOMANS RELIEF CORPS 8 MASS DEP'M'T" marker and flag here.

DeMaranville, Maude See Joseph DeMaranville Monument entry.

DeMaranville, Piercie H. *"PIERCIE H. / SON OF / WILLIAM & KATIE G. / DEMARANVILLE / MARCH 17, 1890 / APRIL 25, 1909"* The first line is carved in relief along an arch.

DeMaranville, William *"WILLIAM / DeMARANVILLE / OCT. 19, 1862 / MAY 21, 1914"* The first line is carved in relief along an arch.

Horr, Benjamin E. *"BENJAMIN E. HORR / Died / Aug 17, 1891 / Aged 72 yrs. / 5 days. / Asleep in Jesus"* The first line is carved along an arch. There are two small cracks at the bottom.

Horr, Benjamin F. Monument *"BENJAMIN F. HORR / 1843 – 1913 / HIS WIFE / MARY A. HORR / 1840 – 1927"* There are floral and geometric designs carved at the top of this monument.

Horr, Chloe A. *"CHLOE ANN. / wife of / Elijah Horr, / died Aug. 12, 1858, / Aged 23 yrs. 6 m's."* The first line is carved in relief. A sculpted scroll is carved at the top of this stone.

Horr, Elijah *"Father, / ELIJAH HORR, / Son of the late / Job & Rhoda Horr, / died Apr. 12, 1889; / Aged 64 yrs. 1 mo. / & 7 d's."* There is a 3 inch crack at the bottom center of this stone.

Horr, Freddie *"OUR LITTLE BOY"* is inscribed along an arch just under the top curved surface of this small stone. *"FREDDIE"* is carved in relief in the center. *"FOR OF SUCH IS THE KINGDOM / OF HEAVEN"* is inscribed at the bottom. *"Son of / Benjamin F. & Mary / Horr / died May 9, 1881 / Aged 8 yrs. 19 d's."* is inscribed on the back.

Horr, Helen M. *"HELEN M. / DAU. OF ELIJAH / & CHLOE A. HORR, / DIED MAR. 10, 1912. / AGED 57 YRS. 11 MOS. / 22 DAYS."* There is a flower and leaf carving at the top of this stone. The first line is carved in relief along an arch.

Horr, Isabel S. *"ISABEL S. HORR / 1869 – 1955"* is inscribed on this slanted, lichen encrusted stone.

Horr, Job *"JOB HORR / died / June 15 1884, / Aged 88 yrs. 4 m's / & 13 days. / Blessed are the dead, who die in the Lord."* The first line is carved in relief along an arch. There is a crack radiating from the center bottom on this stone.

Horr, Justina M. *"Justina M. / dau. of / Benj.ⁿ E. & / Susan H. Horr, / died Nov 13, 1861, Aged 10 years / 9 mo's & 3 d's. /*
     Sweetly our Tina sleeps,

Embraced in Jesus care;
Soon at his glorious coming,
In endless life shall share."

The first line is carved along an arch on this small stone.

Horr, Mary A.   See Benjamin Horr Monument entry.

Horr, Rhoda   *"RHODA, / wife of Job Horr, / died Oct. 14, 1880. / Aged 81 yrs. 1 mo. / & 23 days. / Blessed are the pure in heart / For they shall s__ God"* The first line is carved in relief along an arch. This stone is separated from its base and is leaning against the front of it. A crack radiating from the bottom center of the stone extends through the *&* in the fifth line and the *Ag* in the fourth line. It obliterates the word between *shall* and *God* in the last line.

Horr, Susan A.   *"Susan Annette. / dau. of / Benjⁿ. E. & / Susan H. Horr, / died Oct 31, 1861, / Aged 8 years. / 8 mo's & 16 d's. /*
Rest Nellie till the Saviour
Shall come to bid thee rise,
And call thee with the ransomed
To meet him in the skies."

The first line of this small stone is carved along an arch.

Horr, Susan H.   *"SUSAN H. / Wife of / Benjamin E. Horr / Died Dec. 28, 1893. / Aged 68 yrs. 3 mos. / 4 days. / Peaceful be thy silent slumber."* The first line is carved along an arch. There is a crack running through the words *be thy silent.*

Le Blanc   *"LE BLANC"* is all that is inscribed on this flat, ground level stone.

LeBlanc, Henri P.   *"✝ / HENRI PHILIP LeBLANC / PFC   US ARMY / AUG 30 1930   SEPT 25 2001"* is inscribed on this flat, ground level stone. It was placed directly behind the LeBlanc stone after the initial visit.

Luther, Florence B.   *"L (monogram) / FLORENCE B. / WIFE OF / GEORGE W. LUTHER / BORN AUG. 30, 1864, / DIED APRIL 22, 1926."* Floral designs are carved in shallow relief at the top and bottom of this stone.

Luther, George W.   *"L (monogram) / CAPTAIN / GEORGE W. LUTHER / BORN SEPT. 1. 1851 / DIED FEB. 21. 1917."* The second line is carved along an arch.

Floral designs are carved in shallow relief at the top and bottom of this stone.

Manton, Annie E.   *"ANNIE E. SCOTT / 1904 – 1965"* is inscribed on the front of this monument. Floral designs are carved in the top corners *"ANNIE E. SCOTT / WIFE OF / BERTRAM A. MANTON / MARRIED SEPT. 11, 1941"* is inscribed on the back. A Barnicoat Monuments metal tag is present.

Manton, Beatrice E.   See Bertram Manton Monument entry.

Manton, Bertram A. Monument   *"MANTON / BERTRAM A. MANTON / 1899 – 1967 / HIS WIFE / BEATRICE E. SIVIGNY / 1908 – 1940"* The first line is carved in relief. Ivy leaves are carved in shallow relief at the top. A Plymouth County Police Officer's Association marker is present.

Manton, George B.   *"MANTON / 1928 GEORGE B. 1954"* Floral designs are carved in the top corners. A flag and a James E. Tootell Monument Co. metal tag are present.

Russell, Ethel   *"ETHEL RUSSELL / 1892 – 1974"* is inscribed on this slanted stone.

Vigers, Gladys G.   See James Vigers Monument entry.

Vigers, James J. Jr. Monument   *"JAMES J. VIGERS ᴶᴿ· / 1900 – 1976 / GLADYS G. HIS WIFE / 1899 – 1960"* is inscribed on a large white boulder. A book with the words: *"HISTORY / OF / LAKEVILLE / BY / GLADYS G. VIGERS"* on the cover is carved to the left of the inscription. *"1953"* is inscribed on the book's spine. A flag is placed here yearly in remembrance of her contribution to the town.

Horr Cemetery Map Index

Alphabetical:

By Location:

1 – DeMaranville, Joseph (1848-1923)
    DeMaranville, Chloe A. (1856-1917)
    DeMaranville, Maude (1887-1978)
2 – DeMaranville, Clarence (1896-1917)
3 – DeMaranville, Alton (1885-1901)
4 – DeMaranville, Fred (1882-1897)
5 – Horr, Job (1796-1884)
6 – Horr, Rhoda (1799-1880)
7 – Horr, Elijah (1825-1889)
8 – Horr, Chloe Ann (1835-1858)
9 – Horr, Helen M. (1854-1912)
10 – Luther, George W. (1851-1917)
11 – Luther, Florence B. (1864-1926)
12 – Horr, Benjamin E. (1819-1891)
13 – Horr, Susan H. (1825-1893)
14 – Horr, Justina M. (1851-1861)
15 – Horr, Susan Annette (1853-1861)
16 – Russell, Ethel (1892-1974)

17 – Manton, George B. (1928-1954)
18 – Manton, Bertram A. (1899-1967)
    Manton, Beatrice E. (1908-1940)
19 – Manton, Annie E. (1904-1965)
20 – Horr, Benjamin F. (1843-1913)
    Horr, Mary A. (1840-1927)
21 – Horr, Isabel S. (1869-1955)
22 – Horr, Freddie (1873-1881)
23 – Cobb, Marilyn (1926-1973)
24 – LeBlanc Stone (no dates)
    LeBlanc, Henri P. (1930-2001)
25 – Vigers, James J., Jr. (1900-1976)
    Vigers, Gladys G. (1899-1960)
26 – DeMaranville, William (1862-1914)
27 – DeMaranville, Katie G. (1869-1926)
28 – DeMaranville, Piercie H, (1890-
    1909)

Horr Cemetery Map

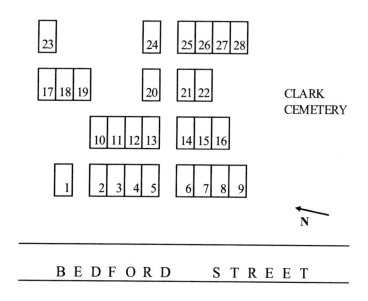

Chapter 10
Howland Cemetery

Howland Cemetery is located between 74 and 76 Howland Road. It sits back from the road, up on a little hill. The dirt road leading to it is blocked off with a chain. A stone wall forms the border on the south and east sides. Four small plots are bordered with a stone post and metal rail fence. Many graves are marked only with fieldstones. No sign was present at the initial visit, but currently one is in place. Most gravestones face northwest, a few face northeast. Gravestones date from 1797 to 2000. The Lakeville Assessor's Office lists this cemetery as town owned, about 1/2 acre in size. Thatcher refers to it as a "Cemetery in woods near Howland Station." Entries were recorded September 15 through October 14, 2000.

Ashley, Alonzo   *"FATHER"* is inscribed on the top slanted surface of this monument. *"ALONZO G. ASHLEY / 1870 – 1911"* is inscribed on the front. Leaf designs are carved in the upper corners. *""Dying is but going Home""* is inscribed at the bottom.

Ashley, Ernest A.   *"ERNEST A. ASHLEY / BORN FEB. 14. 1894 / DIED MAR. 25, 1965 / AGE 71 Y. – 1 M. – 11 D."* *"PERPETUAL CARE"* is inscribed at the bottom of this monument. The first line is carved along an arch. There is a floral design in the upper corners. A Barnicoat Monuments metal tag is present.

Ashley, Jennie G.   *"JENNIE G. ASHLEY / BORN APR. 4, 1908 / DIED FEB. 6, 1988 / AGE 79. - 10M. - 2D."* *"PERPETUAL CARE"* is inscribed at the bottom of this monument. The first line is carved along an arch. There is a floral design in the upper corners. A Barnicoat Monuments metal tag is present.

Ashley, Malcolm G.   *"MALCOLM G. ASHLEY / TECH 5   US ARMY / WORLD WAR II / Jun 26, 1921 ✝ Dec 10 1990"* is embossed on this flat, ground level, metal marker. A veteran's marker and flag are present.

Ashley, Pauline A.   See Thomas M. Ashley Monument entry.

Ashley, Thomas M. Monument   *"Ashley"* is inscribed on the front of this monument below an etching of a bald eagle. *"THOMAS M. ASHLEY / NOV. 26, 1936 – AUG. 29, 2000 / HIS WIFE / PAULINE A. (MEDEIROS) / JUL. 9, 1938 ____ "* is inscribed on the back. A Barnicoat Monuments metal tag is present. This monument was added after the initial visit.

Baker, Abisha R. Monument   *"BAKER"* is inscribed at the top of this flat, lichen encrusted, 0-2 inch high stone. *"ABISHA R / 1807 – 1891 / BETSEY B. / 1809 – 1884"* is inscribed below this on the left side, and *"WILLIAM W. / 1836 – 1890 / MARY H. / 1845 – 1912"* is inscribed below this on the right side. A veteran's marker is present.

Baker, Betsey B.   See Abisha R. Baker Monument entry.

Baker, Judith H.   *"JUDITH H. BAKER / Wife of Simeon Baker / Died APRIL 21, 1880. / Aged 77 yrs."* Note the capital "IL" in April.
"J · B" is inscribed on the footstone.

Baker, Lurana   See William Baker Monument entry.

Baker, Mary H.   See Abisha R. Baker Monument entry.

Baker, Phebe   *"In Memory of / MRS. / PHEBE, / wife of / Josiah Baker. / who died Sept. 15. / 1838. / aged 36 years. /*

> *That once loved form now cold and dead,*
> *Each mournful thought employs;*
> *And nature weeps her comforts fled,*
> *And wither'd all her joys."*

The first line is carved along an arch, and the last line before the poem is carved along a reverse arch. The second line is carved in outline, and the third line is carved in relief.
"P. B." is inscribed on the footstone.

Baker, Samuel, Capt.   *"In memory of / CAPT. SAMUEL BAKER, / who died / Jan. 1, 1851; / aged 73 years."*
"S. B." is inscribed on the footstone.

Baker, Simeon   *"SIMEON BAKER / DIED / March 20, 1880 / AGED 77 Years"*
"S · B" is inscribed on the footstone.

Baker, Simeon D.   *"In memory of / SIMEON D. BAKER. / son of Simeon & / Judith Baker. / who died Nov. 28, / 1846. / in the 14th year / of his age. /*

> *Weep not for me, my parents dear.*
> *Nor sit and shed the silent tear;*
> *But raise your thoughts to joys on high*
> *Where saints immortal never die."*

The second line is carved in shadow. *"E. Warren FR."* is inscribed at the bottom center of this stone.
"S. D. B." is inscribed on the footstone.

Baker, Welthy   *"WELTHY BAKER / Wife of CAP.ᵗ. Samuel / Baker Died July 12, 1860 / Aged 95 yrs."*

"W. B." is inscribed on the footstone.

Baker, William Monument

"WILLIAM BAKER / died / July 26, 1876. / AGED 72 YRS. / LURANA / WIFE of Wᵐ BAKER / DIED MAy 27, 1877 / AGED 76 YRS." is inscribed on the front of this obelisk. The first line is carved along an arch. Note the mix of upper and lower case letters. On the right side is the inscription for their daughter: *"LURANA H. HOWLAND / MAY 10, 1837 / JAN. 30, 1904"* The first line is carved along an arch. There are no inscriptions on the back or the left side. The top of the obelisk was broken about 3½ feet from the top, but it has been successfully repaired. A stone post and metal rail fence surrounds this monument.

Baker, William W.   See Abisha R. Baker Monument entry.
"WM. BAKER / U. S. NAVY" is carved in relief inside a recessed shield shaped area. There are no dates on this second stone. The last line is half buried. *Massachusetts Civil War Soldiers & Sailors, 1861-1865*, Vol. VII, p.571, shows that William W. Baker from Lakeville enlisted in the Navy in 1861 at age 25.

Burgess, James A.   *"BURGESS / 1941"* is inscribed on the horizontal surface of this stone block. Lakeville Vital Records list the death of James A. Burgess on August 8, 1942, at 66 years old.

Cummings, Alonzo G.   *"Erected / to the memory of / ALONZO G. / Son of / Joseph & Susan / T. CUMMINGS. / who died Oct 22, 1850 / Aged 8 mo. & 5 days. /*
Sweet is the rose that budded /
here, to bloom in heaven"
The last three lines on this stone are buried underground. The third line is carved inside a rectangular carved out area.

Cummings, Flora A.   *"Erected / to the memory of / FLORA A. / Dau. of / Joseph & Susan T. / CUMMINGS, / who died Feb 23, 1864; / Aged 2 yrs, 1 mo. / and 8 days. /*
Little Flora too beautiful for earth,
But a fit companion for angels."
"F. A. C." is inscribed on the footstone.

Cummings, Herbert   *"ERECTED / to the memory of / HERBERT F. / Son of Joseph and / Susan T. Cummings. / who died Aug 30, 1852 / Aged 1 yr. and 10 days. /*
Weep not for us our parents dear,
Nor o'er us shed the flowing tear,
I've gone to meet my brothers dear,
In yonder heaven above.

Hard it is to part,
With those we love so dear on earth.
But we will put our trust in him,
Who gave their spirit birth."

The last three lines of the poem are buried underground.
"H. F. C." is inscribed on the footstone.

Cummings, Joseph   *"Erected / to the memory of / JOSEPH CUMMINGS, / who died / in Omaha City / Nebraska, / Aug. 28, 1866: / Aged 42 yrs. 4 m's. / He's gone, but not forgotten."* The third line is carved along an arch. Two cracks radiating from the base have been successfully repaired.
"J. C." is inscribed on this footstone. It is located behind the headstone and to the right within the second line of headstones in the Cummings plot.

Cummings, Joseph L.   *"Erected / to the memory of / JOSEPH L. / Son of / Joseph & Susan / T. CUMMINGS / who died Oct. 19, 1849 / Aged 11 mos. & 20 days"*
"J. L. C." This footstone is leaning against the stone wall on the southwest side.

Cummings, Susan T.   *"SUSAN T. CUMMINGS / WIFE OF / JOSEPH CUMMINGS / APRIL 9, 1825 / APRIL 16, 1904 / OUR MOTHER."* The first line is carved along an arch. This stone is separated from its base, and is leaning against it.

Dean, Deborah   *"MOTHER. / Mrs. / DEBORAH DEAN, / Born Sept. 27, 1782, / Died May 15, / 1850, / Aged 68 years. / "Thou art gone, but not forgotten." / Erected by her daughter Sarah."* The first and third lines are carved in relief.
"D. D." is inscribed on the footstone.

Father   *"FATHER"* is all that is inscribed on this flat, ground level stone. It is located to the left of the Hiram Parry Monument.

Faulkner, Leonard A.   *"✝ / LEONARD ALLEN FAULKNER / SP4 US ARMY / APRIL 16 1937   FEB 19 1997"* is inscribed on this flat, ground level stone. A veteran's marker and flag are present.

Goff, Susan C.   *"SUSAN C. GOFF / 1896 – 1927"* is carved in relief on this stone. Leaf designs are carved in the upper corners.

H., L. B.   *"L. B. H."* is all that is inscribed on this flat, cement block. It is slightly above ground level. This could be just a plot marker.

Howland, Abigail   *"MRS. / ABIGAIL, / wife of / SETH HOWLAND, / died July 24,*
1824, / Æt. 35. /   *She's gone – the voyage of human life is o'er.*
And left a mortal for immortal shore:
Though rough the passage, peaceful is the port,
The bliss is perfect, the probation short;
There wearied virtue shall for refuge fly,
And every tear be wip'd from every eye."

The third line is carved in outline. This slate stone has a small urn and willow carved in relief at the top. An urn topped column is carved in relief on either side of the inscription above the poem.

"A. H. / 1824." is inscribed on the footstone.

Howland, Amelia V.   *"AMELIA V. / daughter of / Jephthah A. & Ruth / Howland, / died April 16, 1851; / aged 5 Yrs. 7 Mos. 22 days. /*

> *Sleep on, sleep on, dear Children sleep, /*
> *Thy Paren'ts will your company shortly keep, /*
> *To sleep with you in beds of dust so still and dark /*
> *Till that blest morn we trust in God no more to par_."*

The first line is carved in shadow. Note the location of the apostrophe in the second line of the poem.

Howland, Anna C.   *"ANNA C. / Wife of / James M. Howland, / Died Oct. 12, 1859; / Aged 37 years. / Blessed are the dead, / that die in the Lord."*
"A. C. H." is inscribed on the footstone.

Howland, Bathshaba   *"In memory of / Bathshaba daug^h- / ter of M^r, Rufus / & M^rs, Bathsheba / Howland she died / Sep^t, 24th, 1791. / in ye 5 ^th, Year of / her age."* A rising sun is carved at the top of this small slate stone. A "d" has been ground down immediately after the name Bathshaba as if the carver had forgotten the space between Bathshaba and daughter. The *h-* is carved directly above the *g* in the second line as the carver ran out of room.
"1791" is inscribed on this broken footstone which is located between her headstone and that of Pardon Howland.

Howland, Bathsheba   *"In Memory of Mrs. Bathshe- / ba, wife of Mr. Rufus Howland / & Dau^tr. of Capt. William Canedy / died April 29th, Æ^t. 56 Year. /*

> *Here lies in silent dust. /*
> *The partner of my joys; /*
> *Her Spirit is with the just /*
> *In more subblime employs. /*
> *Snach't from her loving mate, /*
> *When far advanc'd in life: / ..."*

The rest of the poem is buried in the cement base. An urn and willow are carved at the top. Floral designs are carved on either side. A rope border is carved down the sides. Note the spelling of *subblime*. This slate stone had been broken in the lower right corner and successfully repaired. On the back of this stone is inscribed *"$10"*. Thatcher lists her as Bathsheba Canedy, with her death day as April 20th.

Howland, Benjamin F.   *"In memory of / BENJ. F. / Son of / Jedediah & Susan T. / HOWLAND. / Born Oct. 18, 1833. / Died / Dec. 27, 1862. /*

Many are the hearts that
Mourn his absence.
Erected by his sister Susan."

A veteran's marker and flag are present.

Howland, Charles   *"In memory of / MR. CHARLES HOWLAND, / who died / Aug 8, 1851; / aged 29 yrs. 9 mos. / & 4 ds. /*
> *Oh it is hard to part with one,*
> *We loved so much on earth;*
> *But we will put our trust in him,*
> *Who gave his spirit birth."*

Howland, Charles R.   *"CHARLES R. / Son of / James M. & Anna C. / Howland, / Died June 15, 1853; / Aged 2 yrs. 9 mos. / and 28 days."*
"C. R. H." is inscribed on the footstone.

Howland, Charles R.   *"CHARLES R. HOWLAND / Son of / J. M. & A. C. / Howland, / Died Dec. 19, 1859; / Aged 3 months / and 19 days."* The first line is carved along an arch on this small stone.
"C. R. H." is inscribed on the footstone.

Howland, Chester   See George Howland Stone entry.
Swansea Vital Records show that Chester was born on April 20, 1883, and died on October 24, 1883.

Howland, Florence   *"MOTHER / FLORENCE C. HOWLAND / Born / Aug 25, 1855, / Died Mar. 16, 1900."* The first two lines are carved along an arch, with the first line also carved in relief. There are sculptured scrolls carved at the top of this stone. It shares its base with that of her husband, Lyman Howland. Two cracks are extending up from the bottom.

Howland, George W. Stone   *"GEORGE W. HOWLAND / 1854 – 1888 / SON CHESTER 6 MOS."* is inscribed on this flat, lichen encrusted, ground level stone.

Howland, Harison   *"IN MEMORY / OF / HARISON / son of / Capt. Seth & Abigail / Howland, / who died Nov. 24, / 1838, / Aged 19 years /*
> *Beneath these clods in silent dust,*
> *I sleep where all the living must*
> *Tho joyest with the fairest face*
> *Must shortly lie in this dark place."*

The first line is carved along an arch, and the last line before the poem is carved in a reverse arch. The third line of this stone is carved in outline. The last three lines are buried underground. Note the spelling of *joyest.*
"H. H." is inscribed on the footstone.

Howland, Harrison   *"HARRISON, / son of / Jephthah A. & Ruth / Howland, / Died Oct. 8, 1844; / Aged 1 Yr. 6 Mos. 8 days."* is inscribed on this stone.

Howland, Hope   *"In Memory of Mrs. / HOPE wife of Mr. / Samuel Howland died / Sep.^t 11th AD. 1808. In the / 36th Year of her Age /*
> *Beneath the dust my partner lies*

Secure from all care and strife,
Released from the busy ties,
Of this distresed life"

A willow is carved at top of this slate stone. The first three words are slanted to the left. The words of the poem slant to the right. Note the spelling of *distresed*.

"Mr_ / Hope / Howland" is inscribed on her slate footstone, which is broken into three pieces. These pieces are located on the ground behind her headstone.

Howland, Irean B. "IREAN B. / daughter of / Jephthah A. & Ruth / Howland, / died Sept. 9, 1850; / aged 2 Yrs. 1 Mo. 6 days." The first line is carved in shadow.

Howland, Irene A. "SISTER / IRENE A. / DAUGHTER OF / JAMES M. & ROSENIA J. / HOWLAND / 1872 – 1890 / "We Loved her"" The first line is carved in shallow relief. A floral design is carved on the left side of this monument.

Howland, Irene R. "ERECTED / to the memory of / IRENE R. / daughter of / Jedediah & Susan Howland / who departed this life / Sept 19, 1850; / Aged 20 yrs. 10 mo's & 2 d's /   Friend after friend departs,
            Who hath not lost a friend;
            There is union here of heart,
            That finds not here an end."

This lichen encrusted stone is broken off at ground level, and is lying face up on the ground.

"I. R. H." is inscribed on the footstone.

Howland, James M. "JAMES M. HOWLAND / BORN FEB. 21, 1816 / DIED FEB. 25, 1901" Leaves are carved in shallow relief in the upper corners of this slanted stone.

Howland, James M. "H (monogram) / OUR BROTHER / JAMES M. HOWLAND / 1874 – 1921" is inscribed on this lichen encrusted monument. Ivy and oak leaves are carved in shallow relief on either side of the monogram which is also carved in shallow relief.

Howland, James M. Jr. "JAMES M. JR. / Son of / James M. & Anna C. / Howland, / Died Nov. 27, 1864; / Aged 16 yrs. 5 mos. / and 11 days. / Though lost to sight / to memory dear."

Howland, Jedediah "SACRED / to the memory of / JEDEDIAH HOWLAND / who died / May 28, 1847. / Aged 59 yrs. & 9 mo's. / Sorrow bids us weep / Hope wipes the tear away."

"J. H." is inscribed on the footstone.

Howland, Jeptha A. "JEPTHA A. HOWLAND. / BORN DEC. 1, 1814, / DIED DEC. 17, 1878. / Asleep in Jesus! blessed sleep." There are leaf carvings at the top of this stone.

Howland, Joanna "Miss Joanna Da^{tr} of Mr. / George Howland died / Dec. 2^{d} 1806, Ag'd 15 Years. / Dear youth O may you bear in mind,
            That death the way to you will find;
            Leave firey gusts & seek that shade.

Where youth will bloom & never fade."

A willow is carved above the inscription on this lichen encrusted, slate stone. Note the spelling of *firey.*

"J.__ / 1806" The upper right corner of this slate footstone has exfoliated.

Howland, Joseph L.   *"JOSEPH L. / Son of / James M. & Anna C. / HOWLAND, / Died Mar. 12, 1877; / Aged 22 yrs. 4 mos. /*

> *Dearest Brother thou hast left us*
> *Here, thy loss we deeply feel,*
> *But 'tis God that hath bereft us,*
> *He can all our sorrows heal."*

"J. L. H." is inscribed on the footstone.

Howland, Joshua   *"In Memory of / Mr. JOSHUA HOWLAND, / who died Apl. 11,*
1821: / Æt. 61. /

> *Adieu my friends, a long and sad farewell,*
> *A sene more solemn than the passing bell;*
> *I hope with God in glory I shall bloom,*
> *Where sorrow, sickness, death, can never come.*
> *Consoling thought! dear children dry your tears,*
> *Your friend has gone beyond your anxious fears;*
> *Weep not for me prepare without delay.*
> *To meet that debt you all must shortly pay."*

Note the spelling of the word scene in the second line of the poem. An urn and willow are carved on the top of this slate stone, and columns are carved on the sides of the stone. A flag is present. Note the spelling of *sene.*

Howland, Katharine   *"In MEMORY of / Katharine wife of Mr. Isaac / Howland*
she died Dec. 6ᵗʰ / 1789 in yᵉ 57 yr. of her age /

> *Altho' I am sleeping in the clay*
> *Think on yourselves don't mᵒurn for me,*
> *I hope if God your souls will save*
> *To meet once more beyond the grave"*

This lichen encrusted, slate stone is difficult to read. A carving is present above the inscription, but the lichen hides it.

"Mʳˢ / Katharine / Howland / 1789" is inscribed on the slate footstone. It is located about 14 feet behind and to the left of her headstone.

Howland, Leroy R.   *"HOWLAND"* is inscribed in shallow relief on the top horizontal surface of this monument.   *"LEROY R. / SON OF / LYMAN B. & / FLORENCE C. / JULY 11, 1894 / JAN 30, 1911"* is inscribed on the front. Lichen is growing on the inscriptions.

Howland, Lurana H.   See William Baker Monument entry.

Lakeville Vital Records indicate that she was the daughter of William and Lurana Baker, and the widow of James M. Howland.

Howland, Lyman B.   *"FATHER / LYMAN B. HOWLAND / Born / Dec 1, 1853, / Died Jan. 27, 1903."* The first two lines are carved along an arch, with the first line also carved in relief. There are sculptured scrolls carved on the top of this stone. It shares its base with that of his wife, Florence Howland. His first wife Hannah W.

(Canedy) Howland and their daughter Annie are buried in McCully Cemetery.

Howland, Melissa D.   *"MELISSA DEAN / Daughter of / CAPT. SETH & PHILENA R. / HOWLAND, / Born Sept. 30, 1832. / Died / Sept. 9, 1854. / Though lost to sight to memory de__."* The right side is chipped near the last line. *"M. D. H."* is inscribed on the footstone.

Howland, Oscar V.   *"HOWLAND / OSCAR V. / Nov. 22, 1884 / Nov. 22, 1963"* Flowers are carved at the top of this stone. A Barnicoat Monuments metal tag is present.

Howland, Pardon   *"Pardon Son of M_ / Rufus M^{rs}. Bathsh^a. / Howland he die_ / Aug 24 th 179_ / in y^e 3^d year of hi_ ___"* There is a rising sun carving at the top. This small slate stone is both broken and exfoliating on the right side. Thatcher lists his mother as Bathsheba, and his death year as 1796.

Howland, Phebe   *"In memory of / M^{rs}. Phebe wife of M^r. / Joshua Howland who / died April 11th 1787 in / ye 28th year of her age. /*

> *Tis God that lifts our co^mforts high,*
> *Or sinks them in a grave*
> *He gives and blessed be his name*
> *He takes but what he gave."*

A rising sun is carved at the top of this slate stone.
"M^{rs}. Phebe / Howland" is inscribed on the footstone.

Howland, Philena R.   *"PHILENA R. / Wife of / SETH HOWLAND, / BORN / DEC. 17, 1802, / DIED / May 21, 1878."* The first line is carved in relief along an arch.

Howland, Polly   *"Polly Daugher __ / Mr. Samuel & Mrs. / Hope Howland / __e died Dec. 26th.____ / ____Year of her Age."* A rising sun is carved at the top. This small slate stone is exfoliating. Note the spelling for *Daugher*. Thatcher does not have an entry for her and her death year and age unknown.

Howland, Roby   *"In memory of / ROBY, / dau. of Mr. Malachi & / Mrs. Katurah Howland, / who died / May 13, 1850; / aged 20 years."*

Howland, Rosania J.   *"ROSANIA J. / Wife of / James M. Howland / died June 21, 1877, / Aged 33 yrs. 6 m. /*

Mourn not for the departed one.
For she is now at rest
In her bright home in heaven above
Prepared for all the blest."

"*R. J. H.*" is inscribed on the footstone.

Howland, Ruth   "*Miss. Ruth Da.ʳ of Mr. / George Howland, she died / Nov 30ᵗʰ, 1806. Ag'd 23 Years. / My mourning friends yᵣ tears adieu*
I'm gone & you must follow too;
Keep death familier to yᵣ fight, / ..."
A willow is carved at the top of this slate stone. The rest of this poem is buried in the cement base. Note the spelling of *familier* in the poem.
"*R. H. / 1806."* is inscribed on this slate footstone.

Howland, Seth, Capt.   "*CAPT. / SETH HOWLAND / BORN / July 24, 1789, / DIED / Dec. 23, 1872."*   The second line is carved in relief along an arch. "*HARRINGTON*" is inscribed at the center bottom of the stone.
"*S. H.*" is inscribed on the footstone. The inscribed letters are below ground.

Howland, Shubill G.   "*In memory of / SHUBILL G. / Son of / Jedediah & Susan T. / HOWLAND. / Born June 7, 1818. / Died / March 24, 1867. / Our Brother / Erected by his sister Susan."*   *Massachusetts Civil War Soldiers and Sailors, 1861-1865,* Vol. I, pp. 169 and 439 shows that he enlisted in 1863, and served with the 3ʳᵈ Mass. Infantry, Co. A, and the 4ᵗʰ Mass Calvary, Co B. His name is spelled "Shubael G." in this reference.
"*S. G. H.*" is inscribed on the footstone. It is leaning against the south stone wall.

Howland, Susan T.   "*SACRED / to the memory of / SUSAN T. / Wife of / JEDEDIAH HOWLAND / who died / Feb. 11, 1887, / Aged 93 yrs. 6 mos. / & 19 days. / A tender Mother and faithful friend"*
"*S. T. H.*" is inscribed on the footstone.

Howland, Vera F.   "*VERA F. / Dau of / Lyman B & / Florence Howland / May 26, 1899. / Aug. 1, 1900."*   The first line on this stone is inscribed along an arch. This small stone is lying face up on the ground.

Parry, Herman O.   "*HERMAN O. PARRY / 1915 – 1991"*   There is a carving of a cross, a book and flowers on the left side of this flat, ground level stone.

Parry, Hiram E. Monument   "*HIRAM E. PARRY / 1877 – 1948 / WILHELMINA / WIFE OF / HIRAM E. PARRY / 1879 – 1916"*

Parry, Mary H.   "*MARY H. PARRY / 1919 – 1979 / WIFE OF / HERMAN O. PARRY"*   There is a carving of a cross, an open book, flowers, and a rosary on the left side of this flat, ground level stone.

Parry, Wilhelmina   See Hiram Parry Monument entry.

Partington, Rosena   "*ROSENA J. PARTINGTON / DAUGHTER OF / JAMES AND ROSENA HOWLAND / BORN SEPT. 1, 1868 / DIED SEPT. 12, 1960 / AGE 92 YEARS, 12 DAYS"* "*PERPETUAL CARE"* is inscribed at the bottom center. There are floral designs carved in the upper corners. The first line is carved along an arch.

Peirce, Albert T.   *"SON"* is carved in relief on the top curved surface of this stone. *"ALBERT T. PEIRCE, / 1856 – 1858."* is inscribed on the front. The first line is carved along an arch. This stone had been broken in half below the last line and successfully repaired.

Peirce, Edmund   *"In Memory of / MR.EDMUND PEIRCE, / died Nov. 25, 1823, /*
Æt. 47. /   *His mind was tranquil & serene,*
                  No terrours in his looks were seen,
                  His saviours smiles dispell'd the gloom,
                  And smooth'd his passage to the tomb."

An urn and willow are carved at the top of this slate stone. A curved design is carved as a border halfway down the sides. A second urn and willow carved in a different style are on the back of this stone. The inscription below it has been chiseled off. Note the spelling of *terrours*.

Peirce, Edmund H.   *"FATHER"* is carved in relief on the top curved surface of this stone. *"EDMUND H. PEIRCE, / 1831 – 1884."* is inscribed on the front. The first line is carved along an arch. A veteran's marker and flag are present.

Peirce, M. Margaret   *"MOTHER"* is carved in relief on the top curved surface of this stone. *"M. MARGARET PEIRCE, / 1840 – 1896."* is inscribed on the front. The first line is carved along an arch.

Peirce, Mary H.   *"MARY H. / Dtr. of Edmund & / Welthy Peirce, / died Sep. 2,*
1823, / Æt. 21. /   *Clos'd is the eye of youthfull mirth,*
                  A parent's fondest hopes are fled;
                  Scarce done rejoicing at her birth,
                  E're we must place her with the dead."

An urn and willow are carved at the top of this slate stone. A curved design is carved as a border halfway down the sides. This stone was broken diagonally through the carving and successfully repaired. Note the spelling of *youthfull*.
"M. H. P. / 1823." is inscribed on the slate footstone.

Peirce, Sarah   *"SARAH, / Daught. of Edmund & / Welthy Peirce, / died Nov. 12,*
1832, / Æt. 20. /   *Belov'd in life, she much lamented fell,*
                  And went to rest where saints immortal dwell.
                  Come to my grave my mother dear,
                  Your daughter's dust lies buried here,
                  And when for me you sigh & cry,
                  Remember you are born to die."

There is an urn and willow carving at the top of this slate stone. A curved design is carved as a border halfway down the side.
"S. P. / 1832." is inscribed on this slate footstone. It has been broken in two places and successfully repaired.

Peirce, W. Winifred   *"DAUGHTER"* is carved in relief on the top curved surface of this stone. *"W. WINIFRED PEIRCE / 1858 – 1909."* is inscribed on the front. The first line is carved along an arch. This stone was broken in half through the date line, and successfully repaired.

Sears, Earl   *"In Memory of / MR. / EARL SEARS / who died Jan. 10, / 1842. /*
aged 80 years. /   *The second Adam shall restore*
                          The ruins of the first:
                          Hosanna to that sov'reign power,
                          That new creates our dust."

The first line is carved along an arch and the sixth line is carved along an inverted arch. The second line is carved in outline, and the third line is carved in relief.
"E. S." is inscribed on the footstone. It is lying face up on the ground.

Sears, Judith   *"In memory of / Mrs. / JUDITH. / wife of Earl Sears, / who died*
July 20, / 1846. / aged 91 years. /
                          Jesus, I give my spirit up
                          And trust it in thy hand
                          My dying flesh shall rest in peace
                          And rise at thy..."

The first line is carved along an arch, and the seventh line is carved along an inverted arch. The third line is carved in relief. This stone was broken off and then reburied behind the lower remnant, thus burying the rest of the poem.
"J. S." is inscribed on the footstone.

Terry, Bashabe   *"BASHABE, / Daughter of / Zebedee & Eliza / TERRY, / Died*
Jan. 21, 1832, / Aged / 2 Years."   There is a stone post and metal rail fence surrounding her grave and that of her parents, Zebedee and Eliza Terry. Thatcher lists her age as 12 years.
"B. T." is inscribed on the footstone.

Terry, Eliza   *"ELIZA. / wife of / Zebedee Terry, / died Oct. 14, 1860, / Aged 55*
years."   There is a broken flower and leaf carving at the top of her stone. A stone post and metal rail fence surrounds her grave and that of her husband, Zebedee, and daughter, Bashabe.
"E. T." is inscribed on the footstone.

Terry, Simeon   *"SIMEON TERRY. / Died / May 13, 1880; / Aged 65 years / And 1*
Day."   The first line is carved in relief.
"S. T." is inscribed on the footstone.

Terry, Zebedee   *"ZEBEDEE TERRY. / Died / OCT. 30, 1872, / Aged / 66 years."*

There is a stone post and metal rail fence surrounding his grave and that of his wife, Eliza, and daughter, Bashabe.
"Z. T." is inscribed on the footstone.

Tucker, Elmer E.   See Ida Tucker Stone entry.
Taunton Vital Records list his birth on July 8, 1895.

Tucker, Ida M. Stone   *"IDA M. TUCKER / 1866 – 1920 / SON ELMER E."* is inscribed on this flat, 0-1 inch high marker. Her maiden name was Howland.

Additional Notes:

Thatcher also lists: "Howland, Deborah, wife of George, Oct. 27, 1820, age 63 yrs."

The cemetery cards at the Lakeville Town Hall list only: " ____, Deborah George d. Oct. 27___ broken stone." No stone was found for this person in 2000.

Howland Cemetery Map Index

Alphabetical:

Ashley, Alonzo (1870-1911) – 57
Ashley, Ernest A. (1894-1965) – 38
Ashley, Jennie G. (1908-1988) – 39
Ashley, Malcolm G. (1921-1990) – 37
Ashley, Pauline A. (1938-____) – 40
Ashley, Thomas M. (1936-2000) – 40
Baker, Abisha R. (1807-1891) – 88
Baker, Betsey B. (1809-1884) – 88
Baker, Judith H. (~1803-1880) – 78
Baker, Lurana (~1801-1877) – 81
Baker, Mary H. (1845-1912) – 88
Baker, Phebe (~1802-1838) – 80
Baker, Samuel, Capt. (~1778-1851) – 72
Baker, Simeon (~1803-1880) – 77
Baker, Simeon D. (~1833-1846) – 79
Baker, Welthy (~1765-1860) – 73
Baker, William (~1804-1876) – 81
Baker, William W. (1836-1890) – 87, 88
Burgess, James A. (1876-1942) – 36
Cummings, Alonzo (1850) – 26
Cummings, Flora A. (1862-1864) – 23
Cummings, Herbert (1851-1852) – 24
Cummings, Joseph (1824-1866) – 22, 27
Cummings, Joseph L. (1848-1849) – 25, 29
Cummings, Susan T. (1825-1904) – 21
Dean, Deborah (1782-1850) – 71
Father (no dates) – 85

Faulkner, Leonard A. (1937-1997) – 82
Goff, Susan C. (1896-1927) – 30
H., L. B. (no dates) – 35
Howland, Abigail (~1789-1824) – 10
Howland, Amelia V. (1845-1851) – 6
Howland, Anna C. (~1822-1859) – 48
Howland, Bathshaba (~1787-1791) – 63
Howland, Bathsheba (~1754-1810) – 60
Howland, Benjamin (1833-1862) – 52
Howland, Charles (1821-1851) – 20
Howland, Charles R. (1850-1853) – 45
Howland, Charles R. (1859) – 46
Howland, Chester (1883) – 65
Howland, Florence (1855-1900) – 32
Howland, George W. (1854-1888) – 65
Howland, Harrison (~1819-1838) – 11
Howland, Harrison (1843-1844) – 4
Howland, Hope (~1773-1808) – 59
Howland, Irean B. (1848-1850) – 5
Howland, Irene A. (1872-1890) – 54
Howland, Irene R. (1829-1850) – 44
Howland, James M. (1816-1901) – 47
Howland, James M. (1874-1921) – 55
Howland, James M. Jr. (1848-1864) – 50
Howland, Jedediah (1787-1847) – 42
Howland, Jeptha A. (1814-1878) – 3
Howland, Joanna (~1791-1806) – 69

Howland, Joseph L. (1854-1877) – 51
Howland, Joshua (~1760-1821) – 7
Howland, Katherine (~1733-1789) – 67, 70
Howland, Leroy R. (1894-1911) – 33
Howland, Lurana H. (1837-1904) – 81
Howland, Lyman B. (1853-1903) – 32
Howland, Melissa (1832-1854) – 2
Howland, Oscar V. (1884-1963) – 34
Howland, Pardon (~1794-1796) – 64
Howland, Phebe (~1760-1787) – 8
Howland, Philena R. (1802-1878) – 1
Howland, Roby (~1830-1850) – 19
Howland, Polly (no readable dates) – 58
Howland, Rosania J. (1843-1877) – 49
Howland, Ruth (~1783-1806) – 68
Howland, Seth, Capt. (1789-1872) – 9
Howland, Shubill G. (1818-1867) – 31, 53
Howland, Susan T. (1793-1887) – 43
Howland, Vera F. (1899-1900) – 28
Parry, Herman O. (1915-1991) – 83

Parry, Hiram E. (1877-1948) – 86
Parry, Mary H. (1919-1979) – 84
Parry, Wilhelmina (1879-1916) – 86
Partington, Rosena (1868-1960) – 56
Peirce, Albert T. (1856-1858) – 15
Peirce, Edmund (~1776-1823) – 18
Peirce, Edmund H. (1831-1884) – 12
Peirce, M. Margaret (1840-1896) – 13
Peirce, Mary H. (~1802-1823) – 17
Peirce, Sarah (~1812-1832) – 16
Peirce, W. Winifred (1858-1909) – 14
Sears, Earl (~1762-1842) – 61
Sears, Judith (~1755-1846) – 62
Terry, Bashabe (~1830-1832) – 74
Terry, Eliza (~1805-1860) – 76
Terry, Simeon (1815-1880) – 41
Terry, Zebedee (~1806-1872) – 75
Tucker, Elmer E. (1896-____) – 66
Tucker, Ida M. (1866-1920) – 66

By Location:

1 – Howland, Philena R. (1802-1878)
2 – Howland, Melissa (1832-1854)
3 – Howland, Jeptha A. (1814-1878)
4 – Howland, Harrison (1843-1844)
5 – Howland, Irean B. (1848-1850)
6 – Howland, Amelia V. (1845-1851)
7 – Howland, Joshua (~1760-1821)
8 – Howland, Phebe (~1760-1787)
9 – Howland, Seth, Capt. (1789-1872)
10 – Howland, Abigail (~1789-1824)
11 – Howland, Harison (~1819-1838)
12 – Peirce, Edmund H. (1831-1884)
13 – Peirce, M. Margaret (1840-1896)
14 – Peirce, W. Winifred (1858-1909)
15 – Peirce, Albert T. (1856-1858)
16 – Peirce, Sarah (~1812-1832)
17 – Peirce, Mary H. (~1802-1823)
18 – Peirce, Edmund (~1776-1823)
19 – Howland, Roby (~1830-1850)
20 – Howland, Charles (1821-1851)
21 – Cummings, Susan T. (1825-1904)
22 – Cummings, Joseph (1824-1866)
23 – Cummings, Flora A. (1862-1864)
24 – Cummings, Herbert (1851-1852)
25 – Cummings, Joseph L. (1848-1849)
26 – Cummings, Alonzo C. (1850)
27 – Cummings, Joseph (1824-1866)
28 – Howland, Vera F. (1899-1900)

29 – Cummings, Joseph L. (1848-1849)
30 – Goff, Susan C. (1896-1927)
31 – Howland, Shubill G. (1818-1867)
32 – Howland, Florence (1855-1900)
32 – Howland, Lyman B. (1853-1903)
33 – Howland, Leroy R. (1894-1911)
34 – Howland, Oscar V. (1884-1963)
35 – H., L. B. (no dates)
36 – Burgess, James A. (1876-1942)
37 – Ashley, Malcolm G. (1921-1990)
38 – Ashley, Ernest A. (1894-1965)
39 – Ashley, Jennie G. (1908-1988)
40 – Ashley, Thomas M. (1936-2000)
      Ashley, Pauline A. (1938-____)
41 – Terry. Simeon (1815-1880)
42 – Howland, Jedediah (1787-1847)
43 – Howland, Susan T. (1793-1887)
44 – Howland, Irene R. (1829-1850)
45 – Howland, Charles R. (1850-1853)
46 – Howland, Charles R. (1859)
47 – Howland, James M. (1816-1901)
48 – Howland, Anna C. (~1822-1859)
49 – Howland, Rosania J. (1843-1877)
50 – Howland, James M. Jr. (1848-1864)
51 – Howland, Joseph L. (1854-1877)
52 – Howland, Benjamin (1833-1862)
53 – Howland, Shubill G. (1818-1867)
54 – Howland, Irene A. (1872-1890)

55 – Howland, James M. (1874-1921)
56 – Partington, Rosena (1868-1960)
57 – Ashley, Alonzo (1870-1911)
58 – Howland, Polly (no readable dates)
59 – Howland, Hope (~1773-1808)
60 – Howland, Bathsheba (~1754-1810)
61 – Sears, Earl (~1762-1842)
62 – Sears, Judith (~1755-1846)
63 – Howland, Bathshaba (~1787-1791)
64 – Howland, Pardon (~1794-1796)
65 – Howland, George W. (1854-1888)
    Howland, Chester (1883)
66 – Tucker, Ida M. (1866-1920)
    Tucker, Elmer E. (1896-____)
67 – Howland, Katherine (~1733-1789)
68 – Howland, Ruth (~1783-1806)
69 – Howland, Joanna (~1791-1806)
70 – Howland, Katherine (~1733-1789)
71 – Dean, Deborah (1782-1850)
72 – Baker, Capt. Samuel (~1778-1851)
73 – Baker, Welthy (~1765-1860)

74 – Terry, Bashabe (~1830-1832)
75 – Terry, Zebedee (~1806-1872)
76 – Terry, Eliza (~1805-1860)
77 – Baker, Simeon (~1803-1880)
78 – Baker, Judith H. (~1803-1880)
79 – Baker, Simeon D. (~1833-1846)
80 – Baker, Phebe (~1802-1838)
81 – Baker, William (~1804-1876)
    Baker, Lurana (~1801-1877)
    Howland, Lurana H. (1837-1904)
82 – Faulkner, Leonard A. (1937-1997)
83 – Parry, Herman O. (1915-1991)
84 – Parry, Mary H. (1919-1979)
85 – Father (no dates)
86 – Parry, Hiram E. (1877-1948)
    Parry, Wilhelmina (1879-1916)
87 – Baker, William W. (1836-1890)
88 – Baker, Abisha R. (1807-1891)
    Baker, William W. (1836-1890)
    Baker, Betsey B. (1809-1884)
    Baker, Mary H. (1845-1912)

Edmund Pierce stone, front and back

Howland Cemetery Map

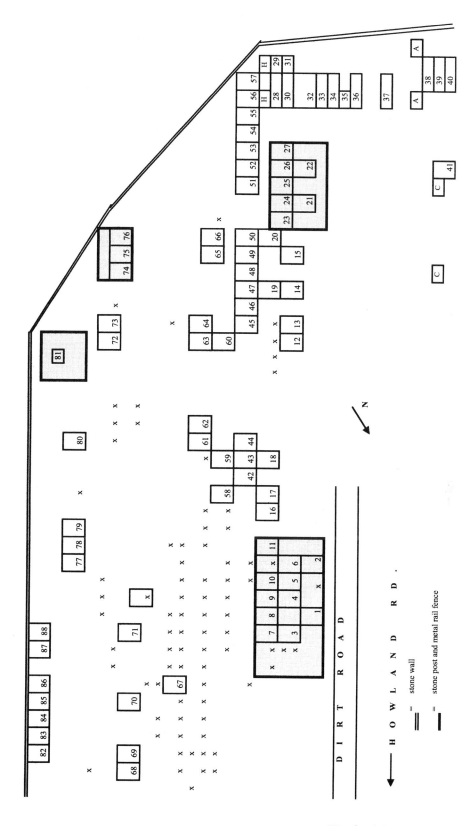

Chapter 11
Indian Shore Cemetery

Indian Shore Cemetery is located north of Betty's Neck Road within town owned property. It is located near the former home of the Mitchell family, the lineal descendants of Chief Tuspaquin. No fencing or sign exist for this cemetery, and its borders cannot be determined. The only stones present are leaning against a tree making even their grave locations impossible to determine. A former resident of the area stated that fieldstones used to mark other Indian graves, but were removed long ago. Gravestones present are dated 1872 and 1875. Thatcher refers to this cemetery as "Graves on Betty's Neck." Entries were recorded April 28, 2000.

Smith, Thomas N. *"Thomas N. Smith / died / March 7, 1872, / Aged 62 years. /*
Mourn not for me, my friends so dear,
Although in death I slumber here;
My days are past my grave you see.
Therefore prepare to follow me."
"T. N. S." is inscribed on the footstone. These stones are leaning against a tree.

Smith, William *"William Smith, / died Feb. 17, 1875, / Aged 61 years."*
"W. S." is inscribed on the footstone. These stones are leaning against a tree.

Additional Notes:

Thatcher also lists the following people as buried here, but their stones were not found:
"Lang, Patty, an indian woman, died previous to 1850"
"Rosier, John, an indian, drowned in Assampsett Pond Feb. 1851, age 57 years, 4 mos."

"Sassamon: A grave on bank of the Pond in the same vicinity, probable that of John Sassamon the first indian missionary – was murdered and pushed under the ice Jan. 29th, 1675."

He also states, "There are a few other unknown graves in this locality."

Thomas Weston's *History of the Town of Middleboro Massachusetts,* p. 17, lists Sassamon's ".... grave is supposed to be in an old Indian burial-ground on the southern shore of Assawompset Pond."

Lang, Patty (d. before 1850)   Smith, Thomas N. (~1810-1872)
Rosier, John (1793-1851)   Smith, William (~1814-1875)
Sassamon (d. 1675)

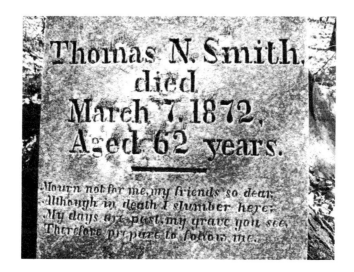

Thomas N. Smith inscription

Chapter 12
Keith Cemetery

Keith Cemetery is located on the south side of County Street, just east of Pierce Avenue. It is surrounded on three sides by a beautiful stone wall. A stone post and metal rail fence forms border along the street. The entrance faces the street, and the sign is in good repair. Gravestones face the center aisle, and date from 1847 to 1977. The Lakeville Assessor's Office lists the cemetery as town owned, 2520 square feet in size. Thatcher calls this a "Cemetery near Canady's Corner on County Road." Entries were recorded April 14, 2000.

Clark, Chloe   *"CHLOE CLARK / Wife of / SAMUEL S. CLARK. / Died Sept. 20, 1863. / In her 77ᵗʰ year. / Shed not for her the bitter tear,*
                   Nor give the heart to vain regret,
                   'Tis but the casket that lies here,
                   The gem that filled it sparkles yet."
The first line is carved in relief along an arch.

Clark, Chloe C.   *"CHLOE C. CLARK / JUNE 18, 1818, / AUG. 20, 1847."* The first line is carved along an arch.

Clark, Samuel S.   *"SAMUEL S. CLARK / DIED / MARCH 14, 1850. / in his 64,*
year. /   *Although his earthly sun has set,*
                       Its light shall linger round us yet,
                       Pure --- radiant --- blest!"
"H. Cobb, F. R." is inscribed on the bottom center. The first line on this textured stone is carved in relief along an arch.

Clark, Stephen C.   *"STEPHEN C. CLARK, / Died / March 8, 1855. / Aged / 28 years. / Not lost but gone before."*

Keith, Alfraetta C.   See Weston E. Keith Monument entry.

Keith, Bethia S.   See Franklin C. Keith Monument entry.
"BETHIA" is inscribed on a small, flat stone, which is located about 2 feet in front of the monument, on the far right.

Keith, Calvin R.   *"CALVIN R."* is carved in relief on the top slanted surface of this small stone. *"FEB. 17, 1846. / APR. 26, 1849."* is inscribed on the front of the stone. *"Son of / Joseph W. & / Judith Keith."* is inscribed on the back of the stone.

Keith, Doris E.   *"DORIS EVELYN KEITH / DAU. OF / W. E. & A. C. KEITH / AUG. 14, 1905. / MAY 13, 1910."* The first line is carved along an arch. Ivy is carved in shallow relief at the top of this small monument.

Keith, Franklin C. Monument   *"KEITH"* is carved in relief on the top slanted surface of this monument. *"FRANKLIN C. KEITH / JULY 7, 1844 – MAY 7, 1907 / JANE A. HIS WIFE / APR. 7, 1848 – MAY 3, 1935 / BETHIA S. / 1884 – 1956 / RUSSELL D. THEIR SON / MAR. 20, 1866 – DEC. 27, 1868"* is inscribed on the front.

Keith, Gertrude E.   *"GERTRUDE EVELYN KEITH / DAU. OF / W. E. & A. C. KEITH / SEPT. 6, 1889, / JULY 23, 1903."* The first line is carved along an arch. Ivy leaves are carved at the top of this small monument.

Keith, Grace E.   See Weston E. Keith Monument entry.
"GRACE" is inscribed on this flat, ground level cement block which is located to the right of the monument.

Keith, Jane A.   See Franklin C. Keith Monument entry.

Keith, Joseph W.   *"FATHER"* is carved in relief on the top slanted surface of the monument. *"JOSEPH W. KEITH / MAY 21, 1797. / APR. 29, 1870"* is inscribed on the front.

Keith, Judith   *"MOTHER"* is carved in relief on the top slanted surface of the monument. *"JUDITH, / WIFE OF / JOSEPH W. KEITH / JANY. 21, 1814 / APRIL 4, 1897"* is inscribed on the front.

Keith, Russell D.   See Franklin C. Keith Monument entry.
"RUSSELL D." is carved in relief on the top slanted surface of this small stone. *"MAR. 20, 1866, / DEC. 27, 1868."* is inscribed on the front. *"Son of / Franklin C. & / Jane A. Keith."* is inscribed on the back.

Keith, Weston E. Monument   *"K (monogram) / KEITH / 1867 WESTON E. 1948 / HIS WIFE / 1868 ALFRAETTA C. 1943 / 1888 GRACE E. 1962"* Leaves are carved in shallow relief on either side of the monogram at the top of the monument.

Simms, Gladys W.   See Harry Simms Monument entry.

Simms, Harry C. Monument   *"SIMMS"* is inscribed at the top of this slanted monument, underneath floral carvings. *"HARRY C. / 1887 1958"* is inscribed on the bottom left, and *"GLADYS W. / 1892 1966"* is inscribed on the bottom right.

Simms, Milton E.   *"MILTON E.SIMMS / 1913 – 1977 / IN LOVING MEMORY"* There are floral carvings in the upper corners of this slanted monument.

Keith Cemetery Index and Map

Alphabetical:

Clark, Chloe (~1787-1863) – 14
Clark, Chloe C. (1818-1847) – 16
Clark, Samuel S. (~1787-1850) – 15
Clark, Stephen C. (~1827-1855) – 10
Keith, Alfraetta C. (1868-1943) – 11
Keith, Bethia S. (1884-1956) – 8, 9
Keith, Calvin R. (1846-1849) – 5
Keith, Doris E. (1905-1910) – 2
Keith, Franklin C. (1844-1907) – 8
Keith, Gertrude E. (1889-1903) – 1
Keith, Grace E. (1888-1962) – 3, 4
Keith, Jane A. (1848-1935) – 8
Keith, Joseph W. (1797-1870) – 11
Keith, Judith (1814-1897) – 10
Keith, Russell D. (1866-1868) – 7, 8
Keith, Weston E. (1867-1948) – 3
Simms, Harry C. (1887-1958) – 6
Simms, Gladys W. (1892-1966) – 6
Simms, Milton E. (1913-1977) – 5

By Location:

1 – Keith, Gertrude E. (1889-1903)
2 – Keith, Doris E. (1905-1910)
3 – Keith, Weston E. (1867-1948)
    Keith, Alfraetta C. (1868-1943)
    Keith, Grace E. (1888-1962)
4 – Keith, Grace E. (1888-1962)
5 – Simms, Milton E. (1913-1977)
6 – Simms, Harry C. (1887-1958)
    Simms, Gladys W. (1892-1966)
7 – Keith, Russell D. (1866-1868)
8 – Keith, Franklin C. (1844-1907)
    Keith, Jane A. (1848-1935)
    Keith, Bethia S. (1884-1956)
    Keith, Russell D. (1866-1868)
9 – Keith, Bethia S. (1884-1956)
10 – Keith, Judith (1814-1897)
11 – Keith, Joseph W. (1797-1870)
12 – Keith, Calvin R. (1846-1849)
13 – Clark, Stephen C. (~1827-1855)
14 – Clark, Chloe (~1787-1863)
15 – Clark, Samuel S. (~1787-1850)
16 – Clark, Chloe C. (1818-1847)

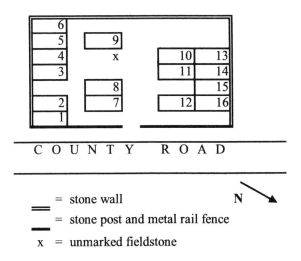

C O U N T Y   R O A D

___ = stone wall   N

▬▬ = stone post and metal rail fence

x = unmarked fieldstone

Chapter 13
Lang Cemetery

Lang Cemetery is located just south of 1 Lang Street. It is surrounded by a stone wall, except for a section along the street where a stone post and metal rail fence forms the border. The sign and two gates face Lang Street. An additional entrance is on the right side, near the rear of the cemetery. Stones face either the front or the rear of the cemetery. Two large and two small plots are surrounded by stone post and metal rail fences. Gravestones date from 1774 to 1998. Lakeville Assessor's Office lists this cemetery as town owned, 65,340 square feet in size. Thatcher lists both Peirce and Pierce surnames as Pierce. He calls this the "Parris Hill Cemetery," and Vigers calls it the "Peirce Cemetery." All Pierce/Peirce entries are listed together alphabetically by given name. Entries were recorded on May 15, 2001.

Anderson, Alfred M. Monument   *"ANDERSON / 1913 ALFRED M.   1955 / HIS WIFE / 1917   THELMA A. ____"* There are floral carvings on the upper corners of this monument.

Anderson, Thelma A.   See Alfred M. Anderson entry.
Lakeville Vital Records list her death on January 17, 1980.

Barry, Ethel T.   *"MOTHER / ETHEL THERESA / CANEDY HOYLE / BARRY / 1887 – 1954"* There are floral designs in the upper corners of this monument. A Richmond Memorials metal tag is present.

Besse, Julia E. Monument   *"CHARRON / JULIA E. CHARRON BESSE / 1865 • 1938 / EVERETT E. CHARRON / 1895 • 1951 / MARIE L. BURROWS / 1880 • 1967"* There are floral designs in the upper corners of this monument

Boardman, Judith   *"BOARDMAN / 1938   JUDITH   1983"* There are floral carvings on the sides of this slanted monument.

Boardman, Roland E.   *" ✝ / ROLAND E BOARDMAN / SP4 US ARMY / NOV 18 1934   DEC 4 1998"* is inscribed on this flat, ground level stone.

Booth, Priscilla   *"In memory of / PRISCILLA / widow of / Guillard Booth, / who died / Dec. 16, 1813: / in her 73d year. /*

> *When Jesus calls the living must _____*
> *To mark our ways, He appoints _____*
> *__ is His voice & I obey the call*
> *Farewell my husband, my children all."*

The second line is carved in relief on this rear facing stone. The last words of the first two lines of the poem are worn away.
"P. B." is inscribed on the footstone. It is located behind and to the far right of the headstone. It faces the rear of the cemetery.

Burrows, Marie L.   See Julia E. Besse Monument entry.

Canedy, Agnes B.   See Thomas W. Canedy Monument entry.

Canedy, Cynthia A.   See Thomas W. Canedy Monument entry.

Canedy, Thomas W. Monument   *"CANEDY / THOMAS W. CANEDY, / 1845 – 1908. / His Wife / CYNTHIA A. PARRIS, / 1848 – 1898 / AGNES B. Their Daughter / 1879 – 1893."* The first line is carved in relief.

Carlin, Patrick   *"PAT'K CARLIN / CO. A. / 4 R. I. INF."* The inscription is carved in relief within a recessed shield shaped area. The first line is carved along an arch. No dates are on this stone. A *"GAR 8 231"* marker, a veteran's marker and a flag are present. Lakeville Vital Records list his death on December 30, 1883, at about 45 years old.

Chace, Edith B.   See Mary J. Chace Monument entry.

Chace, Eliza A.   See John E. Chace Monument entry.
Lakeville Vital Records show Eliza A. Chace died July 10, 1967.

Chace, Harry H.   See John E. Chace Monument entry.
Lakeville Vital Records show Harry Holmes Chace died February 13, 1974.

Chace, John E. Monument   *"1869   JOHN E   1933 / 1873   ELIZA A   ____ / 1899   HARRY H.   ____ / CHACE"* The last line is carved in relief. Floral carvings adorn the top of this monument. There are four metal markers present. The names *"JOHN"* and *"EDITH"* are embossed on two of them, and on the other two markers *"E FREETOWN / GRANGE NO 307"* is embossed. Bound wheat shafts and a scythe are embossed below this.

Chace, Mary J. Monument   *"MOTHER / 1835   MARY J. CHACE   1927 / 1864 WILLIAM F.   1928 / 1893   EDITH B.   1932"* There are floral and geometric designs at the top of this monument.

Chace, William F.   See Mary J. Chace Monument entry.

Charron, Everett E.   See Julia E. Besse Monument entry.
"EVERETT E CHARRON / MASSACHUSETTS / PVT 2   PIONEER INFANTRY / WORLD WAR I / DEC 31, 1895   OCT 23 1951" is inscribed on this flat, ground level stone. It is located to the right of the monument. An American Legion marker, a veteran's marker and flag are present. A Memorial Granite Co. tag is present.

Clark, Harriet   *"HARRIET E. / wife of / Barnabas Clark: / died July 5, 1836. /*
aged 19 Ys. 1 Mo. /   And can it be that she has gone
                        Oh earthly joys how vain:
                        Her spirit fled to world's unknown.
                        Where spirits meet again."
This stone faces the rear of the cemetery. Thatcher lists her death year as 1830.
"H. E. C." This footstone faces the headstone.

Durfee, Sally   *"In memory of / SALLY DURFEE, / who died / Nov. 11, 1827; /*
aged 80 years." This slate stone has a small urn and a willow carved at the top.
Crescent designs are carved down the sides. It faces the rear of the cemetery.

Gomes, Elsie R.   See William P. Gomes Monument entry.

Gomes, William P. Monument   *"GOMES / 1909   WILLIAM P.   1986 / HIS*
WIFE / 1906   ELSIE R.   1976" There is a floral design in the upper left corner of
this slanted monument.

Goodwin, Chester E.   See Ella Goodwin Monument entry.
"CHESTER E." is inscribed on this flat, 1-2 inch high footstone. It is located
behind and to the right of the monument.

Goodwin, Ella Monument   *"GOODWIN"* is inscribed at the top of this
monument. *"ELLA M. / 1880 – 1957"* is inscribed below this on the left, and
"CHESTER E. / 1877 – 1965" is inscribed on the right. Ivy leaves are carved in the
upper corners. A Charles G. Morse Granite Co. metal tag is present.
"ELLA M." is inscribed on this flat 0-3 inch high stone. It is located behind and to
the left of the monument.

Hoard, Isabel P.   See William P. Hoard Monument entry.
"ISABEL P." is inscribed on this flat, ground level stone. It is located behind the
monument, on the left.

Hoard, W. Grant   See William P. Hoard Monument entry.
"W. GRANT" is inscribed on this flat, ground level stone. It is located two rows
behind the monument, on the right.

Hoard, William P. Monument   *"HOARD"* is inscribed on the front of this
monument. A floral design is carved in the upper left corner and two horseshoes
and a pole are carved in the bottom right corner. *"1863   WILLIAM P.   1940 / HIS*
WIFE / 1870   ISABEL P.   1943 / 1889   W. GRANT   1964 / GRANDSON / 1928
WILLIAM T.   1928" is inscribed on the back. A Barnicoat Monuments metal tag is
present.
"WILLIAM P." is inscribed on this flat, ground level stone. It is located behind the
monument, on the right.

Hoard, William T.   See William P. Hoard Monument entry.
"BABY" is all that is inscribed on this flat, ground level stone. It is beginning to be
buried. It is located directly in front of the William P. Hoard Monument, on the left.

Holloway, Isaac   *"ISAAC HOLLOWAY. / Born / July 10, 1770. / Died / Oct. 15,*
1848" This stone faces the rear of the cemetery. Thatcher lists his information as

"died Oct. 15th, 1848, 78 years, 3 mos., 5 days." as if a different stone was present when he did his survey.

"*I. H.*" This footstone is leaning against the back of the headstone.

Holloway, Lois   "*LOIS, / wife of / Isaac Holloway, / died March. 3, 1842, / Æ 72*
years. /   *Blessed are the dead which die in the Lord. /*
           Oh weep not for her she has gone to her rest,
           To the land of the faithful the home of the blest;
           When joy knows no change where the day knows no night
           Where the Glory of God is the fountain of light."

The first line of this rear facing stone is carved in relief.

"*L. H.*" is inscribed on this rear facing footstone. It is located to the left, behind Lois Parish's gravestone.

Mann, Sarah R.   "*SARAH R. MANN / Died Feb. 1, 1890, / Aged 84 years. /*
           Dearst Mother, thou hast left us,
           Here, thy loss we deeply feel,
           But 'tis God that hath bereft us
           He can all our sorrows heal."

The first line is carved along an arch. Note the spelling of *dearst* in the poem.

"*S. R. M.*" is inscribed on the footstone.

Parish, Lois   "*LOIS HOLLOWAY, / Wife of / BENJAMIN PARISH, / Born / May 18, 1795. / Died / Nov. 12, 1858.*" This stone faces the rear of the cemetery. Lois Holloways' footstone is located behind this gravestone.

Pickens, Rachel H. Monument   "*MOTHER. / RACHEL H. PICKENS, / DIED SEPT. 30, 1890, / AGED 86 YRS. 5 MOS. & 3 DYS. / DAUGHTER. / RACHEL. H. PICKENS, / BORN AUG. 29, 1841. / DIED AUG. 12, 1924.*" "*PICKENS.*" is carved in relief on the base.

Pickens, Rachel H.   See Rachel H. Pickens Monument entry.

Pierce, Abbie   See Philip P. Pierce Monument entry.

Peirce, Abiah H.   "*ABIAH H. PEIRCE, / Born Jan. 27, 1792, / Died Feb. 26, 1871, / Aged 79 years 1 mo.*" This stone faces the rear of the cemetery.

Peirce, Abigail H.   See Philip H. Peirce Monument entry.

"*MOTHER*" is carved in relief on the top curved surface of this lichen encrusted footstone. It is located in front of the monument, on the far right.

Peirce, Amey   See Oliver Peirce Monument entry.

"*AMEY, / Wife of / Oliver Peirce Esq. / died Dec. 31, 1825, / Æt. 38. /*
           She hath pass'd away,
           The fair in form, the pure in mind!
           To see the bright the glitering bride,
           Close seated by her Saviour's side!
           O may I find some humble seat,
           Beneath my dear Redeemer's feet."

A sculptured urn is carved at the top of this rear-facing stone. The first line is carved in outline. Note the spelling of *glitering* in the poem. It is located to the right of the monument.

"*A. P.*" is inscribed on this footstone, which is lying face down behind and two plots to the left of the monument.

Peirce, Anna   See Oliver Peirce Monument entry.

"*IN MEMORY OF / ANNA. / wife of / OLIVER PEIRCE ESQ. / who died / Feb. 12, 1847 in / her 69 year. /   To the visions of glory the spirit has fled*
        And left Her body inactive and dead;
        With angelic armies in glory to blaze,
        On Jesus' fair beauty forever to gaze."

An urn is carved in relief at the top of this rear facing stone. The second line is carved in shadow. The last line is buried underground. This stone is located to the left of the monument.

"*A. P.*" is inscribed on the footstone, which is leaning against a stone corner post of the Rachel Pickens plot.

Peirce, Basheba   "*BASHEBA PEIRCE / Died / March 28, 1884, / Aged 85 years.*"
"*B. P.*" is inscribed on the footstone.

Peirce, Betsy   "*In memory of / Betsy Daughter of / Mr. Elkanah & Mrs. / Betsy Peirce, who / died Aug 24th 1802 / Aged 13 m'ts & 18 days.*" A rising sun is carved at the top of this small, slate stone. It is in line with the footstones of the other graves of this row, and faces the rear of the cemetery. Thatcher lists her age at "13 m., 8 days."

Pierce, Betsey H.   "*SISTER*" is carved in relief on the top curved surface of this stone. "*BETSEY H. PIERCE / BORN / Aug. 18, 1841, / DIED / Sept. 9, 1884.*" The first line is carved in relief along an arch.

Peirce, Cynthia   "*CYNTHIA TOBEY, / Wife of / SILAS PEIRCE, / Born / Oct. 23, 1773. / Died / Nov. 25, 1865. / Dearest Mother rest with God.*" This stone shares its base with that of her husband, Silas.
"*C.T.P.*" is inscribed on the footstone.

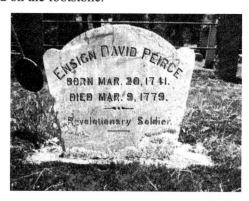

Peirce, David, Ensign   "*ENSIGN DAVID PEIRCE / BORN MAR. 20, 1741. / DIED MAR. 9, 1779. / Revolutionary Soldier*" The first line is carved along an arch. This green, slate stone is tapered at its base and faces the rear of the cemetery. A "*SAR 1775*" marker and flag are here. This stone was not listed by Thatcher.

Peirce, Deliverance   *"In memory of / DELIVERANCE, / wid. of / Isaac Peirce; / who died / Oct. 11, 1801, aged / 87 years."* There is an urn and willow carving at the top of this rear facing, slate stone.

Pierce, Edmund   *"In memory of / EDMUND, / son of Enos / & Lucy Pierce, / who died Dec. 3, / 1845, / Aged 22 years / & 6 mo's. /*

>*He's gone, that manly form has fled,*
>*And left his friends in tears;*
>*Early enrolled among the dead*
>*To sleep till Christ appears."*

The second line is carved in relief. The inscribed surface is recessed on this gravestone. *"E. Warren, F.R."* is inscribed at the bottom right.
"E. P." is inscribed on the footstone.

Peirce, Elizabeth   *"ERECTED / to the memory of / ELIZABETH PEIRCE / who died / Oct. 24, 1845, / Aged 81 years. /*

>*Whilst here below*
>*She had her share of sorrow grief and pain;*
>*No sickness nor distress in death*
>*Will trouble her again."*

The third line is carved in relief on this rear facing stone.
"E. P." is inscribed on the footstone.

Peirce, Elizabeth   *"ERECTED / to the memory of / ELIZABETH / dau. of Ethan & Fanny Peirce: / who died / June 11, 1840; in / her 22 year."* A poem follows but is unreadable due to weathering. An urn and willow are carved in relief at the top of this stone. It is broken at its base and is lying face up behind it. Thatcher lists her death month as January.
"E. P." This footstone is in front of the headstone.

Peirce, Enos   *"In memory of / M^r. Enos Peirce who / died July 29th, 1789 / in y^e 41st Year of his Age /   When the bright morning doth appear*
>*When gabr^{ls} trumpet all shall he__*
>*This sleeping dust will rise again*
>*And with the Sav^r, live & r^{e}ign"*

There is a frond carving at the top of this rear facing, slate stone. A *"SAR 1775"* marker, a veteran's marker and a flag are present.

Pierce, Enos   *"ENOS PIERCE / Born Feb. 11, 1789; / Died April 8, 1868; / Aged 79 yrs. 1 mo. / and 27 days."* This headstone is broken in half along the fourth line and the top section is leaning against the front of the base.
"E. P." This footstone faces its headstone.

Peirce, Enos Monument   *"P"* monogram is inscribed over a sculptured scroll and leaves. *"ENOS PEIRCE / 1811 – 1888 / PEDDY S. PEIRCE / 1824 – 1911"* The first line is carved along an arch. *"THE GIFT OF GOD IS ETERNAL LIFE"* is inscribed on the bottom of this large, rear facing monument. *"JOHN M. PEIRCE / SON OF / E.P. AND P.S. PEIRCE / 1851 – 1863"* is inscribed on the back.

Peirce, Enos   *"ENOS / Son of Enos & / Lucy Peirce / died / Dec. 14, 1836. / aged*

2 y.ʳˢ 8 mo.ˢ / & 26 d.ˢ /   *This lovely bud so young & fair*
                    Call'd hence by early doom
                    Just came to show how sweet a flower"

The poem is only three lines long.

Pierce, Ethan   *"ETHAN PIERCE, / Died / Oct. 9, 1864. / Aged / 78 years, 9 months, / 10 days. / A kind Husband and Father's grave."*
"FATHER" is inscribed on the top horizontal surface of the footstone. *"E. P. / 1864"* is inscribed on the front. It is located in front of the headstone.

Pierce, Ethan E. Monument   *"PIERCE / ETHAN ELBRIDGE PIERCE / JUNE 24 1824 – FEB. 5, 1911 / AGED 86 YRS. 7 MOS. 11 DYS. / WILLIAM CHESTER PIERCE / APRIL 5 1861 – NOV. 13 1942 / AGED 81 YRS. 7 MOS. 8 DYS."* is inscribed on this large monument. The first line is carved in relief. The first two lines are carved along an arch.

Peirce, Eunice R.   *"EUNICE R. PEIRCE / 1865 – 1932"* This monument faces the rear of the cemetery.

Peirce, Eunice R.   See Job Peirce, Esq. Monument entry.

Peirce, Fanny H.   *"FANNY HOARD / Wife of / ETHAN PIERCE, / Died / Feb. 15, 1873; / Aged / 75 years & 8 days. / Your memory shall be with us / until the daybreak, and the / shadows flee away."* This headstone is separated from its base and is located face up behind it. It is broken through between the fifth and sixth lines.
"MOTHER" is inscribed on the top horizontal surface of the footstone. *"F. H. P. / 1873"* is inscribed on the front. It is located in front of the headstone.

Peirce, Fanny P.   See William H. Peirce Monument entry.
"F. P. P." is carved in relief on the top curved surface of this footstone.

Peirce, George   *"In memory of / Mʳ. George Peirce, who / died July 17ᵗʰ, 1774 / in yᵉ 40ᵗʰ Year / of his age."* A rising sun is carved at the top of this small, rear facing, slate stone. The last line is buried underground.
"Mʳ. / George Peirce / 1774." is inscribed on the slate footstone. It is located in another section of the cemetery (see map for location).

Pierce, George W.   *"GEORGE W. / son of / Oliver Pierce Esq. / & Amey his wife / died Feb. 3. 1832. / aged 6 years."* There is no carving on the tympanum. This small stone faces the rear of the cemetery.

Peirce, Hariot   *"Hariot Du'tr of Mr. Free / man & Mrs. Tryphena / Peirce. she died April / 14ᵗʰ 1806 Aged 7 mts / and ten Days"* There is a peeking rising sun carved at the top of this small, rear facing, slate stone. It is located in line with the footstones of the other graves in this row.

Peirce, Harmon   *"HARMON PEIRCE / Born Nov. 17, 1765; / Died Aug. 7, 1809. / Aged 43 yrs. 8 m's / & 20 d's."* This stone faces the rear of the cemetery.

Peirce, Henry   See Philip H. Peirce Monument entry.
"HENRY PEIRCE, / DIED / in Vicksburg, Miss. / June 30, 1882, / Aged 45 yrs. 3

mos. / & 14 days. / Gone but not forgotten." is inscribed on this stone, which is located to the right of the monument. The first line is carved in relief along an arch. A diagonal crack extends from the left side of the fifth line to the bottom right corner. It has been successfully repaired. His wife, Jane M. Peirce, is buried in Strawbridge Cemetery, next to her first husband, David Munroe.
"H. P." This footstone faces the headstone, and has its own base.

Peirce, Hermon   *"HERMON Peirce / Died / February 1, 1912. / Aged 87 years 3 months / & 29 days."*
"H. P." is inscribed on the footstone.

Peirce, Holder   *"__OLDER REED / Son of M.ʳ / Simeon Peirce, / & Lurane his / Wife. Died Feb. / 4ᵗʰ, 1790. In the / 4ᵗʰ. Year of his / Age."* This small, rear facing, slate stone is beginning to exfoliate. Thatcher does not list it. Vigers and the Lang Cemetery chart in the Cemetery Commissions files list his first name as Holder.

Peirce, Infant girl   *"In Memory of / An Infant / daughter of Step'n / & Hope Peirce, / who was Born Apr. / 13, 1848, Died May / 18, Æ. 5 weekls /*
> *Sister thou wast mild & love*
> *Gentle as the summer breeze*
> *Pleasant as the air of evening*
> *When it floats amo'g the trees."*
This stone faces the rear of the cemetery. Notice the spelling of *weekls*.

Peirce, Infant Son   *"A SON of / Ethan & Fanny / Peirce / born Sept. 14 1837 / died the same day."* The death year is carved inside of a rectangular recessed area.

Peirce, Isaac   *"In memory of / M.ʳ ISAAC PEIRCE / who departed this life / Sep.ᵗ 18ᵗʰ 1782, in / yᵉ 77ᵗʰ Year of his age. /*
> *This is the end of all that live,*
> *This is my dark long home*
> *Jesus himself lay in the grave*
> *The house where all must come."*
There is a frond carving at the top of this rear facing, slate stone.

Peirce, James P. Esq.   See Philip H. Peirce Monument entry.

Peirce, Job   *"JOB, / son of Ethan & / Fanny Peirce. / died Jan 26, 1833 / aged 12 days."* *Job* is carved inside of a rectangular recessed area.
"J. P." This footstone is located in front of the headstone.

Peirce, Job, Esq. Monument   *"PEIRCE / JOB PEIRCE ESQ. / SEPT. 2. 1812 – FEB. 17. 1904. / EUNICE R. / HIS WIFE / APRIL 11. 1826 – MARCH 14. 1899."* The first line is carved in relief. There are leaf carvings in the corners of this large, rear-facing monument.

Peirce, John   *"JOHN PEIRCE / Died / September 3, 1884, / Aged 85 years 6 months / & 3 days."*
"J. P." is inscribed on the footstone.

Peirce, John M.   See Enos Peirce Monument entry.

"JOHN M. / Son of Enos & / Peddy S. Peirce / Died Jan. 27, 1863, / Æ 11 y'rs. / As Johnnie said he could trust / himself to die in Jesus we trust / he will rise again when Jesus / calls forth His sleeping saints." On top of this rear facing stone, there is a sculpture of a lamb with a child resting his head on its back.
"J. M. P." is inscribed on the footstone.

Peirce, Judith N. *"JUDITH N. PEIRCE / 1859 – 1918"* This monument faces the rear of the cemetery.

Pierce, Levi *"LEVI PIERCE / Born May 12, 1801, / Died Oct. 1, 1880."* The first line is carved in relief along an arch. A veteran's marker and flag are present.

Pierce, Lucy *"LUCY, / Wife of / ENOS PIERCE, / Born / Nov. 9, 1795. / Died / March 3, 1860."*
"L. P." is inscribed on the footstone.

Pierce, Lucy V. *"LUCY V. / Wife of / LEVI PIERCE, / Born May 16, 1802 / Died Jan. 17, 1859."* The first line is carved in relief along an arch. The stone is broken in half below the inscription. The top half is leaning against the bottom half, which is loose on its base.

Peirce, Lysander *"LYSANDER PEIRCE, / Son of / OLIVER & POLLY / PEIRCE; / Died July 18, / 1856. / Aged 27 years, / 5 months. /*
> *Though lingering pains his bosom lore,*
> *Resigned he kissed the chastening rod:*
> *Each mortal pain with meekness bore,*
> *And smiled in death to meet his God."*

This stone faces the rear of the cemetery.

Peirce, Nancy *"In memor^y of Nancy / (Dau^{tr}. of Mr. Haermon / & M^{rs}, Rachel) Peirce she / died Jan'y 11th 1797 / in ye 2^d Year of her age."* There is a peeking rising sun carving on this small, rear facing stone. Note the spelling of *Haermon*.

Peirce, Oliver Monument *"OLIVER PEIRCE, / Died Aug. 17, 1860. / Aged 74 years. / AMEY, HIS WIFE, / Died Dec. 31, 1825. / Aged 38 years. / POLLY, HIS WIFE, / Died April 26, 1832. / Aged 44 years. / ANNA, HIS WIFE. / Died Feb. 12, 1847. / In her 69th, year"* The first line is carved in relief. An urn sculpture is at the top of this tall, rear-facing monument.

"O. PEIRCE." is inscribed on this footstone. It is located behind the monument leaning against the headstone for Mr. Isaac Peirce.

Peirce, Peddy S. See Enos Peirce Monument entry.

Peirce, Philip H. Monument *"PHILIP H. PEIRCE / BORN MARCH 19, 1807 – DIED MAY 31, 1899. / HIS WIFE / ABIGAIL H. PEIRCE / BORN AUG. 4, 1807 – DIED OCT. 4, 1892."* is inscribed on the front of this large, roofed monument. *"PEIRCE"* is carved in relief on the front base. *"JAMES P. PEIRCE ESQ. / BORN SEPT. 24, 1835 – DIED MAR. 9, 1915 / HENRY PEIRCE / BORN MARCH 16, 1837 – DIED JUNE 30, 1882"* is inscribed on the back.
"FATHER" is carved in relief on the top curved surface of this lichen encrusted stone. It is located in front of the monument, on the right.

Pierce, Philip P. Monument *"PIERCE / PHILIP P. PIERCE / AUG. 29, 1843 – MAY 18, 1900 / ABBIE, HIS WIFE / JUNE 15, 1839 – JULY 16, 1919"* The first line is carved in relief on this large monument.

Pierce, Polly
See Oliver Peirce Monument entry.

> *"POLLY,*
> *wife of*
> *Oliver Pierce Esq.*
> *died April 26, 1832,*
> *Æt. 44.*
>
> *Her tender frame no sorrows knew;*
> *To all on earth she's bid adieu,*
> *Her Saviour beckon'd her away,*
> *To relms of bliss, and endless day."*

An urn is carved in relief at the top of this rear facing stone. The first line is carved in outline. Note the spelling of *relms,* and also the spelling of her last name as compared to the Monument.
"P. P." This footstone is located behind and to the right of this stone.

Peirce, Polly H. *"POLLY H. PEIRCE / 1855 – 1942"* This monument faces the rear of the cemetery.

Peirce, Rachel *"RACHEL / wife of / Harmon Peirce / Born Feb. 1, 1768, / Died Nov. 9, 1856, / Aged 88 yrs, 9 m's. / & 8 d's."* This stone faces the rear of the cemetery.

Peirce, Ruth *"Erected / To the memory of / RUTH, / widow of Enos Peirce, / Died Oct. 9, 1811, / in her 53rd year. /*
> *Peace to thy dusty bed,*
> *Thou lovely sleeping clay;*
> *Here rest thy weary head*
> *'Till the great rising day.*

> *When Gabriels trumpet all shall hear,*
> *Then this sleeping dust shall rise again,*
> *And with her Saviour reign."*

There is no carving in the tympanum on this rear facing, slate stone.

Peirce, Sarah   *"In memory of / M.ʳˢ Sarah, wife of M.ʳ, / George Peirce who died / June 20, 1778, / In yᵉ 41ˢᵗ Year of / her age."* A rising sun is carved at the top of this rear facing, slate stone. The last line is buried underground.
"M.ʳˢ / Sarah Peirce / 1778" This slate footstone is leaning against a stone fence post in another section of the cemetery. See the map for the location.

Peirce, Sarah   *"In MEMORY of / Sarah (Dauʳ. of M., / George & Mˢ, Sarah / Peirce) departed / this life Feb'y 21ˢᵗ, 1784 / in yᵉ 13ᵗʰ Year of her age."* A peeking rising sun is carved at the top of this small, rear facing, slate stone. The last two lines are buried underground. Thatcher lists her death year as 1781, age 12 years.

Peirce, Silas   *"SILAS PEIRCE, / Born / June 5, 1772. / Died / Jan. 20, 1860. / Rest for the weary."* This headstone shares its base with that of his wife, Cynthia.
"S. P." This footstone is lying face up on the ground.

Pierce, William C.   See Ethan Pierce Monument entry.

Peirce, William H. Monument   *"P"* monogram is carved in shallow relief at the top of this large monument. Ivy leaf carvings surround it. *"WILLIAM H. PEIRCE / BORN / OCT. 26, 1819, / DIED / MAY 31, 1896."* is inscribed on the left side. The first line is carved in relief. *"FANNY P. / WIFE OF / WILLIAM H. PEIRCE, / BORN APRIL 14, 1832, / DIED MARCH 25, 1917."* is inscribed on the right. The first line is carved in relief. *"PEIRCE"* is carved in relief on the base.
"W. H. P." is carved in relief on the top arched surface of this 0-2 inch high footstone.

Reed, Benjamin H. Monument   *"BENJAMIN H. REED / 1827 – 1894 / HIS WIFE / EMILY F. SHAW / 1840 – 1927"*

Reed, Charles H.   See Henry B. Reed Monument entry.
"C. H. R." is inscribed in shallow relief on this flat, ground level stone.

Reed, Emily F.   See Benjamin Reed Monument entry.

Reed, Gertrude   See Percy Reed Monument entry.

Reed, Harold P.   See Henry B. Reed Monument entry.
"HAROLD PHILIP REED / MASSACHUSETTS / CPL   68 CO 153 DEPOT BRIGADE / WORLD WAR I / OCT 26 1893   MAY 24 1960" There is a circled cross carved at the top of this flat, ground level stone.

Reed, Helen S.   See Henry B. Reed Monument entry.
"HELEN S. REED / WIFE OF HAROLD / APR. 5, 1896 – DEC. 29, 1996" There is a circled cross carved at the top of this flat, ground level stone.

Reed, Henry B. Monument   *"REED"* is carved in relief on the front of this large, rear facing monument. Ivy leaves and an *"R"* monogram are carved in shallow relief at the top. *"1841 HENRY B. REED 1922 / 1836 PHOEBE A. ʜɪꜱ ᴡɪꜰᴇ 1887 /*

1863   MARY J. REED SHOVE   1931 / 1869   CHARLES H. REED   1954 / 1893 HAROLD P. REED   1960 / 1896   HELEN S. HIS WIFE   1996" is inscribed on the back.

"H. B. R." is inscribed in shallow relief on this flat, ground level stone. It is beginning to be buried. It is located in front of the monument, on the far right.

Reed, Lawrence B.   See Percy Reed Monument entry.

Reed, Percy L. Monument   *"1875   PERCY L. REED   1967 / HIS WIFE / 1874 GERTRUDE E. BROWNELL   1962 / THEIR SON / 1905   LAWRENCE B. REED 1974"*

Reed, Phoebe A.   See Henry B. Reed Monument entry.

"P. A. R." is inscribed in shallow relief on this flat, ground level footstone. It is beginning to be buried.

Reed, Wennie   *"Our Darling / WENNIE,"* is carved on the slanted oval top of this stone. The second line is carved in relief. *"Son of Benj. H. & Emily F. REED / Born Dec. 17, 1864, / Died Aug. 1, 1866."* is carved on the front of the upper base of this small stone.

Robbins, Esther E.   See Orin S. Robbins Monument entry.

Robbins, Hattie C.   *"HATTTIE C. / Dau. of / Orin S. & Esther E. / Robbins. / Born May 16, 1860. / Died / Jan. 28. 1863. / Always so pleasant."* This stone is separated from its base, and is lying face up against it.

Robbins, Orin S. Monument   *"R"* monogram is carved at the top of this monument. *"1829   ORIN S.   1889 / 1842   ESTHER E.   1906 / 1875   WELDON O.   1906 / ROBBINS"* The last line is carved in shallow relief.

Robbins, Weldon O.   See Orin S. Robbins Monument entry.

Settler's Monument   *"IN MEMORY OF THE OLD SETTLERS / AND THOSE WHO CAME LATER / THAT ARE NOW LYING HERE / IN UNMARKED GRAVES / PLACED BY / PIERCE CEMETERY ASSOCIATION / ON LANG STREET."* is embossed on a metal plaque which is attached to this large boulder. A veteran's marker and flag are present.

Sherman, Sarah   *"In memory of / SARAH SHERMAN / daughter of / Nehemiah Sherman / & Deborah his wife / who died Nov. 20, / 1822, / aged 25 years. /*

> *'Far from this world of toil & strife*
> *She's present with the Lord;*
> *The labour of her mortal life*
> *End in a large reward."*
>
> *F. Cooley."*

An urn and willow are carved in relief at the top of this rear facing stone. *"S. S."* is inscribed on the footstone. It is located two rows behind, and to the left of the headstone.

Shove, Mary J.   See Henry B. Reed Monument entry.
"M. J. R. S." is inscribed in shallow relief on this flat, ground level footstone.

Stoddard, George C.   *"GEORGE C. / son of Capt. Elijah / & Persis L. / Stoddard: / died May 2, 1839, / aged 6 years / & 6 mo^s. /*

> *While here below he had his share,*
> *Of sorrow grief and pain:*
> *No sickness nor distressing death*
> *Will trouble him again."*

is inscribed on this small stone.

Webster, John   *"John (Son of M^r. / Nicholas & M^{rs} / Lois) Webster died / March ye 13th 1778. / an Infant."*   There is a frond carving at the top of this small, rear facing, slate stone.

Winslow, Benjamin   *"In Memory of / Mr. BENJAMIN WINSLOW, / who died / Jan. 20th, 1818. / In the 74th Year of his / age. /*

> *Peace to thy dusty bed.*
> *Thou lovely sleeping clay,*
> *Here rest thy weary head,*
> *Till the great rising day."*

An urn is carved at the top of this rear facing, slate stone.
"Mr. B. Winslow. / 1818." is inscribed on this slate footstone.

Winslow, Jirah, Esq.   *"JIRAH WINSLOW ESQ. / Born in / Middleborough / April 17, 1800, / Died in Lakeville, / August 8, 1875, / Aged 75 years, / 3 months & 20 d's."*   The first line is carved in relief along an arch on this rear facing stone.
"J. W."   This footstone has its own base.

Winslow, Phebe   *"In memory of / PHEBE, / wid. of Benjamin / Winslow, who died / May 19, 1838, in / her 79 year. /*

> *Death! Thou hast conquered me,*
> *'Tis by thy dart I'm slain,*
> *But Jesus Christ hath conquered thee,*
> *And I shall rise again."*

An urn and willow are carved at the top of this rear facing, slate stone. It is leaning to the right.
"P. W." is inscribed on this slate footstone.

Winslow, Tisdale *"In / memory of / MR. TISDALE WINSLOW / who died / June 8,*
1827 / aged 25 / years. / I hope one day to reach the shore

Where all my trouble will be o'er,
My wear'ed limb's lie down at ease,
Freed from all trouble or disease."

A sculptured carving of an urn and willow is at the top of this rear facing stone. A
George Thompson swirl is carved below the inscriptions.
"T. W." is inscribed on the footstone.

Worth, Elbridge M. Monument   *"1866   ELBRIDGE M. WORTH   1946 / HIS*
WIFE / 1867   LUELLA C. REED   1945"

Worth, Luella C.   See Elbridge Worth Monument entry.

Additional Notes:

The *1963 Lakeville Town Report* by the Cemetery Commission documents that the
cemetery had been very overgrown and they cleaned it up. "....During the cleaning
up process several markers and fallen stones were removed and cared for. A chart
of the area was prepared, so that these stones can be put back in proper location
when funds are available...." Mansfield reports that at the time, some people did
not like what was being done, and formed the Pierce Cemetery Association, which
took over the care of the cemetery from 1965 to 1974. When they came to put back
the stones they were not sure where they went and it was thought some stones were
missing. They placed the Settlers Monument in the center of the cleared section on
the right to honor those whose graves might now be unmarked. In the Cemetery
Commission files at the Lakeville Town Hall there is an undated "chart" that shows
the positions of the stones in this cemetery. On this map, the stones in the front
enclosed section and near the rear line are mostly in the same positions as they are
today. However, the stones in the enclosed middle section and the open triangular
section on the right are arranged differently. Also, many fieldstone markers from
the section on the right are missing. Identification of the stones on this chart is often
by first name only, with no dates. Many are not identified. Sometimes they are
inaccurate, for example, in the front section, "Edwin Pierce" is listed on the chart
where Edmund Pierce's stone is now. The Freeman stone is listed on the chart

where the stone for Hariot, daughter of Freeman Peirce, is located. A look at Thatcher's work shows that all stones that he listed (those dated prior to 1850) are currently present in the cemetery.

Lang Cemetery Map Index

Alphabetized:

By Location:

48 – Pierce, Polly (~1788-1832)
49 – Peirce, Anna (~1779-1847)
50 – Peirce, Polly H. (1855-1942)
51 – Peirce, Eunice R. (1865-1932)
52 – Peirce, Judith N. (1859-1918)
53 – Peirce, Job, Esq. (1812-1904)
    Peirce, Eunice R. (1826-1899)
54 – Peirce, Amey (~1787-1825)
55 – Peirce, Oliver (~1786-1860)
    Peirce, Amey (~1787-1825)
    Pierce, Polly (~1788-1832)
    Pierce, Anna (~1779-1847)
56 – Pierce, Polly (~1788-1832)
57 – Pierce, Amey (~1787-1825)
58 – Pierce, George W. (~1826-1832)
59 – Peirce, Lysander (1829-1856)
60 – Peirce, Infant girl (1848)
61 – Peirce, Enos (1811-1888)
    Peirce, Peddy S. (1824-1911)
    Peirce, John M. (1851-1863)
62 – Peirce, John M. (1851-1863)
63 – Boardman, Roland E. (1934-1998)
64 – Boardman, Judith (1938-1983)
65 – Anderson, Alfred M. (1913-1955)
    Anderson, Thelma A. (1917-1980)
66 – Chace, John E. (1869-1933)
    Chace, Eliza A. (1873-1967)
    Chace, Harry H. (1899-1974)
67 – Chace, Mary J. (1835-1927)
    Chace, William F. (1864-1928)
    Chace, Edith B. (1893-1932)
68 – Barry, Ethel T. (1887-1954)
69 – Canedy, Thomas W. (1845-1908)
    Canedy, Cynthia A. (1848-1898)
    Canedy, Agnes B. (1879-1893)
70 – Robbins, Hattie C. (1860-1863)
71 – Robbins, Orin S. (1829-1889)
    Robbins, Esther E. (1842-1906)
    Robbins, Weldon O. (1875-1906)
72 – Pierce, Philip P. (1843-1900)
    Pierce, Abbie (1839-1919)
73 – Pierce, Levi (1801-1880)
74 – Pierce, Lucy V. (1802-1859)
75 – Pierce, Betsey H. (1841-1884)
76 – Pickens, Rachel H. (1804-1890)
    Pickens, Rachel H. (1841-1924)

77 – Peirce, Anna (~1779-1847)
78 – Mann, Sarah R. (~1806-1890)
79 – Carlin, Patrick (~1838-1883)
80 – Goodwin, Ella (1880-1957)
    Goodwin, Chester E (1877-1965)
81 – Goodwin, Ella (1880-1957)
82 – Goodwin, Chester E (1877-1965)
83 – Hoard, William T. (1928)
84 – Hoard, William P. (1863-1940)
    Hoard, Isabel P. (1870-1943)
    Hoard, W. Grant (1889-1964)
    Hoard, William T. (1928)
85 – Hoard, Isabel P. (1870-1943)
86 – Hoard, William P. (1863-1940)
87 – Hoard, W. Grant (1889-1964)
88 – Besse, Julia E. (1865-1938)
    Charron, Everett E. (1895-1951)
    Burrows, Marie L. (1880-1967)
89 – Charron, Everett E. (1895-1951)
90 – Gomes, William P. (1909-1986)
    Gomes, Elsie R. (1906-1976)
91 – Reed, Harold P. (1893-1960)
92 – Reed, Helen S. (1896-1996)
93 – Reed, Charles H. (1869-1954)
94 – Reed, Henry B. (1841-1922)
    Reed, Phoebe A. (1836-1887)
    Shove, Mary J. (1863-1931)
    Reed, Charles H. (1869-1954)
    Reed, Harold P. (1893-1960)
    Reed, Helen S. (1896-1996)
95 – Shove, Mary J. (1863-1931)
96 – Reed, Phoebe A. (1836-1887)
97 – Reed, Henry B. (1841-1922)
98 – Holloway, Isaac (1770-1848)
99 – Parish, Lois (1795-1858) – 99
100 – Holloway, Lois (~1770-1842)
101 – Booth, Priscilla (~1741-1813)
102 – Clark, Harriet (1817-1836)
103 – Sherman, Sarah (~1797-1822)
104 – Webster, John (1778)
105 – Booth, Priscilla (~1741-1813)
106 – Peirce, Holder (1787-1790)
107 – Peirce, George (~1735-1774)
108 – Mann, Sarah R. (~1806-1890)
109 – Sherman, Sarah (~1797-1822)
110 – Settler's Monument

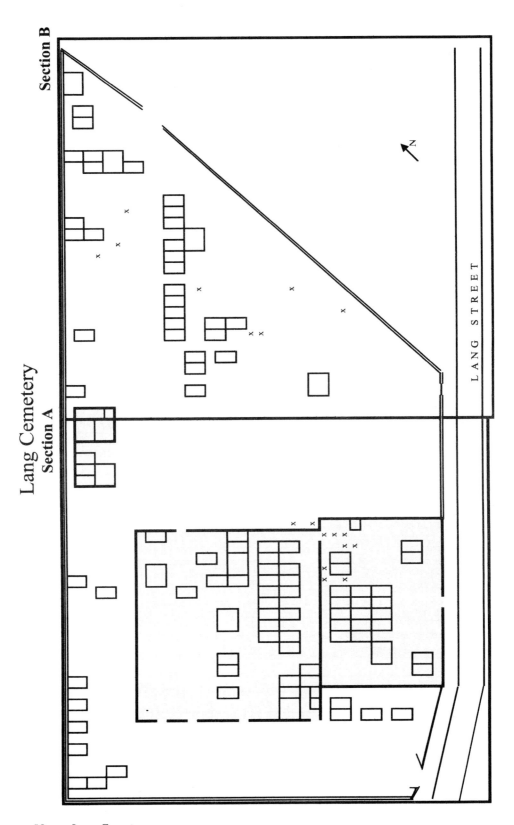

Lang Cemetery

Section B

Section A

LANG STREET

Lang Cemetery
Section A

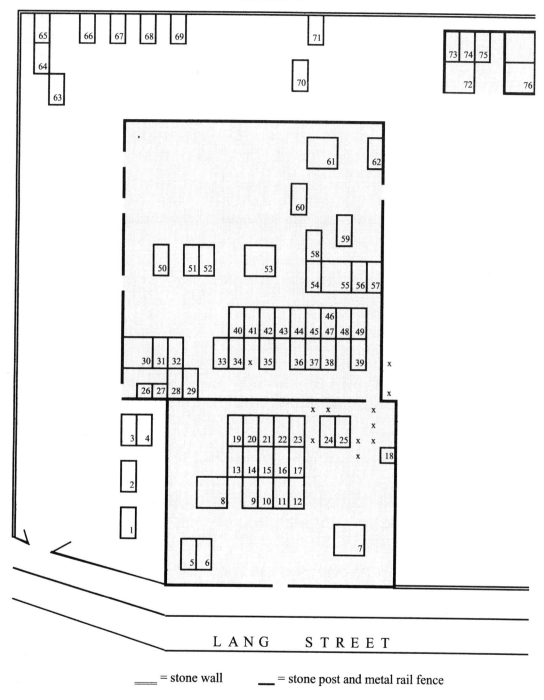

LANG STREET

_____ = stone wall _____ = stone post and metal rail fence

Lang Cemetery
Section B

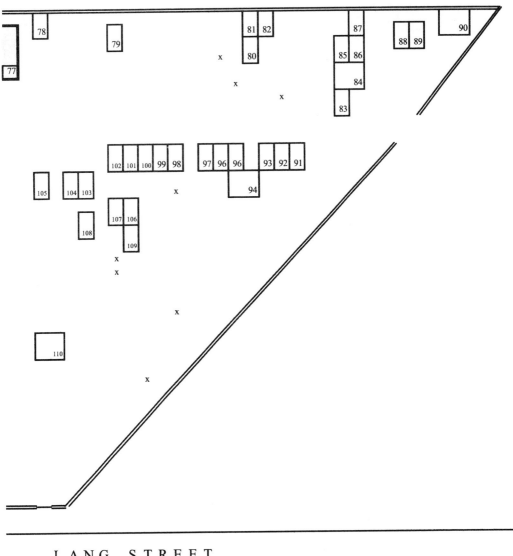

= stone wall   = stone post and metal rail fence

LANG STREET

Lang Cemetery Map in Cemetery Commission Files

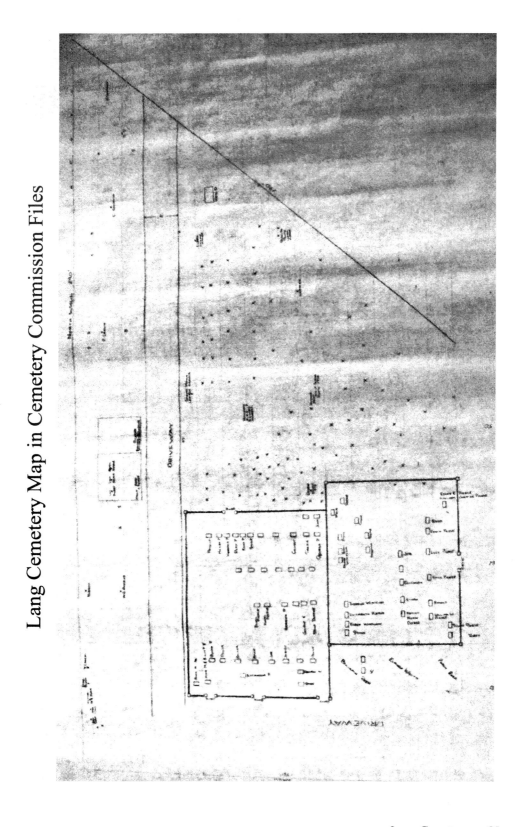

Chapter 14
Malbone Cemetery

Malbone Cemetery is located at the corner of Malbone Street and Emerson Drive. A stone wall, which is in disrepair, extends across the front. No sign was present on the date of transcription, but one was placed later that year. The inscribed surfaces of several slate stones have completely exfoliated. Many unmarked fieldstones are also present. Gravestones face northwest and date from 1785 to 1838. The Lakeville Assessor's Office lists this cemetery as town owned, about 5800 square feet in area. Vigers writes: "the road appears to have been built through the cemetery and perhaps over some graves." Mansfield states that "when the road was constructed the remains of a body was scraped up." Thatcher calls this the "Briggs Cemetery." Entries were recorded May 1, 2000.

Briggs, Daniel   *"In Memory of / M*. *DANIEL BRIGGS / Son of Mr. Malbone Briggs, / & Meribah, his wife / Who died / Oct. 17, 1827. / in the 32. year of / his age."* The tympanum of this slate stone is broken off.

Briggs, Doctor   *"Doctor Briggs / 1821"* is inscribed on this slate footstone. It is lying on the ground face up. No headstone was found. Thatcher lists, "Doctor, son of Malbone & Meribah, died May 26, 1821, age 19 years."

Briggs, Henry W.   *"H. W. B."* is inscribed on this slate footstone, which is lying face up on the ground. Thatcher lists, "Briggs, Henry Williams, son of Henry & Louisa, Apr. 8, 1828, 8 mos., 20 da." He was the son of Louisa Kehoe, see entry below. No headstone was found for him.

Briggs, Job C.   *"In Memory of / MR. JOB C. BRIGGS, / Son of Mr. Malbone Briggs / & Meribah, his wife / Who died / Jan. 20, 1827 / In the 23 year of / his age."* An urn is carved at the top of this lichen encrusted, slate stone. Pieces are missing at the top, and on the right shoulder.

Briggs, Malbone, Jr.   *"In Memory of / Mr. MALBONE BRIGGS.*[Jr.] */ Son of Mr. Malbone Briggs / & Meribah, his wife / Who ___d / July 7, 1826 / in the 36 year / of* *his age."* An urn is carved at the top of this slate stone. The *Jr.* carved on the second line is carved above the *S* in *BRIGGS,* as the carver ran out of room. There is a hole through the stone where the word "died" probably existed, obliterating the first three letters. This stone was broken off at ground level, and placed back in the ground in front of the bottom section. In doing so, the last line is now buried underground. Pieces of slate are missing at the top and on the right shoulder. A veteran's marker and flag are present.

"Mr. / M. Briggs, ^*Jr.** *"* This slate footstone is broken on the left side.

Briggs, Meriba   *"...n mem__ .../ __RS. MERIBA_ ... / daughter... / Mr. Job Ch___ / aged 73 ye___ / Ð 1838"* This slate stone was broken into many pieces. The above inscription was taken from four pieces that had inscriptions on them. Remnants of a willow carving are at the top. Thatcher lists, "Mrs. Meribah Chase, dau of Job, died 1838, age 73 yrs." *Middleborough, Massachusetts Vital Records,* Vol. 2, p. 147 lists her marriage to Malbourn Briggs in 1788.

"M. _" is inscribed on this slate footstone. The right corner is missing.

Briggs, Meribah C.   *"M. C. B."* is inscribed on this slate footstone, which is lying face up on the ground. Thatcher lists, "Briggs, Meribah Chace, dau. of Malbone & Meribah, Feb. 19, 1810, 1 day." No headstone was found for her.

Chase, Deborah   *"In memory of M.ˢ / Deborah (wife of M.ʳ / Job) Chase who died / Dec.ʳ yᵉ 8 ᵗʰ. 1785. in / yᵉ 46 ᵗʰ / Year of her / age. /*
               Remember me as you pass by
               For as you are so once was I
               As I am now so you must be
               Therefore prepare to followᵐᵉ."
A winged angel is carved at the top of this slate stone. Tree outlines are carved down the sides. It is beginning to exfoliate. The carved ran out of room in the last line of the poem, and carved *me* above the *w* in *follow.*

Chase, Job   *"In ME ... / JOB CHA ... / June 17ᵗ ... 94/5 · / in yᵉ 57 ...of his Age. / __ep hither...cast an eye, / ... are to die, / ...you must ..."* The inscribed surface of this slate stone has exfoliated and is split vertically into at least three pieces. The middle piece is missing. Remnants of a frond carving can be seen on what is left of the tympanum on the left side. The above inscription is taken from the pieces on the sides. The death year's last digit is a 4 with a 5 carved over it. Thatcher lists that he died June 17th, 1795, in his 57th year.

"M[r]. JOB / CHASE / died / 1795" is inscribed on this slate footstone. It is located two rows behind the headstone, on the right.

Kehoe, Louisa   *"In memory of / LOUISA, / who departed this life / Oct. 3, 1835; / in the 28 year / of her age. / This stone is erected by her / husband / Thomas Kehoe."* *Vital Records of the Town of Freetown, Massachusetts 1686 Through 1890* lists her as the daughter of Malbone and Meribah (Chase) Briggs. She married Henry Briggs on April 16, 1826. Henry Williams Briggs, listed above, was their child. These records also indicate that Henry Briggs died between 1830 and 1832. She then married Thomas Kehoe on March 20, 1832.

"L. K." is inscribed on the footstone. It is lying face up behind the headstone.

Additional Notes:

Thatcher lists the following people as buried in this cemetery, but no stones were found for them:

"Briggs: Malbon, died Feb. 1st, 1838, in his 76th year.

　　　　John, son of Malbone, died Aug. 13, 1823, age 23 years.

Chase: Mary, widow of Benjamin, Mar. 16, 1786, age 75 yrs."

He also lists: "…a half dozen other graves with stub stones."

Vigers, in 1952, states, "….The grave of Malbone Briggs is one that is between the road and the fence, the stone of which is broken into several pieces. Only part of the inscription can be read: "Sacred to the memory of Mr. Malbone Briggs who…""" This stone remnant was not found in 2000.

No cemetery cards were found at the Lakeville Town Hall for this cemetery.

Malbone Cemetery Map Index

Alphabetical:	By Location:
Briggs, Daniel (~1796-1827) – 3	1 – Briggs, Meribah (~1765-1838)
Briggs, Doctor (~1802-1821) – 8	2 – Kehoe, Louisa (~1808-1835)
Briggs, Henry W. (1827-1828) – 11	3 – Briggs, Daniel (~1796-1827)
Briggs, Job C. (~1805-1827) – 4	4 – Briggs, Job C. (~1805-1827)
Briggs, Malbone, Jr. (~1791-1826) – 7	5 – Chase, Deborah (~1740-1785)
Briggs, Meribah (~1765-1838) – 1	6 – Chase, Job (~1739-1795)
Briggs, Meribah C. (1810) – 10	7 – Briggs, Malbone, Jr. (~1791-1826)
Chase, Deborah (~1740-1785) – 5	8 – Briggs, Doctor (~1802-1821)
Chase, Job (~1739-1795) – 6, 9	9 – Chase, Job (~1739 -1795)
Kehoe, Louisa (~1808-1835) – 2	10 – Briggs, Meribah C. (1810)
	11 – Briggs, Henry W. (1827-1828)

Malbone Cemetery Map

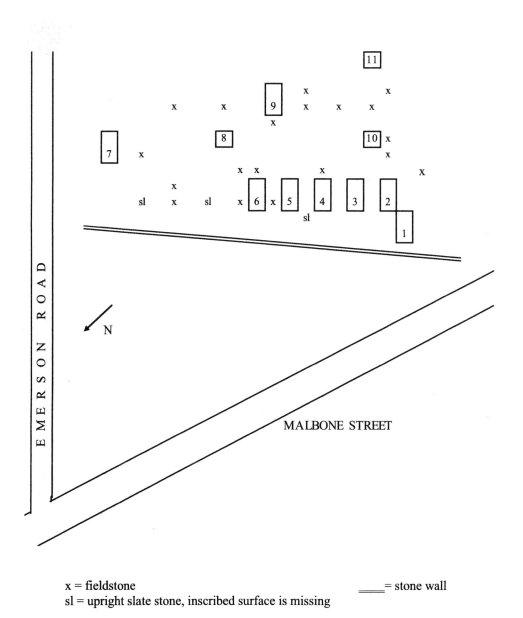

x = fieldstone   ____ = stone wall
sl = upright slate stone, inscribed surface is missing

Chapter 15
McCully Cemetery

McCully Cemetery is located on the east side of Highland Avenue, just south of the bridge over Route 140. It has a stone post and metal rail fence on three sides. A stone wall forms the border on the right side. The entrance to the cemetery faces Highland Road. The sign is in good repair. Many of the head and footstones do not match in material or shape, and several footstones are moved around at the back of the cemetery. The gravestones face northwest, and date from 1787 to 1995. The Lakeville Assessor's Office lists this cemetery as town owned, 12,425 square feet in area. Entries were recorded September 5, 2001.

Ashley, Abigail   *"In memory of / ABIGAIL, / wife of / Luther Ashley; / who died / Jan. 27, 1846, / aged 64 years."*   There is an urn and willow carving at the top of this rectangular slate stone.
"A. A." This footstone faces the headstone.

Ashley, Abigail   *"ABIGAIL / Dr. of / Luther Ashley, / died Oct. 9, 1825, / Æt. 6 yrs."* There is an urn carved at the top this small, rectangular, slate stone.

Ashley, Alsada P.   *"ALSADA P. / WIFE OF / DAVID ASHLEY / Born Dec. 27, 1820. / Died June 19, 1897."* The first line is carved along an arch.
"A. P. / 1898" is inscribed on this footstone. The last line is buried underground. Note the discrepancy in the death year. According to the *Vital Records of the Town of Marshfield, MA, 1841-1910* online database, she died in 1897.

Ashley, Chester Monument   *"ASHLEY"* is inscribed on the center top of this slanted monument. *"CHESTER / OCT. 14. 1863 / DEC. 27, 1954"* is carved on the left side. *"SOPHRONIA A. / JULY 1, 1861 / DEC. 17, 1948"* is carved on the right side. *"MILDRED A. / MAY 4, 1898 – AUG. 26, 1977"* is carved on the bottom center. Flowers are carved in relief on its sides of this lichen encrusted monument.

Ashley, Chloe *"CHLOE, / wife of / Luther Ashley, / died Nov. 6, 1804, / Æt. 23."* There is an urn and willow carving at the top, and curved designs are carved down the sides of this lichen encrusted, slate stone.
"C. A." / 1804." This slate footstone faces the headstone.

Ashley, David *"DAVID ASHLEY. / BORN / Dec. 28, 1807 D. Feb. 13, 1880 / Aged 72 Years, 3 Months."* The first line is carved along an arch.
"D. A / 1880" is inscribed on the footstone.

Ashley, John E. See Mariva G. Ashley Monument entry.

Ashley, Judith S. *"In memory of / JUDITH S. / wife of / David Ashley: / who died / July 27, 1847. / aged 35 years."* An urn and willow are carved at the top of this rectangular, lichen encrusted, slate stone.
"J. S. A." This slate footstone faces the headstone.

Ashley, Lavinia *"In memory of / Mrs. LAVINIA, / wife of / David Ashley, / who died / June 10, 1861, / Aged 55 years."* An urn and willow carving is on the top of this lichen encrusted, slate stone.
"L. H. A." This slate footstone faces the headstone. On the back of this footstone is an angled carving of an urn and willow. The word _acred is inscribed under the urn. It would appear that this is a piece of headstone that has been recycled.

Ashley, Luther *"In Memory of / LUTHER ASHLEY, / died Feb. 13, 1830, / Æt 48."* There is an urn and willow carving at the top. Curved designs are carved on the sides of this lichen encrusted, slate stone.
"L. A. / 1830." This slate footstone faces the headstone.

Ashley, Marcus M. See Mariva G. Ashley Monument entry.

Ashley, Mariva G. Monument *"MARIVA G. / WIFE OF / JOHN E. ASHLEY / BORN MARCH 4, 1849 / DIED AUG. 23, 1901"* is inscribed on the left of this roofed monument. *"JOHN E. ASHLEY / BORN / JULY 31, 1835, / DIED APR. 15, 1913"* is inscribed on the right. *"MARCUS M. ASHLEY / LOST AT SEA IN 1864 AGED 24 YEARS."* is inscribed at the bottom across the width of the monument. The first lines on the right and left side are carved along an arch. A leaf design is carved on the front gable.

Ashley, Mildred A. See Chester Ashley Monument entry.

Ashley, Sophronia A. See Chester Ashley Monument entry.

Ashley, William *"In memory of / WILLIAM ASHLEY, / who died / Oct. 1, 1836, / in his 24 year."* An urn and willow are carved at the top of this lichen encrusted, slate stone. Line designs are carved down the sides.
"W. A." This slate footstone faces the headstone.

Beaton, Abbie E. See Thomas Beaton Monument entry.

Beaton, Thomas C. Monument *"BEATON"* is carved in relief on the front of this large monument. Floral designs are carved in the upper corners. *"THOMAS C. BEATON / 1874 – 1955 / HIS WIFE / ABBIE E. HINDS / 1875 – 1950"* is inscribed on the back. *"PERPETUAL CARE"* is inscribed on the top of the base, on the right side.

Briggs, Betsey *"ERECTED / in memory of / BETSEY, / wife of D.ʳ Elisha Briggs / who died / June 10, 1802 in / her 20 year."* The first line is carved along an arch. The third line is carved in relief. This rectangular stone was broken off 3 inches above the ground and is lying face up behind it. The last line is on the bottom piece, and is carved along an inverted arch. There is evidence of a previous, unsuccessful repair.
"B. B." This footstone faces the headstone.

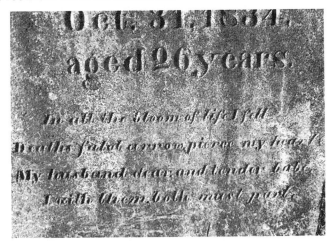

Canedy, Abigail A. *"Erected / to the memory of / ABIGAIL A. / wife of / Capt. John W. Canedy. / who died / Oct. 31, 1834, / aged 26 years. /*
> *In all the bloom of life I fell*
> *Death's fatal arrow, pierce my heart;*
> *My husband dear, and tender babe,*
> *I with them, both must part."*

A sculptured carving of two willows surrounding an urn is at the top of this stone.
"A. A. C." is inscribed on the footstone.

Canedy, Abigail A. W. *"ABIGAIL A. W. CANEDY / BORN / APRIL 19, 1834 / DIED OCT. 12, 1924"* The first line is carved along an arch on this monument.

Canedy, Emery W. *"EMERY WOODBRIDGE CANEDY / BORN / JUNE 23, 1844 / DIED APRIL 2, 1926"* The first line is carved along an arch on this monument.

Canedy, John W., Capt. *"CAPT. / JOHN W. CANEDY / Died / Apr. 29, 1881, / Aged 77 years / 11 mo's & 24 d's."* The second line is carved along an arch. This stone was broken diagonally below the inscription on the left side, but has been successfully repaired. A veteran's marker and flag are present.
"J. W. C." This footstone is face up on the ground, buried under moss.

Canedy, Lucy *"LUCY CANEDY / Wife of / CAPT. / JOHN W. CANEDY / Died / Feb. 16, 1898, / Aged 89 years / 11 mo's & 14 d's."* The first line is carved along an arch.

"L. C." is inscribed on this footstone.

Canedy, Vandalia A. *"VANDALIA AUGUSTA CANEDY / BORN / JUNE 9, 1847 / DIED AUG. 26, 1932"* The first line of this monument is carved along an arch.

Hinds, Elizabeth J. See Stephen V. Hinds Monument entry.
"ELIZABETH" is carved in shallow relief on this flat footstone that is 2-3 inches above ground. It is located to the right of the monument.

Hinds, Ellen P. See Stephen V. Hinds Monument entry.
"MOTHER" is carved in shallow relief on this flat one-inch high footstone. It is located in front of the monument, on the right.

Hinds, Ervin A. See Stephen V. Hinds Monument entry.

Hinds, Ervin A., Jr. See Stephen V. Hinds Monument entry.

Hinds, James P. See Stephen V. Hinds Monument entry.

Hinds, Jennie F. See Stephen V. Hinds Monument entry.
"JENNIE" is carved in shallow relief on this flat, ground level footstone. It is located directly in front of the monument on the right.

Hinds, Stephen V. Monument *"h"* monogram is carved in shallow relief on the front gable of this roofed monument. *"1836 STEPHEN V. HINDS 1917 / HIS WIFE / 1840 ELLEN PIERCE 1928 / DAUGHTER / 1870 JENNIE F. HINDS 1935"* is inscribed below this. *"HINDS"* is carved in relief on the front base. *"ERVIN A. HINDS JR. / 1941 – 1963 / ERVIN A. HINDS / 1907 – 1985"* is inscribed on the right side of this monument. *"1872 JAMES P. HINDS 1951 / HIS WIFE / 1879 ELIZABETH JONES 1932"* is inscribed on the back, and *"PERPETUAL CARE"* is inscribed on the bottom right below this.
"FATHER" is carved in shallow relief on this flat, 2 inch high footstone. It is located in front of the monument, on the far right.

Howland, Annie J. *"ANNIE J. / Dau. of / Lyman B. & / Hannah W. Howland / Born Dec. 14, 1879. / Died May 30. 1891."* The first line is carved along an arch. There is a footstone present, but it contains no inscription.

Howland, Hannah W. *"MOTHER / HANNAH W. CANEDY / Wife of / Lyman B. Howland / Born Sept. 19, 1848 / Died July 20, 1890."* The first line is carved in relief, and the second line is carved along an arch. There is a footstone present, but it contains no inscription. Her husband is buried in Howland Cemetery.

Howland, Luella *"LUELLA HOWLAND / 1887 – 1944"* is inscribed on this lichen encrusted, slanted stone. She was the daughter of Lyman and Hannah Howland.

Kennedy, Cynthia J. *"CYNTHIA J. / KENNEDY / FEB. 6, 1902 / MAR. 3, 1995"* is inscribed on this monument.

Kennedy, Donald R. *"DONALD R. / KENNEDY / MAR. 5, 1933 / SEPT. 21, 1994"* is inscribed on this monument.
"✞ / DONALD ROBERT KENNEDY / SP3 US ARMY / KOREA / MAR 5 1934 SEPT 21 1994" is inscribed on this flat, ground level stone. It is located directly behind the monument. A veteran's marker and flag are present. Note the

discrepancy in the year of birth between the two stones. Lakeville Vital Records list his birth on March 5, 1934.

Kennedy, Edwin A. *"EDWIN A. / KENNEDY / OCT. 24, 1897 / NOV. 23, 1967"* is inscribed on this monument.

McCully, Abigail *"In memory of / ABIGAIL. / wife of Ezra / M°Cully. / who died / Sept. 22, 1843. / aged 41 years."* An urn and willow are carved at the top of this lichen encrusted, slate stone. Curved designs are carved down the sides. *"A. M.ᶜ"* This slate footstone faces the headstone.

McCully, Andrew *"ERECTED / in memory of / ANDREW / who died / June 3, 1843 / ..."* The first line is carved along an arch. The third line is carved in outline. This stone was broken, and reburied behind its base, blocking the rest of the inscription. It was broken and successfully repaired in two other places. It is weathered and very hard to read. Thatcher lists: "McCully, Andrew, died June 3ʳᵈ, 1843, in his 55ᵗʰ year."
"A. Mc." This footstone faces the headstone.

McCully, Andrew, Lieut. *"In MEMORY of Lieuᵗ· / Andrew M°Cully who / died April 23ᵈ, 1790. / in the 43ᵈ, Year of his age. /*
> *My children dear this place draw near*
> *A fathers grave to see;*
> *Not long ago I was with you,*
> *And soon youˡˡ be with me."*

There is a frond carving at the top of this lichen encrusted, slate stone. Tree outlines are carved down the sides. It appears that the *was* in line three of the poem was carved over a ground out *with*. Part of the last line is buried under moss. A veteran's marker and flag are present.
"Lieuᵗ, / Andrew, / M°Cully, / 1790." is inscribed on this slate footstone. The last line is buried underground.

McCully, Annie See Stephen McCully Monument entry.
"ANNIE" is inscribed on this flat, ground level footstone. It is located behind and to the far left of the monument.

McCully, Elizabeth See Stephen McCully Monument entry.
"MOTHER" is inscribed on the top curved surface of this lichen encrusted, upright footstone. It is located behind and to the right of the monument.

McCully, Ezra *"M"* monogram is inscribed at the top of this stone. *"EZRA McCULLY / Died / Mar. 21, 1870, / Æt. 77 yrs. 2 mo / 14 days."* The first line is carved in relief along an arch. *"Bryant & Co."* is inscribed in the lower left corner. This stone has been broken diagonally through the last two lines. The top section is located in front of the bottom section, leaning against it. A repair attempt has failed.
"E. McC." is inscribed on the top curved surface of this upright footstone.

M'Cully, Hannah *"In memory of / HANNAH, / wife of / Ezra M'Cully; / who died / Aug. 30, 1837, / aged 35 years"* The first line is carved along an arch. There is an urn and willow carving at the top of this lichen encrusted, slate stone. Curved designs are carved around the inscription.

"H. MC." This slate footstone faces the headstone.

McCully, Jane *"In MEMORY of / M^{rs}. Jane wife of M^r. John / McCully she died June 3^d. / 1787. Aged 77 Years. /*
> *Remember me as you pass by*
> *Then go thy way, prepare to die."*

A rising sun is carved at the top of this lichen encrusted, slate stone. Tree outlines are carved on the sides.

"M^{rs}, / Jane, / McCully; / 1787." is inscribed on this slate footstone.

McCully, John *"In MEMORY of / Mr John McCully who / died July 28th 1787. / in ye 81st. Year of his age. /*
> *The grave, thy bed blest are ye dead,*
> *That in the Lord thdo die;*
> *For they do rest as God thinks best,*
> *The Soul assends on high."*

There is a frond carving at the top of this lichen encrusted, slate stone. A *"SAR 1775"* marker and flag are present. The *th* in the second line of the poem appears to have been part of the word *that* which was ground down. The word *do* was inscribed on top of the *at*. Note the spelling of *assends*.

"M^r, / John / McCully, / died / 1787." is inscribed on this slate footstone.

McCully, John *"In memory of / MR . JOHN M^cCULLY / who died / July 1, 1829 / aged 85 / years."* There is an urn and willow carving at the top of this slate stone. Swirled designs are carved on the sides, and scalloped designs are carved at the bottom. A *"SAR 1775"* marker and flag are present.

"J. M^cC." This slate footstone faces the headstone.

McCully, Judith *"In memory of / MRS. JUDITH, / wife of / Mr. John M^c. Cully, / who died / Oct. 18, 1834, / aged 64 years."* There is an urn and willow carving at the top of this slate stone. Curved designs are carved down its sides.

"J. M^cC." This slate footstone faces the headstone.

McCully, Lois *"In MEMORY of Mrs. / Lois wid^o. of Mr. Andrew Mc. / Cully, she died Nov. 8th Æ. 1799 / in ye 48th Year of Her Age.*
> *Depart my sighing friends,*
> *And wipe your weeping eyes*
> *Here I must be till Christ desends,*
> *And bids my body rise."*

There is a frond carving at the top of this lichen encrusted, slate stone. The last two lines are buried underground. Notice the spelling of *desends* in the third line of the poem. This stone is starting to split in half, from front to back, on the left side.

"Mrs. / Lois / McCully / died / 1899" is inscribed on this slate footstone. Note the discrepancy in her death year between her head and footstone. *Town of Middleboro Vital Records Index: 1649 – 1945* online through the Middleborough Digital Library has her death year as 1799.

M'Cully, Obed *"In memory of / OBED M'CULLY. / who died / June 11, 1838, / aged 43 years."* The first line is carved along an arch. An urn and willow are carved at the top of this lichen encrusted, slate stone.

"O. M'C." is inscribed on this slate footstone.

McCully, Sidney   See Stephen McCully Monument entry.
"SIDNEY" is inscribed on the top curved surface of this lichen encrusted, upright footstone. It is located behind and to the left of the monument.

McCully, Stephen Monument   *"M"* monogram and ribbon like designs are carved in shallow relief at the top of the front and back of this tall monument. *"STEPHEN McCULLY / BORN AUG. 12, 1804, / DIED OCT. 28, 1898. / ELIZABETH McCULLY / BORN SEPT. 25, 1819, / DIED OCT. 7, 1909"* is inscribed on the front. *"McCULLY"* is carved in relief on the front base. *"SIDNEY McCULLY / BORN JULY 23, 1853, / DIED JAN. 17, 1899. / ANNIE McCULLY / BORN NOV. 14, 1854, / DIED DEC. 6, 1936."* is inscribed on the back. *"C. HARRINGTON / WARREN, R. I."* is inscribed on the back of this monument, on the bottom right.
"FATHER" is inscribed on the top curved surface of this lichen encrusted, upright footstone. It is located directly behind the monument.

Peckins, Abigail   *"MRS. / ABIGAIL. / Wife of / Mr. Thomas Peckins. / died Feb. 25, 1823, / Æt. 68."* The third line is carved in outline. An urn and willow are carved at the top of this lichen encrusted, slate stone. Note the spelling of Pickens.
"A. P. / 1823." This slate footstone faces the headstone. The initials are carved in outline.

Pickens, Abigail   *"In memory of / ABIGAIL, / wife of / George Pickens; / who died / July 13, 1839, / aged 69 years."* An urn and willow are carved at the top of this lichen encrusted, slate stone. A square design is carved down the sides.
"A. P." This slate footstone faces the headstone.

Pickens, Edith   *"EDITH daughter of / Mr. John Pickens and / Anna his wife died / February 2. 1798 / aged 9 months"* An urn and willow are carved at the top of this small, slate stone. It is splitting in half from front to back.
"E. P." This slate footstone is leaning face up against two rocks. It is to the right of her headstone and slightly behind it.

Pickens, George   *"In memory of / GEORGE PICKENS, / who died / April 2, 1849, in / his 82 year."*   An urn and willow are carved at the top of this lichen encrusted, slate stone.
"G. P."   This slate footstone faces the headstone.

Pickens, James   *"Mr. / JAMES PICKENS / died March 22, / 1800 in his 84 / year."*   An urn and willow are carved at the top of this slate stone. A *"SAR 1775"* marker, a veteran's marker and a flag are present.
"Mr. / James / Pickens." is inscribed on this slate footstone.

Pickens, James   *"ERECTED / in / memory / of / MR. JAMES / son of Mr. George / and Mrs. Abigail / Pickens who died / March 5, 1831 / aged 21 years. /*

> *In youth my days are gone and past,*
> *Eternity must count the rest:*
> *My sun is set, my glass is run,*
> *God's holy will on earth is done."*

A sculptured urn and willow are carved at the top of this lichen encrusted, slate stone. Curved designs are carved down the sides. The first three lines are carved along an arch, and the first and fourth lines are carved in outline.
"J. P." is inscribed on this slate footstone.

Pickens, James, Jr.   *"In MEMORY of M^r. / JAMES PICKENS Junr, / who died July 22^d. 1791. / in ye 38th Year of his age. /*

> *This is the end of all that live,*
> *This is my dark long home.*
> *JESUS himself lay in the grave,*
> *The house where all must come."*

There is a frond carving at the top of this slate stone.
"M^r. / James / Pickens, Junr. / 1791" is inscribed on this slate footstone.

Pickens, James, Jun.   *"In / memory of / Mr. JAMES PICKENS jun. / who died / Oct. 23. 1821 / in his 30. / year. /*

> *Not on the Ocean frightful main,*
> *Not on a couch with racking pain*
> *Did death command or bid me fly*
> *To meet my God above the sky;*
> *But on a banefal spot of earth,*
> *I groan,d my last, exhal,d my breath,*
> *Now widow weeps & orphans cry,*
> *My spirit is above the sky*
> *From tears unseen from groans unheard."*

An urn and willow are carved at the top of this slate stone. Scalloped designs are carved down the sides. Note the spelling of *baneful* in the poem and the lowered apostrophe.
"Mr. / J. P. / 1821."   This slate footstone is located face up, to the far right of this row of gravestones. It is almost in line with the other footstones. The headstone for the Shepard son is located where James' footstone should be.

Pickens, Jonathan H.   *"JONATHAN H. PICKENS. / Born / Aug. 15, 1808, / Died /*

Aug. 26, 1880. / Aged 72 Years / & 10 Days." The first line is carved along an arch. *"J. H. P. / 1880"* is inscribed on this upright footstone, which faces its headstone. It has a cement base.

Pickens, Margaret   *"Mrs. / MARGARET PICKENS / wife of Mr. / JAMES PICKENS / died January 28. / 1798 in her 70. / year."* An urn and willow are carved at the top of this lichen encrusted, slate stone. The last line is buried underground.
"Mrs. / Margaret / Pickens." is inscribed on this slate footstone, which faces the front of the cemetery. It is located on the far left, behind Priscilla Shephard's headstone. This stone is made of a different kind of slate than that used for her headstone, but it has the same outline.

Pickens, Mary   *"MARY. / Daught. of / Mr. George Pickens, / died March 5, 1831. / Æt 30."* There is an urn and willow carving at the top of this lichen encrusted, slate stone. Curved designs are carved down the sides.
"M. P. / 1831" is inscribed on this intact slate footstone. There are two other pieces of slate near her footstone, but neither of them have inscriptions on them.

Pickens, Polly   *"Mrs. / POLLY PICKENS / wife of Lieu. / GEORGE PICKENS / died August 19. / 1805 in her 37. / Year."* A simple urn and willow carving at the top of this slate stone.
"Mrs. / Polly / Pickens" There is a 4 inch crack at the top of this slate footstone.

Pickens, Thomas   *"In memory of / THOMAS PICKENS / who died June 7, 1845, / Aged 93 Yrs. /*
> *Hear what the voice from heaven proclaims*
> *For all the pious dead,*
> *Sweet is the Savior of their names,*
> *And soft their sleeping bed."*

This rectangular, slate stone is encrusted with lichen. A *"SAR 1775"* marker, a veteran's marker and flag are present.
"T. P." is inscribed on this slate footstone.

Robbins, Hope   *"HOPE, / Wife of / SETH ROBBINS, / Died Dec. 30, / 1856, / Aged 80 years, / 3 months, & / 2 days."* This red, rectangular slate stone is leaning backwards.
"H. R." is inscribed on this gray, rectangular, slate footstone.

Sawyer, Lydia M.   *"LYDIA M. SAWYER / 1846 – 1882"* is inscribed on this slanted stone.

Shaw, Angie F.   See John Shaw Monument entry.
"A. F. C. S." is carved in shallow relief on this flat, ground level footstone. It is located in front of the monument, on the left.

Shaw, Fred A.   See John Shaw Monument entry.
"F. A. S." is carved in shallow relief on this flat, ground level footstone. It is located directly in front of the monument, on the right.

Shaw, John Monument   *"S"* monogram and ivy leaves are carved in shallow relief at the top of this monument. *"JOHN SHAW / OCT. 25, 1834 – NOV. 23,*

1919 / HIS WIFE / ANGIE F. CANEDY / MAY 3, 1841 – MAR. 7, 1885. / THEIR DAUGHTER / SOPHRONIA M. / SEPT. 18, 1861 – FEB. 24, 1885." is inscribed on the front. *"SHAW"* is carved in relief on the base. *"FRED A. THEIR SON / MAR. 1, 1863 – MAR. 8, 1928 / MARY G. THEIR DAUGHTER / JULY 8, 1864 – OCT. 1, 1938"* is inscribed on the back, and *"KAVANAGH BROS / BOSTON"* is carved in shallow relief on the base on the left side.
"J. S." is carved in shallow relief on this flat, 1 inch high footstone. It is located in front of the monument, on the far left.

Shaw, Mary G.   See John Shaw Monument entry.
"M. G. S." is carved in shallow relief on this flat, ground level footstone. It is located in front of the monument, on the right.

Shaw, Sophronia M.   See John Shaw Monument entry.
"S. M. S." is carved in shallow relief on this flat, ground level footstone. It is located directly in front of the monument, on the left.

Shepard, Infant son   *"In / memory of / a SON of / Thomas &; Priscilla / Shepard, / who died / Aug. 1, 1828."* An urn and willow are carved at the top of this small, slate stone. Note the semicolon in the fourth line. There is a rectangular recessed area in which *a SON of* is inscribed. *SON* is carved in outline.
"S." is carved in outline on this slate footstone. It is located behind and to the right of the headstone.

Shepard, Priscilla   *"In / memory of / PRISCILLA, / wife of / Thomas Shepard. / who died / April 6, 1831, / aged 33 years."* *"Geo. Thompson."* is inscribed on the bottom right of this stone. The third line is carved in outline. An urn and willow are carved at the top of this lichen encrusted, slate stone. Curved designs are carved down the sides.
"P. S." is inscribed on this slate footstone. It is located to the right rear of the headstone.

Washburn, Emery C.   *"EMERY CANEDY WASHBURN / MAY 11, 1912 – MAY 29, 1912"* is inscribed on the top surface of this flat, 6-10 inch high stone.

Washburn, Eugene V.   *"EUGENE V. / WASHBURN / JAN. 16, 1870 / JAN 24, 1941"* is inscribed on this monument.

Washburn, Merle C.   *"MERLE C. / WASHBURN / APR. 29, 1892 / NOV. 9, 1942"* A Mason's symbol is carved in shallow relief at the top of this monument. A *"Middleboro Lodge / B. P. O. E."* marker and flag are present.

Washburn, Olive C. B.   *"OLIVE C. B. / WASHBURN / JAN. 26, 1875 / APR. 11, 1956"* is inscribed on this monument.

Washburn, Thomas E.   *"THOMAS E. / WASHBURN / MAR. 22, 1896 / AUG. 7, 1965"* is inscribed on this monument.

McCully Cemetery Map Index

Alphabetical:

By Location:

1 – Washburn, Eugene V. (1870-1941)
2 – Washburn, Olive C. B. (1875-1956)
3 – Washburn, Thomas E. (1896-1965)
4 – Beaton, Thomas C. (1874-1955)
　　Beaton, Abbie E. (1875-1950)
5 – Washburn, Merle C. (1892-1942)
6 – Kennedy, Cynthia J. (1902-1995)
7 – Kennedy, Edwin A. (1897-1967)
8 – Kennedy, Donald R. (1934-1994)
9 – Washburn, Emery C. (1912)
10 – Kennedy, Donald R. (1934-1994)
11 – Hinds, Jennie F. (1870-1935)
12 – Hinds, Ellen P. (1840-1928)
13 – Hinds, Stephen V. (1836-1917)
14 – Shaw, John (1834-1919)
15 – Shaw, Angie F. (1841-1885)
16 – Shaw, Sophronia M. (1861-1885)
17 – Shaw, Fred A. (1863-1928)
18 – Shaw, Mary G. (1864-1938)
19 – Hinds, Stephen V. (1836-1917)
　　Hinds, Ellen P. (1840-1928)
　　Hinds, Jennie F. (1870-1935)
　　Hinds, Ervin A., Jr. (1941-1963)
　　Hinds, Ervin A. (1907-1985)
　　Hinds, James P. (1872-1951)
　　Hinds, Elizabeth J. (1879-1932)
20 – Hinds, Elizabeth J. (1879-1932)
21 – Shaw, John (1834-1919)
　　Shaw, Angie F. (1841-1885)
　　Shaw, Sophronia M. (1861-1885)
　　Shaw, Fred A. (1863-1928)
　　Shaw, Mary G. (1864-1938)
22 – Canedy, Vandalia A. (1847-1932)
23 – Canedy, Emery W. (1844-1926)
24 – Canedy, Lucy (1808-1898)
25 – Canedy, John W., Capt. (1803-1881)
26 – Canedy, Abigail A. (~1808-1834)
27 – Canedy, Abigail A. W. (1834-1924)
28 – Howland, Annie J. (1879-1891)
29 – Howland, Hannah W. (1848-1890)
30 – Howland, Luella (1887-1944)
31 – McCully, Stephen (1804-1898)
　　McCully, Elizabeth (1819-1909)
　　McCully, Sidney (1853-1899)
　　McCully, Annie (1854-1936)
32 – Ashley, Mariva G. (1849-1901)
　　Ashley, John E. (1835-1913)
　　Ashley, Marcus M. (~1840-1864)
33 – McCully, Annie (1854-1936)

34 – McCully, Sidney (1853-1899)
35 – McCully, Stephen (1804-1898)
36 – McCully, Elizabeth (1819-1909)
37 – McCully, Ezra (1793-1870)
38 – M'Cully, Obed (~1795-1838)
39 – McCully, Abigail (~1802-1843)
40 – M'Cully, Hannah (~1802-1837)
41 – McCully, John (~1744-1829)
42 – McCully, Judith (~1770-1834)
43 – Ashley, Abigail (~1782-1846)
44 – Ashley, Luther (~1782-1830)
45 – Ashley, Chloe (~1781-1804)
46 – McCully, Andrew (~1789-1843)
47 – Briggs, Betsey (~1783-1802)
48 – McCully, Andrew, Lt. (~1748-1790)
49 – McCully, Lois (~1752-1799)
50 – McCully, John (~1707-1787)
51 – McCully, Jane (~1710-1787)
52 – Ashley, Chester (1863-1954)
　　Ashley, Sophronia A. (1861-1948)
　　Ashley, Mildred A. (1898-1977)
53 – Ashley, Alsada P. (1820-1897)
54 – Ashley, David (1807-1880)
55 – Ashley, Lavinia (~1806-1861)
56 – Ashley, Judith (~1812-1847)
57 – Ashley, William (~1812-1836)
58 – Ashley, Abigail (~1819-1825)
59 – Pickens, Thomas (~1752-1845)
60 – Peckins, Abigail (~1755-1823)
61 – Pickens, Abigail (~1770-1839)
62 – Pickens, George (~1768-1849)
63 – Pickens, Jonathan H. (1808-1880)
64 – Pickens, James (~1810-1831)
65 – Pickens, Mary (~1801-1831)
66 – Pickens, James, Jr. (~1792-1821)
67 – Shepard, Priscilla (~1798-1831)
68 – Pickens, Polly (~1769-1805)
69 – Pickens, James, Junr. (~1754-1791)
70 – Pickens, James (~1717-1800)
71 – Pickens, Margaret (~1729-1798)
72 – Pickens, James, Jr. (~1792-1821)
73 – Shepard, Infant son (1828)
74 – Pickens, Margaret (~1729-1798)
75 – Shepard, Infant son (1828)
76 – Sawyer, Lydia M. (1846-1882)
77 – Pickens, Edith (1797-1798)
78 – Pickens, Edith (1797-1798)
79 – Robbins, Hope (~1776-1856)

McCully Cemetery Map

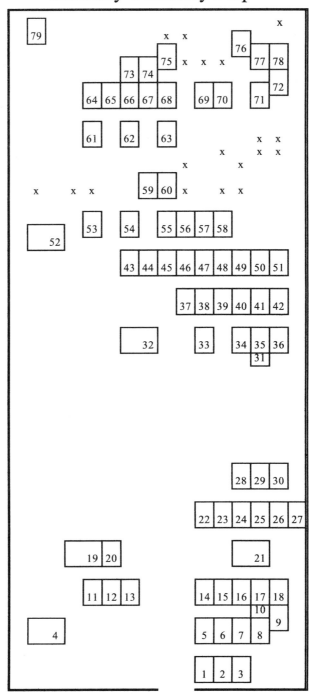

x = fieldstone   ⚌ = stone wall   ▬ = stone post and metal rail fence

H I G H L A N D   R O A D

Chapter 16
Mullein Hill Cemetery

Mullein Hill Cemetery is located just north of Grace Fellowship Foursquare Church, (86 Highland Road), but is owned by Mullein Hill Baptist Church. A stone retaining wall forms the front boundary and part of the right border, and remnants of an old stone post and metal rail fence are on the right and left sides. A chain link fence on the left side has two gates opening into the back section. In the center front of this cemetery is a crypt, belonging to William Canedy. The sign is in good repair, but misspells Mullein. The stones face southeast, and date from 1843 to 2000. The Lakeville Assessor's Office lists the cemetery as half an acre in size. Entries were recorded September 7, 2001.

Abele, Esther M.   *"ESTHER M. W. / ABELE / 1903 – 1998"* is inscribed on this flat, 2 – 4 inch high stone. It was added since the original transcription date.

Aksell, Anna M.   *"ANNA M. AKSELL / WIFE OF / STURE GUSTAV AKSELL / MAR. 13, 1905   NOV. 29, 1993"* A circled cross is carved at the top of this flat, ground level stone.

Aksell, Sture G.   *"STURE GUSTAV AKSELL / COX US NAVY / WORLD WAR II / JULY 5 1908   NOV 18 1980"* A circled cross is carved at the top of this flat, ground level stone. A veteran's marker and flag are present.

Allen, Earnest E.   *"EARNEST E. / Son of / Edgar W. & Olive / ALLEN. / Born July 1, 1869. / Died April 22, 1870. / Asleep in Jesus."* is inscribed on this small, scroll shaped stone.

Andrews, Francis A.   *"FRANCIS A. ANDREWS / 1855 – 1856"* is inscribed on this flat, 4 inch high stone. It is in front of the Winslow Monument, on the left side. It matches the nearby Winslow footstones. He was the grandson of Asa T. Winslow, through his daughter Ann Eliza.

Arbec, Nancy   *"ARBEC /   / NANCY / MAR 1 1951   MAR 1 1988 / PROV.*

31:28" An open book with flowers on either side is carved at the top of this monument. A cross is carved on top of the book. There is space for another inscription above hers. A Tootell Monument Works metal tag is present.

Ashley, Almira F.   See Silas Ashley Monument entry.
"MOTHER" is carved in shallow relief on the top horizontal surface of this footstone. *"A. F. A."* is inscribed on the front. It is located behind the monument, on the right.

Ashley, Arabella   See Luther Ashley Monument entry.
"A" monogram is carved within a double circle at the top of this monument. There are branching designs carved around it. *"ARABELLA / Ashley / Died Aug. 16, 1934, / Aged 83 yrs. 3 mos. & 5 ds."* The first line is carved in relief. It is located slightly behind the monument, on the far left.

Ashley, Benjamin T.   See Calvin Ashley Monument entry.
"BENNIE" is inscribed on the top curved surface of this footstone. *"1884."* is carved on the front. This stone is lying face up, flush with the ground. It is located in front of the monument, on the right.

Ashley, Calvin Monument   *"CALVIN ASHLEY, / SEPT. 28, 1816. / MARCH 24, 1868. / REBECCA C. / HIS WIFE / OCT. 18, 1821, / APRIL 17, 1886."* is inscribed on the front of this textured monument. *"A (monogram)"* is inscribed on the front base, and below it is carved *"ASHLEY"* in relief. *"BENJAMIN T. / FEB. 2, 1858. / OCT. 30, 1884. / LUMAN R. / APRIL 9, 1866. / SEPT. 28, 1884."* is inscribed on the left side of this monument. *"JENNIE R. / JULY 18, 1854. / APRIL 19, 1883. / NETTIE B. / APRIL 2, 1856. / OCT. 8, 1876."* is inscribed on the right side.
> *"... Father, Mother gone.*
> *... brothers borne away,*
> *Our hope is now in God alone,*
> *Whom Heaven and Earth alike obey."* is inscribed on the

back. The monument is very cracked and weathered on this side making some words in the poem unreadable. Geometric designs are at the bottom of all four sides. The urn sculpture from the top of the monument is sitting on the ground on the left side of it.

"FATHER." is inscribed on the top curved surface of this footstone. *"1868."* is inscribed on the front. It is located in front of the monument, on the far left.

Ashley, Elmer   See Luther Ashley Monument entry.

Ashley, Isaiah Stone   *"ISAIAH / Born / Jan. 24, / DIED / Jan. 26, / 1844."* is inscribed on the left side of the stone. *"NOAH / Born / March 24, / DIED / March 25, / 1845."* is inscribed on the right side. *"Sons of Silas P. & Phoebe E."* is inscribed below this in a rectangular recessed area that extends across the width of the stone. *"ASHLEY"* is inscribed on the center bottom. There is a flag present.

Ashley, Jennie R.   See Calvin Ashley Monument entry.
"JENNIE." is inscribed on the top curved surface of this footstone. *"1883."* is inscribed on the front. This stone is lying face up, flush with the ground. It is located in front of the monument, on the left.

Ashley, Laurett S.   See Luther Ashley Monument entry (spelling is Lorett here).
"There is rest in Heaven. / LAURETT S. / Dau. of / Luther & Theodora / Ashley, / died Dec. 28, 1855, / Æ. 11 yrs. 8 mo. 2 d̄." The first line is carved in relief along an arch. A sculptured carving of a left hand, with the index finger and thumb pointing to heaven, is carved between the words *rest* and *in* at the top of this stone. *"L. A."* is inscribed on the footstone.

Ashley, Luman R.   See Calvin Ashley Monument entry.
"LUMAN" is inscribed on the top curved surface of this stone. *"1884."* is inscribed on the front. There are two cracks radiating from the bottom. The stone is lying face up, flush with the ground. It is located in front of the monument, on the right.

Ashley, Luther Monument   This monument is situated at a 45 degree angle from the orientation of the rest of the stones in this cemetery. The front of the monument faces the southeast. *"A (monogram) / LUTHER ASHLEY / MAR. 8, 1814 / FEB. 4, 1895 / THEODORA A. / HIS WIFE / SEPT. 24, 1813 / MAR. 9, 1891"* is inscribed on the front of this monument *"ASHLEY"* is carved in relief on the front base. *"A (monogram) / LORETT S. / APR. 26, 1844 / DEC. 28, 1855 / ELMER / OCT. 17, 1846 / LOST AT SEA, 1864 / ARABELLA / MAY 11, 1851 / AUG. 16, 1934"* is inscribed on the left side. *"S (monogram) / URIAH SAMPSON / JULY 24, 1842 / LOST AT SEA, 1864 / BETSEY J. / HIS WIFE / SEPT. 23, 1842 / SEPT. 28, 1886 / URIAH, THEIR SON / MAY 31, 1864 / JUNE 27, 1880"* is inscribed on the right side. *"SAMPSON"* is carved in relief on the base on the right side. *"WALTER SAMPSON / SON OF / URIAH & BETSEY J. / ASHLEY SAMPSON / DEC 13, 1862 / APR. 23, 1931"* is inscribed on the back.
"L. A." is inscribed on the top horizontal surface of this 1-4 inch high footstone. It is located in front of the monument, on the far left.

Ashley, Nettie B.   See Calvin Ashley Monument entry.
"NETTIE." is inscribed on the top curved surface of this footstone. *"1876."* is inscribed on the front. This stone is lying face up and is beginning to be buried. It is

located in front of the monument, on the left.

Ashley, Noah   *"In / Memory of / NOAH ASHLEY, / who died / Feb. 21, 1843. / aged 55 years / 8 mo. & 3 ds. /*

> *Though dead, he speaks in reason's ear,*
> *And in example lives*
> *His faith and hope and mighty deeds,*
> *Still fresh instructions gives."*

The third line is carved in relief. There is an urn and willow carving at the top of this rectangular gravestone.
"N. A." is inscribed on the footstone.

Ashley, Noah   See Isaiah Ashley Monument entry.

Ashley, Phebe E.   See Silas P. Ashley Monument entry.
"MOTHER" is carved in shallow relief on the top slanted surface of this footstone. *"P. E. A."* is inscribed on the front. It is located behind and to the left of the monument.

Ashley, Rebecca C.   See Calvin Ashley Monument entry.
"MOTHER" is inscribed on the top curved surface of this footstone. *"1886."* is inscribed on the front. It is located in front of the monument, on the far left.

Ashley, Ruth   *"RUTH, / wife of / Noah Ashley, / died Jan. 30, 1867: / Aged 75 yrs. 8 m's. / & 10 d's. / Blessed are the dead which die in the Lord."* The first line is carved in relief.
"R. A." is inscribed on this footstone.

Ashley, Silas P. Monument
"A (monogram) / CAPT. / SILAS P. ASHLEY. / BORN / APR. 4, 1813 / DIED APR. 2, 1897. / PHEBE E. / HIS WIFE / BORN OCT. 15, 1815. / DIED AUG. 11, 1856. / ALMIRA F. / HIS WIFE / BORN MAR. 15, 1826 / DIED MAY 18, 1913." The second line is carved along an arch. *"ASHLEY"* is inscribed on the base of this tall, ornately topped, reddish brown monument. A veteran's marker and flag are present.
"FATHER" is carved in shallow relief on the top slanted surface of this footstone. Lichen obliterates most of the inscription. *"S. P. A."* is inscribed on the front. It is located directly behind the monument.

Ashley, Theodora   See Luther Ashley Monument entry.
"T. A. A." is carved in relief on the top horizontal surface of this 2-4 inch high

footstone. It is located in front of the monument, on the left.

Berthelot, Helen W. *"IN LOVING MEMORY / HELEN W. / BERTHELOT / NOV 29, 1904 – MAY 6, 1996"* is inscribed on this flat, ground level stone.

Bishop, Catherine T. *"B (monogram) / CATHERINE T. / WIFE OF / DEXTER BISHOP, JR. / DIED / JULY 16, 1879, / AGED / 74 YRS. 6 DAYS."* This textured stone shares its base with the stone of her husband.
"C. T. B." This footstone faces the headstone.

Bishop, Dexter, Jr. *"B (monogram) / DEXTER BISHOP, JR . / DIED / APRIL 5,1873, / AGED / 67 YRS. 6 MOS. / 11 DAYS."* *"O. Harrington"* is inscribed on the bottom right. A branching design is carved around the monogram. This textured stone shares its base with that of his wife Catherine T.
"D. B." This footstone was cemented to the base between the two headstones. It is broken off and is located behind the base, leaning face up against it.

Bishop, Dexter, 3ʳᵈ *"DEXTER BISHOP 3ᴰ, / Died / Nov. 13, 1863; / Aged 21 yrs. 2m. / & 13 d's. /*
     When shall we meet again,
     Meet ne'er to sever,
     When will peace wreath her chain,
     Round us forever."
The first line is carved along an arch.
"D. B." This footstone faces the headstone.

Boscombe, David A. *"Boscombe / IN ALL THINGS / GIVE THANKS"* Between the first and second line are carvings of a farm on the right, and pumpkins, corn cobs, corn stalks and a basket of vegetables on the left. *"DAVID A. BOSCOMBE / MAY 25, 1948 – FEB. 22, 1987"* is inscribed on the back. A Barnicoat Monuments metal tag is present.

Canedy, Carrie B. See Elkanah L. Canedy Monument entry.

Canedy, Elizabeth B. See Elkanah L. Canedy Monument entry.

Canedy, Elkanah L. Monument *"CANEDY"* is carved in relief on the front of this large monument. *"C (monogram) / ELKANAH L. CANEDY / 1829 – 1908 / HIS WIFE / ELIZABETH B. WINSLOW / 1843 – 1924 / WALTER S. CANEDY / 1854 – 1918 / HIS WIFE / CARRIE B. STAPLES / 1860 – 1933"* is inscribed on the back. The monogram is carved in shallow relief.

Canedy, Janette *"MOTHER"* is carved in shallow relief on the top curved surface of this monument. *"JANETTE A. CANEDY / BORN / JULY 5, 1837. / DIED / JUNE 30, 1865."* The first line is carved along an arch. This stone shares its base with the gravestones of William and Sophronia Canedy.

Canedy, Sarah E. *"SARAH E. / wife of / Elkanah W. Canedy / Born Apr. 21, 1833. / Died Oct. 7, 1872. / Dear Mother we will meet no more / on earth, / But meet again in Heaven."* There is a 6 inch crack radiating from the center bottom.
"S. E. C." is inscribed on the footstone.

Canedy, Sophronia M. *"MOTHER"* is carved in shallow relief on the top curved surface of this monument. *"SOPHRONIA M. CANEDY / BORN / JUNE 11, 1831. / DIED / JUNE 18, 1859."* The first line is carved along an arch. This stone shares its base with the gravestones of William and Janette Canedy.

Canedy, Walter S.   See Elkanah L. Canedy Monument entry.

Canedy, William Crypt   *"WILLIAM CANEDY. / 1861."* is inscribed on the metal door of this crypt.

Canedy, William   *"FATHER"* is carved in shallow relief on the top curved surface of this monument. *"WILLIAM CANEDY / BORN / JAN. 11, 1824. / DIED / AUG. 13, 1889."* The first line is carved along an arch. This stone shares its base with the gravestones of Sophronia and Janette Canedy.

Caswell, Abigail M.   *"ABIGAIL M. CASWELL / died / Dec. 14, 1916 / Aged 85 years / 8 m's & 14 d's"* The first line is carved along an arch.
"A. M. C." is inscribed on the footstone.

Caswell, Arthur L.   *"ARTHUR L. / Son of Wm H. & / Abigail M. / Caswell, / died Feb. 21, 1862, / Aged 4 yrs. / & 11 m's. / Sleeping here but not forgotten."* The first line is carved in relief.
"A. L. C." is inscribed on the footstone.

Caswell, Betsey H.   *"BETSEY H. / wife of / Abram H. Caswell / died / March 2, 1869; / Aged 28 years / 2 m's. 8 d's.*

> *Sweet is thy rest my loving wife,*
> *Thy spirit dwells with purer life:*
> *While angels watch the sacred place*
> *Which holds thy form in death's embrace."*

The first line is carved in relief along an arch. There is a sculptured carving of a flower at the top. This stone is separated from its base and lying face up behind it. A crack radiating from the center bottom has been repaired. This crack had extended up to the seventh line.
"B. H. C." is inscribed on the footstone.

Caswell, Nathaniel   *"NATHANIEL CASWELL / Died Sept. 20, 1859, / Aged 49 yrs. 1 mo. / & 29 d's."* The first line is carved in relief along an arch.
"N. C." is inscribed on the footstone.

Caswell, Nathaniel   *"NATH'L CASWELL, / died / Nov. 23, 1867, / Aged 86 yrs. 11 m. / & 11 d's."* The first line is carved in relief along an arch.
"N. C." is inscribed on the footstone.

Caswell, Otis W.   *"OTIS W. / Son of W^m. H. & / Abigail M. Caswell, / died March 2, 1862 / Aged 9 yrs. 6 m's / & 2 d's. / 'Oft shall we think of thee.' "* The first line is carved in relief.
"O. W. C." is inscribed on the footstone.

Caswell, Susan   *"SUSAN / wife of / Nathaniel Caswell, / died Sept. 15, 1882, / Aged 76 yrs. 6 m's / & 6 d's."* The first line is carved in relief.
"S. C." is inscribed on the footstone.

Caswell, Theodora *"THEODORA, / wife of / Nathaniel Caswell, / died Jan. 12, 1854, / Aged 69 yrs. 7 m's."* The first line is carved in relief along an arch. *"T. C."* is inscribed on the footstone.

Caswell, William H. *"WILLIAM H. CASWELL / died / Sept. 29, 1886. / Aged 66 years / 6 m's & 27 d's."* The first line is carved along an arch. There is a remnant of a footstone present, but it was broken off at ground level and the top piece is missing. No inscription was found.

Chace, Barbara See Merrill E. Chace Monument entry (listed as Barbara S. on this stone.)\
"BARBARA GURNEY CHACE / JULY 6, 1926 / AUG. 18, 1964" is inscribed on this flat 0-2 inch high stone. It is located to the left of the Merrill Chace Monument. Lakeville Vital Records show her maiden name was Barbara Staples Gurney.

Chace, Merrill E. Monument *"CHACE"* is inscribed on the front of this monument. On the left side, an open book is carved with the words *"HOLY BIBLE"* inscribed on it *"1925 MERRILL E. _____ / 1926 BARBARA S. 1964 / 1918 VICTORIA H. _____"* is inscribed on the back. A Central Monument Co. tag is present.

Chace, Victoria H. See Merrill E. Chace Monument entry.

Clark, Charles H. *"CHARLES H. / Son of / Stephen & / Mary Clark, / died in the / Hospital at / Petersburg Va. / Apr. 26, 1865; / Aged 17 yrs. / 4 m's & 3d's."* The first line is carved along an arch on this 4-foot tall obelisk. There is a *"GAR 8 106"* marker, a veteran's marker and a flag present.

Clark, Mary See Stephen Clark Monument entry.

Clark, Stephen Monument *"STEPHEN CLARK / SEPT. 4, 1814 – MAY 27, 1899. / MARY, HIS WIFE / OCT. 22, 1826 – FEB. 11, 1901."* is inscribed on this roofed monument.

Coleman, Aurelia *"AURELIA COLEMAN / 1796 – 1854"* is inscribed on this flat 0-1 inch high stone. It is located to the immediate left of the Winslow Monument. She was the daughter of Asa and Deborah Winslow

Crump, Laurence N. *"LET ME WALK WITH GOD / LAURENCE N CRUMP / VIRGINIA / EM1 US NAVY / KOREA / JAN 14, 1932 MAY 13 1970"* A circled

cross is carved between the words *me* and *walk* in the first line. A treble cleft and two notes are carved on the left. A veteran's marker and flag are present near this flat, ground level stone.

Dean, Emma   *"EMMA / wife of / Philip C. Dean, / died May 21, 1870; / Aged 42 yrs. 2 m's / & 20 d's."* The first line is carved in relief. This stone is broken in three places under the inscription. It has been successfully repaired.

Dean, Philip C.   *"PHILIP / Philip C. Dean, / died Feb. 3, 1891. / Aged 62 yrs. 11 m's / & 3 d's."* The first line is carved in relief. The bottom right corner of the stone is cracked. A break through the third line has been successfully repaired.

DeMoura, Duane E.   *"DUANE E. / DEMOURA / MAR. 16, 1959 – NOV. 7, 1977 / HE GAVE HIS LIFE FOR A FRIEND / JOHN 15:13."* There are rose carvings in the upper corners of this monument. A Barnicoat Monuments metal tag is present.

DeMoura, Gail M.   See Richard D. Demoura Stone entry.

DeMoura, Jeremy   *"JEREMY DEMOURA / DEC. 19, 1974"* is inscribed on this flat, ground level stone.

DeMoura, Richard D. Stone   *"DEMOURA / 1932 RICHARD D. 1996 / HIS WIFE / 1938 GAIL M. ____ "* is inscribed on this flat, 0-2 inch high stone.

Dubee, Zephrien J.   *"ZEPHRIEN J DUBEE / CPL US ARMY / WORLD WAR II / NOV 8 1921 ✝ JUL 20 1976 "* is embossed on this flat, ground level, brass marker. *"ZEPHRIEN J. DUBEE / NOV. 8, 1921 – JUL. 20, 1976"* There is a floral carving on the left side of this slanted stone. A Barnicoat Monuments metal tag is present. A veteran's marker and flag are present.

Egger Monument   *"EGGER"* is all that is inscribed on this monument. At the top is carved a cranberry scoop with the initials *"J.H.E."* inscribed on it. Cranberry plants are carved in the top corners. A Maver Memorials metal tag is present.

Egger, Annie B.   See Milton W. Egger Monument entry.

Egger, Bruce C.   *"BRUCE COBB / EGGER / 1938 – 1938"* is inscribed on this slanted stone.

Egger, Gertrude M.   *"GERTRUDE M. EGGER / 1905 – 1997"* is inscribed on this flat, ground level stone. It is located in front of the Egger Monument, on the far right.

Egger, Helen R.   See Milton W. Egger Monument entry.

Egger, John H., Jr.   *"JOHN H. EGGER JR. / 1904 – 1991"* is inscribed on this flat, ground level stone. It is located in front of the Egger Monument, on the right.

Egger, Milton W. Monument   *"EGGER"* is carved in relief on the front. A cranberry plant is carved in the top left corner, and a carving of a man scooping cranberries is at the bottom of this monument. *"MILTON WESLEY EGGER / AUG. 18, 1900 – APR. 13, 1968 / HIS WIFE / ANNIE BIRD PARSHLEY / NOV. 14, 1901 – JULY 22, 1966 / HELEN RUTH EGGER / SEPT. 23, 1921 – APR. 4, 1972 / 'TIL JESUS COMES"* is inscribed on the back. A Barnicoat metal tag is present.

Fletcher, Emma J. See Solomon Fletcher Monument entry.

"Mother's darling is in Heaven / EMMA JANE, / Daughter of / Solomon I. & Mary A. / FLETCHER. / Born March 4, 1856 / Died June 19, 1857" The first line is carved along an arch. A sculptured lamb is carved between the first and second lines. This stone is broken below the inscriptions. The top part is lying face up and located to the left of the bottom part which is still in the ground. These pieces are located behind the Fletcher Monument.

"E. J. F." is inscribed on this footstone, which is leaning backwards.

Fletcher, Mary A. See Solomon Fletcher Monument entry.

Fletcher, Solomon Monument *"FLETCHER"* is carved in relief on the front of this monument. *"SOLOMON FLETCHER / 1830 – 1863 / HIS WIFE / MARY A. ANTHONY / 1835 – 1924 / EMMA THEIR DAUGHTER / 1856 – 1857"* is inscribed on the back.

Gagnon, George R. Monument *"GAGNON"* is carved at the top of this slanted monument. Roses are carved on either side. An open book with the inscription *"GEORGE R / 1915 – 1996"* is carved on the left side, and an open book with the inscription *"WINNIFRED E / 1922 – 1981"* is carved on the right side. A heart with the inscription *"MARRIED / FEB. 19, / 1938"* is carved between the two books.

Gagnon, Winnifred E. See George R. Gagnon Monument entry.

Goss, Madison E. *"MADISON ELIZABETH ROBERTSON / GOSS / OCT. 5, 1988 / DAUGHTER OF GEORGE & MARGARET"* A child angel praying is carved on the left side of this flat, ground level stone. It is beginning to be buried.

Gushee Monument *"GUSHEE"* is all that is inscribed on this monument.

Gushee, Miriam F. *"MIRIAM FRANCES GUSHEE / APR. 30, 1928 – DEC. 20, 1980 / ALL THINGS WORK TOGETHER FOR GOOD / TO THEM THAT LOVE GOD. / ROMANS 8.28"* There is a circled cross carved above Miriam's name. This flat, ground level stone is beginning to be buried.

Hannant, Robert W. *"ROBERT WILLIAM HANNANT / MM3 US NAVY / KOREA / 1936 † 1979"* is embossed on this flat, ground level, brass marker. A veteran's marker and flag are present.

Hervey, Abbie M. See Johnathan Hervey Monument entry.

"A. M. H." is inscribed in shallow relief on this flat, ground level footstone that is beginning to be buried. It is located to the left of the monument.

Hervey, Jennie E. See Johnathan Hervey Monument entry.

Hervey, Johnathan Monument *"1849 JOHNATHAN HERVEY 1939 / 1851 ABBIE M. HIS WIFE 1936 / 1869 WILLIAM I. SON 1907 / 1874 JENNIE E. DAU. 1878"* There are floral carvings at the top of this monument. *"HERVEY"* is carved in relief at the bottom. *"PERPETUAL CARE"* is inscribed on the base.

"J. H." is inscribed in shallow relief on this sunken footstone. It is located to the far left of the monument.

Hervey, William I. See Johnathan Hervey Monument entry.

Hinds, Chloe   *"CHLOE / His Wife / DIED / Apr. 21, 1888, / AGED / 82 YRS. 1 Mo."*
This stone shares its base with the gravestone of her husband, Sumner Hinds.

Hinds, Emma May   *"EMMA MAY"* is carved in relief on the top curved surface of
this stone. *"Daughter of / JOHN C. & EVA D. / HINDS. / Died Feb 14, 1881, /
Aged 8 years, 2 mos. / 20 dys. / of such is the kingdom of heaven"* is inscribed on the
front of this rear facing stone.

Hinds, Eva D.   *"H (monogram) / EVA D. / wife of / JOHN C. HINDS, / BORN / JULY
10, 1853, / DIED / FEB. 14, 1881. / Sleeping here but not forgotten."* This stone
shares its base with the stone for John Hinds. A crack on the bottom left has been
successfully repaired.

Hinds, John C.   *"H (monogram) / JOHN C. HINDS, / BORN / MAY 24, 1843. /
DIED / FEB. 22, 1877. / Not lost but gone before."* *"Burt, Taunton"* is inscribed on
the bottom center. This stone shares its base with the stone for Eva Hinds. A crack
on the bottom left has been successfully repaired.
"J. C. H." is inscribed on the footstone.

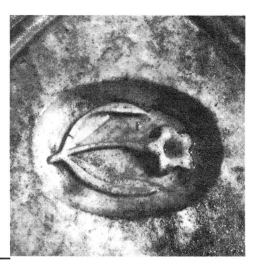

Hinds, Nancy J.   *"NANCY J. / dau. of / Sumner & Chloe / Hinds. / died Oct. 30,
1868: / Aged 27 years / & 3 m's /*

> *Sister thou has gone before us,*
> *And thy Heaven li__ spirit's flown:*
> *Where tears are wiped from every eye,*
> *And sorrow is unknown."*

The first line is carved in relief along an arch. There is a sculptured flower carved at
the top. This stone is separated from its base, and is lying face down in front of it. It
was broken in three places, and a repair was attempted. The repairs of the two
breaks involving the poem have failed. The fourth word in the second line is
unreadable due to these breaks.
"N. J. H." is inscribed on the footstone.

Hinds, Ruth   *"RUTH, / DAUGHTER OF / SUMNER W. & SUSAN L. / HINDS. /
OCTOBER 2 – 3, / 1894. / "A LILY OF A DAY.""*

Hinds, Sumner *"SUMNER HINDS, / DIED / June 15, 1893, / AGED / 86 Yrs., 13 Dys."* This stone shares its base with the gravestone of his wife, Chloe Hinds.

Hinds, William Sumner *"WILLIAM SUMNER HINDS. / January 2, 1835, / May 3, 1905. / "The memory of the just / is blessed.""* The first line is carved along an arch.

Holmes, Bertha A. See Everett A. Holmes Monument entry.

Holmes, Ethyl A. See Everett A. Holmes Monument entry.

Holmes, Everett A. Monument *"HOLMES / EVERETT A. / 1913 – 1984 / HIS WIFE / BERTHA A. / 1921 – 1975"* is inscribed on the front of this monument. *"ETHYL A. HOLMES / 1889 – 1983"* is inscribed on the back. A Barnicoat Monuments metal tag is present.
"EVERETT A. HOLMES / MOMM3   US NAVY / WORLD WAR II / MAY 15 1913 APR 30 1984" is embossed on this flat, ground level, brass plaque. It is beginning to be buried. A veteran's marker and flag are present.

Horton, Linwood W. *"LINWOOD W. HORTON / 1897 – 1897"* is inscribed on this flat, ground level stone. It is beginning to be buried.

Kingsford, Charles H. Monument *"k"* (monogram) is carved in shallow relief at the top of this slanted monument. Ivy leaves are carved in the top corners. *"CHARLES H. KINGSFORD / FEB. 7, 1823, NOV. 19, 1858 / SARAH STAPLES HIS WIFE / APR. 16, 1826, APR. 3, 1916 / CHARLES H. KINGSFORD JR / JUNE 14, 1851, APR. 4 1856"* is inscribed on the slanted surface. *"KINGSFORD"* is carved in relief on the vertical section below this.
"C. H. K." is inscribed in shallow relief on this slanted footstone. It is located to the right of the monument.

Kingsford, Charles H., Jr. See Kingsford Monument.
"C. H. K. JR" is inscribed in shallow relief on this slanted footstone. It is located behind the monument, on the right.

Kingsford, Sarah S. See Kingsford Monument.
"S. S." is inscribed in shallow relief on this slanted footstone. It is located to the left of the monument.

Nix, Barbara See Eley Nix Monument entry.

Nix, Eley Monument *"NIX / ELEY / SEPT. 1919 – OCT. 1993 / HIS WIFE / BARBARA / JUNE. 19, 1930 - ____ / SAFELY HOME"* is inscribed on an open scroll carving. A cross and flowers are carved above this. A Barnicoat Monuments metal tag is present.

Oliveros-Santos, Elaine A. *"IN LOVING MEMORY / ELAINE A. OLIVEROS – SANTOS / OCT. 12 1953 – MAY 8, 1995"* Floral designs are carved in the upper corners. A Barnicoat Monuments metal tag is present.

Parry, Albert E. *"ALBERT E."* is carved in relief on the top slanted surface of this stone. A sculptured carving of flowers is behind it. *"Æ. 3 y'rs. & / 4 mo's. / To good for earth, / to Heaven hath fled / and left our home / in tears. / With Jesus."* is inscribed on the front of this rear facing stone. *"Son of John / E. & Lydia / G. PARRY, / died April / 15, 1862."* is inscribed on the back.

Parry, Charley F. *"GONE HOME / CHARLEY F. / Æ. 12 y'rs. / & 9 mo's. / Think parents while / those tears you shed / How blessed are the / early dead."* is inscribed on the front. Carved on the top of the stone is a lamb sculpture whose head is missing. *"Son of / John E. & / Lydia G. / PARRY, / died March / 29, 1862."* is inscribed on the back.

Parry, John E. Monument This monument is carved to look like two separate stones. *"FATHER"* is carved in relief on the top, left curved surface. *"JOHN E. PARRY, / SEPT. 8, 1820. / MAR. 3, 1900. / AT REST"* is carved on the left front. *"MOTHER"* is carved in relief on the top, right curved surface. *"LYDIA G. PARRY, / NOV. 13, 1828. / MAR. 2, 1900. / RESTING IN JESUS"* is carved on the right front. There are oak leaves carved on the top left, and ivy leaves carved on the top right.

Parry, Lydia G. See John E. Parry Monument entry.

Purvis, Peter S. *"PETER SCOTT / PURVIS / AUG. 12, 1970 / "Suffer the little children, / to come unto me, / and forbid them not: for of / such is the kingdom of God." / Luke 18:16"* There is a lamb sculpture on the top of this stone.

Robbins, Addie M. *"ADDIE M. ROBBINS / MAY 3, 1869 / NOV. 12, 1944"* The first line is carved along an arch.

Robbins, George W. *"GEORGE W. ROBBINS / DIED / JULY 13, 1885, / AGED 51 YEARS."* The first line is carved along an arch.

Robbins, Horace B. *"HORACE B. ROBBINS / DIED / JULY 2, 1886. / AGED 22 YRS. 11 MS. / & 29 DS. / AT REST."* The first line is carved along an arch.

Robbins, John B. *"JOHN B. / Son of Lemuel & / Mary Robbins, / died / Sept. 24, 1868, / Aged 7 yrs. / 6m's & 14 d's. /*
> *He's sleeping now, our angel boy*
> *We've watched him safely home:*
> *A_ shared in our bright world of joy*
> *Where death can never come."*

The first line is carved in relief. The poem is very weathered on this textured stone.

"J. B. R." is inscribed on the footstone.

Robbins, Lemuel   *"FATHER / LEMUEL ROBBINS / DEC. 3, 1826, / FEB. 15, 1901."* The first line is carved in shallow relief. The second line is carved along an arch.

Robbins, Marshall F.   *"MARSHALL F. ROBBINS / NOV. 14, 1865 / NOV. 2, 1905 / WE CHERISH THY MEMORY"* A Mason's symbol is carved in shallow relief at the top of this monument. An Independent Order of Odd Fellows marker is present.

Robbins, Mary   *"MARY, / wife of / Lemuel Robbins / died / July 28, 1869; / Aged 73 yrs. 7 m. /*
    Mother thou art gone to rest,
    And this shall be our prayer;
    That when we reach our journey's end,
    Thy glory we may share."
The first line is carved in relief along an arch. A crack extends from the center bottom of this stone to the last line of the poem.

Robbins, Mary   *"MOTHER / MARY / WIFE OF / LEMUEL ROBBINS / MAY 25, 1834 / FEB. 6, 1918"* The first line is carved in shallow relief and the second line is carved along an arch.

Robbins, Myra A.   *"MYRA A. ROBBINS / SEPT. 30. 1866 / JAN. 31. 1927"* The first line is carved along an arch.

Robbins, Percy   *"PERCY ROBBINS / FEB. 15, 1875 / DEC. 9, 1946"* The first line is carved along an arch. There are three links of a chain carved at the top of this monument.

Sampson, Adrianna B.   See Charles W. Sampson Monument entry.

Sampson, Betsey J.   See Luther Ashley Monument entry.
"S (monogram) / BETSEY J. / Wife of / Uriah Sampson, / Died Sept. 28, 1886, / Aged 44 yrs. & 5 ds. / *A precious one from us has gone,*
    A voice we loved is stilled:
    A place is vacant in our home,
    Which never can be filled."
The first line is carved in relief on this stone. *"HARRINGTON"* is inscribed on the lower right.
"B. S." The inscription on this footstone is buried underground.

Sampson, Charles W. Monument   *"S"* monogram is carved in relief at the top of this monument. *"CHARLES W. SAMPSON / OCT. 2, 1849 – JULY 11, 1929 / HIS WIFE / ADRIANNA B. CANEDY / AUG. 12, 1851 – JAN. 21, 1927"*

Sampson, Uriah   See Luther Ashley Monument entry.
"S (monogram) / URIAH / Son of / Uriah & Betsey J. / Sampson. / Died June 27, 1880, / Aged 16 yrs. & 27 ds." *"HARRINGTON"* is inscribed on the bottom right. The first line is carved in relief.
"U. S." The inscription on the footstone is buried underground.

Sampson, Uriah   See Luther Ashley Monument entry.

Sampson, Walter   See Luther Ashley Monument entry.
"WALTER SAMPSON" is carved in relief on this slanted stone. No dates are present. A veteran's marker and flag are present.

Shaw, Nancy   *"NANCY, / wife of / Zebulon Shaw / Died Dec. 4, 1868 / Æt. 60 yrs.*
10 Mo /   *Sleep Mother, sleep entombed in earth*
                Thy gentle form is sleeping,
                While kindred hearts that know
                    thy worth,
                In anguish deep are weeping."
This stone is textured and beginning to weather.
"N. S." This footstone faces the headstone.

Shaw, Zebulon   *"ZEBULON SHAW / died / Jan. 19, 1882. / Aged 78 yrs. / & 11*
d's. /   *We miss thee dear father, thy fond loving care,*
                But we know in Heaven thou art waiting us there."
The first line is carved along an arch. A crack extends 10 inches up from the base.

Smart, Nicole A.   *"NICOLE A. SMART / JAN. 22 – JAN 23, 1984"* A praying child angel is carved on the left side of this flat, 4-6 inch high stone.

Staples, Abigail   *"ABIGAIL, / wife of / James Staples, / died July 18, 1864; / Aged*
67 yrs. 28 d's. /   *And as we weep above the turf,*
                That rests upon her breast;
                We feel that when she left this earth,
                Her spirit went to rest."
The first line is carved in relief on this textured stone.
"A. S." is inscribed on the footstone.

Staples, Catherine T.   See George B. Staples Monument entry.
"C. T. S." is inscribed on the top slanted surface of this footstone. It is located to the right of the monument.

Staples, Charity S.   *"MOTHER"* is carved in relief on the top curved surface of this stone. *"CHARITY S. STAPLES, / BORN / JAN. 16, 1835. / DIED / DEC. 13, 1909."* There are ivy leaves carved in the top right corner of this stone.

Staples, Charles A.   *"CHARLES ALBERT / Son of / Charles W. & / Charity S. Staples, / Died Sept. 20, 1863; / Aged 4 Y'rs. 3 Mo's. / & 23 d's."* The first line is carved in relief along an arch. There is a small crack at the center bottom.
"C. A. S." This footstone faces the headstone.

Staples, Charles W.   *"FATHER"* is carved in relief on the top, curved surface of this gravestone. *"CHARLES W. STAPLES, / BORN / APR. 20, 1828. / DIED / Oct. 20, 1905."* There are oak leaves carved in the top left corner of this stone.

Staples, George B. Monument   *"S (monogram) / GEO. B. STAPLES / 1831 – 1913 / HIS WIFE / CATHERINE T. / 1833 – 1899 / THEIR SON / WALLACE I. / 1874 – 1878"* is inscribed on the left side of this brown monument. There are no inscriptions on any other side. The "S" monogram is inscribed on all four sides.
"G. B. S." is inscribed on the top slanted surface of this footstone. It is located to

the left of the monument.

Staples, James   *"JAMES STAPLES / Born / July 4, 1799. / Died / May 23. 1885."*
The first line is carved in relief.
"J. S." This footstone is lying face up on the ground.

Staples, Martin K.   *"MARTIN K. STAPLES / 1856 – 1952"* Floral designs are
carved in the upper corners of this slanted monument.

Staples, Wallace I.   See George B. Staples Monument entry.
"WALLACE" is inscribed on the top of this lichen encrusted, slanted footstone. It is
located to the far right of the monument.

Thew, E. Leonice   See Edward J. Thew Monument entry.

Thew, Edward J. Monument   *"THEW"* is inscribed at the top of this slanted
monument. Floral carvings are in the upper corners. *"EDWARD J. / 1904 – 1975"*
is inscribed on the lower left, and *"E. LEONICE / 1915 – 1975"* is inscribed on the
lower right.

Washburn, Abbie J.   *"ABBIE J. / WIFE OF / SALMON M. WASHBURN, / DIED
SEPT. 16, 1863; / AGED 56 Y'RS 3 M'S / & 2 D'S. / Gone Home."* The first line is
carved in relief along an arch. A large crack radiates from the center of this stone
extending up into the last three lines.
"A. J. W." is inscribed on the footstone.

Washburn, Annie L.   See Leroy G. Washburn stone entry.

Washburn, E. Pearl   See George W. Washburn Monument entry.

Washburn, Edgar A. Monument   *"WASHBURN"* is carved in shallow relief on
the top slanted surface of this monument. *"EDGAR A. WASHBURN / 1856 – 1947 /
HIS WIFE / MARIA A. STAPLES / 1866 – 1926"* is inscribed on the front.

Washburn, Esther M.   See Salmon Elbert Washburn Monument entry.
"ESTHER M. / 1880 – 1965" is inscribed on this flat, ground level stone. It is
located behind this monument, on the left.

Washburn, George W. Stone   *"WASHBURN"* is inscribed below floral carvings
on this flat, ground level stone. *"GEORGE W. / 1907 – ____ "* is inscribed on the
lower left, and *"E. PEARL / 1912 – 1974"* is inscribed on the lower right.

Washburn, Helen A.   *"HELEN A. / 1879 – 1904"* is inscribed on this flat 1 inch
high stone. Lakeville Vital Records show that she was the wife of William C.
Washburn.

Washburn, Jerusha W.   *"JERUSHA W. / 1837 – 1916"* is inscribed on this flat,
ground level stone. Lakeville Vital Records show she was the wife of Salmon M.
Washburn.

Washburn, Leroy G. Stone   *"WASHBURN"* is inscribed below floral carvings on
this flat, ground level stone. *"LEROY G. / 1904 – 2000"* is inscribed on the lower
left side, and *"ANNIE L. / 1905 – 1986"* is inscribed on the lower right side.

Washburn, Maria A.   See Edgar A. Washburn Monument entry.

Washburn, Russell I. Monument   *"WASHBURN"* is inscribed across this slanted monument. *"RUSSELL I. / DEC 3, 1909 / JAN. 15, 1993"* is inscribed on the lower left side, and *"S. JEANETTE / MAY 19, 1922 /____"* is inscribed on the lower right side. *"JOHN 3.16"* is inscribed on the center bottom. Floral carvings adorn the upper corners.

Washburn, S. Jeanette   See Russell I. Washburn Monument entry.

Washburn, Salmon E. Monument   *"WASHBURN"* is carved in relief on the front of this large rectangular monument. *"S. ELBERT WASHBURN / 1874 – 1960 / ESTHER MAY WASHBURN / 1880 – 1965"* is carved on the back.
"SALMON E. / 1874 – 1960" is inscribed on this flat, ground level stone. It is located behind the monument and on the left.

Washburn, Salmon M.   *"SALMON M. WASHBURN / DIED / APR. 11, 1863; / AGED 58 Y'RS / 5 M'S & 28 D'S. / Asleep in Jesus"* The first line is carved in relief along an arch. A large crack radiates through the upper base and into the last line.
"S. M. W." This footstone faces the headstone.

Washburn, Salmon M.   *"SALMON M. / 1826 – 1904"* is inscribed on this flat, ground level stone. Lakeville Vital Records show he was the son of Milton S. Washburn and Abigail Keith.

Washburn, Wesley C.   *"WESLEY C. / 1923 – 1923"* is inscribed on this flat, 1 inch high stone. Lakeville Vital Records show he was the son of William C. and Ester Washburn.

Washburn, William C.   *"WILLIAM C. / 1876 – 1962"* is inscribed on this flat, 1 inch high stone. Lakeville Vital Records show he was the son of Salmon & Jerusha Washburn.

Winslow Monument   *"WINSLOW"* is carved in relief on this mammoth, rough cut monument. There are no other inscriptions on it.

Winslow, Addie M.   See Asa Winslow Monument entry.
"A. M. W." is inscribed on this flat, 0-1 inch high footstone. It is located directly behind the monument, two rows back.

Winslow, Alice V.   *"ALICE V. WINSLOW / 1862 – 1960"* is inscribed on this flat, 3-4 inch high stone. It is located in front of the Winslow Monument, on the right.

Winslow, Anna   *"ANNA WINSLOW / 1800 – 1895"* is inscribed on this flat, 5-6 inch high stone. It is located directly in front of the Winslow Monument.

Winslow, Asa Monument   *"ASA   WINSLOW / 1832 – 1908 / HIS WIFE SUSAN / 1836 – 1873 / HIS WIFE LUCY / 1838 – 1901 / ADDIE MAY WINSLOW / 1858 – 1861 / ASA IRVING WINSLOW / 1881 – 1933"*
"A. W." This flat, 1-3 inch high footstone is located behind the monument.

Winslow, Asa I.   See Asa Winslow Monument.
"A. I. W."   This flat 0-1 inch high footstone is located two rows behind the monument, on the right.

Winslow, Asa T.   *"ASA T. WINSLOW / 1798 – 1878"* is inscribed on this flat, 4-6 inch high stone. It is located in front of the Winslow Monument, on the left.

Winslow, Isabella F.   *"ISABELLA F. WINSLOW / 1868 – 1927"* is inscribed on this flat, 1-3 inch high stone. It is located in front of the Winslow Monument, on the right.

Winslow, Isabella V.   *"ISABELLA V. WINSLOW / 1842 – 1865"* This flat, 2-4 inch high stone is located immediately behind the Winslow Monument.

Winslow, Leander   *"LEANDER WINSLOW / 1834 – 1904"* is inscribed on this 2 inch high stone. A *"GAR 8 282"* marker, a veteran's marker, and flag are present. It is located behind the Winslow Monument, on the left. *Massachusetts Civil War Soldiers and Sailors, 1861-1865,* Vol. I, p. 199 shows that he enlisted in 1862 and was in the 3rd Mass Infantry, Co. I.

Winslow, Lucy   See Asa Winslow Monument entry.
"L. W." This flat, 1 inch high footstone is located behind the monument, on the far right.

Winslow, Sallie D.   *"SALLIE D. WINSLOW / 1835 – 1908"* is inscribed on this flat, 4 inch high stone. It is located behind the Winslow Monument, on the right.

Winslow, Susan   See Asa Winslow Monument entry.
"S. W." This flat, 1 inch high footstone is located behind the monument, on the right.

Mullein Hill Cemetery Map Index

Alphabetical:

Robbins, Mary (~1795-1869) – 35
Robbins, Myra A. (1866-1927) – 107
Robbins, Percy (1875-1946) – 120
Sampson, Adrianna B. (1851-1927) – 90
Sampson, Betsey J. (1842-1886) – 112, 113
Sampson, Charles W. (1849-1929) – 90
Sampson, Uriah (1842-1864) – 113
Sampson, Uriah (1864-1880) –111, 113
Sampson, Walter (1862-1931) – 113, 121
Shaw, Nancy (1808-1868) – 76
Shaw, Zebulon (1804-1882) – 75
Smart, Nicole A. (1984) – 142
Staples, Abigail (1797-1864) – 87
Staples, Catherine T. (1833-1899) – 51, 52
Staples, Charity S. (1835-1909) – 74
Staples, Charles A. (1859-1863) – 72
Staples, Charles W. (1828-1905) – 73
Staples, George B. (1831-1913) – 50, 51
Staples, James (1799-1885) – 86
Staples, Martin K. (1856-1952) – 88
Staples, Wallace I. (1874-1878) – 51, 53
Thew, E. Leonice (1915-1975) – 134
Thew, Edward J. (1904-1975) – 134
Washburn, Abbie J. (1807-1863) – 65
Washburn, Annie L. (1905-1986) – 127
Washburn, E. Pearl (1912-1974) – 126
Washburn, Edgar A. (1856-1947) – 89

Washburn, Esther M. (1880-1965) – 81, 96
Washburn, George W. (1907-____) – 126
Washburn, Helen A. (1879-1904) – 85
Washburn, Jerusha W. (1837-1916) – 67
Washburn, Leroy G. (1904-2000) –127
Washburn, Maria A. (1866-1926) – 89
Washburn, Russell I. (1909-1993) – 135
Washburn, S. Jeanette (1922-____) – 135
Washburn, Salmon E. (1874-1960) – 81, 95
Washburn, Salmon M. (1804-1863) – 64
Washburn, Salmon M. (1826-1904) – 66
Washburn, Wesley C. (1923) – 83
Washburn, William C. (1876-1962) – 68
Winslow Monument (no dates) – 15
Winslow, Addie May (1858-1861) – 33, 57
Winslow, Alice V. (1862-1960) – 5
Winslow, Anna (1800-1895) – 3
Winslow, Asa (1832-1908) – 33, 44
Winslow, Asa Irving (1881-1933) – 33, 58
Winslow, Asa T. (1798-1878) – 2
Winslow, Isabella F. (1868-1927) – 4
Winslow, Isabella V. (1842-1865) – 25
Winslow, Leander (1834-1904) – 24
Winslow, Lucy (1838-1901) – 33, 46
Winslow, Sallie D. (1835-1908) – 26
Winslow, Susan (1836-1873) – 33, 45

By Location:

1 – Andrews, Francis A. (1855-1856)
2 – Winslow, Asa T. (1798-1878)
3 – Winslow, Anna (1800-1895)
4 – Winslow, Isabella F. (1868-1927)
5 – Winslow, Alice V. (1862-1960)
6 – Canedy, William crypt (1861)
7 – Hinds, Sumner (1807-1893)
8 – Hinds, Chloe (1806-1888)
9 – Hinds, Nancy J. (1841-1868)
10 – Hinds, William S. (1835-1905)
11 – Allen, Earnest E. (1869-1870)
12 – Canedy, Elkanah L. (1829-1908)
    Canedy, Elizabeth B. (1843-1924)
    Canedy, Walter S. (1854-1918)
    Canedy, Carrie B. (1860-1933)
13 – Fletcher, Solomon (1830-1863)
    Fletcher, Mary A. (1835-1924)
    Fletcher, Emma J. (1856-1857)
14 – Coleman, Aurelia (1796-1854)
15 – Winslow Monument (no dates)
16 – Canedy, Sophronia M. (1831-1859)

17 – Canedy, William (1824-1889)
18 – Canedy, Janette (1837-1865)
19 – Hinds, John C. (1843-1877)
20 – Hinds, Eva D. (1853-1881)
21 – Hinds, Ruth (1894)
22 – Fletcher, Emma J. (1856-1857)
23 – Fletcher, Emma J. (1856-1857)
24 – Winslow, Leander (1834-1904)
25 – Winslow, Isabella V. (1842-1865)
26 – Winslow, Sallie D. (1835-1908)
27 – Hinds, Emma May (1872-1881)
28 – Ashley, Noah (1787-1843)
29 – Ashley, Ruth (1791-1867)
30 – Kingsford, Sarah S. (1826-1916)
31 – Kingsford, Charles H. (1823-1858)
    Kingsford, Sarah S. (1826-1916)
    Kingsford, Charles H. Jr. (1851-1856)
32 – Kingsford, Charles H. (1823-1858)
33 – Winslow, Asa (1832-1908)
    Winslow, Susan (1836-1873)
    Winslow, Lucy (1838-1901)

Winslow, Addie M. (1858-1861)
Winslow, Asa I. (1881-1933)
34 – Clark, Stephen (1814-1899)
Clark, Mary (1826-1901)
35 – Robbins, Mary (~1795-1869)
36 – Parry, John E. (1820-1900)
Parry, Lydia G. (1828-1900)
37 – Bishop, Dexter, Jr. (1805-1873)
38 – Bishop, Catherine T. (1805-1879)
39 – Bishop, Dexter, 3rd (1842-1863)
40 – Caswell, Betsey H. (1840-1869)
41 – Ashley, Isaiah (1844)
Ashley, Noah (1845)
42 – Ashley, Silas P. (1813-1897)
Ashley, Phebe E. (1815-1856)
Ashley, Almira F. (1826-1913)
43 – Kingsford, Charles H., Jr. (1851-1856)
44 – Winslow, Asa (1832-1908)
45 – Winslow, Susan (1836-1873)
46 – Winslow, Lucy (1838-1901)
47 – Robbins, George W. (~1834-1885)
48 – Parry, Charles F. (1849-1862)
49 – Parry, Albert E. (~1858-1862)
50 – Staples, George B. (1831-1913)
51 – Staples, George B. (1831-1913)
Staples, Catherine T. (1833-1899)
Staples, Wallace I. (1874-1878)
52 – Staples, Catherine T. (1833-1899)
53 – Staples, Wallace I. (1874-1878)
54 – Ashley, Phebe E. (1815-1856)
55 – Ashley, Silas P. (1813-1897)
56 – Ashley, Almira F. (1826-1913)
57 – Winslow, Addie M. (1858-1861)
58 – Winslow, Asa I. (1881-1933)
59 – Clark, Charles H. (1847-1865)
60 – Caswell, Susan (1806-1882)
61 – Caswell, Nathaniel (1810-1859)
62 – Caswell, Nathaniel (1780-1867)
63 – Caswell, Theodora (1784-1854)
64 – Washburn, Salmon M. (1804-1863)
65 – Washburn, Abbie J. (1807-1863)
66 – Washburn, Salmon M. (1826-1904)
67 – Washburn, Jerusha W. (1837-1916)
68 – Washburn, William C. (1876-1962)
69 – Berthelot, Helen W. (1904-1996)
70 – Holmes, Everett A. (1913-1984)
71 – Holmes, Everett A. (1913-1984)
Holmes, Bertha (1921-1975)
Holmes, Ethyl (1889-1983)
72 – Staples, Charles A. (1859-1863)
73 – Staples, Charles W. (1828-1905)

74 – Staples, Charity S. (1835-1909)
75 – Shaw, Zebulon (1804-1882)
76 – Shaw, Nancy (1808-1868)
77 – Canedy, Sarah E. (1833-1872)
78 – Caswell, Otis W. (1852-1862)
79 – Caswell, Arthur L. (1857-1862)
80 – Ashley, Laurett S. (1844-1855)
81 – Washburn, Salmon E. (1874-1960)
Washburn, Esther M. (1880-1965)
82 – Abele, Esther M. (1903-1998)
83 – Washburn, Wesley C. (1923)
84 – Horton, Linwood W. (1897)
85 – Washburn, Helen A. (1879-1904)
86 – Staples, James (1799-1885)
87 – Staples, Abigail (1797-1864)
88 – Staples, Martin K. (1856-1952)
89 – Washburn, Edgar A. (1856-1947)
Washburn, Maria A. (1866-1926)
90 – Sampson, Charles W. (1849-1929)
Sampson, Adrianna B. (1851-1927)
91 – Dean, Philip (1828-1891)
92 – Dean, Emma (1828-1870)
93 – Ashley, Luther (1814-1895)
94 – Ashley, Theodora (1813-1891)
95 – Washburn, Salmon E. (1874-1960)
96 – Washburn, Esther M. (1880-1965)
97 – Caswell, Abigail M. (1831-1916)
98 – Caswell, William H. (1820-1886)
99 – Ashley, Calvin (1816-1868)
100 – Ashley, Rebecca C. (1821-1886)
101 – Ashley, Nettie B. (1856-1876)
102 – Ashley, Jennie R. (1854-1883)
103 – Ashley, Luman R. (1866-1884)
104 – Ashley, Benjamin T. (1858-1884)
105 – Robbins, Lemuel (1826-1901)
106 – Robbins, Mary (1834-1918)
107 – Robbins, Myra A. (1866-1927)
108 – Robbins, Addie M. (1869-1944)
109 – Egger, Bruce C. (1938)
110 – Ashley, Arabella (1851-1934)
111 – Sampson, Uriah (1864-1880)
112 – Sampson, Betsey J. (1842-1886)
113 – Ashley, Luther (1814-1895)
Ashley, Theodora (1813-1891)
Ashley, Lorett S. (1844-1855)
Ashley, Elmer (1846-1864)
Ashley, Arabella (1851-1934)
Sampson, Uriah (1842-1864)
Sampson, Betsey J. (1842-1886)
Sampson, Uriah (1864-1880)
Sampson, Walter (1862-1931)

114 – Hervey, Abbie M. (1851-1936)
115 – Hervey, Johnathan (1849-1939)
   Hervey, Abbie M. (1851-1936)
   Hervey, William I. (1869-1907)
   Hervey, Jennie E. (1874-1878)
116 – Ashley, Calvin (1816-1868)
   Ashley, Rebecca C. (1821-1886)
   Ashley, Benjamin T. (1858-1884)
   Ashley, Luman R. (1866-1884)
   Ashley, Jennie R. (1854-1883)
   Ashley, Nettie B. (1856-1876)
117 – Robbins, John B. (1861-1868)
118 – Robbins, Horace B. (1863-1886)
119 – Robbins, Marshall F. (1865-1905)
120 – Robbins, Percy (1875-1946)
121 – Sampson, Walter (1862-1931)
122 – Chace, Barbara G. (1926-1964)
123 – Chace, Merrill E. (1925-____)
   Chace, Barbara S. (1926-1964)
   Chace, Victoria H. (1918-____)
124 – Egger, John H., Jr. (1904-1991)
125 – Egger, Gertrude M. (1905-1997)
126 – Washburn, George W. (1907-____)
   Washburn E. Pearl (1912-1974)
127 – Washburn, Leroy G. (1904-2000)
   Washburn, Annie L. (1905-1986)
128 – Purvis, Peter S. (1970)
129 – DeMoura, Jeremy (1974)

130 – Dubee, Zephrien J. (1921-1976)
131 – Crump, Laurence N. (1932-1970)
132 – Egger Monument (no dates)
133 – Gushee, Miriam F. (1928-1980)
134 – Thew, Edward J. (1904-1975)
   Thew, E. Leonice (1915-1975)
135 – Washburn, Russell I. (1909-1993)
   Washburn, S. Jeanette (1922-____)
136 – Goss, Madison E. (1988)
137 – Aksell, Anna M. (1905-1933)
138 – Aksell , Sture G. (1908-1980)
139 – Hannant, Robert W. (1936-1979)
140 – DeMoura, Richard D. (1932-1996)
   DeMoura , Gail M. (1938-____)
141 – DeMoura, Duane E. (1959-1977)
142 – Smart, Nicole A. (1984)
143 – Nix, Eley (1919-1993)
   Nix, Barbara (1930-____)
144 – Dubee, Zephrien J. (1921-1976)
145 – Egger, Milton W. (1900-1968)
   Egger, Annie B. (1901-1966)
   Egger, Helen R. (1921-1972)
146 – Oliveros-Santos, Elaine (1953-1995)
147 – Gagnon, George R. (1915-1996)
   Gagnon, Winnifred E. (1922-1981)
148 – Arbec, Nancy (1951-1988)
149 – Gushee Monument (no dates)
150 – Boscombe, David A. (1948-1987)

Independent Order of Odd Fellows marker

Mullein Hill Cemetery Map

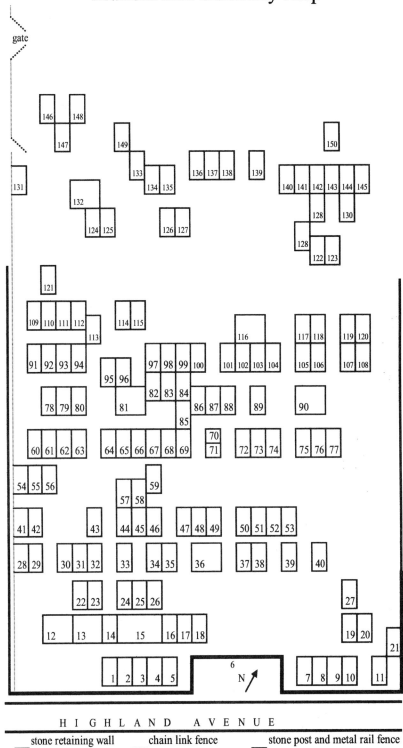

gate

HIGHLAND AVENUE

stone retaining wall   chain link fence   stone post and metal rail fence

Chapter 17
Pickens #1 Cemetery

Pickens #1 Cemetery is located on the west side of Pickens Street, just north of Virginia Drive. It is surrounded on three sides by a stone wall. A stone post and metal rail fence borders the street. This cemetery is unusual in that most of the footstones are in front of the headstones. The sign is in good repair. Gravestones face east, and date from 1830 to 1956. The Lakeville Assessor's Office lists this cemetery as town owned, 1260 square feet in area. Thatcher calls this the "Silas Pickens Cemetery near Elder's Pond" and Vigers calls it "Pickens Cemetery No. 2." Entries were recorded October 29, 1999.

Pickens, Davis Monument   *"PICKENS"* is carved in relief at the top of the monument. *"1835 DAVIS PICKENS 1891 / 1834 PHEBE HOARD HIS WIFE 1899 / 1860 SAMUEL DAVIS 1860 / 1863 MARY HOARD 1902 / 1865 JUDITH CORA PIERCE 1952 / 1868 ETHAN PIERCE 1956"* There are delicate leaf designs carved in the upper corners.
"D. P." This flat, ground level footstone is behind the monument, on the right.

Pickens, John C.   *"IN / memory / of / JOHN C. / son of / Silas Pickens Jr. / & Sally L. his wife: / who died / Aug. 26. 1833, aged / 8 years 1 mo. / 5 days. /*
> *This lovely bud so young and fair,*
> *Call'd home by early doom;*
> *Just came to show how sweet a flower.*
> *In Paradise would bloom."*

The second line is carved along an arch.
"J. C. P." This footstone is in front of the headstone.

Pickens, John F.   *"JOHN F. PICKENS / Died / in the parish of / Morehouse, La., / Nov. 25, 1866. / Aged 31 years, / 7 mos. & 5 days. / Many are the hearts that mourn / his absence."* is inscribed on the front of this stone. *"SON OF / SILAS & SALLY L. / PICKENS."* is inscribed on the back.

"J. F. P." This footstone is in front of the headstone.

Pickens, Josephus   *"JOSEPHUS PICKENS / Born / Sept. 13, 1805, / Died / Oct. 3, 1883."* The first line is carved in relief along an arch. There is a small crack present in the center bottom of the stone. Notice the mix of upper and lower case letters in the second line.
"J. P." This footstone is in front of the headstone.

Pickens, Louisa W.   *"In / memory of / LOUISA W. / dau. of / MR. SILAS and / MRS. SUSANNA / PICKENS / who died / Aug. 25, 1830 / in her 18. / year. /*
> *My tender parents now farewell,*
> *My brothers and sisters too.*
> *With my Saviour now must dwell*
> *And bid you all adieu.*
> *Geo. Thompson"*

There is a George Thompson swirl above his name.
"L. W. P." This footstone is in front of the headstone.

Pickens, Mary H.   See Davis Pickens Monument entry.
"M. H. P." This flat, ground level footstone is located behind the monument, on the left.

Pickens, Phoebe H.   See Davis Pickens Monument entry.
"P. H. P."   This flat, ground level footstone is located directly behind the monument, on the right.

Pickens, Sally L.

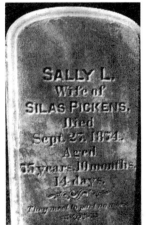

> *"SALLY L.*
> *Wife of*
> *SILAS PICKENS,*
> *Died*
> *Sept. 27, 1874,*
> *Aged*
> *75 years, 10 months,*
> *14 days.*
> *They meet to part no more."*

"S. L. P." This footstone is lying face up in front of the headstone.

Pickens, Sally M.   *"Erected / to the memory / of / SALLY MARIA / dau. of / SILAS PICKENS JR. / and SALLY L. his / wife who died / Dec. 20. 1830 / aged 8 years 2 / mo. and 21 days. /*
> *Here lies a parent's joy,*
> *A mothers tender care:*
> *Though God hath cut her down*
> *He'll raise her fresh and fair."*

A wheel like carving is at the top of this stone. The first two lines are carved along an arch. This stone is leaning backwards.
"S. M. P." is inscribed in outline on this footstone. It is broken off at ground level and lying face up in front of the headstone.

Pickens, Samuel D.   See Davis Pickens Monument entry.
Lakeville Vital Records show that he died February 29, 1860, at 4 months, and 28 days old, and that he was the son of Davis and Phoebe (Hoard) Pickens.
"S. D. P."   This flat, ground level footstone is located directly behind the monument, on the left.

Pickens, Silas, Esq.   *"ERECTED / in memory of / SILAS PICKENS ESQ. / who died / Oct. 25. 1847. / aged 84 years. /*

> *Farewell vain world, I've seen enough of thee*
> *I lived 'till life had no more charm for me.*
> *Then cease my dearest friends, why drop a tear*
> *My wearied limbs will rest in quiet here.*
> *Geo. Thompson"*

The first line is carved in outline, and the third line is carved in relief. This poem was very difficult to read due to weathering. This stone shares a base with his wife Susannah. A *"SAR 1775"* marker and flag are present.
"S. P."   This footstone is in front of the headstone.

Pickens, Silas   *"SILAS PICKENS, / Died / Oct. 8, 1871. / Aged / 75 years, 2 months, / 2 days. / Divided but for a time."*
"S. P."   This footstone is lying face up in front of the headstone.

Pickens, Susannah   *"ERECTED / in memory of / Mrs. SUSANNAH, / widow of / SILAS PICKENS, Esq., / who died / April 28, 1861. / Aged 91 years / 5 mos. 18 days. /*

> *No pain, no grief, no anxious fear,*
> *Invade thy bounds. No mortal woes*
> *Can reach the peaceful sleeper here,*
> *While angels watch the soft repose."*

The first line is carved in outline, and the third line is carved in relief. Her stone shares a base with that of her husband.
"S. P."   This footstone is in front of the headstone.

Pickens, Vodisa H.   *"VODISA H. / wife of / Josephus Pickens, / died Apr. 24, 1872; / Aged 69 yrs, 10 m ˢ⸰."*   The first line is carved in relief along an arch.
"V. H. P."   This footstone is located in front of the headstone.

Pierce, Ethan   See Davis Pickens Monument entry.

Pierce, Judith Cora   See Davis Pickens Monument entry.
"J. C. P."   This flat, ground level footstone is located directly in front of monument, on the right.

SAR marker

Pickens #1 Cemetery Index and Map

Alphabetical:

Pickens, Davis (1835-1891) – 10, 14
Pickens, John C. (1825-1833) – 3
Pickens, John F. (1835-1866) – 4
Pickens, Josephus (1805-1883) – 16
Pickens, Louisa W. (~1813-1830) – 1
Pickens, Mary H. (1863-1902) – 10, 11
Pickens, Phoebe H. (1834-1899) – 10, 13
Pickens, Sally L. (~1798-1874) – 8
Pickens, Sally M. (1822-1830) – 2
Pickens, Samuel D. (1860) – 10, 12
Pickens, Silas, Esq. (~1763-1847) – 7
Pickens, Silas (1796-1871) – 9
Pickens, Susannah (1769-1861) – 6
Pickens, Vodisa H. (1802-1872) – 15
Pierce, Ethan (1868-1956) – 10
Pierce, Judith C. (1865-1952) – 5, 10

By Location:

1 – Pickens, Louisa W. (~1813-1830)
2 – Pickens, Sally M. (1822-1830)
3 – Pickens, John C. (1825-1833)
4 – Pickens, John F. (1835-1866)
5 – Pierce, Judith C. (1865-1952)
6 – Pickens, Susannah (1769-1861)
7 – Pickens, Silas, Esq. (~1763-1847)
8 – Pickens, Sally L. (~1798-1874)
9 – Pickens, Silas (1796-1871)
10 – Pickens, Davis (1835-1891)
    Pickens, Phoebe H. (1834-1899)
    Pickens, Samuel D. (1860)
    Pickens, Mary H. (1863-1902)
    Pierce, Judith C. (1865-1952)
    Pierce, Ethan (1868-1956)
11 – Pickens, Mary H. (1863-1902)
12 – Pickens, Samuel D. (1860)
13 – Pickens, Phoebe H. (1834-1899)
14 – Pickens, Davis (1835-1891)
15 – Pickens, Vodisa H. (1802-1872)
16 – Pickens, Josephus (1805-1883)

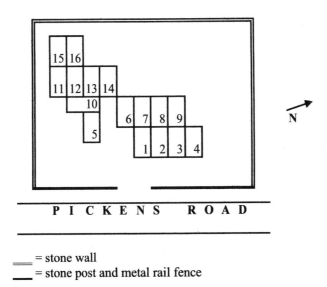

P I C K E N S   R O A D

___ = stone wall
___ = stone post and metal rail fence

Chapter 18
Pickens #2 Cemetery

Pickens #2 Cemetery is located within the James J. Vigers, Jr. Conservation Area which is on Pickens Street, opposite Hill Street. A dirt road leads to the cemetery, which is located about 1,000 feet from Pickens Street. A stone post and metal rail fence surrounds it, and the gate is on the northeast side. No sign is present. Several gravesites are sunken. The gravestones face the surrounding fence, either northwest or southeast. They date from 1840 to 1920. The Lakeville Assessor's Office lists this cemetery as town owned, about 3000 square feet in area. Thatcher calls this the "Zattu Pickens Cemetery," and Vigers calls it "Pickens Cemetery No. 1." Entries were recorded April 14, 2000.

Pickens, Benjamin A. *"BENJAMIN A. PICKENS / BORN / SEPT. 7, 1840, / DIED / FEB. 8, 1920."*

Pickens, Edward P. *"EDWARD P. PICKENS / BORN / OCT. 11, 1837, / DIED / FEB. 8, 1904."*

Pickens, Hope *"HOPE, / Wife of / ZACCHEUS PICKENS, / Died / Sept. 11, 1863, / Aged / 65 years, 7 month. / She always made home happy."* This stone is broken in half horizontally between the second and third lines. The top half is broken in half again vertically through the middle of the words *Hope*, and *Wife*. These two top pieces are leaning against the front of the bottom half.
"H. P." is inscribed on this footstone.

Pickens, Lucinda E. *"In loving remembrance / OF / LUCINDA E. PICKENS / Died Feb. 7, 1888, / Aged 87 years. /*
> *Asleep in Jesus! blessed sleep,*
> *From which none ever wakes to weep,*
> *A calm and undisturbed repose,*
> *Unbroken by the last of foes.*

> *Asleep in Jesus! far from thee,*
> *Thy kindred and their graves may be;*
> *But thine is still a blessed sleep,*
> *From which none ever wakes to weep."*

The first and third lines are carved along an arch. The third line is carved in relief. *"L. E. P."* is inscribed on the footstone.

Pickens, Olive   *"OLIVE PICKENS / BORN / Sept. 21, 1834, / DIED / Sept. 24, 1920."*

Pickens, Rachel   *"ERECTED / in memory of / RACHEL, / wife of / DEA. ZATTU PICKENS; / who died / Dec. 12, 1840, / in / her 79 year."* This stone is lying face up on the ground. The first line is carved along an arch. The third line is carved in relief, and the last line is carved along an inverted arch.
"R. P." is inscribed on the footstone.

Pickens, Zaccheus   *"In Memory of / ZACCHEUS / PICKENS, / Died Jan. 10, 1880, / Aged 84 yrs, 5 mos. / 24 dys. / There remaineth a rest."* The second line is carved in relief along an arch.
"Z. P." is inscribed on the footstone.

Pickens, Zattu, Dea   *"ERECTED / in memory of / DEA. ZATTU / PICKENS, / who died / Oct. 26, 1843, / in / his 78 year."* The first line is carved along an arch. The third and fourth lines are carved in relief. The last line is carved along an inverted arch. This stone is broken in half horizontally along the bottom of the sixth line. The top section is leaning against the back of the lower upright section.

 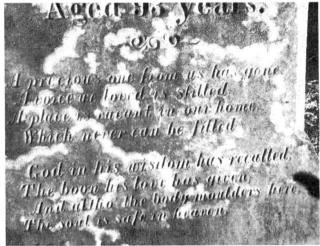

Pickens, Zattu   *"In loving remembrance / OF / ZATTU PICKENS, / Died Oct. 6, 1886, / Aged 93 years. / A precious one from us has gone,*
> *A voice we loved is stilled;*
> *A place is vacant in our home,*
> *Which never can be filled.*

> *God in his wisdom has recalled,*
> *The boon his love has given,*

And altho' the body moulders here,
The soul is safe in heaven."
The first line is carved along an arch. The third line is carved in relief.
"Z. P." is inscribed on the footstone.

Pickens #2 Cemetery Index and Map

Alphabetical:
Pickens, Benjamin A. (1840-1920) – 2
Pickens, Edward P. (1837-1904) – 3
Pickens, Hope (1798-1863) – 6
Pickens, Lucinda (~1801-1888) – 8
Pickens, Olive (1834-1920) – 1
Pickens, Rachel (~1762-1840) – 4
Pickens, Zaccheus (1795-1880) – 7
Pickens, Zattu, Dea. (~1766-1843) – 5
Pickens, Zattu (~1793-1886) – 9

By Location:
1 – Pickens, Olive (1834-1920)
2 – Pickens, Benjamin A. (1840-1920)
3 – Pickens, Edward P. (1837-1904)
4 – Pickens, Rachel (~1762-1840)
5 – Pickens, Zattu, Dea. (~1766-1843)
6 – Pickens, Hope (1798-1863)
7 – Pickens, Zaccheus (1795-1880)
8 – Pickens, Lucinda (~1801-1888)
9 – Pickens, Zattu (~1793-1886)

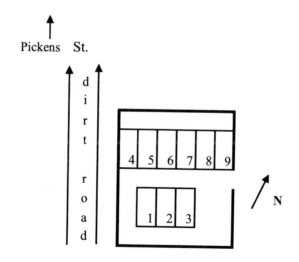

= stone post and metal rail fence

Chapter 19
Pierce Cemetery

Pierce Cemetery is located in Lakeville, but is accessed through the neighboring town of Berkley by way of Route 79, Adams Lane and a field. The cemetery is located about 425 feet south of the juncture of Adams Lane and the railroad tracks. A stone post and metal rail fence surrounds this cemetery. Half of the stone posts are broken, and many of the metal rails are missing. A sign is present and in good repair. The gravestones face northwest, and date from 1755 to 1892. The Lakeville Assessor's Office lists this cemetery as town owned, about 1/4 acre in size. Thatcher calls this the "Peirce and Allen Cemetery," and Vigers calls it the "Peirce and Haskins Cemetery." All Peirce/Pierce entries are listed together alphabetically by given name. Entries were recorded March 27, 2000.

Allen, Abiah   *"ERECTED / to the memory of / ABIAH / wife of / JOHN ALLEN. / died Sept. 8, 1843, / in the 82. year / of her age. /*

>   *Dear children dry those useless tears,*
>   *And wipe your weeping eye;*
>   *We soon shall meet again in love,*
>   *Beyond the starry skies."*

The third line is carved in relief within a rectangular recessed area.
"A. A." is inscribed on the footstone. It is lying face up on the ground.

Allen, Ann   See Joseph Allen Monument entry.
"ANN" This footstone is located behind the monument, on the far right.

Allen, Enos   See Joseph Allen Monument entry.
"ENOS" This footstone is located behind the monument, on the right.

Allen, Esther   See Joseph Allen Monument entry.
"ESTHER" This footstone is located directly behind the monument.

Allen, Esther   See Joseph Allen Monument entry.

"E. A." is inscribed on the footstone. It is broken off at ground level, and lying face down on the ground. It is located directly behind the other Esther Allen footstone.

Allen, Jane See Joseph Allen Monument entry.
"JANE" This footstone is located behind the monument, on the far right.

Allen, John *"ERECTED / to the memory of / JOHN ALLEN / who died / Oct. 20, 1841, / in the 88. year / of his age. /*

> *Thou partner of my youth.*
> *No longer thee, I view;*
> *Death's chilly hand is on my brow.*
> *Accept my last adieu."*

The third line is carved in relief within a rectangular recessed area. There is a *"SAR 1775"* marker, a veteran's marker and flag present at this gravesite.
"J. A." is inscribed on the footstone.

Allen, Joseph Monument *"FATHER / JOSEPH ALLEN / Born / Sept. 29, 1776; / Died / July 5, 1870."* is inscribed on the left side of this double monument. *"MOTHER / ESTHER BABBITT / Wife of / JOSEPH ALLEN. / Born June 7, 1778, / Died Oct. 12, 1862."* is inscribed on the right side. There is a cross sculpture in the middle, and superimposed on the front of the cross is a sculpture of two clasped hands. The word *and* is inscribed under these hands, in line with the first line of the above inscription. *"Children of / JOSEPH & ESTHER / ALLEN"* is inscribed at the top center on the back of this monument. *"JOSEPH, JR. / Born Mar. 5, 1804; / Died June 1804. / JANE / Born June 9, 1812; / Died Mar. 1813. / ANN / Born July 1816; / Died Aug. 1816."* is inscribed on the left side of the back. *"ENOS / Born Aug. 9, 1817; / Died Sept. 12, 1821. / ESTHER / Born Mar. 6, 1809; / Died Oct. 18, 1822. / SAMUEL / Born May 22, 1821; / Died Oct. 19, 1822."* is inscribed on the right side. No birth day is listed for Ann, and no death day is listed for Joseph Jr., Jane or Ann.

Allen, Joseph Jr. See Joseph Allen Monument entry.
"JOSEPH JR." This footstone is located behind the monument, on the far right.

Allen, Samuel See Joseph Allen Monument entry.
"SAMUEL" This footstone is located behind the monument, on the right.

Brown, Thomas *"Here lies the remains / Of / THOMAS, / Son of / Moses &*

Syrena / BROWN, / Died Sept. 15, 1853. / Aged 15 years, 11 Ms. /

> *Farewell my Father,*
> *Farewell my Mother dear*
> *Farewell my Brothers, Sisters*
> *Farewell till we all meet,*
> *Again in that eternal,*
> *World of Joy"*

This stone is very weathered making the poem difficult to read.

Haskins, Laura   *"Laura W. / Wife of / ISAAC HASKINS, / Died / Nov. 14, 1864, / Aged / 28 years, 6 months."* This stone is leaning forward. A veteran's marker and flag are present.

Hatheway, Louisa   *"LOUISA W. PEIRCE, / wife of / WILLIAM R. P. HATHEWAY / died Jan. 26, 1854, / Aged 48 Yrs. 9 Ms. 17 Ds. /*

> *Sleep gently dear mother the calm sleep of death*
> *Sleep gently nor think of the friends thou hast left.*
> *We miss thee dear mother we miss thee below*
> *Yet we would not recall thee to this world of woe."*

The first line is carved in relief along an arch. Notice the spelling of *Hatheway* on this stone is different from that on her son Stephen's stone. Freetown Vital Records list her as being a Hatheway despite the footstone's initials.
"L. W. P." is inscribed on the footstone.

Hathaway, Stephen   *"STEPHEN R. / Son of / William R. P. & Louisa W. / HATHAWAY, / Died Nov. 1, 1856. / Aged / 29 years, 6 months."*
"S. R. H." is inscribed on the footstone.

Peirce, Abraham   *"In MEMORY of M^r. / Abraham Peirce who died / Nov^r, 24th, 1795 in y^e 54th, / Year of his Age. /*

> *This is the end of all that lives*
> *This is my dark long ho___*
> *Jesus himself lay in the grave*
> *The house where all must come."*

A rising sun is carved at the top of this lichen encrusted, slate stone. A veteran's marker and flag are present.

Peirce, Abraham Monument   *"ABRAHAM PEIRCE / SON OF / SIMEON AND HOPE PEIRCE / DIED, DEC. 14, 1879 / AGED 75 YEARS, 5 MONTHS / AND 7 DAYS"* *"PEIRCE"* is carved in relief on the front base of this very large roofed monument. *"MARGARET / (PEIRCE) / WIFE OF / ABRAHAM PEIRCE / BORN, OCT. 12, 1799, / DIED, FEB. 12, 1878"* is inscribed on the left side of the monument. *"LUCY F. / (ASHLEY) / WIFE OF / ABRAHAM PEIRCE / DIED OCT. 10, 1845 / AGED 33 YEARS / 9 MO. & 8 DS."* is inscribed on the right side. The monogram *"P"* is inscribed in shallow relief on the gables of the front and back. Columns are carved in all four corners.
"ABRAHAM PEIRCE" is carved in shallow relief on the top slanted surface of this footstone, which is located behind the monument.

Pierce, Apollos   *"APOLLOS PIERCE, / Born / Oct. 15, 1802. / Died / Jan. 28,*

1865." "J. B. SULLIVAN, Taunton." is inscribed on the center bottom of this stone.

Pierce, Christnia   *"CHRISTNIA, / Wife of / Apollos Pierce, / Born / Aug. 28, 1811. / Died / Aug. 15, 1867."*   This gravestone was broken through the last line, and successfully repaired.

Peirce, Clothier   *"CLOTHIER PEIRCE, / Died / Sept. 23, 1854, / aged / 73 Yrs. 5 Mos. / 11 D'ys."* The first line is carved in shadow.
"C. P." is inscribed on the footstone.

Pierce, Columbus   *"COLUMBUS / Son of / David R. Pierce, / died July 11, 1866. / Aged 24 years."*   The first line is carved along an arch.   A crack in the center bottom has been successfully repaired.   A veteran's marker and flag are present. *Massachusetts Civil War Soldiers & Sailors, 1861-1865*, shows that he served with the 3rd Mass Infantry, Co. G, (Vol. I, p.158), the 22nd Unattached Militia (Vol. V, p. 259), and the U.S. Navy (Vol. VIII, p. 556).
"C. P." is inscribed on the footstone.

Pierce, David B.   *"DAVID B. / Son of / David R. Pierce, / died Jan 7, 1873; / Aged 15 years."* The first line is carved along an arch.   A crack in the center bottom of this stone has been successfully repaired.
"D. B. P." is inscribed on the footstone.

Peirce, David R.   *"DAVID R. PIERCE / died Nov. 7, 1872, / Aged 63 years."*   The first line is carved along an arch.   A crack in the center bottom of this stone has been successfully repaired.
"D. R. P." is inscribed on the footstone.

Peirce, Hope   *"In MEMORY of Miss / Hope Peirce, Dau^{tr}. of M^r. / Abra^m she died April 15th 1800. / In ye 30th Year of her Age. /*

> *Depart my weeping friends*
> *And wipe your streaming eyes*
> *Here I must till Christ descends*
> *And bids my body rise."*

There is a frond carving at the top of this lichen encrusted, slate stone.   The poem was very hard to read due to weathering.
"Miss / Hope / Peirce. / died / 1800." is inscribed on this slate footstone.

Pierce, Hope   *"HOPE, / Wife of / SIMEON PIERCE, / Born Feb. 2, 1772. / Died / May 6, 1857. /*

> *Remember me as you pass by,*
> *As you are now so once was I,*
> *As I am now so you must be,*
> *Prepare yourselves to follow me."*

"D. A. BURT, Taunton." is inscribed on the center bottom of this textured stone. Note that the spelling of Hope's last name differs from the spelling on her husband's gravestone.
"H. P." is inscribed on the footstone.

Peirce, Jemima   *"JEMIMA PEIRCE / DAU^r OF M^r / SAMUEL & M^{rs} / PHEBE PEIRCE / WHO DIED / OCT^r y^{e}16th / 1755 AGED / 19 YEARS __ / MONTHS & / 24 DAYS."*   There is a simple head carving at the top, with semicircular designs carved behind it. Vine carvings are along the sides. This lichen encrusted, slate stone is difficult to read. The area around the number of months she lived is chipped off, but the part that remains suggests a *5*. Thatcher lists her as dying on October 6th, aged 10 years, no months or days listed.

Peirce, Lucy F.   See Abraham Peirce Monument entry.
"LUCY F. / Wife of / Abraham Pierce 2d / died Oct. 10, / 1845, / Aged 33 years / 9 Mo's & 8 D's." is inscribed on a stone located behind and to the right of the monument. The first line is carved in shadow. A sculptured floral carving is at the top. Note the different spelling of her last name on this stone.

Pierce, Luther   *"LUTHER M. / Son of / Abraham & Phebe / PIERCE. / Died Nov. 4. 1822, / aged 19 Yrs. / 8 Mos. & 19 Das. / 'Then shall the dust return to the earth / as it was and the spirit shall return unto / God who gave it.'"*   *"Hathaway, Taunton."* is inscribed at the bottom of the stone. The first line is carved in shadow. *"L. M. P."* is inscribed on the footstone.

Peirce, Lydia   *"LYDIA PEIRCE / wife of / M*.* Abraham Peirce / died May 23, 1817 / Aged 78 years / & 11 months."*   An urn and willow are carved at the top of this lichen encrusted, slate stone. The last two lines are buried underground
"L. Peirce / 1817." is inscribed on this slate footstone. It is broken in half and lying on the ground on the left, behind her grave, between the headstones of Mrs. Lydia Smith and Lydia H. Winslow.

Pierce, Margaret
See Abraham Peirce Monument entry.

"MARGARET
Wife of
ABRAM PIERCE,
Dau. of
Abram & Mary
PIERCE,
Born Oct. 12, 1799;
Died Feb. 12, 1878.
All that live must die
Passing through nature to eternity."
is inscribed on this separate gravestone, which is located behind the monument. Note the different spelling of her last name on this stone.
"M. P." is inscribed on this footstone.

Pierce, Margaret   *"MARGARET, / wife of / DAVID R. PIERCE, / died Aug. 23, 1892, / Aged 74 years. / Ameable, she won all,*
  Intelligent she charmed all,
  Fervant she loved all,
  Dead she saddened all."
The first line is carved along an arch. Note the spelling of *ameable* and *fervent*.
"M. P." is inscribed on the footstone.

Peirce, Phebe *"In memory of M^{rs}, / Phebe, wife of M^r, / Samuel Peirce, who / died Jan. 2^d, 1786, / in ye 83^d Year / of her age. /*
> *Our moments fly apace,*
> *Nor will our minds stay,*
> *Just like a flood our hasty days*
> *Are sweeping us away."*

There is a frond carving at the top of this slate stone, and delicate leaf designs are carved down the sides.
"Mrs. / Phebe / Peirce / 1786." is inscribed on this footstone. There are slivers of slate broken off in the area of her death year. When assembled, they revealed the complete death year.

Pierce, Phebe *"PHEBE HASKINS / Wife of / Abraham Pierce, / died May 16, 1866; / Aged 81 years."* The first line is carved along an arch. A crack at the bottom has been repaired.
"P. H. P." is inscribed on the footstone.

Peirce, Phebe S. *"PHEBE S. PEIRCE / Daughter of / Mr. Abraham Peirce / & Phebe his wife / Died Oct. 28, 1820 / Aged 1 year 11 month & 19 days."* A willow is carved at the top of this slate stone.
"P. S. P. / 1820." is inscribed on this slate footstone.

Peirce, Rebecca *"REBECCA, / Wife of / CLOTHIER PEIRCE, / Died Dec. 13, 1869. / aged / 87 Yrs. 8 Mos. / 24 D'ys."* The first line is carved in shadow.
"R. P." is inscribed on the footstone.

Peirce, Sally E. *"Erected in memory of / SALLY EVANS. / wife of / Simeon Peirce, / died Apr. 6, 1829; / Aged 32 yrs. / Ever in Remembrance."* There is a 5 inch crack at the center bottom of this stone.
"S. E. P." is inscribed on the footstone.

Peirce, Samuel *"In memory of / M^r, Samuel Peirce, / who died June 4th, / 1785. in ye 86th / Year of his age. / Under these silent clods I sleep*
> *In Christ may I arise*
> *And when the angel Gabriel ^{sound}*
> *Meet Jesus in the skies."*

There is a frond carving at the top of this slate stone, and vines are carved down the sides. A veteran's marker and flag are present.
"Mr. / Samuel / Peirce, / 1785." is inscribed on this slate footstone.

Peirce, Sarah *"SARAH. / Wife of / Elijah Peirce, / Died Jan. 30, 1841, / Æ. 51 y'rs 10 mo's / & 12 d's. / Those on earth that knew my name,*
> *I honour them in Heaven;*
> *There my salvation shall be shown*
> *And endless life be given."*

"S. P." is inscribed on the footstone.

Pierce, Sarah H. *"SARAH H. / Dau. of / David R. Pierce, / died Jan. 15. 1850, / in her 10 th year."* The first line is carved along an arch. There is a crack through the center bottom up to the last line.

"S. H. P." is inscribed on the footstone.

Peirce, Simeon   *"SIMEON PEIRCE, / Born / Aug. 6, 1769. / Died / Nov. 17, 1859. / Mark the perfect man and, / behold the upright; for the / end of that man is peace."* *"[D. A. BURT, Taunton.]"* is inscribed in the lower right corner.
"S. P." is inscribed on the footstone.

Smith, Lydia   *"In MEMORY of M^rs. / Lydia, wife of M^r. Edward / Smith y^e Dau_er of M^r. Abra'm Peirce she / died Decr. 10th 1794 in y^e 22^d. / Year of her Age. /*
__ a true gl__ you s_ill here you see
What I am now to marrow you may be."
A rising sun is carved at the top of this lichen encrusted, slate stone. The poem is very difficult to read.
"M^s / Lydia / Smith / 1794." is inscribed on this slate footstone.

Terry, Rebecca   *"REBECCA H. / Wife of / SIMEON TERRY. / Born / Dec. 30, 1815. / Died / April 5, 1865."* is inscribed on this textured stone. The marriage record in *Vital Records of the Town of Freetown, Massachusetts 1686 Through 1890* lists her maiden name as Pierce. Her husband is buried in Howland Cemetery.
"R. H. T." is inscribed on the footstone.

Winslow, Lydia   *"LYDIA H. / Wife of / Frederick Winslow, Jr., / And daughter of / Elijah & Sarah / PIERCE. / Died June 6, 1838. / Aged / 28 years. /*
Thou art gone but not forgotten.

Shed not for her the bitter tear,
Nor give the heart to vain regret,
'Tis but the casket that lies here,
The gem that filled it sparkles yet."
"BURT, Taunton" is inscribed on the bottom right of this stone.
"L. H. W." is inscribed on the footstone.

Additional Notes:

The Lakeville Town Hall cemetery cards list the following people as being buried in this cemetery, but no gravestones were found for them here. Some of their gravestones were located in Lang Cemetery (which was also known as Pierce Cemetery), and some were located in Ward Cemetery (which was also known as Pierce Hill Cemetery).

"Coombs, Julia F. d. Apr. 11, 1914." Lakeville Vital Records indicate that she was the daughter of Jarius H. Shaw and Rebecca Southworth. She was the widow of Clarence Coombs. She died at the age of 69 years, 7 months, and 28 days, and is listed as buried in Pierce Cemetery. There is a stone for her and her husband in Ward Cemetery.

"Goodwin, Chester E. Jr. d. May 17, 1914." Lakeville Vital Records indicate he was the son of Chester E. and Ella Goodwin, who are buried in Lang Cemetery. He died at 1 year, 4 months, and 8 days, and is listed as buried in Peirce Cemetery.

"**Pierce, Abbie** d. July 16, 1919." Lakeville Vital Records indicate that she was the daughter of Luther Ashley and Theodora Caswell. Her husband was Philip Philander Pierce. She died at the age of 80 years, 1 month and 1 day. She is listed as buried in Pierce Cemetery, but she has a stone in Lang Cemetery.

"**Pierce, Fanny P.** d. Mar 25, 1917." Lakeville Vital Records indicate that she is the daughter of Eli Williams of Raynham and Fanny Pickens of Lakeville. She was the widow of William H. Pierce, and she died at the age of 84 years, 11 months, and 11 days. She is listed as buried in Pierce Cemetery, but she has a stone in Lang Cemetery.

"**Peirce, James P.** d. Mar. 9, 1915." Lakeville Vital Records indicate that he was the son of Phillip H. and Abigail Peirce. He died at the age of 79 years, 5 months, and 15 days. He is listed as buried in Pierce Cemetery, but he has a stone in Lang Cemetery.

"**Pierce, Judith Nelson** d. June 21, 1918." Lakeville Vital Records indicate that she was the daughter of Job Peirce of Middleborough and Eunice J. Ellis of Mattapoisett. She died at the age of 58 years, 10 months, and 9 days. She is listed as buried in Pierce Cemetery, but she has a stone in Lang Cemetery.

"**Porter, Josephine** d. July 24, 1915." Lakeville Vital Records indicate that she was the wife of George Porter. She died at the age of 75 years, 9 months, and 17 days, and is listed as buried in Pierce Cemetery. No stone was found here, however there is a stone for Kate Porter, wife of George in Ward Cemetery with this same age and death date. Brockton Vital Records list her name as Josephine Kate Joy at the time of her marriage in 1882.

"**Reed, Henry B.** d. May 22, 1922." Lakeville Vital Records indicate that he was the son of Apollos Reed and Nancy Ransdall. He died at the age of 80 years, 5 months, and 5 days. He is listed as buried in Pierce Cemetery, but he has a stone in Lang Cemetery.

Pierce Cemetery Map Index

Alphabetical:

Allen, Abiah (~1762-1843) – 11
Allen, Ann (1816) – 29, 33
Allen, Enos (1817-1821) – 29, 31
Allen, Esther (1809-1822) – 29, 30
Allen, Esther (1778-1862) – 29, 30
Allen, Jane (1812-1813) – 29, 34
Allen, John (~1754-1841) – 12
Allen, Joseph (1776-1870) – 29
Allen, Joseph, Jr. (1804) – 29, 35
Allen, Samuel (1821-1822) – 29, 32
Brown, Thomas (1837-1853) – 42
Haskins, Laura (1836-1864) – 41

Hathaway, Stephen (1827-1856) – 40
Hatheway, Louisa (1805-1854) – 39
Peirce, Abraham (~1742-1795) – 18
Peirce, Abraham (1804-1879) – 20, 22
Pierce, Apollos (1802-1865) – 6
Pierce, Christnia (1811-1867) – 8
Pierce, Clothier (1781-1854) – 9
Pierce, Columbus (~1842-1866) – 2
Pierce, David B. (~1858-1873) – 1
Pierce, David R. (~1809-1872) – 5
Pierce, Hope (1772-1857) – 16
Pierce, Hope (~1771-1800) – 28

By Location:

Pierce Cemetery Map

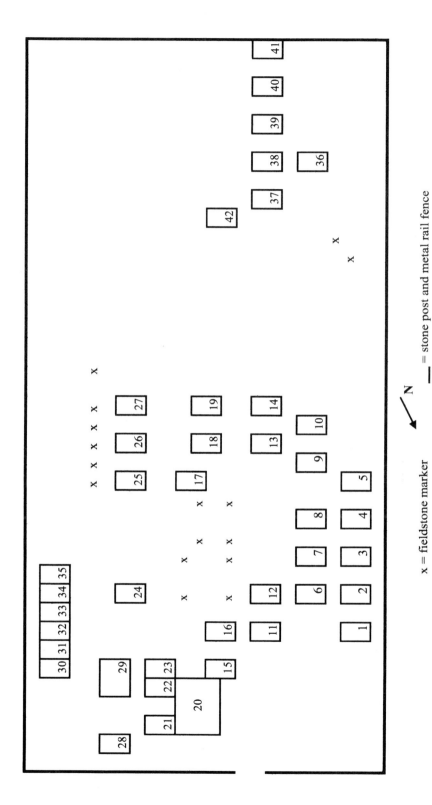

N

x = fieldstone marker

___ = stone post and metal rail fence

Chapter 20
Pond Cemetery

Pond Cemetery is located on Bedford Street (Route 105), 1/4 mile south of Highland Avenue. A stone wall, sometimes retaining, borders the front of the cemetery, and extends back a little on the right side. Wood posts are spaced along the remaining right side and along the back, but no rails are present. On the left side is the Sampson plot which is surrounded by a stone post and metal rail fence. Five additional plots are enclosed in this cemetery. The sign is in good repair. Gravestones face south and west, and date from 1724 to 1998. The Lakeville Assessor's Office lists this cemetery as town owned, 1 acre in size. Vigers states, "...the land was sold by Ebenezer Richmond to Thomas Nelson, his heirs, for use as a burying place, October 14th, 1734, ..." Vigers states it used to be called the "Old Nelson Burying Ground" or the "Nelson Cemetery." Entries were recorded between November 28, 2000, and May 11, 2001.

Alden, Humphrey, Capt. *"IN MEMORY OF / Capt. HUMPHREY ALDEN / who died / June 12, 1844. / Aged 82 y'rs. / ..."* The second line is carved in relief. There are two additional lines on this stone, which are unreadable due to severe weathering. A veteran's marker and flag are present.
"H. A." is inscribed on the footstone.

Alden, Mary *"IN MEMORY OF / Mrs. MARY. / late consort of / Capt. Humphrey Alden / who departed this life / Jan 29, 18__, / Aged 8_ years /...."* The second line is carved in relief. There are two additional lines on this stone, which are unreadable due to severe weathering. Thatcher lists her death year as 1843, and her age as 84.
"M. A." is inscribed on the footstone.

Allen, Parmeliahall *"In Memory of / Pa'meliahall Allen / Dau.'r to M.'r Bezaliel / & M.'rs Parmelia Allen / She Died Jul_ 25 th / 1800 Aged 14 Month.s / Wanting 19 Days."* There is a simple winged head carved at the top of this slate stone. Thatcher lists her and her mother's name as Pamelia, with Hall as the daughter's middle name, but on this stone their names are spelled Parmelia. The daughter's name, Parmeliahall, is inscribed as one word on this stone, but the initials on the footstone are P.H.A.

"*P. H. A.*" is inscribed on this slate footstone.

Bates, Sibel   "*In / memory / of / M͞ʳˢ. Sibel Bates / wife of / Mʳ. Samuel Bates / who died / April 4ᵗʰ 1810 / in the 49 year / of her age /*

> *The body pain'd with sore disease*
> *Till death did on the vitals seize*
> *But now twill moulder in the ground*
> *Till the last trumpets solemn sound*
> *And then we hope in joy complete*
> *Twill rise and the redeemer meet*"

An urn and willow carving is at the top of this tall, tapering, slate stone. Her maiden name was Briggs. A stone post and metal rail fence surrounds this Briggs plot.

"*S. B. / 1810*" is inscribed on this slate footstone, which also tapers to the top.

Belliveau, William   See D. Evelyn Norris Monument entry.

Benton, George S.   "*GEORGE S. / Son of Wᵐ H. & / Lydia A. Benton / died / Feb. 27, 1859: / Æ 2 yrs. 2 mo. / & 7 d's. /*

> *I take these little lambs said he*
> *And fold them on my breast*
> *Protection they shall find in me*
> *In me be ever blest.*"

The last two lines are buried underground.

Benton, Georgie A.   "*Georgie A. / Son of William F. & / Elizabeth Benton / died Sept. 5, 1874. / Aged 2 yrs. 9 m's. / 23 d's / ...*" Ten more lines are inscribed, but only the last two are readable due to severe weathering. "*...But still we trust in higher power, which / "says All is for the best.""*

"*G. A. B.*" is inscribed on the footstone

Bly, John   "*In memory of / Mr. John Bly / who died / Feb. 6. 1808 / aged 48 years.*" A willow is carved at the top of this slate stone. Thatcher lists his last name as Blye.

"*Mr. John Bly*" This slate footstone faces the headstone.

Bly, Margaret   "*In memory of / MARGARET / wife of the late / JOHN BLY. / who died Oct. 4, 1839. / in the 83. Yr. of her age. /*

> *Dear saint thy flesh in hope shall rest.*
> *From sickness, pain, and sorrow free.*
> *Thy soul reclined on Jesus breast.*
> *Who lived and died and rose for thee.*
> *His mercy sanctified thy pain.*
> *His blood washed all thy sins away.*
> *Our loss is thy eternal gain*
> *Thy night is turned to endless day.*"

The second line is carved in relief. A willow is carved in relief at the top of this stone. Thatcher lists her last name as Blye, and her death month as August.

"M. B." is inscribed on the footstone.

Blye, John   *"In Memory of M^r. / John Blye he Died / May $\overset{e}{y}$· 24th 1790 / in $\overset{e}{y}$· 66th Year of / his Age."*   A winged angel is carved at the top of this slate stone. Swirl designs are carved along the edges of the tympanum.   A *"SAR 1775"* marker and flag are present.

"M^r. / John / Blye" is inscribed on this slate footstone.

Booth, Nancy   *"In Memory of / Mrs. NANCY. / wife of / Gilbert Booth / Died Dec. 17, 1844. / Aged 44 Years."*

"N. B." This footstone faces the headstone.

Briggs, Abigail   See Lemuel Briggs Obelisk entry.

"In memory of / Mrs. Abigail wife of / Mr. Lemuel Briggs / she died, Oct. 11. / 1810 / in her 46. Year." is inscribed on a separate stone to the left of the obelisk. An urn and a small willow are carved at the top of this slate stone. A stone post and metal rail fence surrounds this Briggs plot.

"Mrs. / Abigail / Briggs." is inscribed on this slate footstone.

Briggs, Ebenezer   *"Ebenezer Son of / Mr. Ebenezer and / Mrs. Hannah / Briggs died / March 1st 1808 / aged 2 Years 11 / month and 15 days"* An urn with handles is carved at the top of this small, slate stone.

Briggs, Ebenezer, Dea.   *"In memory of / Dea^n. EBENEZER / BRIGGS who died / OCTOBER 26th. AD 1808 / in the 77th. Year / of his age."* An urn with handles is carved at the top of this slate stone. A veteran's marker and flag are present.

"__ / _benezer / Briggs" is inscribed on the footstone. The upper left corner is broken off.

Briggs, Ebenezer Tomb   *"EBENEZER BRIGGS / FAMILY TOMB / 1839"* is inscribed on the stone imbedded in the front of this crypt.

Briggs, Elezebath   *"In Memory of / Elezebath Daugh^{tr} / to M^r. Ebenezer / Briggs & M^{rs}. / Elezebath / his wife who dec^d. / May $\overset{e}{y}$ 5th 1772 / Aged 8 years 7 / months & 19 days."* The last two lines are buried underground. A winged angel is carved at the top of this slate stone. Flower and leaf designs are carved down the sides. It is beginning to exfoliate. Thatcher lists her death month as March, and spells her first name Elizabeth. A footstone is present, but no inscription was found it.

Briggs, Elisabeth *"In memory of / Mrs. Elisabeth widow of / Dea. Ebenezer Briggs / who died Jan. 24. / 1813 in her 80. / year."* There is a carving of an urn and willow above the inscription. This slate stone is broken in several places. A piece from the left side was found in front of the headstone. Letters from the three pieces were used to complete the transcription. Thatcher lists her death day as the 21st of January, and spells her name Elizabeth.
"Mrs. / Elisabeth / Briggs." This slate footstone faces the headstone.

Briggs, Eliza *"ELIZA BRIGGS. / Died Dec. 17, 1885. / Æ 86 yrs. 4 mos. 13 dys."*
"E. B." is inscribed on the footstone.

Briggs, Elizabeth K. *"ELIZABETH K. / Wife of / Capt. Silas Briggs, / Died May 6. 1858. / Æ.85 y'rs & 8 mos."*
"E. K. B." is inscribed on the footstone.

Briggs, Esther See Lemuel Briggs Obelisk entry.
Middleborough Vital Records list her as 79 years old when she died on September 10, 1849.

Briggs, Hannah *"Hannah daughter/ of Mr. Ebenezer / and Mrs. Hannah / Briggs died / November 17th / 1803 aged 7 months / and 24 days."* There is a bottle like urn with handles is carved at the top of this small slate stone. The last line is buried underground. Thatcher did not record the last line.
"1803 / H. B." is inscribed on this small slate footstone.

Briggs, James F. *"JAMES F. BRIGGS, / Died Nov. 7, 1860, / Æ. 48 yrs & 6 mo's"*
"J. F. B." is inscribed on the footstone.

Briggs, Lemuel Obelisk *"In memory of / LEMUEL BRIGGS, / Who was born / June 12, 1764. & / died Aug. 27, 1849. / Aged 85 years."* is inscribed on the front of this obelisk. *"In memory of / ABIGAIL, / Wife of / Lemuel Briggs. / Who died / Oct 11, 1810. / In her 46th year."* is inscribed on the right side. *"In memory of / ESTHER / Wife of / Lemuel Briggs, / Who died Sept. 1849. / Aged 82 years."* is inscribed on the left side. No inscriptions are present on the back. There is no day of death inscribed for Esther. A *"SAR 1775"* marker and flag are present. This plot is enclosed with a stone post and metal rail fence.

Briggs, Melissa *"MELISSA / Daughter of / PELATIAH & PHILENA / BRIGGS / Died / June 22, 1923. / Æ. 76 yrs, 11 mos, 20 dys"*
"M. B." is inscribed on the footstone.

Briggs, Peltiah *"PELTIAH BRIGGS, / Died Apr. 3, 1890, / Æ 88 yrs, 5 mos, 1 day."*
"P.B." is inscribed on the footstone.

Briggs, Philena *"PHILENA / Wife of / PELTIAH BRIGGS, / Died Aug. 4, 1848, / Æ 36 yrs, 11 mos, 20 dys."*
"P. B." is inscribed on the footstone.

Briggs, Rounsevill *"R. B."* is inscribed on this slate footstone. No headstone was found. Thatcher lists: "Rounsevill, son of Abiathar & Joanna, Mar. 8, 1804, 3 yrs., 9 mos., 4 da.." Their child Stephen is buried next to this footstone, so this is probably Rounseville's burial site.

Briggs, Sarah   *"In Memory of M^{rs}. / Sarah Widow of M^r. / David Briggs She / Died April^e_y 4th 1794 / In her 97th year."* A winged angel is carved at the top of this slate stone.
"M^{rs}. / Sarah / Briggs" is inscribed on this slate footstone. It is leaning against the headstone of Mrs. Elizabeth Briggs.

Briggs, Sarah   *"Memnto Mori / In Memory of M^{rs}. / Sar^ah wife of M^r. / Zephaniah Briggs / She Died Janu^{ry} ^e_y 5th. / 1799. In her 61st Year /*

> *My husband & my children dear*
> *Remember me who lies hear*
> *And serve the Lord with all your hear_*
> *That we may meet no more to part `"*

This exfoliating, slate stone has a winged angel carved between the first and second lines. Note the spelling of *Memnto* and *hear*. Middleborough Vital Records show that she was the mother of Lemuel Briggs. A stone post and metal rail fence surrounds this plot.
"M^{rs}. / Sarah / Briggs." is inscribed on the slate footstone.

Briggs, Silas, Capt.   *"CAPT. SILAS BRIGGS, / Died July 1, 1858, / Æ. 87 y'rs & 8 mo's."*
"S. B." is inscribed on the footstone.

Briggs, Stephen   *"In Memory of Steph__ / Son to M^r. Ebenezer / Briggs & M^{rs}. Elezabath / his wife who dec^d. / March y^e 21st, 1771 / Aged one year 10 / months & 17 days."* is inscribed on this small slate stone. A simple winged head is carved at the top. Thatcher lists his death day as the 17th of March, and spells the mother's name as Elizabeth. A footstone is present, but the inscribed surface has exfoliated.

Briggs, Stephen   *"In memory of / Stephen son of / Mr. Abiathar & Mrs. / Joanna Briggs / he died Nov. 5, 1810 / in his 17. year."* An urn and willow are carved at the top of this slate stone. Thatcher lists his death day as the 13th of November.
"Stephen / Briggs." is inscribed on the slate footstone.

Briggs, William   *"WILLIAM BRIGGS, / Died Dec. 22, 1867, / Æ. 51 y'rs & 9 mo's."* is inscribed on this textured stone.
"W. B." is inscribed on the footstone.

Brown, Alvin M.   *"ALVIN M. BROWN. / 1862.   1914."* A rectangular area with floral designs carved around it is above the inscription. Nothing is inscribed within this area.

Brown, Ralph Alvin   *"RALPH ALVIN / SON OF / MR. & MRS. A. M. BROWN, / 1890 – 1901"* is inscribed on the slanted surface of this brown stone. Leaves are carved in relief on the lower vertical surface of the monument.

Chipman, Josiah   See Ebenr. Clark Stone entry. Thatcher lists him as Joshua Clark.

Clark see also **Clarke**. Thatcher's entries are all spelled Clark.

Clark, Abner *"ABNER, / Son of Job P. & / Mary Clark. / died Oct. 7, 1852 / Aged 1 y'r 8 m ᵉ / & 8 d's"* The first line is carved in relief on this textured stone. It appears as if the carver ran out of room on the fifth line. A low cement wall surrounds this Clark/Clarke plot.
"A. C." is inscribed on the footstone.

Clark, Deliverance *"Memento Mori / In Memory of / Mʳˢ Deliverance, wife of / Mʳ. Ezra Clark, who Died / July ᵉ₉ 11 ᵗʰ 1784, In the / 57 ᵗʰ Year of her Age."* A winged angel is carved between the first and second lines. There are several cracks in this slate stone, the largest of which extends from the top of the tympanum to the last line.
"Mʳˢ / Deliverance / Clark" is inscribed on this slate footstone.

Clark, Ebenr. Stone *"EBEN ᴿ CLARK,/ Died, / Dec. 3. 1848. / Æ. 38 years. / JOSIAH, / Son of C. & S. Chipman. / died Dec. 3. 1848. / Æ. 9 y'rs."* The first line is carved in relief. A low cement wall surrounds this Clark / Clarke plot.
"E. C." is inscribed on the footstone.

Clark, Ezra *"Memento Mortis / In Memory of / Mᴿ. EZRA CLARK. / who died July 19 ᵗʰ 1789. / In the 69 ᵗʰ Year of his Age."* A winged angel is carved between the first and second lines on this slate stone.
"Mʳ. / Ezra Clark" is inscribed on this lichen encrusted, slate footstone.

Clark, Ezra *"In memory of Mr. Ezra Clark, / who died / Janʳʸ 17, 1808 in / his 25ᵗʰ year."* A rising sun is carved at the top of this slate stone.
"Mr. / Ezra / Clark." This slate footstone is broken diagonally, below the inscription. The top piece is lying face down next to the bottom section.

Clark, Ezra *"In memory of / Ezra, son of Mr. Elisha / & Mrs. Catherine / Clark, who died June / 21ˢᵗ 1808. Aged 16. / months & 8. days."* A rising sun is carved at the top of this slate stone. A low cement wall surrounds this Clark/Clarke plot.

Clark, Ezra, Lt. *"In Memory of Leu ͭ / Ezra Clark ᵉ₉ 2 ᵈ he / Died Jan ʳʸ yᵉ 22 ᵈ 1793 / In his 45 ᵗʰ Year"* A winged angel is carved at the top of this slate stone. Curved designs are carved along the edge of the tympanum. A *"SAR 1775"* marker and flag are present.
"Leu ͭ / Ezra Clark" is inscribed on the slate footstone.

Clark, Henry See Capt. Horatio G. Clark Stone entry.

Clark, Horatio G., Capt. Stone *"In memory of / CAPT. HORATIO G. CLARK / who died / Jan. 23. 1829 / in his 31. / year. / HENRY CLARK / died Nov. 3. 1819 / at Wainsborough, in / the State of Georgia, in / his 25. year."* There is an urn and willow carving at the top of this slate stone, and columns are carved in relief down the sides. A low cement wall surrounds this Clark/Clarke plot.
"H. G. C. / & / H.C." is inscribed on this slate footstone.

Clark, Joanna *"Memento Mori / In Memory of Mrs Joanna / Daug^r of Mr Ezra Clark / & Mrs Deliverance his / wife who Died Decr ye 14th / 1784 In the 23^d Year of / her Age."* A winged angel is carved between the first and second lines. A diagonal crack runs from the top of the tympanum to the third line. Another crack on the left side extends to the fifth line. Near the bottom, the stone's borders have exfoliated. It appears that the carver ran out of room on the fifth line of this slate stone.
"M^{rs} / Joanna Clar^k" is inscribed on this footstone. It appears that the carver ran out of room on the second line.

Clark, Joanna *"In MEMORY of Miss / Joanna Clark she died / Jan. 6th AD 1808*
Æt 22 /   *With love divine and pu__ delight*
                                 On faith's celestial wing
                                 With sweet repose __ her flight
                                 For Death had left his sting"
A peeking rising sun is carved at the top of this lichen encrusted, slate stone. The last line is buried underground. A low cement wall surrounds this Clark/Clarke plot.
"Miss / Joanna / Clark / died / 1808" is inscribed on the slate footstone.

Clark, Job P. *"In memory of / JOB P. CLARK, / who died / May 17, 1852. / Æ. 46 yrs. & 3 m's."* The second line is carved in relief. A low cement wall surrounds this Clark/Clarke plot.
"J. P. C." is inscribed on the footstone.

Clark, Lydia *"In memory of / Miss Lydia Clark / dau of / Mr. Ezra Clark / & Mrs. Mary his wife / who died / March 29, 1813 / in her 34 year."* A willow is carved at the top. This slate stone was broken diagonally from the third to seventh lines. A repair attempt has failed. The top piece is face up on the ground in front of bottom section.
"Miss. / L. Clark" is inscribed on this slate footstone.

Clark, Mary *"In Memory of M^{rs} / Mary Wife of Leu^t / Ezra Clark ye 2^d She / Died Nov^{mr} ye 6th 1792 / in her 45th Year."* A winged angel head is carved at the top of this lichen encrusted, slate stone. Curved designs are carved along the tympanum.
"M^{rs} / Mary / Clark" is inscribed on this slate footstone.

Clark, Roger *"To the memory of / Mr. / ROGER CLARK / who died / March 19. 1812 / in his 54. / year."* An urn and willow are carved at the top of this slate stone, and small designs are carved down the sides. It was broken diagonally between the second and fourth lines, and successfully repaired. A *"SAR 1775"* marker and flag are present.
"Mr. / Roger / Clark." is inscribed on this slate footstone.

Clark, Xenophon *"In / memory of / XENOPHON CLARK / who died / May 23 1829 / in his 28 / year"* There is an urn and willow carving at the top of this slate stone. Columns are carved in relief on the sides. A George Thompson swirl is carved below the inscription. A low cement wall surrounds this Clark/Clarke plot.
"_ C." is inscribed on this slate footstone. The upper left corner is missing.

Clarke see also **Clark**. Thatcher lists everyone under Clark.

Clarke, Abner, Esq. *"In / memory of / ABNER CLARKE, ESQ. / who died / May 1, 1830, / aged 65 years. / My flesh shall slumber in the ground,*
       Till the last trump of God shall sound
       Then burst the chains with sweet surprise
       And in my Saviours image rise."
There is an urn and willow carving at the top of this slate stone, and scalloped designs are carved down the sides. This stone was broken through the sixth line, and successfully repaired. A veteran's marker and flag are present. A low cement wall surrounds this Clark / Clarke plot.
"A. C." This slate footstone faces the headstone.

Clarke, Alice See James Clarke Monument entry.
"ALICE" is inscribed on this flat, 1 inch high footstone. It is located behind the monument, on the left.

Clarke, Almira *"In memory of / ALMIRA CLARKE / who died / Feb 8, 1834. / aged 30 years."* An urn and willow are carved on this slate stone. There is a diagonal crack below the inscribed area. A low cement wall surrounds this Clark / Clarke plot.
"A. C." is inscribed on this slate footstone.

Clarke, James Monument *"CLARKE"* is carved in relief on the front of this large monument. A leaf design is carved on the left. *"JAMES CLARKE / HIS WIFE / SUSAN (TOWNSEND) / THEIR DAUGHTER / ALICE CLARKE / THEIR SON / JAMES W. CLARKE / EDITH (HATHAWAY) / WIFE OF / BERTRAND HACKETT"* is inscribed on the back. There are no dates on this stone.
"JAMES" is inscribed on this flat, 4-5 inch high footstone.

Clarke, Mary *"Mary dau. of / Mr. Abner & / Mrs. Mary Clarke / died August 15, 1814 / Æt. 4 mos. / & 12 days."* An urn is carved at the top of this small slate stone. A low cement wall surrounds this Clark / Clarke plot.

Clarke, Mary *"In memory of / MARY, / wife of / Abner Clarke Esq ᵣ/ who died / July 23, 1847, in / her 77 year."* An urn and willow are carved at the top of this slate stone. Horizontal lines are carved as the side border. A low cement wall surrounds this Clark / Clarke plot.
"M. C." is inscribed on the slate footstone, which faces the headstone.

Clarke, Richard *"In / memory of / RICHARD CLARKE, / who died / May 20, 1830, / aged 34 years."* An urn and willow are carved at the top of this slate stone. Scalloped designs are carved down the sides. A low cement wall surrounds this Clark / Clarke plot.
"R.C." is inscribed on the slate footstone.

Clarke, Susan T.   See James Clarke Monument entry.
"MOTHER" is inscribed on this flat, 2-3 inch high footstone. It is located behind the monument, on the left.

Coggeshall, Gideon   *"GIDEON / COGGESHALL, / Died Aug. 30, / 1849, / in his 72 year."* This headstone is lying face up on the ground.
"G. C." is inscribed on the footstone. It is located behind the headstone of Silas Townsend, which is two stones to the left.

Cole, Abigail   *"In memory of / Mrs. ABIGAIL / wife of / MR. ANDREW / COLE / who died / Jan. 11. 1830 / Aged 87 years. / Geo. Thompson."* An urn and willow are carved in relief above the inscription. A George Thompson swirl is carved above his name.
"A. C." This footstone faces the headstone.

Cole, Albert L.   *"ALBERT L. / son of Samuel & / Mary Cole, / died Jan. 1, 1866; / Aged 47 yrs. 8m^s"* The first line is carved in shadow. A *"GAR 8 117"* marker and flag are present. *Massachusetts Civil War Soldiers & Sailors, 1861-1865,* shows that he served with the 3rd Mass. Infantry, Co. I, (Vol. I, p. 197), and the 4th Mass. Calvary, Co. B. (Vol. VI, p. 430).
"A. S. C." is inscribed on the footstone. Note the different middle initial from the headstone.

Cole, Andrew   *"In / memory of / MR. / ANDREW COLE · / who died / Jan 20, 1841, / in his 86 $^t_.{}^h$ year."* The third and fourth lines are carved in outline. A *"SAR 1775"* marker and flag are present.
"A. C." This footstone faces the headstone.

Cole, Anna E. Monument   *"D"* monogram is carved in shallow relief at the top of the monument, and ivy leaves are carved on either side. *"DAVIS"* is carved in relief on the base. *"ANNA ELIZA COLE / DIED JAN. 15, 1913 AGED 68 YEARS / ABBIE M. PARKER /   / TIMOTHY K. DAVIS /   "* Lakeville Vital Records show she was the wife of Charles G. Cole. Space is left for inscribing the dates for her siblings Abbie Parker and Timothy Davis.
"A. E. C." is inscribed on the top horizontal surface of this footstone.

Cole, Charles G.   *"C. G. COLE / CO. I, / 3rd MASS. INF."* The above inscription is carved in relief within a recessed shield shaped area. *Middleborough, Massachusetts Vital Records,* Vol. 1, p. 423 lists his birth on February 26, 1825. Taunton Vital Records list his death on February 15, 1883, at 58 years, 11 months, and 20 days old. *Massachusetts Civil War Soldiers and Sailors, 1861-1865,* Vol. I, p. 197, shows that Charles G. Cole enlisted from Lakeville in 1862 at age 38. He served in the 58th Infantry, Co.F also. A veteran's marker and flag are present.

Cole, Isaiah   *"In memory of / Mr. Isaiah Cole / who died / Nov. 9. 1810 / in his 79. Year."* An urn and willow are carved at the top with small curved designs carved down the sides. This slate stone was broken diagonally through the second and third lines, and successfully repaired.
"Mr. / Isaiah Cole" is inscribed on this slate footstone.

Cole, James   *"Memento Mori / In Memory of / M^r. James Cole, Son / of M^r. Isaiah*

& *M.^{rs}/ Eleanor Cole who died / _ug st. 22^d 1779 In the / 23 ^d Year of his Age."* There is a winged angel head carved between the first and second lines on this small, slate stone.

Cole, Lorenzo   *"LORENZO, / son of Samuel / and Mary Cole / died April 10, 1832. / aged 5 mos. and / 5 days."* This slate stone has an urn and willow carving at the top.
"L. C." is inscribed on the slate footstone.

Cole, Martha F.   *"MARTHA F. / Dau. of Job N. & / Abby D. Cole / Died / Nov. 16, 1857, / Æ. 3 yrs. 10 m's / & 27 d's. /*

> *From all the chequered ills Silent*
> *Martha secure doth sleep.*
> *Her little heart no pangs doth know*
> *Her eyes no more shall weep*

Cole, Mary   *"In / memory of / MRS. MARY, / wife of / Mr. Andrew Cole. / who died / Dec 17, 1840. / in her 74th year."* The second line is carved in outline. It is lying face up on the ground and is very weathered.
"M. C." is inscribed on the footstone. It is located two rows behind her headstone, on the right.

Cole, Mary   *"MARY. / wife of / Samuel Cole, / died June 18. 1854, / in her 61 st year."* The first line is carved in relief.
"M. C." This footstone faces headstone.

Cole, Mical   *"In memory of / Mr. Mical Cole / who died Dec, 24 th / 1797. / in his 36 th Year."* A peeking rising sun is carved at the top of this slate stone.
"Mr. M. C." This slate footstone faces the headstone.

Cole, Nancy   *"In memory of / MRS. NANCY wife of / Capt. Nathaniel Cole / who died / Dec. 8, 1828 / in her 68. / year"* An urn and willow are carved at the top of this slate stone. Curved designs are carved down the sides. A George Thompson swirl is carved below the inscription.

Cole, Samuel   *"SAMUEL COLE / Died / Jan. 1, 1872, / Aged / 78 yrs 2 mos."* A veteran's marker and flag are present.

Crane, Carrie I.   See Silas D. Pickens Monument entry.
"CARRIE" is inscribed on this flat, ground level footstone. It is located behind the monument, on the left.

Crowell, Elizabeth F.   *"ELIZABETH FALES / CROWELL / Born Feb. 19, 1816 / Died June 19, 1894: / Daughter of Lemuel / and Betsey Tobey of / New Bedford."*

Cudworth, Arthur A.   See John Cudworth Monument entry.
"ARTHUR" is carved in shallow relief on the top slanted surface of this footstone. It is located in front of the monument, on the left side.

Cudworth, Horace A.   See John Cudworth Monument entry.
"OUR LITTLE HORACE" is inscribed on the top curved surface of this second stone. *"SON OF / JOHN & SARAH C / CUDWORTH, / AGED 2 YRS, 5 MOS. / 24 DAYS."* is carved on the front. There is no death year on this second stone.

Cudworth, Jesse R.   See John Cudworth Monument entry.
"JESSE" is carved in relief on the top slanted surface of this footstone. It is located in front of the monument, on the left. The rear right corner is broken off.

Cudworth, John Monument   *"JOHN CUDWORTH / 1839 – 1921 / SARAH C. HIS WIFE / 1843 – 1909 / ARTHUR A. CUDWORTH / 1889 – 1909."* is inscribed on the front of this monument. *"CUDWORTH"* is carved in relief on the front base. *"HORACE A. CUDWORTH / 1865 – 1867 / JESSE R. CUDWORTH / 1863 – 1936 / ABBY EVELYN / 1878 – 1963"* is inscribed on the back. A veteran's marker and flag are present.
"FATHER" is carved in relief on the top slanted surface of this footstone. It is located in front of the monument, on the right.

Cudworth, Sarah C.   See John Cudworth Monument entry.
"MOTHER" is carved in relief on the top slanted surface of this footstone. It is located in front of the monument, on the right.

Cundell, Benjamin   *"BENJAMIN CUNDELL."* No other inscriptions are present on this stone.
"B. C." is inscribed on the footstone.

Cushing, Lydia   *"In memory of / M^s Lydia Cushing. / wife of / Mr Nathaniel Cushing: / who died July 16th 1790. / In the 55th year / of her age."* A winged angel head is carved at the top of this slate stone.
"L. C. / 1790" This slate footstone faces the headstone. Pieces are broken off at the top.

Davis, Timothy K.   See Anna E. Cole Monument entry.
Rochester Vital Records list his birth on Jan 18, 1850. He was the brother of Anna E. Cole. He is last listed in the annual street listing in the *1927 Lakeville Town Report*. No death record was found.

DeMaranville, Eliza J.   *"MOTHER / ELIZA J. DEMARANVILLE / Nov. 7, 1849 / MAY 8, 1919"* The second line is carved along an arch.

DeMaranville, Jennie   *"JENNIE / Dau. of / JOSIAH & ELIZA J. / DEMARANVILLE / OCT. 8, 1879 / APR. 4, 1880"* is inscribed on this small stone. The first line is carved along a slight arch.

DeMaranville, John   See Josiah DeMaranville Monument entry.

DeMaranville, Josiah   *"FATHER / JOSIAH DEMARANVILLE / APR. 12, 1843 / DEC. 31, 1888"* The second line is carved along an arch.

DeMaranville, Josiah Monument   *"DEMARANVILLE"* is carved in relief on the top slanted surface of this monument. *"JOSIAH DEMARANVILLE / MAY 1, 1821 – SEPT. 23, 1911 / LOUISA DOWNING HIS WIFE / MAY 23, 1825 – JAN. 23, 1916 / JOHN THEIR SON / JAN. 31, 1855 – JAN 30, 1857"* is inscribed on the front.

DeMaranville, Louisa   See Josiah DeMaranville Monument entry.

DeMaranville, Nellie F.   *"NELLIE F. DEMARANVILLE / Oct. 11, 1869 / Oct. 17, 1925"* The first line is carved along an arch.

DeMaranville, Ruby   *"RUBY / Dau. of / JOSIAH & ELIZA J. / DEMARANVILLE / APR. 9, 1874 / OCT. 10, 1874"* is inscribed on this small stone. The first line is carved along a slight arch.

DeMoranville, Allon S.   See Herbert M. DeMoranville Monument entry.

DeMoranville, Charles H.   See Herbert M. DeMoranville Monument entry.

DeMoranville, Eunice   See Herbert M. DeMoranville Monument entry.

DeMoranville, Eunice W.   See Herbert M. DeMoranville Monument entry.

DeMoranville, Herbert M. Monument   *"DEMORANVILLE"* is inscribed on the front of this large monument. There are floral carvings in the upper corners. *"HERBERT M. DEMORANVILLE / SEPT. 23, 1876 – SEPT. 22, 1949 / HIS WIFE / EUNICE W. GRINNELL / APR. 23, 1870 – JUNE 23, 1936 / AUG. 14, 1898 CHARLES H. AUG. 7, 1914 / AUG. 17, 1901 EUNICE OCT. 17, 1901 / MAY 21, 1907 MORRELL SEPT. 3, 1907 / AUG. 25, 1914 ALLON S. SEPT. 30, 1914"* is inscribed on the back of this monument. A Barnicoat Monuments metal tag is present.

DeMoranville, Morrell   See Herbert M. DeMoranville Monument entry.

Downing, Joseph   *"JOSEPH DOWNING, / DIED MAY 30, 1864, / AGED 79 YRS 4 MOS. / 22 DAYS."*

Downing, Sarah   *"SARAH / wife of / JOSEPH DOWNING, / DIED OCT. _, 18__ / AGED __ YRS, 2 MOS."* This stone is very weathered. It is lying face up on the ground. *Vital Records of the Town of Freetown, Massachusetts 1686 through 1890* lists her birth date as August 4, 1789. Vital Records for the Town of Middleborough list her age as 91 years, 2 months old when she died on October 4, 1881.

Downs, Hattie W.   *"HATTIE W. DOWNS / 1879 – 1964"* is inscribed on the top horizontal surface of this 6 inch high stone.

Finney   See also **Phinney**.

Finney, Jonathan   *"In memory of / Mr. JONATHAN FINNEY / who died / April 26. 1822 / in his 73. / year."*   There is an urn and willow carving at the top of this slate stone. Scalloped designs are carved down the sides. Thatcher lists him as Nathan Phinney.

Finney, Meribah   *"MERIBAH. / wife of / Jonathan Finney: / died March 23, 1843. / Æ. 92 years."*
"M. F." is inscribed on the footstone.

Foster, Abigail   *"Memento Mori. / In Memory of / M*^{rs}*. Abigail Foster wife of / M*^{r}*. Nathaniel Foster & Daug*^{tr}*. / of the Rev*^{d}* M*^{r}*. Richard Billings / of Little compton who Died / April 6*th* 1783 · In the 69*th* Year / of her Age ·"*   There is a carving of a winged angel between the first and second lines. There are several diagonal cracks in this slate stone. Thatcher lists her age as "in her 68th year."
"M^{rs}*. / Abigail Foster"* is inscribed on this slate footstone.

Foster, Catharine   *"CATHARINE FOSTER / died / Jan. 15, 1881. / Aged 86 yrs. / 10 m's."*   The first line is carved along an arch. There is a crack radiating from the center bottom. This stone shares its base with that of Mary Foster.
"C. F." is inscribed on the footstone.

Foster, Charles   *"Charles Son of Mr. / Gersham Foster & / Mrs. Jane his wife / died Sep. 29, 1808 / aged 7 years / 1 m."*   This small, lichen encrusted, slate stone has two willows carved at the top. A vertical break in this stone has been successfully repaired. Thatcher's entry does not include the last line.

Foster, Jane   *"In Memory of / Mrs. JANE wife of / Mr. Gershom Foster / who died / August 30. 1820 / in her 64. / year."*   There is an urn and willow carving at the top of this slate stone.
"Mrs. / J. F. / 1820." is inscribed on this slate footstone.   *"T"* is inscribed on the back.

Foster, Marcy   *"In Memory of / Marcy Thatcher / Daugh*^{tr}* to M*^{r}*. / Thomas Foster & / M*^{rs}*. Mary his / Wife Who Dec*^{d}*. / MARCH *^e_y* 22*^{d}* 1773 / Aged 4 Years / & 7 Months"*

A simple winged head is carved at the top of this slate stone. Thatcher lists the death month as January.

"*M F*" is inscribed on this slate footstone.

Foster, Mary   "*MARY FOSTER / died / Feb. 16, 1879, / Aged 89 yrs. / 4 m's.*" The first line is carved along an arch. There is a 6-inch crack extending up from the center bottom. This textured stone shares its base with that of Catharine Foster.

"*M. F.*" is inscribed on the footstone.

Foster, Nathaniel   "*In MEMORY of M^r. Na$_{th}$. / Foster who depa'ted this Life, / Novr. 1st 1793, in the 83^d. / Year of his Age. /*

Under^{this} stone lies zions dust,

At the resurrection of the just,
By virtue of its union with its head,
__all arise to glory that will never fade."

There is a frond carving above the inscription, and semicircular designs are carved down the sides. The carver ran out of room on the first line. The left shoulder and bottom corners of this slate stone are missing. Note the different spellings of his first name between the head and footstones. A "*SAR 1775*" marker and flag are here.

"*M^r. / Nathaniel / Foster / died / 1793*" is inscribed on this slate footstone.

Foster, Nathaniel   "*In Memory of / Nathan__l Son to M^r. / Thomas Foster & / Mrs Mary his / Wife Who Dec^d. / JUNE ^e_y 2^d. 1772 Aged / 8 Years 11 Months / & 22 Days*" A simple winged angel is carved at the top of this slate stone.

"*N F*" is inscribed on this slate footstone.

Fuller, Hannah   "*Erected / in memory of / M^s Hannah Fuller, / wife of Mr John Fuller, / who died Sep$^{!r}$ 13, 1803, / aged 30 years, / 7 months / & 1 day. /*

Fresh as the grass our bodies stand,
And flourish bright & gay;
A blasting wind sweeps o'er the land,
And fades the grass away."

A huge urn is carved in relief on this slate stone, and within it is located the inscription. The poem is carved below the urn. There is a willow carved in shallow relief on the right side. Note the different spellings of her first name between the head and footstones.

"*M^{rs} / Hanah Fuller, / 1803.*"   This slate footstone faces the headstone.

Fuller, Samuel   "*In memory of / SAMUEL FULLER, / Son of Ziba Fuller, / who died / Feb. 16, 1843, / Æ. 45 y'rs & 2 m. / We must all die.*" An urn and willow are carved at the top of this slate stone.

"*S. F.*" is inscribed on this slate footstone.

Fuller, Ziba   "*In memory of / MR. ZIBA FULLER / who died / April 4, 1811, / in his 48th. year.*" There is an urn and willow carving at the top of this slate stone.

"*Z.F.*" This slate footstone faces the headstone.

Gifford, Mary F. S.   "*MARY F. S. GIFFORD / WIFE OF / ELIJAH GIFFORD /*

1820 – 1904."

Grant, Everett F.   *"EVERETT F. GRANT / 1878 – 1972"* This flat, ground level stone is concealed by bushes.

Grant, Harriet P.   *"HARRIET P. GRANT / 1884 – 1971"* This flat, ground level stone is concealed by bushes.

Gurney, Carrie B.   *"CARRIE B. MANTON / WIFE OF / LOUIS R. GURNEY / 1892 – 1914"* A heart is carved in shallow relief on this slanted stone. The inscription is contained within this heart. Leaf and ivy designs are carved in shallow relief on the sides.

Hackett, Edith   See James Clarke Monument entry.
"EDITH" is inscribed on the top horizontal surface of this 5-6 inch high footstone. It is located behind the monument, on the right.

Hall, Arthur S. Monument   *"ARTHUR S. HALL / 1890 – 1966 / HIS WIFE / MILDRED A. (MANTON) / 1894 – 1955"* is inscribed on this slanted monument.

Hall, Arthur S., Sr.   *"ARTHUR S HALL SR. / MASSACHUSETTS / S2 USNRF / WORLD WAR I / OCT 12 1890   FEB 16 1966"* A circled cross is carved at the top of this stone. This flat, ground level marker is beginning to be buried. An American Legion marker and flag are present.

Hall, Carrie L.   *"CARRIE L. HALL / 1916 – 1988"* is inscribed on this flat, ground level stone.

Hall, Mildred A.   See Arthur S. Hall Monument entry.

Hammond, Desire   *"In memory of / Mrs. Desire / wife of / Cap! Christopher Hammond / who died / Nov 1810 / in her 53 year"* A willow tree is carved at the top of this slate stone. No day of death is listed. It is broken diagonally below the last line. The top section is leaning against the bottom piece.
"D. H." is inscribed on this slate footstone.

Hanson, Annie G.   *"ANNIE G. WIFE / OF WILLIAM HANSON / 1886 – 1938"* is inscribed on this flat, ground level stone.

Hanson, William G.   *"WILLIAM G. HANSON / 1875 – 1935"* is inscribed on this flat, ground level stone.

Harding, Hannh   *"Memento Mortis. / In Memory of / Mrs Hannh Harding. / Relict of / Mr Benjamin Harding. / She died July 3^d 1787. / Aged 50 Years 6 Months / & 9 Days."* A winged angel head is carved between the first and second lines on this slate stone. The last line is half buried underground. Thatcher does not include this last line, and he spells her name as Hannah.
"M^{rs} / H. H." is inscribed on this slate footstone.

Harvey, Desire   *"In memory of / MRS. DESIRE, / wife of / Mr. Oliver Harvey, / Died April 18, 1851; / aged 82 yrs. 9 mos. / & 9 ds."*

Harvey, Oliver   *"OLIVER HARVEY, / Born March 5, 1768. / Died Aug. 14, 1855. / Æ. 87 yrs."* The first line is carved in relief on this textured stone.

Haskell, Elisabeth *"Memento Mortis / In Memory of / Mrs. Elisabeth Haskell; / wife of Mr. Seth Haskell / who died June 27 ͭͪ 1784. / In ͤ 27 ͭͪ Year of her* ͣͤͤ·" The first line is inscribed along the top of the tympanum. A winged angel is carved below this on this slate stone. The carver ran out of room on the fourth and sixth lines. Note the period is underneath the condensed *ll* in the fourth line, and the word *age* is elevated in the last line.

Haskell, Seth *"Memento Mortis. / In memory of / Mʳ. Seth Haskell, who / died April 30 ͭͪ 1793. In / his 37 ͭͪ Year."* A winged angel head is carved between the first and second lines on this slate stone. Thatcher lists his death year as 1794. *"Mʳ. / Seth / Haskell."* is inscribed on this slate footstone.

Haskell, Thomas A. Lt. *"In / memory of / Lieut. THOMAS A. HASKELL / who died / May 27. 1816 / in his 29. / year. /*

> *Come view the dwellings of the dead*
> *Ye Mortals born to die*
> *And silent thoughtful tread*
> *Where soon yourselves will lie."*

An urn is carved in relief at the top of this slate stone. The initials *"J H"* are carved under the urn. A George Thompson swirl is carved below the last line. The poem is completely buried underground. A veteran's marker and flag are present.
"Lieu. / Thomas A. / Haskell" This slate footstone faces the headstone. The last line is buried underground.

Haskins, Sarah *"SARAH, / WIFE OF / IRA HASKINS, / 1813 – 1888"*

Hathaway, Benjamin S. *"BENJ. S. HATHAWAY, / Born March 8 ͭͪ 1783, / in Berkley Mass. / Died Oct. 4, 1833; / in Middleboro, Mass. /*

> *Remember you are born to die,*
> *As well as them who here do lie,*
> *Death suddenly on me did call,*
> *May it a warning be to all."*

"B. S. H." is inscribed on the footstone.

Hayes, Susanna See Thomas Hayes Monument entry.

Hayes, Thomas Monument *"HAYES"* is carved in relief on the top slanted surface of this large monument. *"THOMAS HAYES / 1842 – 1918 / HIS WIFE / SUSANNA / 1846 – 1910"* is inscribed on the front. Ivy carvings are in the upper corners.

Henderson, Marjorie W. See Robert E. Henderson Monument entry.

Henderson, Robert E. Monument *"HENDERSON / ROBERT E / JUNE 11, 1907 – MAY 8, 1979 / HIS WIFE / MARJORIE WHITTAKER / JAN. 4, 1914 – FEB. 12, 1998"* is inscribed on this monument.
"ROBERT E HENDERSON / CM 1   US COAST GUARD / WORLD WAR II / JUN 11 1907 ✝ MAY 8 1979" is inscribed on this flat, brass plaque that is beginning to be buried. It is located in front of the monument. A veteran's marker is present.

Hinds, Bartlett *"BARTLETT / son of John & / Olive Hinds / died Apl. 6, 1826 /*

Æt. 15 Yrs." is inscribed on this small stone. It is lying face up on the ground and is very weathered.

Hinds, Catherine   See John Hinds Monument entry.
Middleborough, Massachusetts Vital Records, Vol. 1, p. 336 lists her birth on March 16, 1803 to John and Olive Hinds.

Hinds, Ebenezer, Rev.   *"In memory of / Rev. EBENEZER HINDS / who died / April 19. 1812 / in his 94 year / I have faught a good fight, I have finished / my course, I hae kept the faith, henceforth / there is laid up for me a crown of right_ / eousness."* A willow is carved at the top of this slate stone and diamond shaped designs are carved down the sides. Diagonal cracks are present on the upper third of this stone. Note the spelling of *faught,* and the missing v in the word *hae* in the poem. A *"SAR 1775"* marker and flag are present.
"Rev. Ebenezer Hinds" is inscribed on this lichen encrusted, slate footstone. A willow is carved at the top.

Hinds, Edmund   See John Hinds Monument entry.
Middleborough, Massachusetts Vital Records, Vol. 1, p. 230 lists his birth on October 18, 1787 to John and Olive Hinds.

Hinds, John Monument   *"JOHN HINDS / died Oct. 4, 1830. / Æt. 70. / EDMUND & CATHARINE / HINDS / were lost on their passage / from N.C. to Mass. / March 1828."* An urn and willow are carved at the top of this slate stone. The curved design carved along the sides extends the length of John's inscription only. A *"SAR 1775"* marker and flag are present.
"J. H. / 1830." is inscribed on this slate footstone.

Hinds, Kezia   *"In memory of / Kezia Daugh^{tr}. to / ^e_y Reund Mr Ebenez^r. / Hinds & M^{rs}. Lydia / his wife Died Augst. / ^e_y 12th 1774 Aged 3 / Years 4 Months / & 24 Days / ps 39th mine Age is as / nothing before thee"* A simple winged angel is carved at the top of this slate stone.
"K H" is inscribed on the slate footstone.

Hinds, Leonard   *"LEONARD HINDS, / died Dec. 27, 1859, / Aged 77 years."* is inscribed on this slate stone. There is no carving on the tympanum.
"L. H." is inscribed on the footstone.

Hinds, Lucinda V.   *"LUCINDA V. HINDS / 1805 – 1885"* is inscribed on this flat, 0-2 inches high stone.

Hinds, Lucy   A crumbled stone occupies the place where the headstone would be.
"L. H. / 1824." is inscribed on the footstone. It was broken in half below the inscription and successfully repaired. This is most likely the burial site for the "Lucy Hinds, dau. of John & Olive, Aug. 22, 1824, age 29 years." listed by Thatcher, since this gravesite is located directly behind that of Olive Hinds.

Hinds, Lydia   *"_emento Mori. / __ Memory of / _ydia Dau^{tr} of the Rev^d. / __enezer Hinds & M^{rs}. / ___ia his wife who Died / __gst. ^e_y 22^d. 1780 Aged / _7 Years & 21 Days. /   _o man lieth down, and riseth not /*
                    __ill the Heavens be no more.

_uth consider your latter end,
___ time be wise, make God your friend.
_efore that awfull Day comes on.
When earthly pleasures must be gone."

The slate has exfoliated on the left side of this stone. A winged angel is carved between the first and second lines. Thatcher lists her age at 17 years, and her death month as October. *Middleborough, Massachusetts Vital Records,* Vol. 1, p. 170 lists her as born on August 1, 1763, confirming age as 17 years, but her death month must be August. Note the spelling of *awfull.*

"*M*ˢ· / *Lydia Hinds.*" is inscribed on the footstone. Note her title is Mrs., but no mention is made of a husband.

Hinds, Lydia   "*Sacred to the memory of / Mrs. Lydia wife of the Rev*ᵈ *· / Eben*ʳ*. Hinds, she died / May 12*ᵗʰ *Æ1801. In the / sixty Seven*ᵗʰ *, Year of her Age. /*
Give her of the fruit of her hands /
And let her own work _____ her: / ..."

There is a frond carving at the top of this lichen encrusted, slate stone. Only a few letters can be read on the last two lines of this four line poem. Simple tree designs are carved along the side borders.

"*Mrs. / Lydia / Hinds / died / 1801*" The last line of this slate footstone is buried underground.

Hinds, Nancy   "*NANCY HINDS, / died Oct. 27, 1868, / Aged 84 years.*" is inscribed on this slate stone. There is no carving on the tympanum.

"*Mrs. / N. H.*" is inscribed on this slate footstone.

Hinds, Olive   "*In memory of / OLIVE HINDS, / widow of John Hinds / late of / Middleborough, / who died Dec. 27, 1845, / Aged 77 years. / Blessed are the dead who die in the Lord.*" is inscribed on this slate stone. There is no carving on the tympanum.

"*O. H.*" is inscribed on this slate footstone.

Hinds, Richard   "*In MEMORY of (Richard) / (Son of Elder Eben*ʳ*· & M*ʳˢ*, Lydia) / Hinds, he died dec*ʳ*, 15*ᵗʰ *· 1794. / Aged 17 years 4 m, 4 days. /*
Adieu to this vein world. I cry,
Jesus receive my spirit,
I to the world of glory fly,
Salvation to inherit."

A rising sun with facial features is carved at the top of this slate stone.

"*M*ʳ */ Richard / Hinds / Died / 1794*" is inscribed on this slate footstone.

Hoar, Phebe   "*PHEBE, / wife of / Job Hoar / Died / May 3, 1852. / Æ. 90 y'rs.*" This headstone is lying face up on the ground. Their surname is spelled Horr on her husband's stone.

"*P. H.*" is inscribed on the footstone.

Holmes, Betsey Emma   "*BETSEY EMMA HOLMES / WIFE OF / WILLIAM B. HOLMES / JULY 27, 1852 / SEPT. 10, 1916*" This monument is separated from its base and is lying face up behind it.

Holmes, William B. *"WILLIAM B. HOLMES / JULY 18, 1853 / JUNE 6, 1909"*

Horr, Job *"MR. / JOB HORR, / Died / Sept 8, 1854. / Æ 91 yrs."* This stone is very weathered. Their surname is spelled Hoar on the stone of his wife, Phebe. *"J. H."* is inscribed on the footstone.

Horskins, Waitstill *"In Memory of / Waits^{t}ill Dau^{tr} of / M^r. Jeshermor & M^{rs} / Marcy Horskins / Died Sep^t. ^e_y 2$^d_,$ / 1779 in ^e_y ___$^{th}_.$ / Year of / her Age"* A simple winged head is carved at the top of this slate stone. It has begun to exfoliate at the top and on the right side. The exfoliated piece from the right side is located on the ground in front of this headstone. The number for her age is chipped out and unreadable. This stone is not listed by Thatcher, so her age is unknown.

Hoskins, Hannah *"In Memory of M$^{rs}_{..}$ / Hannah Widow of / M^r. Nathan Hoskins / She Died Nov$^r_{..}$ 17$^{th}_{.}$ / 1800 In her 80$^{th}_{.}$ Year"* A winged angel head is carved at the top of this slate stone. The last line is partially underground. *"M$^{rs}_{..}$ / Hannah / Hoskins."* is inscribed on this slate footstone.

Hoskins, Nathan *"In Memory of M^r. / Nathan Hoskins who / Died May ^e_y 22nd 1778 / in ^e_y 62^d Year / of his Age"* A winged angel is carved at the top of this lichen encrusted, slate stone. *"M^r. / Nathan / Hoskins"* is inscribed on this slate footstone.

Howland, Keturah *"Memento Mori. / In Memory of / Miss Keturah Howland. / Daug$^{tr}_{..}$ of M^r. Joshua & / Mrs Mary Howland who / died Dec^r ^e_y 26th 1784 / In the 24th Year of her / Age."* A winged angel head is carved between the first and second lines. This lichen encrusted, slate stone is difficult to read.

Ingraham, Sarah *"Sacred / to the memory of / SARAH INGRAHAM / wife of / Timothy Ingraham / who died / Oct 28, 1820; / aged 33 years"* There is no carving on the tympanum. *"S. I."* is inscribed on the footstone. This footstone appears to have been switched with that of Timothy Ingraham, two plots to the left.

Ingraham, Timothy *"Sacred / to the memory of / TIMOTHY INGRAHAM / who died / June 17, 1818: / aged 38 years."* There is no carving on the tympanum. *"T. I."* is inscribed on the footstone. This footstone appears to have been switched with that of Sarah Ingraham, two plots to the right.

Jennings, Rex   *"REX JENNINGS / 1885 – 1894."* The first line is carved in relief along an arch. He was the son of Annie Peirce, by her first husband, Daniel Jennings. A low stone wall surrounds this gravestone and that of Frank S. and Annie J. Peirce.

Johnson, Betsey   *"BETSEY / wife of / David B. Johnson / Died / July 28, 1852. / Aged 21 y'rs. Prepare To meet thy God."* A left hand with the index finger pointing up is carved at the top center of this stone. There are floral carvings on the left of this, and a dove flying down on the right. All of these carvings are in relief.
"B. J." is inscribed on the footstone.

Kingman, Hosea   *"HOSEA KINGMAN / BORN / DEC. 14, 1806. / DIED / JAN. 21, 1853."* This monument is separated from its base and is lying face up on the ground. It shares its base with the monument of Phebe, his wife.

Kingman, Phebe   *"PHEBE, / WIFE OF / HOSEA KINGMAN. / BORN JUNE 4, 1806. / DIED JULY 13, 1857."* This monument shares its base with the monument of her husband.

Loner, Hattie M.   *"HATTIE M. LONER / DIED AUG. 31, 1897, / AGE 11 MONTHS, / 17 DAYS."* is inscribed on this flat, sunken, metal marker. A low cement wall surrounds the Cyrus Thrasher plot.

Loner, Laura M.   See Cyrus Thrasher Monument entry.
"LAURA MAY / Aged 9 mos." is inscribed on the slanted front of this stone. *"Dau. Of / William E. & Lydia D. / Loner, / died May 30, 1876"* is inscribed on the back. A low cement wall surrounds the Cyrus Thrasher plot.

Loner, Lydia D.   See Cyrus Thrasher Monument entry. She was the daughter of Cyrus and Hannah Thrasher.

Loner, Lydia W.   See Cyrus Thrasher Monument entry.

Loner, Mabel L.   See Cyrus Thrasher Monument entry.

Loner, William E.   See Cyrus Thrasher Monument entry.
"W. E. LONER / CO. E, / 18th MASS. INF." is carved in relief on this stone within a recessed shield shaped area. A *"Brockton Fire Dept."* marker as well as a veteran's marker and flag are present. *Massachusetts Civil War Soldiers & Sailors, 1861-1865*, Vol. II, p. 376 shows that William E. Loner enlisted in 1862 at age 25. A low cement wall surrounds the Cyrus Thrasher plot.

Macomber, Deborah   The slate headstone is broken off at ground level and is missing. One piece present contains the letters: *"_n mem__"* No other inscriptions were found. This is probably the gravesite for "Macomber, Deborah, dau. of Dea. Joseph, (parts of stone missing)" that is listed by Thatcher. From the other gravestones we can see that John was a Deacon, and Joseph was a Lieutenant. It is unclear whose daughter she was.
"Miss. D_ M_" is inscribed on this slate footstone.

Macomber, Elisabeth   *"Memento Mori. / In Memory of Miss Elisabeth / Macomber Daugr. of Lieut. / Joseph Macomber & Mrs. / Thankful his wife who / Died*

Aug$^{st}_{..}$ ^e_y 28$^{th}_{..}$ 1784. In / the 20th Year of her Age" A winged angel is carved between the first and second lines of this slate stone. Thatcher does not list a title for Joseph in this entry.

"_____ eth / __comber" is inscribed on this slate footstone. Pieces have been broken off at the top and on the left side.

Macomber, Elizabeth *"... / Dec. John Macco___ / who died Jan. 14, 17__ / aged 48 years."* The tympanum of this slate headstone is missing, and most of the inscribed area has exfoliated. Thatcher lists, "Macomber, Elizabeth, wife of Dea. John, Jan. 14, 1775, 48 years." A slate footstone is present, but the top half is missing, and no inscription is present on the remaining section.

Macomber, Hannah *"In / memory of / MISS HANNAH MACOMBER / Dau. of / Mr. Joseph and / Mrs. Thankfull Macomber / who died / March 28. 1827 / aged 46 years."* An urn and willow are carved at the top of the slate stone. The urn is carved in relief. Scalloped designs are carved along the side borders. A diagonal crack under the inscription has been successfully repaired.

"H. M." is inscribed on this slate footstone.

Maccomber, John, Dea. *"In memory of / Dec. JOHN MACCOMBER / _ho died Nov. 9, 1774 / aged 54 years."* The tympanum and the left side of this slate stone have exfoliated. Many cracks are present.

"Dea. / John Maccomber" is inscribed on this slate footstone.

Macomber, Joseph, Lt. *"Memento Mori / In Memory of / Li^{e}u$^!$. Joseph / Macomber he / Died Jan^{ry} 25th 1800 / In his 68th. Year."* A winged angel head is carved between the first and second lines of this slate stone.

"Lieu$^!$. / _oseph / _acombe^r" is inscribed on this slate footstone. It is exfoliating on the left side.

Maccomber, Thankful *"In memory of / Miss. / Thankful Maccomber / daug. of / Dea. John Maccomber / who died Sep. 17, 177_ / aged 22 y_ars."* A small urn on a tall stand is carved in relief at the top of this slate stone. An arched branch is carved in relief around it. This stone is cracking, crumbling, and exfoliating. Thatcher lists her death year as 1774, and her father as Deacon Joseph.

"Miss. T_ M_" is inscribed on this slate footstone.

Macomber, Thankful *"In Memory of / _hankful Wif_ __ / Lieu$^!$. Joseph Macomber / She Died S__$^{tr}_{..}$ / ^e_y 13$^{th}_{..}$ 1794 __ / her 56th. Year."* This slate headstone is broken into two pieces which are lying face up on the ground. The above is taken from the inscriptions on those pieces. She is not listed by Thatcher.

Manning, Arthur A. Monument *"ARTHUR A. MANNING / 1866 – 1927 / LILLIAN I. HIS WIFE / 1883 – 1938 / FREDERICK W. / 1903 – 1903"* A low stone wall surrounds this lone monument.

Manning, Frederick W. See Arthur A. Manning Monument entry.

Manning, Lillian I. See Arthur A. Manning Monument entry.

Manton, Alfred P. Monument *"MANTON / ALFRED P. MANTON / 1865 –*

1944 / HIS WIFE / GEORGIA A. FICKETT / 1872 – 1927" The first line is carved in shallow relief. An ivy design is carved in shallow relief above the inscriptions.

Manton, Georgia A. See Alfred P. Manton Monument entry.

Marshall, Eva G. *"EVA G. MARSHALL / 1905 – 1998"* is inscribed on this flat, 0-1 inch high stone.

Marshall, Russell B. *"RUSSELL B. MARSHALL / 1904 – 1978"* is inscribed on this flat, 0-4 inch high stone.

Maxim, James D. *"JAMES D. MAXIM / CO. D / 5 MASS. INF. / SP. AM. WAR"* The first line is carved along an arch. This inscription is carved in relief within a recessed shield shaped area. A *"Middleboro Lodge / B.P.O.E. / 1274"* marker is present. There is also a Spanish American War marker and flag present. His obituary in *The Middleborough Gazette* 4/17/1936:1 reports that he was 69 years old when he died April 9, 1936.

Maxim, Nellie There is no gravestone here, but there is a *"WOMANS / RELIEF / CORPS / 8 / W. R. C. / E. W. PIERCE"* marker and flag present. Chris Mansfield's veteran's file shows this as the grave of Nellie Maxim. Taunton Vital Records list her birth as Nellie Cummings on October 12, 1864. She married James D. Maxim on February 20, 1888. Her obituary in *The Middleborough Gazette* 11/21/1947:10 reports her death on November 17, 1947, at 82 years old.

Miller, Sarah *"In Memory of / Mr.ˢ Sarah wife / of Mʳ. Joseph / Miller She / died March / ᵉy 24 ᵗʰ 1808 / aged 33 years / & 17 d__"* An urn is carved at the top of this stone, with a simple tree carved on either side. The exfoliated, inscribed section is broken into five pieces. These pieces are lying on the ground, assembled, in front of what remains of the upright section, which is still intact. Thatcher lists her death month as November
"Mʳˢ / Sarah Miller" This slate footstone faces the headstone. It was broken along the word *Sarah* and successfully repaired.

Monroe, Bathsheba *"In Memory of / BATHSHEBA / wife of / Mr. Augustus W. Monroe / Born ... / Died July..."* This stone is very weathered. Thatcher lists her as "Bathsheba Monroe, wife of Augustus, born Oct. 1, 1805, died July 25, 1845."
"B. M." is inscribed on the footstone.

Nelson Monument *"N (monogram) / NELSON"* is all that is inscribed on this large brown monument. The monogram is carved in shallow relief, and the inscription is carved in outlined relief. It is surrounded by floral relief carvings.

Nelson, Abiel S. *"Abiel Smith son of / Mr. Abiel Nelson & / Mrs. Sarah his wife / died Nov. 24, 1811 / Aged 1 year 3 m. / 26 d. /*
> *Scarce the daun of life began*
> *Ere I measur'd out my span."*

A willow is carved at the top of this slate stone. Note the spelling of the word *daun*.

Nelson, Abiel W. See Jeanie C. Nelson Monument entry.
A *"WWP Post 47 GAR"* marker and flag are present. *Massachusetts Civil War*

Soldiers & Sailors, 1861-1865, Vol. II, p.351 shows that he served with the 18th Mass. Infantry as Assistant Surgeon.

"A. W. N." is carved in relief on the top curved surface of this footstone.

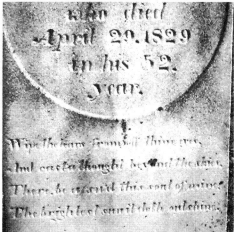

Nelson, Abiel, Dea. *"In / memory of / DEA. ABIEL NELSON / who died / April 29, 1829 / in his 52. / year. / Wipe the tears from off thine eyes,*
And cast a thought beyond the skies,
There be assu'd this soul of mine,
The brightest sun it doth outshine."

An urn and willow are carved in relief at the top on this stone. The third through seventh lines are carved within a recessed semicircular area. Flowers are carved at the top of the shoulders of this stone. A veteran's marker and flag are present
"A. N." is inscribed on the footstone.

Nelson, Abigail *"ABIGAIL, / wife of / Ezra Nelson. / died April 25, 1844. / Aged 66 Years. / Blessed are the dead which die in the Lord"* The first line is carved in relief.
"A. N." is inscribed on the footstone.

Nelson, Abner, Lt. *"Lieut. ABNER NELSON / died Feb. 16. 1816 / in his 62. /*
year. /   *Peace 'tis the Lord Jehovah's hand*
That blasts our joys in death
Changes the visage once so dear
And gathers back the breath"

An urn and willow are carved at the top of this slate stone. The urn is carved in relief. The top of the tympanum has exfoliated. A *"GAR 8 119"* marker, a veteran's marker and flag are present.
"Lieut / Abner / Nelson" is inscribed on the slate footstone.

Nelson, Amos *"HEAR LYES YE / BODY OF AMOS / NELSON AGED V / YEARSDIED / JANVARY YE 17 / 1724"* *"1981"* is carved at the bottom of this replacement stone. Thatcher lists his death day as the 11th of January. The original headstone is located in the Lakeville Historical Society building, on Bedford Street.
"AMOS / NELSON" is inscribed on the slate footstone. It appears to be the original.

It is exfoliating, and missing pieces at the top and the lower right. A carving was present at the top, but most of it is gone.

Nelson, Amos, Dea. *"Memento mortis / In memory of / Deac.ⁿ Amos Nelson / who died Nov.ʳ 11, 1795 In / ___ 53ᵈ Year. /*

> *The sweet remembrance of the just*
> *Shall flourish tho' they sleep in dust."*

A winged angel head is carved at the top of this lichen encrusted slate stone. *"Deac.ⁿ / _mos Nelson"* This slate footstone has exfoliated on the sides.

Nelson, Anna *"In memory of / ANNA wife of / THOMAS NELSON, / who died / Oct. 14, 1828 / aged 87 / years."* An urn and willow are carved in relief at the top of this stone. Flowers are carved on the shoulders. A George Thompson swirl is carved under the inscription.
"A. N." is inscribed on the footstone.

Nelson, C. Eliot *"C. ELIOT / NELSON / 1908 – 1983"* is inscribed in shallow relief on this flat, brown, ground level stone. It matches the Nelson Monument. A Mitchell Memorial Club marker is present.

Nelson, Caroline B. See Elizabeth P. Nelson Monument entry.

Nelson, Charity *"In memory of Mʳˢ, / Charity, wife of Mʳ, / Samuel Nelson, who / died May 4ᵗʰ, 1787. in / yᵉ 37ᵗʰ Year of her / age. /*

> *"Forbear, my Friends. to weep;*
> *Since Death has lost its sting.*
> *Those Christians that in Jesus sleep*
> *Our God will with him bring.""*

A unique scroll design is carved at the top of this slate headstone. Curved designs are carved along the sides.
"Mʳˢ. Charity / Nelson / 1787" is inscribed on this slate footstone.

Nelson, Charles *"_n of Mʳ. Isaa_ / & Mʳˢ. Elizabeth ... / Wife he Died Jun_ / __00 Aged 1 Yea_ ... / & 5 Da__"* This slate stone is exfoliating and missing pieces on all sides. The above is all that is left of the inscription. Thatcher lists, "Nelson, Charles, son of Isaac & Elizabeth, June 18, 1800, 1 yrs., 4 mos., 5 da.."
"C N" is inscribed on this slate footstone.

Nelson, Chloe *"Memento Mortis. / In memory of / Mrs. Chloe Nelson, wife of / the Rev.ᵈ Ebenezer Nelson / who died March 20, 1795. / In her 39 Year"* A winged angel head is carved at the top of this lichen encrusted, slate stone.
"Mrs. / Chloe Nelso_" is inscribed on this slate footstone.

Nelson, Clifton W. *"CLIFTON W / SON OF / SIDNEY T. / 1878 – 1959"* is carved in relief on this flat, brown, 2-3 inch high stone. It matches the Nelson Monument.

Nelson, Cyrus *"CYRUS NELSON / DIED / Nov. 26, 1869, / Æt. 76 yrs. 5 mo."* The first line is carved along an arch.
"C. N." is carved on the top curved surface of this upright footstone.

Nelson, Doris See Thomas Nelson Stone entry.

Nelson, Ebenezer *"I ... / O... / EBE... / NEL... / DEC... / APRIL ... / 1745... / 23 YEARs ... / MONTHs & / 7 DAYs."* This slate headstone is broken into many pieces. Only two pieces had inscriptions on them, and the above is taken from them. Thatcher lists, "Nelson, Ebenezer, died Apr. 1745, age 23 years, 7 days."
"___N / ___5" is all that is left of the inscription on this slate footstone. It is broken at the top and is exfoliating.

Nelson, Eliza *"In memory of / MRS. ELIZA / wife of Mr. Cyrus Nelson / who died / Sept. 18, 1830 / aged 27 years."* The second line is carved in outline. There is no carving on the tympanum.
"E. N." is inscribed on the footstone.

Nelson, Elizabeth *"Mrs. Elizabeth Nelson / wid^o of / Mr. William Nelson / died April 20 1805 in her / 91 year"* A rising sun is carved at the top of this slate stone. It has several cracks and is exfoliating on the sides.
"Mrs / E. Nelson" This slate footstone is exfoliating on the right side.

Nelson, Elizabeth P. *"ELIZABETH PARKHURST / 1846 – 1930"* is carved in relief on this flat, brown, 2-3 inch high stone. It matches the Nelson Monument.

Nelson, Elizabeth P. Monument *"NELSON"* is carved in relief on the top curved surface of this large monument. *"ELIZABETH PEIRCE NELSON * / DEC. 8, 1836 - JULY 29, 1896 / * CAROLINE BAKER NELSON / JUNE 25, 1849 – APRIL 19, 1894 / DAUGHTERS OF JOB PEIRCE NELSON"* There are leaf designs in the upper corners.

Nelson, Emma P. *"EMMA PARKHURST / 1844 – 1881"* is carved in relief on this flat, brown, 4 – 6 inch high stone. It matches the Nelson Monument. Lakeville Vital Records document that her maiden name was Parkhurst, and that she was the wife of Sidney T. Nelson.

Nelson, Emma P. *"EMMA PARKHURST / 1899 – 1899"* is carved in relief on this flat, brown, 1-4 inch high stone. It matches the Nelson Monument. Vital Records of Boston list her as the daughter of Thomas S. and Lillie Nelson.

Nelson, Eunice *"Memento Mori. / In Memory of / Mrs Eunice wife of / Dea^{cn} Amos Nelson / who Died May ye 27th / 1783 ·Aged 39 Years, / 7 Months & 23 Day^s."* A winged angel is carved between the first and second lines. It appears the carver ran out of room on the last line. Thatcher does not include the 23 days in his entry. There are many cracks present on this stone.

Nelson, Ezra *"_n memory ... /_ ^{r}. Ezra Ne___ / who died / in his 30 y..."* is inscribed on the one remaining piece of this broken slate stone. It is lying face up on the ground. *Middleborough, Massachusetts Vital Records,* Vol. 2, p. 11 lists his death on July 25, 1803, at 29 years old, but Thatcher lists his death year as 1805.
"Mr. / Ezra Nelson" is inscribed on this slate footstone, which faces the headstone.

Nelson, Fatima B. *"FATIMA B. NELSON / Aged 63 years."* The inscription is recessed on the front of this stone. The first line is carved in relief along an arch. There is a crack at the bottom center of the stone. *"Wife of / Job P. Nelson, / & dau. of / Ward & Phebe Baker, / of Upton. / Born Jan 23, 1808; / Died Feb. 12, 1871."* is inscribed on the back.

"F. B. N." is inscribed on the footstone.

Nelson, Foxel   *"IN MEMORY OF / Mr FOXEL / NELSON DEC^D / MAY _Y^e 13th 1745 / AGED 28 YEARs / 10 MONTHs & / 21 DAYs."* A simple head is carved at the top of this slate stone. There are stray (practice?) marks carved below the bottom border.
"F. N. / 1745" is inscribed on the slate footstone.

Nelson, Gladys B.   *"GLADYS B. / WIFE OF / SIDNEY P. / 1908-1973"* is carved in relief on this flat, brown, 1-3 inch high stone. It matches the Nelson monument.

Nelson, Hannah   *"In memory of / Mrs. HANNAH / wife of / Mr. Cyrus Nelson / who died / July 20. 1822 in her 21. / year. /*

> *Remember me as you pass by,*
> *As you are now so once was I,*
> *As I am now so you must be,*
> *Prepare for death and follow me.*

An urn and willow are carved in relief at the top of this headstone. *"GEORGE THOMPSON Middleborough."* is carved at the bottom.
"Mrs / H. N. / 1822" is inscribed on the footstone.

Nelson, Hannah   *"In Memory of / WIDOW / HANNAH NELSON. / Who died Nov. 24, 1827. / Æt. 77. /*   *Forbear my friends to weep,*
> *Since death has lost its sting:*
> *For those that do in Jesus sleep,*
> *Our God will with him bring."*

An urn is carved in relief at the top of this stone.
"H. N. / 1827" is inscribed on the footstone.

Nelson, Hiram   *"In memory of / HIRAM NELSON, / who died / Feb. 1, 1838; / Aged 73 years. /*   *Yet again we hope to meet thee*
> *When the lamp of life is fled*
> *Then in heaven with joy to greet thee*
> *Where no farewell tear is shed.*

The second line is carved in relief.
"H. N." is inscribed on the footstone. It is lying face down on the ground.

Nelson, Hope   *"Memento Mori / In Memory of / M^{rs}. Hope, widow of / M^r. Thomas Nelson; / who Died Decr. _y^e, 7th / 1782 · / In the 106th Year / of her Age·"* A winged angel is carved between the first and second lines. There are many vertical cracks in this slate stone.
"M^{rs} / Hope / Nelson" is inscribed on this slate footstone.

Nelson, Hope   *"In / memory of / Mrs. HOPE widow of / Col. John Nelson / who died / Dec. 28, 1820 / in her 85. / year. /*

> *There is a land of pure delight*
> *Where saints immortal reign;*
> *Infinite day excludes the night,*
> *And pleasures banish pain.*
> *There everlasting spring abides,*

And never with'ring flow'rs.
Death like anarrow sea, divide
This heav'nly land from ours."

An urn and willow are carved at the top of this ornate 4-foot tall slate stone. The urn is carved in relief. The first half of the inscription is inscribed on a circular raised area. The poem is inscribed on a rectangular raised area. Underneath the poem is carved a raised pedestal. This stone is in excellent condition. There is no space between *a* and *narrow* in the poem.
"Mrs. / H. N. / 1820" is inscribed on the slate footstone.

Nelson, Horatio, Dea. *"DEA. / HORATIO NELSON. / died / Sept. 11, 1869; / Aged 68 yrs 10 m. / & 8 d's."* The second line is carved along an arch.
"H. N." is inscribed on the footstone.

Nelson, Infant son *"A son of Mr. Abiel / Nelson & Mrs. / Sarah his wife / died Dec. 18, 1807 / Aged 6 days. / To the dark and silent tomb / Soon I hastened from the womb."* A willow is carved at the top of this small, lichen encrusted, slate stone. Thatcher lists his death day as the 8th of December.

Nelson, Irene See Sidney Nelson Stone entry.

Nelson, Jeanie Monument *"✝ / JEANIE C. NELSON / BORN DOVER, N. H. OCT. 1, 1849, / DIED NEW LONDON, CONN. SEPT. 9, 1893. / ABIEL WARD / SON OF / JOB PEIRCE & FATIMA BAKER NELSON / AUG 24, 1835 – DEC. 6, 1913 / ASST. SURG. OF 18TH MASS. VOL. / 47 YRS. PHYS. & SURG. AT NEW LONDON / CONN"* is inscribed on this large monument. A *"WWP Post 47 GAR"* marker and flag are present.

Nelson, Job *"JOB / Son of the late / Dr. Thomas Nelson, / died Oct. 2, 1816: / Æ. 46 yrs."* is inscribed on this textured stone.
"J. N." is inscribed on the footstone.

Nelson, Job Peirce *"JOB PEIRCE NELSON / Aged 56 years."* The inscription is recessed on the front of this stone. The first line is carved in relief along an arch. *"Son of / Abiel & Sarah Nelson / Born Oct 17, 1806; / Died Dec. 3, 1862."* is carved on the back of this stone. A radiating crack at the bottom of the stone has been successfully repaired.
"J. P. N." is inscribed on the footstone.

Nelson, John *"HERE LYES THE / BODY OF / JOHN NELSON / WHO DECEA^D.*

/ JVLY THE 6 th/ 1732 IN ᵉ/ᵧ / 30th YEAR / OF HIS AGE" This thick, lichen encrusted slate stone is out of line with the other headstones in this row. A death's head is carved at the top, and scroll designs are carved on the sides and at the bottom. Thatcher lists his death month as May. His wife, Abiah Haskell is buried in Haskell Cemetery.

"John / Nelson / 1732" is inscribed on this slate footstone.

Nelson, John *"In / memory of / MR. JOHN NELSON / who died / Aug. 10. 1828 / in his 57. / year."* An urn and willow carving is at the top of this slate stone. Curved designs are carved down the sides.

"J. N." is inscribed on this slate footstone.

Nelson, John, Col. *"In memory of / Col. JOHN NELSON / who died September 11, / 1803 in his 66 year."* This slate stone is over 5 feet tall. A vine design is carved on the pointed top and also down the sides. A poem follows but is unreadable due to lichen and weathering. A *"SAR 1775"* marker and flag are present.

"Col. / John Nelson" This slate footstone has many cracks. It was broken diagonally and successfully repaired.

Nelson, Joshua *"Sacred / to the Memory of / JOSHUA S. NELSON / Son of Samuel / & Sarah Nelson / who died Aug. 17, 1831 / in the 17 year / of his age. /*

> *Hope lasts beyond the bounds of time,*
> *When, what we now deplore,*
> *Shall rise in full immortal prime,*
> *And bloom to fade no more.*
>
> *Then cease fond nature cease thy tears*
> *Religion points on high,*
> *Then everlasting spring appears*
> *And Joys which cannot die.*

The lines above the poem are inscribed in outline. There is a willow carved at the top of this tall, textured headstone.

"J. S. N. / 1831" is inscribed in outline on this footstone.

Nelson, Judith *"In Memory of / Judith Daughter / to M^r. Thomas / Nelson & M^{rs}. Anne his / Wife who Dec^d March / ᵉ/ᵧ 31st 176_ Aged 13 / months & 23 days."* A winged simple head carving is at the top of this slate stone. The last two lines are buried underground. The last digit of the death year has been chipped out. Thatcher lists her death year as 1769.

"J. N." is inscribed on this slate footstone.

Nelson, Judith *"Memento Mortis. / In Memory of / M— Judith Nelson wido^w. / of Lie_ Thomas Nelson / who died Jan^{ry}. / 21st 1792 / Aged 82 Years 6 Months / & 17 Days."* A winged angel head is carved between the first and second line. There are numerous vertical cracks in this slate stone, and the slate is beginning to exfoliate.

"Mrs. / Judith Nelson" is inscribed on this slate footstone.

Nelson, Judith *"JUDITH NELSON, / Born / Sept .6, 1769. / Died / Dec. 31, 1858.*
/
> *May my spirit daily rise,*
> *On wings of faith above the skies;*

'Till death shall make my last remove,
To dwell forever with my love."
"*J. N.*" is inscribed on the footstone.

Nelson, Lillie T. "*LILLIE THOMAS / 1873 – 1951*" is carved in relief on this flat, brown, 1-4 inch high stone. It matches the Nelson Monument. Lakeville Vital Records documents the marriage of Lillian M. Thomas and Thomas S. Nelson on October 31, 1898.

Nelson, Mary "*In Memory of / Mary Nelson Daugh ^{tr.} / to Mr. William Nelson / & Mrs. Elisabeth his / wife who Dec^{d.} Aug ^{st.} / ye 9 th 1772 Aged 25 / years 8 Months & / 3 days*" A smiling winged angel is carved in relief at the top of this slate stone. Floral and leaf designs are carved down the sides.
"*Mary Nelson*" is inscribed on this slate footstone.

Nelson, Mary E. "*MARY ELIOT / 1878 – 1953*" is carved in relief on this flat, brown, 1-3 inch high stone. It matches the Nelson Monument. Boston Marriage Records show Mary L. Elliott married Clifton Nelson on November 6, 1904.

Nelson, Mary H. "*ERECTED / IN MEMORY OF / Mary H. Nelson / who died / May 12, 1831 / in the 23 year / of her age.*" The third line is carved in relief.

Nelson, Phebe

"In memory of
PHEBE NELSON,
who died
Aug. 27, 1844,
aged 78 years."

An urn and willow carving is at the top of this thick, slate stone. Thatcher lists her death day as the 17th of August.

"*P. N.*" is inscribed on the footstone.

Nelson, Polly "*In memory of / POLLY, / wife of / Hiram Nelson, / who died / Aug. 15, 1838; / aged 71 years. /*
Then gentle patience smiles on pain,
And dying hope revives again,
Hope wipes the tear from sorrow's eye
And faith points upwards to the sky.
The second line is carved in relief.
"*P. N.*" is inscribed on the footstone.

Nelson, Richard T. "*RICHARD TUCKER / BELOVED SON OF / THOMAS AND DORIS / APR. 1947 – DEC 1950*" is carved in relief on this flat, brown, 0-1 inch high stone. It matches the Nelson Monument. There is a small statue of a cat lying to the right rear of this headstone.

Nelson, Sally   *"ERECTED / In Memory of / SALLY. / Consort of / Samuel Nelson. / who died Jan. 30, 1835. / in the 53 y.r / of her age. /*

> *Cheerful I leave this vale of tears,*
> *Where pains and sorrows grow;*
> *Welcome the day that ends my toils,*
> *And ev'ry scene of woe.*
>
> *No more shall sin disturb my breast*
> *My GOD shall frown no more;*
> *The streams of love divine shall yeald*
> *Transports unknown before."*

The first line is carved along an arch, and the third line is carved in outline. The first eight lines of the inscription are carved within a circle. Floral carvings surround it. A castle is carved in relief at the top of this tall stone. The poem is inscribed on a rectangular panel. Some of the script slants to the right, some to the left. Note the spelling of *yeald* in the poem.

"SALLY / NELSON / 1 $\frac{3}{5}$ *8"* is inscribed on the footstone. The first line is carved along an arch, the second line is carved along an inverted arch.

Nelson, Samuel   *"Sacred / to the Memory of / MR. SAMUEL NELSON. / who died / Sept. 9 1831, in the 53 year / of his age. /*

> *Ye fleeting charm__ of earth farewell,*
> *Your springs of joy are dry*
> *My soul now seeks another home*
> *A brighter world on high.*
>
> *Farewell ye friends whose tender care*
> *Has long engaged my love,*
> *Your fond embrace I now exchange*
> *For better friends above."*

The first seven lines of the inscription are carved within a circle which is surrounded by floral carvings. These letters are carved in outline except for the third line, which is carved in relief. A castle is carved in relief at the top of this tall stone.
"Mr. S. N. / 1831" is inscribed in outline of this footstone.

Nelson, Sarah   *"IN MEMORY OF / MRS. SARAH / widow of / Dea. Abiel / NELSON, / who died Nov. 24. / 1838. / In the 60. year of her age."*   An urn and willow are carved in relief at the top of this stone. The second through seventh lines are carved within a semicircle.
"S. N." is inscribed on the footstone. It is lying face down on the ground.

Nelson, Sidney P. Stone   *"1906   SIDNEY P   1997 / AND WIFE / 1906   IRENE 1994"*   is carved in relief in relief on this flat, brown, 2-4 inch high stone. It matches the Nelson Monument.

Nelson, Sidney T.   *"SIDNEY TUCKER / 1845 – 1919"* is carved in relief on this flat, brown, 3-4 inch high stone. It matches the Nelson Monument.

Nelson, Thomas   *"IN MEMORY / OF M*^{r}* THOMAS / NELSON WHO / DIED*

MARCH / ₑ/ᵧ 28ᵗʰ 1755 / AGED 79 YEARS / 9 MONTHS / A 11 DAYS" A simple head is carved at the top of this lichen encrusted, slate stone. Curved lines are carved in semicircles around the head. Vines are carved along the sides. Note the capital A on the last line.
"T. N. / 1755" is inscribed on the footstone.

Nelson, Thomas *"In memory of / Mr. THOMAS NELSON / who died / Sept. 21, 1819 / in his 81. / year."* An urn is carved in relief at the top of this stone. A *"SAR 1775"* marker and flag are present.
"Mr. / T. N." is inscribed on the footstone.

Nelson, Thomas S. *"THOMAS SIDNEY / SON OF / SIDNEY T. AND EMMA P. / 1874 – 1954"* is carved in relief on this flat, brown, 0-3 inch high stone. It matches the Nelson Monument.

Nelson, Thomas Stone *"1900 THOMAS ___ / SON OF T. S. AND L. T. / AND WIFE / 1913 DORIS WILLIAMS 1993"* is carved in relief on this flat, brown, 0-1 inch high stone. It matches the Nelson Monument. His obituary in *The Middleborough Gazette* 02/01/1996:10 reports his death in Clearwater Florida on January 20, 1996.

Nelson, Thomas, Lt. *"Here Lies buried / Lieᵘᵗ. Thomas Nelson / who Decᵈ. march / yᵉ 7ᵗʰ 1768 / Aged 57 years / 10 months & / 12 days"* A simple head with wild hair is carved at the top of this lichen encrusted, slate stone. Floral and leaf designs are carved along its sides. A veteran's marker and flag are present.
"Lieᵘᵗ. / Thomas Nelson" is inscribed on this slate footstone.

Nelson, William *"_n Memory of / Mʳ. William Nelson / Died Decᵐʳ. ₑ/ᵧ 14ᵗʰ / 1776 Aged 62 Yearˢ. / 6 Months & / 4 Days."* A winged angel is carved at the top. There are several cracks in the slate stone and it is exfoliating on the left side.
"_____ m / _els__" is all that remains of this exfoliating slate footstone.

Nelson, William, Rev. *"In Memory of / Rev. WILLIAM NELSOᴺ / he Died April 11, 1806 / in his 65ᵗʰ Year. /*

> *In Middleborough   had my birth*
> *At ... Education*
> *At Taunton I had my ordination*
> *At Norton my dwelling ___ce*
> *D_m__muth an assylum fo_ . ___health*
> *At Middleborough my exit..."*

This large, lichen encrusted, slate stone is lying on the ground. It is very weathered and chipped. Note the spelling of *asylum*. *The Nelson Family of Plymouth, Middleboro, and Lakeville, Massachusetts* p. 56 has the last six lines as follows:

> "In Middleborough I had my birth
> At Warren my classical education
> At Taunton I had my ordination
> Norton my dwelling place
> Dartmouth an assylum for my health
> At Middleboro my exit and my grave."

It is listed as a large stone over a brick base, but no evidence of a base was found.

Norris, D. Evelyn Monument   *"D. EVELYN NORRIS / 1911 ____ / JAMES E. NORRIS / 1938 ____ / WILLIAM BELLIVEAU / 1931 – 1997 / MERRY MEET, MERRY PART, / MERRY MEET AGAIN..."* is inscribed on this monument.

Norris, James E.   See D. Evelyn Norris Monument entry.

Packard, Infant girl   See Lydia B. Packard Stone entry.

Packard, Lydia B. Stone   *"Here lies / Lydia Barrell Packard, / who died Dec͏ʳ 29, 1793: / aged 5 years & 2 months. / Also in memory of an / Infant. who died Feb. 16, 1792: / aged 1 day. / Dautʳˢ of M͏ʳ. Eliphalet Packard, / the former by his 1ˢᵗ wife, / the latter by his 2ᵈ wife."* A winged angel head is carved at the top of this slate stone. Thatcher lists her middle name as Barrett.
"L. B. P." is inscribed on the slate footstone.

Parker, Abbie M.   See Anna E. Cole Monument entry.
Rochester Vital Records list her birth on June 27, 1846 as Abigail Davis. Lakeville Vital Records list her death on October 13, 1921. She was the widow of William Parker and the sister of Anna E. Cole.

Parkhurst, Helen S. Monument   *"PARKHURST"* is inscribed on the front of this monument and flowers are carved in the top corners. *"PARKHURST"* is inscribed at the top on the back. *"DAUGHTER / HELEN S. / 1889 – 1963"* is inscribed below this on the left side, and *"FATHER / JAMES S. / 1850 – 1938"* is inscribed on the right side. A Barnicoat Monuments metal tag is present.

Parkhurst, James S.   See Helen S. Parkhurst Monument entry.

Peirce, Annie J.   See Frank S. Peirce Monument entry.

Peirce, Ebenezer   *"In memory of / Mr. EBEN ᶻᴿ PEIRCE / who died August 14, 1796 / in his 92 year /   Tho the great God who reigns on high*
                    Has doom,d the race of man to die
                    Yet saints thereby a_e clens,d from sin
                    And shall in glory ____ again"
A frowning angel head with long wings is carved at the top of this slate stone. A crack on the left side extends down to the middle of the poem, obliterating some letters. Note the use of comma in place of an apostrophe. The last two lines are underground.
"Mr. / Eben,ᶻ ͬ Pei___" The upper right corner has exfoliated on this slate footstone.

Peirce, Elizabeth   *"ERECTED / in memory of / ELIZABETH, / wife of / CAPT JOB PEIRCE: / who died / March 22. 1846 / in her 96 year."* The first line is carved along an arch. The third line is carved in outline.
"E. P." is inscribed on the footstone.

Peirce, Frank S. Monument   *"FRANK S. PEIRCE / 1859 – 1902. / ANNIE J. PEIRCE / 1855 – 1931"* A low stone wall surrounds this grave, and that of Rex Jennings, Annie's son from a previous marriage.

Peirce, Henry   *"In memory of / Mr. HENRY PEIRCE / who died / Sep. 1. 1826 / aged 48 years."* An urn and willow are carved at the top of this slate stone, and

scalloped designs are carved on the sides and bottom.
"H. P." is inscribed on the slate footstone.

Peirce, Henry, Capt.   *"In memory of Capt, / Henry Peirce, who / died Jan'y 22^d, 1791. / in y̧^e 48th Year of his / Age. /*

> *Depart my friends,*
> *Wipe off your tears,*
> *Here I must lie,*
> *Till CHRIST appears"*

There is a frond carving at the top of this slate stone. The last line is half buried underground. A *"SAR 1775"* marker and flag are present.
"Capt. / Henry / Peirce / 1791" is inscribed on the slate footstone.

Peirce, Mary   *"Memento Mori. / In Memory of / M^{rs}. Mary Peirce, wife / of M^r. Ebene___ Peirce / She Died Octo^r y^e ___ ___8 / In the 57th Year / of her Age. /*

> *Remember me as you pass by*
> *For as you are so once was I*
> *But as I am so you must be*
> *_heirfore prepare to follow me."*

A detailed winged angel head is carved in relief between the first and second lines. Leaf designs are carved on the sides of the tympanum, and down the sides. Note the spelling of *Theirfore* in the poem. This slate stone was broken diagonally through the first four lines, and successfully repaired, but the repair obliterates part of her given name and the day and year she died. It is exfoliating in the bottom left corner. Thatcher lists, "Mary, wife of Ebenezer, Oct. 5, 1768, in her 57th year."
"M^{rs}. Mary / Peirce" is inscribed on this slate footstone, below a leaf carving.

Peirce, Rhoda   *"Memento Mortis. / In Memory of / Mrs Rhoda Peirce, wife of / M^r. Joseph Peirce Junr., / who died April 2^d. 1788. / In y̧^e 32^d Year of her Age. /*

> *In __r last expireing breath,*
> *She bid farewell to friends,*
> *And welcom'd Death."*

A winged angel head is carved between the first and second line. Note the spelling of *expireing*. The top part of this slate stone is broken off above the second line and is leaning against the back of the bottom part. There are several horizontal cracks present. Thatcher lists her information under the name Joseph Pierce.
"M^{rs}. / Rhoda Peir^{ce}" is inscribed on the slate footstone. The carver ran out of room on the second line.

Peirce, Sarah *"Memento Mori / In Memory of / M.ʳˢ Sarah Peirce / wife of M.ʳ / John Peirce. She / Died Oct.ᵒ ᵉ/ᵧ 25, / 1774 in the 43 ᵈ / Year of ___ / Age"* A detailed winged angel head is carved in relief between the first and second lines. Leaf designs are carved on the sides of the tympanum, and down the sides of this slate stone. The last line is buried underground.

"M.ʳˢ Sarah / Peirce." This slate footstone faces the headstone. A leaf design is carved at the top.

Peirce, Soloma *"In memory of / M.ʳˢ Soloma Daughter / of Elder Hinds & wife / of Capᵗ. Henry Peirce / who died June ye 17ᵗʰ / ...."* The rest of the inscription is buried in cement. A frond carving is at the top of this slate stone. Thatcher lists that she died in "1784 in her 37ᵗʰ year."

"M.ʳˢ Soloma / Peirce / 1784" is inscribed on the slate footstone.

Perkins, Mildred F. *"SCOTTI / MILDRED FRANCES HALL CRAIN / PERKINS / NOV. 13, 1921 – OCT. 29, 1986"* is inscribed on this slanted monument.

Phinney See also Finney.

Phinney, James S. *"MR. / JAMES S. PHINNEY / Died / Sept. 30, 1841. / Aged 58 yrs. / Blessed are the dead that die in the / Lord."* The second line is carved in relief along an arch.

"J. S. P." is inscribed on the footstone.

Phinney, Joanna *"MRS. / JOANNA, / wife of / James S. Phinney / died Aug. 31. 1852, / Aged age 66 yrs. / Blessed are the pure in heart for they / will see God."* The second line is carved in relief along an arch.

"J. P." is inscribed on the footstone.

Phinney, Joseph *"In Memory of / M.ʳ Joseph Phinney. / he Died Aug.ˢᵗ ᵉ/ᵧ 13ᵗʰ / 1793 in ᵉ/ᵧ 77 ᵗʰ Year / of his Age."* A winged angel head is carved at the top of this slate stone. There are several cracks extending through the carving to the first line. A *"SAR 1775"* marker and flag are present.

"M.ʳ / Joseph / Phinney" is inscribed on this slate footstone.

Phinney, Lucinda *"LUCINDA PHINNEY. / died Oct. 16, 1872; / Aged 82 yrs. / & 6 m's."* The first line is carved in relief.

"L. P." is inscribed on the footstone.

Phinney, Lydia *"MIS_ / LYDIA PHINNEY / Died / April 30, 185_ / Aged 80 yrs."* This stone is very weathered. The second line is carved in relief. Lakeville Vital Records show she died in 1854, and was the unmarried daughter of Jonathan.

"L. P." is inscribed on the footstone

Phinney, Phebe *"In Memory of / M.ʳˢ Phebe widow of / M.ʳ Joseph Phinney / She died June ᵉ/ᵧ 10 ᵗʰ / 1796. In her 67 ᵗʰ Year."* A winged angel is carved at the top of this lichen encrusted, slate stone.

"M.ʳˢ / Phebe / Phinney" is inscribed on this slate footstone.

Pickens, Abigail *"SACRED / to the memory of / ABIGAIL. / wife of / STEPHEN B. PICKENS. / died May 4, 1873 / Æ. 84."* There is no carving on the tympanum.

Pickens, Albert G.   *"ALBERT G. PICKENS / Died / Feb 2, 1900, / Aged / 81 yrs. 3 mos. 9 days."*

Pickens, Andrew   *"Memento Mortis. / In Memory of / Mr. Andrew Pickens, / who died March 29 ᵗʰ / 1795. In his 79 ᵗʰ. Year."*   A winged angel head is carved at the top of this slate stone. Several vertical cracks are present. A *"SAR 1775"* marker and flag are present.

Pickens, Arthur L.   See Silas D. Pickens Monument entry.
"ARTHUR" is inscribed on this flat, ground level footstone. It is located behind the monument, on the far left.

Pickens, Elisabeth   *"Memento mortis. / In Memory of / Mrs. Elisabeth Pickens, wife / of Mr. Andrew Pickens. who / died April 4 ᵗʰ. 1795. In / her 82 ᵈ. Year."*   A winged angel head is carved at the top of this lichen encrusted, slate stone. There are several vertical cracks.
"Mrs. Elisab^{eth} / Pickens" is inscribed on this slate footstone. The carver ran out of room on the first line. The *eth* is actually carved above the *ab* in *Elisabeth*. The footstone is lying face up in front of the headstone.

Pickens, Matilda   *"SACRED / to the memory of / MATILDA PICKENS / widow of the late / SAMUEL PICKENS / who died April 13, 1839. / Aged 77 Years."*
"M. P." is inscribed on the footstone.

Pickens, Myra S.   See Silas D. Pickens Monument entry.
"MYRA" is inscribed on this flat, lichen encrusted, ground level footstone. It is located behind the monument, on the far right.
"M. P." is inscribed on a second footstone, which is lying face up in front of the monument.

Pickens, Samuel   *"SACRED / to the memory of / SAMUEL PICKENS. / who died / Feb 12, 1830: / Æt 78."*   A *"SAR 1775"* marker and flag are present.
"S. P." is inscribed on the footstone.

Pickens, Silas D. Monument   *"PICKENS"* is inscribed on the front of this large monument. Floral designs are carved in the lower corners. *"1830   SILAS D. PICKENS   1887 / WIFE / 1831   MYRA SAMPSON   1870 / 1857   ARTHUR L. PICKENS   1941 / 1859   CARRIE I. CRANE   1947 / 1861   ABBIE D. WASHBURN 1947."* is inscribed on the back. A *"GAR 8 415"* marker and flag are present. *Massachusetts Civil War Soldiers & Sailors, 1861-1865,* Vol. VI, p. 167 shows that he served in the 1st Calvary, Co. E.
"SILAS" is inscribed on this flat, lichen encrusted, ground level footstone. It is located directly behind the monument, on the right side.

Pickens, Stephen B.   *"SACRED / to the memory of / Mr. STEPHEN B. PICKENS. / who died Oct. 2, 1825. / Æt. 41."*   There is no carving on the tympanum.

Pickens, Stephen B.   *"ERECTED / in memory of / STEPHEN B. PICKENS / who died / Sept. 22, 1849. in / his 41 year."*   The third line is carved in outline.

Pittsley, Priscilla   *"MOTHER / PRISCILLA PITTSLEY / Died / Feb. 15, 1891 / Aged 75 yrs."*   The second line is carved along an arch.

Plissey, C. Augustus   *"C. AUGUSTUS PLISSEY / 1882 – 1968"* is inscribed on this flat, ground level stone. It is concealed below a large bush.

Pratt, Sally   *"Sacred / to the memory of / MRS. SALLY PRATT / wife of / Dea. Benjamin P. Pratt / who died / in full assurance of faith / March 14, 1842, / in the 53, Yr. of her age."* Middleborough Birth Records online show that she was the daughter of Lemuel and Abigail Briggs. A stone post and metal rail fence surrounds this plot.
"S. P." is inscribed on the footstone.

Pratt, Sarah   *"SACRED / to the memory of / SARAH PRATT / sister of / Dea. Benjamin P. Pratt / who died / May 18, 1849, in / her 66 year."* The third line is carved in outline. This headstone is lying face up on the ground. A stone post and metal rail fence surrounds this Briggs plot.
"S. P." is inscribed on the footstone.

Ramsdell, Minnie E.   *"MINNIE ETTA F."* is inscribed on the top curved surface of this small stone. *"DAU. OF / JAMES E. & ADDIE / RAMSDELL / DIED JULY 22, 1888. / AGED 13 YRS. 4 MO. / 18 DAYS."* is inscribed on the front of this stone.

Richardson, Anna Gove   See Oscar Richardson Monument entry.

Richardson, Oscar Monument   *"RICHARDSON / OSCAR / 1860 – 1940 / HIS WIFE / ANNA GOVE / 1861 – 1941"* There is a carving of a caduceus at the top of this monument, with floral designs carved on either side. This monument is very close to the hill's edge.

Roberts, Infant   *"Infant of / A. J. & E. W. / Roberts."* Lakeville Records show that a female was born on September 8, 1861, and died two days later on September 10, 1861. The parents were Austin J. and Eliza W. Roberts.

Roberts, Infant   *"Infant of / A. J. & E. W. / Roberts."* Lakeville Records indicate that a female was born April 26, 1865, and died two days later on April 28, 1865. The parents were Austin J. and Eliza W. Roberts.

Roberts, Samuel   *"SAMUEL ROBERTS / 1845."*
"S. R." This footstone faces the headstone.

Rogers, Judith   *"JUDITH, / wife of / HARRIS ROGERS, / Died / June 27, 1845, / Aged 53 years."* The first line is carved in relief along an arch.
"J. R." This footstone faces the headstone.

Russell, John   At the initial visit, only the footstone was present. A covered hole was located where the headstone should have been. On a March 4, 2004 revisit, a slate stone was present, encased in cement to repair a diagonal break from the upper right to the lower left side. Some letters were obliterated in the resulting gap. A winged angel is carved on the tympanum, but the top half has exfoliated. The shoulders of the stone have exfoliated as well. Leaf carvings extend down the sides. The inscription reads: *"In Memory __ / M^r. John Russell / of Plymouth / who D_ed at / Middle_oro' April / ^e_y 2^d. 1776 / in _he 42 ^{d} Year / o_ his Age."* Carved in the cement on the back of this stone is: *"IN MEMORY OF / MR JOHN RUFSELL / OF*

PLYMOUTH / WHO DIED AT / MIDDLEBORO APRIL / $\frac{e}{Y}$ 2^d 1776 / IN THE 42^d YEAR / OF HIS AGE."
"M$\underline{r}$. / John / Russell" is inscribed on this slate footstone.

Sampson, Abigail D.   *"ABIGAIL D. / Wife of / URIAH SAMPSON, / Died Feb. 10, 1881; / Aged 71 yrs. 9 mos. / and 7 days."* The first line is carved in relief. This stone shares its base with that of her husband.
"A. D. S." This footstone faces the headstone.

Sampson, Anna   *"ANNA, / wife of / Thomas Sampson, / died Dec. 19, 1863: / Aged 75 yrs. 2 m's. / & 9 d's. / At rest."* is inscribed on this textured stone.
"A. S." is inscribed on the footstone.

Sampson, Betsey   *"BETSEY / wife of / Elias Sampson, / who died / February 15, 1850: / Aged 73 Years."* The first line is carved in shallow relief.
"B. S." This footstone faces the headstone.

Sampson, Betsey

"BETSEY,
dau. of Charles H.
& Louesa B.
Sampson
died Apr. 25, 1862,
Aged 10 yrs. 4 m's
& _ d's"

A broken flower bud is carved in relief at the top. A crack radiating from the base obliterates the number of days. Lakeville Vital Records show she was 10 years, 4 months, and 4 days old when she died.
"B. S." This footstone faces the headstone.

Sampson, Charles H.   The headstone is missing for this grave. This gravestone would have shared its base with Louesa B. Sampson. It is probably the gravesite of Charles H. Sampson, her husband. The cemetery cards at the Lakeville Town Hall list a "Charles H. Sampson b. June 9, 1813, d. Nov. 22, 1867, son of Elias Sampson and Betsey Macomber." Lakeville Vital Records verifies this information.
"C. H. S." is inscribed on the footstone.

Sampson, Ebenezer D.   *"EBENEZER D. SAMPSON / Died / Nov. 10, 1880; / Aged 79 years."* The first line is carved in relief. This gravestone shares its base with the gravestones of Eliza C., Elias, and Ebenezer Sampson, Jr.

Sampson, Ebenezer D., Jr.   *"EBENEZER D. SAMPSON JR. / Son of / Ebenezer D. & Eliza C. / SAMPSON, / Died Feb. 23, 1866; Aged 28 years."* The first line is carved in relief. This gravestone shares its base with the gravestones of Ebenezer D., Eliza C., and Elias Sampson.

Sampson, Elias   *"In memory of / ELIAS SAMPSON / who died / July 31, 1847 / Aged 76 years."* The second line is carved in shallow relief on this weathered stone. *"E. S."* This footstone faces the headstone.

Sampson, Elias   *"ELIAS SAMPSON / Son of / Ebenezer D. & Eliza C. / SAMPSON, / Died in California, / Oct. 1, 1869; / Aged 36 years."* The first line is carved in relief. There are many small cracks on the surface of this stone. This gravestone shares its base with the gravestones of Ebenezer D., Eliza C., and Ebenezer Sampson, Jr.

Sampson, Elias, Jr.   *"ELIAS SAMPSON, JR. / Died / Jan. 19, 1879; / Aged 79 yrs. 10 mos. / and 16 days."* The first line is carved in relief.

Sampson, Eliza   *"ELIZA, / Dau. of Elias & Betsey / Sampson, / Born March 20, 1804; / Died March 9, 1870;"* The first line is carved in relief.
"E. S." is inscribed on the footstone, which faces the headstone.

Sampson, Eliza C.   *"ELIZA C. / Wife of / EBENEZER D. SAMPSON. / Died / June 27, 1896; / Aged 91 years."* The first line is carved in relief. This gravestone shares its base with the gravestones of Ebenezer D., Elias, and Ebenezer Sampson, Jr.

Sampson, Louesa B.   *"LOUESA B. / wife of / Charles H. Sampson, / died Sept. 16, 1874; / Aged 60 yrs. 8 m's / & 24 d's."* The first line is carved along an arch. This stone shares its base with a missing headstone, probably that of Charles H. Sampson. *"L. B. S."* is inscribed on the footstone.

Sampson, Maria Stone   *"MARIA / Wife of / ELIAS SAMPSON JR ., / Died Dec. 2, 1837; / Aged 35 yrs. 2 mos. / Also their Son / WM. BAYLIES / Died Oct. 2, 1837; / Aged 1 mo. 8 days."* The first and seventh lines are carved in relief.

Sampson, Maria J.   *"MARIA JANE / Daughter of / Elias Jr. & Maria / SAMPSON, / Died Aug. 11, 1880; / Aged 55 years. / Blessed are the pure in heart / for they shall see God."* The first line is carved in relief.

Sampson, Sarah R.   *"SARAH R. SAMPSON / MAR. 26, 1838 / FEB. 3, 1899"* There are floral carvings in the upper corners of this stone. The first line is carved in relief along an arch.

Sampson, Uriah   *"URIAH SAMPSON / Died / June 14, 1880: / Aged 73 yrs. 6 mos. / and 9 days."* The first line is carved in relief. This stone shares its base with that of Abigail Sampson, his wife.
"U. S." This footstone faces the headstone.

Sampson, Wm. B.   See Maria Sampson Stone entry.

Sampson, Zilpha B.   *"ZILPHA B. / Wife of / ELIAS SAMPSON, JR. / Died / Feb. 27, 1881; / Aged 74 yrs. 2 mos."* The first line is carved in relief.

Sanderson, Lurana   *"In memory of / LURANA. / wife of / Phineas Sanderson: / who died / Sept. 29. 1851. / in her 74 years."* An urn and willow carving is at the top of this rectangular, slate stone. *Lurana* is inscribed within a rectangular recessed area.
"L. S." This footstone faces the headstone.

Sheafe, Abby Evelyn   See John Cudworth Monument entry.
"ABBY EVELYN / WIDOW OF LLEWELLYN JACOB ATWOOD / AND EDWIN SHEAFE" is inscribed on this flat, 8 inch high stone. It is located behind the monument, on the left. Lakeville Vital Records show she was the daughter of John Cudworth.

Shockley, Almy J.   *"ALMY J. SHOCKLEY. / died / Mar. 24, 1871; / Aged 38 yrs.*
7 m's. /   Kind, generous. devoted. always ready
*   to sacrifice her own happiness for the*
*   good of others. She hath done what she*
*   could and being dead yet speaketh."*
The first line is carved in relief along an arch. There is a 7 inch crack radiating from the center bottom of the stone into the poem.
"A. J. S." is inscribed on the footstone.

Shockley, Andrew Monument   *"SHOCKLEY"* is carved in relief at the top of this monument. *"ANDREW J. SHOCKLEY / 1834 – 1911 / PHEBE J. HIS WIFE / 1836 – 1914 / FRED'K A. SHOCKLEY / 1861 – 1942 / EMMA HIS WIFE / 1862 – 1943"*

Shockley, Averic T.   *"AVERIC T. / DAUGHTER OF / JOSEPH & SARAH / SHOCKLEY / 1840 – 1926"* This stone is separated from its base and is lying face up on top of it.

Shockley, Benjamin F.   *"BENJAMIN F. SHOCKLEY. / Died / Feb. 27, 1900. / Aged 56 yrs."* The first line is carved along an arch. This lichen encrusted stone is separated from its base and is lying face up on top of it.

Shockley, Charles Monument   *"CHARLES SHOCKLEY / 1830 – 1900. / HARRIETT M. / HIS WIFE / 1822 – 1887."* is inscribed on the front of this tall roofed monument. The first line is carved along an arch. *"HATTIE H. / 1860 – 1872. / MARY G. / 1863 – 1880. / CHARLES F. / 1859 – 1882."* is inscribed on the right side. There are no inscriptions on the back or the left side.
"C. S." is inscribed on this flat, ground level footstone. This partially buried stone is located behind the monument, on the left side.

Shockley, Charles Frank   See Charles Shockley Monument entry.
"C. FRANK / SON OF / CHARLES SHOCKLEY." No dates are present on this stone.

Shockley, Emma   See Andrew Shockley Monument entry.
"E. P. S." is inscribed on this flat, ground level footstone

Shockley, Fredrick   See Andrew Shockley Monument entry.
"F. A. S." is inscribed on this flat, ground level footstone

Shockley, Harriett M.   See Charles Shockley Monument entry.
"HARRIET M. / WIFE OF / CHARLES SHOCKLEY" There are no dates on this stone. Note the different spelling of her first name on the monument.

Shockley Hattie H.   See Charles Shockley Monument entry.
"Alive with Christ." is inscribed on the top horizontal surface. An open book is carved on this podium shaped monument. An inscription is evident on the book, but it is too weathered to read. *"HATTIE HORTENSE / Eldest / daughter of / Charles & Harriett / M. Shockley, / Died Aug. 3, 1872: / Aged 13 yrs. 6 d's."* is inscribed on the

front vertical surface. The first line is carved along an arch. Note the discrepancy in her birth year/age from the family monument. Lakeville Vital Records show she was born in 1859 in Illinois. The 1860 Federal Census of Grand Rapids, Illinois lists her as 11 months old on July 7, 1860, confirming her birth year as 1859.

Shockley, John   *"JOHN SHOCKLEY / Died / Sept. 27, 1895. / Aged 73 years."*

Shockley, Joseph   *"JOSEPH / SHOCKLEY, / died Mar. 14, 1863, / Aged 76 yrs. /*
To live is Christ, to die is gain.
Servant of God; well done:
Rest from thy loved employ;
The battle fought, the victory won.
Enter thy Master's joy."
"J. S." is inscribed on the footstone.

Shockley, Mary (Minnie) G.   See Charles Shockley Monument entry.
"MINNIE G. / DAU. OF / CHARLES SHOCKLEY." No dates are present on this stone.

Shockley, Phebe J.   See Andrew J. Shockley Monument entry.

Shockley, Sally Alden   *"SALLY ALDEN, / wife of / Joseph Shockley, / died June 22, 1859. / Aged 63 yrs. / Blessed are the pure in heart for they / shall see God. /*
We're going home, we've had visions bright.
Of that holy land, that world of light.
Where the long dark night of time is past,
And the morn of eternity dawns at last;

Where the weary saint no more shall roam.
But dwell in a happy peaceful home:
Where the brow with sparkling gems is crowned
And the waves of bliss are flowing around."
"S. A. S." is inscribed on the footstone.

Shockley, Wm. Elmer   *"WM. ELMER SHOCKLEY / 1866 – 1939"* The first line is carved along an arch on this slanted monument.

Smith, Abigail   *"In Memory of / Abigail, Daug* *of Cap* */ John Smith & M* *!* */ Abigail his wife. who / died Apriel y* *16. 1789. / Aged 3. Years. 5 Months / & _2 Days."* An hourglass with wings is carved at the top of this stone. A chip is missing before the number 2 in the last line. Thatcher lists her age in days as 12. Note the spelling of *Apriel*.

Smith, Abigail   *"Sacred / to the memory of / MRS. ABIGAIL SMITH / widow of / Cap. John Smith / she died / Dec. 16. 1810 / in her 54. Year."* An urn and willow are carved at the top of this four-foot tall slate stone. Vine designs are carved along the sides and on the bottom. A diagonal crack through the headstone has been successfully repaired. A veteran's marker and flag are present.
"Mrs. / Abigail / Smith" is inscribed on this slate footstone.

Smith, Daniel, Capt. Stone   *"CAPT. DANIEL SMITH, / Born / June 2. 1779. / Died Sept. 8, 1829. / SUSAN, HIS WIFE, / Born / Feb. 3. 1782. / Died Feb. 11, 1868."*

Smith, George E.   *"GEORGE E. / Son of Daniel H. / & Mary A. Smith / died Aug 4, 1856 / Aged 2 yrs. 9 m^s, / 4 d's."* A broken bud is carved in relief above the inscription. The last two lines are buried underground.
"G. E. S." is inscribed on the footstone.

Smith, John, Capt.   *"Sacred / to the memory / OF / Capt. JOHN SMITH. / who died March 6th. / AD 1809. / in his 53 Year. /*

> *My flesh shall slumber in the ground*
> *Till the last trumpets joyfull sound*
> *Then burst the chains with sweet surprise*
> *And in my saviour's image rise."*

An urn and willow carving is at the top of this tall slate stone. Columns are carved on the sides. Note the spelling of *joyfull*. A veteran's marker and flag are present.
"Cap. / John Smith. / 1809" The last line of this slate stone is buried underground.

Smith, Josiah, Lt.   *"In MEMORY of Lieu^t. / Josiah Smit_ who died Augst. / 24th, 1798 in ^e_y 69th. Year / of _is Age /*

> *My _____ en dear this place draw near,*
> *A ____ ers grave to see,*
> *Remember well & bear in mind,*
> *A faithfull friend I left behind."*

A peeking rising sun is carved at the top of this slate stone. Note the spelling of *faithfull*. It has begun to exfoliate and many pieces are present at the base. The inscription was taken from those pieces placed together. A *"SAR 1775"* marker and flag are present. Thatcher lists him without his rank.

Smith, Susan   See Capt. Daniel Smith Stone entry.

Spooner, Alden   *"ALDEN. / Son of / Thomas & Phebe / Spooner. / died Oct, 14, 1849, / Æ. 11 m's / 21 d's."* Thatcher lists his death year as 1845.
"A. S." is inscribed on the footstone.

Spooner, Eleanor   *"_mento mortis / In Memory of / M^{rs}. Eleanor Spooner / who died Octr. ye 21st. / 1786 Aged 54 Years / 1. Month & 17 Days."* The top left corner of this lichen encrusted slate stone has broken off. A winged angel is carved between the first and second lines. The footstone is broken off at ground level. The top inscribed part is missing.

Spooner, Elizabeth S.   See Geo. H. Spooner Monument entry.
"ELIZABETH" is inscribed along an arch on this second stone. It is located behind the monument, on the right.

Spooner, Geo. H. Monument   *"SPOONER."* is carved in relief on the front base of this tall monument. An urn sculpture is at the top. *"GEO. H. SPOONER / DIED / AUG. 3, 1903, / AGED / 61 YRS. 9 MOS. / & 23 DS."* is inscribed on the front. The first line is carved along an arch. *"ELIZABETH S. / WIFE OF / GEO. H. SPOONER. / DIED FEB. 21, 1885, / AGED / 42 YRS. 11 MOS. / & 29 D'S. / DEAR LIZZIE WE HOPE TO / MEET AGAIN, WHERE DEATH / CAN NEVER PART US."* is inscribed on the right side. The first line is carved along an arch. Leaf carvings are present on the bottom above the base on all four sides. There is no inscription on the left side or the back.
"GEORGE" is inscribed along an arch on this stone, which is located behind the monument, on the left.

Spooner, Phebe   *"PHEBE / wife of / Thomas Spooner Jr. / died Nov. 10, 1867; /*
Aged 48 years. /   *Loved One, thou art gone to rest,*
                   And this shall be our prayer
                   That when we reach our journey's end
                   Thy glory we may share."
At the initial visit this headstone was lying face down on the ground. At a subsequent visit, it had been turned over so the inscription could be read. The first line is carved in relief along an arch. This stone has been broken through the poem, and successfully repaired.
"P. S." is inscribed on the footstone.

Spooner, Thomas   *"THOMAS SPOONER / died / Nov. 16, 1898; / Aged 79 years. / Rest after weariness / ease after pain."* The first line is carved in relief along an arch. This stone was broken diagonal through the first four lines. There is no sign of repair, but the two pieces are in place.

Sullivan, Catherine M.   *"CATHERINE M. SULLIVAN / Died / Nov. 19, 1915, / Aged / 73 Years"*

Tallman, Julius C.   *"OUR BABY"* is inscribed on the front of this small, roofed monument. *"JULIUS C. / son of / A. S. & P. W. / TALLMAN / Aug. 24, 1900 / Mar. 27, 1902"* is inscribed on the back.

Thew   *"THEW"* only is inscribed on the front of this large stone. There is a flag present.

Thrasher, Cyrus Monument   *"L (monogram) / 1792   CYRUS THRASHER 1880 / 1807   HANNAH HIS WIFE   1881 / 1837   WILLIAM E. LONER   1888 / 1843 LYDIA D. HIS WIFE   1912 / THEIR CHILDREN / 1875   LAURA M.   1876 / 1871 LYDIA W.   1889 / 1883   MABEL L.   1890 / LONER"* Floral carvings are in the upper corners. A low cement wall surrounds the Cyrus Thrasher plot.

Thrasher, Hannah   See Cyrus Thrasher Monument entry.

Tinkham, Horatio   *"FATHER. / HORATIO TINKHAM. / BORN DEC. 12, 1818. / DIED MAY 5, 1893. / ERECTED BY HIS DAUGHTER."*

Tinkham, J. Elizabeth   *"J. ELIZABETH / Wife of / HORATIO TINKHAM / Died Sept. 13, 1870 / Æt. 45 yrs. 8 mos. / 21 days. /*

> *The orphan group bereaved and sad*
> *Lament: their hopes are fled;*
> *The stricken husband in sorrow clad.*
> *Yearns o'er his cherished dead."*

The first line is carved in relief along an arch. Middleborough Vital Records show her first name was Jane.
"J. E. T." is inscribed on top curved surface of the footstone.

Tobey, Job Townsend   *"JOB TOWNSEND TOBEY / Died / Feb. 11, 1892, / Aged 80 yrs. / 1 mo. 17 days."* The first line is carved along an arch.

Tobey, Maria   *"MARIA, / Wife of / Job T. Tobey, / died April 13, 1876; / Aged 57 yrs & 7 m's"*

Tobey, Martha E.   *"Martha E. / dau. of / Mr. Isaac S. & / Mrs. Rachel Tobey / died Aug 20, 1820 / aged 5 years 4 m. 8 d."* A willow is carved at the top. This slate stone was broken diagonally through the inscribed area, and successfully repaired.

Tobey, Rachel   *"RACHEL TOBEY, / Died / Feb. 11, 1871; / Aged 83 yrs. 9 m's."*

Townsend, Abiel   *"In Memory of / Abiel Son of M*ͬ*. Job & M*ˢ* Rachel / Townsend who died Jan*ʸ*. 15 / 1797 in ye 19 year of his age. /*

> *Death is a debt to nature due*
> *Which I have paid & so must you."*

A winged angel head is carved at the top of this lichen encrusted, slate stone.
"A T / 1797" is inscribed on this slate footstone.

Townsend, Abiel, Lieut.   See John Townsend Stone entry.

Townsend, Anna   *"ANNA, / wife of / John Townsend, / died Aug. 24. 1870; / Aged 54 yrs. 8 m's. / Ever in remembrance."*

Townsend, Daniel B.   *"DANIEL B. / son of Mr. John & / Mrs. Anna Townsend / Died / Sept. 19, 1835; / aged 2 yrs. & 4 mos."* *"M Gallagher."* is inscribed on the bottom right and is buried underground. Thatcher lists his death year as 1805, but *Middleborough, Massachusetts Vital Records,* Vol. 1, p. 431 lists, "Daniel Briggs

Townsend, son of John and Ann born May 19, 1833." This puts his death at 2 years old in 1835.

"D. B. T." This footstone faces the headstone.

Townsend, Hope   "HOPE widow of / SILAS TOWNSEND. / died Oct. 5, 1833. / in the 73 year / of her age." A "SAR 1775" marker and flag are present.

Townsend, Job   "SACRED / to the memory of / JOB TOWNSEND / who died / May 5, 1842 in / his __ year." There is a crack going through the last two lines which makes his death date and age hard to read. Thatcher lists his age as in his "95th year." A "SAR 1775" marker and flag are present.

"J. T." is inscribed on the footstone.

Townsend, John Stone   "In Memory of M^r. / John Townsend who Died / May $_y^e$ 4th 1790 in / his 75 th year / Also In Memory of Lie^{ut}. / Abiel Townsend who was / Killed by an Accidental Shot / at Roxbury Sep^{tr} $_y^e$ 8th 1775 / in his 36th Year." A winged angel is carved at the top of this lichen encrusted, slate stone.

"M^r. / John / Townsend / Lie^{ut}. Abiel / Townsend" is inscribed on this slate footstone. The last line is buried underground.

Townsend, John   "John Townsend, / Aug. 20, 1810, / May 20, 1905."

Townsend, Mary   "In Memory of M^{rs}. / Mary Widow of M^r. / John Townsend. She / Died M__ $_y^e$ 8th 1790 / in her 68th Year." A carving of a winged angel is at the top of this lichen encrusted, slate stone. A chip is missing where the month is carved. The last line is buried underground. Thatcher lists her death month as May.

"M^{rs}. / Mary / Townsend" is inscribed on the footstone.

Townsend, Peace   "SACRED / to the memory of / PEACE, / wife of Job Townsend / who died / Oct. 31, 1844, in / her 86 year." The first line is carved along an arch.

"P. T." is inscribed on the footstone.

Townsend, Rachel   "Memento Mortis. / In Memory of / Mrs Rachel, wife of / M^r. Job Townsend, who / died July 9 th 1787. In $_y^e$ / 29 th Year of her Age." The top of this slate stone is exfoliating, and only the wings are left of a winged angel carving.

"Mrs. / R. T." is inscribed on this slate footstone. It is located in front of Miss Elisabeth Macomber's stone, far from her slate headstone.

"SACRED / to the memory of / RACHEL. / wife of Job Townsend / who died / July 9, 1787 in / her 29 year." is carved on a second stone. The first line is carved along an arch. This headstone is very weathered, and is lying face up on the ground. It is located to the right of her slate headstone.

"R. T." This footstone is lying face up behind the second stone.

Townsend, Silas   "SILAS TOWNSEND / died March 8. 1833. / in the 79. year / of his age"

"S. T." is inscribed on the footstone. It appears his footstone and that of Gideon Coggeshall were switched. Gideon's headstone is two stones to the right.

Tucker, Abigail   "In memory of / ABIGAIL TUCKER / who died / March 2. 1831 / ..." This stone is very weathered and hard to read. It is broken in half under the death year, and the top part is lying on its back, behind the remnant of the base. Her stone is not listed by Thatcher.

"A.T." is inscribed on the footstone.

Walker, Hattie E.   *"Hattie E. / dau. of / Henry & Hannah M. / Walker, / died June 24, 1864; / Aged 11 m's."*

"H. E. W." is inscribed on the footstone. The inscription is buried underground.

Walter, Annie B.   See Lorenzo Walter Monument entry.

Walter, H. Maria   See Lorenzo Walter Monument entry.

"H. M. W." This flat, ground level footstone is located in front of the monument, on the right. Lakeville Vital Records list her first name as Hannah.

Walter, Lorenzo N. Monument   *"WALTER"* is carved in relief on the front of this monument. *"LORENZO N. WALTER 1859 – 1926 / HIS WIVES / H. MARIA 1863 – 1899 / ANNIE B.   1870 – 1905 / LORENZO N. WALTER JR.   1883 – 1902"* is inscribed on the back. Three markers are present at this gravesite: a *"Brockton Fire Dept."* marker and flag, a *"Brockton Fire Dept. in Memoriam"* marker and flag, and a Knights of Pythias marker.

Walter, Lorenzo N., Jr.   See Lorenzo Walter Monument entry.

"L. N. W. JR." This flat, ground level footstone is located behind the monument, on the left.

Ward, Mary W.   *"MARY W. / WIFE OF / C. T. WARD, / & DAU. OF / SAM. & SARAH W. / NELSON, / AUG. 30, 1818. / APR. 22, 1867."*

Washburn, Abbie D.   See Silas D. Pickens Monument entry.

"ABBIE" is inscribed on this flat, ground level footstone. It is located directly behind the monument, on the left.

Westgate, Eunice   *"In memory of / Mrs. Eunice / wife of / Mr. Jonathan Westgate / who died / June 5, 1812 / in her 42 year."* A willow is carved at the top. Both *2*s on this slate stone look like a 9 with a tail. Thatcher lists her death year as 1819. *Middleborough, Massachusetts Vital Records,* Vol. 1, p. 17 lists her death year as 1812.

"Mrs. E. Westgate" is inscribed on the slate footstone.

White, Benjamin   *"BENJAMIN WHITE / Died / July 5, 1881. / Aged 82 yrs. 11 mos. & 22 days."* The first line is carved along an arch.

"B. W." is inscribed on the footstone.

White, Caroline   *"CAROLINE STOCKBRIDGE / Wife of / Benjamin White. / Died Feb. 13, 1896. / Aged 83 yrs. 5 mos."* The first line is carved along an arch.

"C. S. W." is inscribed on the footstone.

White, Elizabeth P.   *"ERECTED / IN MEMORY OF / Mrs. ELIZABETH P. / wife of / Benjamin White / & daughter of / Dea. Abiel Nelson. / who died / Nov. 11, 1831. / in* *the 27. year / of her age."* The third line is carved in relief.

Whitney, Charles C. Monument *"WHITNEY"* is inscribed on the front of this monument. There are leaves carved in the upper corners. *"1895 CHARLES C. 1959 / HIS WIFE / 1899 MYRTLE B. 1977 / 1920 EDNA T. 1926"* is inscribed on the left side of the back. *"1867 EDWARD G. 1934 / HIS WIFE / 1869 ESTHER J. 1936 / 1894 EDWARD T. 1969 / HIS WIFE / 1899 LILLIAN G. 1993"* is inscribed on the right side. *"BARRE / GUILD"* is inscribed in the lower left rear corner. A Barnicoat Monuments metal tag is present.
"CHARLES C. WHITNEY / 1895 – 1959" is inscribed on this flat, ground level stone. It is located in front of the monument, on the far left side.

Whitney, Edna T. See Charles C. Whitney Monument entry.
"EDNA T. WHITNEY / 1920 – 1926" is inscribed on this flat, ground level stone. It is located in front of the monument, on the far left.

Whitney, Edward G. See Charles C. Whitney Monument entry.
"EDWARD G. WHITNEY / 1867 – 1934" is inscribed on this flat, ground level stone. It is located directly in front of the monument, on the left.

Whitney, Edward T. See Charles C. Whitney Monument entry.
"EDWARD T. WHITNEY M.D. / 1894 – 1969" is inscribed on this flat, ground level stone. It is located directly in front of the monument, on the right.
"EDWARD T. WHITNEY / MASSACHUSETTS / PFC US ARMY / WORLD WAR I / FEB 25 1894 – DEC 16 1969" A circled cross is carved above the inscriptions on this flat, ground level stone. This second stone is located to the immediate right of the monument.

Whitney, Esther J. See Charles C. Whitney Monument entry.
"ESTHER J. WHITNEY / 1869 – 1936" is inscribed on this flat, ground level stone. It is located in front of the monument, on the left.

Whitney, Lillian G. See Charles C. Whitney Monument entry.
"LILLIAN G. WHITNEY / 1899 – 1993" is inscribed on this flat, ground level stone. It is located in front of the monument, on the right.

Whitney, Myrtle B. See Charles C. Whitney Monument entry.
"MYRTLE B. WHITNEY / 1899 – 1977" is inscribed on this flat, ground level stone. It is located in front of the monument, on the far left.

Whittaker, Albert Monument *"WHITTAKER / ALBERT / DEC. 29, 1890 – JULY 4, 1975 / HIS WIFE / ETHEL WRIGHT / JULY 29, 1894 – OCT. 1, 1978"*

Whittaker, Ethel Wright See Albert Whittaker Monument entry.

Williams, Betsey S. See Elisha A. Williams Monument entry.

Williams, Elijah *"In / memory of / Mr. ELIJAH WILLIAMS, / who died / July 13. 1818 / in his 74. / year. / Adieu, my friends, a long and sad farewell,*
A scene more solemn than the passing bell,
I hoped with God in glory I should bloom,
Where sorrow, sickness, death can never come,

Consoleing thought! dear partner, dry your tears,
Your friend has gone beyond your anxious fears,
Weep not for me, prepare without delay,
To meet that debt you all must shortly pay."

An urn and willow carving is at the top of this slate stone. Curved designs are carved around the first seven lines, along the sides and below the poem. Note the spelling of *Consoleing* in the poem. A George Thompson swirl is present above the poem. A vertical crack the length of the stone has been successfully repaired. *"Mr / E W / 1818"* is inscribed on the slate footstone.

Williams, Elisha Monument   *"WILLIAMS"* is carved in relief on the top slanted surface of this large monument. *"ELISHA WILLIAMS, / APR. 10, 1837 – MAR. 19, 1900. / BETSEY S. HIS WIFE / JULY 12, 1845 – NOV. 19, 1909."* An oak branch is carved in the top left corner, and ivy leaves are carved in the top right corner.

Williams, Elisha H.   See Narcissus Williams Monument entry.
"FATHER" is carved in relief on the top curved surface of this small stone. *"E. H. W."* is inscribed on the front. It is located in front of the obelisk, on the left.

Williams, Miranda A.   See Narcissus Williams Monument entry.
"MIRANDA" is carved in relief on the top curved surface of this small stone. *"M. A. W."* is inscribed on the front. It is located in front of the obelisk, on the far right.

Williams, Narcissus Obelisk   *"NARCISSUS / Son of / Elisha H. / & Patience / Williams. / and a member / of Co. C. 4th Reg. / Mass. Vol. died / at Brashear City, / La. June 11, 1863; / Aged 29 years / 1 mo. & 28 d's.*
I say to my Mother, and those I hold dear
As fondly my memory they hath _____
Although to the cause, of my Country, I fell
That Death had no teary farewell all was well."
is inscribed on the front surface of this tall, textured obelisk. The first line is carved in relief along an arch. It is weathered, making the poem very difficult to read. *"ELISHA H. / WILLIAMS, / Born / Oct 9, 1806; / Died / Nov. 22, 1895."* is inscribed on the left side. The first two lines on this side are carved in relief. *"PATIENCE, / wife of / Elisha H. / Williams, / Born / Sept. 8, 1795; / Died / Dec. 31, 1874."* is inscribed on the right side. The first line is carved in relief. *"MIRANDA A. / WILLIAMS, / May 10, 1827, / Jan 5, 1902."* is inscribed on the back. A *"GAR 8 116"* marker, a veteran's marker and two flags are present.

Williams, Patience   See Narcissus Williams Monument entry.
"MOTHER" is carved in relief on the top curved surface of this small stone. *"P. B. W."* is carved on the front. It is located in front of the obelisk, on the right.

Williams, Sarah   *"SARAH, / wife of Elijah / WILLIAMS, / died Feb. 6, 1842, / in her 84, year."* There is a simple urn and willow carving at the top of this brown, rectangular, slate stone.
"S. W." is inscribed on this slate footstone. It is different in material and shape than the headstone.

Winslow, Deborah   *"SACRED / to the memory of / DEBORAH, / wife of / ASA*

WINSLOW: / who died / Dec. 23, 1849, in / her 88 year." The third line is carved in relief on this textured stone.

"D. W." is inscribed on the footstone.

Winslow, Hannah   *"In Memory of / MRS. HANNAH / Wife of / Mr. Asa* [T.] *Winslow. / Who died June 29, 1824 / Æt. 26. /*

> *In all the bloom of life I fell,*
> *Death's fatal arrow pierce my heart,*
> *My husband dear & tender babe,*
> *I with them both was call'd to part."*

A sculptured urn is carved at the top. The second line is carved in outline. Her husband is buried in Mullein Hill Cemetery.

"H. W. / 1824" is inscribed on the footstone.

Winslow, Henry P.   *"HENRY P. / Son of Asa & / Deborah Winslow. / died 9 May 1823. / Æt. 20. / ..."* An urn and willow are carved at the top of this slate stone and curved designs are carved down the sides. This stone was broken below the inscription, and reburied in cement. Parts of words are present just above the cement base.

"H. P. W. / 1823" is inscribed on the slate footstone.

Additional Notes:

Thatcher also lists the following, but no stones were found for these people.

"Briggs, Anne S. dau. of Lewis & Betsey July 8, 1807 2nd mo.
Briggs, Sumner – son of Lewis & Betsey July 10, 1807, 10th yr.
Cole, Judith, dau. of Andrew & Abigail Dec. 13, 1786, 7 mos., 19 days.
Cummings, Seth, died May 23 rd, 1844, age 39 years.
Cummings, Two infant Children of Seth & Almeda, Sept. 26th, 1839, Jan. 28, 1843.
Hersey, Elizabeth, dau. of J. S. & Mary A. Oct. 31, 1848 age 15 mos.
Hersey, Amelia, dau. of J. S. & Mary A. Sept. 2, 1849 age 15 weeks.
Sampson, Elisha, son of Abiel M. & Bathsheba, Mar. 1833, 26 Days."

Carving on the Sally Nelson headstone

Pond Cemetery Map Index

Alphabetical:

Alden, Humphrey, Capt. (~1762-1844) – 338

Alden, Mary (~1762-1843) – 339

Allen, Parmeliahall (1799-1800) – 159

Bates, Sibel (~1762-1810) – 256

Belliveau, William (1931-1997) – 321

Benton, George S. (1856-1859) – 354

Benton, Georgie A. 1871-1874) – 353

Bly, John (~1760-1808) – 250

Bly, Margaret (~1757-1839) – 251

Blye, John (~1725-1790) – 252

Booth, Nancy (~1800-1844) – 292

Briggs, Abigail (~1765-1810) – 258, 259

Briggs, Ebenezer (1805-1808) – 194

Briggs, Ebenezer, Dea. (~1732-1808) – 105

Briggs, Ebenezer, Tomb (1839) – 298

Briggs, Elezebath (1763-1772) – 110

Briggs, Elisabeth (~1734-1813) – 106

Briggs, Eliza (1799-1885) – 316

Briggs, Elizabeth K. (1772-1858) – 309

Briggs, Esther (~1767-1849) – 259

Briggs, Hannah (1803) – 195

Briggs, James F. (1812-1860) – 314

Briggs, Lemuel (1764-1849) – 259

Briggs, Melissa (1846-1923) – 311

Briggs, Peltiah (1801-1890) – 313

Briggs, Philena (1811-1848) – 312

Briggs, Rounsevill (1800-1804) – 108

Briggs, Sarah (~1698-1794) – 103

Briggs, Sarah (~1739-1799) – 255

Briggs, Silas, Capt. (1770-1858) – 308

Briggs, Stephen (1769-1771) – 109

Briggs, Stephen (~1794-1810) – 107

Briggs, William (1816-1867) – 315

Brown, Alvin M. (1862-1914) – 327

Brown, Ralph A. (1890-1901) – 326

Chipman, Josiah (~1839-1848) – 285

Clark, Abner (1851-1852) – 283

Clark, Deliverance (~1728-1784) – 130

Clark, Ebenr. (~1810-1848) – 285

Clark, Ezra (~1721-1789) – 129

Clark, Ezra (~1784-1808) – 272

Clark, Ezra (1807-1808) – 275

Clark, Ezra, Lt. (~1749-1793) – 271

Clark, Henry (~1795-1819) – 277

Clark, Horatio, Capt. (~1799-1829) – 277

Clark, Joanna (~1762-1784) – 131

Clark, Joanna (~1786-1808) – 284

Clark, Job P. (1806-1852) – 281

Clark, Lydia (~1780-1813) – 269

Clark, Mary (~1748-1792) – 273

Clark, Roger (~1759-1812) – 157

Clark, Xenophon (~1802-1829) – 280

Clarke, Abner, Esq. (~1765-1830) – 276

Clarke, Alice (no dates) – 143, 158

Clarke, Almira (~1804-1834) – 274

Clarke, James (no dates) – 158

Clarke, James W. (no dates) – 144, 158

Clarke, Mary (~1771-1847) – 278

Clarke, Mary (1814) – 279

Clarke, Richard (~1796-1830) – 282

Clarke, Susan T. (no dates) – 142, 158

Coggeshall, Gideon (~1778-1849) – 288

Cole, Abigail (~1743-1830) – 191

Cole, Albert L. (1818-1866) – 307

Cole, Andrew (~1756-1841) – 192

Cole, Anna Eliza (~1845-1913) – 210

Cole, Charles G. (1824-1883) – 306

Cole, Isaiah (~1732-1810) – 175

Cole, James (~1757-1779) – 176

Cole, Lorenzo (1831-1832) – 303

Cole, Martha F. (1853-1857) – 319

Cole, Mary (~1767-1840) – 160, 190

Cole, Mary (~1794-1854) – 305

Cole, Mical (~1762-1797) –137

Cole, Nancy (~1761-1828) – 174

Cole, Samuel (1793-1872) – 304

Crane, Carrie I. (1859-1947) – 11, 18

Crowell, Elizabeth F. (1816-1894) – 372

Cudworth, Arthur (1889-1909) – 377, 379

Cudworth, Horace A. (1865-1867) – 367, 377

Cudworth, Jesse R. (1863-1936) – 377, 378

Cudworth, John (1839-1921) – 377, 381

Cudworth, Sarah C. (1843-1909) – 377, 380

Cundell, Benjamin (no dates) – 310

Cushing, Lydia (~1736-1790) – 170

Davis, Timothy K. (1850-____) – 210

DeMaranville, Eliza J. (1849-1919) – 363

DeMaranville, Jennie (1879-1880) – 364

DeMaranville, John (1855-1857) – 325

DeMaranville, Josiah (1821-1911) – 325

DeMaranville, Josiah (1843-1888) – 362

DeMaranville, Louisa (1825-1916) – 325

DeMaranville, Nellie F. (1869-1925) – 366

DeMaranville, Ruby (1874) – 365

DeMoranville, Allon S. (1914) – 211

DeMoranville, Charles H. (1898-1914) – 211

DeMoranville, Eunice (1901) – 211

DeMoranville, Eunice W. (1870-1936) – 211

DeMoranville, Herbert M. (1876-1949) – 211

DeMoranville, Morrell (1907) – 211

Downing, Joseph (1785-1864) – 356

Downing, Sarah (1789-1881) – 357

Downs, Hattie W. (1879-1964) – 329

Finney, Jonathan (~1750-1822) – 299

Finney, Meribah (~1751-1843) – 300

Foster, Abigail (~1715-1783) – 206

Foster, Catharine (1794-1881) – 214

Foster, Charles (1801-1808) – 217

Foster, Jane (~1757-1820) – 216

Foster, Marcy (1768-1773) – 125

Foster, Mary (1789-1879) – 215

Foster, Nathaniel (1763-1772) – 126

Foster, Nathaniel (~1711-1793) – 205

Fuller, Hannah (1773-1803) – 228

Fuller, Samuel (1797-1843) – 260

Fuller, Ziba (~1764-1811) – 261

Gifford, Mary F. S. (1820-1904) – 335

Grant, Everett F. (1878-1972) – 149

Grant, Harriet P. (1884-1971) – 148

Gurney, Carrie B. (1892-1914) – 122

Hackett, Edith (no dates) – 158, 173

Hall, Arthur S., Sr. (1890-1966) – 118, 121

Hall, Carrie L. (1916-1988) – 119

Hall, Mildred A. (1894-1955) – 121

Hammond, Desire (~1758-1810) – 161

Hanson, Annie G. (1886-1938) – 146

Hanson, William G. (1875-1935) – 145

Harding, Hannh (1736-1787) – 177

Harvey, Desire (1768-1851) – 244

Harvey, Oliver (1768-1855) – 243

Haskell, Elisabeth (~1758-1784) – 156

Haskell, Seth (~1757-1793) – 155

Haskell, Thomas A., Lt. (~1788-1816) – 165

Haskins, Sarah (1813-1888) – 352

Hathaway, Benjamin S. (1783-1833) – 262

Hayes, Susanna (1846-1910) – 209

Hayes, Thomas (1842-1918) – 209

Henderson, Marjorie W. (1914-1998) – 324

Henderson, Robert (1907-1979) – 323, 324

Hinds, Bartlett (~1811-1826) – 40

Hinds, Catherine (1803-1828) – 28

Hinds, Edmund (1787-1828) – 28

Hinds, Ebenezer, Rev. (~1719-1812) – 26

Hinds, John (~1760-1830) – 28

Hinds, Kezia (1771-1774) – 37

Hinds, Leonard (~1782-1859) – 30

Hinds, Lucinda V. (1805-1885) – 32

Hinds, Lucy (~1795-1824) – 39

Hinds, Lydia (~1763-1780) – 36

Hinds, Lydia (~1735-1801) – 27

Hinds, Nancy (~1784-1868) – 31

Hinds, Olive (~1768-1845) – 29

Hinds, Richard (1777-1794) – 38

Holmes, Betsey E. (1852-1916) – 360

Holmes, William B. (1853-1909) – 359

Horr, Job (~1763-1854) – 111

Hoar, Phebe (~1762-1852) – 112

Horskins, Waitstill (____-1779) – 115

Hoskins, Hannah (~1721-1800) – 134

Hoskins, Nathan (~1717-1778) – 133

Howland, Keturah (~1761-1784) – 178

Ingraham, Sarah (~1787-1820) – 293

Ingraham, Timothy (~1780-1818) – 291

Jennings, Rex (1885-1894) – 207

Johnson, Betsey (~1831-1852) – 358

Kingman, Hosea (1806-1853) – 9

Kingman, Phebe (1806-1857) – 10

Loner, Hattie M. (1896-1897) – 238

Loner, Laura M. (1875-1876) – 239, 240

Loner, Lydia D. (1843-1912) – 239

Loner, Lydia W. (1871-1889) – 239

Loner, Mabel L. (1883-1890) – 239

Loner, William E. (1837-1888) – 239, 241

Macomber, Deborah (no dates) – 232

Macomber, Elisabeth (~1765-1784) – 230

Macomber, Elizabeth (~1727-1775) – 222

Macomber, Hannah (~1781-1827) – 229

Macomber, John Dea. (~1720-1774) – 221

Macomber, Joseph, Lt. (~1733-1800) – 219

Maccomber, Thankful (~1757-1779) – 231

Macomber, Thankful (~1739-1794) – 242

Manning, Arthur A. (1866-1927) – 189

Manning, Frederick W. (1903) – 189

Manning, Lillian I. (1883-1938) – 189

Manton, Alfred P. (1865-1944) – 123

Manton, Georgia A. (1872-1927) – 123

Marshall, Eva G. (1905-1998) – 150

Marshall, Russell B. (1904-1978) – 151

Maxim, James D. (~1867-1936) – 116

Maxim, Nellie (1864-1947) – 117

Miller, Sarah (1775-1808) – 270

Monroe, Bathsheba (1805-1845) – 361

Nelson Monument – 87

Nelson, Abiel Smith (1810-1811) – 76

Nelson, Abiel W. (1835-1913) – 46, 50
Nelson, Abiel, Dea. (~1778-1829) – 68
Nelson, Abigail (~1778-1844) – 65
Nelson, Abner, Lt. (~1755-1816) – 182
Nelson, Amos (~1719-1724) – 51
Nelson, Amos, Dea. (~1743-1795) – 180
Nelson, Anna (~1741-1828) – 59
Nelson, C. Eliot (1908-1983) – 84
Nelson, Caroline B. (1849-1894) – 81
Nelson, Charity (~1751-1787) – 183
Nelson, Charles (1799-1800) – 193
Nelson, Chloe (~1757-1795) – 166
Nelson, Clifton W. (1878-1959) – 89
Nelson, Cyrus (1793-1869) – 72
Nelson, Doris (1913-1993) – 85
Nelson, Ebenezer (~1722-1745) – 48
Nelson, Eliza (~1803-1830) – 74
Nelson, Elizabeth (~1715-1805) – 168
Nelson, Elizabeth P. (1836-1896) – 81
Nelson, Elizabeth P. (1846-1930) – 90
Nelson, Emma P. (1844-1881) – 92
Nelson, Emma P. (1899) – 95
Nelson, Eunice (1743-1783) – 181
Nelson, Ezra (~1774-1803) – 64
Nelson, Fatima B. (1808-1871) – 71
Nelson, Foxel (1716-1745) – 49
Nelson, Gladys B. (1908-1973) – 82
Nelson, Hannah (~1802-1822) – 73
Nelson, Hannah (~1750-1827) – 163
Nelson, Hiram (~1765-1838) – 52
Nelson, Hope (~1677-1782) – 45
Nelson, Hope (~1736-1820) – 55
Nelson, Horatio, Dea. (1800-1869) – 66
Nelson, Infant son (1807) – 75
Nelson, Irene (1906-1994) – 83
Nelson, Jeanie (1849-1893) – 46
Nelson, Job (~1770-1816) – 60
Nelson, Job P. (1806-1862) – 70
Nelson, John (~1703-1732) – 47
Nelson, John (~1772-1828) – 63
Nelson, John, Col. (~1738-1803) – 54
Nelson, Joshua (~1815-1831) – 162
Nelson, Judith (1768-1769) – 67
Nelson, Judith (1709-1792) – 57
Nelson, Judith (1769-1858) – 61
Nelson, Lillie T. (1873-1951) – 94
Nelson, Mary (1746-1772) – 179
Nelson, Mary E. (1878-1953) – 88
Nelson, Mary H. (~1809-1831) – 77
Nelson, Phebe (~1766-1844) – 62
Nelson, Polly (~1767-1838) – 53

Nelson, Richard T. (1947-1950) – 86
Nelson, Sally (~1783-1835) – 154
Nelson, Samuel (~1779-1831) – 153
Nelson, Sarah (~1779-1838) – 69
Nelson, Sidney P. (1906-1997) – 83
Nelson, Sidney T. (1845-1919) – 91
Nelson, Thomas (1675-1755) – 44
Nelson, Thomas (~1739-1819) – 58
Nelson, Thomas (1900-1996) – 85
Nelson, Thomas S. (1874-1954) – 93
Nelson, Thomas, Lt. (1710-1768) – 56
Nelson, William (1714-1776) – 167
Nelson, William, Rev. (~1742-1806) – 164
Norris, D. Evelyn (1911-____) – 321
Norris, James E. (1938-____) – 321
Packard, Infant girl (1792) – 233
Packard, Lydia B. (1788-1793) – 233
Parker, Abbie M. (1846-1921) – 210
Parkhurst, Helen S. (1889-1963) – 127
Parkhurst, James S. (1850-1938) – 127
Peirce, Annie J. (1855-1931) – 208
Peirce, Ebenezer (~1705-1796) – 100
Peirce, Elizabeth (~1751-1846) – 184
Peirce, Frank S. (1859-1902) – 208
Peirce, Henry (~1778-1826) – 43
Peirce, Henry, Capt. (~1744-1791) – 34
Peirce, Mary (~1712-1768) – 101
Peirce, Rhoda (~1757-1788) – 132
Peirce, Sarah (~1732-1774) – 102
Peirce, Soloma (~1748-1784) – 35
Perkins, Mildred (1921-1986) – 120
Phinney, James S. (~1783-1841) – 317
Phinney, Joanna (~1786-1852) – 318
Phinney, Joseph (~1717-1793) – 294
Phinney, Lucinda (~1790-1872) – 302
Phinney, Lydia (~1755-1835) – 301
Phinney, Phebe (~1730-1796) – 295
Pickens, Abigail (~1789-1873) – 249
Pickens, Albert G. (1818-1900) – 246
Pickens, Andrew (~1717-1795) – 224
Pickens, Arthur L. (1857-1941) – 11, 17
Pickens, Elisabeth (~1714-1795) – 225
Pickens, Matilda (~1762-1839) – 235
Pickens, Myra S. (1831-1870) – 11, 21
Pickens, Samuel (~1752-1830) – 234
Pickens, Silas D. (1830-1887) – 11, 20
Pickens, Stephen B. (~1784-1825) – 248
Pickens, Stephen B. (~1809-1849) – 247
Pittsley, Priscilla (~1816-1891) – 355
Plissey, C. Augustus (1882-1968) – 147
Pratt, Sally (~1790-1842) – 257

Pratt, Sarah (~1784-1849) – 254
Ramsdell, Minnie E. F. (1875-1888) – 213
Richardson, Anna G. (1861-1941) – 253
Richardson, Oscar (1860-1940) – 253
Roberts, Infant (1861) – 350
Roberts, Infant (1865) – 351
Roberts, Samuel (____-1845) – 349
Rogers, Judith (~1792-1845) – 104
Russell, John (~1735-1776) – 128
Sampson, Abigail D. (1809-1881) – 13
Sampson, Anna (1788-1863) – 297
Sampson, Betsey (~1777-1850) – 15
Sampson, Betsey (1851-1862) – 25
Sampson, Charles H. (1813-1867) – 22
Sampson, Ebenezer D. (~1801-1880) – 5
Sampson, Ebenezer D., Jr. (~1838-1866) – 8
Sampson, Elias (~1771-1847) – 14
Sampson, Elias (~1833-1869) – 7
Sampson, Elias, Jr. (1799-1879) – 3
Sampson, Eliza (1804-1870) – 16
Sampson, Eliza C. (~1805-1896) – 6
Sampson, Louesa B. (1813-1874) – 23
Sampson, Maria (1802-1837) – 4
Sampson, Maria J. (~1825-1880) – 1
Sampson, Sarah R. (1838-1899) – 24
Sampson, Uriah (1806-1880) – 12
Sampson, Wm. Baylies (1837) – 4
Sampson, Zilpha B. (1806-1881) – 2
Sanderson, Lurana (~1778-1851) – 218
Sheafe, Abby E. (1878-1963) – 374, 377
Shockley, Almy J. (1832-1871) – 345
Shockley, Andrew (1834-1911) – 96
Shockley, Averic T. (1840-1926) – 334
Shockley, Benjamin F. (~1844-1900) – 336
Shockley, Charles (1830-1900) – 340, 344
Shockley, Charles F. (1859-1882) – 344, 348
Shockley, Emma (1862-1943) – 96, 98
Shockley, Fredrick (1861-1942) – 96, 97
Shockley, Harriett M. (1822-1887) – 342, 344
Shockley, Hattie H. (1859-1872) – 344, 346
Shockley, John (~1822-1895) – 337
Shockley, Joseph (~1787-1863) – 341
Shockley, Mary or Minnie G. (1863-1880) – 344, 347
Shockley, Phebe J. (1836-1914) – 96
Shockley, Sally Alden (~1796-1859) – 343
Shockley, Wm. Elmer (1866-1939) – 320
Smith, Abigail (~1757-1810) – 227
Smith, Abigail (1785-1789) – 236
Smith, Daniel, Capt. (1779-1829) – 237

Smith, George E. (1853-1856) – 187
Smith, John, Capt. (~1757-1809) – 226
Smith, Josiah, Lt. (~1730-1798) – 124
Smith, Susan (1782-1868) – 237
Spooner, Alden (1818-1819) – 373
Spooner, Eleanor (1732-1786) – 223
Spooner, Elizabeth (1842-1885) – 264, 265
Spooner, Geo. H. (1841-1903) – 263, 265
Spooner, Phebe (~1819-1867) – 376
Spooner, Thomas (~1819-1898) – 375
Sullivan, Catherine M. (~1842-1915) – 245
Tallman, Julius C. (1900-1902) – 368
Thew Monument (no dates) – 212
Thrasher, Cyrus (1792-1880) – 239
Thrasher, Hannah (1807-1881) – 239
Tinkham, Horatio (1818-1893) – 113
Tinkham, J. Elizabeth (1824-1870) – 114
Tobey, Job Townsend (1811-1892) – 370
Tobey, Maria (1818-1876) – 371
Tobey, Martha E. (1815-1820) – 185
Tobey, Rachel (1787-1871) – 369
Townsend, Abiel (~1779-1797) – 169
Townsend, Abiel, Lt. (~1740-1775) – 135
Townsend, Anna (1815-1870) – 171
Townsend, Daniel B. (1833-1835) – 186
Townsend, Hope (~1761-1833) – 287
Townsend, Job (~1748-1842) – 140
Townsend, John (~1716-1790) – 135
Townsend, John (1810-1905) – 172
Townsend, Mary (~1723-1790) – 136
Townsend, Peace (~1759-1844) – 141
Townsend, Rachel (~1759-1787) – 138, 139, 220
Townsend, Silas (~1754-1833) – 286
Tucker, Abigail (____-1831) – 296
Walker, Hattie E. (1863-1864) – 188
Walter, Annie B. (1870-1905) – 267
Walter, H. Maria (1863-1899) – 267, 268
Walter, Lorenzo N. (1859-1926) – 266, 267
Walter, Lorenzo N., Jr. (1883-1902) – 267
Ward, Mary W. (1818-1867) – 152
Washburn, Abbie D. (1861-1947) – 11, 19
Westgate, Eunice (~1771-1812) – 99
White, Benjamin (1798-1881) – 79
White, Caroline (1812-1896) – 80
White, Elizabeth P. (~1805-1831) – 78
Whitney, Charles C. (1895-1959) – 198, 203
Whitney, Edna T. (1920-1926) – 196, 203
Whitney, Edward G. (1867-1934) – 200, 203
Whitney, Edward T. (1894-1969) – 201, 203, 204

By Location:

70 – Nelson, Job P. (1806-1862)
71 – Nelson, Fatima B. (1808-1871)
72 – Nelson, Cyrus (1793-1869)
73 – Nelson, Hannah (~1802-1822)
74 – Nelson, Eliza (~1803-1830)
75 – Nelson, Infant son (1807)
76 – Nelson, Abiel Smith (1810-1811)
77 – Nelson, Mary H. (~1809-1831)
78 – White, Elizabeth P. (~1805-1831)
79 – White, Benjamin (1798-1881)
80 – White, Caroline (1812-1896)
81 – Nelson, Elizabeth P. (1836-1896)
     Nelson, Caroline B. (1849-1894)
82 – Nelson, Gladys B. (1908-1973)
83 – Nelson, Sidney P. (1906-1997)
     Nelson, Irene (1906-1994)
84 – Nelson, C. Eliot (1908-1983)
85 – Nelson, Thomas (1900-1996)
     Nelson, Doris (1913-1993)
86 – Nelson, Richard T. (1947-1950)
87 – Nelson Monument (no dates)
88 – Nelson, Mary E. (1878-1953)
89 – Nelson, Clifton W. (1878-1959)
90 – Nelson, Elizabeth P. (1846-1930)
91 – Nelson, Sidney T. (1845-1919)
92 – Nelson, Emma P. (1844-1881)
93 – Nelson, Thomas S. (1874-1954)
94 – Nelson, Lillie T. (1873-1951)
95 – Nelson, Emma P. (1899)
96 – Shockley, Andrew (1834-1911)
     Shockley, Phebe J. (1836-1914)
     Shockley, Fredrick (1861-1942)
     Shockley, Emma (1862-1943)
97 – Shockley, Fredrick (1861-1942)
98 – Shockley, Emma (1862-1943)
99 – Westgate, Eunice (~1771-1812)
100 – Peirce, Ebenezer (~1705-1796)
101 – Peirce, Mary (~1712-1768)
102 – Peirce, Sarah (~1732-1774)
103 – Briggs, Sarah (~1698-1794)
104 – Rogers, Judith (~1792-1845)
105 – Briggs, Ebenezer, Dea. (~1732-1808)
106 – Briggs, Elisabeth (~1734-1813)
107 – Briggs, Stephen (~1794-1810)
108 – Briggs, Rounsevill (1800-1804)
109 – Briggs, Stephen (1769-1771)
110 – Briggs, Elezebath (1763-1772)
111 – Horr, Job (~1763-1854)
112 – Hoar, Phebe (~1762-1852)
113 – Tinkham, Horatio (1818-1893)
114 – Tinkham, J. Elizabeth (1824-1870)

115 – Horskins, Waitstill (____-1779)
116 – Maxim, James D. (~1867-1936)
117 – Maxim, Nellie (1864-1947)
118 – Hall, Arthur S., Sr. (1890-1966)
119 – Hall, Carrie L. (1916-1988)
120 – Perkins, Mildred (1921-1986)
121 – Hall, Arthur S., Sr. (1890-1966)
     Hall, Mildred A. (1894-1955)
122 – Gurney, Carrie B. (1892-1914)
123 – Manton, Alfred P. (1865-1944)
     Manton, Georgia A. (1872-1927)
124 – Smith, Josiah, Lt. (~1730-1798)
125 – Foster, Marcy (1768-1773)
126 – Foster, Nathaniel (1763-1772)
127 – Parkhurst, Helen S. (1889-1963)
     Parkhurst, James S. (1850-1938)
128 – Russell, John (~1735-1776)
129 – Clark, Ezra (~1721-1789)
130 – Clark, Deliverance (~1728-1784)
131 – Clark, Joanna (~1762-1784)
132 – Peirce, Rhoda (~1757-1788)
133 – Hoskins, Nathan (~1717-1778)
134 – Hoskins, Hannah (~1721-1800)
135 – Townsend, John (~1716-1790)
     Townsend, Abiel, Lt. (~1740-1775)
136 – Townsend, Mary (~1723-1790)
137 – Cole, Mical (~1762-1797)
138 – Townsend, Rachel (~1759-1787)
139 – Townsend, Rachel (~1759-1787)
140 – Townsend, Job (~1748-1842)
141 – Townsend, Peace (~1759-1844)
142 – Clarke, Susan T. (no dates)
143 – Clarke, Alice (no dates)
144 – Clarke, James W. (no dates)
145 – Hanson, William G. (1875-1935)
146 – Hanson, Annie G. (1886-1938)
147 – Plissey, C. Augustus (1882-1968)
148 – Grant, Harriet P. (1884-1971)
149 – Grant, Everett F. (1878-1972)
150 – Marshall, Eva G. (1905-1998)
151 – Marshall, Russell B. (1904-1978)
152 – Ward, Mary W. (1818-1867)
153 – Nelson, Samuel (~1779-1831)
154 – Nelson, Sally (~1783-1835)
155 – Haskell, Seth (~1757-1793)
156 – Haskell, Elisabeth (~1758-1784)
157 – Clark, Roger (~1759-1812)
158 – Clarke, James (no dates)
     Clarke, Susan T. (no dates)
     Clarke, Alice (no dates)
     Clarke, James W. (no dates)

Hackett, Edith (no dates)
159 – Allen, Parmeliahall (1799-1800)
160 – Cole, Mary (~1767-1840)
161 – Hammond, Desire (~1758-1810)
162 – Nelson, Joshua (~1815-1831)
163 – Nelson, Hannah (~1750-1827)
164 – Nelson, William, Rev. (~1742-1806)
165 – Haskell, Thomas A., Lt. (~1788-1816)
166 – Nelson, Chloe (~1757-1795)
167 – Nelson, William (1714-1776)
168 – Nelson, Elizabeth (~1715-1805)
169 – Townsend, Abiel (~1779-1797)
170 – Cushing, Lydia (~1736-1790)
171 – Townsend, Anna (1815-1870)
172 – Townsend, John (1810-1905)
173 – Hackett, Edith (no dates)
174 – Cole, Nancy (~1761-1828)
175 – Cole, Isaiah (~1732-1810)
176 – Cole, James (~1757-1779)
177 – Harding, Hannh (1736-1787)
178 – Howland, Keturah (~1761-1784)
179 – Nelson, Mary (1746-1772)
180 – Nelson, Amos (~1743-1795)
181 – Nelson, Eunice (1743-1783)
182 – Nelson, Abner (~1755-1816)
183 – Nelson, Charity (~1751-1787)
184 – Peirce, Elizabeth (~1751-1846)
185 – Tobey, Martha E. (1815-1820)
186 – Townsend, Daniel B. (1833-1835)
187 – Smith, George E. (1853-1856)
188 – Walker, Hattie E. (1863-1864)
189 – Manning, Arthur A. (1866-1927)
    Manning, Lillian I. (1883-1938)
    Manning, Frederick W. (1903)
190 – Cole, Mary (~1767-1840)
191 – Cole, Abigail (~1743-1830)
192 – Cole, Andrew (~1756-1841)
193 – Nelson, Charles (1799-1800)
194 – Briggs, Ebenezer (1805-1808)
195 – Briggs, Hannah (1803-1803)
196 – Whitney, Edna T. (1920-1926)
197 – Whitney, Myrtle B. (1899-1977)
198 – Whitney, Charles C. (1895-1959)
199 – Whitney, Esther J. (1869-1936)
200 – Whitney, Edward G. (1867-1934)
201 – Whitney, Edward T. (1894-1969)
202 – Whitney, Lillian G. (1899-1993)
203 – Whitney, Charles C. (1895-1959)
    Whitney, Myrtle B. (1899-1977)
    Whitney, Edna T. (1920-1926)
    Whitney, Edward G. (1867-1934)

    Whitney, Esther J. (1869-1936)
    Whitney, Edward T. (1894-1969)
    Whitney, Lillian G. (1899-1993)
204 – Whitney, Edward T. (1894-1969)
205 – Foster, Nathaniel (~1711-1793)
206 – Foster, Abigail (~1715-1783)
207 – Jennings, Rex (1885-1894)
208 – Peirce, Frank S. (1859-1902)
    Peirce, Annie J. (1855-1931)
209 – Hayes, Thomas (1842-1918)
    Hayes, Susanna (1846-1910)
210 – Cole, Anna Eliza (~1845-1913)
    Parker, Abbie M. (1846-1921)
    Davis, Timothy K. (1850-____)
211 – DeMoranville, Herbert M. (1876-1949)
    DeMoranville, Eunice W. (1870-1936)
    DeMoranville, Charles H. (1898-1914)
    DeMoranville, Eunice (1901)
    DeMoranville, Morrell (1907)
    DeMoranville, Allon S. (1914)
212 – Thew Monument
213 – Ramsdell, Minnie E. F. (1875-1888)
214 – Foster, Catharine (1794-1881)
215 – Foster, Mary (1789-1879)
216 – Foster, Jane (~1757-1820)
217 – Foster, Charles (1801-1808)
218 – Sanderson, Lurana (~1778-1851)
219 – Macomber, Joseph, Lt. (~1733-1800)
220 – Townsend, Rachel, (~1759-1787)
221 – Macomber, John, Dea. (~1720-1774)
222 – Maccomber, Elizabeth (~1727-1775)
223 – Spooner, Eleanor (1732-1786)
224 – Pickens, Andrew (~1717-1795)
225 – Pickens, Elisabeth (~1714-1795)
226 – Smith, John, Capt. (~1757-1809)
227 – Smith, Abigail (~1757-1810)
228 – Fuller, Hannah (1773-1803)
229 – Macomber, Hannah (~1781-1827)
230 – Macomber, Elisabeth (~1765-1784)
231 – Macomber, Thankful (~1757-1779)
232 – Macomber, Deborah (no dates)
233 – Packard, Lydia B. (1788-1793)
    Packard, Infant girl (1792)
234 – Pickens, Samuel (~1752-1830)
235 – Pickens, Matilda (~1762-1839)
236 – Smith, Abigail (1785-1789)
237 – Smith, Daniel, Capt. (1779-1829)
    Smith, Susan (1782-1868)
238 – Loner, Hattie M. (1896-1897)
239 – Thrasher, Cyrus (1792-1880)

Thrasher, Hannah (1807-1881)
Loner, William E. (1837-1888)
Loner, Lydia D. (1843-1912)
Loner, Mabel L. (1883-1890)
Loner, Laura M. (1875-1876)
Loner, Lydia W. (1871-1889)
240 – Loner, Laura M. (1875-1876)
241 – Loner, William E. (1837-1888)
242 – Macomber, Thankful (~1739-1794)
243 – Harvey, Oliver (1768-1855)
244 – Harvey, Desire (1768-1851)
245 – Sullivan, Catherine M. (~1842-1915)
246 – Pickens, Albert G. (1818-1900)
247 – Pickens, Stephen B. (~1809-1849)
248 – Pickens, Stephen B. (~1784-1825)
249 – Pickens, Abigail (~1789-1873)
250 – Bly, John (~1760-1808)
251 – Bly, Margaret (~1757-1839)
252 – Blye, John (~1725-1790)
253 – Richardson, Oscar (1860-1940)
Richardson, Anna G. (1861-1941)
254 – Pratt, Sarah (~1784-1849)
255 – Briggs, Sarah (~1739-1799)
256 – Bates, Sibel (~1762-1810)
257 – Pratt, Sally (~1790-1842)
258 – Briggs, Abigail (~1765-1810)
259 – Briggs, Lemuel (1764-1849)
Briggs, Esther (~1767-1849)
Briggs, Abigail (~1765-1810)
260 – Fuller, Samuel (1797-1843)
261 – Fuller, Ziba (~1764-1811)
262 – Hathaway, Benjamin S. (1783-1833)
263 – Spooner, Geo. H. (1841-1903)
264 – Spooner, Elizabeth S. (1842-1885)
265 – Spooner, Geo. H. (1841-1903)
Spooner, Elizabeth S. (1842-1885)
266 – Walter, Lorenzo N., Jr. (1859-1926)
267 – Walter, Lorenzo N. (1859-1926)
Walter, H. Maria (1863-1899)
Walter, Annie B. (1870-1905)
Walter, Lorenzo N., Jr. (1883-1902)
268 – Walter, H. Maria (1863-1899)
269 – Clark, Lydia (~1780-1813)
270 – Miller, Sarah (1775-1808)
271 – Clark, Ezra, Lt. (~1749-1793)
272 – Clark, Ezra (~1784-1808)
273 – Clark, Mary (~1748-1792)
274 – Clarke, Almira (~1804-1834)
275 – Clark, Ezra (1807-1808)
276 – Clarke, Abner, Esq. (~1765-1830)
277 – Clark, Horatio G., Capt. (~1799-1829)

Clark, Henry (~1795-1819)
278 – Clarke, Mary (~1771-1847)
279 – Clarke, Mary (1814)
280 – Clark, Xenophon (~1802-1829)
281 – Clark, Job P. (1806-1852)
282 – Clarke, Richard (~1796-1830)
283 – Clark, Abner (1851-1852)
284 – Clark, Joanna (~1786-1808)
285 – Clark, Ebenr. (~1810-1848)
Chipman, Josiah (~1839-1848)
286 – Townsend, Silas (~1754-1833)
287 – Townsend, Hope (~1761-1833)
288 – Coggeshall, Gideon (~1778-1849)
289 – Williams, Elijah (~1745-1818)
290 – Williams, Sarah (~1759-1842)
291 – Ingraham, Timothy (~1780-1818)
292 – Booth, Nancy (~1800-1844)
293 – Ingraham, Sarah (~1787-1820)
294 – Phinney, Joseph (~1717-1793)
295 – Phinney, Phebe (~1730-1796)
296 – Tucker, Abigail (____-1831)
297 – Sampson, Anna (1788-1863)
298 – Briggs, Ebenezer Tomb (1839)
299 – Finney, Jonathan (~1750-1822)
300 – Finney, Meribah (~1751-1843)
301 – Phinney, Lydia (~1755-1835)
302 – Phinney, Lucinda (~1790-1872)
303 – Cole, Lorenzo (1831-1832)
304 – Cole, Samuel (1793-1872)
305 – Cole, Mary (~1794-1854)
306 – Cole, Charles G. (1824-1883)
307 – Cole, Albert L. (1818-1866)
308 – Briggs, Silas, Capt. (1770-1858)
309 – Briggs, Elizabeth K. (1772-1858)
310 – Cundell, Benjamin (no dates)
311 – Briggs, Melissa (1846-1923)
312 – Briggs, Philena (1811-1848)
313 – Briggs, Peltiah (1801-1890)
314 – Briggs, James F. (1812-1860)
315 – Briggs, William (1816-1867)
316 – Briggs, Eliza (1799-1885)
317 – Phinney, James S. (~1783-1841)
318 – Phinney, Joanna (~1786-1852)
319 – Cole, Martha F. (1853-1857)
320 – Shockley, Wm. Elmer (1866-1939)
321 – Norris, D. Evelyn (1911-____)
Norris, James E. (1938-____)
Belliveau, William (1931-1997)
322 – Whittaker, Albert (1890-1975)
Whittaker, Ethel Wright (1894-1978)
323 – Henderson, Robert E. (1907-1979)

324 – Henderson, Robert E. (1907-1979)
   Henderson, Marjorie W. (1914-1998)
325 – DeMaranville, Josiah (1821-1911)
   DeMaranville, Louisa (1825-1916)
   DeMaranville, John (1855-1857)
326 – Brown, Ralph A. (1890-1901)
327 – Brown, Alvin M. (1862-1914)
328 – Williams, Elisha (1837-1900)
   Williams, Betsey S. (1845-1909)
329 – Downs, Hattie W. (1879-1964)
330 – Williams, Narcissus (1834-1863)
   Williams, Elisha H. (1806-1895)
   Williams, Patience (1795-1874)
   Williams, Miranda A. (1827-1902)
331 – Williams, Elisha H. (1806-1895)
332 – Williams, Patience (1795-1874)
333 – Williams, Miranda A. (1827-1902)
334 – Shockley, Averic T. (1840-1926)
335 – Gifford, Mary F. S. (1820-1904)
336 – Shockley, Benjamin F. (~1844-1900)
337 – Shockley, John (~1822-1895)
338 – Alden, Humphrey, Capt. (~1762-1844)
339 – Alden, Mary (~1762-1843)
340 – Shockley, Charles (1830-1900)
341 – Shockley, Joseph (~1787-1863)
342 – Shockley, Harriet M. (1822-1887)
343 – Shockley, Sally Alden (~1796-1859)
344 – Shockley, Charles (1830-1900)
   Shockley, Harriett M. (1822-1887)
   Shockley, Hattie H. (1859-1872)
   Shockley, Mary G. (1863-1880)
   Shockley, Charles F. (1859-1882)
345 – Shockley, Almy J. (1832-1871)
346 – Shockley, Hattie H. (1859-1872)
347 – Shockley, Minnie G. (1863-1880)
348 – Shockley, C. Frank (1859-1882)
349 – Roberts, Samuel (____-1845)

350 – Roberts, Infant (1861)
351 – Roberts, Infant (1865)
352 – Haskins, Sarah (1813-1888)
353 – Benton, Georgie A. 1871-1874)
354 – Benton, George S. (1856-1859)
355 – Pittsley, Priscilla (~1816-1891)
356 – Downing, Joseph (1785-1864)
357 – Downing, Sarah (1789-1881)
358 – Johnson, Betsey (~1831-1852)
359 – Holmes, William B. (1853-1909)
360 – Holmes, Betsey Emma (1852-1916)
361 – Monroe, Bathsheba (1805-1845)
362 – DeMaranville, Josiah (1843-1888)
363 – DeMaranville, Eliza J. (1849-1919)
364 – DeMaranville, Jennie (1879-1880)
365 – DeMaranville, Ruby (1874)
366 – DeMaranville, Nellie F. (1869-1925)
367 – Cudworth, Horace (1865-1867)
368 – Tallman, Julius C. (1900-1902)
369 – Tobey, Rachel (1787-1871)
370 – Tobey, Job Townsend (1811-1892)
371 – Tobey, Maria (1818-1876)
372 – Crowell, Elizabeth F. (1816-1894)
373 – Spooner, Alden (1818-1819)
374 – Sheafe, Abby E. (1878-1963)
375 – Spooner, Thomas (~1819-1898)
376 – Spooner, Phebe (~1819-1867)
377 – Cudworth, John (1839-1921)
   Cudworth, Sarah C. (1843-1909)
   Cudworth, Arthur A. (1889-1909)
   Cudworth, Horace A. (1865-1867)
   Cudworth, Jesse R. (1863-1936)
   Sheafe, Abby Evelyn (1878-1963)
378 – Cudworth, Jesse R. (1863-1936)
379 – Cudworth, Arthur A. (1889-1909)
380 – Cudworth, Sarah C. (1843-1909)
381 – Cudworth, John (1839-1921

Pond Cemetery Map Overview

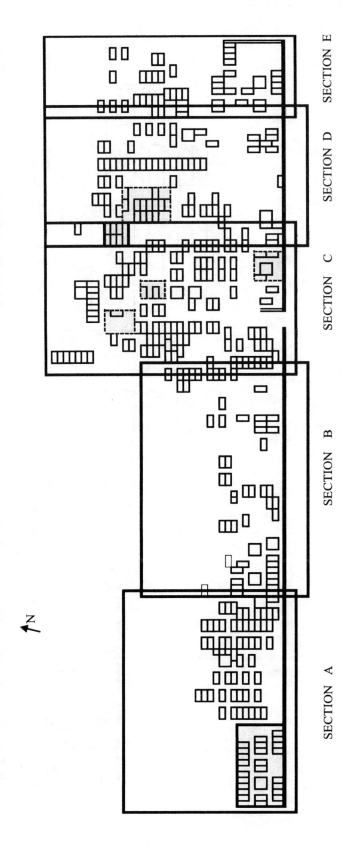

SECTION A   SECTION B   SECTION C   SECTION D   SECTION E

N

Pond Cemetery Map
Section A

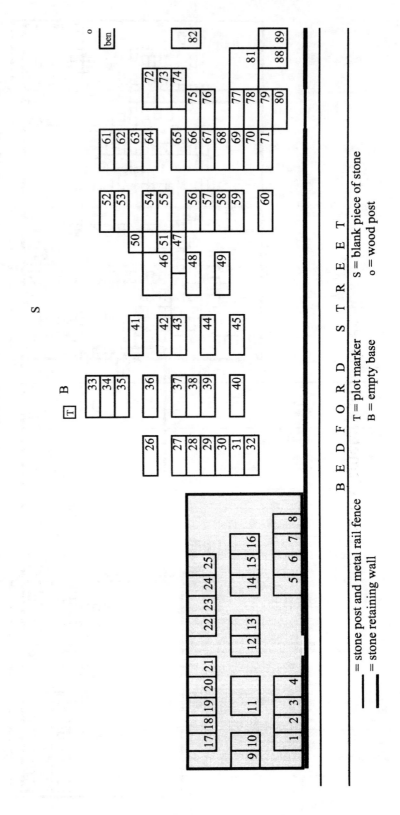

B E D F O R D   S T R E E T

= stone post and metal rail fence
= stone retaining wall

T = plot marker
B = empty base

s = blank piece of stone
o = wood post

Pond Cemetery Map
Section B

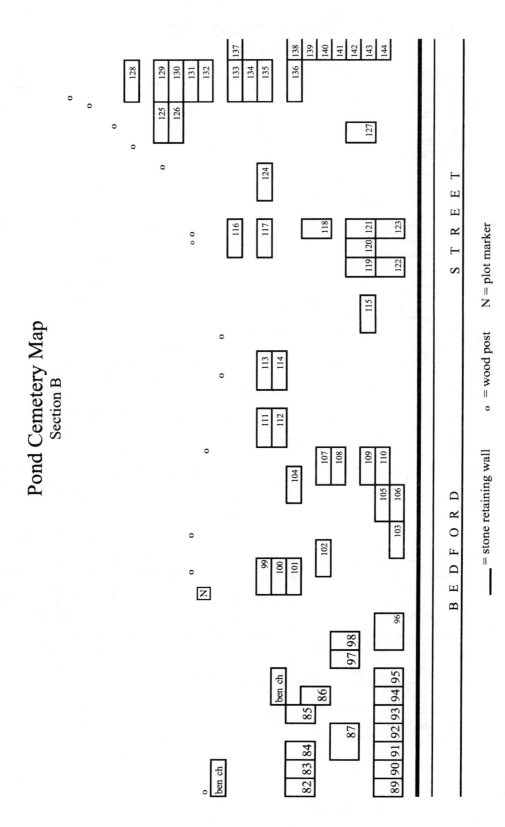

Pond Cemetery Map
Section C

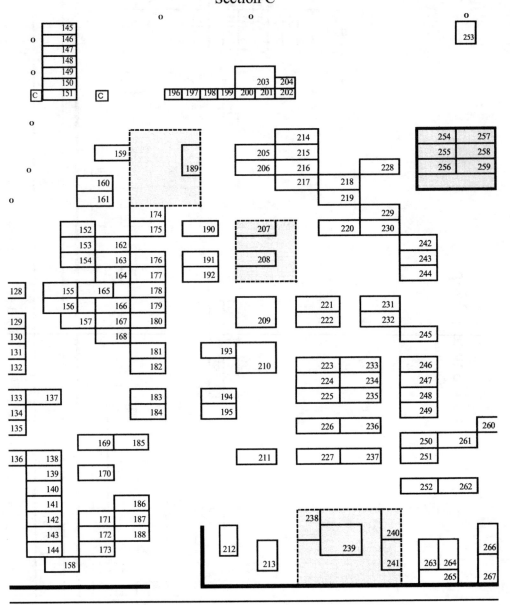

B E D F O R D   S T R E E T

_____ = stone retaining wall   C = plot marker
_____ = stone post and metal rail fence   o = wood post
------- = low cement wall

Pond Cemetery Map
Section D

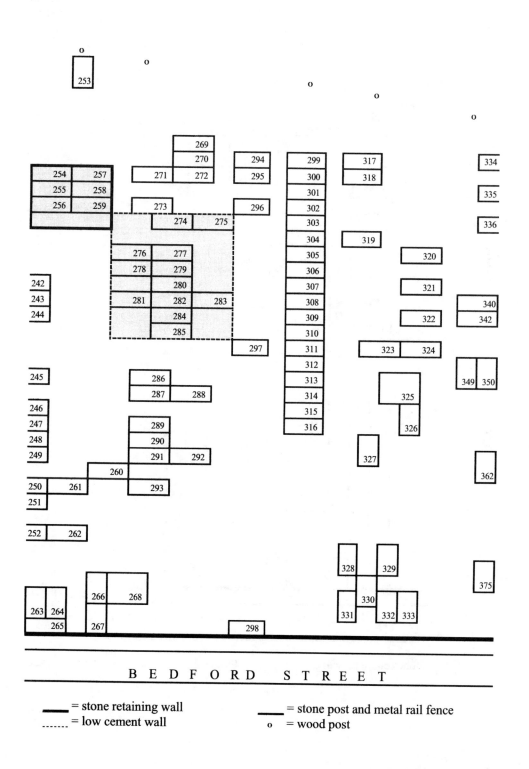

= stone retaining wall
= low cement wall
= stone post and metal rail fence
o = wood post

Pond Cemetery Map
Section E

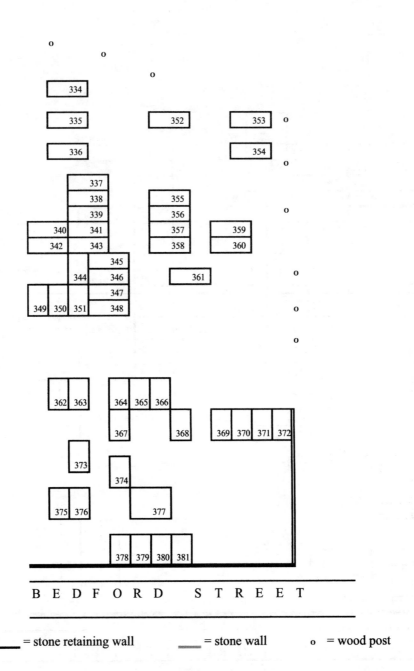

B E D F O R D   S T R E E T

_____ = stone retaining wall   ▭ = stone wall   o = wood post

Chapter 21
Precinct Cemetery

Precinct Cemetery is located at 185 Rhode Island Road. Thompson Hill Cemetery is on the right side. A lone wood post marks the border between the cemeteries. Woods form the border on the left side of the cemetery, and the rear. A white vinyl fence borders the front. A mass of evergreen bushes on the right side of the cemetery is beginning to hide some stones. The sign is in good repair. Most gravestones face southeast. They date from 1951 to present. The Lakeville Assessor's Office lists this cemetery as about 1 acre in size. The land was purchased for use as a town cemetery in 1939. Entries were recorded November 15 and 16, 2001, and updated later through 2003.

Allerdt, Adolph H.   *"ALLERDT"* is inscribed on the front of this monument. *"ADOLPH H. ALLERDT / MAY 18, 1935 – NOV. 8, 1991"* is inscribed on the back. A *"REX"* metal tag is present.

Banks, Donald A.   *"DONALD A / BANKS / MM2 / US NAVY / WORLD WAR II / OCT 12 1908 / SEP 25 1984"* is inscribed on this upright stone. A circled cross is carved at the top. A veteran's marker and flag are present.

Banks, Rita   *"RITA BANKS / MAY 18, 1914 ♦ MAR. 3, 1993"* is inscribed on this black, flat stone. A Raggedy Ann doll is carved on the left. The carved and inscribed areas are painted white.

Benvissuto, Fern F.   *"FERN FRANCES / BENVISSUTO / NOV. 25, 1935 – JAN. 31, 2001 / I'LL WALK / WITH GOD"* is inscribed on this tall cross-shaped monument. There are rose carvings under the arms of the cross. A Barnicoat Monuments metal tag is present.

Berg, Jeannette   *"Jeannette Berg / June 10, 1941 – Dec. 14, 1997"* is written on a Dahlborg-MacNevin Funeral Home marker.

Burch, Anthony R. Monument   *"BURCH / ANTHONY   MARGARET"* is inscribed on the front of this black monument. There is a porcelain portrait above the inscription. Leaf designs are carved on either side of it. *"ANTHONY R. BURCH / 1901- ____ / HIS WIFE / MARGARET E. BURNHAM / 1915 – 1978"* is inscribed on the back of this monument. A Barnicoat Monuments metal tag is present. His obituary in *The Middleborough Gazette* 08/21/1986:23 reports Anthony's death date as Aug. 17, 1986.

Burch, C. Clayton   *"C. CLAYTON BURCH / 1943 – 1998"* is inscribed on this slanted stone. Floral designs and a cross and are carved in the upper left corner.

Burch, Gordon W.   *"GORDON W. BURCH / 1936 – 1963"* is inscribed in the middle of this monument. A relief carving of a lamb is at the top, surrounded by floral carvings on either side. An Albert Richardson metal tag is present. There is an empty base present two plots west of this monument.

Burch, Margaret E.   See Anthony Burch Monument entry.

Burgeson, Ernest H.   See Jason L. Burgeson Monument entry.

Burgeson, Jason L. Monument   *"BURGESON"* is inscribed on the front of this large, black monument. On the left side, there is a carving of two people embracing in the clouds. There are planters carved into its base on both sides. *"JASON L. BURGESON / WORK LIKE YOU DON'T NEED MONEY, / LOVE LIKE YOU'VE NEVER BEEN HURT, / AND DANCE LIKE NO ONE'S WATCHING. / JAY / FEB. 15, 1980 – JUNE 9, 2000 / ERNEST H. BURGESON, III / NOV. 8, 1949 ____ / HIS WIFE / NADINE W. BURGESON / FEB 7, 1951 ____"* is inscribed on the back.
"YOU WILL ALWAYS MEAN THE / WORLD TO ME, AND THE / WORLD IS A BIG PLACE. / SO WHEN YOU THINK I AM / NOT THERE, NOT LISTENING, / NOT WITH YOU, I AM. / J. L. B." is inscribed on this flat, black, ground level stone. It is located in front of the monument, on the left.

Burgeson, Nadine W.   See Jason L. Burgeson Monument entry.

Burnham, Amy L.   See Robert Burnham Monument entry.

Burnham, Arnold M. Monument   *"BURNHAM"* is inscribed on the carving of a scroll at the top of this slanted monument. On a ribbon carving is inscribed *"TOGETHER FOREVER"* with floral carvings underneath. Below this are carved two open books. *"ARNOLD M / SEP. 8, 1923 / APR. 18, 1990"* is inscribed on the pages of the book on the left and *"DORA W. / SEPT 17, 1927 / ____"* is inscribed on the pages of the book on the right. A scene of a horse drawn buggy in the country is carved on the back of this monument. A Barnicoat Monuments metal tag is present.
"FATHER / ARNOLD" is all that is inscribed on this flat, ground level stone. There are flowers carved in the upper corners. It is located directly in front of the monument, on the left.

Burnham, Baby girl   *"BABY / GIRL / BURNHAM / OCT. 1969"* is painted on a rock. Flowers are painted around the inscription.

Burnham, Chester F. Monument   *"BURNHAM"* is inscribed in outline on the front of this monument. There are leaf carvings at the top. *"CHESTER F.*

BURNHAM / JAN. 25, 1909 – NOV. 29, 1961 / NELLIE M. HIS WIFE / JUNE 17, 1908 – JUNE 13, 1993" is inscribed on the back. A Barnicoat Monuments metal tag is present.

"FATHER" is inscribed in outline on this flat, one-inch high stone, which is located in front of the monument, on the right.

Burnham, Constance   See Harold Burnham Monument entry.

Burnham, Dora W.   See Arnold Burnham Monument entry.

Burnham, Gregory A.   *"GREG"* is inscribed in the lower left corner, below a porcelain portrait. Carved in color on the front of the monument is a car driving on a road. The road leads over a rainbow to a cloud in front of the sun. *"GREGORY ADAM / BURNHAM / OCTOBER 5, 1976 / MARCH 14, 1996 / ALWAYS IN OUR HEARTS"* is inscribed on the back. A REX metal tag is present.

"✝ / GREGORY A. BURNHAM / 1976 – 1996 / EGGER & ASHLEY" is embossed on this funeral home marker. It is located in front of the monument.

Burnham, Harold   *"BURNHAM"* is inscribed on the front of this monument. There is a carving of a horse's head on the left and a dog's head on the right. *"BURNHAM / 1936   HAROLD "BABE"   2001 / HIS WIFE / 1938   CONSTANCE (MEACK) ____ / 1962   HAROLD JR. "RAY"   1998"* is inscribed on the back. A Barnicoat Monuments metal tag is present. This monument was placed after the author's initial visit.

Burnham, Harold R., Jr.

See Harold Burnham Monument entry.

> *"Harold R. Burnham Jr.*
> *7·17·62   10 2·98"*

is painted on the front of this white wood cross.

> *"LOVE, LINDA"*

is painted on the back.

Burnham, Kenneth L. Monument   *"BURNHAM"* is carved in outline on the front of the monument. A horse's head, carved within a horseshoe, is on the left. *"In Loving Memory / KENNETH L. BURNHAM / FEB. 6, 1925 – MAR. 8, 1983 / VIRGINIA V. WIFE / APR. 29, 1926 – ____ "* is inscribed on the back. A Barnicoat Monuments metal tag is present.

"FATHER"   This flat, ground level stone is located in front of the monument.

Burnham, Loretta M.   See Robert Burnham Monument entry.

Burnham, Nellie M.   See Chester Burnham Monument entry.

Burnham, Robert W. Monument   *"BURNHAM"* is inscribed on a carving of a scroll. *"ROBERT W. / 1927 - _____"* is inscribed on the lower left. *"LORETTA M. / 1931 - _____"* is inscribed on the lower right. *"ALWAYS TOGETHER"* is inscribed at the center bottom. A couple on a sunset beach is carved above this. The death year 2002 was added for Robert W. after the initial visit. A Barnicoat Monuments metal tag is present.

"HUSBAND FATHER / ROBERT W. BURNHAM SR. / MAR. 23, 1927 – DEC. 31, 2002" is inscribed on this flat, ground level marker. It was added after the initial visit. It is located in front of the monument, on the left side.

Burnham, Robert W. Jr. Monument   *"BURNHAM / Precious Memories / BOBBY AMY"* is inscribed on the front of this monument. There is a porcelain portrait at the top. A country scene of a couple watching the sunset is carved at the bottom. *"OUR LOVE WILL NEVER DIE / ROBERT W. BURNHAM JR. / DEC. 22, 1948 – DEC. 17, 1988 / AMY LOUISE WIFE / SEPT. 22, 1951 _____"* is inscribed on the back. A Barnicoat Monuments metal tag is present.

"ROBeRT BURNHAM JR. / 1948 – 1988" is embossed on this funeral home marker. It is located at ground level in front of the monument, on the left side.

Burnham, Vincent R.   *""DUKE" / VINCENT R . / BURNHAM / AUG. 17, 1921 / SEP. 23, 1994"* A horse is carved in the upper right corner.

Burnham, Virginia V.   See Kenneth Burnham Monument entry.

Cardin, Alice E.   See Herbert H. Thomas Monument entry.
"ALICE / BELOVED MOTHER" This flat, ground level stone faces the rear of the cemetery. It is located directly behind the monument, on the right side.

Cardin, John E.   See Herbert H. Thomas Monument entry.
"JOHNNY / BELOVED BROTHER" This flat, ground level stone faces the rear of the cemetery. It is located directly behind the monument, on the left side.

Cardin, Thomas A.   See Herbert H. Thomas Monument entry.
"TOMMY / BELOVED HUSBAND / AND FATHER" This flat, ground level stone faces the rear of the cemetery. It is located behind the monument, on the right.

Caron, Florence D.   *"FLORENCE D. CARON / 1891 – 1971"* is inscribed on a scroll carving on this flat, partially buried stone.

Caron, Leon N. Sr.   *"LEON NAPOLEON CARON SR / SEA2   US NAVY / WORLD WAR I / APR 21 1897   JAN 10 1978"* is inscribed on this flat, ground level stone that is beginning to be buried. A circled cross is at the top.

Chace, Bertha S.   *"BERTHA S. / CHACE / DEC. 5, 1904 – DEC. 11, 1986"* is inscribed on a scroll carving at the top of the monument. A porcelain portrait is below this and *"In Loving Memory"* is inscribed at the bottom. A carving of a cross and flowers are on the left.

Chace, Florence O.   See Walter R. Chace Monument entry.

Chace, Walter R. Monument   *"CHACE / 1910   WALTER R . 1975 / HIS WIFE / 1913   FLORENCE O. 1988"* is inscribed on this slanted monument. *"Rex"* is carved into the base.

Chambers, John T. Monument *"C* (monogram) */ CHAMBERS / JOHN T. / 1913 – ____ / AND WIFE / MARTHA L. / 1912 – 1982"* The monogram is on the top left side of the monument. Floral carvings are below this. A Barnicoat Monuments metal tag is present. Lakeville Vital Records list his death on November 20, 1996.

Chambers, Martha L. See John Chambers Monument entry.

Colvin, Charles E. See Gertrude Colvin Monument entry.

Colvin, Gertrude E. Monument *"COLVIN"* is inscribed at the top of this 2-4 inch high, flat stone. *"GERTRUDE E. / (MILLER) / 1907 – 1978"* is inscribed on the left side, and *"CHARLES E. / 1902 – 1971"* is inscribed on the right.

Cornell, Barbara A. Monument *"CORNELL / BARBARA   ELLIOT"* is inscribed on the front of this monument. On the left side, there is a carving of a dove flying in the sunlight over flowers. *"ELLIOT E. CORNELL / JUN. 16, 1939 ____ / AND / BARBARA A. CORNELL / SEP. 6, 1952 ____ "* is inscribed on the back of this stone. A Barnicoat Monuments metal tag is present.

Cornell, Bertha A. See Kenneth Cornell Monument entry.

Cornell, Charles E. Monument *"CORNELL / DARLING, I LOVE YOU"* is inscribed on the front of this monument below a carving of praying hands. *"CHARLES E. CORNELL / MAY 18, 1917 – JUL. 6, 1995 / HIS WIFE / FLORENCE L. (PIERCE) / MAY 11, 1920 ____ / GREAT GRANDAUGHTER / MELISSA ANNE / APR. 23, – MAY 24, 1984"* is inscribed on the back. A Barnicoat Monuments metal tag is present. Lakeville Vital Records show that Florence Cornell died on October 29, 2003.

Cornell, Charles S. Monument *"CORNELL"* is carved at the top of this monument. Floral carvings adorn the upper corners. An open book is carved below this. *"CHARLES S. / 1893 – 1967"* is inscribed on the left page and *"JENNIE A. / 1896 – 1980"* is inscribed on the right page. *"THE LORD IS MY SHEPHERD"* is inscribed along the bottom. A Barnicoat Monuments metal tag is present.

Cornell, Elliot E. See Barbara Cornell Monument entry.

Cornell, Ernest *"GOD BLESS OUR ANGEL / BABY / ERNEST / JULY 31 · AUG. 1, 1965"* This flat, ground level stone is beginning to be buried. There is a carving of a praying angel on the left.

Cornell, Florence L. See Charles E. Cornell Monument entry.

Cornell, Gloria M. *"GLORIA M. CORNELL / MAY 22, 1938 / MAR. 15, 1995"* is inscribed on the front of this rear-facing monument. A butterfly flying to flowers along a wooden fence is carved in the lower right corner. *"CORNELL"* is inscribed on the back. Praying hands, an open book and flowers are carved below this. *"MOM AND GRAM"* is carved at the bottom. A Barnicoat metal tag is present

Cornell, Jennie A. See Charles Cornell Monument entry.

Cornell, Jessie M. See Russell Cornell Monument entry.

Cornell, Kenneth M. Monument *"FOREVER IN OUR HEARTS / CORNELL"* is inscribed at the top of this slanted monument. A rose is carved below this.

"KENNETH M. / SEPT. 8, 1922 / AUG. 17, 1992" is inscribed on the lower left side. *"BERTHA A. / DEC. 16, 1927 / NOV. 14, 1990"* is inscribed on the lower right side. A Barnicoat Monuments metal tag is present.

Cornell, Melissa A.   See Charles E. Cornell Monument entry.

Cornell, Paul B. Monument   *"CORNELL / 1928 PAUL B. 1957 / HUSBAND OF / NORMA I. MANTON / 1930 – 1993 / WIFE OF / ERNEST W. MILES / AT REST"* There are floral carvings in the upper corners of this monument.

Cornell, Russell E. Monument   *"CORNELL"* is inscribed across the pages of a carving of an open book. *"RUSSELL E. / 1926 – 1999 / HIS WIFE / JESSIE M. / 1927 – 1998"* is inscribed below this. Ivy leaf carvings are in the upper corners. A Barnicoat Monuments metal tag is present.

Costa, Louis Monument   *"COSTA"* is inscribed on the front of the monument. *"FOREVER IN OUR HEARTS"* is inscribed at the bottom. Two doves are carved in relief within a heart shaped area at the top. Leaves are carved below it. *"LOUIS COSTA / NOV. 15, 1934 ____ / HIS LOVING WIFE / PATRICIA A. (CORNELL) / JUNE 1, 1938 – AUG. 1, 2001"* is inscribed on the back. A Barnicoat Monuments metal tag is present.

Costa, Patricia A.   See Louis Costa Monument entry.

Costa, Rosemarie   *"Sept. 16 1979 Baby girl / Rosemarie Costa / Sept. 16 / 1979"* is written on a wood cross which is lying on the ground. On a revisit in July 2003, this cross was no longer present.

Cotter, Dorothy G.   *"COTTER"* is inscribed on the front of this black stone. An etching of a praying angel in heaven is on the right side. Praying hands are etched in the lower left next to the words *WE LOVE YOU MOM*. *"DOROTHY G. (CORNELL) / COTTER / MAR. 10, 1937 – AUG. 13, 1997 / LOVING / DAUGHTER, SISTER, WIFE / MOTHER AND GRANDMOTHER"* is inscribed on the back. A Barnicoat Monuments metal tag is present.

Cushman, Archie G. Monument   *"CUSHMAN"* is inscribed on the front of this monument. *"ARCHIE GUY / 1882 – 1970"* is inscribed on the left side, and *"BESSIE MAY / 1885 – 1978"* is inscribed on the right. Floral designs are carved in the upper corners. *"BARRE / GUILD"* is inscribed on the top right side of the base.
"A. GUY" is inscribed on this flat, 0-1 inch high footstone. It is located in front of the monument, on the far left.

Cushman, Bessie M.   See Archie Cushman Monument entry.
"BESSIE" is inscribed on this flat, ground level stone. It is located in front of the monument, on the left.

DeCoff, Clifford G. Jr. Monument   *"DECOFF"* is inscribed on the front of this monument above a carving of praying hands and ivy. *"CLIFFORD G. DECOFF JR. / OCT. 23, 1932 ____ / RITA L. HIS WIFE / OCT. 15, 1938 ____ / CLIFFORD I. THEIR SON / SEPT. 13, 1960 – OCT. 18, 1981"* is inscribed on the back. A Barnicoat Monuments metal tag is present.

DeCoff, Clifford I.　See Clifford G. Decoff Monument entry.
"CLIFF / LET THE GOOD TIMES ROLL" is inscribed on this flat, 1 inch high stone. A carving of a man riding a motorcycle is between these two lines. This stone is located in front of the Clifford G. DeCoff, Jr. Monument, on the left.

DeCoff, Rita L.　See Clifford G. DeCoff Monument entry.

DeFreitas, Robert P.　*"IN LOVING MEMORY OF / ROBERT P. DEFREITAS / (BOBBY) / MAY 6, 1949 † NOV. 12, 1989 / BELOVED DAD"* is embossed on a metal plaque which is attached to a slanted, painted stone.
"ROBERT P. / DeFREITAS / MAY 6, 1949 / NOV. 12, 1989" is inscribed on this flat, ground level stone. A carving of a cross in the clouds is on the left side. Below that is a ribbon carving with the words *"IN GOD'S CARE"* is inscribed on it. A floral carving is at the bottom on the left.

Delbene, Roy J., Sr.　*"Roy J. Delbene Sr. / September 30, 1937   ☫ June 20, 2003"* is written on this Dahlborg-MacNevin Funeral Home marker.
"No Farewell Words Were / Spoken, No Time To Say / Goodbye, You Were Gone / Before We Knew It, And / Only God Knows Why" is inscribed on this flat stone, which is located directly in front of the funeral home marker. At the top of this stone, *"ROY J. DELBENE SR. / 9-30-37 – 6-20-03"* is inscribed on a small plaque. These items were placed after the initial visit. A flag is present.

DeLisle, Harold F. Monument　*"DeLISLE"* is inscribed at the top of this black, slanted monument. *"HAROLD F. / DeLISLE / 4 NOVEMBER 1930 / 19 JANUARY 2003"* is inscribed below this, on the left side and *"LUCI M. / FORTUNATO / 7 FEBRUARY 1953 / ____"* is inscribed on the right side. There is a carving of a circular maze below the first line. *"Love is most nearly itself when / Here and now cease to matter"* is inscribed on the back.

DeMoranville, Arthur L.　See Bertram E. DeMoranville Monument entry.

DeMoranville, Bertram E., Jr. Monument　*"DEMORANVILLE"* is inscribed at the top of the monument, below a carving of a cross and flowers. *"BERTRAM E. JR. / 1925 – 1974 / ARTHUR L. / 1929 – 1998 / CLARA L. WIFE / 1926 – ____"* is inscribed in outline below this. *"BERTRAM E. SR. / 1904 – 1987 / JESSIE M. WIFE / 1906 – 1995"* is inscribed in outline on the back. A Barnicoat Monuments metal tag is present.

DeMoranville, Bertram E., Sr.   See Bertram E. DeMoranville, Jr. Monument entry.

DeMoranville, Clara L.   See Bertram E. DeMoranville, Jr. Monument entry.

DeMoranville, Jessie M.   See Bertram E. DeMoranville, Jr. Monument entry

DeMoranville, Shirley F.   *"SHIRLEY F. (WESTGATE) / DEMORANVILLE / NOV. 2, 1937 MAY 29, 1997"* is embossed on a metal marker which is attached to a painted cement block.   *"✝ / SHIRLEY DeMORANVILLE / 1937 – 1997 / EGGER'S FUNERAL HOME"* is embossed on a marker at the foot of the gravesite.

Doyle, Cody C.   *"CODY CHRISTOPHER / DOYLE / JULY 21, 1998"* A praying child angel is carved on the left side of this small stone. It faces the right side of the cemetery.

Dunlevy, Brendan M.   See Thomas W. Dunlevy Monument entry.
"Brandon M. Dunlevy / March 22, 1992 – Oct 6, 1992" is written on a Dahlborg-MacNevin Funeral Home marker which is located near the front of the monument.

Dunlevy, Karin E.   See Thomas W. Dunlevy Monument entry.

Dunlevy, Thomas W., Jr. Monument   *"DUNLEVY"* is inscribed on the front of this monument. There is a cross carved above the inscription, with shamrocks on either side. *"THOMAS W. DUNLEVY JR. / JAN. 4, 1965 ____ / HIS WIFE / KARIN E. SERGIO / FEB. 2, 1962 – OCT. 26, 1998 / BELOVED SON / BRENDAN MATTHEW / MAR. 22, 1992 – OCT. 6, 1992"* is inscribed on the back. A Mason's symbol is carved above these inscriptions.

Ebert, Jacqueline L.   *"Ebert / JACQUELINE LEE / CHAMBERS / MAY 6, 1949 – NOV. 2, 1985 / BELOVED DAUGHTER / OF / JOHN T. & MARTHA L. / THOSE WHO KNEW HER / LOVED HER"* Flowers and mushrooms are carved at the top of this rear facing stone. A smiley face is carved on the bottom right. A Barnicoat Monuments metal tag is present.

Ferguson, Sherrie L.   *"FERGUSON"* is inscribed on the front of this monument. Praying hands and roses are carved in the upper corners. *"BELOVED DAUGHTER AND SISTER / SHERRIE L. FERGUSON / NOV. 21, 1967 – JAN. 9, 1996"* is inscribed on the back. A Barnicoat Monuments metal tag is present.
"SHERRIE" is inscribed on this flat, ground level stone. It is located to the left of the monument.

Fortunato-DeLisle, Luci M.   See Harold F. DeLisle Monument entry.

Freitas, Joseph   *"JOSEPH FREITAS / 1942 – 1961 / OUR ANGEL"* A half sculptured cross on its side and a branch carving are at the top of this monument.

Gates, Eileen S. Monument   *"GATES"* is inscribed on the front of this monument. On the left is carved a cross, a rosary, a rose, and an open book with *"IN GODS CARE"* inscribed on it. *"EILEEN S. / 1950 – ____ "* is inscribed on the bottom left and *"LAWRENCE D. / 1948 – 1990"* is inscribed on the bottom right. A Barnicoat Monuments metal tag is present. A Mitchell Memorial Club marker and flag are present.

Gates, Ida A. Monument   *"GATES"* is inscribed at the top of this slanted monument. Ivy carvings are on either side below this. *"IDA ANN / 1893 – 1977"* is inscribed on the left side, and *"LEONARD / 1887 – 1960"* is inscribed on the right side. *"NAVY VETERAN'S WW I"* is inscribed across the bottom.
"IDA / ANN / GATES / Y1 / US NAVY / WORLD WAR I / 1893 / 1977" is inscribed on this upright stone. There is a circled cross at the top. A veteran's marker and flag are present. It is located directly in front of the monument, on the left.

Gates, Lawrence D.   See Eileen Gates Monument entry.

Gates, Leonard   See Ida Gates Monument entry.
"LEONARD / GATES / ILLINOIS / AS / USNRF / WORLD WAR I / MARCH 19 1887 / FEBRUARY 12 1960" There is a circled cross at the top of this upright stone. A veteran's marker and flag are present. It is located directly in front of the monument, on the right.

Gay, Harold M.   *"HAROLD M GAY / HM2   US NAVY / KOREA / AUG 26 1930 APR 2 1986"* is inscribed on this flat, ground level stone. A veteran's marker and flag are present.

Hawes, Benjamin Monument   *"HAWES"* is inscribed at the top of this monument with a cross and a rose carved on either side. *"OUR LOVE FOR YOU WILL LAST FOREVER"* is inscribed at the bottom. *"BENJAMIN HAWES / JUNE 21, 1915 ____ / HIS WIFE / BARBARA L. HAWES / JAN. 26, 1918 – APR. 5, 1983"* is inscribed on the back. A Barnicoat Monuments metal tag is present.

Hawes, Barbara L.   See Benjamin Hawes Monument entry.

Hayward, George A.   See Annie Kelly Monument entry.

Holcomb, Willis C.

"WILLIS COBB
HOLCOMB
MASSACHUSETTS
PHM lc US NAVY
WORLD WAR I
AUGUST 9 1889
MARCH 20 1947"
There is a relief carving of a cross within a recessed circle at the top of this upright stone. A veteran's marker and flag are present

Johnson, Frederick T. Marker   *"JOHNSON / FREDERICK T. / AUG. 24, 1937 – JUL. 4, 1992 / HIS WIFE / PATRICIA J. (O'BRIAN) / MAY 7, 1935 ____ "* A dog is carved in the upper left corner, and a cat is carved in the upper right corner.

Johnson, Patricia J.   See Frederick Johnson Monument entry.

Jones, A. Frederick Monument   *"JONES"* is embossed in the center of this flat, ground level, bronze monument. *"A. FREDERICK / 1898 – 1979"* is embossed on a separate metal plaque at the bottom left side, and *"MABEL R. M. / 1911 – 1983"* is embossed on a separate metal plaque on the right. There is a vase holder at the top, with ivy embossed around it. Ivy is also embossed in the upper corners. The monument is beginning to be buried.

Jones, Alberta M.   See George Jones Monument entry.
"MOM / 1932 1990 / FROM ALL YOUR CHILDREN" is embossed on a small metal plaque. It is attached to a ground level cement base and is located directly in front of the monument, on the left.

Jones, George E. Monument   *"JONES"* is inscribed in outline underneath a carving of a tractor-trailer. *"GEORGE EVERETT / 1928 – 1987 / HIS WIFE / ALBERTA MAY / 1932 – 1990"* is inscribed at the bottom. A Barnicoat Monuments metal tag is present.
"GEORGE EVERETT JONES / PVT   US ARMY / WORLD WAR II / SEP 18 1928 JUL 23 1987" is inscribed on this flat, ground level stone, which is beginning to be buried. A circled cross is carved at the top of this stone. A veteran's marker and flag are present. It is located in front of the monument, on the left.

Jones, Mabel R. M.   See A. Frederick Jones Monument entry.

Judson, Dorothy L.   See Williard Judson Monument entry.
"MOM" is inscribed on this flat, ground level stone, which is beginning to be buried. It is located in front of the Willard Judson Monument, on the right.

Judson, Irma D.   See Kenneth H. Judson Monument entry.

Judson, Kenneth H. Stone   *"KENNETH H. JUDSON / SEP. 23, 1908 – AUG. 3, 1987 / WIFE / IRMA D. (CUSHMAN) / JUN. 29, 1909 ____ "* is inscribed on this flat, ground level stone.

Judson, Williard E. Monument   *"JUDSON"* is inscribed on the front of this monument. There are floral designs carved in the upper corners. *"1904 WILLIARD E. JUDSON 1986 / HIS WIFE / 1909 DOROTHY L. MANTON 1964"* is inscribed on the back.
"DAD" is inscribed on this flat, ground level marker which is beginning to be buried. This stone is in front of and to the left of the monument.

Kaminski, Adam B. Monument   *"KAMINSKI / 1914 ADAM B. ____ / HIS WIFE / 1922 BERNICE A. ____ "* Floral carvings adorn the upper corners of this slanted monument.

Kaminski, Bernice A.   See Adam Kaminski Monument entry.

Keefe, Pamela L.   *"IN LOVING MEMORY OF / PAMELA LEE KEEFE / APRIL 9, 1960 / JANUARY 28, 2003 / WIFE MOTHER AND FRIEND"* is inscribed on this flat, ground level marker. An angel is carved on the left. This stone was placed after the initial visit.

Keen, Pamela K.   *"PAMELA KAY KEEN / FEB. 20, 1955 / OCT. 25, 1969"* is inscribed on this flat, ground level stone. It is beginning to be buried.

Kelly, Annie H. Monument   *"ANNIE HACKETT KELLY / 1892 – 1963 / GEORGE A. HAYWARD / 1915 – 1983"*

Lee, John H.   See Minnie Lee Monument entry.

"JOHN HALE LEE / CBM US NAVY / WORLD WAR II / 1902   1980" A circled cross is carved at the top of this flat, ground level stone. This rear facing stone is beginning to be buried. A flag is present.

Lee, Minnie B. Monument   *"LEE"* is carved in relief on this large, black monument which faces the rear of the cemetery. *"MINNIE B. / 1911 – 1981"* is inscribed on the bottom left, and *"JOHN HALE / 1902 – 1980"* is inscribed on the bottom right. A Barnicoat Monuments metal tag is present.

Lentini, Alfred   *"LENTINI / ALFRED LENTINI M. D. / JULY 27, 1914 – MAY 9, 1996 / MEDICAL EXAMINER / WHATSOEVER A MAN SOWETH, THAT SHALL HE ALSO REAP. / CHARITY EDIFIETH; ENVIETH NOT, THINKETH NO EVIL; / LET ALL THINGS BE DONE WITH CHARITY."* The first line is carved in relief. A caduceus is carved at the top center of this stone. Oak leaves and acorns are carved in the upper corners. A Middleboro Lodge #1274 BPOE marker and flag are present.

LeVesque, Paul S., Jr.   *"LeVesque / (TURK – TRAPPER)"* is inscribed on the front of this monument. A football helmet is carved at the top. *"LeVESQUE / PAUL SOLOMON JR. / 1964 – 1985 / BELOVED SON OF / PAUL AND JANICE"* is inscribed on the back. A Barnicoat Monuments metal tag is present.

Lewis, Thomas M.   *"LEWIS"* is inscribed on the front of this monument along with carvings of a cross, Mary praying and flowers. *"1969 THOMAS M. 1987"* is inscribed on the back. A Taunton Monument Co. metal tag is present.

Maddox, Amos G. Monument   *"MADDOX"* is inscribed on the front of this monument. A harness racer is carved under the inscription. *"In Loving Memory / AMOS G. MADDOX / 1930   (NOBBY)   1983 / HIS WIFE / MURIEL E. MEACK / 1931 ____"* is inscribed on the back. A Barnicoat Monuments metal tag is present.

Maddox, Muriel E.   See Amos Maddox Monument entry.

Maher, Ada M.   See John Maher Monument entry.

Maher, Howard S.   *"HOWARD S. MAHER"* is embossed on a metal plaque that is attached to this large white rock. No dates are present. His obituary in *The Middleborough Gazette* 12/15/1963:11 reports his death on December 1, 1963, at 61 years old. His wife, Mary E. Maher, who died April 17, 1998, age 87, is buried to his right without a headstone.

Maher, John J. Monument   *"MAHER"* is inscribed on the front of this monument. Floral carvings adorn the upper corners, but large evergreens obscure them. *"1886   JOHN J. MAHER   1948 / 1885   ADA M. HIS WIFE   1969"* is inscribed on the back. An A. F. Richmond metal tag is present.

Martowska, Anthony P. Monument   *"MARTOWSKA / ANTHONY P. / NOV. 29, 1925 – JUNE 10, 1999 / HIS WIFE / AGNES P. RUSSIS / MAR. 18, 1930 – ____"* A cross and rose are carved in the upper corners. A veteran's marker and flag are present. A Rex metal tag is present.

Martowska, Agnes P.   See Anthony Martowska Monument entry.

Mason, James R.   *"MASON"* is inscribed on this heart shaped monument. *"OUR DAD / 1940 JAMES R. 1975"* is inscribed below this. Metal flower vases are attached to the monument on either side.

Mastera, Matt   The figure of Jesus with outstretched arms is carved on the front of this monument. *"MATT MASTERA / FEB. 6, 1958 – JUN. 29, 1982"* is inscribed on the back. Above this inscription is attached a black diamond shaped stone upon which is carved a motorcycle. An S. Barnicoat metal tag is present.

Maynard, Sally   See Wil Maynard Monument entry.

Maynard, Wil Monument   *"MAYNARD / WIL AND SALLY"* is all that is inscribed on this large stone. A veteran's marker and flag are present. Lakeville Vital Records indicate that Wilfred Maynard died June 5, 1986, at 60 years old.

McDonald, David C. Monument   *"McDONALD / DAVID C. 'KETCHA LATER MA' / MAR. 5, 1956 – JAN. 12, 1979 / RHONDA JEAN McDONALD / MAR. 1, 1956 – JAN. 6, 1968"* There are floral carvings along the sides. A carving of a dove flying down from the sun is on the top left. A Barnicoat Monuments metal tag is present.

McDonald, Rhonda J.   See David McDonald Monument entry.

Meack, Arthur M. Monument   *"MEACK"* is inscribed on the front of this monument. There are leaf carvings at the top. *"1910 ARTHUR M. MEACK 1981 / HIS WIFE / 1911 GERTRUDE L. PARRIS 1942"* is inscribed on the back. A Barnicoat Monuments metal tag is present.
"FATHER" is inscribed on this flat, ground level stone. It is located in front of the monument, on the right.

Meack, Arthur M., Jr. Monument   *"MEACK"* is inscribed on the front of this monument. *"ARTHUR M. JR. / 1936 – 2001"* is inscribed on the lower left corner. *"JANE C. / 1938 – ____ "* is inscribed on the lower right. Praying hands and flowers are carved between the inscriptions. *"IN GOD'S CARE"* is inscribed below the carving. An S. Barnicoat metal tag is present. Arthur's death year was added since the initial visit.

Meack, Cindy   *"CINDY / NOV. 17, 1960 / JUNE 16, 1962"* is inscribed on this flat, 1-3 inch high stone. A child angel sitting with a baby lamb is carved in the lower left corner of this stone. It is located in front of the Arthur M. Meack Monument, on the left side.

Meack, Gertrude L. See Arthur Meack Monument entry.
"MOTHER" is inscribed on this flat, ground level stone. It is located in front of the monument, on the far right.

Meack, Jane C. See Arthur Meack, Jr. Monument entry.

Meack, Ralph E. *"RALPH E. MEACK / MAY 10, 1914 / MAY, 18, 1963"* is inscribed on this slanted stone.

Meack, Ralph E., Jr. Monument *"MEACK / RALPH E. JR. / DEC. 24, 1936 ____ / HIS WIFE / ROBERTA M. / NOV. 26, 1938 ____"* Floral carvings adorn the upper corners. A Barnicoat Monuments metal tag is present. His obituary in *The Middleborough Gazette* 07/06/2000:8 reports his death on June 29, 2000.

Meack, Roberta M. See Ralph Meack, Jr. Monument entry.

Meack, Shirley H. *"SHIRLEY H. MEACK / AUG. 26, 1928 / SEPT. 4, 1994"* is inscribed on this slanted monument. The death date was added after the initial visit.

Miles, Norma I. See Paul B. Cornell Monument entry.
Manton was her maiden name, Paul Cornell was her first husband, and Earnest Miles was her second husband.

Mooney, Joseph A. Monument *"MOONEY / JOSEPH A. / 1925 + 1983 / PATRICIA A. / 1930 + 1999"* is inscribed on this slanted stone. Praying hands are carved in the upper left corner.

Mooney, Patricia A. See Joseph Mooney Monument entry.

Morris, Isabel G. *"LOVING MOTHER / ISABEL G. MORRIS / 1911 – 1993"* A carving of a cross is above the inscription and floral designs adorn the upper corners. A REX metal tag is present.

Morris, John *"FATHER / JOHN MORRIS / 1906 – 1989"* is inscribed on this slanted stone.

Netto, Violet M. *"VIOLET MAE / (MASON) NETTO / 1923 – 1965"* A floral carving is above the inscription.

Noonan, Gerald A. See June Noonan Monument entry.

Noonan, June M. Monument *"NOONAN"* is inscribed on this slanted monument. *"JUNE M. / 1914 ____"* is inscribed on the lower left side, and *"GERALD A. / 1924 – ____"* is inscribed on the lower right. Floral designs are carved in the upper corners.

Norris, John H. *"JOHN H. NORRIS / 1904 – 1984"* is inscribed on this flat, 0 – 2 inch high stone.

Orrall, Archie B. Monument *"ORRALL / 1886 ARCHIE B. 1978 / HIS WIFE / 1886 JOSEPHINE C. 1978"* Floral carvings adorn the upper corners. An A. F. Richmond metal tag is present.

Orrall, Josephine C.   See Archie Orrall Monument entry.

Osborne Monument   *"OSBORNE"* is all that is inscribed on this stone. Floral carvings adorn the upper corners.

Osborne, Charles W.   *"OSBORNE / CHARLES WALTER / 1934   1991"* Ivy is carved on either side of this slanted stone.

Osborne, Evelyn M.   *"EVELYN M. / 1889 – 1973"* is inscribed on this flat, ground level stone, which is beginning to be buried. This stone is located in front of the Osborne Monument, on the left. Lakeville Vital Records indicate that she was the wife of William Dennis Osborne.

Osborne, Gertrude E.   *"GERTRUDE E. / 1901 – 1953"* is inscribed on this flat, ground level stone. It is hidden under evergreen bushes. She was the wife of David G. Osborne, and the daughter-in-law of William D. Osborne. This stone is located in front of the Osborne Monument, on the right.

Osborne, William D.   *"WILLIAM D. / 1883 – 1963"* is inscribed on this flat, ground level stone. The Lakeville Vital Records list his name as William Dennis Osborne. This stone is located in front of the Osborne Monument, on the far left.

Peabody, Nelly D. Monument   *"PEABODY"* is inscribed at the top of this slanted monument. Praying hands are carved on the left. *"MOSTEST"* is shallowly carved below this. *"NELLY D. / APR. 23, 1919 / APR. 17, 1997"* is inscribed on the lower left, and *"ROBERT L. / DEC. 22, 1913, / MAY 31, 1988"* is inscribed on the lower right. A Barnicoat metal tag is present.

Peabody, Robert L.   See Nelly Peabody Monument entry.

Pereira, Dolores   *"DOLORES / PEREIRA / 1930 – 2002"* is inscribed on this flat, ground level stone. It was not present on the initial visit.

Perry, Francis D. Monument   *"FOREVER IN OUR HEARTS"* is inscribed on a ribbon carving. *"SONNY" / FRANCIS D. PERRY / APR. 19, 1936 – MAY 11, 1997 / BELOVED WIFE / LOIS I. (PITTSLEY) / MAR. 9, 1943 ____ "* is carved below this. At the top is carved a cross with a rosary and roses around it.

Perry, Lois I.   See Francis Perry Monument entry.

Perry, Jeffrey N.   See James N. Pittsley, Sr. Monument entry.

Perry, John F.   *"✝ / FOREVER IN OUR HEARTS / "JON" / JOHN F. PERRY / DEC. 7, 1962 – OCT. 31, 1996"* is inscribed on this black monument. A race car is carved on the lower left.

Pierce, Gertrude C.   *"PIERCE / GERTRUDE C. / 1899 – 1966 / MOTHER"* Praying hands are carved above the inscription, and floral designs adorn the upper corners. A Barnicoat Monuments metal tag is present.

Pittsley, Eliza F.   *"ELIZA F. PITTSLEY / 1891 – 1954"* is inscribed on this flat, ground level stone, which is beginning to be buried.

Pittsley, Doris L.   See James N. Pittsley, Sr. Monument entry.

Pittsley, James N., Sr. Monument *"PITTSLEY"* is inscribed at the top of this monument. A village with a church is carved below this. *"1901 JAMES N. PITTSLEY SR. 1995 / HIS WIFE / 1912 DORIS L. (MEACK) 1964"* is inscribed at the bottom. *"JEFFREY N. PERRY / SEP. 6, 1967 – JUL. 2, 1968"* is inscribed on the top surface of the base, on left side of this monument. An S. Barnicoat metal tag is present.

Rego, Anna J. *"ANNA J. REGO / DEC. 27, 1931 / NOV. 5, 2000"* is inscribed on this teardrop shaped monument. A praying angel is etched in the lower right. The sun and clouds are etched on the upper left. A stone vase is attached to the base on the right.

Rego, Leonard *"FOREVER IN OUR HEARTS / LEONARD REGO / FEB. 3, 1931 – APR. 25, 1997"* A painted relief carving of a deer and a tree are on the lower left side. A painted carving of a race car is on the lower right.

Reynolds, Ada M. *"REYNOLDS"* is inscribed on the front of this monument with shamrock carvings in the upper corners. *"FOREVER IN OUR HEARTS"* is inscribed on the back, with shamrocks carved on either side. *"MOTHER / REYNOLDS / ADA MAY / MAR. 17, 1933 – JUL. 15, 2002"* is inscribed below this.
"MOM / WE LOVE YOU / AND MISS YOU" is inscribed on this flat stone immediately behind this monument. At the top of this rear facing stone is a collage of photos.

Reynolds, Annie M. Monument *"REYNOLDS"* is inscribed at the top of this monument, with floral designs carved on either side. *"1901 ANNIE M. 1951 / 1898 MAURICE A. 1971"* is inscribed on the back.

Reynolds, Barry L. *"BARRY L. / REYNOLDS / JAN. 20, 1946 – MAR. 1, 1995"* is inscribed on this flat, ground level stone.
"BARRY REYNOLDS / LOVE YOU / 1946 1995" is painted on this upright fieldstone. A pipe is painted between the dates. It is located behind the above stone.

Reynolds, Daisy *"DAISY"* is all that is inscribed on this flat, ground level stone. It is beginning to be buried. Her obituary in *The Middleborough Gazette* 01/21/1971:7 reports her death on January 13, 1971, at 36 years old. She was the wife of Sheldon Reynolds.

Reynolds, Dale A. See Rita Reynolds Monument entry.

Reynolds, Derek M. *"DEREK MARK / REYNOLDS / NOV. 20, 1988"* A praying child angel is carved on the left side of this small stone. It faces the right side of the cemetery. A Barnicoat Monuments metal tag is present.

Reynolds, Leon E. Monument *"REYNOLDS"* is inscribed above a carved scene of a hunter resting near a lake. *"JUST RESTING"* is inscribed below the carving. *"LEON E. REYNOLDS / JUN 6, 1923 – OCT. 14, 1988 / HIS WIFE / MARJORIE L. (MEACK) / DEC. 19, 1923 ____"* is inscribed on the back. A Barnicoat Monuments metal tag is present.
"✝ / LEON EUGENE REYNOLDS / PFC US ARMY / WORLD WAR II / JUN 6 1923 OCT 14 1988" is inscribed on this flat, ground level stone. It is located in front of the monument, on the right side. A veteran's marker and flag are present.

Reynolds, Leon F. Monument   *"REYNOLDS"* is inscribed on the front of this monument. Floral designs are carved in the upper corners. *"1900   LEON F. REYNOLDS 1959 / 1903 LUELLA M. HIS WIFE   1980"* is inscribed on the back. An Albert F. Richmond Memorials metal tag is present.
"FATHER / FROM CHILDREN" is inscribed on this flat, ground level stone. It is beginning to be buried. It is located in front of the monument, on the far right.

Reynolds, Lillian L.   See O. Nelson, Jr. Reynolds Monument entry.

Reynolds, Luella M.   See Leon F. Reynolds Monument entry.
"MOTHER / FROM CHILDREN" is inscribed on this flat, ground level stone. It is located in front of the monument, on the right.

Reynolds, Kathleen V.   See Stephen Reynolds Monument entry.

Reynolds, Marcia L.   See Maynard Reynolds Monument entry.

Reynolds, Marion L.   See Walter Reynolds Monument entry.

Reynolds, Marjorie L.   See Leon E. Reynolds Monument entry.

Reynolds, Maurice A.   See Annie Reynolds Monument entry.

Reynolds, Maurice A., Jr.

"FOREVER IN OUR HEARTS
"SONNY"
MAURICE A. JR.
REYNOLDS
SEPT. 17, 1935
MAR. 8, 1991"

A painted horse head is carved within a horseshoe in the upper right corner of this slanted stone.

Reynolds, Maynard W. Monument   *"REYNOLDS"* is carved in outline at the top of this monument, above a carving of a valley farm scene. *"MAYNARD W. / MAR. 29, 1936 ____"* is inscribed in the lower left, and *"MARCIA L. / MAR. 14, 1943 – APR. 12, 1988"* is inscribed in the lower right. An American flag is present. A Barnicoat Monuments metal tag is present.

Reynolds, Nancy V.   *"REYNOLDS"* is inscribed on the front of the monument. A carving of a cross, flowers and Mary praying is at the top. *"PRAY FOR US"* is inscribed on a ribbon carving below this. *"NANCY V. REYNOLDS / DEC 5, 1907 / DEC. 27, 1961"* is inscribed on the back.
"MOTHER" is inscribed on this flat, ground level stone. It is located in front of the monument.

Reynolds, O. Nelson Jr. Monument   *"REYNOLDS / O. NELSON JR / JAN. 12, 1928 – FEB. 2, 1995 / LOVING WIFE / LILLIAN L. / JAN. 2, 1925 – APR. 7, 1992"* A Barnicoat metal tag is present.

Reynolds, Rita V. Monument   *"REYNOLDS / RITA V. / 1941 – ___ / DAUGHTER / DALE ANN / 1963 – ___ "* On the left is carved a cross, a rose, and an open book with the words *"IN GOD'S CARE"* inscribed on its pages. A Barnicoat Monuments metal tag is present.

Reynolds, Stephen F. Monument   *"REYNOLDS"* is inscribed on this heart shaped monument. A cross and a rose are carved behind this inscription. *"LOVE FOREVER / AND ALWAYS"* is inscribed at the bottom of the heart. Below the heart, *"STEPHEN F. / 1944 – 1983"* is inscribed on the bottom left, and *"KATHLEEN V. / 1944 – ___ "* is inscribed on the bottom right. A porcelain portrait is in the upper right corner.

Reynolds, Suzanne   *"MAMA / SUZANNE / 1940 – 1970 / FROM CHILDREN"* is inscribed on this flat, ground level stone, which is beginning to be buried. Lakeville Vital Records list her name as Suzanne Cora Reynolds, the wife of Richard W.

Reynolds, Thelma A. Monument   *"THELMA A. / REYNOLDS / 1920 – 1972 / 1911 LOVE GEORGE 1982"* is inscribed on this monument.
"THELMA A. / REYNOLDS / JULY 19, 1920 – FEB. 23, 1973 / LOVE GEO." is inscribed on this flat, ground level stone. It is located in front of the monument. Note the discrepancy between the death years.

Reynolds, George   See Thelma Reynolds Monument entry.

Reynolds, Walter A. Monument   *"REYNOLDS / 1927   WALTER A.   ___ / HIS WIFE / 1931   MARION L.   1977"* Ivy is carved in the upper corners.

Richards, Delphine A.   See Frederick Richards Monument entry.

Richards, DeWitt L. Monument   *"RICHARDS / De WITT L. / JUN. 3, 1935 – SEPT. 27, 2000 / HIS WIFE / GRACE A. (DEMORANVILLE) / MAY 6, 1934 – MAY 7, 2002"* A dog is carved in the lower left corner of this rear facing stone. Grace's death date was added since the initial visit. A Barnicoat Monuments metal tag is present.

Richards, Donald N., Sr. Monument   *"RICHARDS"* is inscribed on the front of this rear facing monument. A racing greyhound is carved in the upper left corner. A royal flush in hearts is carved on the lower right. *"DONALD N. RICHARDS Sr. / JUNE. 29, 1944 – DEC. 16, 1986 / DOROTHY BELOVED WIFE / DEC. 23, 1945 – JUL. 27, 1988"* is inscribed on the back. A Barnicoat Monuments metal tag is present.

Richards, Dorothy   See Donald Richards, Sr. Monument entry.

Richards, Grace A.   See DeWitt Richards Monument entry.

Richards, Frederick E. Monument   *"RICHARDS"* is inscribed on the front of monument which faces the rear of the cemetery. *"FREDERICK E. "JUGGIE" JR. / 1939 – 1984 / DELPHINE A. "DELLA" / 1940 – 1995"* is inscribed on the back. A carving of a racing greyhound is at the top.

Richards, Nancy L.   *"RICHARDS"* is inscribed on the front of this black monument. There is an etching of two people with a dove overhead. Two open hands extend from the clouds below a rainbow. *"SAFELY HOME"* is inscribed at the bottom. *"NANCY L. / JUNE 21, 1938 / MAY 22, 2002"* is inscribed on the right side on the back. This stone was placed after the initial visit.

Rijo, George R. Monument   *"FOREVER IN OUR HEARTS / RIJO / GEORGE R. / 1926 – 1999 / BELOVED WIFE / HILDA M. / 1923 – 2001"* A cross and floral designs are carved at the top of this stone. A Barnicoat Monuments metal tag is present. Hilda's death year was added after the initial visit.
"✝ / GEORGE R RIJO / PFC   US ARMY / WORLD WAR II / APR 23 1926   MAY 12 1999" is inscribed on this flat, ground level stone. It is located in front of the monument, on the far left, and is beginning to be buried.

Rijo, Hilda M.   See George Rijo Monument entry.

Romaska, Irene T.   *"IRENE T. ROMASKA / 1912 – 1978"* is inscribed on this flat, 3 inch high stone.

Rose-Mello, Tasha T.   *"Tasha T. / Rose – Mello / Apr. 9 1965 / Dec. 5, 2000"* is inscribed inside a heart outline on this small 1 inch high flat stone. A boulder with *"ROSE"* inscribed on it is behind this marker. A bench is present in front of the boulder upon which is inscribed:

> *"If tears could build a stairway,*
> *and memories a lane,*
> *I'd walk right up to heaven*
> *and bring you home again."*

An upright stone on the left is inscribed with:

> *"No Farewell Words Were*
> *Spoken, No Time To Say*
> *Goodbye, You Were Gone*
> *Before We Knew It, And*
> *Only God Knows Why."*

Rubadou, Mary I.   *"RUBADOU / MARY IDA / JAN. 18, 1925   OCT. 17, 1984 / TOGETHER ALWAYS."* A cross with flowers and an open book are carved on the left side of this slanted stone.

Russis, William C.   *"✝ / WILLIAM CHARLES RUSSIS / A1C   US AIR FORCE / KOREA / FEB 27 1929   OCT 23 2001"* is inscribed on this flat, ground level stone. A veteran's marker and flag are present. This stone was placed after the initial visit.

Santos, Cora L.   *"DADDY'S GIRL / CORA LEE SANTOS / DECEMBER 22, 1990"* is embossed on a metal plaque, which is attached to a ground level stone.

Shuman, Mary T. Monument   *"SHUMAN"* is inscribed in outline on the front of this rear facing monument. A cross and a rose are carved at the top. *"MARY T. SHUMAN / 1908 – 1976 / SISTER / WINIFRED V. SHUMAN / 1913 – 1979"* is inscribed on the back. A Barnicoat Monuments metal tag is present.

Shuman, Winifred V.   See Mary Shuman Monument entry.

Simms, Alexander Monument   *"SIMMS / ALEXANDER / AUG. 9, 1908 – DEC. 9, 1990 / HIS WIFE / ELIZABETH / MAR. 30, 1912 ____"* Praying hands are carved at the top center of this monument. Floral designs adorn the upper corners. A Barnicoat metal tag is present. The *Social Security Death Index* lists Elizabeth's death on October 1, 2002.

Simms, Elizabeth   See Alexander Simms Monument entry.

Simpson, Beatrice E.   See Harry Simpson Monument entry.
"MOTHER" is inscribed on this flat, ground level stone. It is located in front of the monument, on the right.

Simpson, Harry W. Monument   *"SIMPSON"* is inscribed on a ribbon carving on the front of this stone. There are floral carvings on the left. *"HARRY W. SIMPSON / 1922 – 1996 / HIS WIFE / BEATRICE E. DeMORANVILLE / 1920 – 1971"* is carved on the back. *"TAMMY"* is inscribed below a carving of a dog at the bottom. A Barnicoat Monuments metal tag is present.
"✟ / HARRY W SIMPSON / PFC   US ARMY / WORLD WAR II / APR 5 1922   DEC 17 1996" is inscribed on this flat, ground level stone. The last line is beginning to be buried. It is located in front of the monument, on the right. A veteran's marker and flag are present.

Sisson, Bettylou   *"MOTHER / BETTYLOU SISSON / FEB. 21, 1940 – APR. 3, 1983"* is inscribed within a heart shaped outline. A carving of a cross and flowers is behind the inscription. There is a carving of a horse in a valley on the lower left. A Barnicoat Monuments metal tag is present.

Sisson, Phillip G.   *"PHILLIP G. / SISSON / 1930 – 1988"* is inscribed on this flat, ground level stone. A carving of a horse's head is on the left.

Souza Monument   *"SOUZA"* is all that is carved on this stone. The carved letters are painted white. A Barnicoat Monuments metal tag is present.

Souza, E. J.   *"SOUZA / E. J. / 1925 – ____"* is inscribed on the front of this monument. *"WHAT IS – IS / WHAT WAS – IS NOT"* is inscribed on the back. The carved letters and numbers on the front and back are painted white. A Barnicoat Monuments metal tag is present.

St. Don, Eva M.   *"ST. DON / EVA M. / MAR. 30, 1945 / DEC. 9, 1973"*   At the top of this monument is a carving of a cross lying on an open book, with flowers underneath. An Albert F. Richmond Memorials metal tag is present.

Taylor, Gertrude R.   See Roy Taylor Monument entry.

Taylor, J. Roy Monument   *"TAYLOR"* is embossed at the top of this metal plaque. *"J. ROY / 1899 – 1993 / "PUP""* is inscribed on the left side, and *"LOU / 1907 – 1998 / "NANA""* is inscribed on the right side. Her death date is embossed on a separate metal plate, which is screwed onto the plaque. *"WITH LOVE / KELLY, KERRY, KEMMY, JIM"* is embossed at the bottom center. Shamrocks are embossed in its four corners. This metal plaque is attached to the slanted front of a stone, which has an ornate metal cross attached at the top.

Taylor, Lou   See J. Roy Taylor Monument entry.

Taylor, Roy W. Monument   *"TAYLOR"* is inscribed at the top of this slanted monument. A cross and flowers are carved on either side of the inscription. A rosary is carved below it. *"ROY WM / 1886 ____ "* is inscribed on the left side, and *"GERTRUDE R. / 1903 · 1974"* is inscribed on the right. Lakeville Vital Records list Roy's death on April 22, 1977.

Thomas, Alice L.   See Herbert H. Thomas Monument entry.

Thomas, Arnold G.   *"ARNOLD G. "PETE" / THOMAS / 1920 – 1985"* A porcelain portrait is attached to this slanted stone above the inscription. A veteran's marker and flag are present.
"ARNOLD GORDON THOMAS / PVT   US ARMY / KOREA / OCT 15 1920   OCT 15 1985" is inscribed on this flat, ground level stone. It is located directly in front of his monument.

Thomas, Harry Monument   *"THOMAS / HARRY   PHYLLIS"* is inscribed on the front of this monument. Praying hands and a floral design are carved at the top. *"HARRY G. THOMAS JR. / FEB. 24, 1932 ____ / BELOVED WIFE / PHYLLIS M. (BURNHAM) / JAN. 17, 1934 ____ "* is inscribed on the back. A Barnicoat Monuments metal tag is present.

Thomas, Herbert H. Monument   *"THOMAS"* is inscribed at the top of this monument, above a carving of a vase of flowers. *"HERBERT H. / 1893 – 1969"* is inscribed on the left side of the vase, and *"ALICE L. / 1893 – 1965"* is inscribed on the right. *"MAY THEIR SOULS REST IN PEACE"* is inscribed below the vase. *"JOHN ERIC CARDIN / JUNE 22, 1954 – AUG. 22, 1978 / ALICE E. CARDIN / MAY 18, 1918 – SEPT. 3, 1988 / THOMAS A. CARDIN / OCT. 28, 1942 – OCT. 31, 1988"* is inscribed on the back.

Thomas, Herbert H. Jr.   *"HERBERT H. JR. / THOMAS / 1916 – 1979"* is inscribed on this slanted stone.

Thomas, Herbert H. III Monument   *"THOMAS"* is inscribed on this black monument below a porcelain portrait. A scene of deer at a lake is etched below this. *"BELOVED HUSBAND AND FATHER / HERBERT H. THOMAS III / MAR. 11, 1939 – OCT. 3, 2001 / BELOVED WIFE AND MOTHER / MURIEL L. (SOUZA) / FEB. 24, 1932 ____ "* is inscribed on the back. A Barnicoat Monuments metal tag is present. This stone was placed after the initial visit.

Thomas, Phyllis   See Harry Thomas Monument entry.

Thomas, Roberta   *"ROBERTA / 1921 – 1958"* is inscribed on this slanted stone. Lakeville Vital Records show that she was the wife of Herbert Thomas, Jr.

Thompson, Margaret A.   *"IN LOVING MEMORY OF / MARGARET A. / THOMPSON / MAR. 31, 1940 / MAY 1, 2001"* is inscribed on a black, teardrop shaped stone. The sun, peeking through the clouds, is etched at the top. A girl angel with a fawn and flowers is etched at the lower right. A stone vase is attached to the base on the right side. A Barnicoat Monuments metal tag is present.

VanSchelt, Virginia   *"VIRGINIA / VAN SCHELT / JULY 18, 1927 / JUNE 6, 2002"* is inscribed on this slanted stone. Floral designs adorn the upper corners. This stone was placed after the initial visit.

Vera, Alma B.   See Edmund Vera Monument entry.

Vera, Edmund H. Monument   *"EDMUND H. VERA / MAR. 5, 1912 – SEP. 13, 1983 / WIFE / ALMA B. (CUSHMAN) / MAR. 8, 1913 – JAN 13, 1997"* is inscribed on this one-inch high, flat stone. A veteran's marker and flag are present.

Vigers, James J., III Stone   *"JAMES J. VIGERS III / NOV. 10, 1927 – MAR. 30, 1992 / WIFE / LILLIAN E. (CUSHMAN) / DEC. 16, 1915 ____"* is inscribed on this flat stone, which is beginning to be buried. A veteran's marker and flag are present.

Vigers, Lillian E.   See James J. Vigers Stone entry.

Wambolt, Avis L.   See Newell Wambolt Monument entry.
"MOM / FOREVER IN OUR HEARTS" is carved in outline on this flat, ground level stone. A cross surrounded by flowers is carved at the top. This stone is located in front of the monument, on the right.

Wambolt, Newell I. Monument   *"WAMBOLT"* is carved in outline under a carved and outlined cross. There are floral designs on the sides of the cross. *"1920 NEWELL I. WAMBOLT 1961 / HIS WIFE / 1915 AVIS L. DEMORANVILLE 1986"* is inscribed on the back. A World War II marker and flag as well as a veteran's marker and flag are present. A Barnicoat Monuments metal tag is present.
"✝ / NEWELL ISSAC WAMBOLT / MASSACHUSETTS / COX   USNR / WORLD WAR II / APRIL 13 1920   SEPT 27 1961" is embossed on this flat, ground level, metal marker. A World War II marker and flag are present. It is located in front of the monument on the far right.

Watts, Muriel A. C.   See Raymond Watts Monument entry.

Watts, Raymond Monument   *"Watts / IN LOVING MEMORY / RAYMOND / SEPT. 29, 1929 – AUG. 13, 1984 / BELOVED WIFE / MURIEL A. C. / NOV. 27, 1934 ____"* is inscribed on this rear facing monument. A Mason's symbol is carved at the top, and rose carvings adorn the upper corners. A Barnicoat Monuments metal tag is present.
"RAYMOND WATTS / US ARMY / KOREA / SEPT. 29, 1929   ✝ AUG 13 1984" is embossed on this flat, rear facing, metal marker. A veteran's marker and flag are present. It is located directly in front of the monument.

Westgate, Barbara A.   See Lawrence Westgate Monument entry.

Westgate, Beverly A.   *"BEVERLY A. WESTGATE / 1932 – 2002 / EGGER'S FUNERAL HOME"* is inscribed on this funeral home marker. It is located just left of the Bertha S. Chace Monument.

Westgate, Carrie L.   See Clarence Westgate Monument entry.

Westgate, Clara E.   See William S. Westgate Monument entry.

Westgate, Clarence M. Monument   *"WESTGATE"* is inscribed at the top of this monument. A rose carving is below this on the left. *"BEYOND THE SUNSET."* is inscribed on the bottom. *"CLARENCE M. WESTGATE / SEPT. 4, 1902 – SEPT. 24, 1988 / HIS WIFE / CARRIE L. DEMORANVILLE / JULY 27, 1906 – AUG. 18, 1994"* is inscribed on the back.

Westgate, Inez L. Monument   *"WESTGATE"* is inscribed on a carved scroll on the front of this monument. Floral designs are carved around it. An open book is carved on the top horizontal surface of this monument. *"INEZ L. / 1898 – 1980"* is inscribed on the left page, and *"IRVING B. / 1894 – 1969"* is inscribed on the right page. A Barnicoat Monuments metal tag is present.

Westgate, Irving B.   See Inez Westgate monument entry.

Westgate, Jennie Monument   *"WESTGATE"* is inscribed on the front of this monument. Floral carvings adorn the upper corners. *"JENNIE   MERRILL"* is inscribed on the bottom. *"MERRILL M. WESTGATE / 1917 – 1967 / JENNIE M. HIS WIFE / 1903 – 1971"* is inscribed on the back.

Westgate, Lawrence W. Monument   *"WESTGATE"* is inscribed on the front of the monument. Ivy leaves are carved in the upper corners. *"1934 LAWRENCE W. ____ / HIS WIFE / 1935 BARBARA A. 1958"* is inscribed on the back. A Hancock Monument Co. metal tag is present.

Westgate, Leslie Monument   *"WESTGATE / In Loving Memory"* is inscribed on a carved scroll on the front of this monument. On the left is carved a cross with flowers at its base. There is a porcelain portrait under the scroll. *"LESLIE   SHIRLY / TOGETHER AS ONE, FOREVER"* is inscribed at the bottom. Between their names is a heart carving with *"MARRIED / APR. 3, / 1954"* inscribed inside. *"LESLIE A.*

WESTGATE / MAR. 28, 1937 ____ / SHIRLY E. HIS WIFE / FEB. 29, 1936 – MAY 31, 1986" is inscribed on the back. A metal flower vase is attached to the right side of the base.

Westgate, Merrill   See Jennie Westgate Monument entry.

Westgate, Shirly E.   See Leslie Westgate Monument entry.

Westgate, Walter W. Jr.   *"WALTER W. JR. / WESTGATE / JAN. 1, 1968 – FEB. 11, 1989"* is inscribed on a scroll carving. A cross, floral design and praying hands are carved above it. *"WALK WITH GOD / YOU'RE NOT ALONE / TAKE HIS HAND / NOW YOU'RE HOME / WE'LL SEE YOU SON / SOMEDAY AND THEN / WE'LL ALL BE TOGETHER / A FAMILY AGAIN."* is inscribed below the scroll on this black monument. A Barnicoat metal tag is present.

Westgate, William S. Monument   *A "W"* monogram is carved at the top of this monument. *"IN LOVING MEMORY OF"* is inscribed on a ribbon carving beneath it, and floral carvings surround them both. *"WESTGATE / 1873   WILLIAM S.   1957 / 1884   CLARA E.   1966"* is inscribed below this. A Charles G. Morse Granite Co. metal tag is present.

Westgate, Scott   *"BABY SCOTT / JUNE 16   JUNE 18 / 1961"* There is a floral carving between the birth and death dates on this flat, ground level stone. His stone is located directly behind the Lawrence W. Westgate Monument. Lakeville Vital Records show that he was Lawrence's son.

Wray, Dorothy E.   *"FOREVER IN OUR HEARTS"* is inscribed at the top of this heart shaped monument. *"DOROTHY E. WRAY / APR. 28, 1934 – JUN. 13, 1995"* is inscribed on a scroll carving. Two rose stems are carved below the inscription. A Barnicoat Monuments metal tag is present.

Zielke, Beatrice C.   *"BEATRICE C. / ZIELKE / JUNE 27, 1931 – OCT. 6, 1996"* is inscribed on this flat, ground level stone, which faces the rear of the cemetery. It is located directly in front of Jacqueline Ebert's monument.

Alfred Lentini Monument

Precinct Cemetery Map Index

Alphabetical:

Allerdt, Adolph H. (1935-1991) – 84
Banks, Donald A. (1908-1984) – 159
Banks, Rita (1914-1993) – 160
Benvissuto, Fern F. (1935-2001) – 182
Berg, Jeannette (1941-1997) – 191
Burch, Anthony R. (1901-1986) – 175
Burch, C. Clayton (1943-1998) – 181
Burch, Gordon W. (1936-1963) – 185
Burch, Margaret E. (1915-1978) – 175
Burgeson, Ernest H. (1949-____) – 33
Burgeson, Jason L. (1980-2000) – 32, 33
Burgeson, Nadine W. (1951-____) – 33
Burnham, Amy L. (1951-____) – 19
Burnham, Arnold M. (1923-1990) – 29, 30
Burnham, Baby Girl (1969) – 163
Burnham, Chester F. (1909-1961) – 92, 96
Burnham, Constance (1938-____) – 46
Burnham, Dora W. (1927-____) – 30
Burnham, Gregory A. (1976-1996) – 18, 20
Burnham, Harold (1936-2001) – 46
Burnham, Harold R., Jr. (1962-1998) – 46, 47
Burnham, Kenneth L. (1925-1983) – 99, 103
Burnham, Loretta M. (1931-____) – 28
Burnham, Nellie M. (1908-1993) – 96
Burnham, Robert W., Sr. (1927-2002) – 26, 28
Burnham, Robert W., Jr. (1948-1988) – 17, 19
Burnham, Vincent R. (1921-1994) – 176
Burnham, Virginia V. (1926-____) – 103
Cardin, Alice E. (1918-1988) – 129, 133
Cardin, John E. (1954-1978) – 129, 132
Cardin, Thomas A. (1942-1988) – 129, 134
Caron, Florence D. (1891-1971) – 156
Caron, Leon N. Sr. (1897-1978) – 155
Chace, Bertha S. (1904-1986) – 154
Chace, Florence O. (1913-1988) – 80
Chace, Walter R. (1910-1975) – 80
Chambers, John T. (1913-____) – 124
Chambers, Martha L. (1912-1982) – 124
Colvin, Charles E. (1902-1971) – 88
Colvin, Gertrude E. (1907-1978) – 88
Cornell, Barbara A. (1952-____) – 15
Cornell, Bertha A. (1927-1990) – 45
Cornell, Charles E. (1917-1995) – 106
Cornell, Charles S. (1893-1967) – 152

Cornell, Elliot E. (1939-____) – 15
Cornell, Ernest (1965) – 151
Cornell, Florence L. (1920-____) – 106
Cornell, Gloria M. (1938-1995) – 116
Cornell, Jennie A. (1896-1980) – 152
Cornell, Jessie M. (1927-1998) – 115
Cornell, Kenneth M (1922-1992) – 45
Cornell, Melissa A. (1984) – 106
Cornell, Paul B. (1928-1957) – 149
Cornell, Russell E. (1926-1999) – 115
Costa, Louis (1934-____) – 153
Costa, Patricia A. (1938-2001) – 153
Costa, Rosemarie (1979) – 127
Cotter, Dorothy G. (1937-1997) – 105
Cushman, Archie G. (1882-1970) – 56, 62
Cushman, Bessie M. (1885-1978) – 57, 62
DeCoff, Clifford G. Jr. (1932-___) – 111
DeCoff, Clifford I. (1960-1981) – 107, 111
DeCoff, Rita L. (1938-____) – 111
DeFreitas, Robert P. (1949-1989) – 16
Delbene, Roy J., Sr. (1937-2003) – 171
DeLisle, Harold F. (1930-2003) – 183
DeMoranville, Arthur L. (1929-1998) – 109
DeMoranville, Bertram E., Jr. (1925-1974) – 109
DeMoranville, Bertram E., Sr. (1904-1987)– 109
DeMoranville, Clara L. (1926-____) – 109
DeMoranville, Jessie M. (1906-1995) – 109
DeMoranville, Shirley F. (1937-1997) – 110
Doyle, Cody C. (1998) – 12
Dunlevy, Brendan M. (1992) – 190
Dunlevy, Karin E. (1962-1998) – 190
Dunlevy, Thomas W., Jr. (1965-____) – 190
Ebert, Jacqueline L. (1949-1985) – 117
Ferguson, Sherrie L. (1967-1996) – 177, 178
Fortunato-DeLisle, Luci M. (1953-____) – 183
Freitas, Joseph (1942-1961) – 90
Gates, Eileen S. (1950-____) – 48
Gates, Ida A. (1893-1977) – 82, 85
Gates, Lawrence D. (1948-1990) –48
Gates, Leonard (1887-1960) – 83, 85
Gay, Harold M. (1930-1986) – 112
Hawes, Barbara L. (1918-1983) – 157
Hawes, Benjamin (1915-____) – 157
Hayward, George A. (1915-1983) – 60

Holcomb, Willis C. (1899-1947) – 162
Johnson, Frederick T. (1937-1992) – 21
Johnson, Patricia J. (1935-____) – 21
Jones, A. Frederick (1898-1979) – 38
Jones, Alberta M. (1932-1990) – 51, 52
Jones, George E. (1928-1987) – 50, 52
Jones, Mabel R. M. (1911-1983) – 38
Judson, Dorothy L. (1909-1964) – 64, 67
Judson, Irma D. (1909-____) – 58
Judson, Kenneth H. (1908-1987) – 58
Judson, Williard E. (1904-1986) – 63, 67
Kaminski, Adam B. (1914-____) – 39
Kaminski, Bernice A. (1922-____) – 39
Keefe, Pamela L. (1960-2003) – 189
Keen, Pamela K. (1955-1969) – 192
Kelly, Annie H. (1892-1963) – 60
Lee, John H. (1902-1980) – 121, 125
Lee, Minnie B. (1911-1981) – 121
Lentini, Alfred (1914-1996) – 55
LeVesque, Paul S., Jr. (1964-1985) – 174
Lewis, Thomas M. (1969-1987) – 36
Maddox, Amos G. (1930-1983) – 158
Maddox, Muriel E. (1931-____) – 158
Maher, Ada M. (1885-1969) – 136
Maher, Howard S. (1902-1963) – 137
Maher, John J. (1886-1948) – 136
Martowska, Agnes P. (1930-____) – 186
Martowska, Anthony P. (1925-1999) – 186
Mason, James R. (1940-1975) – 74
Mastera, Matt (1958-1982) – 69
Maynard, Sally (no dates) – 168
Maynard, Wil (~1926-1986) – 168
McDonald, David C. (1956-1979) – 193
McDonald, Rhonda J. (1956-1968) – 193
Meack, Arthur M. (1910-1981) – 165, 167
Meack, Arthur M., Jr. (1936-____) – 40
Meack, Cindy (1960-1962) – 164
Meack, Gertrude L. (1911-1942) – 166, 167
Meack, Jane C. (1938-____) – 40
Meack, Ralph E. (1914-1963) – 95
Meack, Ralph E., Jr. (1936-____) – 41
Meack, Roberta M. (1938-____) – 41
Meack, Shirley H. (1928-1994) – 94
Miles, Norma I. (1930-1993) – 149
Mooney, Joseph A. (1925-1983) – 27
Mooney, Patricia A. (1930-1999) – 27
Morris, Isabel G. (1911-1993) – 76
Morris, John (1906-1989) – 75
Netto, Violet M. (1923-1965) – 70
Noonan, Gerald A. (1924-____) – 161
Noonan, June M. (1914-____) – 161

Norris, John H. (1904-1984) – 170
Orrall, Archie B. (1886-1978) – 135
Orrall, Josephine C. (1886-1978) – 135
Osborne Monument – 146
Osborne, Charles W. (1934-1991) – 172
Osborne, Evelyn M. (1889-1973) – 145
Osborne, Gertrude E. (1901-1953) – 144
Osborne, William D. (1883-1963) – 140
Peabody, Nelly D. (1919-1997) – 37
Peabody, Robert (1913-1988) – 37
Pereira, Dolores (1930-2002) – 71
Perry, Francis D. (1936-1997) – 187
Perry, Jeffrey N. (1967-1968) – 7
Perry, John F. (1962-1996) – 6
Perry, Lois I. (1943-____) – 187
Pierce, Gertrude C. (1899-1966) – 108
Pittsley, Doris L. (1912-1964) – 7
Pittsley, Eliza F. (1891-1954) – 179
Pittsley, James N., Sr. (1901-1995) – 7
Rego, Anna J. (1931-2000) – 42
Rego, Leonard (1931-1997) – 43
Reynolds, Ada M. (1933-2002) – 14
Reynolds, Annie M. (1901-1951) – 139
Reynolds, Barry L. (1946-1995) – 24
Reynolds, Daisy (~1935-1971) – 78
Reynolds, Dale A. (1963-____) – 4
Reynolds, Derek M. (1988) – 13
Reynolds, George (1911-1982) – 141
Reynolds, Kathleen V. (1944-____) – 25
Reynolds, Leon E. (1923-1988) – 22, 23
Reynolds, Leon F. (1900-1959) – 73, 79
Reynolds, Lillian L. (1925-1992) – 101
Reynolds, Luella M. (1903-1980) – 72, 79
Reynolds, Marcia L. (1943-1988) – 31
Reynolds, Marion L. (1931-1977) – 89
Reynolds, Marjorie L. (1923-____) – 23
Reynolds, Maurice A. (1898-1971) – 139
Reynolds, Maurice A., Jr. (1935-1991)– 143
Reynolds, Maynard W. (1936-____) – 31
Reynolds, Nancy V. (1907-1961) – 97, 102
Reynolds, O. Nelson Jr. (1928-1995) – 101
Reynolds, Rita V. (1941-____) – 4
Reynolds, Stephen F. (1944-1983) – 25
Reynolds, Suzanne (1940-1970) – 77
Reynolds, Thelma A. (1920-1973) – 138, 141
Reynolds, Walter A. (1927-____) – 89
Richards, Delphine A. (1940-1995) – 119
Richards, Donald N., Sr. (1944-1986) – 113
Richards, Dorothy (1945-1988) – 113

Richards, DeWitt L. (1935-2000) – 114
Richards, Frederick E. (1939-1984) – 119
Richards, Grace A. (1934-2002) – 114
Richards, Nancy L. (1938-2002) – 54
Rijo, George R. (1926-1999) – 86, 91
Rijo, Hilda M. (1923-____) – 91
Romaska, Irene T. (1912-1978) – 81
Rose-Mello, Tasha T. (1965-2000) – 194
Rubadou, Mary I. (1925-1984) – 104
Russis, William C. (1929-2001) – 180
Santos, Cora L. (____-1990) – 49
Shuman, Mary T. (1908-1976) – 120
Shuman, Winifred V. (1913-1979) – 120
Simms, Alexander (1908-1990) – 98
Simms, Elizabeth (1912-2002) – 98
Simpson, Beatrice E. (1920-1971) – 2, 5
Simpson, Harry W. (1922-1996) – 3, 5
Sisson, Bettylou (1940-1983) – 100
Sisson, Phillip G. (1930-1988) – 169
Souza Monument – 35
Souza, E. J. (1925-____) – 34
St. Don, Eva M. (1945-1973) – 142
Taylor, Gertrude R. (1903-1974) – 1
Taylor, J. Roy (1899-1993) – 87
Taylor, Lou (1907-1998) – 87
Taylor, Roy W. (1886-1977) – 1
Thomas, Alice L. (1893-1965) – 129
Thomas, Arnold G. (1920-1985) – 126, 128
Thomas, Harry (1932-____) – 93
Thomas, Herbert H. (1893-1969) – 129
Thomas, Herbert H., Jr. (1916-1979) – 131

Thomas, Herbert H., III (1931-2001) – 53
Thomas, Muriel L. (1932-____) – 53
Thomas, Phyllis (1934-____) – 93
Thomas, Roberta (1921 – 1958) – 130
Thompson, Margaret A. (1940-2001) – 188
VanSchelt, Virginia (1927-2002) – 184
Vera, Alma B. (1913-1997) – 61
Vera, Edmund H. (1912-1983) – 61
Vigers, James J., III (1927-1992) –59
Vigers, Lillian E. (1915-____) – 59
Wambolt, Avis L. (1915-1986) – 65, 68
Wambolt, Newell I. (1920-1961) – 66, 68
Watts, Muriel A. C. (1934-____) – 122
Watts, Raymond (1929-1984) – 122, 123
Westgate, Barbara A. (1935-1958) – 148
Westgate, Carrie L. (1906-1994) – 10
Westgate, Clara E. (1884-1966) – 147
Westgate, Clarence M. (1902-1988) – 10
Westgate, Inez L. (1898-1980) – 9
Westgate, Irving B. (1894-1969) – 9
Westgate, Jennie (1903-1971) – 8
Westgate, Lawrence W. (1934-____) – 148
Westgate, Leslie (1937-____) – 11
Westgate, Merrill (1917-1967) – 8
Westgate, Scott (1961) – 150
Westgate, Shirly E. (1936-1986) – 11
Westgate, Walter W., Jr. (1968-1989) – 173
Westgate, William S. (1873-1957) – 147
Wray, Dorothy E. (1934-1995) – 44
Zielke, Beatrice C. (1931-1996) – 118

Funeral Home Marker for Jeannette Berg

Precinct Cemetery Map Index

By Location:

1 – Taylor, Roy W. (1886-1977)
Taylor, Gertrude R. (1903-1974)
2 – Simpson, Beatrice E. (1920-1971)
3 – Simpson, Harry W. (1922-1996)
4 – Reynolds, Rita V. (1941-____)
Reynolds, Dale A. (1963-____)
5 – Simpson, Harry W. (1922-1996)
Simpson, Beatrice E. (1920-1971)
6 – Perry, John F. (1962-1996)
7 – Pittsley, James N., Sr. (1901-1995)
Pittsley, Doris L. (1912-1964)
Perry, Jeffrey N. (1967-1968)
8 – Westgate, Jennie (1903-1971)
Westgate, Merrill (1917-1967)
9 – Westgate, Inez L. (1898-1980)
Westgate, Irving B. (1894-1969)
10 – Westgate, Clarence M. (1902-1988)
Westgate, Carrie L. (1906-1994)
11 – Westgate, Leslie (1937-____)
Westgate, Shirly E. (1936-1986)
12 – Doyle, Cody C. (1998)
13 – Reynolds, Derek M. (1988)
14 – Reynolds, Ada M. (1933-2002)
15 – Cornell, Barbara A. (1952-____)
Cornell, Elliot E. (1939-____)
16 – DeFreitas, Robert P. (1949-1989)
17 – Burnham, Robert W. Jr. (1948-1988)
18 – Burnham, Gregory A. (1976-1996)
19 – Burnham, Robert W., Jr. (1948-1988)
Burnham, Amy L. (1951-____)
20 – Burnham, Gregory A. (1976-1996)
21 – Johnson, Frederick T. (1937-1992)
Johnson, Patricia J. (1935-____)
22 – Reynolds, Leon E. (1923-1988)
23 – Reynolds, Leon E. (1923-1988)
Reynolds, Marjorie L. (1923-____)
24 – Reynolds, Barry L. (1946-1995)
25 – Reynolds, Stephen F. (1944-1983)
Reynolds, Kathleen V. (1944-____)
26 – Burnham, Robert W., Sr. (1927-2002)
27 – Mooney, Joseph A. (1925-1983)
Mooney, Patricia A. (1930-1999)
28 – Burnham, Robert W. (1927-2002)
Burnham, Loretta M. (1931-____)
29 – Burnham, Arnold M. (1923-1990)
30 – Burnham, Arnold M. (1923-1990)
Burnham, Dora W. (1927-____)
31 – Reynolds, Maynard W. (1936-____)

Reynolds, Marcia L. (1943-1988)
32 – Burgeson, Jason L. (1980-2000)
33 – Burgeson, Jason L. (1980-2000)
Burgeson, Ernest H. (1949-____)
Burgeson, Nadine W. (1951-____)
34 – Souza, E. J. (1925-____)
35 – Souza Monument
36 – Lewis, Thomas M. (1969-1987)
37 – Peabody, Nelly D. (1919-1997)
Peabody, Robert (1913-1988)
38 – Jones, A. Frederick (1898-1979)
Jones, Mabel R. M. (1911-1983)
39 – Kaminski, Adam B. (1914-____)
Kaminski, Bernice A. (1922-____)
40 – Meack, Arthur M., Jr. (1936-____)
Meack, Jane C. (1938-____)
41 – Meack, Ralph E., Jr. (1936-____)
Meack, Roberta M. (1938-____)
42 – Rego, Anna J. (1931-2000)
43 – Rego, Leonard (1931-1997)
44 – Wray, Dorothy E. (1934-1995)
45 – Cornell, Kenneth M (1922-1992)
Cornell, Bertha A. (1927-1990)
46 – Burnham, Harold (1936-2001)
Burnham, Constance (1938-____)
Burnham, Harold R., Jr. (1962-1998)
47 – Burnham, Harold R., Jr. (1962-1998)
48 – Gates, Eileen S. (1950-____)
Gates, Lawrence D. (1948-1990)
49 – Santos, Cora L. (____-1990)
50 – Jones, George E. (1928-1987)
51 – Jones, Alberta M. (1932-1990)
52 – Jones, George E. (1928-1987)
Jones, Alberta M. (1932-1990)
53 – Thomas, Herbert H., III (1931-2001)
Thomas, Muriel L. (1932-____)
54 – Richards, Nancy L. (1938-2002)
55 – Lentini, Alfred (1914-1996)
56 – Cushman, Archie G. (1882-1970)
57 – Cushman, Bessie M. (1885-1978)
58 – Judson, Kenneth H. (1908-1987)
Judson, Irma D. (1909-____)
59 – Vigers, James J., III (1927-1992)
Vigers, Lillian E. (1915-____)
60 – Kelly, Annie H. (1892-1963)
Hayward, George A. (1915-1983)
61 – Vera, Edmund H. (1912-1983)
Vera, Alma B. (1913-1997)

62 – Cushman, Archie G. (1882-1970)
   Cushman, Bessie M. (1885-1978)
63 – Judson, Williard E. (1904-1986)
64 – Judson, Dorothy L. (1909-1964)
65 – Wambolt, Avis L. (1915-1986)
66 – Wambolt, Newell I. (1920-1961)
67 – Judson, Williard E. (1904-1986)
   Judson, Dorothy L. (1909-1964)
68 – Wambolt, Newell I. (1920-1961)
   Wambolt, Avis L. (1915-1986)
69 – Mastera, Matt (1958-1982)
70 – Netto, Violet M. (1923-1965)
71 – Pereira, Dolores (1930-2002)
72 – Reynolds, Luella M. (1903-1980)
73 – Reynolds, Leon F. (1900-1959)
74 – Mason, James R. (1940-1975)
75 – Morris, John (1906-1989)
76 – Morris, Isabel G. (1911-1993)
77 – Reynolds, Suzanne (1940-1970)
78 – Reynolds, Daisy (~1935-1971)
79 – Reynolds, Leon F. (1900-1959)
   Reynolds, Luella M. (1903-1980)
80 – Chace, Walter R. (1910-1975)
   Chace, Florence O. (1913-1988)
81 – Romaska, Irene T. (1912-1978)
82 – Gates, Ida A. (1893-1977)
83 – Gates, Leonard (1887-1960)
84 – Allerdt, Adolph H. (1935-1991)
85 – Gates, Ida A. (1893-1977)
   Gates, Leonard (1887-1960)
86 – Rijo, George R. (1926-1999)
87 – Taylor, J. Roy (1899-1993)
   Taylor, Lou (1907-1998)
88 – Colvin, Gertrude E. (1907-1978)
   Colvin, Charles E. (1902-1971)
89 – Reynolds, Walter A. (1927-____)
   Reynolds, Marion L. (1931-1977)
90 – Freitas, Joseph (1942-1961)
91 – Rijo, George R. (1926-1999)
   Rijo, Hilda M. (1923-____)
92 – Burnham, Chester F. (1909-1961)
93 – Thomas, Harry (1932-____)
   Thomas, Phyllis (1934-____)
94 – Meack, Shirley H. (1928-1994)
95 – Meack, Ralph E. (1914-1963)
96 – Burnham, Chester F. (1909-1961)
   Burnham, Nellie M. (1908-1993)
97 – Reynolds, Nancy V. (1907-1961)
98 – Simms, Alexander (1908-1990)
   Simms, Elizabeth (1912-2002)
99 – Burnham, Kenneth L. (1925-1983)

100 – Sisson, Bettylou (1940-1983)
101 – Reynolds, O. Nelson Jr. (1928-1995)
   Reynolds, Lillian L. (1925-1992)
102 – Reynolds, Nancy V. (1907-1961)
103 – Burnham, Kenneth L. (1925-1983)
   Burnham, Virginia V. (1926-____)
104 – Rubadou, Mary I. (1925-1984)
105 – Cotter, Dorothy G. (1937-1997)
106 – Cornell, Charles E. (1917-1995)
   Cornell, Florence L. (1920-____)
106 – Cornell, Melissa A. (1984)
107 – DeCoff, Clifford G. Jr. (1932-____)
108 – Pierce, Gertrude C. (1899-1966)
109 – DeMoranville, Bertram E., Jr (1925-1974)
   DeMoranville, Arthur L. (1929-1998)
   DeMoranville, Clara L. (1926-____)
   DeMoranville, Bertram E., Sr. (1904-1987)
   DeMoranville, Jessie M. (1906-1995)
110 – DeMoranville, Shirley F. (1937-1997)
111 – DeCoff, Clifford G. Jr. (1932-____)
   DeCoff, Rita L. (1938-____)
   DeCoff, Clifford I. (1960-1981)
112 – Gay, Harold M. (1930-1986)
113 – Richards, Donald N., Sr. (1944-1986)
   Richards, Dorothy (1945-1988)
114 – Richards, DeWitt L. (1935-2000)
   Richards, Grace A. (1934-2002)
115 – Cornell, Russell E. (1926-1999)
   Cornell, Jessie M. (1927-1998)
116 – Cornell, Gloria M. (1938-1995)
117 – Ebert, Jacqueline L. (1949-1985)
118 – Zielke, Beatrice C. (1931-1996)
119 – Richards, Frederick E. (1939-1984)
   Richards, Delphine A. (1940-1995)
120 – Shuman, Mary T. (1908-1976)
   Shuman, Winifred V. (1913-1979)
121 – Lee, Minnie B. (1911-1981)
   Lee, John H. (1902-1980)
122 – Watts, Raymond (1929-1984)
   Watts, Muriel A. C. (1934-____)
123 – Watts, Raymond (1929-1984)
124 – Chambers, John T. (1913-____)
   Chambers, Martha L. (1912-1982)
125 – Lee, John H. (1902-1980)
126 – Thomas, Arnold G. (1920-1985)
127 – Costa, Rosemarie (1979)
128 – Thomas, Arnold G. (1920-1985)
129 – Thomas, Herbert H. (1893-1969)
   Thomas, Alice L. (1893-1965)

Cardin, John E. (1954-1978)
Cardin, Alice E. (1918-1988)
Cardin, Thomas A. (1942-1988)
130 – Thomas, Roberta (1921 – 1958)
131 – Thomas, Herbert H., Jr. (1916-1979)
132 – Cardin, John E. (1954-1978)
133 – Cardin, Alice E. (1918-1988)
134 – Cardin, Thomas A. (1942-1988)
135 – Orrall, Archie B. (1886-1978)
135 – Orrall, Josephine C. (1886-1978)
136 – Maher, John J. (1886-1948)
Maher, Ada M. (1885-1969)
137 – Maher, Howard S. (1902-1963)
138 – Reynolds, Thelma A. (1920-1973)
139 – Reynolds, Annie M. (1901-1951)
Reynolds, Maurice A. (1898-1971)
140 – Osborne, William D. (1883-1963)
141 – Reynolds, Thelma A. (1920-1973)
Reynolds, George (1911-1982)
142 – St. Don, Eva M. (1945-1973)
143 – Reynolds, Maurice A., Jr. (1935-1991)
144 – Osborne, Gertrude E. (1901-1953)
145 – Osborne, Evelyn M. (1889-1973)
146 – Osborne Monument
147 – Westgate, William S. (1873-1957)
Westgate, Clara E. (1884-1966)
148 – Westgate, Lawrence W. (1934-____)
Westgate, Barbara A. (1935-1958)
149 – Cornell, Paul B. (1928-1957)
Miles, Norma I. (1930-1993)
150 – Westgate, Scott (1961)
151 – Cornell, Ernest (1965)
152 – Cornell, Charles S. (1893-1967)
Cornell, Jennie A. (1896-1980)
153 – Costa, Louis (1934-____)
Costa, Patricia A. (1938-2001)
154 – Chace, Bertha S. (1904-1986)
155 – Caron, Leon N. Sr. (1897-1978)
156 – Caron, Florence D. (1891-1971)
157 – Hawes, Benjamin (1915-____)
Hawes, Barbara L. (1918-1983)
158 – Maddox, Amos G. (1930-1983)
Maddox, Muriel E. (1931-____)
159 – Banks, Donald A. (1908-1984)
160 – Banks, Rita (1914-1993)

161 – Noonan, June M (1914-____)
Noonan, Gerald A. (1924-____)
162 – Holcomb, Willis C. (1899-1947)
163 – Burnham, Baby Girl (1969)
164 – Meack, Cindy (1960-1962)
165 – Meack, Arthur M. (1910-1981)
166 – Meack, Gertrude L. (1911-1942)
167 – Meack, Arthur M. (1910-1981)
Meack, Gertrude L. (1911-1942)
168 – Maynard, Wil (~1926-1986)
Maynard, Sally (no dates)
169 – Sisson, Phillip G. (1930-1988)
170 – Norris, John H. (1904-1984)
171 – Delbene, Roy J., Sr. (1937-2003)
172 – Osborne, Charles W. (1934-1991)
173 – Westgate, Walter W., Jr. (1968-1989)
174 – LeVesque, Paul S., Jr. (1964-1985)
175 – Burch, Anthony R. (1901-1986)
Burch, Margaret E. (1915-1978)
176 – Burnham, Vincent R. (1921-1994)
177 – Ferguson, Sherrie L. (1967-1996)
178 – Ferguson, Sherrie L. (1967-1996)
179 – Pittsley, Eliza F. (1891-1954)
180 – Russis, William C. (1929-2001)
181 – Burch, C. Clayton (1943-1998)
182 – Benvissuto, Fern F. (1935-2001)
183 – DeLisle, Harold F. (1930-2003)
Fortunato-DeLisle, Luci M. (1953-____)
184 – VanSchelt, Virginia (1927-2002)
185 – Burch, Gordon W. (1936-1963)
186 – Martowska, Anthony P. (1925-1999)
Martowska, Agnes P. (1930-____)
187 – Perry, Francis D. (1936-1997)
Perry, Lois I. (1943-____)
188 – Thompson, Margaret A. (1940-2001)
189 – Keefe, Pamela L. (1960-2003)
190 – Dunlevy, Thomas W., Jr. (1965-____)
Dunlevy, Karin E. (1962-1998)
Dunlevy, Brendan M. (1992)
191 – Berg, Jeannette (1941-1997)
192 – Keen, Pamela K. (1955-1969)
193 – McDonald, David C. (1956-1979)
McDonald, Rhonda J. (1956-1968)
194 – Rose-Mello, Tasha T. (1965-2000)

Precinct Cemetery Map
Overview

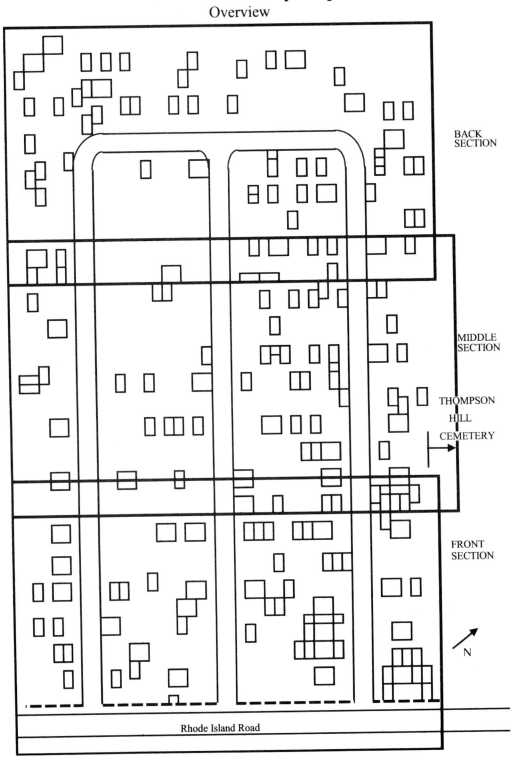

BACK
SECTION

MIDDLE
SECTION

THOMPSON

HILL

CEMETERY

FRONT
SECTION

N

Rhode Island Road

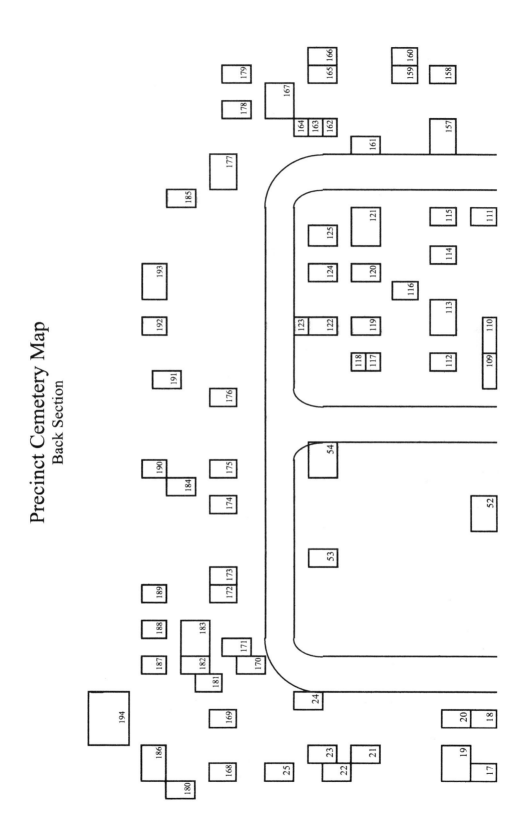

Precinct Cemetery Map
Back Section

Precinct Cemetery Map
Middle Section

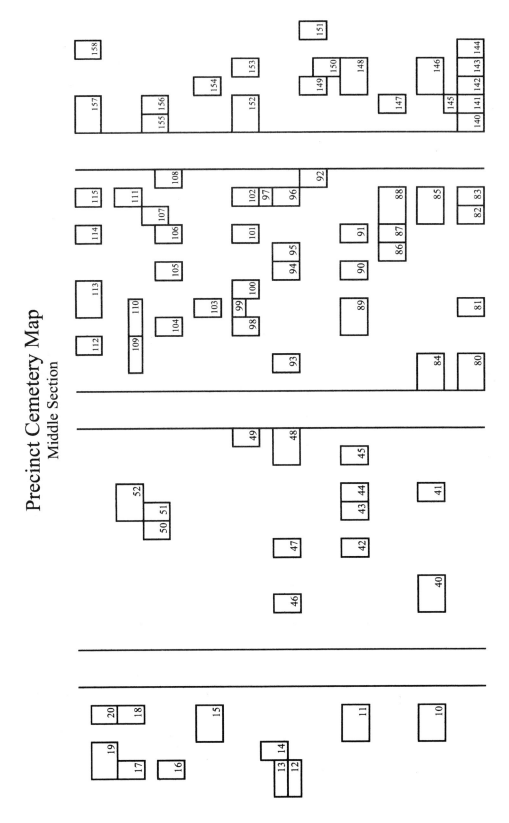

Precinct Cemetery Map
Front Section

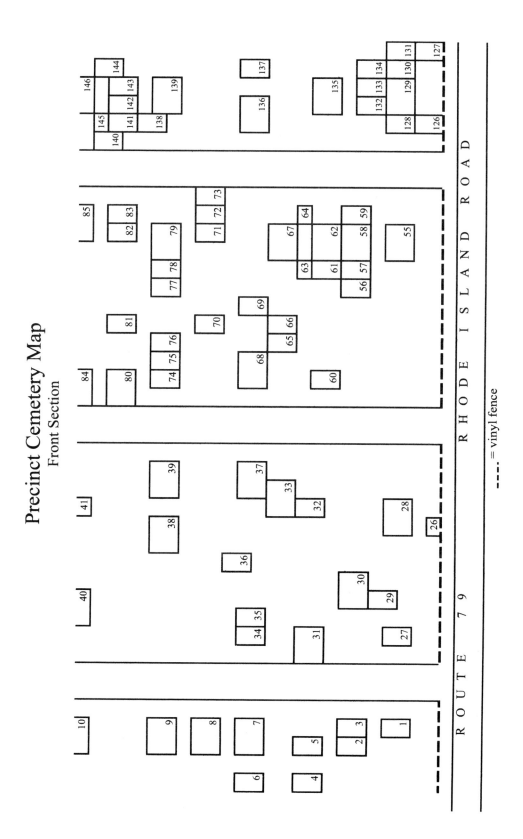

Chapter 22
Race Course Cemetery

Race Course Cemetery is located between the driveways for 12 and 14 Race Course Road, next to the street. There is no fencing or any other type of border around this wooded area, and no sign is present. Only two inscribed gravestones are present in this cemetery, but there are several other fieldstones that may signify additional graves. Gravestones face northwest, and date 1778 and 1802. The Lakeville Assessor's Office lists this cemetery as located on private property. However, the deed has an "easement for cemetery purposes" on approximately 1/3 acre. Thatcher refers to this cemetery as "Graves in field on opposite side of "Race-course" road." It has also been called "Veteran's Graves" in the *1965 Lakeville Town Report*. Entries were recorded March 8, 2000.

Ammon   *"⚜ / AMMON / CONTINENTAL LINE / REVOLUTIONARY WAR / 1752 1778"* is inscribed on this flat, ground level marker. A veteran's marker and flag are present.

Booth, John   *"⚜ / JOHN BOOTH / CONTINENTAL LINE / REVOLUTIONARY WAR / 1728   1802"* is inscribed on this flat, 1 inch high marker. A veteran's marker and flag are present.

Additional Notes:

Thatcher lists the following people as being buried here:
"Ammon: a Negro, belonged to Capt. William Canedy, Mar. 30, 1778, in his 29th year."
"Booth: John, died Nov. 30, 1802, in his 74th year."
"Booth, Lydia, wife of John, Mar. 28, 1784, 52nd year."

Because Thatcher's research predate the movement of gravestones in this town, it is the opinion of this author that the above three people are actually buried in Race Course Cemetery despite the fact that they have gravestones in other cemeteries. (John and Lydia Booth's footstones are in Booth #1 Cemetery and their headstones are in Booth #2 Cemetery. A headstone for Ammon is in Thompson Hill Cemetery.) Vigers (1952) lists Ammon, John and Lydia Booth's gravestones as being in Race Course Cemetery as recently as 1952.

Race Course Cemetery Index and Map

Ammon (1752-1778) – 2
Booth, John (1728-1802) – 1
x = other unmarked stones

1 – Booth, John (1728-1802)
2 – Ammon (1752-1778)

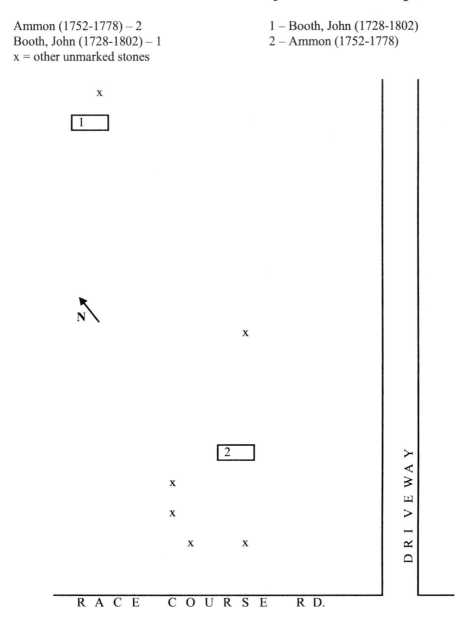

Chapter 23
Reynolds Cemetery

This cemetery is located on private property, about 100 yards behind, and to the right of the house at 184 County Street. A stone wall forms one border of this cemetery. Its size is unknown. No sign is present. One fieldstone appears to be squared off at the top, and another has an "S" carved on it. No other inscriptions were found. Stones face northwest. Thatcher described it as "A dozen more graves with rough stones as markers on land and near house of John E. Staunton, near Lake View, Long Pond, Lakeville near Freetown line. Supposed to be the old Reynolds family burying place." Entries were recorded September 21, 2006.

Reynolds Cemetery Map

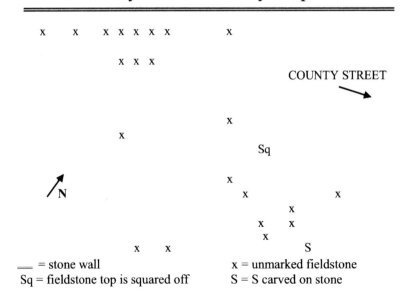

= stone wall   x = unmarked fieldstone
Sq = fieldstone top is squared off   S = S carved on stone

Chapter 24
Richmond Cemetery

Richmond Cemetery is located on the northwest corner of Cross Street and Taunton Street. A vinyl fence surrounds this cemetery, and its entrance is on Taunton Street. The sign is in good repair. Several unmarked footstones are present on the left side of the cemetery. It is unknown if these stones mark graves, or just plots. Gravestones face south, and date from 1821 to 1999. The Lakeville Assessor's Office lists this cemetery as town owned, 11,400 square feet in size. Thatcher calls this a "Cemetery at North Lakeville." Entries were recorded March 8, 2000.

Aldrich, John R. *"FATHER"* is inscribed in shallow relief on the top curved surface of the stone. *"JOHN R. ALDRICH / AUG. 3, 1838, / OCT. 17, 1906. / REST, SWEET REST"* is inscribed on the front. Flower and leaf designs are carved in shallow relief above the inscription.

Aldrich, Sarah E. *"MOTHER"* is carved in shallow relief on the top curved surface of this stone. *"SARAH ELLEN, / WIFE OF / JOHN R. ALDRICH, / APR. 21, 1842, / AUG. 27, 1899. / HE GIVETH HIS BELOVED SLEEP."* is inscribed on the front. Flower and leaf designs are carved in shallow relief above the inscription.

Auger, Grace R. See Herbert M. Haskins Monument entry.
"GRACE" This flat, ground level stone is located to the far left of the monument. Lakeville Vital Records show that she was the wife of Alfred E. Auger, and her middle name was Richmond.

Back, Aurilla J. *"AURILLA JANE / Daut. of / George & Sarah S. / BACK / Died Oct 11, 1856 / Æ. 1 y'r, 3 m's, / & 22 d's. / ..."* is inscribed on this small textured stone. The first line is carved in relief along an arch. A two-line inscription follows, but is unreadable due to the weathering. Lakeville Vital Records verify her death information.

Back, George   *"GEORGE BACK / died / Aug. 8, 1881. / Aged 61 years. / Peacefully sleeping."*   The first line is carved in relief along an arch.   A *"GAR 8 234"* marker and flag are present at this gravesite. *Massachusetts Civil War Soldiers & Sailors, 1861-1865,* Vol. IV, p. 129 shows that he served with the 40th Infantry, Co. F., and the 22 Veteran's Reserve Corp, Co. D.

Back, Sarah S.   *"SARAH S. / Wife of / George Back. / and widow of / B. M. Dunham, / Died Feb. 16, 1887, / Aged 75 yrs. 4 m's. / Gone but not forgotten."*   The first line is carved in relief along an arch.

Dunham, Amanda P.   See D. Frances Dunham Monument entry.

Dunham, Barnaba M.   *"BARNABA M. DUNHAM / died / May 27. / 1851. / Aged 51 years. / There is sweet rest in Heaven"*   The first line is carved in relief along an arch.

Dunham, D. Frances Monument   This monument is carved to appear as two separate headstones at the top, but is actually one stone. *"D. FRANCES / died / Feb. 8, 1862; / Aged 18 yrs. / & 3 m's."* is inscribed on the left side, and *"AMANDA P. / died / Feb. 7, 1862; / Aged 13 yrs. / & 9 m's."* is inscribed on the right. *"Daughters of / Barnaba M. & Sarah S. Dunham. / A Mother's Love still lingers round thy graves."* is inscribed on the bottom half of the monument, across the entire width. The first line on each side is carved in relief along an arch.

Dunham, Edwin O. Monument   A sculptured scroll is carved on the slanted surface of this lichen encrusted monument. *"EDWIN O. DUNHAM / 1845 – 1906. / HIS WIFE / S. LIZZIE LEONARD / 1848 – 1919."* is carved in relief on this scroll. *"DUNHAM"* is carved in relief on the front of the base of this monument.

Dunham, Erastus R.   *"ERASTUS R. / son of Barnaba M. / & Sarah S. Dunham. / died March 30, 1840. / Æ 1 Month / & 18 D's."*   The first line is carved in outline. The two-line poem that follows is unreadable due to weathering.   *"Warren, Fall River?"* is inscribed on the bottom of this stone.

Dunham, S. Lizzie   See Edwin Dunham Monument entry.
Lakeville Vital Records show that her name was Sarah Elizabeth   She was the daughter of Jefferson Leonard and Sarah Tinkham.   She was 72 years and 7 days old when she died on June 26, 1919.

Dunham, William Morton   *"WILLIAM MORTON, / Son of / Barnaba M. & Sarah S. / DUNHAM, / 1st Sergeant Co. C. 7th Mass., Vol. / Born Jan. 15, 1829. / Killed at the Battle of / Fredericksburg, Va., / May 3, 1863.*

> *Rest soldier in thy honored grave,*
> *Thy duty nobly done,*
> *Long as thy Country's banners wave,*
> *The land whos life thou died to save,*
> *Shall bless the Memory of the brave,*
> *And prize her patriot Son."*

"BURT, Taunton." is inscribed at the bottom of this stone.   Note the spelling of *whos*

in the poem. A *"GAR 8 103"* marker and flag are present. *Massachusetts Civil War Soldiers & Sailors, 1861-1865,* Vol. I, p. 482 confirms he was with the 7th Infantry, Co. C.

Gifford, Allen R.   See David B. Monroe Monument entry.
His information was added after the original transcription date. There is no footstone present for him.

Gifford, Mildred L.   See David B. Monroe Monument entry.
"M. L. G." is inscribed on this flat, 1-2 inch high footstone, which is located in front of the monument, on the left. It was added after the transcription date.

Gifford, Richmond M.   See David B. Monroe Monument entry.
"R. M. G." This flat, 2-3 inch high footstone is located in front of the monument on the far left. It was added after the transcription date.

Harlow, Elvira J.   See Foster Harlow Monument entry.

Harlow, Foster A. Monument   *"FOSTER A. HARLOW / 1832 – 1909 / ELVIRA J. / HIS WIFE / 1837 – 1912"* The first line is carved along an arch.

Harlow, Lena   *"Little LENA. / Died July 26, 1863. / Aged / 3 yrs. 5 months, / 19 days."* Underneath the first line is a sculptured carving of a dove. The last line on this stone is buried underground. This stone is leaning forward due to the pressure of yucca plants behind it.

Haskins, Abbie B.   See Herbert M. Haskins Monument entry.

Haskins, Charles T.   See Herbert M. Haskins Monument entry.

Haskins, Clarence T.   See Herbert M. Haskins Monument entry.

Haskins, Herbert M. Monument   *"HERBERT M. HASKINS / FEB. 24, 1858 – FEB. 14, 1946 / IDA J. WASHBURN HIS WIFE / MAY 24, 1862 – APR. 21, 1938 / GRACE R. AUGER THEIR DAUGHTER / MAY 23, 1891 – AUG. 17, 1951 / LESTER W. HASKINS / JULY 2, 1886 – JAN. 3, 1962"* is inscribed on the front of this monument. *"HASKINS"* is carved in relief on the front base. *"MARTIN K. HASKINS / MAY 31, 1816 – OCT. 7, 1891 / ABBIE B. HIS WIFE / MAR. 23, 1821 – MAR. 29, 1914 / CHARLES T. / JUNE 17, 1848 – NOV. 9, 1853 / CLARENCE T. / JUNE 17, 1848 – NOV. 18, 1853"* is inscribed on the back.
"FATHER" This flat, ground level stone is located to the left of the monument.

Haskins, Ida J.   See Herbert M. Haskins Monument entry.
"MOTHER" This flat, ground level stone is located to the immediate left of the monument.

Haskins, Lester W.   See Herbert M. Haskins Monument entry.
"LESTER W. HASKINS / MASSACHUSETTS / CPL CO A 8 DIV SUPPLY TN / WORLD WAR I / JULY 2, 1886 – JAN 3, 1962" This flat, ground level stone is located to the very far left of the monument. It is beginning to be buried. A circled cross is carved at the top. An American Legion marker and a flag are present.

Haskins, Martin K.   See Herbert M. Haskins Monument entry.

Haskins, Russell L.   *"RUSSELL L. HASKINS / NOV 12, 1898 – MAY 2, 1969"* is inscribed on this flat, ground level stone. This lichen encrusted stone is beginning to be buried. Lakeville Vital Records show that he was the son of Herbert and Ida Haskins.

Hinkley, Aaron A.   See Benjamin Hinkley Monument entry.

Hinkley, Benjamin Monument   *"HINKLEY"* is carved in relief on front of this monument. *"BENJAMIN HINKLEY / 1793 – 1885 / AARON A. HINKLEY / 1826 – 1906"* is inscribed on the back on the left side, and *"SARAH HINKLEY / 1801 – 1884 / JULIA A. HINKLEY / 1823 – 1908"* is inscribed on the right side. *"CLARENCE HERBERT HINKLEY / 1854 – 5 MOS."* is inscribed across the bottom. Remnants of four 8 inch square stone post are at the corners of this Hinkley plot. They vary in height from 0 to 6 inches.

Hinkley, Clarence H.   See Benjamin Hinkley Monument entry.

Hinkley, Julia A.   See Benjamin Hinkley Monument entry.

Hinkley, Sarah   See Benjamin Hinkley Monument entry.

Keelin, Jennie E.   *"JENNIE E. (COTTI) / Feb. 7, 1909 – ____ / WIFE OF RUSSELL HASKINS / AND FRANCIS KEELIN"* is inscribed on this flat, lichen encrusted, ground level stone.

Lang, Stella M.   *"STELLA M. LANG / DAUGHTER OF / HERBERT & IDA HASKINS / JUNE 2, 1894 – NOV 8, 1976"* This flat, ground level stone is beginning to be buried.

Macomber, Gideon   *"GIDEON MACOMBER / died / Oct. 27, 1852; / Aged 74."* The first line is carved along an arch.

Macomber, Huldah   *"HULDAH, / wife of / Gideon Macomber. / died / April 29, 1849. / Aged 66."* The first line is carved along an arch.

McFarlin Rock   *"M ^C,, FARLIN"* is embossed on a metal plaque that is attached to this large white boulder. It is located behind the McFarlin graves.

McFarlin, Pamelia F. C.   *"1880 ✝ 1915 / PAMELIA F. C. MCFARLIN"* is embossed on this flat, ground level, metal plaque that is beginning to be buried. A circle of embossed floral designs surround the upper half of the cross. It is located in front of the McFarlin Rock.

McFarlin, Sampson   *"✝ / SAMPSON McFARLIN / MASSACHUSETTS / PVT CO D 5 REGT MASS INF / SPANISH AMERICAN WAR / SEPT 22 1877   DEC 29 1957"* is embossed on this flat metal plaque. It is in front of the McFarlin Rock. A Spanish American War Veteran marker, a veteran's marker and a flag are present at this site.

Miller, Adino R.   *"In memory of / ADINO R. MILLER, / who died / Oct. 5, 1835, / in his 28 Year."* An urn and willow carving is at the top of this slate stone. Designs are carved down the sides.

Miller, Almira   See Samuel Miller Monument entry.

Miller, Betsey   See Samuel Miller Monument entry.

Miller, Charles   See Samuel Miller Monument entry.

Miller, Earnest   See Samuel Miller Monument entry.

Miller, Helen   See Samuel Miller Monument entry.

Miller, Joseph   See Samuel Miller Monument entry.

Miller, Josie   See Samuel Miller Monument entry.

Miller, Mary   See Samuel Miller Monument entry.
The inscription for Mary's death year is not completely filled in.   Lakeville Vital Records list her death on January 28, 1901, at 79 years, 5 months, and 20 days old.

Miller, Samuel Monument   *"MILLER"* is carved in relief on the first line of this monument. Below this, *"SAMUEL 1818 · 1900 / HIS WIFE / ALMIRA 1822 · 1904 / HELEN 1849 · 1908 / EARNEST 1849 · 1866 / BETSEY 1859 · 1965"* is inscribed on the left side, and *"JOSEPH 1821 · 1881 / HIS WIFE / MARY 1822 · 190_ / JOSIE 1848 · 1868 / STANLEY 1865 · 1865 / CHARLES 1853 · 1860"* is inscribed on the right side. The last digit in Mary's death year is left blank.

Miller, Stanley   See Samuel Miller Monument entry.

Monroe, David B. Monument
"DAVID B. MONROE / 1834 – 1920 / HIS WIFE / SAMANTHA L. MONROE / 1836 – 1919 / MABEL H. MONROE / 1873 – 1963" is inscribed on the front of this monument.   *"MONROE"* is carved in relief at the bottom. *"INFANT. / JAN. 10, 1859. – JAN. 11, 1859. / LIZZIE M. / JAN. 5, 1860. – SEPT. 11, 1869. / HORACE C. / JUNE 18, 1863. – NOV. 27, 1863. / MATTIE W. / JULY 15, 1866. – NOV. 24, 1867. / CHILDREN OF DAVID B. AND / SAMANTHA L. MONROE."* is inscribed on the right side. *"RICHMOND M. / 1914 – 1984 / HIS WIFE / MILDRED L. / 1920 – ____ / SON / ALLEN R. / 1938 – 1999"* is inscribed on the left side, with *"GIFFORD"* inscribed on the base. There are no inscriptions on the back. This monument has a pointed top with  designs carved below it on all four sides. A low stone wall forms the border of this plot on the front and right sides.
"D. B. M." is carved in shallow relief on this flat 0-2 inch high footstone. It is located in front of the monument, on the far right.

Monroe, Horace C.   See David B. Monroe Monument entry.

Monroe, Infant   See David B. Monroe Monument entry.

Monroe, Lizzie M.   See David B. Monroe Monument entry.

Monroe, Mabel H.   See David B. Monroe Monument entry.
"M. H. M." is carved in shallow relief on this flat, 1-2 inch high footstone. It is located to the right of the monument.

Monroe, Mattie W.   See David B. Monroe Monument entry.

Monroe, Samantha L.   See David B. Monroe Monument entry.
"S. L. M." is carved in shallow relief on this flat, ground level stone. It is located in front of the monument, on the right.

Reed, James S. Monument   *"REED"* is carved in relief on the top slanted surface of this monument. *"JAMES S. REED / 1857 – 1933 / HIS WIFE / MARY F. REYNOLDS / 1848 – 1928"* is inscribed on the front.

Reed, Mary F.   See James Reed Monument entry.

Richmond, Abigail   *"ABIGAIL / wife of / William Richmond. / died Dec. 14, 1880. / Aged 80 yrs. 3 m's."* The first line is carved in relief along an arch.

Richmond, Aurelia J.   See Sally R. Richmond Obelisk entry.
"AURILIA J." is inscribed on the top slanted surface of this stone. *"Richmond."* is inscribed on the front. It is located to the right of the obelisk. A crack runs through the center of this stone in the front, but it does not extend to the back.

Richmond, Benjamin, Dea.   *"As the Just / tribute of respect this stone / is erected"* is inscribed along the sides and above a relief carving of an urn and four willows. The side inscriptions are very weathered. *"In / memory of / DEA. BENJAMIN / RICHMOND / who died Jan. 20, 1830 / Æ. 46 years. /*

> *His mind was tranquil and serene,*
> *No terrours in his looks were seen;*
> *His Savior's smiles dispell'd the gloom,*
> *And smooth'd his passage to the tomb.*
> *Consoling that dear partner dry your tears*

> *Your friend has gone beyond your anxious fears*
> *Weep not for me, prepare without delay!*
> *To meet that debt you all must shortly pay."*

The first word of the poem is inscribed within a recessed rectangle. The last line of the poem is beginning to be buried. Note the spelling of *terrours*.

Richmond, Deborah   *"DEBORAH RICHMOND, / Wife / Of / WILLIAM RICHMOND, / Died Sept 18, 1857, / Aged / 79 years."* The first line of this textured stone is carved in relief along an arch. *"BURT, Taunton."* is inscribed on the bottom left.

Richmond, Dorothy C.   See Winston Richmond Monument entry.

Richmond, Eleazer Obelisk   *"RICHMOND"* is inscribed on the front base of this tall obelisk. *"ELEAZER RICHMOND / Born Feb. 19, 1804, / Died Oct. 10, 1876."* is inscribed on the right side. The first line is carved in relief along an arch. *"SALLY R. / Wife of / Eleazer Richmond / Born Oct. 8, 1809. / Died June 6, 1874."* is inscribed on the left side. The first line is carved in relief along an arch. *"Aurelia J. / Dau. of Eleazer & / Sally R. Richmond, / died Dec. 29, 1833; / Aged 7 m's, 24 d's"* is inscribed on the back.
"ELEAZER" is carved in relief along an arch on the top slanted surface of this stone. *"RICHMOND."* is inscribed on the front. It is located on the left side of the monument.

Richmond, Joseph, Dea.   *"Sacred to the / memory of Dea". / JOSEPH RICHMOND / who died January / 23. Æ. 1821. In the 65 / year of his age. /*
> *Blessed are the dead which die*
> *in the Lord from henceforth you*
> *saith the Spirit, that they may*
> *rest from their labours, and*
> *their works do follow them."*

An urn and willow are carved at the top of this rectangular stone. Whorls are carved on either side. A fan shaped carving is in the upper corners of the inscribed area.

Richmond, Phebe   *"SACRED / to the memory of / PHEBE, / wife of / Dea. Joseph Richmond / who died / Feb. 7, 1839. in her / 84 year. /*
> *Remember me as you pass by.*
> *As you are now, so once was I;*
> *As I am now so you must be,*
> *Prepare for death & follow me."*

An urn and willow are carved in relief at the top of this rectangular stone. The third line is carved in outline.

Richmond, Prudence W.   *"As the Just / tribute of respect this stone / is erected."* is inscribed along the sides and above a relief carving of an urn and four willows. *"In / memory of / PRUDENCE W. / RICHMOND / who died / Nov. 30, 1831 / in her 21. year. /*
> *Could virtue, modesty and worth*
> *Secure our mortal breath,*
> *The tenant of this narrow cell*
> *Had been exempt from death.*

> *Though these could not prolong her life*
> *To her the grave was given.*
> *To feel her virtues join'd by faith,*
> *'T would raise her soule to heaven."*

Note the spelling of *soule* in the poem.

Richmond, Sally R. See Eleazer Richmond Obelisk entry.
"SALLY R." is carved in relief along an arch on the top slanted surface of this stone. *"RICHMOND."* is carved on the front. It is located to the far left side of the monument.

Richmond, William *"WILLIAM RICHMOND, / died / Nov. 25, 1849, / aged / 75 years."* The first line is carved in relief along an arch. *"Hathaway, Taunton."* is inscribed on the bottom left corner.

Richmond, William *"WILLIAM RICHMOND / died / Apr. 27, 1873, / Aged 75 years / & 4 m's."* The first line is carved in relief along an arch on this textured stone.

Richmond, Winston D. Monument *"IN LOVING MEMORY"* is inscribed at the top of this monument. Ivy carvings are on either side. *"RICHMOND / 1904   WINSTON D.   1986 / 1905   DOROTHY CHOATE   1977"* is inscribed below this. A Quincy Memorial Co. metal tag is present.

Robinson, Gertrude M. See Godfrey W. Robinson Monument entry.
"GERTRUDE" is carved in shallow relief on this 0-4 inch high footstone. It is located behind and to the left of the monument.

Robinson, Godfrey W. Monument *"ROBINSON"* is carved in relief along an arch at the top of this monument. *"GODFREY W. ROBINSON / 1863 – 1956 / NELLIE J. HIS WIFE / 1869 – 1948 / GERTRUDE M. THEIR DAU. / 1888 – 1924"* is inscribed below this. The first line is carved along an arch. A Quincy Memorial Co. metal tag is present.
"GODFREY" is carved in shallow relief on this 0-1 inch high footstone. It is located behind the monument on the right.

Robinson, Nellie J. See Godfrey W. Robinson Monument entry.
"NELLIE" is carved in shallow relief on this 0-4 inches high footstone. It is located directly behind the monument.

Washburn, Benjamin L. Monument *"THIS / CENOTAPH IS ERECTED IN SWEET / REMEMBRANCE OF / BENJAMIN LEONARD, / Born July 24. 1837, / Died at Folly Island, S.C. Sept. 20, 1863. / GEORGE. / Born Feb. 15. 1841. / Died at Florence, S.C. Oct. 19, 1864. / Members Co. A. 40th Regt., Mass. Vols. / Sons of LEONARD & ELIZABETH WASHBURN. / Sleep on Brave Soldiers."* A *"GAR 8 100"*, a *"GAR 8 101"* and a veteran's marker and flag are present. *Massachusetts Civil War Soldiers & Sailors, 1861-1865,* Vol. IV, p. 112 lists them under "Washburne."

Washburne, C. Everett *"C. EVERETT WASHBURNE / DIED / Apr. 30, 1870. / Æt. 31 yrs. 2mos. / 4 days."* The first line is carved in relief along an arch. A relief carving of a Mason's symbol is at the top of this stone. Below this is a sculptured carving of a flower. A *"GAR 8 232"* marker, a veteran's marker and flag are present. *Massachusetts Civil War Soldiers & Sailors, 1861-1865,* Vol. I, p. 497 lists him with the 7th Infantry, Co. F. as Everett Washburn.

Washburn, Elizabeth   *"MOTHER"* is carved in relief on the top curved surface of this stone. *"ELIZABETH. / Wife of / Leonard Washburn, / Died July 24, 1891. / Aged 77 yrs. / 11 mos. / Resting at home."* is carved on the front. The first line is carved along an arch. Columns are carved on the sides of this stone. This gravestone and that of Leonard Washburn share the same base.

Washburn, George   See Benjamin L. Washburn Monument entry.

Washburn, Hannah E.   *"HANNAH E. / WIFE OF / BENJAMIN L. WASHBURN / Dec. 12, 1837 / Mar. 20, 1919"*

Washburn, Leonard   *"FATHER"* is carved in relief on the top curved surface of this stone. *"LEONARD WASHBURN / Died / Jan. 13, 1888. / Aged 74 yrs. / Gone but not forgotten."* is inscribed on the front. The first line is carved along an arch. There are columns carved on the sides. This gravestone and that of Elizabeth Washburn share the same base.

Richmond Cemetery Map Index

Alphabetical:

Miller, Mary (1822-1901) – 57
Miller, Samuel (1818-1900) – 57
Miller, Stanley (1865) – 57
Monroe, David B. (1834-1920) – 52, 53
Monroe, Horace C. (1863) – 53
Monroe, Infant (1859) – 53
Monroe, Lizzie M. (1860-1869) – 53
Monroe, Mabel H. (1873-1963) – 53, 54
Monroe, Mattie W. (1866-1867) – 53
Monroe, Samantha (1836-1919) – 51, 53
Reed, James S. (1857-1933) – 38
Reed, Mary F. (1848-1928) – 38
Richmond, Abigail (1800-1880) – 32
Richmond, Aurelia (1833) – 41, 42
Richmond, Benjamin, Dea. (~1784-1830) – 3
Richmond, Deborah (~1778-1857) – 6
Richmond, Dorothy C. (1905-1977) – 8

Richmond, Eleazer (1804-1876) – 40, 41
Richmond, Joseph, Dea. (~1757-1821) – 1
Richmond, Phebe (~1756-1839) – 2
Richmond, Prudence W. (~1811-1831) – 4
Richmond, Sally R. (1809-1874) – 39, 41
Richmond, William (~1774-1849) – 5
Richmond, William (~1797-1873) – 31
Richmond, Winston D. (1904-1986) – 8
Robinson, Gertrude (1888-1924) – 22, 35
Robinson, Godfrey (1863-1956) – 22, 37
Robinson, Nellie J. (1869-1948) – 22, 36
Washburn, Benjamin L. (1837-1863) – 46
Washburne, C. Everett (1839-1870) – 45
Washburn, Elizabeth (1813-1891) – 44
Washburn, George (1841-1864) – 46
Washburn, Hannah E. (1837-1919) – 47
Washburn, Leonard (~1814-1888) – 43

By Location:

1 – Richmond, Joseph, Dea. (~1757-1821)
2 – Richmond, Phebe (~1756-1839)
3 – Richmond, Benjamin, Dea.(~1784-1830)
4 – Richmond, Prudence W. (~1811-1831)
5 – Richmond, William (~1774-1849)
6 – Richmond, Deborah (~1778-1857)
7 – Dunham, Edwin O. (1845-1906)
    Dunham, S. Lizzie (1848-1919)
8 – Richmond, Winston D. (1904-1986)
    Richmond, Dorothy C. (1905-1977)
9 – McFarlin, Pamelia (1880-1915)
10 – McFarlin, Sampson (1877-1957)
11 – McFarlin Rock
12 – Miller, Adino R. (~1808-1835)
13 – Dunham, William M. (1829-1863)
14 – Dunham, D. Frances (1843-1862)
    Dunham, Amanda P. (1848-1862)
15 – Back, Aurilla J. (1855-1856)
16 – Dunham, Erastus (1840)
17 – Dunham, Barnaba M. (~1800-1851)
18 – Back, George (~1820-1881)
19 – Back, Sarah S. (1811-1887)
20 – Aldrich, John R. (1838-1906)
21 – Aldrich, Sarah E. (1842-1899)
22 – Robinson, Godfrey (1863-1956)
    Robinson, Nellie J. (1869-1948)
    Robinson, Gertrude (1888-1924)
23 – Keelin, Jennie E. (1909-   )
24 – Haskins, Russell (1898-1969)
25 – Lang, Stella M. (1894-1976)
26 – Haskins, Lester W. (1886-1962)

27 – Auger, Grace R. (1891-1951)
28 – Haskins, Herbert M. (1858-1946)
29 – Haskins, Ida J. (1862-1938)
30 – Haskins, Herbert M. (1858-1946)
    Haskins, Ida J. (1862-1938)
    Auger, Grace R. (1891-1951)
    Haskins, Lester W. (1886-1962)
    Haskins, Martin K. (1816-1891)
    Haskins, Abbie B. (1821-1914)
    Haskins, Charles T. (1848-1853)
    Haskins, Clarence T. (1848-1853)
31 – Richmond, William (~1797-1873)
32 – Richmond, Abigail (1800-1880)
33 – Macomber, Gideon (~1778-1852)
34 – Macomber, Huldah (1783-1849)
35 – Robinson, Gertrude (1888-1924)
36 – Robinson, Nellie J. (1869-1948)
37 – Robinson, Godfrey (1863-1956)
38 – Reed, James S. (1857-1933)
    Reed, Mary F. (1848-1928)
39 – Richmond, Sally R. (1809-1874)
40 – Richmond, Eleazer (1804-1876)
41 – Richmond, Sally R. (1809-1874)
    Richmond, Eleazer (1804-1876)
    Richmond, Aurelia (1833)
42 – Richmond, Aurelia (1833)
43 – Washburn, Leonard (~1814-1888)
44 – Washburn, Elizabeth (1813-1891)
45 – Washburne, C. Everett (1839-1870)
46 – Washburn, Benjamin L. (1837-1863)
    Washburn, George (1841-1864)

47 –Washburn Hannah E. (1837-1919)
48 – Hinkley, Benjamin (1793-1885)
    Hinkley, Sarah (1801-1884)
    Hinkley, Aaron A. (1826-1906)
    Hinkley, Julia A. (1823-1908)
    Hinkley, Clarence H. (1854)
49 – Gifford, Richmond (1914-1984)
50 – Gifford, Mildred L. (1920-   )
51 – Monroe, Samantha (1836-1919)
52 – Monroe, David B. (1834-1920)
53 – Monroe, David B. (1834-1920)
    Monroe, Samantha (1836-1919)
    Monroe, Mabel H. (1873-1963)
    Gifford, Richmond M. (1914-1984)
    Gifford, Mildred L. (1920-____)
    Gifford, Allen R. (1938-1999)
    Monroe, Infant (1859)

    Monroe, Lizzie M. (1860-1869)
    Monroe, Horace C. (1863)
    Monroe, Mattie W. (1866-1867)
54 – Monroe, Mabel H. (1873-1963)
55 – Harlow, Foster A. (1832-1909)
    Harlow, Elvira J. (1837-1912)
56 – Harlow, Lena (1860-1863)
57 – Miller, Samuel (1818-1900)
    Miller, Almira (1822-1904)
    Miller, Helen (1849-1908)
    Miller, Earnest (1849-1866)
    Miller, Betsey (1859-1965)
    Miller, Joseph (1821-1881)
    Miller, Mary (1822-1901)
    Miller, Josie (1848-1868)
    Miller, Stanley (1865)
    Miller, Charles (1853-1860)

Richmond Cemetery Map

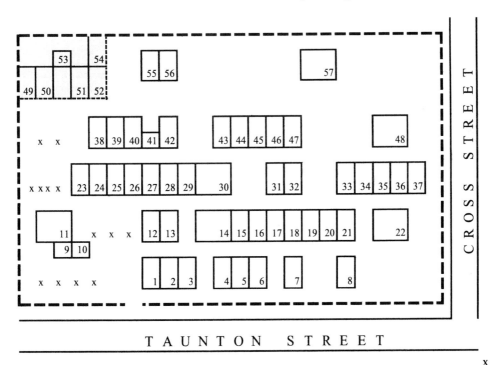

x = unmarked stone   ▪▪▪▪ = plastic fence   ...... = low concrete wall

Chapter 25
Robbins Cemetery

At first glance, Robbins Cemetery appears to be the side yard of a private residence. Right of way to it is the driveway for 17 Race Course Road. The cemetery is straight ahead when the driveway turns to the right. It was used as a pauper's cemetery, and many more people are buried here than there are stones. The *1964 Lakeville Town Report* indicates that there were "32 sunken graves" present at that time. A partial list of people buried in this cemetery without a marker is included below. Vigers states it is on land formerly owned by Zebulon L. Canedy, and was deeded to the Town of Lakeville on February 17, 1902, by James P. Pierce. Although no fence exists for this cemetery, four stone posts still mark its corners. No sign is present, but a pole for a sign is at the street, west of the driveway. Gravestones face northwest, and date from 1848 to 1923. The Lakeville Assessor's Office lists this cemetery as town owned, about 12,000 square feet in area. Thatcher calls this a "Cemetery on so called "Race-course" road, in bushes way back from road." Vigers calls it the "Pauper Cemetery." It was also called "Citizens Cemetery" in the *1968 Lakeville Town Report*. Entries were recorded April 14, 2000.

Gillogly, Jerry L. *"IN LOVING MEMORY / JERRY LeROSS GILLOGLY / MAR. 3, 1939 – JUL. 4, 1966"* is inscribed on this flat, 8-12 inch high stone. A flag is present. This stone was added during the summer of 2006, replacing the unmarked fieldstone, which was present in 2000.

Morris, Frank *"FRANK MORRIS / 1897 – 1923 / AN EMPLOYEE OF Z. L. CANEDY."*

Ramsdell, John *"In Memory of / JOHN RAMSDELL / died / Jan. 7, 1856, in / his 70 year."* An urn and willow carving is at the top of this lichen encrusted, slate stone.
"J. R." is inscribed on this slate footstone.

Ramsdell, Sarah   *"In memory of / SARAH, / wife of / JOHN RAMSDELL, / who died / Jan. 24, 1848, in / her 61 year."*   An urn and willow carving is at the top of this slate stone.
"S. R." is inscribed on this slate footstone. It is lying face up on the ground.

Robbins, Samuel   *"SAMUEL ROBBINS / BORN / FEB. 13, 1793 / DIED / DEC. 18, 1854"* A *"SAR 1775"* marker and a flag are present.

Additional Notes:

The cemetery cards at the Lakeville Town Hall list the following people as being buried in this cemetery, but no gravestones are present for them:

"Athanas, John d. Mar. 17, 1916
Faushanes, Nicholas d. June 3, 1919
Helle, Mary K. d. Sept. 21, 1919
Hooper, Denzall d. Mar 7, 1915
Jakishart, Sophia d. Apr. 20, 1915
Keraluk, Antonio d. Nov. 18, 1919
Machael, Charles d. June 27, 1919
Martinson, Alexander J. d. Dec. 22,
    1919

McPherson, Esther d. May 17, 1915
Niemi, Oscar d. Oct. 27, 1916
Olson, August d. Sept. 30, 1919
Olson, Otto d. Oct. 21, 1915
Salme, Sannie d. July 3, 1919
Sarenson, Inga d. Sept. 30, 1915
Wains, Mary d. Feb. 27, 1919"

Robbins Cemetery Index and Map

Gillogly, Jerry L. (1939-1966) – 5
Morris, Frank (1897-1923) – 3
Ramsdell, John (~1787-1856) – 1
Ramsdell, Sarah (~1788-1848) – 2
Robbins, Samuel (1793-1854) – 4

1 – Ramsdell, John (~1787-1856)
2 – Ramsdell, Sarah (~1788-1848)
3 – Morris, Frank (1897-1923)
4 – Robbins, Samuel (1793-1854)
5 – Gillogly, Jerry L. (1939-1966)

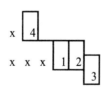

x = upright fieldstone   ☐ = upright stone posts

Chapter 26
Royal Wampanoag Cemetery

Royal Wampanoag Cemetery is located on the west side of Bedford Street, 0.3 miles north of the Freetown line. It is located on property owned by the City of New Bedford. There is no fence present, and the sign is in good repair. The gravestones in this cemetery appear to face Little Quittacus Pond (west). Only one gravestone is inscribed, and one fieldstone appears to have initials on it. There are many fieldstone markers, some of which have shells, rocks, and feathers near them. Marked graves range from 1794 to 1812. Thatcher calls this the "Indian Cemetery." Entries were recorded May 25, 2000.

Squeen, Jean Stone   *"In me... / who died Apr_... / he ... Also / ... / who died ... / in h ... 6 year... / Lydi_... _queen native / W... / D..."* is all that can be read on this broken stone. There are many shells, rocks, and bones in front of this gravestone. Thatcher lists a more complete transcription: "To the Memory of Jean Squeen, who died April 13th, 1794 in the 23rd year of her age. Also of Benjamin who died at sea April 22nd, 1799, in his 26th year. Children of Lydia Squeen a native" "When earth was made and time began / Death was decreed fate of Man."

Squeen, Benjamin   See Jean Squeen Monument entry.

T, F   " F T " is inscribed on a fieldstone. Thatcher lists: "I. F. (Israel Felix)" Perhaps this is that stone.

Wamsley, Lydia   Behind and to the left of the Jean Squeen stone is a pine tree. There is a picture of an Indian child, some feathers and two straps of leather tied to the tree. Inscribed on the leather straps is:

"LYDIA WAMSLEY / 1740 – 1812 / TUSPAQUIN"
"WHEN EARTH WAS MADE AND TIME BEGAN
DEATH WAS DECREED THE FATE OF MAN"

Thatcher lists: "To the Memory of Lidia Squeen, who died in 1811, age 72" "In God the poor & helpless find / A Judge most just, a parent kind." He adds "This was doubtless Lydia Tuspaquin, who married a Wamsley and who was drowned in Asswampsett Pond and was the mother of Jean & Benjamin Squeen." Note the difference in year of death.

Thatcher states that "there are other graves here whose stones are entirely demolished."

Royal Wampanoag Cemetery Index and Map

Squeen, Jean (~1772-1794) – 2
Squeen, Benjamin (~1774-1799) – 2
T, I – 1
Wamsley, Lydia S. (1740-1812) – 2

1 – T, I
2 – Squeen, Benjamin (~1774-1799)
    Squeen, Jean (~1772-1794)
    Wamsley, Lydia S. (1740-1812)

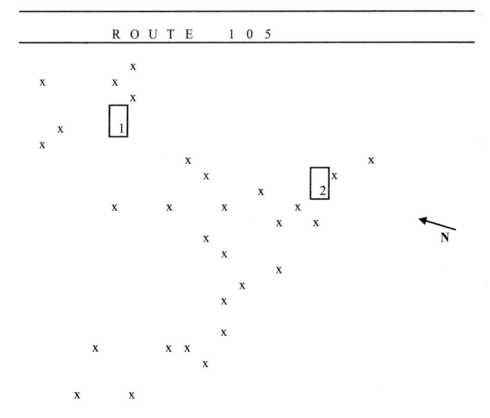

Chapter 27
Sampson Cemetery

Sampson Cemetery is located on the west side of Bedford Street (Route 18), just north of the Old Town Hall at the intersection of Routes 18 and 105. It is bordered on the front with a cement post and metal rail fence. This fence used to continue halfway down the sides, but in 2006, it was extended to the rear on both sides. The back is open. The sign is in good repair. Gravestones face east, and date from 1845 to present. Vigers states that over time, "…parcels have been added, the land being donated by the Boston Council of Boy Scouts and by Ethan A. Peirce. On March 1, 1944, the Sampson Cemetery Association was organized: Susan Goodridge, president, N. Merrill Sampson, vice-president, M. Alma Sampson, secretary and treasurer, trustees: Leslie H. Norton, Wallace C. Wilkie and N. Merrill Sampson." The Lakeville Assessor's Office lists this private cemetery as being 56,628 square feet in size. Thatcher calls this the "Cemetery near the Town House." Entries were recorded November 19 and 27, 2001. This cemetery was subsequently revisited to update the listings through 2003.

Abbaticola, Frank A. Monument   *"ABBATICOLA"* is inscribed on the front of this monument. *"ONE DAY AT A TIME"* is inscribed at the bottom center. A cross and flowers are carved on the left. *"FRANK A. ABBATICOLA / MAY 8, 1925 OCT. 18, 2001 / HIS WIFE / LUISA M. (NARDONE) / SEPT. 9, 1924 ____ "* is inscribed on the back. A veteran's marker and flag are present. A Barnicoat Monuments metal tag is present.

Abbaticola, Luisa M.   See Frank Abbaticola Monument entry.

Agnew, John H. Monument   *"AGNEW"* is inscribed on the front of the monument. *"JACK   PAT"* is inscribed in the bottom corners. There is a picture of the Sacred Heart of Jesus etched on the upper left, and a rose on the upper right. *"JOHN H. AGNEW / MAY 2, 1923 – FEB. 3, 1996 / LOVING WIFE / PATRICIA M.*

AGNEW / JUNE 2, 1941 _____" is inscribed on the back. An American flag is present. A Barnicoat Monuments metal tag is present.
"✝ / JOHN H AGNEW / TM1 US NAVY / WORLD WAR II / MAY 2 1923 FEB 3 1996" is inscribed on this flat, ground level stone. It is located directly in front of the monument, on the left.

Agnew, Patricia M.   See John H. Agnew monument entry.

Ahr, Linda S.   See William Ahr Monument entry.

Ahr, William A. Monument   *"AHR / WILLIAM A. / DEC. 4, 1950 – MAY 12, 1998 / LINDA S. / MAR. 8, 1950 – _____"* A carving of golf bag with clubs is at the top of this monument. Rose carvings are in the upper corners. A metal REX tag is present.

Alden, Myles S. Monument   *"NEITHER DEATH NOR LIFE NOR ANY OTHER THING / SHALL SEPARATE US FROM THE LOVE OF GOD / ROMANS 8.38,39. / MYLES STANDISH ALDEN / 1897 – 1964 / PERSIS (TAYLOR) HIS WIFE / 1900 – 1995"* is inscribed on this slanted monument.

Alden, Persis   See Myles S. Alden Monument entry.

Alvilhiera, Frank B.   *"FRANK B. ALVILHIERA / JUL. 5, 1936 – MAR. 31, 1992"* Oak leaves and acorns are carved on the bottom of this flat, ground level stone, which is beginning to be buried.

Angers-Handy Monument   *"ANGERS"* is inscribed on the front of this monument. *"HANDY"* is inscribed on the back.

Angers, Eleanor M.   *"ELEANOR MARIE ANGERS / JAN. 5, 1933 – MAY 3, 2003"* is inscribed on this flat, ground level stone. It is located in front of the Angers-Handy Monument, on the left.

Angers, Lois F.   See Paul Angers Stone entry.

Angers, Paul A. Stone   *"ANGERS"* is inscribed at the top of this flat, 4-6 inch high stone. A cross is carved on either side. *"PAUL A. / 1901 – 1984"* is inscribed on the bottom left side, and *"LOIS F. / 1909 – 1985"* is inscribed on the bottom right side. It is located in front of the Angers-Handy Monument, on the far left.

Arenburg, Julia   See N. Merrill Sampson Monument entry.

Arrington, Frank Monument   *"ARRINGTON"* is inscribed at the top of this monument, and floral carvings are in the upper corners. Below this, *"FRANK / 1890 – 1976"* is inscribed on the left side, and *"LILLA / 1891 – 1969"* is inscribed on the right. *"MAGNUSON"* is inscribed at the top on the back of this monument. Below this, *"EARL R. / 1911 – 1998"* is inscribed on the left, and *"ARLINE E. / 1920 – _____"* is inscribed on the right. All of the inscriptions on this monument are carved in outline. Flowers are carved in the upper corners on both sides. A metal Barnicoat Monuments tag is present.

Arrington, Lilla   See Frank Arrington Monument entry.

Aschiero, Carlo   *"CARLO ASCHIERO / 1891 – 1968"* is inscribed on this flat, ground level stone. It is located directly behind the Van Lenten-Aschiero Monument, on the right.

Aschiero, Margherita L. *"WIFE OF CARLO / MARGHERITA L. ASCHIERO / 1893 – 1994"* is inscribed on this flat, ground level stone, which is beginning to be buried. It is located directly behind the Van Lenten-Aschiero Monument, on the left.

Austin, Alice S. See George Austin Monument entry.

Austin, George R. Monument *"Austin"* is carved in outline on the front of this monument. There are floral carvings in the upper corners. *"GEORGE R. AUSTIN / JUNE 19, 1911 – DEC. 6, 1990 / HIS WIFE / ALICE S. GOODELL / JAN. 2, 1910 – JUN. 25, 2000"* is inscribed on the back.

Babbitt Monument *"BABBITT"* is carved in relief on the front of this monument. There are floral carvings in the upper corners. No other inscriptions are present.

Babbitt, David L. *"DAVID L. BABBITT / 1889 – 1949"* is inscribed on this flat, ground level stone, which is beginning to be buried. It is located to the far right of the Babbitt Monument.

Bailey-Flanders Rock *"BAILEY / FLANDERS"* is all that is inscribed on this large boulder.

Bailey, Edward B. C. *"EDWARD B. C. BAILEY / 1898   1973"* is inscribed on this flat, ground level stone. A Mason's symbol is carved between the birth and death years. It is located in front of the Bailey-Flanders Rock, on the left. A veteran's marker and flag are present.

Bailey, Lauretta F. *"LAURETTA F. BAILEY / 1901 – 1972"* is inscribed on this flat, ground level stone. It is located directly in front of the Bailey-Flanders Rock, on the left.

Barlow, Grace C. See Hanna Barlow Monument entry.

Barlow, Hanna E. Monument *"Hanna Elizabeth Barlow / ✝ / Grace Caroline Barlow"* is written on a funeral home marker.
"BARLOW / HANNAH ELIZABETH / OCT. 29, 2001 – OCT. 31, 2001 / GRACE CAROLINE / OCT. 29, 2001 – OCT. 30, 2001 / BELOVED DAUGHTERS OF / MICHAEL AND LAURIE" is inscribed on this monument, which was placed after the initial visit. Child angels are carved in the upper corners.

Barron, Barbara See Thomas Barron Monument entry.

Barron, Thomas F. Monument *"BARRON / THOMAS F. BARRON / OCT. 22, 1924 – JUL. 15, 1987 / HIS WIFE / BARBARA (GILLIS) / MAY 5, 1925 – FEB. 17, 2002"* A veteran's marker and flag are present. A Barnicoat Monuments metal tag is present.
"THOMAS F BARRON / SFC US ARMY / WORLD WAR II   KOREA / OCT 22 1924 JUL 15 1987" is inscribed on this flat, ground level stone. A circled cross is carved at the top. It is located directly in front of the monument.

Barry, Lillian *"ANGELS SING THEE TO REST"* is inscribed on a small scroll carving at the top of this monument. *"BARRY / LILLIAN / APR. 5, 1928 – OCT. 16, 1999"* is carved below this. A praying angel is carved above flowers on the left. A Barnicoat Monuments metal tag is present.

Battistelli, Avis E. See Joseph Battistelli Monument entry.

Battistelli, Joseph Monument *"BATTISTELLI"* is inscribed on the front of this monument. A colored picture of the sun setting over the ocean with sailboats, birds, and a lighthouse is etched on the front, above the inscription. *"JOSEPH BATTISTELLI / MAY 26, 1927 – NOV. 2, 1996 / BELOVED WIFE / AVIS E. BATTISTELLI / DEC. 10, 1916 – ____"* is inscribed on the back. A Barnicoat Monuments metal tag is present.
"JOSEPH / BATTISTELLI / 1927 – 1996" is inscribed on this flat, ground level stone. It is located directly in front of the monument, on the left.

Bavin, Charette *"BABY / CHARETTE BAVIN / JUNE 30, 1984"* is inscribed on this flat, 1-2 inch high stone. Praying hands are carved on the left.

Bavin, Katherine See William Bavin Monument entry.

Bavin, William A. Monument *"BAVIN"* is inscribed in outline at the top of the monument. *"WILLIAM A. / 1920 – 1976"* is inscribed on the bottom left, and *"KATHERINE / 1924 – ____"* is inscribed on the bottom right. Praying hands are carved over a cross on the left. Flowers are carved at the bottom of the cross.

Beard, Cathy M. See N. Merrill Sampson Monument entry.

Beard, H. Deborah See N. Merrill Sampson Monument entry.

Beard, James M. See N. Merrill Sampson Monument entry.

Bednar, Charlotte E. See Francis Prifogle Monument entry.

Bednar, Julius J. See Francis Prifogle Monument entry.

Beech, Aaron H. Monument *"BEECH"* is inscribed in outline at the top of the monument. *"FOREVER IN OUR HEARTS / HENRY   FRANCES"* is inscribed at the bottom. Rose carvings are in the upper corners. A scene of a person walking in a pasture is carved below the first line. *"AARON H. BEECH JR. / MAR. 8, 1919 ____ / BELOVED WIFE / FRANCES V. (GAUL) / MAY 11, 1920 – JUN. 29, 1994"* is inscribed on the back. A Barnicoat Monuments metal tag is present.

Beech, Frances V. See Aaron Beech Monument entry.

Beech, Margaret P. See Roger E. Beech Monument entry.

Beech, Marjorie H. See Roger C. Beech Monument entry.

Beech, Roger C. Monument *"BEECH"* is inscribed on a carved scroll on the front of this monument. Floral carvings are behind it. *"ROGER C. BEECH / JUL. 20, 1895 – JAN. 2, 1988 / BELOVED WIFE / MARJORIE H. (WASHBURN) / JUN. 14, 1903 – MAR. 26, 1998"* is inscribed on the back. An open book is carved on the top horizontal surface. A Barnicoat Monuments metal tag is present. A veteran's marker and flag are present.

"⚜ / ROGER C. BEECH / PVT   US ARMY / WORLD WAR I / JUL 20 1895   JAN 2 1988" is inscribed on this flat, ground level stone. It is located in front of the monument, on the left

Beech, Roger E. Monument   *"BEECH"* is inscribed on the front of this monument. Floral carvings are in the upper corners. *"MAR. 20, 1922   ROGER E. BEECH _____ / SEPT. 13, 1923   MARGARET PEARL BEECH _____ / OCT. 29, 1947   MARY ELIZABETH ROGERS   AUG. 15, 1993"* is inscribed on the back. A Barnicoat Monuments metal tag is present.

Begin, Edward E.   See Margaret L. Begin Monument entry.

Begin, Margaret L. Monument   *"BEGIN"* is inscribed below a carved cross on the front of this monument. *"MARGARET L. / SEP. 29, 1915 / _____ "* is inscribed on the lower left, and *"EDWARD E. / JUL. 6, 1915 / MAR. 17, 2002"* is inscribed on the lower right. Daffodils are carved on the upper corners. A Barnicoat Monuments metal tag is present. This monument was not present at the initial visit.

Belben, Kenneth E.   *"KENNETH E. BELBEN / SSGT   US ARMY / WORLD WAR II / OCT 12 1922   FEB 6 1984"* is inscribed on this flat, sunken stone. A circled cross is carved above the inscriptions. It is located directly behind the Freeman Monument, on the right. A veteran's marker and flag are present.

Belben, Myra E.   *"MOTHER / MYRA E. BELBEN / 1919 – 1976"* is inscribed on this flat, ground level stone. It is located directly in front of the Freeman Monument, on the right.

Benson, Gladys   *"GLADYS"* is inscribed on this flat, ground level stone. It is located to the far right of the Wilkie Monument. Only her name is inscribed on the left side of this stone. The *Social Security Death Index* lists her birth in October 1908 and death on June 30, 1998.

Berry, Barbara B.   See Francis N. Berry Monument entry.

Berry, Francis N. Monument   *"BERRY"* is inscribed on the front of this monument. Floral carvings are in the upper corners. *"FRANCIS N. BERRY / SEP. 28, 1926 – SEP. 25, 1992 / HIS WIFE / BARBARA B. (DUNHAM) / AUG. 24, 1928 – _____ "* is inscribed on the back.
"⚜ / FRANCIS NATHANIEL BERRY / COX US NAVY / WORLD WAR II / SEP 28 1926 SEP 25 1992" is inscribed on this flat, ground level stone. A veteran's marker and flag are present. It is located directly in front of the monument, on the right.

Bessey, Isa M.   See Norman Given Monument entry.

Bessey, Lloyd   See Norman Given Monument entry.

Biasiucci, Domenic A.   See John Biasiucci Monument entry.

Biasiucci, Infant son   *"BIASIUCCI / BABY BOY / JUNE 13, 1974"* is inscribed on this flat, ground level stone.

Biasiucci, John J. Monument   *"IN LOVING MEMORY / BIASIUCCI / JOHN J. / JUL. 26, 1929 –JUL. 17, 1994 / HIS WIFE / VIOLET / JUN. 26, 1931 _____ "* is inscribed on the front of this monument. Flowers and a cross are carved in the upper corners. *"DOMENIC A. BIASIUCCI / AUG. 5, 1952 – NOV. 29, 1996 / JOHN J. BIASIUCCI JR. / FEB. 10, 1951 – DEC. 18, 2002"* is inscribed on the back. The last two lines were added after the initial visit. A Barnicoat Monuments metal tag is present.

Biasiucci, John J., Jr.   See John Biasiucci Monument entry.

Biasiucci, Violet   See John Biasiucci Monument entry.

Bock, Pauline T.   See Roland Bock Monument entry.

Bock, Roland A. Monument   *"BOCK"* is inscribed on the front of this black monument. Ivy vines are carved on the sides. *"ROLAND A. E. BOCK / FEB. 5, 1924 – JULY 30, 1990 / HIS WIFE / PAULINE T. BOCK / JAN. 19, 1928 ____ / Parents of / Donald, Diane, David, Nancy / Paula, Karl – Peter"* is inscribed on the back.
"✝ / ROLAND A E BOCK / PFC   US ARMY / WORLD WAR II / FEB 5 1924   JUL 30 1990" is inscribed on this flat, ground level stone, which is beginning to be buried. It is located directly in front of the monument, on the left.

Bollesen, Sandra Lee   *"SANDRA LEE / BOLLESEN / 1958 – 1964"* is inscribed on this slanted stone. A cross is carved in the upper right corner, and a praying child angel is carved in the bottom left corner.

Bowers, Robert E.   *"BOWERS"* is inscribed on the front of this monument. A scene with a snow skier and a water skier is carved below it. *"ROBERT E. BOWERS / 1911 – 1987"* is inscribed on the back. A veteran's marker and flag are present.
"ROBERT E. BOWERS / T SGT   US ARMY / WORLD WAR II / JUL 19 1911   MAY 14 1987" is inscribed on this flat, ground level stone, which is beginning to be buried. It is located directly in front of the monument, on the left.

Bowles, Cuthbert   *"CUTHBERT / 1898 – 1973"* is inscribed on this flat, rear facing stone, which is beginning to be buried. It is located directly behind the Mosher-Bowles Monument, on the right.

Bowles, Verna C.   *"VERNA C. / 1899 – 1949"* is inscribed on this flat, ground level stone, which faces the rear of the cemetery. It is located directly behind the Mosher-Bowles Monument, on the left. Lakeville Vital Records show her maiden name was Mosher.

Bradford, Joseph E.   *"LOVING MEMORY"* is inscribed on a carved scroll on the top of this monument. *"BRADFORD / 1898   JOSEPH E.   1952"* is inscribed below this. Floral carvings are in the upper corners. A Memorial Granite Co. metal tag is present.

Brienzo, Dennis M.   See Mikelino Brienzo Monument entry.

Brienzo, Irene A.   See Mikelino Brienzo Monument entry.
"GRAM / IRENE A. BRIENZO" is inscribed on this flat, ground level stone. There is a cross carved on the left side. It is located directly in front of the monument, on the left.

Brienzo, Leona A.   See Mikelino Brienzo Monument entry.

Brienzo, Mikelino D. Monument   *"BRIENZO"* is inscribed in outline on the front of this monument, with floral carvings in the upper corners. *"MIKELINO D. BRIENZO / 1917 – 1988 / HIS WIFE / IRENE A. LeBEAU BRIENZO / 1917 – 1993 / DENNIS M. BRIENZO / 1942 – ____ / HIS WIFE / LEONA A. KNIGHT FEARING BRIENZO / 1947 – ____ "* is inscribed on the back. A copy of a Lakeville, MA police sergeant's badge is attached to the stone to the right of the first line.
"LAKEVILLE POLICE / DET. SERGEANT / "MIKE" BRIENZO" is inscribed on this flat, ground level stone. A cross is carved on the left side. It is located directly in front of the monument, on the right.

Brown, Edward J. Monument   *"BROWN / EDWARD J. / MAY 31, 1935 – OCT. 29, 1997 / HIS WIFE / MARGARET M. / OCT. 31, 1944 ____ / FOREVER IN OUR HEARTS"* There is a painted floral carving in the upper left corner. A metal REX tag is present.

Brown, Margaret M.   See Edward Brown Monument entry.

Brune, Everett W. Monument   *"BRUNE"* is inscribed on the front of this monument. A scene of a lighthouse with a sailboat nearing the shoreline is carved on the front. *"1909   EVERETT W.   1983 / HIS WIFE / 1909   PEARL F.   1989"* is inscribed on the back. A Taunton Monument Co. metal tag is present.

Brune, Pearl F.   See Everett Brune Monument entry.

Buckley, Christopher Monument   *"Buckley"* is inscribed on the front of this monument. *"Together we shared / more joy than pain / The walk has ended / the love remains"* is inscribed on the left. A cancer ribbon is carved in the upper left corner. An etched road leads from flowers in the lower left corner, to a church in the upper right corner. *"CHRISTOPHER BUCKLEY / SEPT. 14, 1960 ____ / LYNN BUCKLEY / AUG. 8, 1960 – Oct. 18, 2003"* is inscribed on the back.

Buckley, Lynn   See Christopher Buckley Monument.
A funeral home marker with her name, picture and dates is present.

Bump, Bathsheba M.   See Josiah B. Bump Monument entry.

"*B. M. B.*" is carved in relief on the top horizontal surface of this 1-foot high stone. It is in front of the monument, on the right.

Bump, Caroline   "*CAROLINE / Wife of / J. CLARK BUMP, / Born Mar. 13, 1820; / Died Dec. 19, 1881. / A faithful wife and / loving mother.*" The first line is carved in relief. Her stone shares its base with that of her husband, J. Clark Bump. "*C. B.*" is inscribed on the footstone.

Bump, Clara K.   "*CLARA K. BUMP / DAUGHTER OF / THOMAS W. & / NANCY J. BUMP / NOV. 18, 1849 / JAN. 26, 1931*"

Bump, Jonathan C.   "*J. CLARK BUMP / Born / Sept. 10, 1819, / Died / July 14, 1890.*" The first line is carved in relief. This stone shares its base with that of Caroline, his wife. Lakeville Vital Records show his first name was Jonathan. "*J. C. B.*" is inscribed on the footstone.

Bump, Josiah B. Monument   "*B*" monogram is carved in shallow relief at the top on the front and back of this monument. Designs are carved around it. "*JOSIAH BISBEE BUMP / BORN FEB. 3, 1826, / DIED MAY. 8, 1898. / BATHSHEBA M. / HIS WIFE / BORN OCT. 4, 1825. / DIED MAY 13, 1907.*" is inscribed on the front. "*BUMP*" is carved in relief on the front of the base. "*RALPH P. EATON / 1883 – 1963 / HIS WIFE / HARRIETTE B. / 1880 – 1944*" is inscribed on the back. "*J. B. B.*" is carved in relief on the top horizontal surface of this one-foot high footstone. It is located in front of the monument, on the left.

Bump, Nancy J.   "*NANCY J. / WIFE OF / THOMAS W. BUMP / DEC. 3, 1828. / MAR. 8, 1906. / ASLEEP IN JESUS.*"

Bump, Susan M.   "*SUSAN MYRA / Dau. of / J. Clark and / Caroline Bump, / Born / Feb. 18, 1856; / Died Sept. 15, 1862.*" This small stone is separated from its base and is leaning against the front of it. It shares this base with the stone of her sister, Susan Warren Bump. "*S. M. B.*" This footstone faces the grave.

Bump, Susan W.   "*SUSAN WARREN / Dau. of / J. Clark and / Caroline Bump, / Born / July 31, 1840; / Died Dec. 2, 1845.*" This small stone is separated from its base, and is leaning against the front of it. It shares this base with the stone of her sister, Susan Myra Bump. The last line is buried underground.

"S.W.B." is inscribed on this footstone, which faces the grave.

Bump, Thomas W. *"THOMAS W. BUMP / MAY 7, 1828. / FEB. 25, 1913."*

Buttermore, Richard L. *"BUTTERMORE / SEND ME LORD"* is inscribed on the front of this black monument. There is a carving of a Maltese cross above the inscription. *"RICHARD L. BUTTERMORE / JUL. 17, 1929 – FEB. 14, 1994 / HUSBAND OF / SANDRA A. (COPELAND)"* is inscribed on the back.

Caldwell, Bernice W. See Russell Caldwell Jr., Monument entry.

Caldwell, Jeannette L. See Russell Caldwell, Jr. Monument entry.

Caldwell, Russell E., Jr. Monument *"CALDWELL"* is carved in outline at the top of this monument. *"RUSSELL E. JR. / 1934 – 1973 / HIS WIFE / JEANNETTE L. / 1935 – ____ "* is inscribed below this. *"MOE"* is inscribed in outline on the bottom left, and floral carvings are carved on the top left. *"CALDWELL"* is carved in outline at the top on the back of this monument, with *"RUSSELL E. SR. / 1911 – 1998 / HIS WIFE / BERNICE W. / 1910 – 1987"* inscribed below it. There is a badge with the inscription *"Chief / Lakeville / Massachusetts"* attached to the monument at the beginning of the second line.

Caldwell, Russell E., Sr. See Russell Caldwell, Jr. Monument entry.

Case, Betsy See James Case Monument entry.

Case, James W. Monument *"CASE"* is inscribed at the top of this monument. *"JIM   Precious Moments   BETSY"* is inscribed on the bottom. A scene of a couple looking out over a lake is carved on the front. *"JAMES W. CASE / MAY 8, 1932 ____ / HIS WIFE / BETSY (KENDALL) / JUL. 24, 1929 – APR. 5, 1989"* is inscribed on the back. A Barnicoat Monuments metal tag is present.

Chadwick Monument *"CHADWICK"* is carved in outline on this slanted monument. No other inscriptions are present.

Chadwick, Ruth M. *"RUTH M. / 1911 – 1998"* is inscribed on this flat, ground level stone. It is located directly in front of the Chadwick Monument, on the left.

Chadwick, William H. *"WILLIAM H. / 1903 – 1967"* is inscribed on this flat, 0-1 inch high stone. It is located in front of Ruth Chadwick's footstone.

Chiuppi, Lorna M. See Peter Chiuppi Monument entry.

Chiuppi, Peter Monument *"Chiuppi"* is inscribed in outline on the front of this monument. A rose carving is on the left side. *"PETER CHIUPPI / APR. 12, 1906 – SEP. 21, 1984 / LORNA M. HIS WIFE / JUL. 3, 1909 – MAY 24, 1995"* is inscribed in outline on the back. A Barnicoat Monuments metal tag is present. A Middleboro Lodge #1274 BPOE marker and flag is present.

Churchill, Helen L. See John V. Churchill Monument entry.

Churchill, John A. See John V. Churchill Monument entry.
"JACK" is inscribed on this flat, ground level stone, which is beginning to be buried. It is located behind the monument on the left.

Churchill, John V. Monument *"1920 JOHN V. CHURCHILL 1992 / 1928 HELEN L. HIS WIFE ___ / 1955 JOHN A. THEIR SON 1973"* is inscribed on this slanted monument. A veteran's marker and flag are present.
"JOHN VINCENT CHURCHILL / BM2 US NAVY / WORLD WAR II / JUL 19 1920 ✝ DEC 31 1992" is embossed on this flat, metal marker which is beginning to be buried. It is located directly in front of the monument, on the right.

Clark, Eunice J. See Warren Clark Monument entry.

Clark Lois G. See Warren Clark Monument entry.

Clark, Phyllis Y. See Warren Clark Monument entry.

Clark, Warren W. Monument *"CLARK"* is inscribed on the front of this monument. A country scene with a covered bridge is carved below this. *"WARREN W. CLARK / MAR. 15, 1907 – MAR. 14, 1985 / EUNICE J. HIS WIFE / DEC. 4, 1907 – OCT. 13, 1987 / PHYLLIS Y. CLARK / JUN. 23, 1936 ___ / LOIS G. CLARK / MAR. 4, 1943 ___ "* is inscribed on the back. A Barnicoat Monuments metal tag is present.

Coelho, Arnold Monument *"COELHO"* is inscribed on a carving of an open book. Floral designs are carved around it, and a cross is carved above it. *"IN LOVING MEMORY / ARNOLD VERA"* is inscribed below this. *"ARNOLD M. COELHO / 1911 – 1977 / VERA M. HIS WIFE / 1919 – 1987 / ARNOLD M. JR. / MAR. 31, 1939 – MAY 9, 2001 / DOROTHY L. HIS WIFE / OCT. 18, 1939 – FEB. 6, 1999."* is inscribed on the back. A Barnicoat Monuments metal tag is present.

Coelho, Arnold M., Jr. See Arnold Coelho Monument entry.

Coelho, Dorothy L. See Arnold Coelho Monument entry.

Coelho, Michael J. *"MICHAEL J. COELHO / OCT. 31, 1980 / DEC. 8, 1980"* is inscribed on this flat, 3 inch high stone. It is located to the left of the Arnold Coelho Monument.

Coelho, Vera M. See Arnold Coelho Monument entry.

Conant, Charles A. Monument *"CONANT / 1919 CHARLES A. 1999 / HIS WIFE / 1925 RUTH E. 1985"* A cross and floral designs are carved in the upper corners. *"RICHARD A. / JAN. 28, 1960 – SEP. 28, 2000"* is inscribed on the back. A veteran's marker and flag are present.
"✝ / CHARLES A. CONANT / TEC 4 US ARMY / WORLD WAR II / MAY 8 1919 OCT 1 1999 / PURPLE HEART" is inscribed on this flat, ground level stone. It is located in front of the monument.

Conant, Richard A. See Charles A. Conant Monument entry.

Conant, Ruth E. See Charles A. Conant Monument entry.

Cook, Jane W. See Malcolm Cook Monument entry.

Cook, Malcolm A. Monument *"COOK"* is carved in outline on the front of this monument. An open book is carved below this. *"MALCOLM A. / 1918 – 1989"* is inscribed on the left page, and *"JANE W. / 1915 – 1981"* is inscribed on the right page. There is a carving of a cross and flowers on the left. A Barnicoat Monuments metal tag is present.

"MALCOLM A. COOK / 1ST LT   US ARMY AIR CORPS / WORLD WAR II / MAR 29 1918   ✝   NOV 14 1989" is embossed on this flat, metal marker which is beginning to be buried. It is located directly in front of the monument, on the left. A veteran's marker and flag are present.

Cordeiro, James F. Monument   *"CORDEIRO"* is inscribed on the front of this circular monument. *"IN LOVING MEMORY OF DAU. DONNA"* is inscribed on the bottom. Praying hands and a rose are carved on the left. *"JAMES F. CORDEIRO / JUL. 11, 1924 – NOV. 6, 1983 / MILDRED H. HIS WIFE / MAY 23, 1925 ____ / JAMES H. THEIR SON / APR. 15, 1946 ____"* is inscribed on the back. A veteran's marker and flag are present. A Barnicoat Monuments metal tag is present. Lakeville Vital Records list the death of Donna Cordeiro on August 17, 1971, at 16 years, 8 months, and 30 days old. She is listed as being buried in King Burial Grounds in Taunton.

"JAMES F. CORDEIRO / PFC US ARMY / WORLD WAR II / JUL 11 1924   NOV 6 1983" is inscribed on this flat, sunken stone. It is located directly in front of monument, on the left.

Cordeiro, James H.   See James F. Cordeiro Monument entry.

Cordeiro, Mildred H.   See James F. Cordeiro Monument entry.

Crocker, Sarah S.

> *"SARAH S.*
> *Wife of*
> *Harvey Crocker,*
> *& dau. of Thomas W.*
> *& Nancy J. Bump,*
> *died Mar. 17, 1876;*
> *Aged 24 yrs, 4 m's.*
> *Blessed are the p___ of heart; for they*
> *shall ___ God"*

The first line is carved in relief along an arch. A sculptured left hand pointing up is carved at the top of this stone. A crack radiates from the center bottom to the second last line.

"S. S. C." is inscribed on the footstone.

Dean, Helen A.   See John H. Nelson Monument entry.

"H. A. D." is inscribed on this flat, 3 inch high footstone, which faces the rear of the cemetery. It is located directly behind the John Nelson Monument, on the left.

Delano   *"DELANO"* is carved in outline on the front of this monument. A Mason's symbol carved at the top. A Barnicoat Monuments metal tag is present. This monument has since been moved to a cemetery in another town.

DeMoranville, Donald E.   See Donald O. DeMoranville Monument entry.
"DONNIE" is inscribed on this flat, ground level stone. It is located in front of the monument, on the right.

DeMoranville, Donald O. Monument   *"DEMORANVILLE"* is inscribed on the front of this monument. A calla lily is carved on either side of the inscription. A saw and hammer are carved in relief within a circle at the top of this monument. *"DONALD OSCAR DEMORANVILLE / APR. 24, 1931 – JAN. 16, 1992 / DONALD EDWARD DEMORANVILLE / DEC. 13, 1956 – MAR. 9, 1986 / BABY STEPHEN OCT 11 – 14, 1955"* is inscribed on the back. A Barnicoat Monuments metal tag is present.
"✝ / DONALD OSCAR DEMORANVILLE / CPL   US ARMY / KOREA / APR 24 1931   JAN 16 1992" is inscribed on this flat, ground level stone. It is located directly in front of the monument, on the left.

DeMoranville, Howell G. Monument   *"DEMORANVILLE"* is inscribed on the front of this monument. Calla lilies are carved along the sides. A Mason's symbol is carved at the top. *"HOWELL G. DEMORANVILLE / 1904   1978 / HIS WIFE / ORA M. GABREY / 1904   1962"* is inscribed in the upper left corner on the back. There is a star between their birth and death dates. A Barnicoat Monuments metal tag is present.

DeMoranville, Ida L.   See Oscar DeMoranville Monument entry.

DeMoranville, Lorraine L.   See Philip DeMoranville Monument entry.

DeMoranville, Merrill Monument   *"DEMORANVILLE"* is inscribed on the front of this monument. *"MERRILL"* and *"ROWENA"* are inscribed on the bottom corners. A Mason's symbol is carved at the top with three linked chains underneath. Roses are carved in the upper corners. *"MERRILL V. DEMORANVILLE / JAN. 10, 1910   DEC. 12, 1970 / HIS WIFE / ROWENA M. BABBITT / JUNE 25, 1911 – MAR. 27, 1995"* is inscribed on the back. A treble clef, staff and sixteenth note are carved between his birth and death year. A Barnicoat Monuments metal tag is present.

DeMoranville, Ora M.   See Howell DeMoranville Monument entry.

DeMoranville, Oscar F. Monument   *"DEMORANVILLE"* is inscribed on the front of this monument. Calla lilies are carved on either side. *"OSCAR F. DEMORANVILLE / 1897 – 1947 / IDA L. HIS WIFE / 1900 – 1986"* is inscribed on the back. A Barnicoat Monuments metal tag is present.

DeMoranville, Philip L. Monument   *"DEMORANVILLE"* is inscribed in outline on the front of this monument. *"PHILIP LORRAINE YVETTE / FAMILIES ARE FOREVER"* is inscribed at the bottom, below a floral carving. *"PHILIP L. DEMORANVILLE / JUN. 9, 1944 ____ / HIS WIFE / LORRAINE LEBLANC / FEB. 23, 1946 ____ / OUR DAUGHTER / YVETTE LORRAINE / DEC. 27, 1975   NOV. 12, 1985"* is inscribed on the back. A heart is carved in relief between Yvette's birth and death years. A Barnicoat Monuments metal tag is present.

DeMoranville, Rowena   See Merrill DeMoranville Monument entry.

DeMoranville, Stephen   See Donald O DeMoranville Monument entry.

"OUR BABY / STEPHEN / OCT. 11-14, 1955" is inscribed on this flat, ground level stone. A lamb is carved in the lower left corner. It is located behind the monument, on the right.

DeMoranville, Yvette L.   See Philip DeMoranville Monument entry.

DesRoche, William J.   *"DESROCHE"* is inscribed on the front of the monument with a mountain lake scene etched underneath. *"WILLIAM J. DESROCHE / MAY 9, 1953 – JAN. 7, 1998"* is inscribed on the back. A Maver Memorial metal tag is present.

Devlin, Victoria L.   *"VICKI / VICTORIA LEE DEVLIN / AUG. 27, 1981 – JAN. 3, 1990 / SOMEONE SPECIAL"* is inscribed on this heart shaped monument. A cross and red roses are carved behind this inscription. A Bárnicoat Monuments metal tag is present.

Dextraze, Jeannette Monument   *"JEANNETTE DEXTRAZE / 1907 – 1994 / GEORGE F. ROSE / 1929 – 1997"* A rose within two hearts is carved on the left side. A Barnicoat Monuments metal tag is present. A Middleboro Lodge #1274 BPOE marker and flag are present.

DiCarlo, John J.   *"JOHN J. DiCARLO / JUL 24, 1963 – JUL. 16, 1995"* is inscribed on this flat, ground level stone. *"IN LOVING MEMORY"* is inscribed on a carved open book in the upper right corner, and a cross is carved in the upper left corner. A carving of a scuba diver is on the lower left, and a carving of a man on a sled is on the lower right. A Dahlborg-MacNevin Funeral Home marker is present for him.. A Middleboro Lodge #1274 BPOE marker and flag are present.

Dill, Ernest E.   See Edgar Peck Monument entry.
"ERNEST" is inscribed on this flat, ground level stone. It is located behind the monument, on the far right.

Dill, Linda   *"LINDA / 1949 – 1951"* is inscribed on this flat, ground level stone, which is beginning to be buried. It faces the rear of the cemetery. It is located behind the Edgar Peck Monument, on the far left.

Dill, Louise G.   See Edgar Peck Monument entry.

Dill, Ruth E.   See Edgar Peck Monument entry.
"RUTH" is inscribed on this flat, ground level stone, which is beginning to be buried. It is located behind the monument, on the far right.

Dill, Thomas G.   See Edgar Peck Monument entry.
"THOMAS G DILL / SGT   US ARMY / WORLD WAR I / NOV 1, 1894   OCT 10 1983" is inscribed on this flat, ground level stone, which is beginning to be buried. It is located behind the Edgar Peck Monument, on the right. A veteran's marker and flag are present.

Dillon, Brenda C.   See Elwyn G. Dillon Monument entry.

Dillon, Elwyn G. Monument   *"Elwyn G. Dillon / August 7, 1934   May 7, 2001"* is written on a Dahlborg-MacNevin Funeral Home marker. It was replaced by the monument and stone listed below after the initial visit.

"DILLON / ELWYN "JERRY" / AUG. 7, 1934 – MAY 7, 2001 / HIS WIFE / BRENDA COLLINS SAMPSON / DEC. 26, 1944 ____" is inscribed on this monument. Floral carvings are in the upper corners. A veteran's marker and flag are present.
"ELWYN G. DILLON / US ARMY / AUG 7 1934   MAY 7 2001" is inscribed on this flat, ground level stone. It is located directly in front of the monument, on the left.

Dixon, Travis A.   *"DIXON"* is inscribed on the front of the monument. The Great Seal of the United States is carved in the upper left corner. *"TRAVIS A. / SEP. 6, 1936 / NOV. 12, 1998 / BUDDY"* is inscribed on the lower left side. An Army Master Parachutist insignia is carved above the inscription. A veteran's marker and flag are present. A Barnicoat Monuments metal tag is present.
"TRAVIS ADRIAN DIXON / US ARMY / MSGT   US AIR FORCE / VIETNAM / SEP 6 1936   NOV 12 1998" is inscribed on this flat, ground level stone. It is located directly in front of the monument, on the left.

Doucet, Catherine T.   See Rene Doucet Monument entry.

Doucet, Rene E. Monument   *"DOUCET / TOGETHER FOREVER"* is inscribed on one of two overlapping hearts. Floral carvings are on the left side of this heart. On the base is carved *"RENE E. / 1930 – 1978"* is carved on the left. *"CATHERINE T. / 1934 – 1993"* is carved on the right. A veteran's marker and flag are present.
"✞ / RENE E DOUCET / US NAVY / WORLD WAR II / AUG 13 1930   MAY 20 1978" is inscribed on this flat, ground level stone, which is beginning to be buried. It is located directly in front of the monument, on the left.

Draghetti, Alexander J.   See George Elliott Monument entry.

Draghetti, Elisabeth M.   See Raymond Draghetti Monument entry.

Draghetti, Phyllis   See George Elliott Monument entry.

Draghetti, Raymond L. Monument   *"Draghetti"* is carved in outline on the front of this monument. Leaves are carved in a row along the bottom. *"RAYMOND L. DRAGHETTI / JULY 15, 1905 – DEC. 10, 1986 / HIS WIFE / ELISABETH MOORE SAVAGE / OCT. 19, 1914 – NOV. 17, 1974"* is inscribed on the back. A veteran's marker and flag are present. A Barnicoat Monuments metal tag is present.

Eaton, Harriett E.   See Josiah B. Bump Monument entry.
"WIFE / HARRIETTE" is carved in shallow relief on this flat, 3-4 inch high stone. It faces the rear of the cemetery and is located behind the monument, on the right.

Eaton, Ralph P.   See Josiah B. Bump Monument entry.
"RALPH P. / EATON" is carved in shallow relief on this flat, ground level stone. This rear facing footstone is located directly behind the monument, on the right.

Elliott, Carrie S.   See George Elliott Monument entry.

Elliott, George V. Monument   *"ELLIOTT / 1884   GEORGE V.   1958 / 1884 CARRIE S.   1963"* is inscribed on the front of this monument. Floral carvings are in the upper corners. *"ALEXANDER J. DRAGHETTI / 1900 – 1969 / HIS WIFE / PHYLLIS (ELLIOTT) / 1913 – 1992 / ARTHUR L. GUIDOBONI / 1912 – 1988 / HIS WIFE / LELIA S. (ELLIOTT) / 1914 – 1973"* is inscribed on the back. A Middleboro

Lodge #1274 BPOE Lodge marker and flag are present.

England, Frank E. Monument *"ENGLAND / 1901 FRANK E. 1976 / HIS WIFE / 1902 HELEN E. 1967"* A Mason's symbol is carved at the top of this monument. Floral carvings are in the upper corners. A veteran's marker and flag are present.

England, Helen E. See Frank England Monument entry.

Erickson, Caroline See Herbert England Monument entry.

Erickson, Herbert F. Monument *"ERICKSON / 1895 HERBERT F. 1974 / 1894 CAROLINE E. HIS WIFE 1967"* There are floral carvings at the top of this monument. A R. L. Linton metal tag is present.

Estey Monument *"ESTEY / TOGETHER FOREVER"* is embossed on this metal marker which is attached to a slanted monument. Floral carvings are embossed on the sides and surround the center vase at the top. A book is embossed to the right of the first line with the words *"HOLY BIBLE"* embossed on it. An eagle with *"FOE"* embossed underneath it is on the left. The places for name plaques are empty.

Fidler, Edna M. See John A. Fidler Monument entry.

Fidler, John A. Monument *"FIDLER / DEMORANVILLE"* is carved in outline on the front of this hexagonal monument. A pine branch is carved on the left. *"1915 JOHN A. FIDLER 1979 / HIS WIFE / EDNA M. LEES"* is carved in outline on the back. A veteran's marker and flag are present.
"JOHN ARTHUR FIDLER / SF1 US NAVY / WWII KOREA VIETNAM / APR 4 1915 ✝ JUN 3 1979" is embossed on this flat, metal marker. It is located directly in front of the monument, on the left.

Fitting, David L. Monument *"Fitting"* is inscribed on the front of this monument. A cross is carved on the left. *"DAVID L. / 1920 – 1998 / HIS WIFE / MILDRED B. / 1922 – ____ / DAUGHTER / 1951 MARIE MACKIEWICZ 2002"* is inscribed on the back. The last line was added after the initial visit. A veteran's marker and flag, a Knights of Columbus marker and K of C flag are present. A Barnicoat Monuments metal tag is present.
"✝ / DAVID L FITTING / CSM US ARMY / WORLD WAR II / AUG 18 1920 SEP 1 1998" is inscribed on this flat, ground level stone. It is located directly in front of the monument, on the left, and is beginning to be buried.

Fitting, Mildred B. See David Fitting Monument entry.

Flanders, Lauretta M.   *"LAURETTA M. FLANDERS / 1921 – 1994"* is inscribed on this flat, ground level stone. It is located directly in front of the Bailey-Flanders Monument, on the right.

Fontano, Margaret M.   See Nicholas Fontano Monument entry.

Fontano, Nicholas J. Monument   *"FONTANO / IN LOVING MEMORY / NICHOLAS J. / 1915 – 1995 / HIS LOVING WIFE / MARGARET M. / 1924 – ____"* Floral carvings are in the upper corners. A World War II marker and flag are present. A Barnicoat Monuments metal tag is present.
"✝ / NICHOLAS J FONTANO / PVT   US ARMY / WORLD WAR II / AUG 23 1915 MAY 22 1995" is inscribed on this flat, ground level stone. It is beginning to be buried. It is located directly in front of the monument, on the left.

Foster, B. Warren Monument   *"FOSTER"* is inscribed on the front of this monument. A floral wreath is carved on the left side. *"B. WARREN FOSTER / JUN. 3, 1925 – MAR. 17, 1985 / BELOVED WIFE / ELINOR L. / JUN. 26, 1929 ____"* is inscribed on the back, on the right side. The left side is blank. A Mason's symbol is carved at the top. A World War II marker and flag are present.
"B WARREN FOSTER / US NAVY / 1925   1985" is inscribed on this flat, ground level stone that faces the rear of the cemetery. It is located behind the monument, on the left.

Foster, Elinor L.   See B. Warren Foster Monument entry.

Franklin, Charles H. Monument   *"✝ FRANKLIN ✝"* is inscribed at the top of the monument, below a carving of the BPOE symbol. *"CHARLES   AT REST MARY A."* is inscribed along the bottom. Rose carvings extend down the sides. *"✝ / 1911   CHARLES H. FRANKLIN   1997 / 1931   MARY A. HIS WIFE   1965 / 1955 SYLVESTER V. FRANKLIN   1974"* is inscribed on the back. Cement planters are on the either side of this monument. A Barnicoat Monuments metal tag is present.

Franklin, Mary A.   See Charles H. Franklin Monument entry.

Franklin, Sylvester V.   See Charles H. Franklin Monument entry.

Freeman Monument   *"FREEMAN"* is the only inscription on this monument. Ivy carvings are on either side. An open book is carved on the top horizontal surface. A veteran's marker and flag are present. A Barnicoat Monuments metal tag is present.

Frizzell, Euphemia B.   See Walter Frizzell Monument entry.

Frizzell, Harold E.   See Walter Frizzell Monument entry.

Frizzell, Suzanne M.   See Walter Frizzell Monument entry.

Frizzell, Walter R. Monument   *"FRIZZELL"* is inscribed on the front of this monument. Floral carvings are at the top. *"WALTER R. FRIZZELL / 1875 – 1955 / WIFE – EUPHEMIA B. / 1879 – 1963 / HAROLD E. FRIZZELL / 1905 – 1999 / WIFE – SUZANNE M. / 1909 – 1986"* is inscribed on the back.

Fuller, Peter G.   See Myrtle Walsh Monument entry.

Fuller, Sandra R.   See Myrtle Walsh Monument entry.

Galego, Carol L.   See John Galego Monument entry.

Galego, John E. Monument   *"GALEGO / TOGETHER FOREVER / JOHN   CAROL"* is inscribed on the front of this tall, tapering monument. A cross and Star of David are carved in relief at the top. Below this, a building is carved in relief with the words *"DEVELOPER   ROOFER   CONTRACTOR"* encircling it. *"JOHN E. GALEGO / SEP. 22, 1942 – DEC. 20, 1989 / HIS WIFE / CAROL L. (ESTNER) / AUG. 3, 1944 ____ "* is inscribed on the back. Above the inscription is a carving of a ball, racquet, horseshoe, and swimmer. A boat named *"Carol Lee"* is carved below the inscription.

Gamache, Alexander R.   *"ALEXANDER ROBERT / GAMACHE / MAY 12, 1993 – NOV. 14, 1994"* An angel carrying away a child is carved on the front of this monument, above the inscription. A Barnicoat Monuments metal tag is present.

Gamache, Elyana L.   See Ronald S. Garbitt Monument entry

Gamache, Olivia A.   See Ronald S. Garbitt Monument entry

Garbitt, Rita A.   See Ronald S. Garbitt Monument entry.

Garbitt, Ronald S. Monument   *"GARBITT / RONALD S. / MAR. 8, 1950 ____ / RITA ALMA / FEB. 2, 1952 ____ "* is inscribed on the front of this monument with flowers carved in the upper corners. *"GAMACHE / TWIN DAUGHTERS / OLIVIA ALMA, ELYANA LOUISE DEC. 10, 2003"* is inscribed on the back. Angels are carved in the upper corners. This monument was placed after the initial visit.

Gibney, Arthur J. Monument   *"GIBNEY"* is inscribed on the front of this monument. *"ARTHUR J. / 1907 – 1990"* is inscribed on the bottom left, and *"LUCILLE E. / 1906 – 1990"* is inscribed on the bottom right. A Middleboro Lodge #1274 BPOE marker and flag are present. A Barnicoat Monuments tag is present.

Gibney, Lucille E.   See Arthur Gibney Monument entry.

Gilker, Joanne   *"IN MEMORY OF / JOANNE (MENDALL) / GILKER / OCT. 15, 1923 – SEP. 25, 1988"* is inscribed on this flat stone, which is beginning to be buried.

Given, Edward   See Norman Given Monument entry.

Given, Mabel   See Norman Given Monument entry.

Given, Norman Monument   *"GIVEN"* in inscribed on the front of this monument, above a carving of an open book. *"NORMAN / 1903 – 1978"* is inscribed on the pages on the left side of this book, *"EDWARD / 1873 – 1954"* is inscribed in the center, and *"MABEL / 1871 – 1951"* is inscribed on the right side. *"BESSEY"* is inscribed on the back of this monument above a carving of an open book. *"LLOYD / 1902 – 1960"* is inscribed on the left side of this book, and *"ISA M. / 1905 – 1972"* is inscribed on the right side. A veteran's marker and flag, and an American Legion marker and flag are present.

Goodridge, Elsie F.   *"ELSIE F. GOODRIDGE / 1883 – 1930"* is inscribed on this flat, 0-1 inch high stone. The lower left side is beginning to be buried.

Goodridge, Ono M. Stone   *"GOODRIDGE"* is inscribed on this flat, 0-2 inch high stone. Below this, *"ONO M. / 1880 – 1961"* is inscribed on the left side, and *"SUSAN F. / 1884 – 1975"* is inscribed on the right.

Goodridge, Susan F.   See Ono Goodridge Monument entry.

Goodwin, Chester E., Jr. Monument   *"GOODWIN"* is inscribed on the front of this monument. Floral carvings are in the upper corners. A Mason's symbol is carved at the top. *"CHESTER E. GOODWIN JR. / 1919 – 1993 / HIS WIFE – EDITH E. (WILLIAMS) / 1923 – 1962 / FRANK B. WILLIAMS / 1868 – 1939 / HIS WIFE – BERTHA M. (ROUNDS) / 1881 – 1964"* is inscribed on the back. A veteran's marker and flag are present.
"✝ / CHESTER EDWIN GOODWIN JR / PFC   US ARMY / WORLD WAR II / DEC 14 1919   JAN 14 1993" is inscribed on this flat, sunken stone. It is located to the right of the monument.
"CHESTER E." This flat, ground level stone is located in front of the monument, on the right.

Goodwin, Edith E.   See Chester Goodwin, Jr. Monument entry.
"EDITH E." This flat, ground level stone is located directly in front of the monument, on the right. An Order of the Eastern Star symbol is carved at the top.

Gray, Arthur W. Monument   *"GRAY"* is inscribed on the front of this monument. A cross, rosary and a rose are carved behind this. *"ARTHUR W. / NOV. 24, 1949 / ____ "* is inscribed on the bottom left, and *"MARY A. / DEC. 4, 1949 / ____ "* is inscribed on the bottom right. *"FOREVER IN OUR HEARTS"* is inscribed on a ribbon carving on the back, around an etched picture of Renee. *"RENEE / NOV. 23, 1972   AUG. 11, 1995"* is inscribed below this. A circular design is carved between her birth and death dates. A Barnicoat Monuments metal tag is present.

Gray, Mary A.   See Arthur Gray Monument entry.

Gray, Renee   See Arthur Gray Monument entry.
"IN GOD'S CARE / RENEE" This flat, ground level stone faces the rear of the cemetery. It is located directly behind the monument, on the left.

Griffith, Harold L. Monument   *"GRIFFITH"* is carved in relief on the front of this monument. Floral carvings are at the bottom. *"HAROLD S.   LILLIAN M. VIRGINIA Y.   HAROLD L."* is inscribed on the base. *"GRIFFITH"* is inscribed on the back at the top. *"HAROLD L. / 1911   1965 / HIS WIFE / VIRGINIA Y. / 1913 ____ "* is inscribed on the left side, and *"HAROLD S. / 1888 – 1958 / HIS WIFE / LILLIAN M. / 1888 – 1956"* is inscribed on the right. A Mason's symbol is carved between Harold L.'s dates, and a star between Virginia's dates. A Middleboro Lodge #1274 BPOE marker and flag are present. A Barnicoat Monuments metal tag is present.

Griffith, Harold S.   See Harold L. Griffith Monument entry.

Griffith, Lillian M.   See Harold L. Griffith Monument entry.

Griffith, Virginia Y.   See Harold L. Griffith Monument entry.

Gudmundsson, Diana   *"GUDMUNDSSON"* is inscribed in shadow on the center section of this wide, three part monument. A picture of the couple is etched above the inscription. On the lower left is a carving of two hearts touching, and on the lower right are carved the hands of a chiropractor. *"DIANA / APRIL 14, 1952 / ____"* is inscribed on the left section of this monument   *"GUDMUNDUR / AUGUST 30, 1951 / OCTOBER 13, 1996"* is inscribed on the right section. There are sculptured rose carvings in the outer upper corners on the front and back.

Gudmundsson, Gudmundur   See Diana Gudmundsson Monument entry.
"DOCTOR / "GOODY"" is inscribed in outline on this flat, ground level stone. A caduceus is carved on the lower left. This stone is located directly in front of monument, on the right.

Guidoboni, Arthur L.   See George Elliott Monument entry.

Guidoboni, Lelia S.   See George Elliott Monument entry.

Hall, Arthur S., Jr. Monument   *"HALL"* is inscribed on the front of this monument. Floral carvings are in the upper corners. *"ARTHUR S. HALL JR. / MAR. 11, 1917 ____ / HELEN F. HIS WIFE / SEPT. 20, 1919 – DEC. 30, 1987"* is inscribed on the back. A Maver Memorials metal tag is present.

Hall, Helen F.   See Arthur Hall Monument entry.
"HELEN" is inscribed on this flat, ground level stone, which is beginning to be buried. It is located directly in front of the monument, on the right.

Hamilton, Harry W. Monument   *"HAMILTON"* is inscribed on the front of this monument. Calla lilies are carved in the upper corners. *"HARRY W. / 1908 – ____"* is inscribed on the bottom left, and *"LILLIAN R. /1909 – ____"* is inscribed on the bottom right. A Barnicoat Monuments metal tag is present.

Hamilton, Lillian R.   See Harry Hamilton Monument entry.

Handy, George M.   *"GEORGE MELVIN HANDY / MASSACHUSETTS / PFC US MARINE CORPS RES / WORLD WAR II / SEP 6 1924 DEC 5 1956"* This flat, ground level stone is located behind the Angers-Handy Monument, on the far left. A cross is carved in relief within a circle at the top of this stone. A veteran's marker and flag are present.

Handy, Marion F.   *"MARION FAITH HANDY / AUG. 14, 1927 – ____"* is inscribed on this flat, ground level stone. It is located behind the Angers-Handy Monument, on the left. It was placed after the initial visit.

Haskins, Amy M.   See John Haskins Monument entry.
"AMY MARIE / JUNE 4, 1978 – DEC. 23, 1980 / DAUGHTER OF / JOHN AND BARBARA" A praying child is carved on the left side and floral designs are carved in the upper right corner. This slanted stone is located directly behind the monument, on the left.

Haskins, John S. Monument   *"Haskins"* is carved in outline on the front of the monument. Roses are carved in the upper corners. *"1924   JOHN S. HASKINS ____ / 1927   VIRGINIA D. HIS WIFE ____ / 1978   AMY MARIE   1980"* is carved in outline on the back. A Barnicoat Monuments metal tag is present.

Haskins, Virginia D.   See John Haskins Monument entry.

Heifner, Dorothy J.   See Alden Perry Monument entry.

Heifner, Tilden O.   See Alden Perry Monument entry.

Holmes, Standish F.   *"✠ / STANDISH F. HOLMES / SSGT   US AIR FORCE / KOREA / DEC 18 1928   SEP 5 2000"* is inscribed on this flat, ground level stone. A veteran's marker and flag are present.

Jewell, Peter R.   *"JEWELL"* is inscribed in outline on the front of this monument. There are floral carvings below this. *"OUR BELOVED SON / PETER R. JEWELL / JUN. 4, 1971 – JAN. 25, 1988 / WE MISS YOU NOW, OUR HEARTS ARE SORE. / AS TIME GOES BY WE MISS YOU MORE, / YOUR LOVING SMILE, YOUR GENTLE FACE, / NO ONE CAN FILL YOUR VACANT PLACE."* is inscribed on the back.
"PETER" is inscribed on this flat, ground level stone. A shoe is carved below this. This rear facing stone is located behind the monument, on the right.

Johnson, Grace A.   See Robert F. Johnson Monument entry.

Johnson, Robert F. Monument   *"Johnson / ROBERT F. / 1926   1981 / HIS WIFE / GRACE A. VINTON / 1925 – ____ "* is carved in outline on the front of this monument. A Mason's symbol is carved between his birth and death dates. *"CHARTER MEMBER L. F. D. / CHIEF 1964 –1981 / HIGHWAY SURVEYOR 1973 – 1981"* is inscribed at the bottom. A fireman's hat with *"CHIEF / L. F. D."* on the front of it is carved above the inscriptions. A veteran's marker and flag are present.
"ROBERT FRANKLIN JOHNSON / MOMM1   US NAVY / WORLD WAR II / MAR 1 1926   MAY 27 1981" A circled cross is carved at the top of this flat, ground level stone. It is located directly in front of the monument, on the left.

Kelley, Eunice M.   *"KELLEY"* is inscribed on the front of this monument. A BPOE symbol is carved above this. A short musical score is carved in the upper left corner, and a porcelain portrait is in the upper right corner. *"EUNICE M. KELLEY / JULY 2, 1935 ____ "* is inscribed on the back. A Barnicoat Monuments metal tag is present.

King, Elizabeth C.   See William King Monument entry.

King, James E.   See William King Monument entry.

King, William Monument   *"KING"* is inscribed on the front of this monument, underneath an etching of Leonardo da Vinci's Last Supper. *"WILLIAM / JULY 10, 1913 / JAN. 29, 1970"* is inscribed on the bottom left. *"ELIZABETH C. / NOV. 22, 1913 / DEC. 5, 2001"* is inscribed on the bottom center, and *"JAMES E. / NOV. 19, 1936 / ____"* is inscribed on the bottom right. A Barnicoat Monuments metal tag is present. This monument was placed after the initial visit.
"WILLIAM KING / 1913 – 1970" is inscribed on this flat, ground level stone. It is beginning to be buried along the edges.

Kinsman, Alice E.   See Reginald Kinsman Monument entry.

Kinsman, Reginald F. Monument   *"KINSMAN / REGINALD F. / 1916 – ____ / HIS WIFE / ALICE E. (BEECH) / 1922 – ____"* is inscribed on this slanted monument. A calla lily and a bird are carved on the left, and a single leaf is carved on the lower right. A Barnicoat Monuments metal tag is present.

LaFave, Charles A.   See Perfica LaFave Monument entry.
"✝ / CHARLES A LaFAVE / S SGT   US ARMY / WORLD WAR II / MAR 24 1921 OCT 17 2000 / BELOVED HUSBAND" is inscribed on this flat, ground level stone. It is located directly in front of the monument, on the right.

LaFave, Perfica Monument   *"LaFave"* is inscribed on the front of this monument. *""PAT" / Perfica (Augusta) / May 4, 1920 / ____"* is inscribed on the lower left, and *""AL" / Charles A. / Mar. 24, 1921 / Oct. 17, 2000"* is inscribed on the lower right. Floral carvings adorn the upper corners. A veteran's marker and flag are present. A Barnicoat Monuments metal tag is present.

LaJeunesse, Marion   See Theodore LaJeunesse Monument entry.

LaJeunesse, Theodore V. Monument   *"LAJEUNESSE"* is inscribed on a carved banner at the top of this monument. Below this is carved a cross with a rosary on it, with flowers at its base. On either side is carved an open book. *"THEODORE V. / 1918 – 1993"* is inscribed on the left book, and *"MARION (ASACKER) / 1920 – ____"* is inscribed on the right book. A stone planter is attached to the base on the right side. A veteran's marker and flag are present. A Barnicoat Monuments metal tag is present.
"✝ / THEODORE V LaJEUNESSE / TEC 4   US ARMY / WORLD WAR II / APR 18 1918   DEC 23 1993" This flat, ground level stone is beginning to be buried. It is located directly in front of the monument, on the left.

Lang, Charles M. Monument   *"LANG"* is carved in relief on the front of this monument. Floral carvings are in the upper corners. *"CHARLES M°NEIL LANG / APR. 6, 1921 – DEC. 15, 2000 / HIS WIFE / MARY ELIZABETH SOUSA / DEC. 1, 1927 – FEB. 24, 2001 / SCOTT ALLEN LANG / SEPT. 24, 1957 – MAR. 3, 2003"* is inscribed on the back. A Maver Memorials metal tag is present. The last two lines were added after the initial visit.
"DAD" This flat, ground level stone is located directly in front of the monument, on the left.

Lang, Mary E.   See Charles Lang Monument entry.
"MOM" This flat, ground level stone is located directly in front of the monument,

on the right.

Lewoczko, Myron M. Monument   *"LEWOCZKO"* is inscribed on the front of this monument. Below this is inscribed *"MYRON M. / LOVING HUSBAND / MAY 8, 1925 / _____"* on the left side, and *"BEVERLY I. / (PORELL) / JAN. 25, 1932 / SEPT. 4, 2003"* on the right. Floral carvings are on the left side. A cross is carved on the lower right side with a purple sash around it. This monument was not present at the initial visit.

Lima, Beulah H.   See Joseph Lima Monument entry.

Lima, Joseph Jr. Monument   *"LIMA"* is inscribed on this slanted monument. *"JOSEPH JR. / 1920 – 2003"* is inscribed on the lower left, and *"BEULAH H. / 1927 – 1993"* is inscribed on the lower right. Floral carvings adorn the upper corners. *"BELOVED SON / MICHAEL LIMA / 1953 – 2001"* is inscribed on the back. The inscription for Michael, and Joseph's death year were added after the initial visit.

Lima, Michael   See Joseph Lima Monument entry.

Linton, Alton H. Monument   *"LINTON / ALTON H. / FEB. 21, 1909 – JAN. 24, 1992 / MYRA H. (STANDISH) / OCT 10, 1908 – AUG. 20, 1995"* Floral carvings adorn the upper corners. A Barnicoat Monuments metal tag is present.

Linton, Myra H.   See Alton Linton Monument entry.

Lomasney, Thomas L.   *"THOMAS L. LOMASNEY / 1946 – 1973 / IF WE BE DEAD WITH CHIRST – / WE SHALL ALSO LIVE WITH HIM / Rom.. 6:8"* is inscribed on this flat, slate stone, which is set into a ground level rock.

Longworth-Neville Monument   *"LONGWORTH"* is carved in relief on the front of this monument. *"NEVILLE"* is carved in relief on the back. No other inscriptions are present. Floral carvings adorn the upper corners on both sides of the monument.

Longworth, Grace A.   *"MOTHER / GRACE A. / 1908 – 1982"* is inscribed on this flat, ground level stone, which is beginning to be buried. Lakeville Vital Records for her husband Luther show her maiden name was Neville.

Longworth, Luther J.   *"FATHER / LUTHER J. / 1908 – 1950"* is inscribed on this flat, ground level stone, which is beginning to be buried. Lakeville Vital

Records show his last name was Longworth.

Lucas, Emma R.   See Eli Williams Obelisk entry.
"E. R. L." is carved in shallow relief on the top curved surface of this 3-5 inch tall footstone. It is located behind the obelisk, on the left, and faces the rear of the cemetery.

Lucas, Samuel W.   See Eli Williams Obelisk entry.
"S. W. L." is carved in shallow relief on the top curved surface of this 5-7 inch high footstone. This rear facing footstone is located behind the obelisk, on the far left.

Lun, Mae W.   *"In Loving Memory of / MAE W. LUN / 1928 – 1978"* This flat, ground level stone is beginning to be buried. Rose carvings are on the sides.

Mackiewicz, Marie   See David Fitting Monument entry.

MacLeod, Donald Y. Stone   *"MAC LEOD"* is inscribed on this flat, ground level stone. *"DONALD Y. / MAR. 25, 1916 / ____ "* is inscribed below this on the left, and *"GENEVIEVE L. / MAR. 24, 1923 / DEC. 11, 2002"* is inscribed on the right. This stone was placed after the initial visit.

MacLeod, Genevieve L.   See Donald Y. MacLeod Monument entry.

Maddigan, Annette L.   See Charles L. Reed, Jr. Monument entry.

Magnuson, Arline R.   See Frank Arrington Monument entry.

Magnuson, Earl R.   *"EARL RUSSELL MAGNUSON / 1ST SGT   US ARMY / WORLD WAR II / MAY 8 1911   NOV 13 1998"* is inscribed on this flat, ground level stone. A veteran's marker and flag are present.

Magnuson, Earl R.   See Frank Arrington Monument entry.

Mahoney, Daniel E.   See James F. Mahoney, Jr. Monument entry.

Mahoney, James F., Jr. Monument   *"MAHONEY / JAMES F. JR. / JAN. 23, 1925 ____ / LOVING WIFE / MARGARET C. (DeROMA) / APR. 12, 1923 – NOV. 3, 1996"* is inscribed on the front of this monument. Floral carvings are in the upper corners. *"DANIEL E. / JAN. 28, 1970 – JAN. 29, 2001"* has been added on the back of this monument since the initial visit. A Barnicoat Monuments metal tag is present.

Mahoney, Margaret C.   See James Mahoney Monument entry.

Marcos, Antone V. Monument   *"MARCOS"* is inscribed on the front of this monument. *"TONY   LORRAINE"* is inscribed below a carved scene of a deer in a meadow and a bird in a tree. *"ANTONE V MARCOS / SEP. 11, 1919 – JUN. 18, 1992 / BELOVED WIFE / LORRAINE E. (BRADSHAW) / JUL. 3, 1925 ____ "* is carved on the back. A veteran's marker and flag, and a Middleboro Lodge #1274 BPOE marker and flag are present. A Barnicoat Monuments metal tag is present.
"✟ / ANTONE V MARCOS / CPL   US ARMY / WORLD WAR II / SEP 11 1919   JUN 18 1992" This flat, ground level stone is located on the left, directly in front of the monument.

Marcos, Lorraine   See Antone Marcos Monument entry.

Marques, John F.   See Shirley Marques Monument entry.

Marques, Shirley R. Monument   *"MARQUES"* is inscribed on the front of this monument, below a carved BPOE symbol. *"SHIRLEY R. / APR. 4, 1930 / DEC. 18, 1987"* is inscribed on the lower left, and *"JOHN F. / APR. 25, 1927 / DEC. 21, 1993"* is inscribed on the lower right. Floral carvings adorn the upper corners. A Barnicoat Monuments metal tag is present.

Marshall, Alice M.   See Harry H. C. Marshall Monument entry.

Marshall, Douglas P.   *"DOUGLAS PERSHING MARSHALL / TEC 5   US ARMY / WORLD WAR II / 1918   1978"* A circled cross is carved at the top of this stone. This flat, ground level stone is beginning to be buried.

Marshall, F. Rita   See Harry Marshall Monument entry.

Marshall, Harold C.   See Harry H. C. Marshall Monument entry.

Marshall, Harry H. Monument   *"MARSHALL"* is inscribed in outline on the front of this monument. Floral carvings adorn the upper corners. *"MARSHALL / HARRY H. / 1889 – 1972 / HIS WIFE / F. RITA / 1893 – 1969"* is inscribed on the back, on the left side. A veteran's marker and flag, and a Mitchell Memorial Club marker and flag are present.

Marshall, Harry H. C. Monument   *"MARSHALL"* is inscribed at the top of this monument, below floral carvings. *"1914   HARRY H. C.   1963 / 1919   ALICE M. ____"* is inscribed on a carving of an open book. *"MARSHALL / HAROLD C. / 1943 – 2002 / INEZ E. / 1945 ____"* is inscribed on the back. The inscription for Alice, Harold C. and Inez were added after the initial visit. A Middleboro Lodge #1274 BPOE marker and flag are present.

Marshall, Inez E.   See Harry H. C. Marshall Monument entry.

Marston, Howard W. Monument   *"MARSTON"* is carved in outline on the front of this monument. *"HOWARD W. / 1909   1995"* is carved in outline on the bottom left, and *"LAURA M. / 1914 – ____"* is carved in outline on the bottom right. Floral carvings are in the upper corners. There is a Mason's symbol between Howard's birth and death years.

Marston, Laura M.   See Howard W. Marston Monument entry.

Mastera, Elizabeth H.   See Melvyn F. Mastera Monument entry.

Mastera, Melvyn F. Monument   *"BUFFY / MASTERA"* is inscribed on the front of this monument. There are floral carvings on either side. Holes for pots are present in the base on either side of the monument. *"1910   MELVYN F. MASTERA 1983 / 1913   ELIZABETH H. HIS WIFE   1969"* is inscribed on the back. A Barnicoat Monuments metal tag is present.

McEachern, Francis   *"FRANCIS / MCEACHERN / JULY 1, 1928 – DEC. 4, 1995 / TO LIVE IN HEARTS WE LEAVE BEHIND / IS NOT TO DIE"* A cross and ivy vines are carved at the top. A Barnicoat Monuments metal tag is present.

Medeiros, Alice I.   See Arthur Medeiros Monument entry.

Medeiros, Arthur Monument   *"✞ / MEDEIROS"* is inscribed in outline on the front of this monument. *"IN LOVING MEMORY"* is inscribed on the bottom. Floral carvings adorn the upper corners. *"1912 ARTHUR MEDEIROS 1970 / 1918 ALICE I. (CARLSON) 1999"* is inscribed on the back. A Barnicoat Monuments metal tag is present.

Medeiros, C. Margaret   See James N. Medeiros Monument entry.

Medeiros, James N. Monument   *"MEDEIROS / JIMMY MARGIE"* is carved in outline on the front of this monument. A sculptured rose is carved in the upper left corner. *"JAMES N. MEDEIROS / MAY 27, 1925 – DEC. 16, 1996 / HIS WIFE / C. MARGARET (NORRIS) / SEP. 30, 1923 – OCT. 9, 1990"* is carved in outline on the back. There is a WWII Veteran's marker, a Middleboro Lodge #1274 BPOE marker and a flag present. A Barnicoat Monuments metal tag is present.

Meleedy, Bernadette D.   See William J. Meleedy, Jr. Monument entry.

Meleedy, William J. Jr. Monument   *"MELEEDY"* is inscribed on the front of this monument. *"WILLIAM J. JR. / AUG. 5, 1930 / MAR. 13, 2003"* is inscribed on the bottom left, and *"BERNADETTE D. / JUNE 25, 1935 / JUNE 8, 1997"* is inscribed on the bottom right. Sculptured roses are carved in the upper corners. William's death date has been added since the initial visit. A Barnicoat Monuments metal tag is present.
"WILLIAM J MELEEDY / CPL US ARMY / KOREA / AUG 5 1930 MAR 13 2003" is inscribed on this flat, ground level stone. This stone was added since the initial visit.

Mendall, Eleanor B. Monument   *"MENDALL / ELEANOR THEODORE"* is inscribed on the front of this monument. *"THEODORE F. MENDALL / OCT. 27, 1894 – NOV. 15, 1981 / HIS WIFE / ELEANOR B. MONROE / NOV. 28, 1893 – APR. 1, 1984"* is inscribed on the back.

Mendall, Theodore F.   See Eleanor Mendall Monument entry.

Michaud, Lee J.   *"MICHAUD"* is inscribed at the top of this slanted monument, with a cross and floral carvings on either side. *"ALWAYS IN OUR HEARTS"* is inscribed on a banner below this. *"LEE JAMES / MAY 7, 1993 – NOV. 8, 2000"* is inscribed on the back. A Maver Memorials metal tag is present. A veteran's marker and flag are present.
"LEE JAMES" is inscribed on this flat, ground level stone. A carving of a bow and arrow is in the upper left corner, a cross is carved in the upper right corner. Cowboy boots are carved in the lower left corner, and a motorcycle is carved in the lower right corner. It is located directly in front of the monument, on the left.

Mills Monument   *"MILLS"* is inscribed on the front and back of this monument. Floral carvings are in the upper corners on the front. No other inscriptions are present.

Mills, Beatrice A.   *"WIFE / BEATRICE A. / 1898 – 1977"* is inscribed on this flat, ground level marker. It is located directly in front of the Mills Monument, on the right. Lakeville Vital Records show that she was the second wife of Robert J. Mills.

Mills, George E. *"HUSBAND / GEORGE E. / 1905 – 1979"* is inscribed on this flat, ground level stone, which is beginning to be buried. This rear facing stone is located behind the Mills Monument on the far right. Lakeville Vital Records confirm his last name is Mills.

Mills, Helen *"WIFE / HELEN / 1904 – 1964"* This flat, ground level stone faces the rear of the cemetery. It is located behind the Mills Monument, on the right. Lakeville Vital Records show she was the wife of George E. Mills.

Mills, Margarette J. *"WIFE / MARGARETTE J. / 1883 – 1947"* is inscribed on this flat, ground level stone. This stone is located in front of the Mills Monument, on the right. Lakeville Vital Records show she was the wife of Robert J. Mills.

Mills, Marguerite A. See Stanley R. Mills Monument entry.

Mills, Robert J. *"HUSBAND / ROBERT J. / 1881 – 1957"* This flat 1 inch high stone is located in front of the Mills Monument, on the far right. Lakeville Vital Records show that he was the husband of Margarette and Beatrice Mills.

Mills, Robert J. Sr. *"✝ / ROBERT JOHN MILLS Sr / SN   US NAVY / JAN 31 1938   AUG 6 1989"* This flat, ground level stone is beginning to be buried. A veteran's marker and flag are present. It is located directly behind the Mills Monument, on the right.

Mills, Stanley R. Monument *"MILLS"* is inscribed on the front of this monument. *"STANLEY R. / JAN. 11, 1907 / MAY 18, 1981"* is inscribed on the bottom left, and *"MARGUERITE A. B. / JUL. 10, 1910 / ____"* is inscribed on the bottom right. A Barnicoat Monuments metal tag is present.

Moffett, Patti L. Monument *"MOFFETT"* is carved in outline along an arch on the front of this black monument. There is a carving of a cloverleaf with an arrow through it on the lower left. *"✝ / PATTI LOU MOFFETT / NOV. 11, 1937 – OCT. 17, 1995 / BELOVED WIFE OF / RAYMOND J. MOFFETT / AUG. 20, 1931 ____"* is inscribed on the back. *"CHILDREN / SHAWN, CASEY, GILLIAN"* is inscribed at the bottom. A Rex metal tag is present.

Moffett, Raymond J. See Patti Moffett Monument entry.

Morelli, Pete *"PETE / 1956 – 2000"* is all that is inscribed on this flat, ground level stone. A dove is carved in the upper left corner.

Mosher-Bowles Monument *"MOSHER"* is carved in relief on the front of this monument. *"BOWLES"* is carved in relief on the back. Floral carvings are in the upper corners of both the front and back of the monument.

Mosher, Harriet M. *"HARRIET M. / 1878 – 1944"* This flat, ground level stone is located directly in front of the Mosher-Bowles Monument, on the right. Lakeville Vital Records list her as the wife of Trask Mosher.

Mosher, Trask S. *"TRASK S. / 1875 – 1967"* This flat, ground level stone is beginning to be buried. It is located directly in front of the Mosher-Bowles

Monument, on the left. Lakeville Vital Records show that his name was Trask Sherwood Mosher.

Mosier, Harold W., Jr. *"MOSIER / In Loving Memory / HAROLD W. JR. / NOV. 9, 1922 – MAY 8, 1972"* A rose is carved between the second and third lines, on the left. A Barnicoat Monuments metal tag is present.
"HAROLD W MOSIER Jr / MASSACHUSETTS / BMC US NAVY / WORLD WAR II KOREA / NOV 9, 1922 MAY 8 1972" is inscribed on this sunken, flat metal marker. A veteran's marker and flag are present. It is located directly in front of the monument, on the left.

Nelson, Hannah K. See John H. Nelson Monument entry.

Nelson, John H. Monument
"NELSON" is carved in relief on the top slanted surface of this monument. *"JOHN H. NELSON / FEB. 7, 1829 – DEC. 15, 1912 / MARY D. WILLIAMS / HIS WIFE / JULY 28, 1836 – APR. 5, 1930 / HANNAH K. NELSON / SEPT. 9, 1860 – MAY 4, 1949 / MARY L. NELSON / JULY 26, 1870 – SEPT. 9, 1953"* is inscribed on the front. *"HELEN A. WILLIAMS / WIFE OF / JAMES I. DEAN / MAR. 3, 1848 – APR. 12, 1928"* is inscribed on the back.
"J. H. N." is inscribed on this flat, ground level stone. It is located in front of the monument, on the far right.

Nelson, Mary D. See John H. Nelson Monument entry.
"M. D. W. N." This flat, ground level stone is located in front of the monument, on the right.

Nelson, Mary L. See John H. Nelson Monument entry.

Neville, Alice M. *"MOTHER / ALICE M. / 1880 – 1951"* is inscribed on this flat, ground level stone, which beginning to be buried. It is broken in the upper left corner. It is located behind the Longworth-Neville Monument on the right.

Neville, Anna E. See John Neville Monument entry.

Neville, John D. Monument *"JOHN D. NEVILLE / 1910 – 1988 / ANNA E. HIS WIFE / 1910 – ____"* This flat, ground level stone faces the rear of the cemetery and is beginning to be buried on the right side. It is located directly behind the Longworth-Neville Monument, on the left.

Norris, Alice See Harry Norris Monument entry.

Norris, Harry G. Monument *"NORRIS"* is inscribed in outline on the front of

the monument. Leaves are carved in the upper corners. *"HARRY G. NORRIS /
1908____ / HIS WIFE / ALICE ELDRIDGE / 1910 – 2002"* is inscribed on the back.

Northcott, George H. Monument   *"NORTHCOTT, / GEORGE H. / 1875 – 1951 /
MABEL S. / 1881 – 1960"* Floral carvings adorn the top corners.

Northcott, Henry S.   *"HENRY S. / NORTHCOTT / 1909 – 1935"*

Northcott, Mabel S.   See George H. Northcott Monument entry.

Norton, Charles F.   See Leslie Norton Monument entry.

Norton, Claire C.   See Leslie Norton Monument entry.

Norton, Julia S.   See Leslie Norton Monument entry.

Norton, Leslie H. Monument   *"NORTON"* is carved in outline on the front of the
monument. A relief carving of the Mason's symbol is above this, with ivy carvings
on either side. *"1891   LESLIE HOWARD   1966 / HIS WIFE / 1896   JULIA
SAMPSON   1987 / 1921   WINTHROP HOWARD   1946 / U. S. N. R. / 1922
CHARLES FREDERICK   1922" "1927   MERRILL S. NORTON   ____ / HIS WIFE /
1932   CLAIRE CALDWELL   ____"* is inscribed on the back. A veteran's marker
and flag are present.

Norton, Merrill S.   See Leslie Norton Monument entry.

Norton, Winthrop H.   See Leslie Norton Monument entry.

O'Neill, Bonnie   See Robert J. O'Neill Stone entry.

O'Neill, Robert J. Stone   *"O'NEILL / ROBERT J. / SEP. 15, 1962   ____ / HIS
WIFE / BONNIE (CALDWELL) / JUN. 15, 1963 – OCT. 12, 2003"* A carving of the
Tasmanian Devil is in the upper left corner of this flat, ground level stone.

Owen, Arthur S., Jr.   *" ✝ / ARTHUR S OWEN JR / PFC   US ARMY / KOREA /
JULY 15 1928   MAR 4 2002"* This flat, ground level marker faces the rear of the
cemetery. A veteran's marker and flag are present.

Owen, Arthur S., Sr. Monument   *"OWEN"* is inscribed on the front of this
slanted monument. *"1897   ARTHUR S. OWEN SR.   1969 / 1897   JENNIE K. HIS
WIFE   1986"* is inscribed on the back.
*"ARTHUR SHERMAN OWEN / MASSACHUSETTS / S2   USNRF / WORLD WAR I
/ JAN 24 1897   SEPT 30 1969"* is inscribed on this flat, 1-2 inch high stone. It is
located directly in front of the monument.

Owen, Jennie K.   See Arthur Owen Monument entry.

Panettieri, Maria P.   See Pietro Panettieri Monument entry.

Panettieri, Pietro Monument   *"PANETTIERI"* is inscribed on the front of this
monument. *"PIETRO / JULY 12, 1939 / ____"* is inscribed on the bottom left, and
"MARIA P. / APRIL 18, 1946 / ____" is inscribed on the bottom right. *" SILVA /
ANTONIETTA SILVA MOTHER / OCT. 19, 1926 – APRIL 24, 1996"* is inscribed on
the back. A carving of the Virgin Mary is to the left of the first line. A porcelain
portrait with *"ANTONIETTA BARRAGO"* embossed below it is to the left of the last

two lines. Barrago was her maiden name. Crosses are carved in the upper corners of both the front and the back of the monument.

Paulson, Ann Marie Monument   *"PAULSON"* is inscribed in the center front of this large black monument. *"ANN MARIE (GRANEY) / JAN 8, 1954 / _____"* is inscribed below this on the left side, and *"PHILIP DURNIN / DEC 7, 1948 / AUG 1, 2000"* is inscribed on the right side. A porcelain portrait of the couple is present between these two inscriptions with the words *"MARRIED / JULY 17, 1982"* inscribed underneath. In the top left corner, two books are carved with the titles *"SCIENCE"* and *"HISTORY"* on their spines. A lamp is sitting on top of the books. There is a heart carving at the top center of the monument, with a silhouette of a couple painted inside. On the right is an etching of the couple. The beginning of the musical score for "Ode to Joy" is carved at the bottom of the monument. Attached to the right side of the monument is a stone bench. Attached to the base on the left side of the monument, is a rectangular stone planter with etchings of Revolutionary War shooters on three sides. *"XITH Mass. Reg."* is inscribed on a flag in the scene on the back of this planter. A heart shaped porcelain portrait of the couple is on the back of the monument, at the top. Angels are etched in the upper corners. Below this are various etchings of Revolutionary War reenactors. *"This is no ordinary person you are dealing with"* is inscribed on the bottom. A Knights of Columbus marker and flag are present.

Paulson, Phillip D.   See Ann Marie Paulson Monument entry.
"Phillip D. Paulson / December 7, 1948 ✞ August 1, 2000" is written on a Dahlborg-MacNevin Funeral Home marker.

Peck, David   *"DAVID / 1940 – 1951"* is inscribed on this flat, ground level stone, which is beginning to be buried. Lakeville Vital Records list his last name was Peck.

Peck, Edgar C. Monument   *"PECK"* is carved in relief on the front of this monument. *"1870   EDGAR C.   1955 / HIS WIFE / 1874   MYRTIE A.   1955"* is inscribed below this. Floral designs are carved in the upper corners. *"DILL"* is carved in relief on the back. *"1894   THOMAS G.   1983 / 1904   RUTH E. WIFE 1994 / 1925   ERNEST E. SON   1994 / 1927   LOUISE G. DAU.   _____"* is inscribed below this.
"EDGAR" is inscribed on this flat, ground level stone, which is beginning to be buried on the left side. It is located in front of the monument on the far left.

Peck, Harold S.   *"HAROLD S. / PECK / 1909 – 1977"* is inscribed on this flat, sunken stone.

Peck, Hazel   *"HAZEL L. / HIS WIFE / 1912 – 1989"* is inscribed on this flat, ground level stone, which is beginning to be buried. Hazel was the wife of Harold S. Peck.

Peck, Myrtie A.   See Edgar Peck Monument entry.
"MYRTIE" This flat, ground level stone is located in front of the monument, on the left. The lower left corner is beginning to be buried.

Pember, Frances C.   See Henry L. Pember Monument entry.

Pember, Henry L. Monument *"HENRY L. / FEB. 26, 1880 – OCT. 16, 1979 / HIS WIFE / FRANCES C. / NOV. 23, 1884 – MAR. 3, 1959"* is inscribed on the southeast side of this square monument, which is rotated 45 degrees from the line of graves. A Mason's symbol is carved above the inscription. *"PEMBER"* is carved in relief on the base. *"GEORGE F. / APR. 4, 1874 – MAY 26, 1947 / HIS WIFE / LOUISA J. / MAY 6, 1881 – JAN. 16, 1927 / HIS WIFE, JESSIE / FEB. 9, 1885 – NOV. 26, 1951"* is inscribed on the northeast side. A wreath is carved above the inscription. *"REED"* is carved in relief on the base of this side. There are no inscriptions on the other two sides.

Perry, Alden C. Monument *"PERRY / HEIFNER"* is inscribed on the rough cut front of this monument. *"ALDEN C. PERRY / JAN. 28, 1911 – MAY 1, 1993 / MARION E. HIS WIFE / JUNE 1, 1910 – MAR. 11, 1974 / TILDEN O. HEIFNER / JUNE 28, 1908 – DEC. 24, 1997 / DOROTHY J. HIS WIFE / NOV. 5, 1918 – MAR. 14, 2002"* is inscribed on the smooth back. Birds and flowers are carved in the top left corner on the back. Dorothy's death date was added after the initial visit. A veteran's marker and flag are present.
"ALDEN CHESTER PERRY / BORN JAN 28 1911 DIED MAY 1, 1993 AGE 82 YEARS." is written on a Nickerson Bourne Funeral Home marker.
"ALDEN C PERRY / MOMM 2   US NAVY / WORLD WAR II / JAN 28 1911   ✝ MAY 1 1993" is embossed on this flat, ground level metal marker.

Perry, Marion E.   See Alden Perry Monument entry.

Person, Mary P.   See Robert Person Monument entry.

Person, Robert F. Monument   *"PERSON"* is inscribed at the top of this monument. A scene of a deer near water is carved below this on the front. *"GIG"* is inscribed on the lower left. *"ROBERT F. PERSON / APR. 15, 1933 – DEC. 27, 1990 / MARY P. BELOVED WIFE / APR. 18, 1938 ____"* is inscribed on the back. A Barnicoat Monuments metal tag is present.

Pierce, Ina A.   *"INA. A. / 1890 – 1980"* is inscribed on this flat, ground level stone, which is beginning to be buried. It is located in front of the Babbitt Monument, on the right. David Babbitt was her second husband.

Plissey, Clara C.   See Harry F. Plissey Monument entry.

Plissey, Harry F. Monument   *"PLISSEY"* is inscribed on the front of this monument. Floral carvings adorn the upper corners. *"HARRY F. PLISSEY / 1880 – 1966 / MARY E. HIS WIFE / 1887 – 1962 / HARRY F. PLISSEY JR. / 1922 – 1990 / CLARA C. HIS WIFE / 1923 – 1989"* is inscribed on the back. A R. L. Linton metal tag is present.

Plissey, Harry F., Jr.   See Harry F. Plissey Monument entry.

Plissey, Mary E.   See Harry F. Plissey Monument entry.

Porell, David G.   See Donald Porell Monument entry.

Porell, Donald E. Monument   *"✝ / PORELL / DONALD ERNEST / JAN. 25, 1932 – AUG. 20, 2000 / HIS LOVING WIFE / JOAN MARIE (DiCARLO) / DEC. 18, 1939 ___ "* is inscribed on the center section of this wide, three part monument. A floral arrangement is carved on the bottom. *"THEIR CHILDREN / DAVID GEORGE / DEC. 16, 1966 /___ / JOSEPH DONALD / DEC. 15, 1967 / ____"* is inscribed on the left section, and *"THEIR CHILDREN / DONNA MARIE / JUL. 2, 1962 / ____ ROBERT MATTHEW / OCT. 28, 1974 / ____"* is inscribed on the right section. Floral carvings adorn the upper outer corners.
"✝ / DONALD E PORELL / CPL   US ARMY / KOREA / JAN 25 1932   AUG 20 2000" is inscribed on this flat, ground level stone. It is located directly in front of the monument, on the left. A *"KOREAN VETERAN"* marker and flag are present.
"DONALD E. PORELL / JAN. 25, 1932 – AUG. 20, 2000" is inscribed on this second stone. This flat, ground level stone is located directly in front of the above stone. Both are beginning to be buried.

Porell, Donna M.   See Donald Porell Monument entry.

Porell, Joan M.   See Donald Porell Monument entry.

Porell, Joseph D.   See Donald Porell Monument entry.

Porell, Robert M.   See Donald Porell Monument entry.

Prifogle, Charlotte   See Francis Prifogle Monument entry.

Prifogle, Francis E. Monument   *"PRIFOGLE"* is inscribed on the front of this monument. *"FRANCIS E. / 1908 – 1980"* is inscribed on the bottom left, and *"CHARLOTTE / 1922 – 2002"* is inscribed on the bottom right. The death year for Charlotte was added after the initial visit. *"BEDNAR"* is inscribed on the back of the monument. *"JULIUS J. / 1895 – 1984"* is inscribed on the bottom left, and *"CHARLOTTE E. / 1896 – 1989"* is inscribed on the bottom right. A Barnicoat Monuments metal tag is present.

Reed, Charles L. Monument   *"REED"* is inscribed on the front of this monument. Floral carvings adorn the upper corners. *"CHARLES L. REED / 1888 – 1956 / WIFE – ELIZABETH M. / 1891 – 1974"* is inscribed on the back. An R. L. Linton metal tag is present.
"FATHER" This flat 2-4 inch high stone is located to the left of the monument.

Reed, Charles L., Jr. Monument   *"REED"* is inscribed in outline on the front of this monument. Floral carvings are in the upper corners.   *"FATHER"* and

"*MOTHER*" are inscribed in outline on the bottom front corners. "*CHARLES L. REED JR. / JUNE 11, 1915 – NOV. 29, 1971 / HIS WIFE / ELEANOR A. DEMORANVILLE / MAY 3, 1918 – APR. 21, 1986 / DAUGHTER / ANNETTE L. MADDIGAN / MAR. 20, 1940 – MAR. 29, 1994*" is inscribed on the back. "*ANNETTE*" is inscribed in outline on the lower left. A Middleboro Lodge #1274 BPOE marker and flag are present.

Reed, Eleanor A.   See Charles L. Reed, Jr. Monument entry.

Reed, Elizabeth M.   See Charles Reed Monument entry.
"*MOTHER*" This flat, 2-4 inch high stone is located to the right of the monument.

Reed, George F.   See Henry L. Pember Monument entry.

Reed, Jessie   See Henry L. Pember Monument entry.

Reed, Louisa J.   See Henry L. Pember Monument entry.

Reposa, Todd M.   "*REPOSA / INFANT SON / 1974   TODD MATTHEW   1974*" is inscribed on the front of this monument. A cross and floral carvings are in the upper corners. A medallion from the General Society of Mayflower Descendants is at the top of this monument. An A. Souza & Sons metal tag is present.

Rinkus, James R.   See Shirley Rinkus Monument entry.

Rinkus, Shirley A. Monument   "*RINKUS*" is inscribed in outline on the front of this monument. "*SHIRLEY A. / SEP. 16, 1934 / APR. 11, 2001 / BELOVED GRANDMOTHER*" is inscribed below this on the left, and "*JAMES R. / NOV. 11, 1932 / ____ / BELOVED GRANDFATHER*" is inscribed on the right. Floral carvings are in the upper corners. A Barnicoat Monuments metal tag is present

Roby, Mildred J.   See Waldo Roby Monument entry.

Roby, Waldo N. Monument   "*ROBY*" is inscribed on a carved scroll at the top of this monument. Two open books are carved on either side of a carving of a church. "*WALDO NATHAN / MAR. 26, 1932 / ____*" is inscribed on the left book, and "*MILDRED JANE / MAR. 15, 1935 / DEC. 24, 1992*" is inscribed on the right book. "*IN MY FATHER'S HOUSE*" and "*ARE MANY MANSIONS*" are inscribed on two separate scroll carvings below these books. A Mason's symbol is carved above Waldo's book, and an Order of the Eastern Star symbol is carved above Mildred's book.

Rogers, Mary E.   See Roger E. Beech Monument entry.
"*ROGERS / MARY ELIZABETH (BEECH) / "BETTY" / WIFE OF JIM, / MOTHER OF KARYN AND JULIE*" is inscribed on this slanted monument. Floral carvings are in the upper corners. This second monument is located in front of the Roger Beech Monument, on the right.

Rose, George F.   See Jeannette Dextraze Monument entry.

Sampson, Abiel M.   "*ABIEL M. SAMPSON, / Died March 4, / 1867. / Aged 70 years, 3 mo's / & 1 day.*" This stone shares its base with the stone of Bathsheba Sampson.

Sampson, Angeline *"ANGELINE SAMPSON, / DIED APR. 9, 1897. / AGED 65 YRS. 9 MOS. / 3 DAYS."*

Sampson, Ardelia B. See Eugene H. Sampson Monument entry.

Sampson, Bathsheba N.

"BATHSHEBA N.
widow of
Abiel M. Sampson,
died Dec. 24, 1877;
Aged 79 years, 6 m's
& 19 d's.

She made home happy."

This stone shares its base with the stone of Abiel Sampson.

Sampson, Emmeline See John Sampson Monument entry.
"E. S" is carved in relief on the top horizontal surface of this one-foot high footstone. It is located in front of the monument, on the far right.

Sampson, Eugene H. Monument *"S" (monogram) / "SAMPSON"* is inscribed in shallow relief on the front of the monument. *"EUGENE H. SAMPSON / 1856 – 1930 / HIS WIFE / ARDELIA B. SAMPSON / 1871 – 1955 / HELEN SAMPSON / 1900 – 1976"* is inscribed on the back. *"EUGENE H. SAMPSON JR. / APR. 19, – MAY 3, 1893"* is inscribed below this at the bottom.

Sampson, Eugene H., Jr. Sec Eugene H. Sampson Monument entry.

Sampson, Francis E. *"FRANCIS E. SAMPSON / JAN. 22, 1832 / MARCH 22, 1906"* The first line is carved along an arch.

Sampson, Helen See Eugene H. Sampson Monument entry.

Sampson, Horatio N. *"HORATIO N. SAMPSON. / DIED AUG. 18, 1913. / AGED 75 YRS. 3 MOS. / 3 DAYS."* is inscribed on this textured stone. A veteran's marker and flag are present. A *"GAR 8 387"* marker is present. *Massachusetts Civil War Soldiers & Sailors, 1861-1865,* Vol. I, p. 240 shows that Horatio N. Sampson served with the 4th Infantry, Company C.

Sampson, Isaac Monument *"ISAAC SAMPSON / 1826 – 1919 / JULIA SAMPSON / 1831 – 1904"* is inscribed on the front of this large monument. *"SAMPSON"* is carved in relief on the base.

Sampson, James B. See John Sampson Monument entry.
"J. B. S" is carved in relief on the top horizontal surface of this one-foot high stone. It is located in front of the monument, on the right. A *"GAR 8 99"* marker, a veteran's marker and flag are present. *Massachusetts Civil War Soldiers & Sailors, 1861-1865,* Vol. II, p. 40 shows that James B. Sampson served with the 12th Infantry, Co. F.

Sampson, James M., Lt. Monument *"LIEUT. / JAMES M. SAMPSON / BORN JUNE 19, 1834, / DIED JAN. 5, 1902. / SARAH B. / HIS WIFE / BORN JAN. 31, 1831, / DIED MAR. 16, 1872. / PHEBE J. / HIS WIFE / BORN APR. 1, 1824, / DIED AUG. 15, 1890."* is inscribed on the front of this tall, square, roofed monument. *"SAMPSON"* is carved in relief on the front base only. *"JENNIE THATCHER / DAU. OF / JAMES M. & SARAH B. / SAMPSON / BORN FEB. 14, 1860 / DIED DEC. 29, 1934"* is inscribed on the right side. *"LIEUT. SAMPSON, / A SOLDIER IN THE WAR / OF THE REBELLION. / 1861 – 1865. / CO. C. 4TH REGT. M. V. M. / HE WAS TRUE TO THE FLAG."* is inscribed on the left side. There is no inscription on the back of this monument.
"J. M. S." is carved in shallow relief on the top curved surface of this 4-6 inch high stone. It is located in front of the monument, on the far left. A veteran's marker and flag are present as well as a *"GAR 8 251"* marker.

Sampson, Jennie T. See Lieut. James M. Sampson Monument entry.
"J. T. S." is carved in shallow relief on the top curved surface of this 3-5 inch high stone. It is located in front of the monument, on the far right.

Sampson, John Monument *"JOHN SAMPSON / DIED MAY 7. 1865 / AGED 68 YRS. / 8 MOS. 11 DYS / PHEBE D. / WIFE OF / JOHN SAMPSON / DIED APR. 20. 1865 / AGED 69 YRS. / 5 MOS. 20 DYS."* is inscribed on the southeast side of this tall obelisk. It is rotated 45 degrees from the line of graves. *"LIEUT. JAMES B. / SON OF / JOHN & PHEBE D. / SAMPSON / DIED FEB. 11, 1865. / AGED 28 YRS. / 5 MOS. 22 DYS. / EMMELINE / DAUGHTER OF / JOHN & PHEBE D / SAMPSON / DIED FEB. 3, 1826. / AGED 3 YRS. 5 MOS. 21 DYS."* is inscribed on the northeast side. There are no inscriptions on the other two sides.
"J. S" is carved in relief on the top horizontal surface of this one-foot high footstone. It is located in front of the monument, on the far left.

Sampson, Julia See Isaac Sampson Monument entry.

Sampson, M. Alma See N. Merrill Sampson Monument entry.

Sampson, N. Merrill Monument *"SAMPSON"* is carved in outline on the front of this monument. *"1894 N. MERRILL 1985 / HIS WIFE / 1896 M. ALMA 1989"* is inscribed below this. A sculpted rose is carved along the left side. A Mason's symbol is carved on the left side of the second line, with an Order of the Eastern Star symbol on the right side. *"1938 JAMES M. BEARD _____ / HIS WIFE / 1939 H. DEBORAH 1991 / JULIA ARENBURG / FEB. 20 1918 – AUG. 6, 1999"* is inscribed on the back. *"CATHY MAY BEARD / OCT. 13, 1960 – DEC. 8, 1960"* is inscribed below this at the bottom. A Barnicoat Monuments metal tag is present.

Sampson, Nathaniel Monument *"NATHANIEL SAMPSON / 1798 – 1890 / ZILPAH T. SAMPSON / 1802 – 1853."* is inscribed on the front of this large monument. *"SAMPSON"* is carved in relief on the base.

Sampson, Phebe D. See John Sampson Monument entry.
"P. D. S" is carved in relief on the top horizontal surface of this one-foot high stone. It is located in front of the monument, on the left.

Sampson, Phebe J. See Lieut. James M. Sampson Monument entry.

"P. J. S." is carved in shallow relief on the top curved surface of this 4-6 high stone. It is located directly in front of the monument, on the right.

Sampson, Sarah B.   See Lieut. James M. Sampson Monument entry.
"S. B. S." is carved in shallow relief on the top curved surface of this 4-6 inch high stone. It is located directly in front of the monument, on the left.

Sampson, Sarah E.

"SARAH E. PEARY
WIFE OF
FRANCIS E. SAMPSON
SEPT 7, 1840
MAY 31, 1930"
The first line is carved along an arch. Cracks on the lower left side of the stone and its base have been successfully repaired. A crack extending through the right side of the base has not been repaired.

Sampson, Zilpah   See Nathaniel Sampson Monument entry.

Sanderson, Marjorie T.   *"MARJORIE TAYLOR / SANDERSON / 1894 – 1978"* is inscribed on this flat, sunken stone.

Schlageter, Gerhard P. Monument   *"BLESSED MOTHER PRAY FOR US"* is inscribed on a ribbon carving. A carving of the Virgin Mary is above this. A sculptured rose extends below and to the right of this carving. *"SCHLAGETER"* is inscribed near the bottom. *"GERHARD P. SCHLAGETER / OCT. 15, 1939 – MAR. 14, 1995 / HIS BELOVED WIFE / NOELLA T. SCHLAGETER / FEB. 23, 1945 ____ "* is inscribed on the back. A veteran's marker and flag, and a Middleboro Lodge #1274 BPOE marker and flag are present.
"✝ / GERHARD P SCHLAGETER / SP5   US ARMY / OCT 15 1939   MAR 14 1995" is inscribed on this flat, ground level stone.

Schlageter, Noella T.   See Gerhard Schlageter Monument entry.

Shaughnessey, Arline R.   See Charles W. Shaughnessey Monument entry.

Shaughnessey, Charles W. Monument   *"SHAUGHNESSEY / CHARLES W. / 1921 – ____ / AND WIFE / ARLINE R. / 1927 – ____ "* A rose carving is at the top of this black monument. A Barnicoat Monuments metal tag is present.

Sherman, Eunice M.   See Gardner Sherman Monument entry.

Sherman, Gardner P. Monument   *"SHERMAN"* is inscribed on the front of this monument. *"GARDNER P. SHERMAN / JUL. 31, 1922   ____ / LOVING WIFE / EUNICE M. (GOODELL) / NOV. 4, 1923   ____ "* is inscribed on the back. A Barnicoat Monuments metal tag is present.

Shing, Lee G. Monument   *"Shing"* in inscribed in outline at the top of this monument. *"IN LOVING MEMORY"* is inscribed on a ribbon carving below this.

A carving of a cross and flowers is on the left. *"LEE G. / 1892 – 1973"* is inscribed on the bottom left. *"TOY S. / 1892 – 1988"* is inscribed on the bottom right. Chinese characters are carved in the center of the last two lines. A Barnicoat Monuments metal tag is present.

Shing, Toy S. See Lee Shing Monument entry.

Silva, Antonietta See Pietro Panettieri Monument entry.
"MOTHER" is inscribed on this flat, ground level stone, which faces the rear of the cemetery. It is located directly behind the monument, on the right.

Silvia, Joseph L. Monument *"SILVIA"* is inscribed on this heart shaped monument. A cross with IHS inscribed on it and a rose are carved behind this inscription. *"JOSEPH L. / 1914 – 1990"* is inscribed on the left side of the base, and *"PATRICIA / 1923 – 1986"* is inscribed on the right side.

Silvia, Patricia See Joseph Silvia Monument entry.

Smith, Robert B. Monument *"SMITH"* is inscribed on the front of this monument. Floral carvings adorn in the upper corners. *"ROBERT B. SMITH / 1908 – 1995 / HIS WIFE / VIRGINIA C. / 1908 – 1998"* is inscribed on the back.
"ROBERT" is inscribed on this flat, ground level footstone. It is located in front of the monument, on the left.

Smith, Virginia C. See Robert Smith Monument entry.
"VIRGINIA" is inscribed on this flat, ground level stone. It is located in front of the monument, on the right.

Souza, Manuel F. Monument *"IN GODS CARE"* is inscribed along an arch at the top. *"SOUZA"* is inscribed on a carving of an open book. A flower is carved to the left of it. *"1913   MANUEL F.   1987 / HIS WIFE / 1915   RUTH BIRDSALL ____ "* is inscribed at the bottom.

Souza, Ruth B. See Manuel Souza Monument entry.

Sowerby, Bernice M. Monument *"S (monogram) / SOWERBY"* is inscribed in outline at the top of this monument. *"BERNICE M / 1911 – 1997"* is inscribed on the lower left. *"EDGAR C. / 1909 – 1978"* is inscribed on the lower right. Floral designs are carved in the upper corners. A Barnicoat Monuments metal tag is present.

Sowerby, Edgar C. See Bernice Sowerby Monument entry.

St. Pierre, Edna See Herbert St. Pierre Monument entry.

St. Pierre, Herbert Monument *"ST. PIERRE / 1897   HERBERT   1970 / 1911 EDNA   1986"* A cross surrounded by flowers is carved at the top. A Hancock Monuments metal tag is present.

Steidinger, Loretta M. *"STEIDINGER"* is inscribed on a banner at the top of this heart shaped monument. On the heart are carved a rose on the left, an airplane on the lower right, and a female golfer on the bottom. *"LORETTA M. / SEP. 26, 1946 / OCT. 15, 1999"* is inscribed on the lower left side of the base. A Barnicoat

Monuments metal tag is present.

Sullivan, George C. Monument *"SULLIVAN / GEORGE C. / 1913 – 1976 / KATHERINE M. / 1918 – 1977"* is inscribed on this slanted monument.

Sullivan, Katherine M. See George Sullivan Monument entry.

Taylor, Deborah See Gordon Taylor Monument entry.

Taylor, Gordon Rock *"TAYLOR / 1898 GORDON 1968 / 1900 DEBORAH 1988"* is inscribed on this white boulder. A veteran's marker and flag are present. *"✝ / GORDON TAYLOR / MASSACHUSETTS / MM2 USNRF / WORLD WAR I / JAN 3 1899 MAY 6 1968"* is embossed on this flat, ground level, metal marker which is embedded in a stone base. Note the difference in his birth year between the two stones. The *Social Security Death Index* lists his birth year as 1899.

Taylor, Pauline, J. See Robert Taylor Monument entry.

Taylor, Robert J. Monument *"✝ / TAYLOR"* is inscribed on the front of this monument. Floral carvings are in the upper corners. *"ROBERT J. TAYLOR / FEB. 6, 1943 ____ / PAULINE JOHNSON TAYLOR / AUG. 19, 1943 – APR. 30, 1983"* is inscribed on the back. A Barnicoat Monuments metal tag is present.

Tobojka, Cynthia L. See Kenneth Tobojka Monument entry.

Tobojka, Kenneth R. Monument *"TOBOJKA / Precious Memories / 12·11·1943 KENNETH R. 1·18·1999 / 9·20·1947 CYNTHIA L. ____"* A carving of a couple under a tree is on the left side of the monument.

Valler, Clifton S. Sr. Monument *"FOREVER IN OUR HEARTS / VALLER"* is inscribed at the top center of this monument. *"CLIFTON S. SR. / HUSBAND / DEC. 23, 1924 - JAN. 19, 1995"* is inscribed on the bottom left and *"LILLIAN C. / SHING / MAR. 1, 1923 – OCT. 8, 1998"* is inscribed on the bottom right. Cowboy boots are carved on the far left, and a rose is carved on the far right side of this flat, ground level stone.

Valler, Lillian C. See Clinton Valler Monument entry.

Van Lenten-Aschiero Monument *"VAN LENTEN / ASCHIERO"* is inscribed on the front of this monument. A stone planter is located on the left side. A Barnicoat metal tag is present.

Varnum, Elizabeth See Sumner Vernum Monument entry.

Vernum, Sumner T. Monument *"VARNUM / 1904 SUMNER T. 1980 / HIS WIFE / 1908 ELIZABETH M. 1986"* Floral carvings adorn the upper corners. A Mason's symbol is carved at the top of this monument. A Barnicoat Monuments metal tag is present.

Vickery, Susan P. *"SUSAN PYE VICKERY / 1942 – 1996"* is inscribed on this flat, ground level stone, which is beginning to be buried.

Vieira, Joan M. *"Joan M. Vieira / July 16, 1964 December 12, 2000"* is written on this Dahlborg-MacNevin Funeral Home marker.

"JULY 16, 1964   JOAN THIBEAULT VIEIRA   DEC 12, 2000 / AMONG THE ANGELS" is inscribed on the front of this table monument. It was placed after the initial visit.

Vigers, Earle R. Monument   *"VIGERS"* is carved in outline on the front of this monument which is carved in the shape of an upright book. A pine branch is carved on the left side. *"BOOK / OF / LIFE"* is inscribed on the spine of this book monument. *"EARLE R. VIGERS / 1924 – 2002 / HIS WIFE / MARTHA E. DeMORANVILLE / 1935 – ___ / MICHAEL K. VIGERS / 1955 – 1972"* is inscribed on the back. A Barnicoat Monuments metal tag is present.

Vigers, Martha E.   See Earle Vigers Monument entry.

Vigers, Michael K.   See Earle Vigers Monument entry.
"MIKE" is inscribed on this flat, 0-1 inch high stone. A man holding a lamb and a shepherd's hook is carved on the left side. It is located directly behind the monument.

Vinal, Maurice L. Monument   *"VINAL / MAURICE L. / 1887 – 1956 / WILHELMINA B. / 1882 – 1970"* is inscribed on this slanted monument.

Vinal, Wilhelmina B.   See Maurice L. Vinal Monument entry.

Waller, John I. Monument   *"WALLER / JOHN I. / NOV. 27, 1915 – DEC. 30, 1953 / MYRTLE A."* The Great Seal of the United States is carved at the top. Floral carvings adorn the upper corners.

Waller, Myrtle A.   See John Waller Monument entry.

Walsh, Myrtle E. Monument   *"✝ / WALSH"* is inscribed in outline at the top of this monument. A single rose is carved on either side of the cross. Two open books are carved at the bottom of the monument. *"MYRTLE E. (LONG) / AUG. 25, 1912 / MAY 9, 2001"* is inscribed on the left book, and *"PATRICK R. / MAR. 16, 1912 / DEC. 22, 1997"* is inscribed on the right book *"FULLER"* is inscribed in outline on the back. Below this are carved two open books. *"PETER G. / DEC. 11, 1946 / ____"* is inscribed on the left book, and *"SANDRA R. / (WALSH) / JUN. 24, 1945 / ____"* is inscribed on the right book. A Barnicoat Monuments metal tag is present.

Walsh, Patrick R.   See Myrtle Walsh Monument entry.

Warburton, Ethel M.   See Lester J. Warburton Monument entry.

Warburton, Lester J. Monument   *"WARBURTON"* is inscribed in outline on the front of this monument. *"WE LOVE YOU ALL OVER THE WORLD"* is inscribed at the bottom. Floral carvings are in the upper corners. *"LESTER J. WARBURTON / APR. 3, 1920 (2-4-3) AUG. 21, 1998 / ETHEL M. BELOVED WIFE / JUN. 25, 1920 (2-4-3) JAN. 20, 1988"* A Barnicoat Monuments metal tag is present.
"✝ / LESTER J WARBURTON / EM2   US NAVY / WORLD WAR II / APR 3 1920 AUG 22 1998" is inscribed on this flat, ground level stone. It is located directly in front of the monument, on the left.

Washburn, Grace H.   See Merle Washburn Monument entry.
"GRACE" This flat, ground level marker is located directly in front of the

monument, on the left.

Washburn, Laura   See Wallace Washburn Monument entry.

Washburn, Merle C. Monument   *"WASHBURN / MERLE C / MAR. 22, 1914 – MAY 5, 1997 / HIS WIFE / GRACE H. / JAN. 31, 1915 – DEC. 22, 1988"* An Order of the Eastern Star symbol is carved in the upper left corner and a Shriner's symbol is carved in the upper right corner. A Middleboro Lodge #1274 BPOE marker and flag are present. A Barnicoat Monuments metal tag is present.
"MERLE" is inscribed on this flat, ground level stone, which is beginning to be buried. It is located directly in front of the monument, on the right.

Washburn, Wallace E. Monument   *"WASHBURN / WALLACE E. / 1902 – 1996 / BELOVED WIFE / LAURA / 1902 – 1991"* A Barnicoat Monuments metal tag is present.

Welch, Isabelle   See Kenneth Welch Monument entry.

Welch, Kenneth W. Monument   *"WELCH / 1918   KENNETH W.   1983 / 1914 ISABELLE   1994"* A veteran's marker and flag are present.
"KENNETH W. WELCH / SGT   US ARMY / WORLD WAR II / JAN 8 1918   DEC 21 1983" is inscribed on this flat, ground level stone, which is beginning to be buried. A circled cross is carved at the top.

White, Donald A.   See Helen White Monument entry.
"✝ / DONALD A WHITE / SP4 US ARMY / FEB 5 1941   OCT 6 1998" is inscribed on this flat, ground level stone, which is beginning to be buried. A veteran's marker and flag are present. It is located directly in front of the monument, on the right.

White, Gertrude   See Richard White Monument entry.

White, Helen Monument   *"WHITE"* is inscribed in the center of this monument. *"HELEN / MAY 8, 1943 ____ "* is inscribed on the bottom left, and *"DONALD A. / FEB. 5, 1941 – OCT. 6, 1998"* is inscribed on the bottom right. Floral carvings are in the upper corners. A Middleboro Lodge #1274 BPOE marker and flag are present. A Barnicoat Monuments metal tag is present.

White, Richard H. Monument   *"RICHARD H. WHITE / 1916 – ____ / HIS WIFE / GERTRUDE (DUPRĒ) / 1918 – 2000"* is inscribed on this slanted monument.

Whitman, Edith I.   See Wayne Whitman Monument entry.

Whitman, Wayne L. Monument   *"WHITMAN"* is inscribed on the front of this monument. Floral carvings adorn the upper corners. *"WAYNE L. WHITMAN / JULY 27, 1893 – JAN. 28, 1973 / EDITH I. HIS WIFE / JUNE 12, 1892 – FEB. 25, 1977"* is inscribed on the back. An Albert F. Richmond metal tag is present.

Wilding, Archibald V.   *"ARCHIBALD V. / WILDING / 1912 – 1994"* is inscribed on this flat, ground level stone, which is beginning to be buried.

Wilkie, Emily B.   See Leroy Wilkie Monument entry.
"EMILY" is inscribed on this flat, ground level stone. It is located in front of the monument, on the left.

Wilkie, Leroy G. Monument   *"WILKIE"* is inscribed on the front of this monument. Floral designs are carved along the sides. *"1887   LEROY G. WILKIE 1968 / 1889   EMILY B. HIS WIFE   1973 / 1907   WALLACE C. WILKIE   1992 / 1908   NORMA B. HIS WIFE   1986"* is inscribed on the back.
"LEROY" This flat, ground level stone is located in front of the monument, on the left.

Wilkie, Norma B.   See Leroy Wilkie Monument entry.
"NORMA – WALLACE" is inscribed on this flat, ground level stone. It is located to the immediate right of the Wilkie Monument.

Wilkie, Wallace C.   See Leroy Wilkie Monument entry.
"NORMA – WALLACE" is inscribed on this flat, ground level stone. It is located to the immediate right of the Wilkie Monument.

Williams, Bertha M.   See Chester Goodwin, Jr. Monument entry.
"BERTHA M. WILLIAMS / 1881 – 1964" is inscribed on this flat, ground level stone. The stone is tilted so that one side is 1 inch above ground and the other is 1 inch below ground. It is located directly in front of the monument, on the left.

Williams, Eli Obelisk
"ELI WILLIAMS / BORN APR. 12, 1796, / DIED DEC. 6, 1885. / FANNY / HIS WIFE / BORN MAY 15, 1802, / DIED OCT. 13, 1892." is inscribed on the front of this tall obelisk. *"SAMUEL W. / LUCAS / DEC. 19, 1861, / MAR. 1, 1940. / EMMA R. / HIS WIFE / DEC. 3, 1867 / NOV. 16, 1947"* is inscribed on the left side. *"ELI W. WILLIAMS / BORN OCT. 12, 1830, / DIED FEB. 19, 1907. / EMELINE F. / HIS WIFE / BORN DEC. 16, 1835, / DIED DEC. 9, 1889."* is inscribed on the right side. *"HERBERT W. WILLIAMS / OCT. 14, 1859 / DEC. 22, 1915"* is inscribed on the back with the first line carved along an arch. *"WILLIAMS"* is carved in relief on the front base only.

"E. W." is carved in shallow relief on the top curved surface of this 4-7 inch high stone. It is located in front of the obelisk, on the left. A veteran's marker and flag, and a veteran's *"1812"* marker and flag are present.

Williams, Eli W.   See Eli Williams Obelisk entry.
"E. W. W." is carved in shallow relief on the top, curved surface of this 2-5 inch high stone. It is located in front of the obelisk, on the right.

Williams, Emeline F.   See Eli Williams Obelisk entry.
"E. F. W." is carved in shallow relief on the top curved surface of this 0-2 inch high stone. It is located in front of the obelisk, on the far right.

Williams, Fanny   See Eli Williams Obelisk entry.
"F. W." is carved in shallow relief on the top curved surface of this 3-6 inch high stone. It is located directly in front of the obelisk, on the right.

Williams, Frank B.   See Chester Goodwin, Jr. Monument entry.
"FRANK B. WILLIAMS / 1868 – 1939" is inscribed on this flat, 1-4 inch high stone. It is located in front of the monument, on the left.

Williams, Herbert W.   See Eli Williams Obelisk entry.
"H. W. W." is inscribed in shallow relief on the top curved surface of this 4-6 inch footstone. This rear facing stone is located behind the obelisk, on the right.

Winter, Arthur Monument   *"WINTER"* is inscribed in outline on the front of this monument. *"ARTHUR / 1883 – 1964"* is inscribed on the bottom left, *"REGINALD / 1900 – 1972"* is inscribed on the bottom center, and *"ETHEL / 1894 – 1980"* is inscribed on the bottom right side. Ivy carvings are in the upper corners. A Central Monument metal tag is present.

Winter, Ethel   See Arthur Winter Monument entry.

Winter, Reginald   See Arthur Winter Monument entry.

Wylie, Mary J., Dr.   See Robert J. Wylie Monument entry.

Wylie, Mary T.   See Robert J. Wylie Monument entry.

Wylie, Robert J. Monument   *"WYLIE"* is inscribed on the front of this monument, underneath a carving of an American flag. Floral carvings are in the upper corners. *"ROBERT J. / JULY 10, 1914 / DEC. 27, 1996"* is inscribed on the bottom left, and *"MARY T. / JULY 8, 1915 / MAR. 1, 2001"* is inscribed on the bottom right. *"DAUGHTER / DR. M. J. WYLIE PH.D. / FEB 10, 1958 – JUN. 9, 2002 / BELOVED WIFE OF / "NIP" PIRES"* is inscribed on the back. The *Social Security Death Index* lists her first name as Mary. A Barnicoat Monuments metal tag is present.

Lee Shing Monument

Sampson Cemetery Map Index

Alphabetical:

Chiuppi, Lorna M. (1909-1995) – 9
Chiuppi, Peter (1906-1984) – 9
Churchill, Helen L. (1928-____) – 27
Churchill, John A. (1955-1973) – 27, 87
Churchill, John V. (1920-1992) – 26, 27
Clark, Eunice J. (1907-1987) – 110
Clark, Lois G. (1943-____) – 110
Clark, Phyllis Y. (1936-____) – 110
Clark, Warren W. (1907-1985) – 110
Coelho, Arnold (1911-1977) – 16
Coelho, Arnold M., Jr. (1939-2001) – 16
Coelho, Dorothy I. (1939-1999) – 16
Coelho, Michael J. (1980) – 15
Coelho, Vera M. (1919-1987) – 16
Conant, Charles A. (1919-1999) – 1, 2
Conant, Richard A. (1960-2000) – 2
Conant, Ruth E. (1925-1985) – 2
Cook, Jane W. (1915-1981) – 113
Cook, Malcolm A. (1918-1989) – 112, 113
Cordeiro, Donna (1954-1971) – 69
Cordeiro, James F. (1924-1983) – 68, 69
Cordeiro, James H. (1946-____) – 69
Cordeiro, Mildred H. (1925-____) – 69
Crocker, Sarah S. (1851-1876) – 252
Dean, Helen A (1848-1928) – 239, 240
Delano Monument – 265
DeMoranville, Donald E. (1956-1986) –
        187, 188
DeMoranville, Donald O. (1931-1992) –
        186, 188
DeMoranville, Howell G. (1904-1978) –
        136
DeMoranville, Ida L. (1900-1986) – 117
DeMoranville, Lorraine L. (1946-____) –
        135
DeMoranville, Merrill (1910-1970) – 98
DeMoranville, Ora M. (1904-1962) – 136
DeMoranville, Oscar F. (1897-1947) – 117
DeMoranville, Philip L. (1944-____) – 135
DeMoranville, Rowena (1911-1995) – 98
DeMoranville, Stephen (1955) – 188, 189
DeMoranville, Yvette L. (1975-1985) – 135
DesRoche, William J. (1953-1998) – 303
Devlin, Victoria L. (1981-1990) – 61
Dextraze, Jeannette (1907-1994) – 5
DiCarlo, John J. (1963-1995) – 263, 264
Dill, Ernest E. (1925-1994) – 231, 235
Dill, Linda (1949-1951) – 227
Dill, Louise G. (1927-2003) – 231
Dill, Ruth E. (1904-1994) – 231, 234
Dill, Thomas G. (1894-1983) – 231, 233

Dillon, Brenda (1944-____) – 295
Dillon, Elwyn G. (1934-2001) – 294, 195
Dixon, Travis A. (1936-1998) – 283, 284
Doucet, Catherine T. (1934-1993) – 315
Doucet, Rene E. (1930-1978) – 314, 315
Draghetti, Alexander J. (1900-1969) – 146
Draghetti, Elisabeth M. (1914-1974) – 80
Draghetti, Phyllis (1913-1992) – 146
Draghetti, Raymond L. (1905-1986) – 80
Eaton, Harriett E. (1880-1944) – 47, 105
Eaton, Ralph P. (1883-1963) – 47, 104
Elliott, Carrie S. (1884-1963) – 146
Elliott, George V. (1884-1958) – 146
England, Frank E. (1901-1976) – 131
England, Helen E. (1902-1967) – 131
Erickson, Caroline (1894-1967) – 130
Erickson, Herbert F. (1895-1974) – 130
Estey Monument – 62
Fidler, Edna M. (no dates) – 18
Fidler, John A. (1915-1979) – 17, 18
Fitting, David L. (1920-1998) – 291, 292
Fitting, Mildred B. (1922-____) – 292
Flanders, Lauretta M. (1921-1994) – 120
Fontano, Margaret M. (1924-____) – 281
Fontano, Nicholas J. (1915-1995) – 280,
        281
Foster, B. Warren (1925-1985) – 179, 180
Foster, Elinor L. (1929-____) – 179
Franklin, Charles H. (1911-1997) – 29
Franklin, Mary A. (1931-1965) – 29
Franklin, Sylvester V. (1955-1974) – 29
Freeman Monument – 76
Frizzell, Euphemia B. (1879-1963) – 216
Frizzell, Harold E. (1905-1999) – 216
Frizzell, Suzanne M. (1909-1986) – 216
Frizzell, Walter R. (1875-1955) – 216
Fuller, Peter G. (1946-____) – 324
Fuller, Sandra R. (1945-____) – 324
Galego, Carol L. (1944-____) – 108
Galego, John E. (1942-1989) – 108
Gamache, Alexander R. (1993-1994) – 276
Gamache, Elyana L. (2003) – 311
Gamache, Olivia A. (2003) – 311
Garbitt, Rita A. (1952-____) – 311
Garbitt, Ronald D. (1950-____) – 311
Gibney, Arthur J. (1907-1990) – 72
Gibney, Lucille E. (1906-1990) – 72
Gilker, Joanne (1923-1988) – 209
Given, Edward (1873-1954) – 140
Given, Mabel (1871-1951) – 140
Given, Norman (1903-1978) – 140

Mills, Robert J. (1881-1957) – 42
Mills, Robert J. Sr. (1938-1989) – 100
Mills, Stanley R. (1907-1981) – 12
Moffett, Patti L. (1937-1995) – 318
Moffett, Raymond J. (1931-____) – 318
Morelli, Pete (1956-2000) – 106
Mosher-Bowles Monument – 248
Mosher, Harriet M. (1878-1944) – 247
Mosher, Trask S. (1875-1967) – 246
Mosier, Harold W., Jr. (1922-1972) – 184, 185
Nelson, Hannah K. (1860-1949) – 239
Nelson, John H. (1829-1912) – 239, 241
Nelson, Mary D. (1836-1930) – 238, 239
Nelson, Mary L. (1870-1953) – 239
Neville, Alice M. (1880-1951) – 144
Neville, Anna E. (1910-____) – 142
Neville, John D. (1910-1988) – 142
Norris, Alice (1910-2002) – 205
Norris, Harry G. (1908-____) – 205
Northcott, George H. (1875-1951) – 167
Northcott, Henry S. (1909-1935) – 168
Northcott, Mabel S. (1881-1960) – 167
Norton, Charles F. (1922) – 170
Norton, Claire C. (1932-____) – 170
Norton, Julia S. (1896-1987) – 170
Norton, Leslie H. (1891-1966) – 170
Norton, Merrill S. (1927-____) – 170
Norton, Winthrop H. (1921-1946) – 170
O'Neill, Bonnie (1963-2003) – 20
O'Neill, Robert J. (1962-____) – 20
Owen, Arthur S., Jr. (1928-2002) – 196
Owen, Arthur S., Sr. (1897-1969) – 194, 195
Owen, Jennie K. (1897-1986) – 195
Panettieri, Maria P. (1946-____) – 266
Panettieri, Pietro (1939-____) – 266
Paulson, Ann M. (1954-____) – 306
Paulson, Phillip D. (1948-2000) – 306
Peck, David (1940-1951) – 232
Peck, Edgar C. (1870-1955) – 231, 226
Peck, Harold S. (1909-1977) – 229
Peck, Hazel L. (1912-1989) – 230
Peck, Myrtie A. (1874-1955) – 228, 231
Pember, Frances C. (1884-1959) – 45
Pember, Henry L. (1880-1979) – 45
Perry, Alden C. (1911-1993) – 200, 201
Perry, Marion E. (1910-1974) – 201
Person, Mary P. (1938-____) – 67
Person, Robert F. (1933-1990) – 67
Pierce, Ina A. (1890-1980) – 36

Plissey, Clara C. (1923-1989) – 44
Plissey, Harry F. (1880-1966) – 44
Plissey, Harry F., Jr. (1922-1990) – 44
Plissey, Mary E. (1887-1962) – 44
Porell, David G. (1966-____) – 300
Porell, Donald E. (1932-2000) – 298, 299, 300
Porell, Donna M. (1962-____) – 300
Porell, Joan M. (1939-____) – 300
Porell, Joseph D. (1967-____) – 300
Porell, Robert M. (1974-____) – 300
Prifogle, Charlotte (1922-2002) – 114
Prifogle, Francis E. (1908-1980) – 114
Reed, Charles L. (1888-1956) – 214, 215
Reed, Charles L., Jr. (1915-1971) – 96
Reed, Eleanor A. (1918-1986) – 96
Reed, Elizabeth M. (1891-1974) – 215, 217
Reed, George F. (1874-1947) – 45
Reed, Jessie (1885-1951) – 45
Reed, Louisa J. (1881-1927) – 45
Reposa, Todd M. (1974) – 79
Rinkus, James R. (1932-____) – 178
Rinkus, Shirley A. (1934-2001) – 178
Roby, Mildred J. (1935-1992) – 277
Roby, Waldo N. (1932-____) – 277
Rogers, Mary E. (1947-1993) – 34, 97
Rose, George F. (1929-1997) – 5
Sampson, Abiel M. (1796-1867) – 49
Sampson, Angeline (1831-1897) – 51
Sampson, Ardelia B. (1871-1955) – 169
Sampson, Bathsheba N. (1798-1877) – 50
Sampson, Emmeline (1822-1826) – 55, 57
Sampson, Eugene H. (1856-1930) – 169
Sampson, Eugene H., Jr. (1893) – 169
Sampson, Francis E. (1832-1906) – 165
Sampson, Helen (1900-1976) – 169
Sampson, Horatio N. (1838-1913) – 52
Sampson, Isaac (1826-1919) – 59
Sampson, James B., Lt. (1836-1865) – 55, 56
Sampson, James M., Lt. (1834-1902) – 152, 155
Sampson, Jennie T. (1860-1934) – 155, 156
Sampson, John (1796-1865) – 53, 55
Sampson, Julia (1831-1904) – 59
Sampson, M. Alma (1896-1989) – 60
Sampson, N. Merrill (1894-1985) – 60
Sampson, Nathaniel (1798-1890) – 58
Sampson, Phebe D. (1795-1865) – 54, 55
Sampson, Phebe J. (1824-1890) – 154, 155
Sampson, Sarah B. (1831-1872) – 153, 155

Sampson, Sarah E. (1840-1930) – 166
Sampson, Zilpah (1802-1853) – 58
Sanderson, Marjorie T. (1894-1978) – 183
Schlageter, Gerhard P. (1939-1995) – 312, 313
Schlageter, Noella T. (1945-___) – 313
Shaughnessey, Arline R. (1927-___) – 3
Shaughnessey, Charles W. (1921-___) – 3
Sherman, Eunice M. (1923-___) – 273
Sherman, Gardner P. (1922-___) – 273
Shing, Lee G. (1892-1973) – 127
Shing, Toy S. (1892-1988) – 127
Silva, Antonietta (1926-1996) – 266, 267
Silvia, Joseph L. (1914-1990) – 109
Silvia, Patricia (1923-1986) – 109
Smith, Robert B. (1908-1995) – 124, 126
Smith, Virginia C. (1908-1998) – 125, 126
Souza, Manuel F. (1913-1987) – 208
Souza, Ruth B. (1915-___) – 208
Sowerby, Bernice M. (1911-1997) – 218
Sowerby, Edgar C. (1909-1978) – 218
St. Pierre, Edna (1911-1986) – 25
St. Pierre, Herbert (1897-1970) – 25
Steidinger, Loretta M. (1946-1999) – 270
Sullivan, George C. (1913-1976) – 103
Sullivan, Katherine M. (1918-1977) – 103
Taylor, Deborah (1900-1988) – 198
Taylor, Gordon (1899-1968) – 197, 198
Taylor, Pauline, J. (1943-1983) –111
Taylor, Robert J. (1943-___) – 111
Tobojka, Cynthia L. (1947-___) – 309
Tobojka, Kenneth R. (1943-1999) – 309
Valler, Clifton S. Sr. (1924-1995) – 128
Valler, Lillian C. (1923-1998) – 128
Van Lenten-Aschiero Monument – 202
Vernum, Elizabeth (1908-1986) – 78
Vernum, Sumner T. (1904-1980) – 78
Vickery, Susan P. (1942-1996) – 182
Vieira, Joan M. (1964-2000) – 310
Vigers, Earle R. (1924-2002) – 190
Vigers, Martha E. (1935-___) – 190

Vigers, Michael K. (1955-1972) – 190, 191
Vinal, Maurice L. (1887-1956) – 38
Vinal, Wilhelmina B. (1882-1970) – 38
Waller, John I. (1915-1953) – 139
Waller, Myrtle A. (no dates) – 139
Walsh, Myrtle E. (1912-2001) – 324
Walsh, Patrick R. (1912-1997) – 324
Warburton, Ethel M. (1920-1988) – 23
Warburton, Lester J. (1920-1998) – 22, 23
Washburn, Grace H. (1915-1988) – 81, 84
Washburn, Laura (1902-1991) – 88
Washburn, Merle C. (1914-1997) – 83, 84
Washburn, Wallace E. (1902-1996) – 88
Welch, Isabelle (1914-1994) – 86
Welch, Kenneth W. (1918-1983) – 85, 86
White, Donald A. (1941-1998) – 304, 305
White, Gertrude (1918-2000) – 326
White, Helen (1943-___) – 305
White, Richard H. (1916-___) – 326
Whitman, Edith I. (1892-1977) – 91
Whitman, Wayne L. (1893-1973) – 91
Wilding, Archibald V. (1912-1994) – 287
Wilkie, Emily B. (1889-1973) – 148, 149
Wilkie, Leroy G. (1887-1968) – 147, 149
Wilkie, Norma B. (1908-1986) – 149, 150
Wilkie, Wallace C. (1907-1992) – 149, 150
Williams, Bertha M. (1881-1964) – 221, 223
Williams, Eli (1796-1885) – 157, 161
Williams, Eli W. (1830-1907) – 161, 162
Williams, Emeline F. (1835-1889) – 161, 164
Williams, Fanny (1802-1892) – 160, 161
Williams, Frank B. (1868-1939) – 220, 223
Williams, Herbert W. (1859-1915) – 161, 163
Winter, Arthur (1883-1964) – 31
Winter, Ethel (1894-1980) – 31
Winter, Reginald (1900-1972) – 31
Wylie, Mary J., Dr. (1958-2002) – 290
Wylie, Mary T. (1915-2001) – 290
Wylie, Robert J. (1914-1996) – 290

Sampson Cemetery Map Index

By Location:

1 – Conant, Charles A. (1919-1999)

2 – Conant, Charles A. (1919-1999)
Conant, Ruth E. (1925-1985)
Conant, Richard A. (1960-2000)

3 – Shaughnessey, Charles W. (1921-____)
Shaughnessey, Arline R. (1927-____)

4 – Medeiros, James N. (1925-1996)
Medeiros, C. Margaret (1923-1990)

5 – Dextraze, Jeannette (1907-1994)
Rose, George F. (1929-1997)

6 – Brienzo, Irene A. (1917-1993)

7 – Brienzo, Mikelino D. (1917-1988)

8 – Brienzo, Mikelino D. (1917-1988)
Brienzo, Irene A. (1917-1993)
Brienzo, Dennis M. (1942-____)
Brienzo, Leona A. (1947-____)

9 – Chiuppi, Peter (1906-1984)
Chiuppi, Lorna M. (1909-1995)

10 – Johnson, Robert F. (1926-1981)

11 – Johnson, Robert F. (1926-1981)
Johnson, Grace A. (1925-____)

12 – Mills, Stanley R. (1907-1981)
Mills, Marguerite A. (1910-____)

13 – Meleedy, William J. Jr. (1930-2003)

14 – Meleedy, William J. Jr. (1930-2003)
Meleedy, Bernadette D. (1935-1997)

15 – Coelho, Michael J. (1980)

16 – Coelho, Arnold (1911-1977)
Coelho, Vera M. (1919-1987)
Coelho, Arnold M., Jr. (1939-2001)
Coelho, Dorothy I. (1939-1999)

17 – Fidler, John A. (1915-1979)

18 – Fidler, John A. (1915-1979)
Fidler, Edna M. (no dates)

19 – Linton, Alton H. (1909-1992)
Linton, Myra H. (1908-1995)

20 – O'Neill, Robert J. (1962-____)
O'Neill, Bonnie (1963-2003)

21 – Caldwell, Russell E., Jr. (1934-1973)
Caldwell, Jeannette L. (1935-____)
Caldwell, Russell E., Sr. (1911-1998)
Caldwell, Bernice W. (1910-1987)

22 – Warburton, Lester J. (1920-1998)

23 – Warburton, Lester J. (1920-1998)
Warburton, Ethel M. (1920-1988)

24 – Arrington, Frank (1890-1976)
Arrington, Lilla (1891-1969)
Magnuson, Earl R. (1911-1998)

Magnuson, Arline E. (1920-____)

25 – St. Pierre, Herbert (1897-1970)
St. Pierre, Edna (1911-1986)

26 – Churchill, John V. (1920-1992)

27 – Churchill, John V. (1920-1992)
Churchill, Helen L. (1928-____)
Churchill, John A. (1955-1973)

28 – Marston, Howard W. (1909-1995)
Marston, Laura M. (1914-____)

29 – Franklin, Charles H. (1911-1997)
Franklin, Mary A. (1931-1965)
Franklin, Sylvester V. (1955-1974)

30 – Alden, Myles S. (1897-1964)
Alden, Persis (1900-1995)

31 – Winter, Arthur (1883-1964)
Winter, Reginald (1900-1972)
Winter, Ethel (1894-1980)

32 – Beech, Roger C. (1895-1988)

33 – Beech, Roger C. (1895-1988)
Beech, Marjorie H. (1903-1998)

34 – Rogers, Mary E. (1947-1993)

35 – Babbitt Monument

36 – Pierce, Ina A. (1890-1980)

37 – Babbitt, David L. (1889-1949)

38 – Vinal, Maurice L. (1887-1956)
Vinal, Wilhelmina B. (1882-1970)

39 – Mills, Beatrice A. (1898-1977)

40 – Mills Monument

41 – Mills, Margarette J. (1883-1947)

42 – Mills, Robert J. (1881-1957)

43 – Mastera, Melvyn F. (1910-1983)
Mastera, Elizabeth H. (1913-1969)

44 – Plissey, Harry F. (1880-1966)
Plissey, Mary E. (1887-1962)
Plissey, Harry F., Jr. (1922-1990)
Plissey, Clara C. (1923-1989)

45 – Pember, Henry L. (1880-1979)
Pember, Frances C. (1884-1959)
Reed, George F. (1874-1947)
Reed, Louisa J. (1881-1927)
Reed, Jessie (1885-1951)

46 – Bump, Josiah B. (1826-1898)

47 – Bump, Josiah B. (1826-1898)
Bump, Bathsheba M. (1825-1907)
Eaton, Ralph P. (1883-1963)
Eaton, Harriett E. (1880-1944)

48 – Bump, Bathsheba M. (1825-1907)

49 – Sampson, Abiel M. (1796-1867)

50 – Sampson, Bathsheba N. (1798-1877)
51 – Sampson, Angeline (1831-1897)
52 – Sampson, Horatio N. (1838-1913)
53 – Sampson, John (1796-1865)
54 – Sampson, Phebe D. (1795-1865)
55 – Sampson, John (1796-1865)
    Sampson, Phebe D. (1795-1865)
    Sampson, James B., Lt. (1836-1865)
    Sampson, Emmeline (1822-1826)
56 – Sampson, James B. (1836-1865)
57 – Sampson, Emmeline (1822-1826)
58 – Sampson, Nathaniel (1798-1890)
    Sampson, Zilpah (1802-1853)
59 – Sampson, Isaac (1826-1919)
    Sampson, Julia (1831-1904)
60 – Sampson, N. Merrill (1894-1985)
    Sampson, M. Alma (1896-1989)
    Beard, James M. (1938-____)
    Beard, H. Deborah (1939-1991)
    Arenburg, Julia (1918-1999)
    Beard, Cathy M. (1960)
61 – Devlin, Victoria L. (1981-1990)
62 – Estey Monument
63 – MacLeod, Donald Y. (1916-____)
    MacLeod, Genevieve L. (1923-2002)
64 – Jewell, Peter R. (1971-1988)
65 – Jewell, Peter R. (1971-1988)
66 – Abbaticola, Frank A. (1925-2001)
    Abbaticola, Luisa M. (1924-____)
67 – Person, Robert F. (1933-1990)
    Person, Mary P. (1938- ___)
68 – Cordeiro, James F. (1924-1983)
69 – Cordeiro, Donna (1954-1971)
    Cordeiro, James F. (1924-1983)
    Cordeiro, Mildred H. (1925-____)
    Cordeiro, James H. (1946-____)
70 – Bavin, Charette (1984) – 126
71 – Bavin, William A. (1920-1976)
    Bavin, Katherine (1924-____)
72 – Gibney, Arthur J. (1907-1990)
    Gibney, Lucille E. (1906-1990)
73 – Hall, Helen F. (1919-1987)
74 – Hall, Arthur S., Jr. (1917-____)
    Hall, Helen F. (1919-1987)
75 – Belben, Myra E. (1919-1976)
76 – Freeman Monument
77 – Belben, Kenneth E. (1922-1984)
78 – Vernum, Sumner T. (1904-1980)
    Vernum, Elizabeth (1908-1986)
79 – Reposa, Todd M. (1974)
80 – Draghetti, Raymond L. (1905-1986)

    Draghetti, Elisabeth M. (1914-1974)
81 – Washburn, Grace H. (1915-1988)
82 – Magnuson, Earl R. (1911-1998)
83 – Washburn, Merle C. (1914-1997)
84 – Washburn, Merle C. (1914-1997)
    Washburn, Grace H. (1915-1988)
85 – Welch, Kenneth W. (1918-1983)
86 – Welch, Kenneth W. (1918-1983)
    Welch, Isabelle (1914-1994)
87 – Churchill, John A. (1955-1973)
88 – Washburn, Wallace E. (1902-1996)
    Washburn, Laura (1902-1991)
89 – King, William (1913-1970)
90 – King, William (1913-1970)
    King, Elizabeth C. (1913-2001)
    King, James E. (1936-____)
91 – Whitman, Wayne L. (1893-1973)
    Whitman, Edith I. (1892-1977)
92 – Chadwick, William H. (1903-1967)
93 – Chadwick, Ruth M. (1911 – 1998)
94 – Chadwick Monument
95 – Lomasney, Thomas L. (1946-1973)
96 – Reed, Charles L., Jr. (1915-1971)
    Reed, Eleanor A. (1918-1986)
    Maddigan, Annette L. (1940-1994)
97 – Beech, Roger E. (1922-____)
    Beech, Margaret P. (1923-____)
    Rogers, Mary E. (1947-1993)
98 – DeMoranville, Merrill (1910-1970)
    DeMoranville, Rowena (1911-1995)
99 – Marques, Shirley R. (1930-1987)
    Marques, John F. (1927-1993)
100 – Mills, Robert J. Sr. (1938-1989)
101 – Mills, Helen (1904-1964)
102 – Mills, George E. (1905-1979)
103 – Sullivan, George C. (1913-1976)
    Sullivan, Katherine M. (1918-1977)
104 – Eaton, Ralph P. (1883-1963)
105 – Eaton, Harriett E. (1880-1944)
106 – Morelli, Pete (1956-2000)
107 – Case, James W. (1932-____)
    Case, Betsy (1929-1989)
108 – Galego, John E. (1942-1989)
    Galego, Carol L. (1944-____)
109 – Silvia, Joseph L. (1914-1990)
    Silvia, Patricia (1923-1986)
110 – Clark, Warren W. (1907-1985)
    Clark, Eunice J. (1907-1987)
    Clark, Phyllis Y. (1936-____)
    Clark, Lois G. (1943-____)
111 – Taylor, Robert J. (1943-____)

Taylor, Pauline, J. (1943-1983)
112 – Cook, Malcolm A. (1918-1989)
113 – Cook, Malcolm A. (1918-1989)
Cook, Jane W. (1915-1981)
114 – Prifogle, Francis E. (1908-1980)
Prifogle, Charlotte (1922-2002)
Bednar, Julius J. (1895-1984)
Bednar, Charlotte E. (1896-1989)
115 – Berry, Francis N. (1926-1992)
116 – Berry, Francis N. (1926-1992)
Berry, Barbara B. (1928-____)
117 – DeMoranville, Oscar F. (1897-1947)
DeMoranville, Ida L. (1900-1986)
118 – Bailey, Edward B. C. (1898-1973)
119 – Bailey, Lauretta F. (1901-1972)
120 – Flanders, Lauretta M. (1921-1994)
121 – Bailey-Flanders Monument
122 – Bowers, Robert E. (1911-1987)
123 – Bowers, Robert E. (1911-1987)
124 – Smith, Robert B. (1908-1995)
125 – Smith, Virginia C. (1908-1998)
126 – Smith, Robert B. (1908-1995)
Smith, Virginia C. (1908-1998)
127 – Shing, Lee G. (1892-1973)
Shing, Toy S. (1892-1988)
128 – Valler, Clifton S. Sr. (1924-1995)
Valler, Lillian C. (1923-1998)
129 – Lun, Mae W. (1928-1978)
130 – Erickson, Herbert F. (1895-1974)
Erickson, Caroline (1894-1967)
131 – England, Frank E. (1901-1976)
England, Helen E. (1902-1967)
132 – Marshall, Douglas P. (1918-1978)
133 – Marshall, Harry H. (1889-1972)
Marshall, F. Rita (1893-1969)
134 – Holmes, Standish F. (1928-2000)
135 – DeMoranville, Philip L. (1944-____)
DeMoranville, Lorraine L. (1946-____)
DeMoranville, Yvette L. (1975-1985)
136 – DeMoranville, Howell G. (1904-1978)
DeMoranville, Ora M. (1904-1962)
137 – Biasiucci, Infant (1974)
138 – Marshall, Harry H. C. (1914-1963)
Marshall, Alice M. (1919-____)
Marshall, Harold C. (1943-2002)
Marshall, Inez E. (1945-____)
139 – Waller, John I. (1915-1953)
Waller, Myrtle A. (no dates)
140 – Given, Norman (1903-1978)

Given, Edward (1873-1954)
Given, Mabel (1871-1951)
Bessey, Lloyd (1902-1960)
Bessey, Isa M. (1905-1972)
141 – Longworth-Neville Monument
142 – Neville, John D. (1910-1988)
Neville, Anna E. (1910-____)
143 – Longworth, Luther J. (1908-1950)
144 – Neville, Alice M. (1880-1951)
145 – Longworth, Grace A. (1908 – 1982)
146 – Elliott, George V. (1884-1958)
Elliott, Carrie S. (1884-1963)
Draghetti, Alexander J. (1900-1969)
Draghetti, Phyllis (1913-1992)
Guidoboni, Arthur L. (1912-1988)
Guidoboni, Lelia S. (1914-1973)
147 – Wilkie, Leroy G. (1887-1968)
148 – Wilkie, Emily B. (1889-1973)
149 – Wilkie, Leroy G. (1887-1968)
Wilkie, Emily B. (1889-1973)
Wilkie, Wallace C. (1907-1992)
Wilkie, Norma B. (1908-1986)
150 – Wilkie, Norma B. (1908-1986)
Wilkie, Wallace C. (1907-1992)
151 – Benson, Gladys (1908-1998)
152 – Sampson, James M., Lt. (1834-1902)
153 – Sampson, Sarah B. (1831-1872)
154 – Sampson, Phebe J. (1824-1890)
155 – Sampson, James M., Lt. (1834-1902)
Sampson, Sarah B. (1831-1872)
Sampson, Phebe J. (1824-1890)
Sampson, Jennie T. (1860-1934)
156 – Sampson, Jennie T. (1860-1934)
157 – Williams, Eli (1796-1885)
158 – Lucas, Samuel W. (1861-1940)
159 – Lucas, Emma R. (1867-1947)
160 – Williams, Fanny (1802-1892)
161 – Williams, Eli (1796-1885)
Williams, Fanny (1802-1892)
Lucas, Samuel W. (1861-1940)
Lucas, Emma R. (1867-1947)
Williams, Eli W. (1830-1907)
Williams, Emeline F. (1835-1889)
Williams, Herbert W. (1859-1915)
162 – Williams, Eli W. (1830-1907)
163 – Williams, Herbert W. (1859-1915)
164 – Williams, Emeline F. (1835-1889)
165 – Sampson, Francis E. (1832-1906)
166 – Sampson, Sarah E. (1840-1930)
167 – Northcott, George H. (1875-1951)
Northcott, Mabel S. (1881-1960)

168 – Northcott, Henry S. (1909-1935)
169 – Sampson, Eugene H. (1856-1930)
    Sampson, Ardelia B. (1871-1955)
    Sampson, Helen (1900-1976)
    Sampson, Eugene H., Jr. (1893)
170 – Norton, Leslie H. (1891-1966)
    Norton, Julia S. (1896-1987)
    Norton, Winthrop H. (1921-1946)
    Norton, Charles F. (1922)
    Norton, Merrill S. (1927-____)
    Norton, Claire C. (1932-____)
171 – Bock, Roland A. (1924-1990)
172 – Bock, Roland A. (1924-1990)
    Bock, Pauline T. (1928-____)
173 – Marcos, Antone V. (1919-1992)
174 – Marcos, Antone V. (1919-1992)
    Marcos, Lorraine E. (1925-____)
175 – Mahoney, James F., Jr. (1925-____)
    Mahoney, Margaret C. (1923-1996)
    Mahoney, Daniel E. (1970-2001)
176 – Barron, Thomas F. (1924-1987)
177 – Barron, Thomas F. (1924-1987)
    Barron, Barbara (1925-2002)
178 – Rinkus, Shirley A. (1934-2001)
    Rinkus, James R. (1932-____)
179 – Foster, B. Warren (1925-1985)
    Foster, Elinor L. (1929-____)
180 – Foster, B. Warren (1925-1985)
181 – Brune, Everett W. (1909-1983)
    Brune, Pearl F. (1909-1989)
182 – Vickery, Susan P. (1942-1996)
183 – Sanderson, Marjorie T. (1894-1978)
184 – Mosier, Harold W., Jr. (1922-1972)
185 – Mosier, Harold W., Jr. (1922-1972)
186 – DeMoranville, Donald O. (1931-1992)
187 – DeMoranville, Donald E. (1956-1986)
188 – DeMoranville, Donald O. (1931-1992)
    DeMoranville, Donald E. (1956-1986)
    DeMoranville, Stephen (1955)
189 – DeMoranville, Stephen (1955)
190 – Vigers, Earle R. (1924-2002)
    Vigers, Martha E. (1935-____)
    Vigers, Michael K. (1955-1972)
191 – Vigers, Michael K. (1955-1972)
192 – Haskins, John S. (1924-____)
    Haskins, Virginia D. (1927-____)
    Haskins, Amy M. (1978-1980)

193 – Haskins, Amy M. (1978-1980)
194 – Owen, Arthur S., Sr. (1897-1969)
195 – Owen, Arthur S., Sr. (1897-1969)
    Owen, Jennie K. (1897-1986)
196 – Owen, Arthur S., Jr. (1928-2002)
197 – Taylor, Gordon (1899-1968)
198 – Taylor, Gordon (1899-1968)
    Taylor, Deborah (1900-1988)
199 – Medeiros, Arthur (1912-1970)
    Medeiros, Alice I. (1918-1999)
200 – Perry, Alden C. (1911-1993)
201 – Perry, Alden C. (1911-1993)
    Perry, Marion E. (1910-1974)
    Heifner, Tilden B. (1908-1997)
    Heifner, Dorothy J. (1918-2002)
202 – Van Lenten-Aschiero Monument
203 – Aschiero, Margherita L. (1893-1994)
204 – Aschiero, Carlo (1891-1968)
205 – Norris, Harry G. (1908-____)
    Norris, Alice (1910-2002)
206 – Austin, George R. (1911-1990)
    Austin, Alice S. (1910-2000)
207 – Bollesen, Sandra Lee (1958-1964)
208 – Souza, Manuel F. (1913-1987)
    Souza, Ruth B. (1915- ____)
209 – Gilker, Joanne (1923-1988)
210 – Mendall, Eleanor B. (1893-1984)
    Mendall, Theodore F. (1894-1981)
211 – Hamilton, Harry W. (1908-____)
    Hamilton, Lillian R. (1909-____)
212 – Alvilhiera, Frank B. (1936-1992)
213 – Bradford, Joseph E. (1898-1952)
214 – Reed, Charles L. (1888-1956)
215 – Reed, Charles L. (1888-1956)
    Reed, Elizabeth M. (1891-1974)
216 – Frizzell, Walter R. (1875-1955)
    Frizzell, Euphemia B. (1879-1963)
    Frizzell, Harold E. (1905-1999)
    Frizzell, Suzanne M. (1909-1986)
217 – Reed, Elizabeth M. (1891-1974)
218 – Sowerby, Bernice M. (1911-1997)
    Sowerby, Edgar C. (1909-1978)
219 – Griffith, Harold L. (1911-1965)
    Griffith, Virginia Y. (1913-____)
    Griffith, Harold S. (1888-1958)
    Griffith, Lillian M. (1888-1956)
220 – Williams, Frank B. (1868-1939)
221 – Williams, Bertha M. (1881-1964)
222 – Goodwin, Edith E. (1923-1962)
223 – Goodwin, Chester E., Jr. (1919-1993)
    Goodwin, Edith E. (1923-1962)

Williams, Frank B. (1868-1939)
Williams, Bertha M. (1881-1964)
224 – Goodwin, Chester E., Jr. (1919-1993)
225 – Goodwin, Chester E., Jr. (1919-1993)
226 – Peck, Edgar C. (1870-1955)
227 – Dill, Linda (1949-1951)
228 – Peck, Myrtie A. (1874-1955)
229 – Peck, Harold S. (1909-1977)
230 – Peck, Hazel L. (1912-1989)
231 – Peck, Edgar C. (1870-1955)
Peck, Myrtie A. (1874-1955)
Dill, Thomas G. (1894-1983)
Dill, Ruth E. (1904-1994)
Dill, Ernest E. (1925-1994)
Dill, Louise G. (1927-2003)
232 – Peck, David (1940-1951)
233 – Dill, Thomas G. (1894-1983)
234 – Dill, Ruth E. (1904-1994)
235 – Dill, Ernest E. (1925-1994)
236 – Goodridge, Elsie F. (1883-1930)
237 – Goodridge, Ono M. (1880-1961)
Goodridge, Susan F. (1884-1975)
238 – Nelson, Mary D. (1836-1930)
239 – Nelson, John H. (1829-1912)
Nelson, Mary D. (1836-1930)
Nelson, Hannah K. (1860-1949)
Nelson, Mary L. (1870-1953)
Dean, Helen A. (1848-1928)
240 – Dean, Helen A. (1848-1928)
241 – Nelson, John H. (1829-1912)
242 – Bump, Jonathan C. (1819-1890)
243 – Bump, Susan M. (1856-1862)
244 – Bump, Caroline (1820-1881)
245 – Bump, Susan W. (1840-1845)
246 – Mosher, Trask S. (1875-1967)
247 – Mosher, Harriet M. (1878-1944)
248 – Mosher-Bowles Monument
249 – Bowles, Verna C. (1899-1949)
250 – Bowles, Cuthbert (1898-1973)
251 – Bump, Nancy J. (1828-1906)
252 – Crocker, Sarah S. (1851-1876)
253 – Bump, Thomas W. (1828-1913)
254 – Bump, Clara K. (1849-1931)
255 – Angers, Paul A. (1901-1984)
Angers, Lois F. (1909-1985)
256 – Handy, George M. (1924-1956)
257 – Handy, Marion F. (1927-___)
258 – Angers, Eleanor M. (1933-2003)
259 – Angers-Handy Monument
260 – Begin, Margaret L. (1915-___)
Begin, Edward E. (1915-2002)

261 – Gray, Arthur W. (1949-___)
Gray, Mary A. (1949-___)
Gray, Renee (1972-1995)
262 – Gray, Renee (1972-1995)
263 – DiCarlo, John J. (1963-1995)
264 – DiCarlo, John J. (1963-1995)
265 – Delano Monument
266 – Panettieri, Pietro (1939-___)
Panettieri, Maria P. (1946-___)
Silva, Antonietta (1926-1996)
267 – Silva, Antonietta (1926-1996)
268 – Battistelli, Joseph (1927-1996)
269 – Battistelli, Joseph (1927-1996)
Battistelli, Avis E. (1916-___)
270 – Steidinger, Loretta M. (1946-1999)
271 – LaFave, Charles A. (1921-2000)
272 – LaFave, Perfica (1920-___)
LaFave, Charles A. (1921-2000)
273 – Sherman, Gardner P. (1922-___)
Sherman, Eunice M. (1923-___)
274 – Agnew, John H. (1923-1996)
275 – Agnew, John H. (1923-1996)
Agnew, Patricia M. (1941-___)
276 – Gamache, Alexander R. (1993-1994)
277 – Roby, Waldo N. (1932-___)
Roby, Mildred J. (1935-1992)
278 – LaJeunesse, Theodore V. (1918-
1993)
279 – LaJeunesse, Theodore V. (1918-
1993)
LaJeunesse, Marion (1920-___)
280 – Fontano, Nicholas J. (1915-1995)
281 – Fontano, Nicholas J. (1915-1995)
Fontano, Margaret M. (1924-___)
282 – Beech, Aaron H. (1919-___)
Beech, Frances V. (1920-1994)
283 – Dixon, Travis A. (1936-1998)
284 – Dixon, Travis A. (1936-1998)
285 – Lima, Joseph Jr. (1920-2003)
Lima, Beulah H. (1927-1993)
Lima, Michael (1953-2001)
286 – McEachern, Francis (1928-1995)
287 – Wilding, Archibald V. (1912-1994)
288 – Biasiucci, John J. (1929-1994)
Biasiucci, Violet (1931-___)
Biasiucci, Domenic A. (1952-1996)
Biasiucci, John J., Jr. (1951-2002)
289 – Kinsman, Reginald F. (1916-___)
Kinsman, Alice E. (1922-___)
290 – Wylie, Robert J. (1914-1996)
Wylie, Mary T. (1915-2001)

Wylie, Mary J., Dr. (1958-2002)
291 – Fitting, David L. (1920-1998)
292 – Fitting, David L. (1920-1998)
Fitting, Mildred B. (1922-____)
292 – Mackiewicz, Marie (1951-2002)
293 – Buttermore, Richard L. (1929-1994)
294 – Dillon, Elwyn G. (1934-2001)
295 – Dillon, Elwyn G. (1934-2001)
Dillon, Brenda (1944-____)
296 – Gudmundsson, Gudmundur (1951-1996)
297 – Gudmundsson, Diana (1952-____)
Gudmundsson, Gudmundur (1951-1996)
298 – Porell, Donald E. (1932-2000)
299 – Porell, Donald E. (1932-2000)
300 – Porell, Donald E. (1932-2000)
Porell, Joan M. (1939-____)
Porell, David G. (1966-____)
Porell, Joseph D. (1967-____)
Porell, Donna M. (1962-____)
Porell, Robert M. (1974-____)
301 – Brown, Edward J. (1935-1997)
Brown, Margaret M. (1944-____)
302 – Ahr, Linda S. (1950-____)
Ahr, William A. (1950-1998)
303 – DesRoche, William J. (1953-1998)
304 – White, Donald A. (1941-1998)
305 – White, Helen (1943-____)
White, Donald A. (1941-1998)
306 – Paulson, Ann M. (1954-____)
Paulson, Phillip D. (1948-2000)
307 – Barlow, Hanna E. (2001)
Barlow, Grace C. (2001)

308 – Barry, Lillian (1928-1999)
309 – Tobojka, Kenneth R. (1943-1999)
Tobojka, Cynthia L. (1947-____)
310 – Vieira, Joan M. (1964-2000)
311 – Garbitt, Ronald S. (1950-____)
Garbitt, Rita A. (1952-____)
Gamache, Olivia A. (2003)
Gamache, Elyana L. (2003)
312 – Schlageter, Gerhard P. (1939-1995)
313 – Schlageter, Gerhard P. (1939-1995)
Schlageter, Noella T. (1945-__)
314 – Doucet, Rene E. (1930-1978)
315 – Doucet, Rene E. (1930-1978)
Doucet, Catherine T. (1934-1993)
316 – Michaud, Lee J. (1993-2000)
317 – Michaud, Lee J. (1993-2000)
318 – Moffett, Patti L. (1937-1995)
Moffett, Raymond J. (1931-____)
319 – Lewoczko, Myron M. (1925-____)
Lewoczko, Beverly I. (1932-2003)
320 – Kelley, Eunice M. (1935-____)
321 – Lang, Charles M. (1921-2000)
322 – Lang, Mary E. (1927-2001)
323 – Lang, Charles M. (1921-2000)
Lang, Mary E. (1927-2001)
Lang, Scott A. (1957-2003)
324 – Walsh, Myrtle E. (1912-2001)
Walsh, Patrick R. (1912-1997)
Fuller, Peter G. (1946-____)
Fuller, Sandra R. (1945-____)
325 – Buckley, Christopher (1960-____)
Buckley, Lynn (1960-2003)
326 – White, Richard H. (1916-____)
White, Gertrude (1918-2000)

Middleboro Lodge #1274 BPOE marker
(The Benevolent and Protective Order of the Elks)

Sampson Cemetery Map Overview

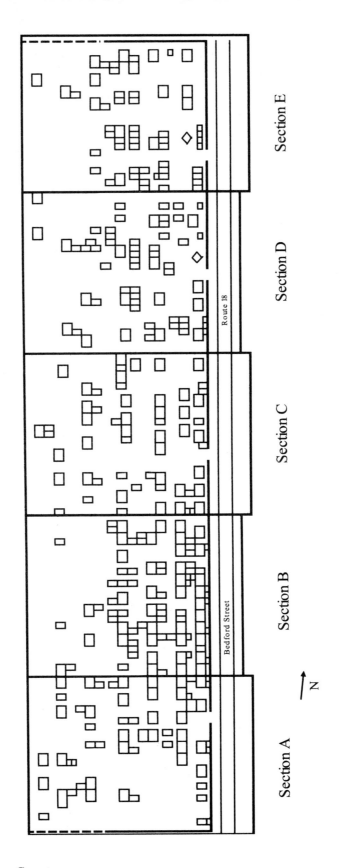

Section A   Section B   Section C   Section D   Section E

Bedford Street

Route 18

N

Sampson Cemetery Map
Section A

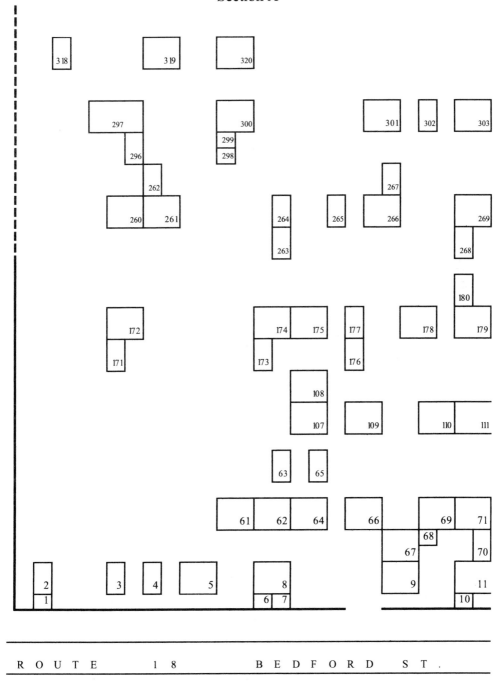

ROUTE   18   BEDFORD   ST.

____ = stone post and metal rail fence   .____= stone post and metal rail addition in 2006

Sampson Cemetery Map
Section B

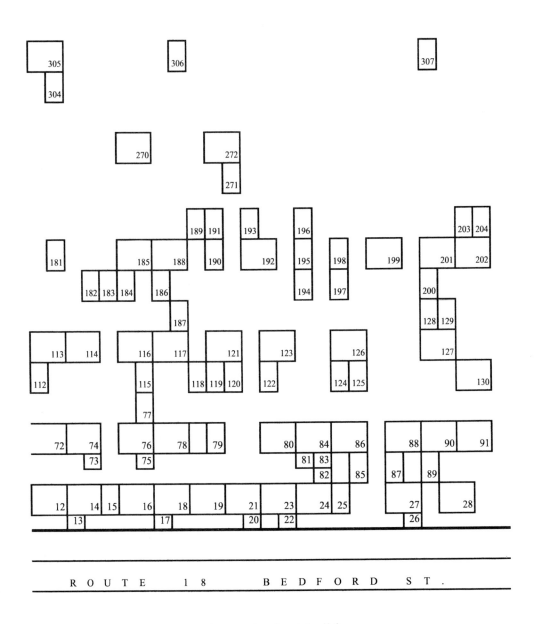

= stone post and metal rail fence

Sampson Cemetery Map
Section C

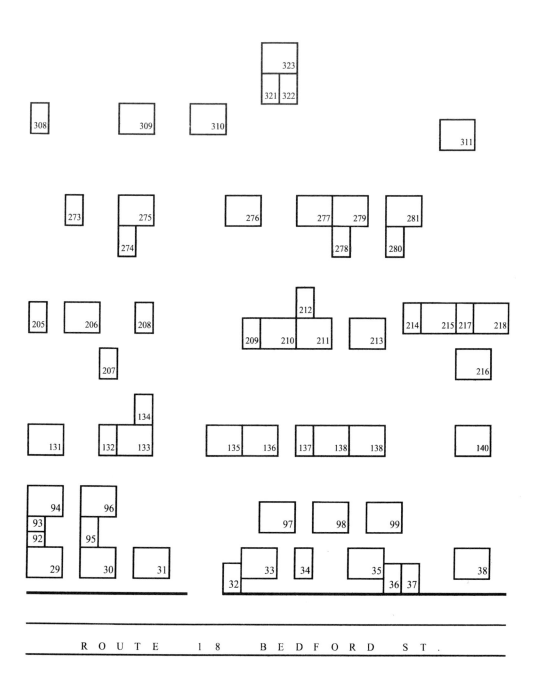

___ = stone post and metal rail fence

Sampson Cemetery Map
Section D

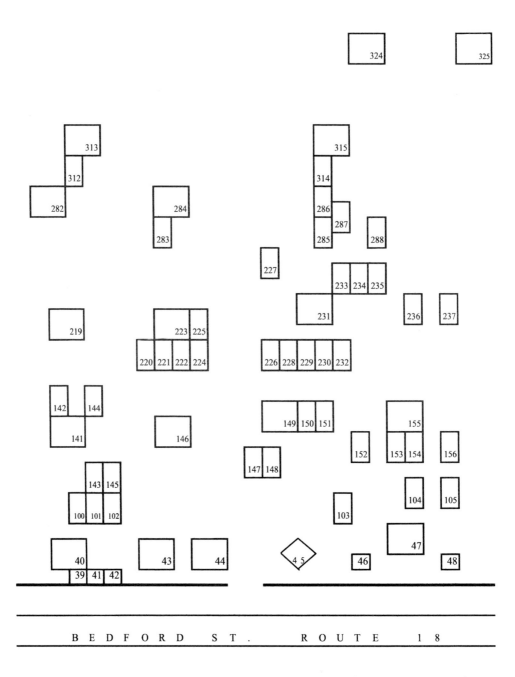

____ = stone post and metal rail fence

Sampson Cemetery Map
Section E

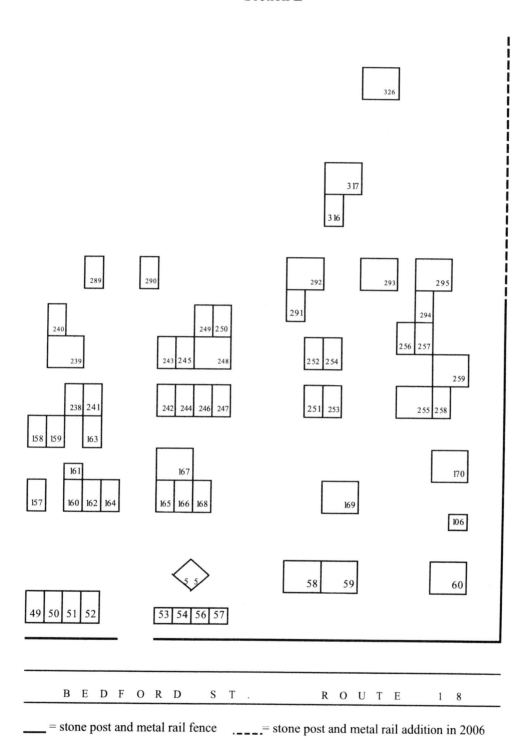

BEDFORD   ST .   R O U T E   1 8

_____ = stone post and metal rail fence   ._ _ _. = stone post and metal rail addition in 2006

Chapter 28
Smallpox Cemetery

Smallpox Cemetery is located at 97 County Street on private property. Only one gravestone, dated 1840, was found. It is leaning upside down against the only standing stone post left of a stone post and metal rail fence. Two other stone posts are lying on the ground nearby, but no rails are present. The ground had been bulldozed 10 feet west of the location of the gravestone for construction of a cranberry bog. There are lots of rocks and boulders around this site, prohibiting any determination as to whether they are marking graves, or just debris from the construction site. There is a stone wall that separates the rear portion of this property from the bog area. The current homeowner stated that this stone wall formed the western boundary of the cemetery at one time. The intact stone post is about 10 feet to the east, and 10 feet south of where this wall ends. Rail holes in this post are only on the south side, indicating to the author that the gate to the cemetery was north of the post, and part of the cemetery extended south from there. However, the current homeowner believed that post to be the southeast corner post of the cemetery. He also stated the cemetery was about 10 by 20 feet or so, and that there were fieldstones marking other graves. No sign is present. Thatcher calls this the "Enoch Davis Cemetery." The entry was recorded April 14, 2000.

Davis, Beulah   *"In memory of / Mrs. Beulah / wife of / Mr. Enoch Davis / who died with / the small pox. / Jan. 7, 1840: In her 61 year. /*
> *Ye living men as you pass by*
> *As you are now so wonce was I;*
> *As I am now soon you shall be,*
> *Prepare for deth and follow me."*

Notice the spelling of *wonce* and *deth* in the poem.

Thatcher lists additionally one unmarked grave.
Gladys Vigers' *History of Lakeville* p. 219 lists Beulah's husband, Enoch, who died in 1843, as being buried in this cemetery without a headstone.

Chapter 29
Strobridge Cemetery

Strobridge Cemetery is located between 60 and 62 Kingman Avenue. A stone wall surrounds it. There are two areas partitioned off with stone posts and metal rails. The sign is present and in good repair. Gravestones face southwest, and date from 1822 to 2000. The Lakeville Assessor's Office lists this cemetery as town owned, measuring 40,582 square feet in size. In 1978 an adjoining plot of land to the east was acquired for use as a cemetery, but has yet to be developed. It measures a little over an acre. Thatcher calls this the "Cemetery between McFall Hill and Mullain Hill." Entries were recorded on October 26, 2000.

Barker, Daniel W.   *"DANIEL W. BARKER / Died / Jan. 21, 1906. / Aged 63 years."* The first line is carved along an arch. There is a crack radiating from the center bottom of this stone.

Barker, Elmer   *"ELMER BARKER / DIED / Aug. 17, 1895, / Age 4 Months / and 18 days."* The first line is carved along an arch.

Barker, Emma B.   *"EMMA B. BARKER, / Wife of DANIEL W. BARKER / Died / Nov. 26, 1896, / Aged 37 years, / And 7 months"* *"HARRINGTON."* is inscribed on the bottom right corner of the stone. The first two lines are carved along an arch. The second line looks like it was added later. This stone is separated from its base and is leaning against it.

Barker, Florence E.   *"FLORENCE E. BARKER / Died / Feb. 17, 1906, / Aged 14 years."* The first line is carved along an arch.

Barker, Ruby A.   *"RUBY A. BARKER / DIED / Aug. 23, 1897, / Age 9 Months / and 14 days."* The first line is carved along an arch. Floral carvings are in the upper corners.

Bassett, Caleb   *"C. B."* This footstone is in line with the other headstones, and to the right of the stone for Mary Bassett. This is probably the footstone for Caleb Bassett, her husband. His death notice in *The Middleborough Gazette* 08/25/1860:2 reports his death on August 17, 1860, at 73 years, and 5 months old.

Bassett, Mary   *"In memory of / MARY, / Wife of / Caleb Bassett, / who died Aug. 15, 1841, / in the 51st year / of her age. /*
> *She has bidden farewell to the shores of time*
> *She has gone from earth to a happier clime*
> *She has left her husband, the children of her love*
> *And joined the communion of spirits above."*

"Warren." is inscribed at the bottom of this stone. The poem is hard to read due to weathering.

Bullock, Sarah W.   *"SARAH W. BULLOCK / 1833 – 1904 / AT REST."*
"S. W. B." is inscribed on the footstone.

Cardno, Georgianna S.   See John Cardno Monument entry.

Cardno, John W. Monument   *"CARDNO / 1869 JOHN W. 1930 / HIS WIFE / 1859 GEORGIANNA S. 1942"* Floral designs are carved at the top of this monument.

Carver, Gilbert W.   *"Father / GILBERT W. CARVER / BORN / Sept. 1, 1839, / Died Sept. 15, 1887, / Aged 48 yrs. 14 d's. / Gone but not forgotten."* The second line is carved along an arch. A *"GAR 3"* marker and flag are present. *Massachusetts Civil War Soldiers & Sailors, 1861-1865*, Vol. I, p. 196 shows that he served with the 3rd Infantry, Co. I.

Carver, Harry H.   *"HARRY H."* is carved in relief on the top slanted surface of the stone. *"SON OF / FRANK H. & CARRIE W. / CARVER. / BORN OCT. 20, 1887, / DIED JUNE 20, 1890. / OUR ONLY TREASURE"* is inscribed on the front.

Carver, James A.   *"Brother / JAMES A. CARVER / BORN / Dec. 11, 1862, / Died Jan. 30, 1890. / Aged 28 y's, 1 mo. 19d's / Gone but not forgotten."* The second line is carved along an arch. *"C. HARRINGTON / WARREN R.I."* is carved on the bottom right corner of this stone. It is hidden when the stone is in the base.

Carver, Maybell   *"MOTHER / MAYBELL CARVER / 1878 – 1966"* A cross, an open book and grapes are carved in the upper left corner of this flat, ground level stone.

Colrick, Luella E. *"LUELLA E. BARKER / WIFE OF / JOHN F. COLRICK / 1888 – 1950 / WELL DONE."*

Dow, David F. See Frank J. Dow Monument entry.
"DAVID F. DOW / SGT US ARMY / KOREA / MAY 16, 1933 MAR. 27, 2000" is inscribed on this flat, ground level stone. A *"Korean War"* marker and flag are present.

Dow, Elsie M. See Frank J. Dow Monument entry.

Dow, Frank J. Monument *"DOW"* is inscribed on the front of this monument. Rose branches are carved in the upper corners. *"FRANK JAMES DOW / SEPT. 3, 1902 – MAR. 22, 1993 / HIS WIFE / ELSIE MAY McFARLANE / DEC. 10, 1899 – DEC. 12, 1976"* is inscribed on the back. *"DAVID E. DOW / MAY 16, 1933 – MAR. 27, 2000"* was added to this stone after the initial visit. A Barnicoat Monuments metal tag is present.

Evans, Marion Y. *"EVANS"* is inscribed on the front of this monument. *"MARION YOUNG EVANS / OCT. 10, 1903 – SEPT. 30, 1976"* is inscribed on the back. A Barnicoat Monuments metal tag is present.
"MARION YOUNG EVANS / 1903 – 1976" is inscribed on this flat, ground level stone. It is located in front of the monument, on the right.

Hunt, Thomas *"THOS. HUNT / CO. F / 7 MASS. INF."* is carved in relief inside a recessed shield shaped area. No dates are inscribed on it. *Massachusetts Civil War Soldiers & Sailors, 1861-1865*, Vol. I, p. 496 shows that he enlisted in 1861 at age 29. Taunton Vital Records list his death on February 15, 1886, at 53 years, 1 month and 1 day old. A *"GAR 8 233"* marker and flag are present.

I *"I."* is the only inscription on this stone, which faces the rear of the cemetery. It is located to the right of Eva Towns' gravestone.

Johnson, Amelia F. See Gustaf Johnson Monument entry.
"A. F. J." is inscribed on this flat, ground level marker which is located behind the monument, on the left.

Johnson, Gustaf E. Monument *"JOHNSON"* is inscribed on the front of this monument underneath carvings of a cross and a rose. *"GUSTAF E. JOHNSON / MAR. 6, 1913 – JAN. 31, 1991 / AMELIA F. HIS WIFE / JAN. 23, 1919 ____"* is inscribed on the back. A Barnicoat Monuments metal tag is present.
"G. E. J." is inscribed on this flat, ground level marker which is located directly behind the monument.

Jones, Mary Jane *"MARY JANE JONES / 1874 – 1941"* This flat, sunken stone is located to the immediate right of the George H. Thatcher Monument.

McGee, Andrew *"ANDREW McGEE, / Died / Sept. 17, 1871. / Aged / 78 years / Left an earthly for a Heavenly home." "W. H. JACKSON & CO. TAUNTON,"* is inscribed in the bottom left corner. A Mason's symbol is carved in relief at the top.

This stone is separated from its base and leaning against it.

McGee, Ann   *"In memory of / ANN, / Wife of / Andrew A. McGee, / DIED / JULY 22, 1879, / Aged 83 yrs, 5 mos. / 20 dys. / "Blessed are the dead who die in the Lord.""* *"C. HARRINGTON / WARREN"* is inscribed in the lower right corner. The first line is carved along an arch, and the second line is carved in relief. This stone is broken in half through the death date. The top half is in front of the base, leaning against it and the bottom half is lying face up behind the base.

Munroe, David B. Monument   *"IN MEMORY OF / DAVID B. MUNROE / 1837 – 1864 / JANE M. PIERCE / 1839 – 1926 / MARY MUNROE / 1863 – 1865 / AT REST"* This monument is separated from its base, and is lying face up behind it. It is too heavy to be lifted to check for inscriptions on the back.

Munroe, Mary   See David B. Munroe Monument entry.
Lakeville Vital Records list her death on June 8, 1865, at 2 years old. She was the daughter of David and Jane Munroe (later Pierce).

Nickerson, Benjamin   *"FATHER"* is inscribed on the top curved surface of this stone. *"BENJ. C. NICKERSON / Born / Oct. 20, 1814, / Died / March 7, 1909."*

Nickerson, Frances A.   *"FRANCES A. / Daughter of / Benjamin C. & Joanna G. / NICKERSON, / Born Aug. 15, 1852. / Died / Aug. 31, 1878."* *"BURT & CO. Taunton."* is inscribed at the bottom of this stone.

Nickerson, Joanna   *"MOTHER"* is inscribed on the top curved surface of this stone. *"JOANNA, / Wife of / BENJ. C. NICKERSON, / Born / Oct. 8, 1812, / Died / April 10, 1885."* *"BURT & CO. Taunton"* is inscribed on the upper base.

Parris, Betsey   *"BETSEY, / wife of / Dea. Enos Parris / died / July 28, 1881, / in her 83rd year."* This stone shares a second base with the gravestone of her husband. There is a crack radiating from the bottom center.

Parris, Caleb B.   *"CALEB B. PARRIS / Died / Feb. 19, 1900, / Aged 66 years 5 / months 16 days. / SOLDIER IN THE CIVIL WAR."* A flag is present. *Massachusetts Civil War Soldiers & Sailors, 1861-1865*, Vol. I, p. 198, shows that he served with the 3rd Infantry, Company I.

Parris, Enos, Dea.   *"DEA. / ENOS PARRIS. / died / Mar. 3, 1852. / in his 59th year."* This stone shares a second base with the gravestone of his wife, Betsey. There is a small crack at the bottom of this gravestone.

Parris, Enos   *"ENOS PARRIS, / Died / Dec. 12, 1898, / In the 72nd year / of his age."* The first line is carved along an arch.

Parris, Henry B.   *"HENRY B. PARRIS / AGED 14 YEARS"* There is a carving of an oak leaf above the inscription. There are no dates on this stone. Taunton Vital Records list his birth on November 9, 1867, the son of Caleb and Margaret Parris. Lakeville Vital Records list his death on April 19, 1882.

Parris, Job P.   *"JOB P. PARRIS / BORN / April 11, 1790, / DIED / Sept. 4, 1878, / Aged 88 yrs. 4 mos. / 23 days."* There is a metal shield shaped marker present with the inscription: *"GOOD / SAMARITAN / NO. 18 / F L T / I.O.O.F."*

Parris, Sabra P. *"MOTHER / SABRA P. PARRIS / 1814 – 1895. / At rest."* The first line is carved along an arch.

Parris, Susan T. *"SUSAN T. / dau. of / WILLIAM C. & SABRA / PARRIS, / died / Oct. 3, 1851, in / her 16 year."* The first line is carved in outline.

Parris, Susanna *"In memory of / SUSANNA, / wife of / JOB PARRIS, / who died / Oct. 8, 1851, in / her 68 year."* An urn and willow carving is at the top of this rectangular, slate stone, and square designs are carved down the sides. This is the only slate gravestone in this cemetery.

Parris, Sylvanus *"SYLVANUS, / Son of / Sylvanus & Lydia / PARRIS, / Died Sept. 28, 1852, / Æ. 32 Yrs. 9 Mos. /*
> *Why do we mourn departing friends,*
> *Or shake at deaths alarms,*
> *'Tis but the voice that Jesus sends,*
> *To call them to his arms."*

Parris, William C. *"FATHER / WILLIAM C. PARRIS / 1812 – 1888. / At rest."* The first line is carved along an arch.

Parris, William J. *"WM. J. PARRIS / U.S. NAVY"* The above inscription is carved in relief within a recessed shield shaped area. There are no dates on this stone. A *"GAR 8 342"* marker and flag are present. *Massachusetts Civil War Soldiers & Sailors, 1861-1865*, Vol. VII, p. 534 reports that he served on the USS Sabine and Niagara. *Middleborough, Massachusetts Vital Records*, Vol. 1, p. 426 lists his birth on March. 14, 1838 to William C. and Sabra Parris. Lakeville Vital Records document that William J. Parris died on November 21, 1909, at the Old Soldier's Home in Chelsea, Mass.

Peirce, Elizabeth *"ELIZABETH PEIRCE / died / Feb. 6, 1915, / in her 83$\underline{rd}$ year."* The first line is carved along an arch.

Peirce, John E. *"JOHN E. PEIRCE / died / Aug. 5, 1916, / in his 47$\underline{th}$ year."*

Pierce, Jane M. See David B. Munroe Monument entry.
Lakeville Vital Records show that her father was Andrew McGee, and her first husband was David Munroe. She married Henry Peirce February 17, 1872. He is buried in Lang Cemetery, with his parents. Note the difference in spelling between her last name and that of Henry.

Reed, Abigail *"ABiGAiL REED / Born Jan. 24, 1800 / Died March 22, 1840 / Aged 40 Yrs. 1 M. 27 D. / there is Rest for you."* Note the mix of lower and upper case letters. This stone and that of her husband, Apollos, share the same base.

Reed, Apollos, Capt. *"Capt. APOLLOS REED / Born April 17, 1791. / Died Aug. 20, 1863. / Aged 72 Yrs. 4 M. 3 D. / There is Rest for the Weary."* Note the mix of lower and upper case letters. The third number in the death year is a backward 6. This stone is separated from its base, and is broken in half under the inscription. The upper half is lying face up behind the base, and the lower part is leaning against it. This stone shares the same base with the headstone for his wife, Abigail.

Reed, Infant son *"Infant Son / of / J.E. & S.A. / Reed / Aged 13 days."* Lakeville Vital Records indicate a male infant was born to John and Susan Reed on September 3, 1863, and died on September 15.

Reed, John E. See John E. Reed Monument entry.

Reed, John E. Monument *"JOHN E. REED / 1831 – 1873 / HIS WIFE / SUSAN A. SHAW / 1836 – 1928 / THEIR SON / JOHN E. / 1873 – 1957."* is inscribed on the front of this large monument.
"JOHN E. REED / died / Jan. 23, 1873: / Aged 41 yrs. 6 ms. /
> *A light is from our household gone,*
> *A voice we loved is still,*
> *A place is vacant on our hearth,*
> *Which never can be filled."* is inscribed on this stone, which
is located in front of the monument, on the far left. The first line is carved in relief along an arch. A crack extends up from the center bottom of the stone.

Reed, Susan A. See John E. Reed Monument entry.
"SUSAN" is inscribed on this flat, lichen encrusted, 4-6 inch high, stone. It is located in front of the monument, on the left.

Simmons, Jennie A. *"DAUGHTER / JENNIE A. CARVER / SIMMONS / 1911 – 1985"* A cross, an open book and grapes are carved in the upper left corner of this flat, ground level stone.

Staples, Bethiah K. Stone

> *"BETHIAH K.*
> *Wife of*
> *ELIAS STAPLES.*
> *Died Apr. 16, 1857;*
> *Aged 62 Y'rs, 4 Mo's,*
> *CALEB FRANCIS.*
> *Son of*
> *Elias & Bethiah K.*
> *STAPLES,*
> *Died Dec. 20, 1831;*
> *Aged 6 Y'rs. 7 Mo's."*

This stone shares its base with the stone of her husband.

Staples, Caleb F. See Bethiah Staples Monument entry.

Staples, Elias *"ELIAS STAPLES. / Died Sept. 12, 1862: / Aged 66 Y'rs. 8 Mo's. / & 3 days.* This stone shares its base with the headstone for his wife, Bethiah K.

Stevens, Charles H. M. *"CHARLES H. M. / Son of Charles & / Olive K. Stevens. / Died / June 7, 1852; / aged 9 ms. & 24 ds."*
"C. H. M. S." is inscribed on the footstone.

Stevens, Olive K. *"In memory of / OLIVE K. / wife of / CHARLES STEVENS / Born Oct. 28, 1825, / Died June 3, 1854, / aged 28 years / 7 Ms. 6 Ds."* *"Hathaway,*

Taunton" is inscribed on the bottom left. This stone is lying face up on the ground. It is broken along the fourth line, which is carved in relief.

"O. K. S." is inscribed on the footstone.

Strobridge, Elizabeth *"In memory of / MISS ELIZABETH / STROBRIDGE, / who died / Nov. 18, 1848, / aged 62 years."*

"E. S." is inscribed on the footstone, but the inscription is buried underground.

Strobridge, Harriet *"HARRIET, / Wife of / Thomas Strobridge, / Died Feb. 5, 1881, / Aged 88 yrs. 10 mos."* There is no footstone present. Her headstone is in line with the footstones of the other graves in this row. It was probably moved due to the large cedar tree growing where her headstone should be.

Strobridge, Harriet M. *"In memory of / HARRIET M. / Dau. of Thomas & / Harriet Strobridge / Born / Feb. 25, 1816; / Died / Nov. 15, 1831; / aged 15 yrs 8 ms / & 19 ds."* Thatcher lists her death day as the 16th.

"H. M. S." is inscribed on the footstone.

Strobridge, Henry *"In memory of / HENRY STROBRIDGE, / who died Jan. 22, / 1842, / in his 82nd year."*

"H. S." is inscribed on the footstone.

Strobridge, John *"In memory of / JOHN STROBRIDGE / who died / April 22, 1834, / in his 40 year."*

"J. S." is inscribed on the footstone.

Strobridge, Thomas *"In memory of / THOMAS STROBRIDGE, / Born / Aug. 21, 1788, / Died / Nov. 7, 1851, / aged 63 yrs. 2 mos. / & 16 ds."*

"T. S." is inscribed on the footstone.

Strobridge, Thomas H. *"THOMAS HENRY, / son of / Thomas & Harriet / STROBRIDGE, / Born Nov. 3, 1830, / Died July 17, 1855, / aged 24 years / & 8 Mos."*

"T. H. S." is inscribed on the footstone.

Strobridge, Zilpah *"In memory of / ZILPAH, / wife of / Henry Strobridge, / who died / Oct. 8, 1833, / in her 75 year."*

"Z. S." is inscribed on the footstone.

T., J. W. P. *"J. W. P. T."* This flat, lichen encrusted, ground level stone is in line with the headstones. No dates are present. A fieldstone serves as its footstone.

Thatcher, Florence A. See George H. Thatcher Monument entry.

"F. A. T." This flat, lichen encrusted, ground level stone is located directly in front of the monument, on the left.

Thatcher, George H. Monument *"THATCHER / YOUNG / GEORGE H. THATCHER / 1864 – 1935 / FLORENCE A. HIS WIFE / 1871 – 1942 / JOHN B. YOUNG / 1836 – 1895 / FLORA HIS WIFE / 1836 – 1924"* Curved designs are carved at the top of this monument.

"G. H. T." This lichen encrusted, ground level stone is located in front of the monument, on the left.

Tinkham, Albert D. *"ALBERT D. / Son of / Dennis & Elizabeth / TINKHAM, / Born Mar. 10, 1852, / Died Sept. 19, 1852."* The first line on this small stone is carved in relief along an arch.

Tinkham, Caleb, Dea. *"DEA. / CALEB TINKHAM, / Born / April 25, 1786, / Died / July 12, 1865. / Thou art gone, but not forgotten."* *"C. T."* is inscribed on the footstone.

Tinkham, Caleb, Jr. *"CALEB TINKHAM, JR. / Son of Caleb & / Joanna Tinkham; / Born May 22, 1819, / Died May 16, 1840."* *"Hathaway"* is inscribed on the bottom left of this stone. *"C. T."* is inscribed on the footstone.

Tinkham, Deborah *"DEBORAH, / daughter of Caleb & / Joanna Tinkham; / Born Jan. 13, 1815, / Died July 12, 1835."* *"D. T."* is inscribed on the footstone.

Tinkham, Dennis *"FATHER"* is carved in relief on the top curved surface of this stone. *"DENNIS TINKHAM / BORN / March 13, 1821, / DIED / May 27, 1910."* is inscribed on the front. The first line is carved in relief along an arch. There is a crack in the stone in the lower left corner. *"D. T."* is inscribed on the footstone, but the inscription is buried.

Tinkham, Elizabeth P. *"MOTHER"* is carved in relief on the top curved surface. *"ELIZABETH PARRY / Wife of / DENNIS TINKHAM, / BORN / Feb. 18, 1823, / DIED / Nov. 23, 1883. / Asleep in Jesus."* is inscribed on the front. The first line is carved in relief along an arch. *"E. P. T."* is inscribed on the footstone, but the inscription is buried.

Tinkham, James *"JAMES TINKHAM, / Born / March 18, 1827. / Died / April 6, 1898."*

Tinkham, Joanna *"JOANNA, / wife of / Dea. Caleb Tinkham; / & daughter of John & / Anna Peckens; / Born Oct. 13, 1781, / Died Sept. 5, 1838."* Note the spelling of *Peckens*. *"J. T."* is inscribed on the footstone.

Tinkham, John F. *"JOHN F. / Son of James & / Mary A. Tinkham / Born Feb. 18, / Died Feb. 19, 1850"* is inscribed on this small stone.

Tinkham, Mary A. *"MARY A. PARIS, / Wife of / JAMES TINKHAM, / Born / March 12, 1827. / Died / Sept. 19, 1896."* *"J. B. SULLIVAN, Taunton."* is inscribed on the base.

Tinkham, William *"WILLIAM, / Son of Caleb & / Joanna Tinkham; / Born Dec. 16, 1811. / Died Aug. 9, 1822."* is inscribed on this small stone.

Towns, Eva A. *"EVA A. REED, / Beloved Daughter of / John E. & Susan A. / REED. / Wife of / Fred A. Towns. / Nov. 16, 1867, / Nov. 19, 1911."* This stone is separated from its base and leaning against the front of it. Floral and leaf carvings are at the top. A small stone with only the letter "I" inscribed on the back is located to the right of her stone.

Trefethen, George T. *"HUSBAND FATHER / GEORGE THOMAS / TREFETHEN / 1912 – 1990"* A cross, an open book, and a grapes are carved in the upper left corner of this flat, ground level stone.

Trefethen, Lois M. *"LOIS M. TREFETHEN / 1948 – 1950"* is inscribed on this flat, ground level stone.

Trefethen, Marion *"WIFE – MOTHER / MARION CARVER / TREFETHEN / 1913 – 1987"* A cross, an open book, and a grapes are carved in the upper left corner of this flat, ground level stone.

Twombly, Julia M.

> *"JULIA M.*
> *Wife of*
> *Daniel Twombly,*
> *& Dau. of*
> *Apollos & Abigail*
> *Reed,*
> *died Jan. 5, 1873,*
> *Aged 43 yrs, 8 m's*
> *& 16 d's."*

The first line is carved in relief along an arch. This stone is separated from its base and leaning against the front of it.

Walker, Edgar A. *"EDGAR A. / Son of / Allen C. & Bethiah K. / WALKER, / Died Oct. 1, 1863; / Aged 12 Y'rs. 7 Mos. / & 6 d's. / Suffer little children to come unto me."* This stone shares its base with that of Luella G. Walker, his sister.

Walker, Luella G. *"LUELLA G. / Dau. of / Allen C. & Bethiah K. / WALKER. / Died Mar. 17, 1865; / Aged 6 Y'rs. 3 Mo's, / & 17 d's. / Of such is the Kingdom of Heaven"* This stone shares its base with that of Edgar A. Walker, her brother.

Wilcox, Bradford *"BRADFORD WILCOX / died / June 28, 1882 / Aged 66 yrs. 4 m's / & 28 d's."* The first line is carved along an arch. There is a crack in the center bottom of the stone.

Wilcox, Ruby A. *"RUBY A. PARRIS, / Widow of / BRADFORD WILCOX, / died / March 11, 1887, / Aged 65 yrs. 5 mos. / & 5 ds."* The first line is carved along an arch. Lakeville Vital Records show that she was the daughter of Enos and Betsy Parris. Her last name is listed as Butts in the records, although the name is not on her gravestone. Dartmouth Vital Records list her marriage to Peleg C. Butts on June 11, 1884.

Williams, Dorothy See Frank Williams Monument entry.
"D. L. W." This flat, ground level stone is located in front of the monument, on the left.

Williams, Elizabeth See Frank Williams Monument entry.
"E. M. W." This flat, ground level stone is located on the right, directly in front of the monument.

Williams, Frank Monument   "*WILLIAMS*" is inscribed on the front of this monument. Floral carvings adorn the upper corners. "*1836   FRANK WILLIAMS 1917 / 1838   MARY A. HIS WIFE   1917 / 1881   JOHN S.   1963 / 1890 ELIZABETH M. HIS WIFE   1949 / 1908   DOROTHY L. WILLIAMS   1986*" is inscribed on the back.
"*F. W.*" This flat, ground level stone is located in front of the monument, on the right.

Williams, James F.   "*J. F. W.*" This footstone is located in front of and to the farthest right of Frank Williams Monument. His obituary in *The Middleborough Gazette* 02/05/1953:9 reports that he was the son of Frank and Mary Williams and was 55 years old when he died on January 29, 1953.

Williams, John S.   See Frank Williams Monument entry.
"*J. S. W.*" This flat, ground level stone is located directly in front of the monument, on the left.

Williams, Mary A.   See Frank Williams Monument entry.
"*M. A. W.*" This flat, ground level stone is located in front of the monument, on the far right.

Young, Flora   See George H. Thatcher Monument entry.
"*F. Y.*" This flat, ground level stone is located in front of the monument, on the left. It is beginning to be buried.

Young, John B.   See George H. Thatcher Monument entry.
"*J. B. Y.*" This flat, lichen encrusted, ground level stone is located directly in front of the monument, on the right.

Additional Notes:

Between the stones of Daniel W. Barker, and John E. Peirce, there is a stone vase on top of a cement block. A stone base is located in front of it. It is unclear if this marks a grave.

Strobridge Cemetery Map Index

Alphabetical:

Dow, Elsie M. (1899-1976) – 28
Dow, Frank J. (1902-1993) – 28
Evans, Marion Y. (1903-1976) – 1, 6
Hunt, Thomas (1833-1886) – 42
I. (no dates) – 23
Johnson, Amelia F. (1919-____) – 14, 17
Johnson, Gustaf E. (1913-1991) – 14, 18
Jones, Mary Jane (1874-1941) – 8
McGee, Andrew (~1793-1871) – 33
McGee, Ann (1796-1879) – 34
Munroe, David B. (1837-1864) – 35
Munroe, Mary (1863-1865) – 35
Nickerson, Benjamin (1814-1909) – 30
Nickerson, Frances A. (1852-1878) – 32
Nickerson, Joanna (1812-1885) – 31
Parris, Betsey (1799-1881) – 75
Parris, Caleb B. (1833-1900) – 37
Parris, Enos, Dea. (~1794-1852) – 74
Parris, Enos (~1827-1898) – 76
Parris, Henry B. (~1868-1882) – 36
Parris, Job P. (1790-1878) – 72
Parris, Sabra P. (1814-1895) – 86
Parris, Susan T. (~1836-1851) – 92
Parris, Susanna (~1784-1851) – 73
Parris, Sylvanus (1819-1852) – 93
Parris, William C (1812-1888) – 85
Parris, William J. (1838-1909) – 91
Peirce, Elizabeth (~1833-1915) – 80
Peirce, John E. (~1870-1916) – 89
Pierce, Jane M. (1839-1926) – 35
Reed, Abigail (1800-1840) – 26
Reed, Apollos, Capt. (1791-1863) – 25
Reed, Infant son (1863) – 21
Reed, John E. (1873-1957) – 24
Reed, John E. (1831-1873) – 19, 24
Reed, Susan A. (1836-1928) – 20, 24
Simmons, Jennie A. (1911-1985) – 71
Staples, Bethiah K. (1794-1857) – 39
Staples, Caleb F. (1825-1831) – 39
Staples, Elias (1796-1862) – 38
Stevens, Charles H. M. (1851-1852) – 46

Stevens, Olive K. (1825-1854) – 43
Strobridge, Elizabeth (~1786-1848) – 48
Strobridge, Harriet (1792-1881) – 50
Strobridge, Harriet M. (1816-1831) – 51
Strobridge, Henry (~1761-1842) – 44
Strobridge, John (~1795-1834) – 47
Strobridge, Thomas (1788-1851) – 49
Strobridge, Thomas H. (1830-1855) – 52
Strobridge, Zilpah (~1759-1833) – 45
Thatcher, Florence A. (1871-1942) – 3, 7
Thatcher, George H. (1864-1935) – 2, 7
Tinkham, Albert D. (1852) – 60
Tinkham, Caleb, Dea. (1786-1865) – 56
Tinkham, Caleb Jr. (1819-1840) – 53
Tinkham, Deborah (1815-1835) – 54
Tinkham, Dennis (1821-1910) – 58
Tinkham, Elizabeth (1823-1883) – 59
Tinkham, James (1827-1898) – 64
Tinkham, Joanna (1781-1838) – 55
Tinkham, John F. (1850) – 66
T., J. W. P. (no dates) – 65
Tinkham, Mary (1827-1896) – 63
Tinkham, William (1811-1822) – 57
Towns, Eva A. (1867-1911) – 22
Trefethen, George T. (1912-1990) – 84
Trefethen, Lois M. (1948-1950) – 82
Trefethen, Marion (1913-1987) – 83
Twombly, Julia M. (1829-1873) – 27
Walker, Edgar A. (1851-1863) – 40
Walker, Luella G. (1858-1865) – 41
Wilcox, Bradford (1816-1882) – 78
Wilcox, Ruby A. (1821-1887) – 79
Williams, Dorothy L. (1908-1986) – 9, 15
Williams, Elizabeth M. (1890-1949) – 11, 15
Williams, Frank (1836-1917) – 12, 15
Williams, James F. (~1898-1953) – 16
Williams, John S. (1881-1963) – 10, 15
Williams, Mary A. (1838-1917) – 13, 15
Young, Flora (1836-1924) – 5, 7
Young, John B. (1836-1895) – 4, 7

By Location:

1 – Evans, Marion Y. (1903-1976)
2 – Thatcher, George H. (1864-1935)
3 – Thatcher, Florence A. (1871-1942)
4 – Young, John B. (1836-1895)
5 – Young, Flora (1836-1924)
6 – Evans, Marion Y. (1903-1976)

7 – Thatcher, George H. (1864-1935)
    Thatcher, Florence A. (1871-1942)
    Young, John B. (1836-1895)
    Young, Flora (1836-1924)
8 – Jones, Mary Jane (1874-1941)
9 – Williams, Dorothy L. (1908-1986)

10 – Williams, John S. (1881-1963)
11 – Williams, Elizabeth M. (1890-1949)
12 – Williams, Frank (1836-1917)
13 – Williams, Mary A. (1838-1917)
14 – Johnson, Gustaf E. (1913-1991)
     Johnson, Amelia F. (1919-____)
15 – Williams, Frank (1836-1917)
     Williams, Mary A. (1838-1917)
     Williams, John S. (1881-1963)
     Williams, Elizabeth M. (1890-1949)
     Williams, Dorothy L. (1908-1986)
16 – Williams, James F. (~1898-1953)
17 – Johnson, Amelia F. (1919-____)
18 – Johnson, Gustaf E. (1913-1991)
19 – Reed, John E. (1831-1873)
20 – Reed, Susan A. (1836-1928)
21 – Reed, Infant son (1863)
22 – Towns, Eva A. (1867-1911)
23 – I. (no dates)
24 – Reed, John E. (1831-1873)
     Reed, Susan A. (1836-1928)
     Reed, John E. (1873-1957)
25 – Reed, Apollos, Capt. (1791-1863)
26 – Reed, Abigail (1800-1840)
27 – Twombly, Julia M. (1829-1873)
28 – Dow, Frank J. (1902-1993)
     Dow, Elsie M. (1899-1976)
     Dow, David F. (1933-2000)
29 – Dow, David F. (1933-2000)
30 – Nickerson, Benjamin (1814-1909)
31 – Nickerson, Joanna (1812-1885)
32 – Nickerson, Frances A. (1852-1878)
33 – McGee, Andrew (~1793-1871)
34 – McGee, Ann (1796-1879)
35 – Munroe, David B. (1837-1864)
     Pierce, Jane M. (1839-1926)
     Munroe, Mary (1863-1865)
36 – Parris, Henry B. (~1868-1882)
37 – Parris, Caleb B. (1833-1900)
38 – Staples, Elias (1796-1862)
39 – Staples, Bethiah K. (1794-1857)
     Staples, Caleb F. (1825-1831)
40 – Walker, Edgar A. (1851-1863)
41 – Walker, Luella G. (1858-1865)
42 – Hunt, Thomas (1833-1886)
43 – Stevens, Olive K. (1825-1854)
44 – Strobridge, Henry (~1761-1842)
45 – Strobridge, Zilpah (~1759-1833)
46 – Stevens, Charles H. M. (1851-1852)
47 – Strobridge, John (~1795-1834)

48 – Strobridge, Elizabeth (~1786-1848)
49 – Strobridge, Thomas (1788-1851)
50 – Strobridge, Harriet (1792-1881)
51 – Strobridge, Harriet M. (1816-1831)
52 – Strobridge, Thomas H. (1830-1855)
53 – Tinkham, Caleb Jr. (1819-1840)
54 – Tinkham, Deborah (1815-1835)
55 – Tinkham, Joanna (1781-1838)
56 – Tinkham, Caleb, Dea. (1786-1865)
57 – Tinkham, William (1811-1822)
58 – Tinkham, Dennis (1821-1910)
59 – Tinkham, Elizabeth (1823-1883)
60 – Tinkham, Albert D. (1852)
61 – Bassett, Mary (~1791-1841)
62 – Bassett, Caleb (1787-1860)
63 – Tinkham, Mary (1827-1896)
64 – Tinkham, James (1827-1898)
65 – T., J. W. P. (no dates)
66 – Tinkham, John F. (1850)
67 – Bullock, Sarah W. (1833-1904)
68 – Carver, Gilbert W. (1839-1887)
69 – Carver, James A. (1862-1890)
70 – Carver, Maybell (1878-1966)
71 – Simmons, Jennie A. (1911-1985)
72 – Parris, Job P. (1790-1878)
73 – Parris, Susanna (~1784-1851)
74 – Parris, Enos, Dea. (~1794-1852)
75 – Parris, Betsey (1799-1881)
76 – Parris, Enos (~1827-1898)
77 – Colrick, Luella E. (1888-1950)
78 – Wilcox, Bradford (1816-1882)
79 – Wilcox, Ruby A. (1821-1887)
80 – Peirce, Elizabeth (~1833-1915)
81 – Carver, Harry H. (1887-1890)
82 – Trefethen, Lois M. (1948-1950)
83 – Trefethen, Marion (1913-1987)
84 – Trefethen, George T. (1912-1990)
85 – Parris, William C (1812-1888)
86 – Parris, Sabra P. (1814-1895)
87 – Barker, Emma B. (1859-1896)
88 – Barker, Daniel W. (~1843-1906)
89 – Peirce, John E. (~1870-1916)
90 – Cardno, John W. (1869-1930)
     Cardno, Georgianna S. (1859-1942)
91 – Parris, William J. (1838-1909)
92 – Parris, Susan T. (~1836-1851)
93 – Parris, Sylvanus (1819-1852)
94 – Barker, Elmer (1895)
95 – Barker, Ruby A. (1896-1897)
96 – Barker, Florence E. (~1892-1906)

Strobridge Cemetery Map
Front Section

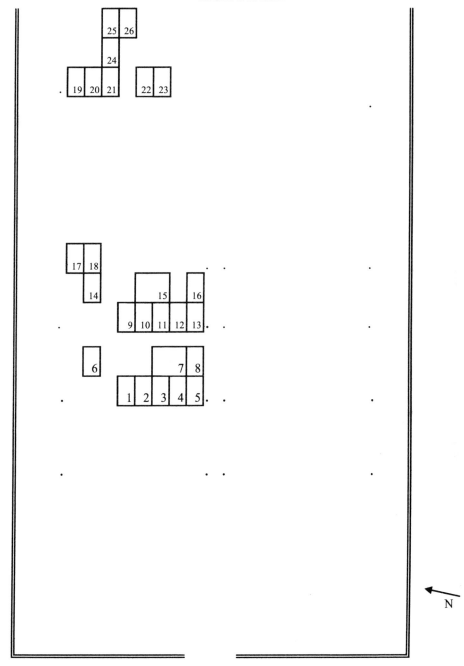

KINGMAN STREET

= stone wall   . = plot markers

Strobridge Cemetery Map
Back Section

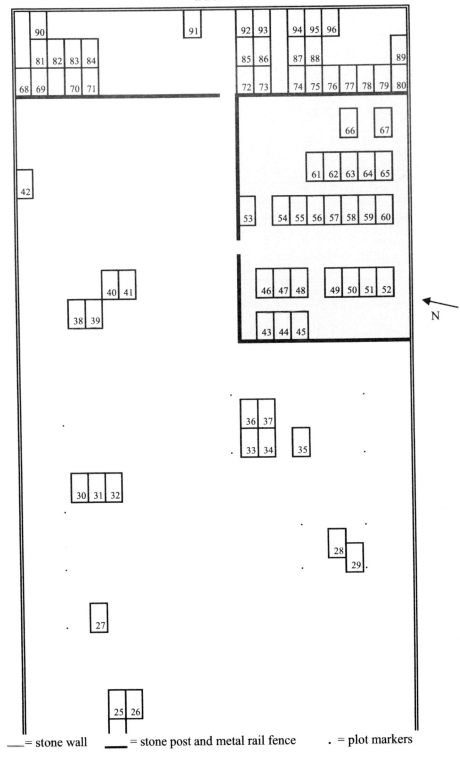

___= stone wall   ___ = stone post and metal rail fence   . = plot markers

Chapter 30
Thompson Hill Cemetery

Thompson Hill Cemetery is located at 185 Rhode Island Road. Precinct Cemetery is on the left, and a lone wood post marks the border between them. A vinyl fence borders the front of the cemetery, and a stone wall borders the rear. Remnants of a wood post and metal rail fence are on the right side. The sign is in good repair. There are two masses of evergreen bushes in this cemetery. A footstone was found hidden inside one of the bushes. These bushes are so overgrown it is impossible to determine whether more gravestones exist within them. Unless stated otherwise, headstones face the front of the cemetery, and footstones face the rear. Graves date from 1711 to present. The records at the Lakeville Assessor's Office show that this cemetery was acquired from the Lakeville United Church of Christ in 1972. It measures about 3 acres. Entries were made between September 24 and November 8, 2001.

____, Alton   *"ALTON"* is inscribed on this flat, ground level footstone. A low concrete wall surrounds this plot for William H. Burnham.

____, Son   *"SON"* is inscribed on this flat, six-inch square stone. The words *"ROCK / OF / AGES"* are inscribed within a circle on the bottom right side. It is located in front of the back wall of the cemetery.

____, Lois   *"LOIS"* is inscribed on this flat, ground level stone. It is located to the right of the Chester Burnham plot. To the right of this stone is an empty stone base.

Allen, Clara M.   See John G. Allen Monument entry.
"CLARA" is inscribed on this flat, ground level stone. It is located in front of the monument, on the left.

Allen, John G. Monument   *"ALLEN"* is inscribed on the front of this monument. Floral carvings are on the sides. *"JOHN G. ALLEN / 1886 – 1972 / CLARA M. HIS WIFE / 1888 – 1968 / AND CHILDREN"* is inscribed on the back. An Albert F.

Richmond Memorials metal tag is present.

"JOHN G." is inscribed on this flat, ground level stone. It is located directly in front of the monument, on the right.

Ammon *"__ Memory __ / Ammon a Negro / Man belong^d to / Cap! William Canedy, / he Died March y̆^e / 30 .^th 1778 in y̆^e 29 .^th / Year of his Age."* *"1881"* is carved on the bottom left. This rear facing, slate stone is encased in cement. The top and shoulders are missing. According to Mansfield's research, this stone had been moved from Race Course Cemetery, where his body lies. A flat, ground level stone currently marks his grave at that cemetery.

Andrews, E. Frank See George M. DeMaranville Monument entry.
"FRANK EDWARD ANDREWS / US ARMY / WORLD WAR II / JUL 18 1924 NOV 19 1984" is inscribed on this flat, ground level stone. A circled cross is carved at the top of this rear facing stone. A veteran's marker and flag are present. It is located directly behind the monument, on the right.

Andrews, Mildred See George M. DeMaranville Monument entry.
"MILDRED" is carved on this black, ground level footstone. It faces the rear of the cemetery and is located directly behind the monument, on the left.

Ashley, Asenath L. *"ASENATH L. ASHLEY / 1839 – 1908"* This flat, 0-2 inch high stone faces the rear of the cemetery. She was the wife of John C. Ashley.

Ashley, Henry A. *"HENRY ALSON, / Son of John C. & / A. L. Ashley, / died Apr. 22, 1864. / Aged 3 yrs. 1 m. / & 15 d's."* There is a relief carving of a broken bud at the top of this stone. The stone is leaning backwards, and faces the rear of the cemetery. A crack is present which extends from the bottom up through the last two lines.

Ashley, Infant *"Infant Daughter / of John C. & / Aseneth L. Ashley"* This stone is lying face up on the ground behind Henry A. Ashley's stone. Lakeville Vital Records list a female born to John and Aseneth Ashley on August 11, 1866. No death record is listed. On her mother's gravestone, the name is spelled *Asenath*.

Ashley, John C. *"J. C. ASHLEY / CO. C. / 4 MASS. INF."* is carved in relief within a recessed shield shaped area. There are no dates on this rear facing stone. A veteran's marker and flag are present. His first name was obtained from his children's gravestones. *Massachusetts Civil War Soldiers and Sailors, 1861-1865,* Vol. I, p. 238 lists him as being 25 when he enlisted in 1862. Lakeville Vital Records list his death on June 18, 1897, at 59 years, 8 months, and 8 days old.

B., C. *"C. B."* is crudely inscribed on this rough-cut fieldstone.

Ball, Ida C. *"IDA CASWELL BALL / 1900 1938"* This flat, ground level stone is beginning to be buried. It faces the rear of the cemetery and is beneath a large evergreen bush.

Barrows, Ebenezer *"In Memory of M_ / Ebenezer Barrows w__ / died Apri_ 2_____ / in y̆^e 9__ Year __ / his Ag_."* An angel with upright wings is carved at the top of this rear facing stone. The right side is missing. A crack runs from the top to the bottom near the center of this slate stone, and there is an additional crack that joins it in the tympanum. The last line is buried underground. A *"SAR 1775"* marker and flag are present. Thatcher lists his information as "died April 23, 17__; in his 90th year." *Middleborough, Massachusetts Vital Records,* Vol. 2, p. 9 lists his birth on July 27, 1702. *Vital Records of Taunton, Bristol Co. MA to the end of the year 1849,* Vol. III, p. 26 lists his burial date as April 25, 1792.

"Mr / Ebenezer Barrows" is inscribed on this slate footstone. The inscription is buried underground.

Barrows, Esther *"In / memory of / MRS. ESTHER wife of / Mr. George Barrows / who died / Dec. 14. 1809 / in her 44 · / year."* This rear facing, slate stone has an urn and willow carving at the top. Designs are carved down the sides.
"E. B." is inscribed on the slate footstone.

Barrows, George *"In / memory of / MR. GEORGE BARROWS / who died / Nov. 30. 1826 / in his 75. / year."* This rear facing slate stone has an urn and a willow carved at the top. Scalloped designs are carved down the sides.
"G. B." is inscribed on the slate footstone.

Barrows, John, Capt. *"Memento Mori / _n Memory of / _ap[t]. John Barrows, / who Died Nov[r]. y̆, 30th. / 1782 · In the 40th. Year / of his Age · /*
Naked as from the earth we came
And crept to life at first.
We to the earth return again,
And mingle with our dust."
There has been some exfoliation on the left side of this rear facing, slate stone. The first line is carved along an arch at the top of the tympanum. A winged angel is carved below this. The last two lines are buried underground. A *"SAR 1775"* marker, and a veteran's marker and flag are present.
"_ap[t]. / J. Barrows" is inscribed on the slate footstone. It is located face up on the ground in front of the headstone for Sarah Shaw.

Barrows, Mary *"IN MEMORY OF / MARY BARROWS, / (DAUGH[r] OF M[r] / EBEN[r] & M[rs] / SARAH BARR[O]WS) / WHO DIED MAY / y̆ 22nd 1759 IN / y̆ 19th YEAR OF / HER AGE"* There is a simple head carving at the top of this slate stone, with semicircular rows of small curved designs behind it. A leaf carving extends down the sides of this lichen encrusted, rear facing stone.
"M. __ / 1759" The upper right corner of this slate footstone is chipped off.

Barrows, Sarah *"Here lies / Mrs. Sarah, widow of / Mr. Ebenezer Barrows. / Died June 9th, 1793. / Aged 88 Years."* A peeking rising sun is carved at the top of this rear facing, slate stone. Thatcher lists her as being in her "88th year"
"Mrs. S, Barrows / 1793" is inscribed on the footstone. The last line is buried underground.

Barrows, Susannah *"_N MEMORY OF / SUSANNAH BARR- / OWS, DAU[tr] OF M[r]. / EBEN[r]. BARROWS & / M[rs] SARAH HIS / WIFE, DEC[D] MAY y̆ / 17: 1749 IN y̆ 14th / YEAR OF HER AGE."* There is a simple head carving at the top of this rear facing, slate stone. The shoulders have begun to exfoliate. Note the carving of the

NN in *SUSANNAH, AR* in *SARAH* and *YEAR* and the *HE* in *HER* are overlapped. *"S B / 1749"* is inscribed on the slate footstone.

Bassett, Bethiah   *"In memory of / BETHIAH, / wife of / Dea. Caleb Bassett; / who died / April 19, 1832, in / her 70 year."* The first line is carved along an arch. This rectangular slate stone has an urn and willow carving at the top. There are two horizontal cracks and two diagonal cracks running through the stone. Small, shallow designs are carved in a circle around the inscription.
"B. B." This slate footstone is located in front of the headstone.

Bassett, Caleb, Dea

> *"In memory of*
> *DEA. CALEB*
> *BASSETT,*
> *who died*
> *March 27, 1841, in*
> *his 84 year."*

The first line is carved along an arch. An urn and willow carving is at the top of this rectangular slate stone. Small, shallow designs are carved in a circle around the inscription. Thatcher lists 1844 as his death year.
"C. B." This slate footstone is located in front of the headstone.

Bassett, Lewis   *"In Memory of / LEWIS, / Son of Caleb Bassett / died May 11, 1822, / Æt. 32."* An urn is carved at the top of this lichen encrusted, slate stone.

Bassett, Sarah M.   *"SARAH M. / Wife of / Mr. Keith Bassett, / died Aug. 30, 1830,*
/ Æt 34. /
> *Unveil thy bosom faithful tomb,*
> *Take this new treasure to thy trust;*
> *And give these sacred relicks room,*
> *To slumber in the silent dust.*
> *B. Leonard Bridger.."*

An urn and willow are carved on this lichen-encrusted, slate stone. The first line is carved in outline. Note the spelling of *relicks*.
"S. M. B. / 1830." This slate footstone is located in front of the headstone. The first line is carved in partial outline.

Blackman, Lucy   *"To the memory of / LUCY BLACKMAN, / who died / July 15, 1860, / Aged 68 yrs."* is inscribed on this textured stone.
"L. B." This footstone is located in front of the headstone.

Braley, Serena J.   *"SERENA J. KEYES / WIDOW OF D. B. CASWELL / WIFE OF E. R. BRALEY / BORN DEC. 5, 1860 / DIED APRIL 16, 1927"* is embossed on a metal plaque which is attached to this rear facing stone. Circular designs are carved at the top of the stone.

Briggs, Anna M.   *"ANNA M. BRIGGS / Daughter of / DANIEL & JULIA / BRIGGS. / Died Feb. 12, 1884, / In the 61ˢᵗ year / of her age."* The first line is carved along an arch. *"ANNA"* is carved in relief on the back. A low concrete wall surrounds this Montgomery plot.

Briggs, Daniel   See Julia Briggs Monument entry.

Briggs, Julia Monument   *"MOTHER. / JULIA MONTGOMERY / wife of / DANIEL BRIGGS. / Feb. 7, 1798, / Apr. 6, 1880. / At rest. / DANIEL BRIGGS. / Died Jan. 20, 1849, / Aged 53 yrs."* The second line is carved along an arch. *"JULIA"* is carved in relief on the back of this stone. A low concrete wall surrounds this Montgomery plot.

Burnham, Ada E.   See Chester W. Burnham Monument entry.
"MOTHER" is inscribed on this flat, ground level stone. It is located in front of the Chester Burnham Monument, on the left. A low concrete wall surrounds this plot.

Burnham, Amelia M.   *"BABY"* is inscribed on the top curved surface of this stone. *"AMELIA M. / BURNHAM / BORN DEC. 6, 1946 / DIED DEC. 6, 1946"* is inscribed on the front. A low cement wall surrounds this plot which includes the Gilbert Westgate Monument and the Charles H. Westgate Monument.

Burnham, Bessie   *"BESSIE"* is inscribed on this broken, flat, ground level stone. A low concrete wall surrounds this plot for William H. Burnham. Taunton Vital Records list the birth of Bessie Olive Burnham, daughter of William and Annie Burnham, on January 30, 1909, and her death on April 29, 1909.

Burnham, Chester W. Monument   *"BURNHAM / CHESTER W. BURNHAM / 1890 – 1954 / ADA E. HIS WIFE / 1894 – 1979"* A lamp is carved in the lower left corner. Flowers are carved on the left side and at the bottom of this monument. An Albert F. Richmond metal tag is present. A low concrete wall surrounds this plot.
"FATHER" is inscribed on this flat, ground level stone. It is located in front of the monument, on the far left.

Burnham, Harry L.   *"HARRY L. BURNHAM / 1896 – 1978"* A low concrete wall surrounds this slanted stone and Mary Burnham's stone.

Burnham, Mary V.   *"WIFE / MARY V. BURNHAM / 1894 – 1938"* Floral carvings adorn the upper corners of this slanted stone. A low concrete wall surrounds it and Harry Burnham's stone.

Burnham, William H. Monument   *"BURNHAM / 1865   WILLIAM H.   1943 / DIETRICH / 1873   ANNA M.   1930"* A low concrete wall surrounds this plot for William H. Burnham.

Burr, George J.   *"GEORGE J. BURR, / died Oct. 31, 1859, / Aged 32 yrs. 9 mo. /*
> *Dearest Husband thou hast left me,*
> *Here my loss I deeply feel:*
> *But 'tis God who has bereft me.*
> *He can all my sorrows heal."*

The first line is carved in shadow. An open book is carved in relief at the top. The words inscribed on the pages are unreadable due to weathering. This tall, textured stone faces the rear of the cemetery.

"*G. J. B.*" is inscribed on the footstone.

Burrell, Lony   "*LONY BURRELL / 1797 – 1876*" is inscribed on the slanted surface of this small rear facing, stone. There are floral designs in the upper corners.

C., D.   "*D C*" is crudely carved on this rear facing fieldstone. The *D* is carved backwards.

C., T.   "*T C*" is crudely carved on this fieldstone.

Cain, George S.   "*GEORGE STAPLES / son of / Capt. Samuel & Serena / Cain. / died Aug. 21, 1840, / aged 11 years. /*

> *His mind was tranquil and serene*
> *No terrors in his looks were seen*
> *His Saviour's smiles dispell'd the gloom*
> *And smooth'd his passage to the tomb."*

This stone is broken off at ground level and is lying face up behind the bottom portion.

"*G. S. C.*" This footstone is located in front of the headstone.

Cain, Lucy   "*LUCY, / Wife of / SAMUEL CAIN. / Born June 24, 1777. / Died April 10, 1856. /*

> *A faithful wife, a mother dear.*
> *In quiet rest reposes here.*
> *No sorrow clouds her thoughtful brow,*
> *Or breaks her peaceful slumbers now.*
> *For through a kind Redeemer's love,*
> *Her spirit dwells with God above."*

The first line is carved in relief on this rear facing stone.

"*L. C.*" is inscribed on the footstone.

Cain, Samuel   "*SAMUEL CAIN, / Born / Sept. 21, 1772, / Died / Aug. 31, 1857. /*

> *When trembling limbs refuse their weight,*
> *And films slow gathering dim the sight,*
> *And clouds obscure the mental light,*
> *'Tis nature's precious boon to die."*

The first line is carved in relief on this rear facing stone.

"*S. C.*" is inscribed on the footstone.

Cain, Samuel   "*SAMUEL CAIN, / Born / Jan 1, 1801. / Died / Sept. 6, 1876. / Angels bore his gentle spirit, / Where the living waters flow.*" The first line is carved in shadow on this rear facing stone. It is separated from its base, and is placed in the ground behind it.

"*S. C.*" This footstone is leaning against the front of the headstone.

Cain, Serena   "*SERENA, / Wife of / SAMUEL CAIN; / Born Aug. 14, 1803, / Died Oct. 5, 1857. /*

> *Sharp were her pains her trials long,*
> *Her faith was great her patience strong.*
> *No murmuring thought disturbed her breast,*
> *What Jesus ordered: she thought best.*
> *Then weep not for the loved one fled,*

To realms more pure a home more fair:
And call not the departed dead!
She lives she loves, she waits you there."

The first line is carved in shadow on this rear facing stone. It is separated from its base, and is placed in the ground behind it.

"S. C." This footstone is leaning against the front of the headstone.

Canedy, Barnabas   *"Barnabas / Canedy. / 1785."* is inscribed on this slate footstone, which faces the front of the cemetery. No headstone is present. There is a leaf or tree carving in the tympanum. The very top of it is broken off and missing. Thatcher lists him as the "son of Noble & Hope, Nov. 30, 1785, 8 da."

Canedy, Barnebus, Ens.   *"In Memory of / Ens^n. Barnebus, / Canedy who / Died Jan^{ry} / ^e_y 22^d 1776 / Aged 41 / Years."* A winged angel is carved at the top of this rear facing, slate stone. Floral and leaf carvings are on the sides. This lichen encrusted stone is beginning to exfoliate. The last line is buried underground.

"Ens^n. / Barnebu^s / Canedy" is inscribed on the slate footstone.

Canedy, Charity   *"In MEMORY of Mrs. CHARITY / widow of Capt. William Canedy & / Dautr of Elkanah Leonard Esq,r. / she Departed this Life Oct'r 13th Æ D. 1805. / in the 74th Year of her Age. /*

Under these clods the body lies
The soul triumphs above the skes
No sore temptations reach the place
Nor guilt to hide the Saviours face
When the bright morning doth appear
When gabriels trumpit all shall hear
This sleeping dust shall rise again
And with the Saviour li_e and reig_."

A leaning tree is carved at the top of this large, rear facing, slate stone. Semicircular designs are carved above the inscription and on the sides. The *D* of *Departed* is carved backwards. Note the different spellings for *skes*, and *trumpit*.

"Mrs / CH^{A}RITY / CANADY / died 1805" is inscribed on this large footstone. Note the different spellings of *Canedy* on the head and footstones.

Canedy, Elizabeth   *"In Memory of M^{rs} / Elizabeth Widow of / Esqr. William Canedy / She died May ^e_y 5th 1780 / in ^e_y 79th Year of her Age."* A winged angel is carved at the top of this rear facing, slate stone.

"Mrs / Elizabe_h / Canedy" This slate footstone is broken in half diagonally through the last two lines. It faces the headstone.

Canedy, Elkanah L.   *"Elkanah / Leonard Son of / Cap Noble & Mrs. Hope / Canedy. he died Oct. 19th 1800. / Aged nine months & nine Days /*

'Tis God that lifts our comforts high,
Or sinks them in the grave
He gives, and blessed be his name,
He takes but what he gave."

This lichen-encrusted slate stone faces the rear of the cemetery.

"Elkanah / Leonard / Canedy / died / 1800" is inscribed on the footstone. The last

line is partially underground.

Canedy, Hope   *"In memory of / MRS. HOPE wife of / Capt. Noble Canedy / who died / July 10. 1829, / in her 68. / year /*

> *'Tis finish'd the conflict is past,*
> *The heav'n born sperit is fled;*
> *Her wish is accomplish'd at last,*
> *And now she's entomb'd with the dead."*

"Geo. Thompson" is inscribed at the bottom. An urn and willow are carved in relief at the top of this slate stone. Curved designs extend down its sides. George Thompson's tornado like swirl is carved below the poem. The *d* in *Canedy* has a vertical tail like the "y" next to it. Note the spelling of *sperit* in the poem. An exfoliated footstone is present in front of the headstone. No inscribed pieces were found.

Canedy, Mary B.   *"MARY B. / DAU. OF / ZEBULON L. & / OLIVE CANEDY; / died / April 14, 1832, / aged 14 years."* The first line is carved in relief. Thatcher lists her death year as 1832/33.
"M. B. C." is inscribed on the footstone, which is located in front of the headstone.

Canedy, William, Capt.   *"Sacred to the MEMORY of / Cap. WILLIAM CANEDY / who departed this Life March 26th, / Æ 1804 in ye 75th Year of his Age /*

> *With love divine and pure delight,*
> *On faiths ceelestial wing,*
> *With sweet repose he took his flight*
> *For death had lost his sting*
> *Great God I won thy sentence just*
> *And yield my body to the dust."*

There is a frond carving at the top of this large, lichen encrusted, rear facing, slate stone. Tree outlines are carved along the sides. Note the spelling of *ceelestial*. A *"SAR 1775"* marker and flag are present.
"Cap't / William / Canedy / died March 26th, / 1804." is inscribed on this large, slate footstone.

Canedy, William, Esq.   *"In Memory of / William Canedy Esq. / Who Dec^d. JUNE y^e · 23^d. / 1774 in ye 86th. Year / of his Age.*

> *Silent the Warrior lies: He Shall no more*
> *Scurge the wild Natives of the eastern Shore*
> *His honorable Titles with Him fall;*
> *He leaves behind him friends & earthly all.*
> *His Soul immortal, was it calm'd with Peace*
> *Before he fled: his joy Shall never cease.*
> *Go widow'd Consort. trust in GOD most High.*
> *Children bereav'd to Heaven for Grace now cry,*
> *That after Death to Glory you may rise above ye Sky.*
>   *REPLACED 1913"*

This rear facing, slate, replacement stone has a smiling winged angel carved in relief at the top. Leaf designs are carved in relief down the sides.

"William / Canedy Esqr. / Dec^d. 1774" is inscribed on this original slate footstone.

Caswell, Abiah   *"Miss ABIAH dau. of / Mr. DAVID and / Mrs. ANNES CASWELL / died April 2. 1817 / in her 32. / year."* An urn and willow are carved at the top of this lichen encrusted, rear facing, slate stone. Curved designs are carved along the sides and above the inscription. A George Thompson swirl is carved under the last line.

Caswell, Abigail W.   See Abraham Caswell Monument entry.
"ABBY" is inscribed on the top slanted and curved surface of this footstone. It is 4 inches high and faces the rear of the cemetery. It is located directly in front of the Abraham Caswell Monument, on the left.

Caswell, Abraham   See Abraham Caswell Monument entry.
"ABRAHAM CASWELL / died / Feb. 24, 1859, / Aged 68 yrs. / & 24 d's. /

He is not dead our father dear.
And when our life is ended here,
We'll meet again to part no more,
From th'loved of earth who've gone before."

The first line is carved in relief along an arch. This textured stone is located to the left of the Abraham Caswell Monument. An empty base is located behind and to the left of this stone.
"A. C." This footstone is located in front of the headstone.

Caswell, Abraham Monument   *"ABRAHAM CASWELL / BORN / MAR. 12, / 1816, DIED / APR. 11, 1880. / HIS WIVES / PHEBE HOWLAND / BORN / FEB. 29, / 1816, DIED / SEPT. 22, 1848. / ABIGAIL W. BRADFORD / BORN / JUNE 14, 1817. / DIED JUNE 16, 1888."* is inscribed on the southwest side of this tall gable roofed monument. It is rotated 45 degrees from the front of the cemetery. *"CASWELL."* is inscribed on the upper base. The first, sixth, seventh, and twelfth lines are carved along an arch. Part of the "1" in Abigail's death day is broken off, making it look like a period. Part of the "E" in her death month is broken off also. *"ABRAHAM CASWELL / BORN / JAN. 31, / 1791 DIED / FEB. 24, 1859. / HIS WIFE / ELIZA CHASE / BORN / JUNE 26, / 1796, DIED / MAR. 19, 1884."* is inscribed on the northwest side of this monument. The first, sixth and seventh lines are carved along an arch. *"MARY JANE / BORN / OCT. 8, 1843, DIED / MAR. 26, 1881. / DAU. OF ABRAHAM & / PHEBE CASWELL."* is inscribed on the southeast side of this monument. The first line is carved along an arch. All inscriptions on this monument are carved in relief. Designs are carved at the top of this textured monument on all four sides. No inscription is present on the northeast side.

Caswell, Annis   *"In memory of / MRS. ANNIS / wife of Mr. David Caswell / who died / Sept. 13, 1830, / in her 75 year."* This rear facing, slate stone has an urn and willow carving at the top. Curved designs are carved down its sides.

Caswell, Belony W.   *"BELONY W. / Son of / Martin L. & Celia S. / CASWELL. / Died March 10. / 1856. / Aged 4 months. / 6 days."* This stone faces the rear of the cemetery.
"B. W. C." is inscribed on the footstone.

Caswell, Benj. W.   See Ella M. Caswell Monument entry.

Caswell, David   *"In / memory of / MR. DAVID CASWELL / who died / Jan. 22. 1825 / in his 84. / year."* An urn and willow are carved at the top of this rear facing, slate stone, and designs are carved down the sides. The left part of this stone was broken vertically and successfully repaired. A crack runs through the carving at the top. All of the *2's* carved on this stone looks like a 9 with a tail.

Caswell, David   *"DAVID CASWELL / Died Sept. 7, 1837; / in his 59 th year. / "Say ye to the righteous, that it shall / be well with him.""* There is a low stone post and metal rail fence surrounding this grave, and that of Phebe J. and Lois Caswell. *"D. C."* This footstone is located in front of the headstone.

Caswell, David B.

"DAVID B. CASWELL. DIED NOV. 1, 1894. AGED 31 YRS. 1 MO. 17 DAYS."

Floral and leaf carvings are present at the top of this rear facing stone.

Caswell, Edward T. Monument   *"C (monogram) / EDWARD T. CASWELL / 1868 – 1948 / GRACE M. HIS WIFE / 1870 – 1927"* Floral carvings adorn the upper corners of this rear facing stone.

Caswell, Eliab   *"ELIAB CASWELL / died March 15, 1873; / Aged 72 years, / 11 mos. & 15 d's. / This is not our home."* This stone faces the rear of the cemetery.

Caswell, Eliza   *"ELIZA, / Wife of / ELIAB CASWELL, / Died / Aug. 11, 1860. / Aged / 61 years, 4 months, / 9 days. / Thou art gone, but not forgotten."* *"D. A. BURT, Taunton."* is inscribed on the bottom right. This stone faces the rear of the cemetery.

Caswell, Eliza C.   See Abraham Caswell Monument entry.

Caswell, Ella M. Monument   *"CASWELL"* is inscribed at the top of this slanted, 4-6 inch high stone. *"ELLA M / 1865 – 1943"* is inscribed on the left below this, and *"BENJ W / 1860 – 1942"* is inscribed on the right. Floral carvings are in the upper corners of this pebbled stone.

Caswell, Grace M.   See Edward T. Caswell Monument entry.

Caswell, Kenneth E.   *"Caswell"* is inscribed in outline on the front of this monument. *"Kenneth E. / Caswell / 1907 – 1977"* is inscribed in outline on the back. Floral carvings are carved above this. A Barnicoat Monuments metal tag is present.

Caswell, Kenneth M.   See Stanley C. Simmons Monument entry.

"KENNETH" is inscribed on this flat, 1 inch high footstone. It is located behind the monument, on the right.

Caswell, Leavitt C.   See Stanley C. Simmons Monument entry.
"LEAVITT" is inscribed on this flat, 2 inch high footstone. It is located in front of the monument, on the far right.

Caswell, Lois   *"LOIS, / wife of / David Caswell, / died Jan. 24, 1868; / in her 84 th year. / "Because I live ye shall live also.""* There is a low stone post and metal rail fence surrounding this grave, and that of David and Phebe J. Caswell.
"L. C." This footstone is located in front of the headstone.

Caswell, Lucy   *"Miss LUCY dau. of / Mr. DAVID and / Mrs. ANNES CASWELL. / died July 12, 1808 / in her 31. / year."* An urn and willow are carved at the top of this rear facing, slate stone. Curved designs are carved below this and on the sides. The *2* in the inscription resembles a 9 with a tail. A George Thompson swirl is carved under the last line.

Caswell, Lucy P.   *"LUCY P. / dau. of David & Lois / Caswell, / died Aug. 8, 1872; / Aged 60 yrs. 10 m's / & 12 d's. / She was the light of home."* This headstone faces the rear of the cemetery.
"L. P. C." is inscribed on the footstone.

Caswell, Mary E.   *"MARY ELIZA. / Daughter of / Belony C. & Mary R. / CASWELL. / Died Oct, 1, 1855. / Aged 1 year. 3 Mos. / 24 days. /*
> *Sleep on dear child,*
> *And take thy rest;*
> *For such as thee.*
> *Our Saviour blest."*

"D. A. BURT. Taunton." is inscribed on the bottom right. This stone is broken off at ground level, and is lying face up behind the bottom portion.
"M. E. C." This footstone is located in front of the headstone.

Caswell, Mary Jane   *"C (monogram) / MARY JANE / 1828 – 1903 / WIDOW OF / ELIAB CASWELL"* This stone faces the rear of the cemetery.

Caswell, Mary Jane   See Abraham Caswell Monument entry.

Caswell, Nettie P.   See Stanley C. Simmons Monument entry.
"NETTIE" is inscribed on this flat, 4-5 inch high footstone. It is located in front of the monument, on the right.

Caswell, Phebe H.   See Abraham Caswell Monument entry.

Caswell, Phebe J.   *"SACRED / to the memory of / PHEBE J. / wife of Horatio L. / Caswell; / who died / Sept. 25, 1842, in / her 22 year."* The first line is carved along an arch, and the last line is carved along an upside down arch. The third line is carved in relief. There is a low stone post and metal rail fence surrounding this grave, and that of David and Lois Caswell.
"P. J. C." This footstone is lying face up on the ground in front of the headstone.

Caswell, Richard B. Jr., Rev.   *"REV. RICHARD B. / CASWELL JR / 1943 –*

1971" is inscribed on this flat, 2-4 inch high stone.

Caswell, Richard B. Sr. Monument   *"CASWELL"* is inscribed on the front of this monument. Floral carvings adorn the upper corners. *"RICHARD B. CASWELL $^{SR.}$ / 1909 – 1985 / S. HELEN HIS WIFE / 1918 – 2001"* is inscribed on the back.

Caswell, S. Helen   See Richard B. Caswell, Sr. Monument entry.

Caswell, Sarah M.   See Stanley C. Simmons Monument entry.
"SARAH M. CHANDLER / WIFE OF / STETSON CASWELL / APR. 30, 1837 / MAY. 29, 1915" is inscribed on this stone, which is located in front of the monument, on the left. The first line is carved along an arch. The stone, with its base still attached, is lying on its back. The gravestone is at ground level, but its base extends 2 inches above ground.
"SARAH" is inscribed on the top of this flat, 4-5 inch high footstone. It is directly in front of the headstone.

Caswell, Stetson   See Stanley C. Simmons Monument entry.
"STETSON CASWELL / JUNE 3, 1823, / MARCH 30, 1902. / Gone but not forgotten." The first line is carved along an arch. This stone is lying face up in front of the monument, on the far left. Note the two different birth dates. *Middleborough, Massachusetts Vital Records,* Vol. 1, p. 386 list his birth year as 1823.
"STETSON" is inscribed on the top horizontal surface of this 6-inch high footstone. It is located directly in front of his headstone.

Churchill, Chloe J.   *"CHLOE J. / Wife of / George W. Churchill, / died May 15, 1877, / Aged 62 years. / Gone Home."*
"C. J. C." This footstone is located in front of the headstone.

Churchill, Libeus C.   *"LIBEUS C. CHURCHILL / BORN / APR. 25, 1811, / DIED / JAN. 24, 1892. / GONE HOME."*

Churchill, Malancy J.   *"MALANCY J. / WIFE OF / LIBEUS CHURCHILL, / JULY 14, 1810. / JAN. 30. 1886. / AT REST."*

Churchill, Sarah   *"SARAH, / Wife of / Zebedee Churchill, / died July 6, 1874, / Aged 84 years."*
"S. C." This footstone is located in front of the headstone.

Cobb, Harriet   *"HARRIET N. COBB, / DIED MAY 20, 1882. / AGED 65 YRS. 7 MOS. / 24 DAYS."* Designs are carved in the upper corners of this small stone.

Cornell, Russell E., Jr.   *"OUR BABY / RUSSELL E. / CORNELL JR. / 1946 1947"* A lamb is carved between the birth and death year on this flat, ground level stone.

Crafts, Thomas, Rev.   *"In Memory / of the / REV. THOMAS CRAFTS, / who died Feb. 27, 1819. / In the 61 Year of his Age, / & 33 of his / Ministry. / "The fruit of the righteous is a tree of life / And he that winneth soul is wise.""   "-B. Leonard, Sc. Bridge'."* is inscribed at the bottom. An urn and willow carving is at the top of this green, lichen encrusted, slate stone. Zigzag designs are carved around the urn and willow, and columns are carved on the sides.

"*T. C. / 1819.*" A leaf design is carved at the top. This dark slate footstone is located in front of the headstone.

Crane, Betsey A.   See Gershom Crane Monument entry.
Information listed by Thatcher suggests that a different gravestone was present during his survey: "dau. of Gershom & Sally, May 10, 1846, 28 yrs., 27 da."
"*B. A. C.*" is carved in relief on the top curved surface of this upright footstone. It is located to the left of the monument.

Crane, Caroline   See Gershom Crane Monument entry.
Information listed by Thatcher suggests that a different gravestone was present during his survey: "dau. of Gershom & Sally, July 17, 1846, 29 yrs., 6 m., 17 da."
"*C. C.*" is carved in relief on the top curved surface of this upright footstone. It is located to the far left of the monument.

Crane, Ebenezer   See Gershom Crane Monument entry.
"*E. C.*" is carved in shallow relief on the top curved surface of this upright footstone. It is located behind the monument, on the far left.

Crane, Gershom Monument   "*GERSHOM CRANE, / AUG. 28, 1778 – JAN. 22, 1848. / SALLY CRANE, / MAY 29, 1795 – FEB. 27, 1875, / CHILDREN / CAROLINE / JAN. 1, 1817 – JULY 17, 1846. / BETSEY ALLEN / APR. 13, 1818 – MAY 10, 1846. / EBENEZER / NOV. 2, 1820 – MAR. 22, 1899.*" is inscribed on the front of this monument "*CRANE*" is carved in relief on the front base. "*WILLIAM STROBRIDGE, / MARCH 14, 1762 – SEPT. 5, 1842. / HIS WIFE / HANNAH STROBRIDGE, / SEPT. 7, 1760 – JULY 30, 1826.*" is inscribed on the back. "*C. HARRINGTON*" is inscribed in lower left corner on the back. Designs are carved at the top and in the upper corners of the inscribed area on both the front and back of this monument. Thatcher's listing of the gravestones of Betsey and Caroline Crane, and William and Hannah Strobridge suggest that they had individual stones when he did his survey. Sally Crane was the daughter of William and Hannah Strobridge.

Crane, Sally   See Gershom Crane Monument entry.
"*S. C.*" is carved in shallow relief on the top curved surface of this upright footstone. It is located behind the monument, on the left.

Crossman, LeRoy P. Monument   "*CROSSMAN*" is inscribed on the front of this monument. Ivy leaves are carved on the left side. "*WHERE YOU STAND I ONCE STOOD*" is carved on the bottom. "*LEROY P. / NOV. 8, 1922 – MAY 7, 1983 / WIFE / STELLA P. (PESTANA) / MAY 28, 1925 ___ / LEROY R. / FEB. 12, 1944 ___ / KRISTIN LYNN ISAACSEN / APRIL 29, 1987 / LOTTIE E. WORDELL / FEBRUARY 12 – 13, 1968*" is inscribed on the back. A Barnicoat Monuments metal tag is present. An empty 36" x 12" base is located in front of the monument.

Crossman, LeRoy R.   See LeRoy P. Crossman Monument entry.

Crossman, Stella P.   See LeRoy P. Crossman Monument entry.

Dean, Barney T.   See Henry A. Dean Monument entry.
Massachusetts Civil War Soldiers and Sailors, 1861-1865, Vol. I, p. 495 shows that Barney T. Dean, of Taunton enlisted with the 7th Infantry, Co. F. in 1861.

Dean, Betsey See Henry A. Dean Monument entry.
The information listed by Thatcher suggests that a different gravestone was present during his survey: "wife of Henry A., Nov. 19, 1840, age 26 years."

Dean, Drusilla Monument *"MOTHER / DRUSILLA DEAN / JULY 3, 1831 / JUNE 27, 1905"* is inscribed on the left side of the monument, below ivy carvings. *"FATHER / JAMES A. DEAN / FEB. 14, 1830 / MAR. 10, 1908"* is inscribed on the right side, under oak leaf carvings. The first line on both sides is carved in relief. *"DEAN"* is carved in relief on the base.

Dean, Henry A. Monument *"D* (monogram) */ 1816,   HENRY A. DEAN,   1898. / 1814,   BETSEY, HIS WIFE,   1840. / 1820,   JULIA, HIS WIFE,   1869."* is inscribed on the front of this monument. Carvings surround the monogram, and separate it from the inscription below it. *"DEAN"* is inscribed on the base. *"1840   BARNEY T. DEAN   1928 / 1852,   RHODA FRANCES DEAN,   1913."* is inscribed on the back. *"F. Hanson"* is carved on the right side of this monument, at the bottom. The information for Betsey Dean in Thatcher's work suggests that she a separate stone before this monument was erected.

Dean, James A. See Drusilla Dean Monument entry.

Dean, Joshua, Rev. See Mary M. Dean Monument entry.

Dean, Julia See Henry A. Dean Monument entry.
"J. D." This footstone is located behind the monument, on the left.

Dean, Julia M. *"JULIA M. / Daughter of Henry A. & / Julia Dean, / died Aug. 30, 1846; / aged / 16 months & 5 days."* This small stone faces the rear of the cemetery.

Dean, Mary M. Monument *"MARY MONTGOMERY / wife of / REV. JOSHUA DEAN. / Oct. 26, 1788, / Mar. 27, 1843. / REV. JOSHUA DEAN / July 16, 1788, / July 12, 1824."* The first line is carved along an arch on this rear facing stone. *"MARY"* is carved in relief on the back with a *"D"* (monogram) carved at the bottom. *"Blessed are the dead which die in the Lord."* is inscribed on the upper base. Thatcher also lists her under her maiden name Montgomery. A low concrete wall surrounds this Montgomery plot.

Dean, Rhoda F. See Henry A. Dean Monument entry.

DeMaranville, E. May See George M. DeMaranville Monument entry.
"E. MAY" is carved in relief on this flat, black, ground level stone. There are leaf designs above and below the inscriptions. It is located in directly in front of the monument. Her obituary in *The Middleborough Gazette* 10/27/1977:19 shows her first name was Eliza.

DeMaranville, George M. Monument *"DEMARANVILLE / 1870   GEORGE M. 1949 / HIS WIFE / 1872   MABEL A. PARRY   1936 / 1893   E. MAY DAU.   1977 / SISTER / 1872   FLORA M. MATTESON   1966"* is inscribed on the front of this monument. The first line is carved in relief. *"ANDREWS / FORREST / 1886 JOHN A.   1948 / 1899   JOSEPHINE HIS WIFE   1992 / 1924   E. FRANK   1984 / 1925   MILDRED A. HIS WIFE   1994 / 1927   JOHN A.   1994 / 1928   LOUISE K. HIS WIFE   ____"* is inscribed on the back. The first two lines are carved in relief.

The death year for Mildred was added after the initial visit.

"FATHER" is carved in relief on this flat, ground level stone. Leaf designs are carved above and below the inscription. It is located in front of the George M. DeMaranville Monument on the far left.

DeMaranville, Mabel A. See George M. DeMaranville Monument entry.

"MOTHER" is carved in relief on this flat, ground level stone. Leaf designs are carved above and below the inscription. It is located in front of the monument, on the left.

DeMoranville, Charles E. *"CHARLES EDWARD / DeMORANVILLE / JAN. 16, 1964"* is inscribed on this flat, ground level stone. It is located just inside the low stone wall on the left in front of the Gerald C. DeMoranville Monument.

DeMoranville, Deborah F. See Shoman DeMoranville Monument entry.

DeMoranville, Evelyn L. See Gerald C. DeMoranville Monument entry.

DeMoranville, Frederick E. Monument *"DeMORANVILLE"* is carved on the front of the monument. Floral carvings are at the top. *"DeMORANVILLE / FREDERICK E. / 1875 – 1970 / HIS WIFE / ROSE A. / 1876 – 1962"* is inscribed on the back. A Barnicoat Monuments metal tag is present.

DeMoranville, Gerald C. Monument

> *"DEMORANVILLE*
> *1916   GERALD C.   1964*
> *HIS WIFE*
> *1918   EVELYN L.   1970"*

is inscribed on a carving of an open book. Above this is carved a cross lying on grapevines. A low stone wall surrounds this DeMoranville plot. A Barnicoat Monuments metal tag is present.
"GERALD C. DeMORANVILLE / 1916 – 1964 / EGGER FUNERAL HOME" is embossed on a marker located behind the monument, on the left. A wreath is embossed at the top.

DeMoranville, Harriet E. See Jesse H. DeMoranville Monument entry.

DeMoranville, Inez L. *"DeMORANVILLE"* is inscribed at the top of this monument. *"INEZ L. /1917 · 1974"* is inscribed on the bottom left, and *"JESSE N. / 1914 · 1965"* is inscribed on the bottom right. Ivy is carved in the upper corners. A low stone wall surrounds this DeMoranville plot.

DeMoranville, James F. *"JAMES F. / DeMORANVILLE / MAY 24, 1948 / AUG. 5, 1988"* is inscribed on the front of this black monument, below a carving of a motorcycle. *"HE HAS ACHIEVED SUCCESS / WHO HAS LIVED WELL, LAUGHED / OFTEN AND LOVED MUCH; WHO / HAS GAINED THE RESPECT OF / INTELLIGENT MEN AND THE LOVE / OF LITTLE CHILDREN, WHO / HAS FILLED HIS NICHE AND / ACCOMPLISHED HIS TASK; WHO / HAS TRIED*

EVERYTHING ONCE / IN LIFE, AND LEFT THE WORLD / BETTER THAN HE FOUND IT." is inscribed on the back. A low stone wall surrounds this DeMoranville plot.

DeMoranville, Jamie F. *"JAMIE F. / DEMORANVILLE / MAR. 25, 1978 / NOV. 22, 2003"* is inscribed on the top slanted surface of this monument. *"FESTER"* is inscribed on the vertical front, and *"SON OF / JAMES AND SANDRA"* is inscribed on the base. It was placed after the initial transcription. A low stone wall surrounds this DeMoranville plot.

DeMoranville, Jesse H. Monument *"DEMORANVILLE / JESSE HARRIET"* is inscribed on the front of this monument. There is a carving of a cabin in the woods at the top. *"JESSE H. / MAY 30, 1942 – JAN. 13, 1993 / BELOVED WIFE AND MOTHER / HARRIET E. / MAR. 7, 1941 – OCT. 20, 1985"* is inscribed on the back. *"REX / MT WKS."* is carved in the right side of the base.

DeMoranville, Jesse N. See Inez L. DeMoranville Monument entry.

DeMoranville, Leo F. Jr. See Leo F. DeMoranville Monument entry.
"DARLING" is inscribed on the top slanted surface of this stone. *"LEO F. / DEMORANVILLE JR. / 1945 – 1948"* is inscribed on the front.

DeMoranville, Leo F. Monument *"DEMORANVILLE / LEO FREDERICK / NOV. 21 1923 – NOV. 14, 1998 / HIS SON / LEO F. JR. 1945 – 1948"* There is a carving of a meadow with deer below the inscription. A Barnicoat Monuments metal tag is present. A ground level stone border surrounds this monument, and the stone of Leo DeMoranville, Jr. An empty 39" x 16" base is located to the right of the monument.
"⊹ / LEO F DEMORANVILLE / CPL US ARMY AIR FORCE / WORLD WAR II / NOV 21 1923 NOV 14 1998" is inscribed on this flat, ground level stone.

DeMoranville, Myron V. *"MYRON V. DEMORANVILLE / 1877 – 1965 / EGGER'S FUNERAL HOME"* is embossed on this marker. A wreath is embossed at the top.

DeMoranville, Rose A. See Frederick E. DeMoranville Monument entry.

DeMoranville, Shoman A. Monument *"D (monogram) / 1850 SHOMAN A. 1882 / HIS WIFE / 1852 DEBORAH F. 1928 / DEMORANVILLE"* The last line is carved in relief at the bottom of the stone. Maple leaves are carved at the top. A *"GAR 3"* marker is present. He is not listed in the *Massachusetts Civil War Soldiers & Sailors, 1861-1865.*

Dietrich, Anna M. See William H. Burnham Monument entry.
"MOTHER" is inscribed on this flat, ground level stone. There are ivy leaves in the upper left corner. A low concrete wall surrounds this plot for William H. Burnham.

Dugan, Nellie F. *"In Loving Memory of / NELLIE FROST DUGAN / 1878 – 1916"* Floral carvings are in the top left and the bottom right corners of this flat, ground level stone. This rear facing stone is beginning to be buried.

Dushane, Adeline See Francis Dushane Monument entry.

Dushane, Chauncey E.   See Francis Dushane Monument entry.

Dushane, Francis Monument   *"DUSHANE"* is inscribed on the front of this monument. There are floral carvings in the upper corners. *"1815   FRANCIS DUSHANE   1902 / 1836   ADELINE HIS WIFE   1914 / 1872   FRANK E.   1908 / 1873   CHAUNCEY E.   1911 / 1879   MINNIE HIS WIFE   1906"* is inscribed on the back. An A. F. Richmond Memorial metal tag is present.

Dushane, Frank E.   See Francis Dushane Monument entry.

Dushane, Minnie   See Francis Dushane Monument entry.

Eaton, Agusta S.   *"AGUSTA S. EATON / Died / Aug. 18, 1893, / Aged 69."* The first line of this rear facing stone is inscribed along an arch.

Ellis, M. Maude   See Reuben Westgate Monument entry.

Ellis, Thomas P.   See Reuben Westgate Monument entry.

Elms, Abner   *"In memory of / ABNER ELMS. / who died March 1, 1836, in / his 72 year."* An urn and willow carving is at the top of this lichen encrusted, rear facing, slate stone. Small horizontal carvings extend down the sides.
"A. E." is inscribed on the footstone.

Elmes, Anner E.   *"Memento Mori. / In Memory of M^{rs}. / Anner wife of M^r. / Abner Elmes who died / march $_y^e$ 16th 1788 / in $_y^e$ 23^d Year of her / Age."* There is a winged angel carved between the first and second lines. This rear facing stone has a 2 inch square chunk of stone missing in the middle of the second last line. There are two stained areas on the carving. Note the lower case m in March.
"M^s. / Anner E. / Elmes" is inscribed on the footstone.

Elmes, Cyrus   *"CYRUS ELMES; / Died / July 17, 1864. / Aged / 63 years"*
"C. E." is inscribed on this footstone, which is located in front of the headstone.

Elmes, Cyrus O.   See Marshall B. Williams Monument entry.
Lakeville Vital Records list the death of Cyrus Elmes on December 30, 1903, at 77 years, 11 months, and 12 days old.

Elmes, Phebe   *"In memory of / PHEBE, / widow of / Abner Elmes, / who died / April 19, 1849, / in her 81st. Yr."* The second line is carved in shadow on this rear facing stone.
"P. E." This footstone faces the rear of the cemetery.

Elmes, Phebe A.   *"... __r of / ... Elmes. / ... 1850. / ... year.. / ... ds."* This weathered, textured stone is broken in two places. The top pieces are lying face up behind the remnant that is still in the ground. The above is all that can be read from it. Taunton Vital Records show that Phebe A. Elmes, daughter of Cyrus died on July 6, 1850, at 7 years old
"P. A. E." This footstone is lying face down on the ground.

Elmes, Nancy C.   See Marshall B. Williams Monument entry.
Taunton Vital Records list the death of Nancy Copeland Elmes on December 14, 1900, at 68 years, 9 months, and 3 days old.

Elmes, Silence   *"SILENCE, / Wife of / CYRUS ELMES. / Died / June 28, 1865, / Aged / 62 years. / An angel whispered to my Mother / And she slept."* is inscribed on this textured stone.
"S. E." This leaning footstone is located in front of the headstone.

Forrest, John A.   See George M. DeMaranville Monument entry.
"FATHER" is carved in relief on this black, ground level, rear facing footstone. Leaf designs are carved at the top and bottom. It is located behind the monument, on the far left side.

Forrest, John A. Stone   See George M. DeMaranville Monument entry.
"JOHN A. FORREST / HIS WIFE / LOUISE K. FORREST" is carved in relief on this ground level, rear facing stone. It is located to the right of the monument.

Forrest, Josephine   See George M. DeMaranville Monument entry.
"MOTHER" is carved in relief on this black, ground level, rear facing footstone. It is located behind the monument, on the left side.

Forrest, Louise K.   See George M. DeMaranville Monument entry.
See John A. Forrest Stone entry.

Fredette, Alfred J.   *"ALFRED J. FREDETTE / 1868 – 1955"* is inscribed on this flat, ground level stone.

French, Hadon   *"___ori / ___ory of M^{rs}.. / ___n French, wife / __ _^{r}. John French Ju^r / who died July y^e 18th / Ð. 1787 Aged 46 Years / 10 Months & 4 Days."* This rear facing, slate stone was broken diagonally from the tympanum to the fifth line. The left piece is missing. The first line was carved at the top of the tympanum, with a winged carving underneath. Thatcher lists her first name as Hadon.

Gay, Bradley Monument   *"GAY / 1866   BRADLEY L.   1948 / HIS WIFE / 1868 KATHERINE B.   1948 / 1894   EDNA R   1941 / 1890   LEWIS   1942 / 1900 HORACE F.   1974"* The first line is carved in relief. Floral carvings adorn the upper corners of this rear facing monument. An Albert F. Richmond metal tag is present.

Gay, Edna R.   See Bradley Gay Monument entry.

Gay, Horace F.   See Bradley Gay Monument entry.

Gay, Katherine B.   See Bradley Gay Monument entry.

Gay, Lewis   See Bradley Gay Monument entry.
"LEWIS GAY / 1890 – 1942" is embossed on this small, ground level funeral home marker. It is located to the left of the monument.

Gibbs, Dennis   *"Dennis Son of Mr. Elisha / & Mrs. Gibbs he died / Feb 6, 1811. / Aged 9 mts, / & 25 days. /*

> *Here lies a parents joy,*
> *A mother's tender care*
> *Tho' God has cut him down*
> *He'll raise him fresh & fair."*

An urn and willow carving is at the top of this rear facing, slate stone. Pieces are

missing at the top and left side of the tympanum. The third line of the poem contains ground down remnants of *He'll*, underneath the word *Tho* as if the carver skipped the third line, and then attempted to correct the error. Upon the revisit in 2003, this stone was face up on the ground.
"D. C." is inscribed on the slate footstone.

Gibbs, Elisha *"In memory of / MR. ELISHA GIBBS, / who died / Oct. 30, 1831, / in his 63, year."* There is an urn and willow carving at the top of this rear facing, slate stone. Located west of this stone is a piece of a slate tympanum which is placed in the ground on its right side. *"Memento Mori"* is inscribed above a carved angel. No other pieces were found.
"E. G." is inscribed on the slate footstone.

Goodwin, Sarah P. *"SARAH PICKENS GOODWIN / JAN. 18, 1798 / JAN. 9, 1827 / NOR SCULPTURED BRASS, / NOR MONUMENTAL STONE CAN ADD TO / HER IN WHOM THE VIRTUES SHONE"* This stone faces the rear of the cemetery.

H., F. *"F. H."* is inscribed on this flat stone that is beginning to be buried. It is located behind and to the left of the Montgomery Monument, next to Rosseter Hopkins' stone.

Hacket, John, Elder *"In Memory of Eld^r / John Hacket / who Dec^d Novem^r / y^e 11$^{\underline{th}}$ 1767 In / y^e 79$^{\underline{th}}$ year of / his Age."* A winged angel is carved at the top, and floral carvings are carved down the sides of this rear facing, slate stone.
"Eld^r / John Hacket" is inscribed on the slate footstone.

Hall, Abigail *"HE_ ... / L_ ... / ABIGAIL HALL / WAY_ ... AGED / _E_ ... / 1747"* is all that can be read on this crudely carved fieldstone. Thatcher lists her as "Hall, Abigail, Feb. 27, 1747"

Haskell, George E. *"GEORGE / E / HASKELL"* White metal letters are attached to this upright, cement stone. No dates are present. A flag is present.

Haskins, Adam J. *"OUR BABY A. J. / ADAM JAMES / HASKINS / MAY 11, 1993 / SON OF EDWARD AND SHERI"* A praying child angel is carved on the left side of this flat stone. A low cement wall encloses this stone and the Westgate Monuments.

Haskins, Albert *"ERECTED / to the memory of / ALBERT, / son of Dea. Andrew & / Lydia B. Haskins; / who died / Nov. 28. 1837. / aged 11 years. /*
>
> *Sleep on dear Albert in thy silent tomb*
> *Sleep on 'till our incarnate God shall come.*
> *Then burst thy tomb, with the triumphant rise*
> *To join the ransom'd millions in the skies."*

Haskins, Amelia K. *"AMELIA K. / Wife of / APOLLOS HASKINS, / Died Oct. 24, 1885, / Aged 81 Yrs. 27 Days. / Dear Mother we miss thee, but / our loss is thy gain."* The last two lines are buried underground on this rear facing stone.
"A. K. H." is inscribed on the footstone.

Haskins, Andrew, Dea. Monument *"DEA. / ANDREW HASKINS / died Oct. 26,*

1855, / aged 66 years. / LYDIA B. HASKINS. / died Jan. 4, 1841, / aged 47 years. / Erected / to the memory of / a beloved Father & Mother, / by their Children." The second and fifth lines are carved in relief on this rear facing stone. Thatcher lists her as in her 47th year.

"*A. H. & L. B. H.*" This footstone is located in front the headstone, on the right.

Haskins, Apollos   "*APOLLOS HASKINS, / Died / April 23, 1865. / Aged / 68 years, 4 months, / 29 days. / The Righteous shall go into Life Eternal.*"   "*BURT, Taunton*" is inscribed on the center bottom of this rear facing stone.

"*A. H.*" is inscribed on the footstone.

Haskins, Austin   "*AUSTIN HASKINS, / DIED MAR 23, 1908 / AGED 77YRS. 7MO. 22DS. / To Live in Hearts we leave be- / hind is not to die.*" This stone shares its lower base with the stone of Betsey S. Haskins. A low concrete wall surrounds the family plot.

Haskins, Betsey S.   "*BETSEY S. ATWOOD / WIFE OF / AUSTIN HASKINS, / DIED APR. 11, 1905. / AGED 69 YRS, 2 MOS, 14 DS. / He giveth his beloved sleep.*" This stone shares its lower base with that of Austin Haskins. A low concrete wall surrounds the family plot.

Haskins, Elmore P.   "*ELMORE P. HASKINS / SON OF / ORVILLE AND LYDIA B. / HASKINS / DEC. 10, 1849, / APR. 24, 1930.*" A low concrete wall surrounds this family plot.

Haskins, Emily A.   "*EMILY A. / Daughter of / Mr. Apollos Haskins Esq. & / Mrs. Amelia K. his wife. / Died April 5, 1850; / aged 12 yrs. 8 mos. & 28 ds. /*

> *And when this feeble stammering tongue,*
> *Lies silent in the grave:*
> *Then with a nobler sweeter song,*
> *I'll sing his power to save.*"

This stone faces the rear of the cemetery.

Haskins, Hannah   "*In / memory of / MRS. HANNAH wife of / Mr. Joshua Haskins / who died / Nov. 11. 1820 / in her 64. / year.*" An urn and willow are carved at the top of this rear facing stone, and scalloped designs are carved down the sides. The *2* in her death year looks like a 9 with a tail. There are horizontal cracks through the willow carving, and a steep through and through diagonal crack under the inscription. This slate stone shares a cement base with Joshua Haskins.

"*H. H.*" There is a horizontal crack in the middle of this slate footstone.

Haskins, Harriot   "*In memory of / HARRIOT / HASKINS, / who died / Aug. 23, 1834, / aged 20 years. / Her mind was tranquil and serene,*

> *No terrour in her looks were seen;*
> *Her Saviour's smiles dispell'd the gloom,*
> *And smooth'd her passage to the tomb.*"

This stone faces the rear of the cemetery. Note the spelling of *terrour* in the poem.

"*H. H.*" is inscribed on the footstone.

Haskins, Joseph C.   "*JOSEPH C. HASKINS, / BORN IN MIDDLEBORO, / JUNE 16, 1817. / DIED IN NEW BEDFORD, / OCT. 8, 1904.*" A low concrete wall surrounds this family plot.

Haskins, Joshua   *"ERECTED / in memory of / JOSHUA HASKINS / who died / Aug. 31, 1849. in / his 95 year."* *"G. Thompson"* is carved in the lower right corner. The first line is carved in shadow, and the third line is carved in outline. This rear facing stone shares its cement base with that of Hannah Haskins. There is a *"SAR 1775"* marker and flag present.
"J. H." is inscribed on the footstone.

Haskins, Joshua, Jr.   *"JOSHUA HASKINS JR.. / Died / Aug. 1, 1861, / Aged 77 yrs."* The first line is carved in shadow along an arch. This rear facing stone shares its base with that of Rebecca and Serena Haskins.
"J. H." is inscribed on the footstone.

Haskins, Levi   *"LEVI HASKINS, / Born Mar. 28, 1794 / Died Apr. 4, 1862 / Beloved in life, lamented in death."* The first line is carved in relief. A wide 3½ inch long crack radiates from the center bottom. The base has a 2½ inch crack in it also. A veteran's marker and flag are present.
"L. H." is inscribed on the footstone.

Haskins, Levi H.   *"LEVI H. / SON OF / LEVI & MARY / HASKINS, / DIED FEB. 29, 1908. / AGED 73 YRS. 9 MOS. / 7 DAYS. / A GOOD MAN IN WHOM WAS / NO GUILE"* The first line is carved in relief. There is a palm tree carved on the left of this stone. In *The Middleborough Gazette,* 3/6/1908:1, his Death Notice reports that he died in Detroit, Michigan.

Haskins, Lydia B.   See Dea. Andrew Haskins Monument entry.
"L. B. H." This footstone is located in front of the headstone, on the left side.

Haskins, Lydia B.   *"LYDIA B. KINSLEY. / Wife of / Orville Haskins. / Died May 7, 1887. / Aged 68 yrs. 3 ms / & 11 days."* The first line is carved along an arch. This stone shares a base with the stone of her husband. A low concrete wall surrounds this family plot.

Haskins, Martha   *"In memory of / MARTHA / dau. of Apollos & / Amelia K. Haskins / who died / Oct. 15, 1831 / Æt. 1 year, 7 mo. / & 12 days."* This stone faces the rear of the cemetery.

Haskins, Mary   *"MARY, / widow of / Levi Haskins, / died Sept. 26, 1871; / Aged 68 years. / Ever cherished will be thy memory."* The first line is carved in relief. The repair of a 4 inch crack radiating from the center bottom has failed.
"M. H." is inscribed on the footstone.

Haskins, Mary K.   *"MARY KINSLEY, / wife of / Joseph C. / HASKINS, / born July 31, 1821, / died in New Bedford / March 21, 1860, /*

> *Life's jeaurney is oe'r,*
> *And thy soul is at rest:*
> *For Jesus hath taken thee,*
> *Home with the blest."*

The first line is carved in relief along an arch. Notice the spelling of *jeaurney.*

Haskins, Mary S.   *"MARY S. / Dau. of / Levi & Mary / HASKINS, / Died Oct. 18, 1884. / Aged 55 yrs. 2 ms / & 21 days."*   The first line is carved in relief. There is a 4½ inch crack radiating from the center bottom. A repair attempt has failed.

Haskins, Mirick   *"Cut of in the morning of life / Mr. Mirick Haskins / who died September 30 th. / 1810 in the 24 th. Year / of his age. /*

> *One dieth in his full strength*
> *while his bones are moisten'd with marrow*
> *My flesh shall slumber in the ground,*
> *Till the last trumpets joyful sound*
> *Then burst the bars with sweet surprise,*
> *And in my Saviour's im_ge rise."*

There is a wide urn, and a willow carving at the top of this slate stone. Notice the spelling of *of* in the first line. This stone was broken off below the inscription and reburied in front of the piece in the ground. The last three lines are buried underground. A crack radiates from the bottom to the second line. A small, third piece (containing *Th* and *And* from the last two lines of the poem) was found on the ground in front of the broken base.
"Mr. / Mirick / Haskins." is inscribed on the slate footstone.

Haskins, Orin E.   *"ORIN E. HASKINS, / Born Jan. 6, 1845 / Died Apr. 30, 1922"*   The first line is carved in relief.

Haskins, Orville   *"ORVILLE HASKINS / Died / Feb. 19, 1893. / Aged 77 yrs. 7 mos / & 15 days."*   The first line is carved along an arch. A diagonal crack in the lower right corner extends through to the back of this stone. This stone shares its second base with that of his wife, Lydia. A low concrete wall surrounds this family plot.

Haskins, Rebecca S.   *"ERECTED / in memory of / REBECCA S. / wife of / JOSHUA HASKINS JR. / who died / Aug 21, 1839. / aged 49 years."*   The first line is inscribed along an arch, and the last line is carved in a reverse arch. The third line is carved in relief. This rear facing stone shares its base with that of Serena and Joshua Haskins.
"R. S. H." is inscribed on the footstone.

Haskins, Serena   *"Cut of in early life / Mrs. Serena wife of / Mr. Joshua Haskins jur. / who died / February 12 th. 1809 / in the 23. Year / of her age."*   A wide urn and a willow carved at the top of this rear facing, slate stone. Notice the spelling of *of* in the first line. There are two diagonal cracks on the left side extending to the second line from the bottom. This stone shares its base with that of Rebecca and Joshua Haskins.

"Mrs. / Serena / Haskins" The last line on this slate footstone is buried underground.

Hopkins, Bertha *"BERTHA"* is carved in relief on the top curved surface of this stone. *"June 14, 1868, / Aug. 14, 1868."* is inscribed on the front. This stone shares its base with Sadie and Rosseter's stones. Vital Records for the City of Somerville show she was the daughter of William H. and Fanny A. Hopkins.

Hopkins, Charles W. Monument *"CHARLES / CHARLES WATSON / SON OF / Wm H. & FANNY A. / HOPKINS / OCT. 16, 1861 / MAR. 19, 1929"* The first line is carved in relief. *"ELLA T. HIS WIFE / 1865 – 1951 / FANNY HIS DAUGHTER / 1888 – 1952"* is inscribed on the back

Hopkins, Ella T. See Charles W. Hopkins Monument entry.

Hopkins, Fanny See Charles W. Hopkins Monument entry.

Hopkins, Fanny A. *"MOTHER / FANNY A. CASWELL / WIFE OF / WILLIAM H. HOPKINS / JAN 22. 1821 / OCT. 22. 1879"* The first line is carved in relief. This stone has shifted forward and to the left on its base.

Hopkins, Fanny M. *"MARIA / FANNY MARIA / DAUGHTER OF / Wm H. & FANNY A. / HOPKINS / JAN. 8, 1847, / MAR. 7, 1922."* The first line is carved in relief.

Hopkins, Lydia A. *"LYDIA / LYDIA ANN / DAUGHTER OF / Wm H. & FANNY A. / HOPKINS / APR. 24, 1849 / DEC. 2, 1900"* The first line is carved in relief. It appears that her stone has shifted to the left on its base.

Hopkins, Lydia E. *"LYDIA / LYDIA E. CASWELL / WIFE OF / WILLIAM H. HOPKINS / FEB. 22, 1825, / JAN. 17, 1909."* The first line is carved in relief.

Hopkins, Rosseter *"ROSSETER"* is carved in relief on the top curved surface of this stone. *"Mar. 9, 1843, / July 21, 1843."* is inscribed on the front. This stone shares its base with that of Bertha and Sadie Hopkins. *Vital Records of Taunton, Bristol Co., MA to the end of the Year 1849*, Vol. III, p. 110 lists his name as William Roseter (sic), son of William H. Hopkins.

Hopkins, Sadie *"SADIE"* is carved in relief on the top curved surface of this stone. *"Sept. 10, 1855, / Feb. 16, 1856."* is inscribed on the front. This stone shares its base with that of Bertha and Rosseter's stones. Lakeville Vital Records show Sarah A Hopkins was the daughter of William and Fanny Hopkins.

Hopkins, William H. *"FATHER / WILLIAM HARTWELL / HOPKINS / AUG. 8, 1820 / SEPT. 18, 1902"* The first line is carved in relief. This stone is shifted to the left on its base.

Hopkins, William H. *"WILLIAM / WILLIAM HARTWELL / SON OF / Wm H. & FANNY A. / HOPKINS / NOV. 25, 1844, / JUNE 22, 1909."* The first line is carved in relief.

Isaacsen, Kristin L.   See LeRoy P. Crossman Monument entry.

Jones, Consider   *"Mr. CONSIDER JONES / died March 20. 1820 / in his 80. / year."* An urn and willow carving is at the top of this rear facing, slate stone. A veteran's marker and flag are present.

Jones, Patience   *"In memory of / PATIENCE, / wid. of / Consider Jones; / who died / July 28. 1847, / aged 86 years."* There is an urn and willow carving at the top of this lichen encrusted, rear facing, slate stone. A near horizontal crack is present between the second and third lines. This stone was removed from the cemetery sometime in June or July of 2006.

Jones, Paul L. Monument   *"J (monogram) / PAUL LEWIS JONES / 1820 – 1900. / SARAH MARIA FROST / HIS WIFE / 1828 – 1854."* *"JONES"* is carved in relief on the base.

Jones, Sarah M.   See Paul Jones Monument entry.

King, Bathsheba   *"Memento Mori / In memory of Bathsheba / Daughter of Capt. Josiah King / and Bathsheba his wife ^e_y / Adopted Daughter of ^e_y Rev^r. M^r. / _aleb Turner who died / June ^e_y 9th. 1788 in ^e_y 11th. / Year of her Age."* The first line is carved along an arch on this crumbling, rear facing stone. A winged angel is carved between the first and second lines. This slate stone has exfoliated at the top and two of the exfoliated pieces are located on the ground in front of the stone. There is a footstone present, but it is crumbled into many pieces and no inscription was found. Thatcher lists her under both King and Turner.

King, Mary C.   *"MARY C. HASKINS / Wife of / SILAS S. KING, / June 29, 1824. / Oct. 29, 1866."* This stone shares a second base with that of her husband, Silas S. King. A low concrete wall surrounds this Orville Haskins family plot.

King, Silas S.   *"SILAS S. KING / Aug. 22. 1818. / Feb. 13, 1890."* This stone shares a second base with the stone of his wife, Mary C. A low concrete wall surrounds this Orville Haskins family plot.

Kinsley, Alvin E.   *"ALVIN E. / son of / Unite & Susanna / KINSLEY. / died Nov. 5, 1841 / aged 15 years. / Thy early dust shall rest from sorrow free, Here oft parental tears shall rest on thee."* This stone is lying face up on the ground.

Kinsley, Betsey   *"BETSEY KINSLEY / DIED / Feb. 24, 1906, / aged 82 yrs. 1 mo. / At rest."* The first line is carved along an arch.

Kinsley, John   *"JOHN KINSLEY / DIED   / Aug. 13, 1899, / aged 70 yrs, 4 mo. / He giveth His beloved sleep."* The first line is carved along an arch. The headstone is beginning to crack at the bottom, and it is loose on its base despite evidence of repair. The upper base is cracked through the middle, and is beginning to crumble.

Kinsley, Sarah   *"SARAH, / dau. of Unite and / Susanna Kinsley: / died / Feb. 9, 1833, / aged 11 months."* is inscribed on this small stone.

Kinsley, Susanna A. *"SUSANNA ALDEN / widow of / Unite Kinsley, / died Aug. 10, 1875. / Aged 80 yrs. 8 m's. / He doeth all things well."* The first line is carved along an arch. There is a 3½ inch crack on the bottom front of this textured stone. A veteran's marker and two flags are present.

Kinsley, Unite *"UNITE KINSLEY, / died Apr. 9, 1833; / Aged 41 yrs, 8 m's. / Death is swallowed up in victory"* The first line is carved along an arch. There is a 7 inch crack radiating from the center bottom.

Leonaid, E. L.

*"E L · LEONAiD
DiED MARCH 1911"*

is inscribed on a metal plate which is nailed and screwed to this flat, ground level stone. It faces the rear of the cemetery. Notice the *i*'s are in lower case.

Leonard, Anna *"ANNA. / Daughter of / Gideon & Hannah / LEONARD. / Died Feb. 17, 1863. / Aged / 71 years."* is inscribed on this rear facing stone. *"A. L."* This footstone faces the headstone.

Leonard, child

*"·HERE·LIES·
A·CHILD·OF
ELKANAH·LEON
ARD·DIED·IN ·THE
YEAR·1711·"*

This crudely carved stone faces the rear of the cemetery. Notice the letters H and E in *HERE* and *THE* are overlapped. Dots separate the words on this stone.

Leonard, Deliverance *"In Memory of Mr.ˢ / Deliverance Leonard, / the wife of Mʳ. / Elkanah Leonard Junʳ / who Decᵈ Decemʳ. / yᵉ 25 ᵗʰ 1751 Aged / 28 years 6 months / & 12 Days·"* A winged angel is carved at the top of this slate stone, and floral carvings extend down the sides. The last two lines of this lichen encrusted, rear facing stone are buried underground.

Leonard, Elisabeth *"Memento Mori. / In memory of M.ʳˢ / Elisabeth widow of / the Hon. Elkanah / Leonard Esqʳ. who / died Decʳ. ẏ 16 ᵗʰ 1780 / in ẏ 77 ᵗʰ Year of her age."* The first line is carved along an arch at the top of this stone. A winged angel is carved below this. Trees are carved down the sides of this lichen encrusted, rear facing, slate stone. Part of the left shoulder is missing. A poem follows, but is unreadable due to lichen growth and weathering. Thatcher lists her death day as December 6ᵗʰ, and spells her name as Elizabeth.

"M^{rs} / Elisabeth / Leonard / 1780" is inscribed on the slate footstone.

Leonard, Elizabeth *"In Memory of M^{rs} / Elizabeth Leonard wife / of Mr Joseph Leonard who / died Dec. 1st 1791 in ye 38th / Year of her Age. /*

Hark! h^{e}ar the trumpet's solemn sound,
Proclaim the mournful theme;
Go tell the nations I have found,
That death is not a dream.
The stream of death has roll'd me down,
To dwell with silent clay,
My body now must lie alone,
Till the great rising day."

There is a smiling, winged angel carved at the top of this rear facing, slate stone. The last two lines are buried underground.
"Mrs. Elizabeth / Leonard" is inscribed on this slate footstone.

Leonard, Elkanah *"·HERE·LISE· / ·THE·BODY·OF· / ·ELKANAH·LEON / ARD·AGED·38·DIED / ·IN·THE·YEAR·1714 / DECEMBER·y^{e}·29"* This tall, thin, rear facing stone is crudely inscribed. Note the spelling *LISE* and the dots separating the words on this stone. The letters *H* and *E* in *THE* are overlapped. A footstone is present. It is broken off at the top and no inscription was found on it.

Leonard, Elkanah Esq. *"Sic transit Gloria Mundi. / In memory of / the Hon. Elkanah Leonard / Esqr who died July y^{e} 24th / 1777 in y^{e} 74th Year / of his age. /*

Under these silent clods I sleep
In CHRIST may I arise
And when the angel Gabriel sounds,
Meet Jesus in skies."

The first line is carved along an arch at the top of this slate stone. A frowning, winged angel with a spike of hair is carved below this. Trees are carved along the sides. The last line is buried underground.
"Elkanah Leonard / Esqr / 1777" is inscribed on this lichen encrusted, slate footstone.

Leonard, Gideon *"Mr. GIDEON LEONARD / died July 17. 1811 / in his 55. / year."* An urn and willow carving is at the top of this rear facing, slate stone. A diagonal crack extends through the tympanum.

Leonard, Gideon *"GIDEON LEONARD / Died / Oct. 23, 1872, / Aged / 82 yrs, 11 mo. 12 ds."* The first line of this rear facing stone is carved along an arch.

Leonard, Hannah *"In memory of / HANNAH, / wife of / Zebulon Leonard: / who died / June 30, 1796. / in her 65 year."* This stone faces the rear of the cemetery.

Leonard, Hannah *"HANNAH. / Wife of / GIDEON LEONARD. / Died / May 13, 1840. / Aged / 81 years."* This stone faces the rear of the cemetery.
"H. L." This footstone faces the headstone.

Leonard, Henry *"HENRY·LEO / NARD·BORN· / AND·DIED·IN· / ·THE·1714"* This crudely carved stone faces the rear of the cemetery. Notice the dots separating the words, and the overlapping of the letters *H* and *E* in the word *THE*. The word *YEAR* is missing in the last line. A footstone is present, but it contains no inscription.

Leonard, Joseph *"In Memory of / JOSEPH LEONARD, / who died / March 20, 1844, / Æ. 91."* This stone faces the rear of the cemetery. A footstone is present, but there is no inscription on it.

Leonard, Joseph J. C. *"JOSEPH J. C. / LEONARD, / died June 24, 1872. / Aged 70 years, / 10 m's, 28 d's."* There is a vertical 7½ inch crack at the center bottom of this stone. Its repair has failed.
"J. J. C. L." is inscribed on the footstone.

Leonard, Joseph O. L. *"In Memory of Joseph / Oliver L. son of M^r. / Joseph Leonard & M^{rs}, / Elizabeth his wife / who died Feb. 8th / 1792 in $_y^e$ 4th Month / of his / Age."* A peeking rising sun is carved on this rear facing, slate stone. The last five lines are buried underground.

Leonard, Lydia *"LYDIA LEONARD / Died / July 25, 1874. / Aged 70."* The first line on this rear facing stone is carved along an arch.

Leonard, Thomas *"THOMAS·LEON / A"* is all that is inscribed on this crudely carved, rear facing stone. Thatcher lists his last name as Leonard.

Leonard, Timothy M. *"TIMOTHY M. LEONARD / Died / April 13, 1854 / aged 54 y'rs."* The first line is carved in relief along an arch. The last line of this rear facing stone is buried underground.

Leonard, Zebulon *"In memory of / ZEBULON / LEONARD, / who died / Nov. 29, 1794, in / his 66 year. / Ye friends that weep around my grave,*
> *Compose your minds to rest,*
> *Prepare, with me, for sudden death,*
> *And live forever bless,d."*
This stone faces the rear of the cemetery. Note the lowered apostrophe in the poem.

Leonard, Zilpha *"In Memory of / ZILPHA. / wife of / Joseph Leonard, / who died / April 20, 1827; / Æ. 61."* This stone faces the rear of the cemetery. A footstone is present, but there is no inscription on it.

MacAulay, Annie M. *"M (monogram) / ANNIE M. MACAULAY / 1872 – 1946"* Floral designs are carved in the upper corners of this rear facing stone.

Manchester, Horace A *"H. A. MANCHESTER / 21 CO. / MASS. INF."* is carved in relief within a recessed shield shaped area on this rear facing stone. A *"GAR 8 344"* marker, and a veteran's marker and flag are present. *Massachusetts Civil War Soldiers & Sailors, 1861-1865,* Vol. V, p. 286 shows that Horace A. Manchester from Fall River enlisted in 1864 at age 21. Lakeville Vital Records list his death on December 1, 1910, at 68 years, and 1 day old.

Matteson, Flora M. See George M. DeMaranville Monument entry.
"FLORA" is carved in relief on this black, flat, ground level stone. There are leaf designs carved above and below the inscriptions. It is located in front of the monument, on the far right.

McCully, Martha *"IN MEMORY OF / MARTHA MCCULLY / (DAUGH^{r} OF M^{r} / JOHN & MR^{s} / JEAN MCCULLY) / WHO DIED JAN^{r} / $^{e}_{y}$ 13th 1760 IN / $^{e}_{y}$ 21st YEAR OF / HER AGE"* A simple head is carved at the top of this lichen encrusted, rear facing, slate stone. Curved designs are carved in semicircles behind it. Vine carvings extend down the sides. Note the overlapping of the L's in *MCCULLY*. The last two lines are buried underground.
"M M / 1760" The top right corner of this slate footstone is chipped.

Meack, Timothy *"TIMOTHY W. MEACK / NOV. 20 – NOV. 22, 1960"* is inscribed on this flat, 0-2 inch high stone. It is located behind the Chester W. Burnham Monument, on the far right. A flying bird is carved on the upper left. A low cement wall surrounds this plot.

Merick, Roxana *"Roxana D___r of Mr. / John $^{&}$ Mrs. ____ Merick / died July ___ 1808. Aged / F__ Mont..."* A willow is carved at the top of this small, lichen encrusted, rear facing, slate stone. It is very weathered, especially in the center. The poem that follows is unreadable. Thatcher lists her mother's name as Betsey, and her death date as July 18, 1808, aged 5 months.
"R. M / 1808" is inscribed on the footstone.

Miller, Joanna *"IN MEMORY OF / Mrs JOANNA MILLER / (WIFE OF Mr JOHN / MILLER) WHO DIED / SEP^{T} $^{e}_{y}$ 2ND 1758 / IN $^{e}_{y}$ 27th YEAR / OF HER AGE."* A simple head is carved at the top of this rear facing, slate stone and curved designs are carved in semicircles behind it. Vine designs are carved down the sides. Note the overlapping Ls in *MILLER*.
"_ M / 1758" This slate footstone has exfoliated on the upper left.

Miller, Rhoda *"Death / dissolves the / dearest connections / In memory of / Mrs, Rhoda Miller / wife of / Mr, Samuel Miller / who died April 7th 1801 / in her 41st year. /*

> *When we have past life's tragic scenes*
> *And paid the debt of natures due*
> *Earth must recieve our mortal part*
> *To mou'der t'ill we rise anew"*

The first three lines are inscribed within the top triangular area of this rear facing,

slate stone. Note the spelling of *recieve* in the third line of the poem, and the placement of the apostrophe in *t'ill* in the last line.
"___ / Rho_ Miller" The top half of this footstone has exfoliated.

Miller, Susa S.   *"In memo'y of / Susa,S,dau,ʳof Mr / Samuel Miller / & Mrs. Rhoda his / wife who died / july 3 ,ᵈ 1801 aged / 11 months & 3 days"* A rising sun is carved at the top of this rear facing, slate stone. Many cracks are present.

Montgomery Monument   *"MONTGOMERY"* is carved in relief on the base of this large, rear facing monument. Leaves are carved in the upper corners on the front and back. A low concrete wall surrounds the Montgomery plot.

Montgomery, Anna S.   *"ANNA SAMPSON / wife of / HUGH MONTGOMERY: / Died Dec. 29, 1828, / Æt. 64 yrs. /*
> *Her mind was tranquil and serene.*
> *No terrors in her looks were seen.*
> *Her Saviour's smiles dispell'd the gloom,*
> *And smooth'd her passage to the tomb."*

The first line is carved along an arch. This rear facing stone shares its base with that of her husband. *"ANNA"* is carved in relief on the back.

Montgomery, Augustus   *"AUGUSTUS / Son of / JOHN MONTGOMERY, / And his wife, / MARGARET HENRY. / Died Sept. yᵉ 14ᵗʰ 1782, / In his 3ᵈ year."* The first line is carved along an arch. This stone is not centered on its base.
"AUGUSTUS" is carved in relief on the back of this stone.

Montgomery, Fannie   *"FANNIE WASHBURN. / Daughter of / John F. & Isadore L. / MONTGOMERY. / July 13, 1876. / Dec. 28, 1891. / Blessed are the pure in heart / For they shall see God."* is inscribed on the front of this stone. The first line is carved along an arch. *"FANNIE"* is carved in relief on the back. A sculptured carving of a morning glory is carved above this. *"M"* monogram is carved below the inscription, and *"W. H. JACKSON, Taunton."* inscribed on the base.

Montgomery, Hugh   *"HUGH MONTGOMERY / Mar. 23, 1802, / Mar. 13, 1883. / Grad. B. U. 1826. / Member of Mass. Bar. / 1832 – 1883."* The first line is carved along an arch. *"HUGH"* is carved in relief on the back of this stone. A leaf sculpture is carved above it, and an *"M"* monogram is inscribed at the bottom.

Montgomery, Hugh   *"HUGH MONTGOMERY / Died Mar. 17, 1835. / In the 80th*
year / of his age. /   *Rest, friend, in peaceful silence rest.*
                             No voice shall reach thine ear.
                             Till God in judgement dress'd,
                             Shall call the nations to appear."
The first line is carved along an arch. This rear facing stone shares its base with that of his wife, Anna. *"HUGH"* is carved in relief on the back. A *"SAR 1775"* marker and flag are present.

Montgomery, Isadore L.   *"ISADORE L. PHILLIPS / Wife of / JOHN F. MONTGOMERY / Aug. 20, 1852. / April 29, 1916."* This stone shares its base with that of her husband. *"ISADORE"* is inscribed on the back of this stone. *"TAUNTO."* is inscribed below this on the lower right corner of the upper base.

Montgomery, James   *"JAMES MONTGOMERY / Died Jan. 4, 1849, / Aged 41 yrs."* The first line is carved along an arch. *"JAMES"* is carved in relief on the back of this stone.

Montgomery, John   *"ELDER JOHN MONTGOMERY. / Died Oct. y[e] 19th, Æ. / 1787. / Being in y[e] 80 [th] year / of his age. /*
                             Praises on tombs are _i__es vainly spent
                             This man's good name is his monument."
The first line is carved along an arch. This rear facing stone shares its base with his wife, Mary S. The stone is weathered, and the poem is hard to read. *"M"* (monogram) is carved at the top on the back of this stone. *"JOHN"* is carved in relief below it.

Montgomery, John   *"JOHN MONTGOMERY / Aug. 29, 1799, / June 9, 1881."* The first line is carved along an arch. This rear facing stone shares its base with that of his wife, Mary Ann. *"JOHN"* is carved in relief on the back of this stone. Sculptured oak leaves are carved above it.

Montgomery, John F.   *"JOHN F. MONTGOMERY / Sept. 6, 1843. / June 5, 1918."* This stone shares its base with the stone of his wife, Isadore. *"JOHN FRANCIS"* is inscribed on the back. *"J. B. SULLIVAN SON"* is inscribed below this, on the lower right corner of the upper base.

Montgomery, Mary A.   *"MARY A. MONTGOMERY / 1847 – 1935"* *"MARY"* is inscribed on the back of this stone.

Montgomery, Mary Ann   *"MARY ANN [WASHBURN,] / Wife of / JOHN MONTGOMERY. / Sept. 3, 1804. / July 26, 1886."* The first line is carved along an arch. This rear facing stone shares its base with that of her husband. *"MARY ANN"* is carved in relief on the back. Sculptured ivy leaves are carved above this.

Montgomery, Mary S.   *"MARY STROBRIDGE / wife of / JOHN MONTGOMERY. / Died May y[e] 16th, 1790, / In y[e] 73[d] year / of her age."* The first line is carved along an arch. Her stone shares its base with the stone of her husband,

John. *"MARY"* is carved in relief on the back of this rear facing stone.

Montgomery, Nancy   *"NANCY MONTGOMERY / Nov. 10, 1789. / Mar. 9. 1881."*
The first line is carved along an arch. *"NANCY"* is carved in relief on the back.

Montgomery, Rebecca   *"REBECCA MONTGOMERY / Died May 14, 1798. / in
her 39ᵗʰ year. /   This dust which here doth lie confined,
                          Shall rise again and be refined,
                          And shall our glorious Saviour see,
                          And live her doom'd eternity."*
The first line is carved along an arch. The stone is loose on the base. *"REBECCA"*
is carved in relief on the back.

Montgomery, Samuel, Dr.   *"Dʀ. SAMUEL MONTGOMERY / Died May y ᵉ 22 ᵈ,
Ɐ. 1787. / In y ᵉ 34 ᵗʰ year / of his age."* The first line is carved along an arch. The
stone is loose on its base. *"SAMUEL"* is carved in relief on the back.

Montgomery, William   *"WILLIAM MONTGOMEERY / Died June 23, 1804, / In
his 38ᵗʰ year."* The first line is inscribed along an arch. *"WILLIAM"* is carved in
relief on the back of this stone.

Montgomery, William   *"WILLIAM MONTGOMERY. / July 17, 1804. / April 30,
1898."* The first line is carved along an arch. *"WILLIAM ."* is carved in relief on
the back of this stone. A sculptured carving of an oak leaf branch is carved above
this, and an *"M"* monogram is carved at the bottom.

Moranville, Alice M.   See Edson V. Moranville Monument entry.
"ALICE" is inscribed on this flat, ground level stone. It is located in front of the
monument, on the far left.

Moranville, Bernice L.   See Edson V. Moranville Monument entry.
"BERNICE" is inscribed on this flat, ground level stone. It is located directly in
front of the monument, on the left.

Moranville, Dennis L.   See Edson V. Moranville Monument entry.
"DENNIS" is inscribed on this flat, ground level stone. It is located directly in front
of the monument, on the right. It was placed after the initial visit.

Moranville, Edson V. Monument   *"IN LOVING MEMORY / 1869 EDSON V. 1944
/ HIS WIFE / 1881 ALICE M. 1947 / 1911 RUSSELL S. 1949 / 1902 BERNICE
L. 1978 / 1942 DENNIS L. 2002 / MORANVILLE"* is inscribed on the front of
this monument. *"1841 LUCANA J. 1929 / 1870 FLORA E. 1933"* is inscribed
on the back.
"EDSON" is inscribed on this flat, ground level stone. It is located behind the
monument, on the left.

Moranville, Flora E.   See Edson V. Moranville Monument entry.
"FLORA" is inscribed on this flat, ground level stone. It is located directly behind
the monument, on the left.

Moranville, Jarvis R.   *"JARVIS R. MORANVILLE / APR. 3, 1838 / FEB. 21, 1908
/ GONE BUT NOT FORGOTTEN"* The first line is carved along an arch.

Moranville, Lucana J.   See Edson V. Moranville Monument entry.
"LUCANA" is inscribed on this flat, ground level stone. It is located directly behind of the monument, on the right.

Moranville, Russell S.   See Edson V. Moranville Monument entry.
"RUSSELL" is inscribed on this flat, ground level stone. It is located in front of the monument, on the left.

Morse, Rose A.   *"ROSE A. MORSE / 1901 – 1971"* is inscribed on this slanted stone, which faces the rear of the cemetery.

Morton, Alice M. Monument   *"ALICE M. MORTON / 1863 – 1942 / HIRAM F. ROGERS / 1860 – 1891 / DAUS. RUBY – R. GRACE / 1889 – 1892   1882 – 1900"* Floral designs are carved in partial relief in the upper corners.

Muthow, Benno Monument   *"MUTHOW"* is carved in relief on the slanted top surface on this monument. *"BENNO MUTHOW / 1865 – 1940 / SARAH HIS WIFE / 1870 – 1922"* is carved on the front. Ivy leaves are carved in relief in the top left corner, and oak leaves are carved in relief in the top right corner. A low cement wall surrounds the Muthow gravestones.
"BENNO" is inscribed in shallow relief on a 2-4 inch high slanted footstone.

Muthow, Sarah   See Benno Muthow Monument entry.
"SARAH" is inscribed in shallow relief on this 2-4 inch high slanted footstone.

Nelson, Susan A.   *"SUSAN A. KINSLEY, / Wife of / WILLIAM W. NELSON, / Born / Dec. 20, 1816. / Died / Jan. 18, 1860. /*

> *Dearest mother thou hast left us.*
> *Here thy loss we deeply feel.*
> *But 'tis God that hath bereft us.*
> *He can all our sorrows heal."*

Nelson, Susan F.

> *"SUSAN FRANCES,*
> *Dau. of / William W.*
> *& Susan A. K.*
> *NELSON,*
> *died Feb. 5, 1862,*
> *Aged 20 yrs. 7 $\frac{m's}{}$.*
> *We wept to see her die,*
> *We mourn her abscence yet;*
> *We hope to meet her in the sky,*
> *And all our _____ forget."*

The first line is carved in relief along an arch on this stone. Note the spelling of *abscence*. The top of this stone forms a pointed arch. A crack radiates from the base, obliterating the missing word in the last line of the poem. The base is broken in half.

Nelson, William W.   *"ERECTED / in memory of / WILLIAM W. / NELSON, / who died / Nov. 29, 1844. / aged 33 years. /*

> *Has death another trophy now,*
> *And is a father dead*
> *Behold a family bereaved*
> *And weeping for their dead."*

The first line is carved along an arch. The third and fourth lines are carved in relief. The seventh line is carved along a reverse arch.

Paddock, Elisabeth   *"In Memory of Mr.ˢ / Elisabeth Paddock / yᵉ 3ᵈ wife to Mʳ. / Joseph Paddock / who Decᵈ Decemʳ. yᵉ / 19 ᵗʰ 1761 in ᵧᵉ 62ᵈ / year of her Age."* This rear facing stone has a winged angel carved at the top and floral designs carved down the sides. Part of the left border of this slate stone is broken off. The last three lines are buried underground. Thatcher lists her death day as December 10.
"Mrˢ. Elisabeth / Paddock" This footstone is lying face down in front of the headstone for Lydia Paddock.

Paddock, Joseph   *"In Memory of / Mʳ. Joseph Paddock / who Decᵈ April / yᵉ. 10 ᵗʰ 1768. / In yᵉ. 69 ᵗʰ year of / his Age."* A winged angel is carved at the top of this rear facing, slate stone. Floral designs are carved down the sides.
"Joseph / Paddock" is inscribed on the footstone. The top right side has exfoliated.

Paddock, Josiah   *"In / memory of / Mr. JOSIAH PADDOCK / who died / April 17. 1815 / aged 54 / years"* An urn and willow carving is at the top of this rear facing, slate stone. The top half of the urn is carved in relief. Small crescent carvings encircle the inscription, and are also carved at the top, bottom and sides of the inscribed area. A diagonal crack extends through the second line.

Paddock, Lydia   *"In / memory of / Mrs. LYDIA widow of / Mr. Thomas Paddock / who died / August 22. 1807 / in her 77. / year."* This rear facing, slate stone is leaning to the right. An urn and willow are carved in relief at the top. Small crescent carvings encircle the inscription, and are also carved at the top, bottom and side edges of the inscribed area.

Page, Carlton A.   *"CARLTON A. PAGE, / BORN JULY 19, 1853, / DIED AUG. 14 1854."* Curved designs are carved in the upper corners of this rear facing stone. A footstone is present, but there is no inscription on it.

Page, Homer A.   *"HOMER A. PAGE, / BORN SEPT. 24, 1862, / DIED OCT. 1, 1862"* Curved designs are carved in the upper corners of this rear facing stone. A footstone is present, but there is no inscription on it.

Page, Infant Daughter   *"A DAUGHTER / DIED AT BIRTH / MARCH 6, 1842."* Curved designs are carved in the upper corners of this rear facing stone. Thatcher lists her as the daughter of John B. and Susannah Page.

Page, John B.   *"FATHER"* is carved in shallow relief on the top slanted surface of this rear facing stone. *"JOHN B. PAGE, / BORN AUG. 14, 1820, / DIED AUG. 27, 1890."* is inscribed on the front.

Page, Susannah   *"MOTHER"* is carved in shallow relief on the top slanted surface of this rear facing stone. *"SUSANNAH PAGE, / BORN APR. 10, 1821, / DIED MAY 13, 1866."* is inscribed on the front. Curved designs are carved in the upper corners.

Page, Susannah A. *"SUSANNAH A. PAGE, / BORN JULY 7, 1848, / DIED AUG. 8, 1848."* Curved designs are carved in the upper corners of this rear facing stone. A footstone is present, but there is no inscription on it. Thatcher lists her as the daughter of John B. and Sarah Page.

Page, Susannah M. *"SUSANNAH M. PAGE, / BORN OCT. 15, 1857, /DIED JULY 13, 1858."* Curved designs are carved in the upper corners of this rear facing stone.

Perkins, Charity *"In memory of MR^S. / Charity Perkins DEC^d. / late wife of Jabez Perkins of / Norwich Esqr Born April 1685 / & Dyed at Middlebarough feb^r. 29th / 1759 in ye 74th year of / her Age / Lyes Buried by her first / husband M^r.Elkanah Leonard"* A simple head with wild hair is carved at the top of this rear facing, slate stone. There are many diagonal cracks present. A flower is carved at the top of the shoulders, and leaf designs are carved down the sides. Note the spelling of *dyed*, *Middlebarough* and *lyes*.
"MR^S. / Charity Perkins" is inscribed on this slate footstone.

Perry, George H. Monument *"REV. AND MRS. GEORGE H. PERRY / SERVED THIS PRECINCT / 1897 – 1908"* is inscribed on this slanted stone. Lakeville Vital Records list his death on November 12, 1917, at 73 years, 1 month, and 17 days old.

Perry, Anna A. See George H. Perry Monument entry.
Lakeville Vital Records list her name as Anna Augusta (Benjamin) Perry. She died March 5, 1916, at 69 years, 9 months, and 29 days old.

Pickens, Archie H. See Henry C. Pickens Monument entry.
"ARCHIE" is inscribed on the top slanted surface of this 8 inch high footstone. It is located to the left of the monument. Lakeville Vital Records list his birth on May 29, 1869 and his death on September 25 that same year.

Pickens, Grissel *"In memory of Miss / Grissel ... Pickens / Dau^r ... John Pick / ens & Mrs. Ruth his / wife who died April / 1 1779 ... 26 year / ..."* This lichen encrusted, slate stone is broken diagonally through the right shoulder. The break has been successfully repaired. Lichen obliterates the carving in the tympanum as well as the last two lines on this rear facing stone.
"Miss / Grissel Bally / Pickens" is inscribed on the slate footstone.

Pickens, Henry C. Monument *"P (monogram) / HENRY C. PICKENS / DIED APRIL 10, 1911 / SOPHIA A. HIS WIFE / DIED MAY 23, 1890"* is inscribed on the front of this monument. *"P (monogram) / ARCHIE H. PICKENS / DIED SEPT. 25, 1869 / S. IRVING PICKENS / DIED OCT. 27, 1955"* is inscribed on the back. Vital Records index cards at the Middleborough Town Clerk's Office list Henry's birth date as January 19, 1838.
"HENRY" is carved in shallow relief on this flat footstone. It is located in front of the monument, on the left and is beginning to be buried.

Pickens, John *"In memory of / Mr, John Pickens / who died Feb^{ry} 21 / 1798 in his*

80 year /

> *Death frees the saint from sin & pain*
> *Their souls ascend to GOD above*
> *Their dust shall rise and live again*
> *And reign in everlasting love"*

There are many small cracks in this lichen encrusted, rear facing, slate stone. Only a branch can be seen in the carving at the top, as the rest is obliterated by the lichen or exfoliation. The first three lines of the poem extend into the side border. A *"SAR 1775"* marker, a veteran's marker and flag are present.

"Mr. / John Pickens" The left shoulder of this slate footstone is missing.

Pickens, John *"In memory of John / Son of Mr. __ttu / Pickens & Mrs. Rachel / his wife who died / Octo^r 8th 1798 in his / 8 Year. / Come weeping parents..."* This small, lichen encrusted, slate stone faces the rear of the cemetery. Lichen obliterates all but a part of the left wing of the carving in the tympanum. Thatcher lists him as "John, son of Zattu & Rachel." His parents are buried in Pickens #2 Cemetery.

Pickens, Mary *"In Memory of Mary / Daughter of M^r. James / & M^rs. Margaret Pickens. / She died / Oc^tr. 27th. 1781. / in ẙ 14th. Year of her age."* This small slate stone faces the rear of the cemetery. A frond carving is at the top.

"M. P. / 1781" is inscribed on the footstone. The last line is buried underground.

Pickens, Ruth *"In memory of ___ / Ruth Pickens wife ___ / Mr. ₁ohn Pickens w__ / died ₁an^ry. 4th 1798 in / her 73 year /*   *high*

> *Through the great GOD who reigns on*
> *Has doom'd the race of man to die*
> *Yet saints thereby are cleans'd from sin*
> *And shall in glory rise again"*

An urn and a leaning tree are carved at the top of this rear facing, slate stone. The carver ran out of room on the first line of the poem, thus *high* is carved above that line. The stone is exfoliating on the upper right side.

Pickens, S. Irving See Henry C. Pickens Monument entry.
"IRVING" is carved in shallow relief on this flat 0-¾ inch high stone. It is located to the right of the monument. His obituary in *The Middleborough Gazette* 11/03/1955:3 reports that he was 83 years old when he died on October 27, 1955.

Pickens, Sarah *"SARAH PICKENS / DIED: SEPT^r. 8 1765 / AGED 16, 9, 10"*
There is a simple head carving at the top of this small, slate stone. The last line is buried underground. A fieldstone is present as its footstone.

Pickens, Sophia A. See Henry C. Pickens Monument entry.
"SOPHIA" is carved in shallow relief on this flat, 1 inch high stone. It is located in front of the monument, on the far left. Lakeville Vital Records show she was 53 years, 7 months, and 18 days old when she died.

Pierce, Eben S. Monument *"EBEN STROBRIDGE / SON OF / JAMES & / MARY PIERCE / BORN / JULY 12, 1850 / DIED / MAY 3, 1857 / JAMES ALTON / SON OF / JAMES & / MARY PIERCE / BORN / OCT. 10, 1857 / DIED / OCT. 9, 1878"* is inscribed on the front of this tall obelisk. The first line is carved along an arch. *"J. PIERCE."* is carved in relief on the front base. *"JAMES PIERCE / BORN*

/ FEB. 11, 1821, / DIED OCT. 23, 1889. / HIS WIFE / MARY STROBRIDGE / JUNE 6. 1829 / OCT. 19, 1912" is inscribed on the right side. The first line is carved along an arch. *"MARY ELLA / DAUGHTER OF / JAMES & MARY / PIERCE / BORN DEC. 24, 1856 / DIED AUG. 26, 1930"* is inscribed on the back. The first line is carved along an arch. There are no inscriptions on the left side. Geometric designs are carved in the upper corners on all sides.

"EBEN S. / Son of / JAMES & MARY / PIERCE. / Born / July 12, 1850, / Died / May 3, 1857. / Not mortal now but cherub bright, / He's left this world for realms of light." "[D. A. BURT, Taunton.]" is inscribed in the lower right corner of this rear facing stone. The first and fourth lines are carved in shadow. There is a broken floral sculpture on the top of this small stone. A crack extends down from this sculpture several inches. Its repair has failed.

"E. S. P." This footstone is lying face upon the ground. This rear facing stone is located in front of the monument, on the far right.

Pierce, James   See Eben. Pierce Monument entry.
"JAMES" is inscribed in shallow relief on this flat, ground level stone. It is located behind the monument, on the far right.

Pierce, James A.   See Eben. Pierce Monument entry.
"J. A. P." This footstone is located in front of the monument, on the right.

Pierce, Mary   See Eben. Pierce Monument entry.

Pierce, Mary E.   See Eben. Pierce Monument entry.
"ELLA" is inscribed in shallow relief on this flat, lichen encrusted, ground level stone. It is located behind the monument, on the left.

Pittsley, Kenneth E.   *"✝ / KENNETH E. PITTSLEY / 3 YRS. 2 MOS."* This flat, ground level stone is beginning to be buried. Lakeville Vital Records list his death on November 12, 1916. He was the son of Albert E. & Edna (Burnham) Pittsley.

Poak, James   *"IN MEMORY OF / Mr JAMES POAK. / SON OF Mr SAMUEL & M^{rs} / JENNET POAK: / DIED MAY ^e_y 5th/ 1749 IN ^e_y 38th / YEAR OF HIS AGE."* This rear facing, slate stone has a simple head carving at the top. Note the condensed letters in *JENNET*, and *YEAR*.
"J P / 1749" is inscribed on the slate footstone. It is in line with the other footstones, but overgrown bushes hide its presence.

Poak, Jennet   *"IN MEMORY OF / Mrs JENNET POAK, / WIFE OF M^r / SAMUEL POAK / DIED MAY ^e_y / 8TH 1749 AGED / 68 YEARS."* There is a simple head carving at the top of this rear facing, slate stone. The right shoulder is broken off. Note the overlapping N's in her name.
"J P / 1749" is inscribed on the slate footstone.

Poak, Martha   *"IN MEMORY OF / Mrs MARTHA POAK / $^{e}_{y}$ DAU ^{tr} OF M^{r} / SAMUEL & M^{rs} / JENNET POAK / DIED MAY $^{e}_{y}$ 21ST / 1749 IN $^{e}_{y}$ 41ST / YEAR OF HER AGE."* This rear facing, slate stone has a simple head carving at the top. The last line is buried underground. Note the condensed letters in *MARTHA*, *JENNET*, and *YEAR*. She is remembered as Mrs., but no husband is mentioned.
"M P / 1749" is inscribed on the slate footstone.

Poak, Samuel   *"IN MEMORY OF / Mr SAMUEL POAK, / DIED JULY $^{e}_{y}$ 26 / 1747 IN $^{e}_{y}$ · 86 / YEAR OF HIS / AGE."* A simple head carving is at the top of this lichen encrusted, rear facing, slate stone.
"__ S P / 1747" The top left corner is chipped off of this slate footstone.

Porter, Charles A. Monument   *"PORTER"* is inscribed on the front of the monument. There are floral carvings in the upper corners. *"1836   CHARLES A. 1910 / 1840   MARY E.   1908 / 1860   CLARA O.   1903 / 1870   CHARLES F. 1870 / 1881   HATTIE C.   1881"* is inscribed on the back. An Albert F. Richmond Memorials metal tag is present.

Porter, Charles F.   See Charles A. Porter Monument entry.

Porter, Clara O.   See Charles A. Porter Monument entry.

Porter, Hattie C.   See Charles A. Porter Monument entry.

Porter, Mary E.   See Charles A. Porter Monument entry.

R., E.   *"e R"* is crudely carved on this fieldstone.

R., G.   *"G R"* is crudely carved on this fieldstone.

R., M. E.   *"BABY / M. E. R."* This crudely carved concrete stone faces the rear of the cemetery. The word *BABY* is surrounded by small white stones.

R., S.   *"S R / 1756"* is crudely carved in this rear facing fieldstone. Thatcher lists this stone under the name of Richmond. A fieldstone serves as the footstone.

Ramsdell, Anna   *"ANNA."* is inscribed on the top slanted surface of this small stone. *"Dau. of / S. C. & H. A. / Ramsdell. / died / Aug. 3, 1867, / Æ. 6 m's."* is inscribed on the front. A crack radiating from the center bottom extends through the last two lines.
"A. R." is inscribed on the top slanted surface of the footstone.

Ramsdell, Hepsy A.   *"HEPSY A. / wife of / Stephen C. Ramsdell / died Jan. 27, 1867; / Aged 18 years."* The first line is inscribed along an arch. There is an 8 inch crack at the center bottom.
"H. A. R." is inscribed on the footstone.

Ramsdell, Mary M.   *"MARY M. COGGESHALL / wife of / Stephen C. Ramsdell / Died Nov. 26, 1910; / Aged 80 yrs. 2 ms."* Two cracks at the base of this stone have been successfully repaired.
"M. M. R." is inscribed on the footstone. The inscription is buried underground.

Ramsdell, Stephen C.   *"STEPHEN C. RAMSDELL / died / Feb. 24, 1873; / Aged*

50 years." This stone had been broken horizontally below the inscription. This break and a crack radiating from the center bottom have been successfully repaired. *Massachusetts Civil War Soldiers & Sailors, 1861-1865,* Vol. V, p. 259 shows a Stephen C. Ramsdell, age 42, resident of Freetown enlisting in 1864.
"S. C. R." is inscribed on the footstone. The inscription is half buried.

Reed, Abraham W.   *"ABRAHAM W. / Son of / John C. & / Irena R. Reed, / died Apr. 16, 1840. / Aged 6 years / 5 ms. & 15 ds."* This small stone is very weathered.
"A. W. R." This footstone faces the headstone.

Reed, Charles   *"In memory / of / Mr CHARLES REED / who / died December / 1ˢᵗ 1810 / in his 75ᵗʰ Year"* An urn and willow carving is at the top of this rear facing, slate stone. A geometric design is carved along the outer edges. A veteran's marker and flag are present.
"Mr. / Charles Reed" is inscribed on the slate footstone.

Reed, Elisabeth   *"Memento Mortis / In memory of / Mrs. Elisabeth Reed daugᵗʳ. / of Mr. Charles Reed, & / Mrs. Zilpah his wife who / died Febʳʸ. 12ᵗʰ. 1793, Aged 29 / Years 1 Months & 17 Days. /*

> *Affliction sore long time I bore*
> *Physicians skill was vain*
> *Till God was pleas'd to give me ease*
> *And free me from my pain."*

A winged angel is carved at the top of this lichen encrusted, rear facing, slate stone. Note no mention is made of a husband, yet she is called Mrs.

Reed, Irena R.   *"In memory of / IRENA R. / wife of / John C. Reed / who died / Oct. 26, 1835, / in her 25 year."*
"I. R. R." This footstone is located to the right of the headstone.

Reed, Isaac N.   *"ISAAC NEWTON, / Son of / John C. & Irene R. / REED, / Born March 27, 1835. / Died / Nov. 5, 1859."* *"D. A. BURT."* is inscribed on the bottom right side of this stone.
"I. N. R." is inscribed on the footstone. The inscription is buried underground.

Reed, Lois   *"LOIS REED, / Died / March 14, 1855, / aged 90 years."* This stone faces the rear of the cemetery.
"L. R." This footstone faces the headstone.

Reed, Nathan   *"NATHAN REED, / DIED / Dec. 10, 1800. / aged 34 yrs."* The last line of this rear facing stone is buried underground. A footstone is present, but there is no inscription on it.

Reed, Zilphia   *"In memory of / Mrs Zilphia wife of / Mr. Charles Reed / who died March 4ᵗʰ. / 1808 in her / 68 year."* is inscribed underneath a carving of a rising sun. Small designs are carved down the sides. Many cracks are present on this rear facing, slate stone.

Reynolds, Ellery J.   *"ELLERY JOHN / 1964 – 1969"* is crudely carved in a ground level block of cement which faces the rear of the cemetery. His stone is located behind the John Wordell Monument. He was the grandchild of John and Lottie Wordell.

Reynolds, Hannah M.   *"HANNAH M. / 1871 – 1941 / REYNOLDS"* Floral carvings are in the upper corners of this monument. It is leaning to the right. A low cement wall surrounds this large plot which contains only her gravestone.

Ricard, Arthur H. Monument   *"RICARD / CASWELL"* is inscribed on the front of this black monument. An etching of a couple sitting on a bench, watching a sunset is below this. *"ARTHUR H. RICARD / OCT. 23, 1942 – JUL. 29, 2003 / HIS LOVING WIFE / ESTHER R. (CASWELL) / JUL. 5, 1949 ____"* is inscribed on the back.

Richards, Fred E. Monument   *"RICHARDS"* is carved in relief on the front of this monument. Floral carvings are in the upper corners. *"FRED E. RICHARDS / 1901 – 1960 / HAZEL A. HIS WIFE / 1913 – 1970"* is carved on the back. An Albert F. Richmond Memorials metal tag is present.
"____ – 1960" is embossed on this metal marker. *"EGGER FUNERAL HOME"* is embossed at the bottom. It is located in front of the monument.

Richards, Hazel A.   See Fred E. Richards Monument entry.
This blank funeral home marker, is located between Lynn Ann's stone and Fred's funeral home marker.

Richards, Lynn Ann   *"LYNN ANN / RICHARDS / APR. 19, 1963"* is inscribed on this flat, ground level stone.

Richmond, Allen   *"Father / In memory of / ALLEN RICHMOND / who died / April 18, 1862 / Aged 84 yrs. 3 m's / & 8 d's. / Gone to rest."* This rear facing stone appears to have been recently put back into its base. There is the outline of the stone in dead grass behind it.
"A. R." is inscribed on the footstone.

Richmond, Elisabeth   *"In memory of / M.ʳˢ Elisabeth widow / of Deacon Edward / Richmond who died / Octᶠ 10 ᵗʰ 1782 in yᵉ 81ˢᵗ. / Year of her age. / Th_ ancient wife of M ʳ / Samuel Shaw"* is inscribed on this lichen encrusted, rear facing, slate stone. Exfoliation and lichen have obliterated the carving on the tympanum. Thatcher spells her first name as "Elizabeth". He lists her as both Richmond and Shaw.
"M.ʳˢ / Elisabeth / Richmond / 1782." is inscribed on the slate footstone.

Richmond, Jones   *"In memory of / JONES. / son of Allen & / Nancy Richmond / who died / Nov. 25, 1833; / aged 9 years."* This stone faces the rear of the cemetery. A footstone is lying in place on the ground, but no inscription was found. Thatcher lists his first name as John.

Richmond, Joseph, Deacon   *"Memento mortis / Sacred to the Memory of / DEACᴺ. JOSEPH RICHMOND / who died July 19ᵗʰ 1792 In the / 69ᵗʰ Year of his Age / ..."* A winged angel is carved at the top of this lichen encrusted, rear facing, slate stone. Lichen obliterates most of the four line poem which follows. Thatcher lists his death day as July 10ᵗʰ.
"D__ / Joseph Richmond" is inscribed on this lichen encrusted, slate footstone.

Richmond, Nancy   *"In Memory of / NANCY, / wife of / Allen Richmond, / who died / Nov. 17, 1855; / Æ. 69 y'rs ./ Blessed are they that keep my ways."* The second and fourth lines are carved in relief on this rear facing stone.
"N. R." is inscribed on the footstone. It is broken in half along the inscription.

Richmond, Prudence   *"Memento Mortis / In Memory of / Mrs. Prudence Richmo^nd. / wife of / Lieu.^t Joseph Richmond, / who died June 27th. 1789. / In her 32^d Year."* A winged angel is carved at the top of this rear facing, slate stone. There are numerous cracks present. The carver ran out of room on the third line.
"M^rs. / _rudence / _ichmond." is inscribed on the slate footstone. A piece of slate is missing on the left side.

Richmond, Rufus   *"In Memory of Mr. Rufu_ / Richmond Jun. Son of Mr. / Rufus Richmond who died / Dec 15, 1795 in his 23 year /*

> *My youthful friends attend and view*
> *A youth once gay and blith like you.*
> *Remember death.   Soon you must be*
> *Lodg'd in the silent grave with me."*

An urn and willow are carved in the tympanum, but the top half of it has exfoliated. The last two lines of the poem are underground. This lichen encrusted, slate stone faces the rear of the cemetery. Note the spelling of *blith*.
"R. _" is inscribed on the slate footstone. Its right shoulder has exfoliated. Beginning on the same line, *"Mr. /_hi_"* appears to be carved less deeply, and perhaps ground down. This appears to be a recycled footstone.

Richmond, Sarah   *"SARAH / RiCHMOND / DIED 1761"* is crudely carved on this rear facing fieldstone. The *D*'s are all carved backwards. The *I* in *DIED* has a horizontal line carved midway through it. Note the lower case *i* in her last name. The stone leans to the right. A fieldstone serves as the footstone.

Roche, Nicholas   *"This Monumental stone is erected / in Memory of / Mr. NICHOLAS ROCHE, / Who died Oct. the 31st. 1808. / Aged 85 Years. / He was born in the Kingdom of Ireland, / and came from thence to America in the days / of his youth; where by indefatigable / industry, he accumulated / an handsome fortune; / a valuable part of which he bequeathed / for the support of the gospel Ministry, / in this and some of the adjacent / Congregational Societies. / He gave several large bequests to individuals; / and the remaining part of his estate, / he directed his executors to distribute, according / to their judgment amongst the / "sober hone_t and industrious poor." / The deceased sustained, through life, an / irreproachable moral character. / The virtues which he practised, and the / judicious distribution / which he made of his valuable property, more / than any posthumous eulogium, speak his / praise."* This table monument is on a solid block base. An urn and two crossed branches are carved at the top. This stone is weathered in the center. Note the backward quotation mark before *sober*.

Rogers, Hiram   *"HIRAM ROGERS, / BORN / MAY 10, 1827. / DIED / NOV. 16. 1885."* A veteran's marker and flag are present. *Massachusetts Civil War Soldiers and Sailors, 1861-1865,* Vol. I, p. 484 shows that he was in the 7th Co. C, the 20th Co. K, and the 37th Co. I Massachusetts Infantries.

Rogers, Hiram F.   See Alice M. Morton Monument entry.
"HIRAM F. ROGERS / BORN / OCT. 10, 1860 / DIED / JUNE 17, 1891" This stone is located to the right of the monument.

Rogers, R. Grace   See Alice M. Morton Monument entry.
Lakeville Vital Records show her first name was Roxanna.

Rogers, Ruby   See Alice M. Morton Monument entry.

Rogers, Ruby A.   *"MOTHER. / RUBY A. / Wife of / HIRAM ROGERS, / Died Aug. 30, 1864. / Aged 43 yrs. / 6 mos."* The second line is carved in relief.

S., B.   *"B S / HEYR LIEZ / THE BODY OF HIM"* The S is carved backwards. Note the spelling of *HEYR LIEZ*. This inscribed fieldstone faces the rear of the cemetery. A blank, slate stone serves as the footstone.

Sampson, Anna   *"In memory of / Mrs. Anna / wid⁰. of / Mr. Uriah Sampson / who died / Aug. 26. 1801 / in her 73 year"* A willow is carved at the top of this rear facing, slate stone. Diamond shaped carvings form the border on the sides. A vertical crack 11 inches long runs from the bottom half of the carving to the bottom of line three. Notice the different spelling of *Sampson* on her stone verses *Samson* on Uriah's stone.
"Mrs. Anna Sampson" A willow is carved at the top of this slate footstone.

Sampson, Daniel   *"In memory of / Daniel Sampson / who died / July 14. 1814. / aged 39 years 6 m. 11 d."* A willow is carved at the top of this tall, rectangular, rear facing, slate stone. A hand pointing heavenward is carved on either side of it. Thatcher lists his age in days as one, and his first name as David.
"Mr. Daniel Sampson" is inscribed on the footstone. A simple carving of a leafless tree is at the top.

Samson, Deborah   *"In Memory of Deborah / Dauʳ to Docʳ John / Samson & Mˢ. Deborah / his Wife She died Oct. / ʃ 24ᵗʰ 1792 Aged 1 Year / 10 Months 7 Days."* This slate stone is broken diagonally from the left side of the tympanum to the fourth line. The top part is located behind the upright bottom part. An exfoliated piece is located in front of this rear facing stone. A winged angel is carved at the top. Thatcher and her parents' gravestones spell their surname *Sampson*.

Sampson, Deborah   *"ERECTED / In Memory of / DEBORAH, / widow of / Dr. John Sampson, / who died Oct. 2, 1844 / in the 85 th year / of her age."* The first line is carved along an arch, and the last line is carved along a reverse arch. This stone faces the rear of the cemetery.
"D. S." This footstone is separated from the base, and leaning face up against it.

Sampson, Deliverance   *"ERECTED / in memory of / DELIVERANCE, / wife of / ISAAC SAMPSON: / who died / Feb. 9, 1821, in / her 58 year."* The first line is inscribed in outline. The third line is carved in relief. *"G. Thompson."* is inscribed in the lower right corner.
"D. S." This footstone is broken off at ground level and lying face up behind the section still in the ground.

Sampson, Emeline   *"EMELINE dau. of / Mr. John Sampson Jr. / & Mrs. Phebe*

his wife / died Feb. 3. 1826 / aged 3 years & 6 / months." An urn and willow carving is at the top of this small stone. A deeply carved rectangle is below the urn. This slate stone is broken off at ground level, and is lying face down behind the piece still in the ground. It is beginning to be buried.
"E. S." is inscribed on the slate footstone.

Sampson, Ezra *"Ezra son of Mr. Isaac / Sampson & Mrs. / Deliverence his wife / died Sep. / 4. 1802 / aged 1 year 10 m."* A willow is carved at the top of this rear facing, slate stone. Note the spelling of *Deliverence* differs from the spelling on his mother's stone.

Sampson, Isaac *"Isaac son of Mr. Isaac / Sampson & Mrs. Delivere. / nce his wife died / Aug. 21. 1808 / Aged 13 years 9 m."* There is a willow carved at the top of this rear facing, slate stone. A rope like design is carved along the sides. Note the hyphen is lowered, and the spelling of *Deliverence* differs from the spelling on his mother's stone.
"I. S." is inscribed on the footstone, which is lying face up on the ground.

Sampson, Isaac

> *"ERECTED*
> *in memory of*
> *ISAAC SAMPSON,*
> *who died*
> *Dec 7, 1846, in*
> *his 85 year."*

This 4-foot tall stone faces the rear of the cemetery. The first line is inscribed in outline, and the third line is carved in relief. *"G. Thompson."* is inscribed in the lower right corner.
"I. S." is inscribed on the footstone.

Sampson, John, Dr. *"ERECTED / in / memory of / Doct. JOHN / SAMPSON / who died / May 20, 1830 / in his 80 year."* The first and third lines are carved along an arch. The fourth and fifth lines are carved in outline. This stone faces the rear of the cemetery. A veteran's marker and flag are present.
"J. S." is inscribed on the footstone.

Samson, Nathaniel *"In Memory of / M^r. Nathani^{e}l Samson / Died Sep$^{t.r}$. y^e / 13th 1778 In y^e / 60th. year of his / Age."* A winged angel is carved at the top of this rear facing, slate stone. A veteran's marker and flag are present.
"Mr / __thaniel / ____ " This slate footstone is broken in half horizontally with the top piece lying face down in front of the bottom piece. A previous repair has failed. This stone has exfoliated on the left side and at the bottom.

Samson, Uriah *"R_member Death / In Memory of M^r. __IAH SAMSON / who died May y^e 11$^{t.h}$. / 1790 in y^e 73^d Year / of his Age."* This stone is broken off diagonally at the bottom, and the top piece is leaning against the bottom piece. The tympanum of this rear facing stone is missing.

"M.ʳ Uriah Samson" is inscribed on the slate footstone.

Sears, Elkanah Capt. *"SACRED / to the memory of / Capt. ELKANAH / SEARS. / who died / March 18, 1838, in / his 74 year."* The first line of this rear facing stone is carved along an arch. A veteran's marker and flag are present.
"E. S." is inscribed on the footstone.

Sears, Mary *"IN MEMORY OF / M ʳˢ MARY SEARS, / WHO DIED DECEM - / BER ẙᵉ 5ᵀᴴ 1771 / IN ẙ35ᵗʰ YEAR / OF HER AGE / WIFE OF M ʳ / ZEBEDEE SEARS / & DAUTʳ OF / ELKANAH LENARD / ESqʳ"* A simple head is carved at the top, with a curved design carved in semicircles around it. A vine carving runs down the sides of this rear facing stone. The slate is beginning to exfoliate on the right shoulder. The last line is buried underground. A flag is present.
"M S / 1771" is inscribed on the slate footstone.

Sears, Remember *"In memory of / Mrs. Remember Sears / wife of / Mr. Leonard Sears / who died Febʳʸ 26. 1803, / in her 28 ᵗʰ Year."* A peeking rising sun with a nose is carved at the top of this lichen encrusted, rear facing, slate stone.
"Mrs. / Remember Sears" is inscribed on this slate footstone, which faces the grave.

Sears, Zebedee *"Zebedee Sears / ___d Janʳʸ ẙᵉ 30ᵗʰ 1779 / 45ᵗʰ Year of his Age. / ... and spends a tear, / ..."* There is just a small piece remaining of this slate headstone, and it is stuck in the ground on its left side.
"...Zeb... / Sears" This footstone, which faces the headstone, has a heart carved at the top. It has exfoliated on the right and left sides.

Shaw, Abraham *"In memory of / Mr. Abraham Shaw; / who died / July 8 1808: / in his 79. year."* An urn and willow carving is at the top of this rear facing, slate stone. A rope carving borders the tympanum, and a ribbon carving runs down the sides. A *"SAR 1775"* marker, a veteran's marker, and flag are present.
"Mr. / Abraham / Shaw." The left shoulder of this slate footstone is broken off.

Shaw, Abraham *"ABRAHAM SHAW / DIED NOV. 8, 1822 / AGED 34 YEARS."* This stone shares its base with the stone of Abraham Shaw, Jr.

Shaw, Abraham, Jr. *"ABRAHAM SHAW, JR / DIED JUNE 18, 1901 / AGED 79 YEARS."* This stone shares its base with the stone of his father.

Shaw, Betsey *"SACRED / To / the memory of / BETSEY SHAW / wife of John Shaw, / who died / Jan. 15, 1854, / in the 84 year of her Age. / MY MOTHER."* *"F. Silvers / Newport, RI."* is inscribed in the lower right corner of the stone. The first and fourth lines are carved in relief. This stone is broken off at its base, and is lying face down in front of it.

Shaw, Desire *"Memento Mori. / In Memory of / M ʳˢ. Desire wife to / Ens ⁿ. Samuel Shaw / who Died May ẙ 6 ᵗʰ. 1772 / in the 65 ᵗʰ. Year of / her Age."* A winged angel is carved between the first and second lines on this rear facing, slate stone.
"M ʳˢ. / Desire Shaw" is inscribed on the slate footstone.

Shaw, Samuel, Ensign *"Here Lies buried / Ensigⁿ Samuel Shaw, / who Decᵈ June ẙᵉ 2 ᵈ. / 1768 In ẙᵉ / 62ᵈ year of / his Age."* A winged angel is carved at the top of this

lichen encrusted, rear facing, slate stone. Flowers and leaves are carved down the sides. A veteran's marker and flag are present.
"Ensig^n / Samuel Shaw / 1768" is inscribed on this lichen encrusted, slate footstone.

Shaw, Sarah *"In memory of / Mrs. Sarah, wife of / Mr. Abraham Shaw; / who died / April 13. 1804: / in her 71. year."* An urn and willow carving is at the top of this rear facing, slate stone. A rope border is carved on the tympanum, and there is a ribbon carving down the sides.
"Mrs. / Sarah. Shaw" The shoulders of this slate footstone have begun to exfoliate.

Shaw, Susanna *"SUSANNA SHAW / BORN / SEPT. 10, 1754 / DIED / JANY. 1836"*

Shaw, Zebedee *"In memory of / ZEBEDEE SHAW, / who died / June 17, 1838, in / his 67 year."* An urn and willow carving is at the top of this lichen encrusted, rear facing, slate stone.
"Z. S." is inscribed on the slate footstone.

Shove, Betsey *"In / memory of / Mrs. BETSEY widow of / Edward Shove Esq. & / dau. of Mr. Josiah Paddock / who died June 21. 1817 / in her 25. / year."* This rear facing slate, stone has an urn and willow carving at the top. Small crescent designs are carved along the sides and the top of the inscription, and also encircle it. She is listed by Thatcher as both Betsey Paddock and Betsey Shove.

Shove, Eliza P. *"ELIZA PADDOCK SHOVE / Daughter of / EDWARD & BETSY / SHOVE / Born Nov. 29, 1810, / Died Apr. 9, 1884."* The first line is carved along an arch. This rear facing stone is leaning backwards.

Simmons, Methyl D. See Stanley C. Simmons Monument entry.
"METHYL" is inscribed on this 1 inch high footstone. It is located behind the monument, on the left.

Simmons, Stanley C. Monument *"CASWELL"* is inscribed on the front of this monument. Floral carvings adorn the upper corners. *"1896 STANLEY C. SIMMONS 1978 / 1901 METHYL D. SIMMONS 1941 / 1898 KENNETH MERRILL CASWELL 1898 / 1864 NETTIE PAGE CASWELL 1931 / 1860 LEAVITT CHANDLER CASWELL 1946 / 1803 STETSON CASWELL 1902 / 1837 SARAH M. CHANDLER CASWELL 1915"* is inscribed on the back.
"STANLEY" is inscribed on this 1-3 inch high footstone. It is located behind the monument, on the right.

Simon, Ben *"IN MEMORY OF / BEN SIMON. / the last male of the / Native Indians / of Middleboro. / He was a Revolutionary / Soldier and died in / May 1831 aged 80 / years."* The above is inscribed on a separate stone that has been attached to the front of this small obelisk. A veteran's marker and flag are present.

Smith, Elisabeth *"In Memory of Mrs. / Elisabeth Wife of / Mr Nathaniel Smith / Died February ye 1st / A. D. 1772 / In the 72^d year / of her age."* There is a frond carving at the top and down the sides of this lichen encrusted, rear facing, slate stone. The 2s on this stone look like 9s. Thatcher spells her name as Elizabeth.
"M^s / Elisabeth Smith / 1772" is inscribed on the slate footstone.

Smith, Lydia *"In memory of / Mrs LYDIA SMITH / widow of Capt. Nathaniel /*

Smith. She died Nov. 13 th / 1790 in y^e 87 th year / of her age." An urn and willow carving is at the top of this lichen encrusted, rear facing, slate stone.
"Mrs. Lydia Sm___" is inscribed on the lichen encrusted, slate footstone. The right side has exfoliated.

Smith, Nathaniel   "Memento Mortis. / In Memory of / Mr. Nathaniel Smith, / who died Sep ^{t}. 10 th. 1782. In y^e / 82 ^{d}. Year of his Age. /
>   Remember me as you pass by,
>   For as you are so once was I.
>   As I am now so you must be,
>   Therefore prepare to follow me."

A winged angel is carved at the top of this rear facing, slate stone.
"___haniel / Smith" The top and sides of this slate footstone have exfoliated.

Smith, Nathaniel, Capt.   "Memento Mori / In Memory of / Cap ^{t}. Nathaniel Smith, / who Died Jan ^{ry}. 10 th. 1777 · / In the 82 nd Year / of his Age
>   Reader stand still and spend a tear,
>   Think on the dust that slumber here;
>   And when you read the fate of me
>   Think on the glass that runs for thee."

The first line is carved along the top of the tympanum. A winged angel is carved between the first and second lines on this rear facing, slate stone.
"Cap ^{t}. / N. S." is inscribed on the slate footstone.

Smith, Polley   "In Memory of / Polley ... / Molley ... / who died ... / ye 28, 1786. Aged 6 / Months & 27 days." A winged hourglass is carved at the top of this small, rear facing, slate stone. The stone is broken off near ground level, and the top piece is lying face down behind the piece still in the ground. A third, blank piece of slate is lying nearby. The last three lines are buried underground. Thatcher lists her as the daughter of John and Molley, and her death month as December.
The slate footstone is broken off at ground level. No inscribed pieces were found.

Smith, Polly   "In Memory of Polly, / Daug ^{tr}. of M ^{r}. John & / M ^{rs}. Molly Smith who / Died April y^e 18 th. 1782 / Aged 10 Months & 18 Days /
>   What shall we do when Death is sent
>   God takes away but what He lent;
>   ___must Die God gives the call
>   ___ arly life by Death must fall."

A winged angel is carved at the top of this rear facing, slate stone. The top right side of the tympanum has begun to exfoliate. A piece is missing on the lower left.
"_. S." This slate footstone is chipped in the upper left corner.

Smith, Rachel   "In Memory of / Rachel Daughter / of M ^{r} Abial Smith & / Lydia his wife Died / _____ y^e / AD 1772 in y^e 17 th / year of her age." There is a frond carving at the top and down the sides of this slate stone. It is broken between the first and second lines, and the fifth and sixth lines. The top two pieces are buried under the sod, face up, in front of the bottom part. Thatcher lists her as dying in January 1772, no day given.
"Rachel / Smith / 1772" The last line on this slate footstone is buried underground.

Smith, Susanna   *"In Memory of / Mr.ͤ Susanna Smith the / wife of Cap ͭ. / Nathaniel Smith who / Dec.ᵈ may ͤ_y_ 17 ͭʰ / 1768. Aged 73 yearˢ / 1 month & 18 days."* A simple head with wild hair is carved at the top of this rear facing, slate stone. Floral and leaf designs are carved on the sides. It appears the carver ran out of room with the sixth line. Note May is not capitalized.
"Mrs. / S. S." is inscribed on the slate footstone.

Southworth, Ebenezer   *"S... / decᵈ... / 16ᵗʰ 1___ ... / in ÿͤ. / of his ... / ..."* is all that can be read on the remnant of this rear facing, slate stone. The tympanum, top, and right side have exfoliated, leaving very little of the inscription left. A leaf design is carved on the left side. It is the same design as that on Elizabeth Southworth's stone, which is west of it. Thatcher lists, "Southworth, Ebenezer, died May 6ᵗʰ, 1751, in his 35ᵗʰ year." A footstone is present, but the top is missing, and no inscription was found on what remains.

Southworth, Elizabeth   *"Here lies buried / M ͬˢ _lizabeth ÿͤ / Wife to MR / Ebenezer Southworth / who decᵈ JULY ÿ / ... _ 55 in ÿͤ / ... / ... her / age."* A simple head with hair standing on end is carved at the top of this rear facing, slate stone. Leaf designs are carved down the sides. This stone has exfoliated in several places. Thatcher lists, "Southworth, Elizabeth, wife of Ebenezer, July 18, 1755, 31st year."
"MRˢ / E S" is inscribed on the slate footstone.

Staples, Edward F. Monument   *"S"* monogram is carved in shallow relief at the top of this monument. It is surrounded by carved ivy leaves. *"STAPLES / EDWARD F. STAPLES / 1846 – 1931"* is inscribed on the front. The first line is carved in relief. *"REV. CALEB TURNER / 1735 – 1803 / PHOEBE HIS WIFE / 1738 – 1818 / CALEB TURNER JR. / 1805 – 1890 / ALMIRA HIS WIFE / 1810 – 1885 / POLLY TURNER / 1820 – 1904"* is inscribed on the back.

Staples, Hannah   *"HANNAH, / wife of Paul Staples, / DIED / Jan. 16, 1842, / Æt. 58."* The first and third lines are carved in relief. A sculptured carving of a right hand, with index finger pointing up, is carved at the top of this rear facing, textured stone.
"H" is all that was found inscribed on the pieces of this crumbled footstone.

Staples, Paul   *"PAUL STAPLES / DIED / May 29, 1853, / Æt. 67. /*
It is the hope, the blissful hope,
Which Jesus's grace has given,

The hope when days and years are past,
We all...."

The first and second lines are carved in relief. A sculptured carving of a right hand, with index finger pointing up, is carved at the top of this rear facing, textured stone. The stone is broken off at ground level and reburied directly behind the piece in the ground. The rest of the poem is blocked by this piece of stone.
"P. S." This footstone is beginning to crumble.

Staples, Sarah *"SARAH / Second wife of / Paul Staples, / died Aug. 4, 1865, / in*
her 84 th year. /   *Mother thou art gone to rest,*
                      And this shall be our prayer,
                      That when we reach our journey's end
                      Thy glory we may share."
Note the space between *84* and *th.*
"S. S." is inscribed on the footstone.

Strobridge?, ___ *"...e /...April ^e_y 14 th / ..._ged 4 .../ one _onth /... _ays..."* This slate stone is broken into many small fragments. Pieced together, the above inscription is all that can be obtained. These remnants are located to the left of the stone for Jane Strobridge (d. 1762). Thatcher does not list a stone that matches the above partial information.

Strobridge, B. Frank See Strobridge Children Monument entry.

Strobridge, Benjamin *"In Memory of / BENJAMIN STROBRIDGE, / Who died*
Sep. 25, 1827, / Æt. 61. / Where friends depart or where their ashes fall,
              It matters not to die in Christ is all."
This rear facing, slate stone has an urn and willow carving at the top. Curved designs are carved down the sides.
"B. S. / 1827." is inscribed on the slate footstone. The top of the footstone is pointed, whereas the headstone has a rounded tympanum.

Strobridge, Benjamin H. See Strobridge Children Monument entry.
Massachusetts Civil War Soldiers & Sailors, 1861-1865, Vol. I, p. 196 shows that he was a Corporal with the 3rd Infantry, Co. I.

Strobridge, Chattie H. See Strobridge Children Monument entry.

Strobridge Children Monument *"CHILDREN OF / B. H. & O. D. /*
STROBRIDGE, / INFANT / BORN & DIED 1858 / MYRA E. / 1859 – 1864 /
CHATTIE H. / 1858 – 1880 / B. FRANK / 1848 – 1881 / NELLIE C. / 1860 – 1882."
is inscribed on the front of this tall, four sided monument. *"EDDIE WESTON /*
1881 – 1882" is inscribed on the left side. *"BENJAMIN H. STROBRIDGE / 1822 –*
1888 / OLIVE D. / HIS WIFE / 1827 – 1907" is inscribed on the back of this roofed monument. The first line is carved along an arch. There are no inscriptions on the right side.

Strobridge, Ebenezer Monument *"Ebenezer / Strobridge, / 1792 – 1849. / Polly*
/ Myrick, / his wife / 1800 – 1827. / Susan / Paull, / his widow / 1802 – 1878." is inscribed on the front of this tall obelisk. *"STROBRIDGE"* is inscribed on the front base. *"Ebenezer / Agustus, / 1821 – 1829. / Phebe / Myrick, / 1825 - 1831. /*

Children of / Ebenezer / & Polly M. / Strobridge." is inscribed on the right side. *"Ebenezer / Son of / Ebenezer & / Susan P. / Strobridge, / 1834 – 1839."* is inscribed on the left side. There is no inscription on the back of this obelisk. *"E. S."* This rear facing footstone is located directly behind the obelisk.

Strobridge, Ebenezer   See Ebenezer Strobridge Monument entry.
"E. S." This footstone is located in front of the monument, on the far right.

Strobridge, Ebenezer A.   See Ebenezer Strobridge Monument entry.
"E. A. S." This footstone is located in front of the monument, on the right.

Strobridge, Eddie W.   See Strobridge Children Monument entry.

Strobridge, Elisabeth   *"Mento Mortis / In Memory o_ / Mrs. Elisabeth Strobridge / wife of Mr. Benjamin Stro- / bridge, who died in childbed / Feb.ʳʸ 3ᵈ 1792. In her 25 ᵗʰ. / Year. /*
In silent dust Mrs. Strobridge lies.
Her child lies by her side,
In early Years her months did end,
With Days full sattisfi_d."
A winged angel is carved at the top of this rear facing, slate stone. Many cracks are present, and the right shoulder has exfoliated. Note the spelling of *sattisfied*.
"Mrs. / Elisabeth / Strobridge" is inscribed on this slate footstone, which faces the headstone. The right and left sides are chipped.

Strobridge, Hannah   See Gershom Crane Monument entry.
Information listed by Thatcher suggests that a different gravestone was present during his survey: "wife of William & dau. of Ebenezer Crane Esq., died July 30ᵗʰ, 1826, in her 66ᵗʰ year."
"H. S." is carved in shallow relief on the top curved surface of this upright footstone. It is located directly behind the monument, on the left.

Strobridge, Henry   *"Memento Mortis. / In memory of / Mr. Henry Strobridge, who / died Nov.ʳ 7ᵗʰ 1795. In his 74. Yeḏ /*
Look oh! my offsprings, see my friends,
The mandate, which our Saviour sends,
See how the living now are hurld
Before the Judge of all the _orld"
The first line is inscribed along an arch at the top of the tympanum. A winged angel is carved below it on this lichen encrusted, rear facing, slate stone. Many cracks are present. A veteran's marker and flag are present. Note the spelling of *hurld*.
"Mr. / Henry Strobridg_" is inscribed on this slate footstone.

Strobridge, Infant Dau.   See Strobridge Children Monument entry.
"INFANT, / Dau. of / B. H. & Olive D. / Strobridge. / Transplanted from earth, / To bloom in Heaven." This textured stone faces the rear of the cemetery, and has no dates on it. It is located in front on the monument, on the far right. This stone is for the infant mentioned on the monument. Lakeville Vital Records show that she was the twin of Chattie H. (Charity Hathaway Strobridge), and died two days after their birth on July 28, 1857. Note this birth year differs from the monument.

Strobridge, James   *"Memento Mori / In Memory of / Mʳ James Strobridge / he*

Died Feb.*ry* *ỹe* *7th* / *1773* · *in the 79 th year / of his age"* The first line is inscribed along an arch at the top of the tympanum. A winged angel is carved below this. Floral and leaf designs are carved down the sides of this rear facing stone. This reddish, slate stone is very smooth and appears to be a replacement stone. Thatcher lists that he died in February 1777, in his 78th year.

Strobridge, Jane *"In Memory of / Jane Daugh*.*tr* / *to M*.*r* *James / & M*.*rs* *Mary / Strobridge / Who Dec*.*d* / *June ỹe* · *26th* / *1762 Aged / 6 Days."* A simple head with wings is carved at the top of this rear facing, slate stone. This lichen encrusted stone is exfoliating on the sides. The last line is half buried. Thatcher lists her death as January 20th.

Strobridge, Jane *"Erected in Memory of / Mrs. JANE wido' of / Mr. Henry Strobridge / She died Feb. 28 th, / 1815. In the 84 th, / Year of her / Age."* This rear facing, slate stone has a flat topped urn and unique willow carved at the top. A curved design is carved down the sides. Several vertical cracks are present.
"JAN_ / ..." This slate footstone has exfoliated on the right side. It was broken off near ground level and is reburied behind the lower piece, blocking the rest of the inscription.

Strobridge, Jean *"IN MEMORY / OF MRS JEAN / STROBRIDGE WHO / DIED FEB* *r* *ỹe* *17th* / *1759 IN ỹe* *32nd YEAR OF HER / AGE / SHE WAS ỹe* / *WIFE OF M*r WIL / LIAM STROBRIDGE"* This lichen encrusted, rear facing, slate stone has a simple head carving at the top, and vine carvings down its sides.
"_ S. / 1759" The top left corner of this rectangular, slate footstone is missing.

Strobridg, Margaret *"Memento Mori. / In Memory of / M*.*rs* *Margaret wife of / M*.*r* *William Strobridg / who Died Dec*.*r* *ỹe* *8* .*th*1776. / In the 83d Year of her Age."* The first line is carved along an arch at the top of the tympanum. A carving of a winged angel is below this. The last line is buried underground on this rear facing, slate stone. Note the spelling of Strobridge. The carver ran out of room on the fourth line and the g is carved directly above the d.

Strobridge, Myra E. See Strobridge Children Monument entry.
"MYRA E. / Dau. of / B. H. & Olive D. / Strobridge. / Born Dec. 29, 1858. / Died Jan. 5, 1864. /

           Like a beautiful flower,
           Our darling was given,
           To bud on earth,
           And blossom in Heaven."

This small stone is located in front of the monument, on the right. Note the difference in birth year on this stone from the monument. Lakeville Vital Records confirm a female born to Benjamin and Olive on December 29, 1858.

Strobridge, Nellie C. See Strobridge Children Monument entry.

Strobridge, Olive D. See Strobridge Children Monument entry.

Strobridge, Phebe M. See Ebenezer Strobridge Monument entry.
"P. M. S." This footstone is located directly in front of the monument.

Strobridge, Polly M. See Ebenezer Strobridge Monument entry.

"P. M. S." is inscribed on this rear facing footstone. It is located behind the monument, on the far right.

Strobredg, Robert, Lieut. *"In Memory of Lieu.̲ / ROBERT STROBREDG / who departed this life / Aug.̲ ͭ ̲ͤ 14ᵗʰ AD 1790 / in ̲ͤ 39ᵗʰ Year of his / Age /*
>*My flesh shall slumber in the ground*
>*Till the Arch Angel ...*
>*Shall wake my dust and __ it rise*
>*To join my Soul and mount the skies."*

An hourglass with wings is carved above a winged angel at the top of this rear facing stone. Flower stems are carved in the lower corners of the tympanum. Scalloped designs are carved down the sides. This lichen encrusted, slate stone is exfoliating and part of the poem is unreadable because of this. *"_phas Tomson _cu..."* is inscribed on the bottom right of this stone. A *"SAR 1775"* marker and flag are present.
"___ / _obert Strobredg" This lichen encrusted slate footstone is exfoliating.

Strobridge, Sarah *"In / memory of / MRS. SARAH widow of / Mr. William Strobridge / who died / Oct. 3, 1817 / in her 90. / year."* An urn and willow carving is at the top of this rear facing, slate stone. Curved designs are carved down the sides. The stone has a near vertical crack on the right side that has been successfully repaired.

Strobridge, Susan P. See Ebenezer Strobridge Monument entry.
"S. P. S." This rear facing footstone is located behind the monument, on the left.

Strobridge, Thomas *"...EMORY OF / _HOMAS STROBR_ / IDGE, DEC^D AUGUSᵀ / yᵉ 6:ˢᵀ 1724 In yᵉ / 25ᵗʰ YEAR OF HIS / AGE"* The tympanum and shoulders of this lichen encrusted, rear facing, slate stone are missing.

Strobridge, Thomas *"IN MEMORY OF / Mͬ THOMAS / STROBRIDGE SON / OF Mͬ WILLIAM / & Mͬˢ MARGRET / STROBRIDGE / DIED APRIL ȳ 26 / 1749 IN ȳ 23ᵈ / YEAR OF HIS AGE."* A simple head is carved at the top of this rear facing, slate stone. Note the spelling of *MARGRET* and the overlap of the ME in *MEMORY*, LL in *WILLIAM* and the AR in *YEAR*
"T S / 1749" is inscribed on the slate footstone.

Strobridge, Thomas *"Memento Mori / In Memory of Mͬ. Thomas / son of Mͬ. William / Strobridge Junͬ & Mͬˢ Jane / his wife who Died Feb.ͬʸ 19 ͭʰ. / 1777 · In the 26ͭʰ. Year of / His Age."* A winged angel is carved between the first and second lines of this lichen encrusted, rear facing, slate stone.
"Mr. / Thomas / Strobridge" is inscribed on the slate footstone.

Strowbridg, William *"Memento Mori. / In Memory of / Mͬ William Strowbridg / who Died Novͬ ȳ / 14 ͭʰ. 1777 · / In the / 87 ͭʰ Year of his / Age."* The first line is carved along an arch at the top of the tympanum. A winged angel is carved below this on this rear facing, slate stone. Note the spelling of *Strowbridg*. Pieces of the border are missing on the lower right side. Below the angel carving is a circular depression with discoloration around it (a bullet hole?). A footstone is present, but exfoliation has removed the inscribed surface.

Strobridge, William   *"In Memory of / M^r. William Strobridge / who died April 1, 1797 in ẙ 73 / year of his age."* This lichen encrusted, rear facing, slate stone has a winged angel carved at the top.
"M. Wm Strobridge / 1797" is inscribed on the slate footstone.

Strobridge, William   See Gershom Crane Monument entry.
Information listed by Thatcher suggests that a different gravestone was present during his survey: "died Sept. 5th, 1842, in his 81st year."
"W. S." is carved in shallow relief on the top curved surface of this upright footstone. It is located directly behind the monument, on the right.

Sweatt, Emma C.

"EMMA C.
Only child of O. H. & M. E.
SWEATT,
Died Aug. 16, 1869.
Aged 1 yr. 4 mos."

The first line is carved in relief along an arch. A sculptured carving of a rosebud is at the bottom. A piece is broken off on the left side. This oval stone has broken off its crumbled pedestal and is resting upon it.

Tatro, Andrew M. Monument   *"TATRO"* is inscribed at the top of this monument underneath ivy leaf carvings. *"ANDREW M. / 1875 – 1933"* is inscribed below this on the left side, and *"ROSE E. / 1876 – 1968"* is inscribed on the right side.
"FATHER" is carved in relief on this flat, rear facing, ground level footstone. It is located behind and to the left of the Andrew Tatro Monument.

Tatro, Rose E.   See Andrew M. Tatro Monument entry.
"MOTHER" is inscribed on this flat, rear facing, ground level footstone. It is located behind and to the right of the Andrew Tatro Monument.

Tetro, Francis   *"FRANCIS TETRO / CO. B. / 10 N.H. INF."* is carved in relief within a recessed shield shaped area. A veteran's marker and flag are present. Lakeville Vital Records list his death on December 22, 1899, at 73 years old.

Thomas, Sabrina   *"SABRINA THOMAS, / died Aug. 7, 1871. / Aged 66 years."* This stone faces the rear of the cemetery.
"S. T." is inscribed on the footstone.

Thompson, Joanna   *"In memory of / JOANNA, / wife of / Nathaniel Thompson / who died / Oct. 2, 1837, / aged 52 years."* An urn and willow carving is at the top of this rear facing, slate stone. A simple line design is carved down the sides. A shallow crack runs through the death date.
"J. T." is inscribed on this slate footstone. No headstone was found in front of it. This is probably the footstone for Joanna Thompson's slate headstone, which is

located two plots to the east.

"JOANNA / wife of / NATHANIEL THOMPSON, / Died Oct. 2. 1837; / Aged 52 Y'rs 3 Mos / and 8 Days." is inscribed on this second stone. The first line is carved in relief along an arch. This stone also faces the rear of the cemetery, and is located in front of and to the left of the slate stone.

"J. T." is inscribed on the footstone.

Thompson, John *"JOHN TINKHAM, / son of / Nathaniel & / Joanna Thompson, / died / Feb. 19, 1832, / aged 6 years."* An urn and willow carving is at the top of this rectangular, rear facing, slate stone. Rectangular designs are carved down the sides. Thatcher lists his death day as the 9th.

"J. T. T." This footstone faces the headstone.

Thompson, Nathaniel *"NATHANIEL THOMPSON, / Died / May 2, 1856; / Aged 78 Y'rs 11 Mo's / and 24 Days"* The first line is carved in relief along an arch. This stone faces the rear of the cemetery.

"N. T." is inscribed on the footstone.

Thompson, Phebe *"PHEBE THOMPSON / died / May 30, 1850, / aged 79 Yrs."* The first line of this rear facing stone is carved in shadow.

"P T" is inscribed on the footstone.

Thompson, Sally *"To the / memory of / Mrs. Sally Thompson / wife of Mr. / Isaac Thompson / who died / November 4. 1809 / in her 27. Year."* An urn and willow carving is at the top of this rear facing, slate stone. A chain is carved on the borders of the tympanum. A thin scalloped border is carved below the carving, and around the inscription.

"Mrs. / Sally / Thompson" is inscribed on the slate footstone.

Thomson, Samuel *"In Memory of / Samuel Son to M[r] / Nathaniel Thomso[n]. / & M[s]. Phebe his / Wife Who Dec[d]. / June y[e] 19th / 1774 Aged / 17 Months / & one Day"* A simple head with wings is carved at the top of this slate stone. The footstone is a rough piece of slate. Note the spelling of Thompson.

Thresher, Edwin C. See Stephen M. Thresher Monument entry.

"EDDIE" is carved in relief on the front of this small, lichen encrusted stone. Curved designs are carved above this. *"T"* (monogram) is carved in relief at the bottom center. *"To God belongs the choicest work of his hand."* is inscribed on the vertical surface of the upper base. There are two cracks radiating from the bottom through the width of the stone. The center crack extends to his name, and the crack on the right side extends about 2½ inches. *"EDDIE C. / Son of / Stephen M. & Ellen / THRESHER, / Died Jan. 8, 1877. / Aged 2 yrs. 4 m's."* is inscribed on the back. The first line is carved along an arch. The back of the stone is very weathered.

Thresher, Elias C. *"ELIAS C. / son of / Job & Mary / Thresher, / died April 1, 1868; / Aged 37 yrs. 5 m's. / We wept ... die*

> *We mourn ... yet*
> *We hope...the sky*
> *And all ... forget."*

The first line of this weathered stone is carved in relief along an arch. A crack

radiates from the center bottom through the poem. It has been successfully repaired, but the repair material obliterates the words in the center of the poem.
"E. C. T." is inscribed on the footstone.

Thresher, Ellen A. See Stephen M. Thresher Monument entry.

Thresher, George E. *"BROTHER"* is carved in relief on the top slanted surface. *"GEORGE E. THRESHER / Born / Jan. 22, 1833, / Died Jan. 21, 1906."* is inscribed on the front. The first line is carved in relief along an arch. The two cracks at its base have been repaired successfully. This stone shares a second base with the stone of Mary A. Thresher.

Thresher, Israel *"ISRAEL THRESHER / Died / June 25, 1882, / Aged 80 years. / 2 mos."* The first line is carved along an arch. A 1½ inch crack radiates from the center bottom.

Thresher, Job P. *"JOB P. THRESHER / died March 28, 1878, / Aged 78 years."* The first line is carved in relief along an arch. This stone shares its base with that of his wife, Mary B. Thresher.
"J. P. T." is inscribed on the footstone. The inscription is buried.

Thresher, Mary A. *"SISTER"* is carved in relief on the top slanted surface. *"MARY A. THRESHER / Born / Jan. 2, 1827. / Died Nov. 14, 1912."* The first line is carved in relief along an arch. Two cracks at its base have been successfully repaired. This stone shares a second base with the gravestone of George E. Thresher.

Thresher, Mary B. *"MARY B. / widow of / Job P. Thresher, / Died Dec. 29, 1882, / Aged 84 years / & 10 m's."* The first line is carved in relief along an arch. There is a repaired crack at the bottom of this stone. This stone shares its base with her husband's stone.
"M. B. T." is inscribed on the footstone.

Thresher, Mary W. *"MARY W. / wife of / ISRAEL THRESHER / Died Oct. 9, 1898 / Aged 93 yrs. 6 mo. / 21 days"* The first line is carved along an arch.

Thresher, Phebe A. *"PHEBE A. / wife of / Elias C. Thresher, / Died June 26, 1896, / Aged 68 yrs. 2 mos."* The first line is carved in relief along an arch.

Thresher, Stephen M. Monument *"THRESHER"* is carved in relief on the top slanted surface. *"STEPHEN M. / SEPT. 4, 1840 – OCT. 14, 1900 / ELLEN ATWOOD HIS WIFE / OCT. 18, 1841 – OCT. 2, 1916 / EDWIN C. / SEPT. 5, 1874 – JAN. 8, 1877"* Overgrown evergreen bushes on the left side are beginning to encroach on this monument.

Tilson, Timothy *"Memento Mori. / In Memory of / MR Timothy Tilson / who Died Sep^t. ye 12 th / 1780 · In the 74 th Year / of his Age."* The first line is carved along an arch at the top of this lichen encrusted, rear facing, slate stone. A winged angel is carved below this. There are two, crumbling stone pieces in the ground where a footstone should be. No inscription was found on them.

Tinkham, Caleb *"Erected in Memory of / Mr. Caleb Tinkham who / died July 5 th*

*Æ*D. 1798. / in *ȳ*ᵉ 60 Year of his Age /
> *The mighty conqurer shall appear*
> *High on a royal seat,*
> *And death the last of all his foes,*
> *Lie vanquish'd at his feet."*

A peeking rising sun with a nose is carved on the tympanum of this rear facing, slate stone. The last line is buried underground. Note the spelling of *conqurer*.
"Mr. / Caleb / Tinkham" is inscribed on this rectangular, slate footstone.

Tinkham, Elisha *"In Memory of / ELISHA TINKHAM. / Who died / Aug. 28. 1868. / Aged / 76 years, 7 days."*
"E. T." This footstone is in front of the headstone.

Tinkham, Elisha H. *"ELISHA H. TINKHAM, / Died / Sept. 5, 1893, / Aged / 76 years, 8 months."* The first line is carved along an arch. *"W. H. Jackson, Taunton"* is inscribed at the center bottom of this stone. This stone is loose on its base.

Tinkham, Francis M. See Mary J. Tinkham Monument entry.

Tinkham, Hilkiah *"In Memory of / Mʳ. Hilkiah Son of Mʳ. / Peter & Mʳˢ. Mary / Tinkham. he Died / Decʳ. ȳᵉ25 ᵗʰ 1773 / In the 23ᵈ Year / of his Age."* A winged angel is carved in relief at the top of this rear facing, slate stone. Floral and leaf designs are carved along the sides. The last line is buried underground.

Tinkham, Jeremiah *"JEREMIAH TINKHAM, / Born / Aug. 18, 1778, / Died / Oct. 21, 1858."* A break through the third line has been successfully repaired.
"J. T." This footstone is located in front of the headstone.

Tinkham, Jeremiah E. *"JEREMIAH E. son of / Mr. Jeremiah and / Mrs. Nabby Tinkham / died July 25. 1825. / Æt. 2 years 1 mo. / & 10 days."* This rear facing stone has an urn and willow carving at the top. Small designs are carved down its sides. A vertical crack the height of the stone is present to the right of the midline. Although there is no sign of repair, this small stone appears to be holding together.

Tinkham, Mary J. Monument *"T"* monogram is carved at the top of this monument, with vine designs carved on either side of it. Below this, *"MARY J. TINKHAM / 1830, – 1894."* is inscribed on the left side, and *"FRANCIS M. TINKHAM / 1819, – 1892."* is inscribed on the right side.

Tinkham, Nabby *"In memory of / NABBY, / wife of / Jeremiah Tinkham; / who died / March 1, 1838, / aged 51 years / & 9 moˢ."* An urn and willow are carved at the top of this stone. Horizontal lines are carved as the side border of this stone.
"N. T." This slate footstone is located in front of the headstone.

Tinkham, Rhoda *"In memory of / RHODA. / wife of / Elisha Tinkham, / who died / Feb. 16, 1848, / aged 53 Yrs."* *"Hathaway, Taunton"* is inscribed in the lower left corner of this stone.
"R. T." This footstone is located in front of the headstone.

Townsend, Betsey *"SACRED / to the memory of / BETSEY, / wife of / John Townsend, / who died / Dec. 31, 1804; / in her 60 year."* This stone faces the rear of the cemetery.

"B. T." is inscribed on the footstone.

Townsend, John
"SACRED / to the memory of / JOHN TOWNSEND, / who died / May 6, 1835 / in his 92 year." "Geo. Thompson" is inscribed at the bottom of this rear facing stone within a mushroom like carving. A "SAR 1775" marker and flag, and a veteran's marker and flag are present.
"J. T." is inscribed on the footstone.

Turner, Almira   See Edward F. Staples Monument entry.

Turner, Caleb Jr.   See Edward F. Staples Monument entry.

Turner, Caleb, Rev.   See Edward F. Staples Monument entry.
"... / ... monumental ... / In memory of / __verand CALEB TURN__ / He _as ... in Conecticut, May 9th / 1733... Education / ...Yale College / Ordain'd Pastoral Office in the 2d Church o_ / ... Middleborough Jul_ 5th, 1761 / Whe_ __ serv'd in the Christian Ministry 41 Years / __ departed this life Sep. 11th AD 1803 / In the 71 Year of his Age / He was / The kind affectionate Consort of / Mrs. PHEBE TURNER, / A friend to pure undefil'd Religion / And Morality / A Father to the poor / Charitable & benevolent to all / Mankind./ But / ..." The rest of the inscription is too weathered to read. This collapsed table monument is lying on the ground. It is broken in the upper left corner. Note the spelling of *Conecticut*. Note his birth year differs between the two stones.

Turner, Josiah R.   "JOSIAH R. / son of / Mr. Caleb & Mrs. / Polly Turner / died Aug. 16, 1823 / aged 6 years 11 m. 18 d. /
> Come view the dwelling of the dead
> Ye mortals born to die
> And silent solemn thoughtful tread
> Where soon yourselves must lie."

An urn and willow carving is at the top of this rear facing, slate stone. The urn is sitting on a carved rectangle with fan designs carved in the corners.

Turner, Phebe/Phoebe   See Edward F. Staples Monument entry.
"In / memory of / Mrs. PHEBE / widow of / Rev.d CALEB TURNER A. M. / who died / August 25, 1818 / in her 79, / year. /
> Hear what the voice from heaven proclaims
> For all the pious dead.
> Sweet is thy savour of their names,
> And soft their sleeping bed."

There is an urn carving at the top of this table monument. There are designs along the sides, top and bottom. Thatcher lists her death day as August 5th. Note that her birth year differs between the two stones.

Turner, Philip   "Philip son of / Mr. Caleb and / Mrs. Polly Turner / died Feb. 13. 1806 / aged 6 months / & 7 days." There is an urn carved at the top of this small slate stone. Wavy lines are carved as a border on this rear facing stone.

Turner, Philip   *"Philip son of / Mr. Caleb and / Mrs. Polly Turner / died Oct. 22. 1818 / aged 7 years / & 11 months. / Here lies the hope of a fond / Mother and the blasted expe- / ctation of an indulgent Fath- / er."* An urn is carved at the top of this rear facing, slate stone. Wavy lines are carved down the sides. A George Thompson swirl is carved above the poem.

Turner, Polly   See Edward F. Staples Monument entry.

Walker, Phebe   *"Sacred to the Memory of / Mrs. Phebe wido of Col. / Eln^{a}than Walker she died / April 3^d ÆD 1803 in ÿ^e 80th. / Year of her Age. /*
             This is the end of all that live
             This ^{is} my dark long home,
             Jesus himself lay in the g^{r}ave
             The house where all must come."
There is a frond carving at the top of this lichen encrusted, rear facing, slate stone. *"...er / _ied / 1803."* The left side of this slate footstone is missing.

Warren, Anna   *"In Memory of / Mrs Anna wife of / Mr John Warren / who Died Jan^{ry}.^e_y 8th. / 1770 Aged 69 Years & / 11 Months."* A winged angel is carved at the top of this lichen encrusted, rear facing, slate stone. The last line is buried underground.
"M^s / Anna Warren." is inscribed on this slate footstone.

Washburn, Amos, Capt.   *"CAPT. / AMOS WASHBURN, / died Oct. 14, 1794; / aged 52 y'rs."* A veteran's marker and flag are present near this rear facing stone. A footstone is present, but there is no inscription on it.

Washburn, Amos, Esq.   *"AMOS WASHBURN / ESQ. / died Aug. 4, 1853; / Aged 79 years."* This stone faces the rear of the cemetery.
"A. W." is inscribed on the top horizontal surface of this footstone.

Washburn, Betsy   *"BETSY WASHBURN. / died April 12, 1845, / aged 82 years."* This stone is very weathered. A footstone is present, but it contains no inscription.

Washburn, Charles E.   *"CHARLES E. WASHBURN / died / March 2, 1880, / Aged 61 years."* The first line of this rear facing stone is carved along an arch.
"C. E. W." is inscribed on the footstone.

Washburn, Charles F.   *"In memory of / Charles F. son of / Mr. Luther & Mrs. / Hannah Washburn / he died Sep. 23 / 1810 / Aged 1 Year 10 Mo. / 3 Days"* A rising sun is carved on the lichen encrusted tympanum. The last three lines are buried underground on this small, rear facing, slate stone.

Washburn, Charlotte   *"CHARLOTTE WASHBURN, / Died / May 5, 1854. / Aged 38 years."* The first line is carved along an arch on this rear facing stone.
"C. W. M." is inscribed on the footstone.

Washburn, Christiana W.   *"CHRISTIANA W. / Wife of / JAMES WASHBURN / Born / August 7, 1827. / Died / November 8, 1904."* This stone faces the rear of the cemetery.

Washburn, Cyrus *"CYRUS WASHBURN / Died / Aug. 17, 1875. / Aged 69 Yrs. 9 mo's."* This stone faces the rear of the cemetery.
"C. W." is inscribed on the footstone.

Washburn, Emily A. *"In memory of / Emily A, daug. of / Luther & Hannah / WASHBURN, / who died Feb. 11, 1815 / Æt. 3 y'rs / 11 months."* This rear facing, slate stone has a curved design carved at the top, and a scalloped line carved around its edges. The last line is buried underground.

Washburn, Francis *"FRANCIS WASHBURN / died / May 5, 1892, / Aged 74 years."* The first line is carved along an arch. This textured stone faces the rear of the cemetery.

Washburn, Hannah F. *"HANNAH F. / WIFE OF / LUTHER WASHBURN, ESQ. / DIED / Oct. 26, 1853. / Aged 68 years."* This stone faces the rear of the cemetery.
"H. F. W." is inscribed on the top horizontal surface of this footstone.

Washburn, James *"JAMES WASHBURN, / Born / Dec. 20, 1820, / Died / April 19, 1897."* is inscribed on this rear facing stone.

Washburn, James Esq. *"In / memory of / JAMES WASHBURN Esq. / who died / Nov. 19. 1815 / aged 48 / years."* An urn and willow are carved at the top of this lichen encrusted, rear facing, slate stone. A George Thompson swirl is carved under the last line. Small, carved designs are carved below the tympanum, on the sides, and in a circle around the inscription. They also outline an area where a poem could be placed, although none is present. A veteran's marker and flag are present.
"Esq. / J. W." is inscribed on this slate footstone.

Washburn, Joshua *"In / memory of / Mr. JOSHUA WASHBURN / who died / May 2, 1818 / aged 39 / years."* There is an urn and willow carving at the top of this lichen encrusted, rear facing, slate stone. A George Thompson swirl is carved below the last line. Small, carved designs are carved below the tympanum, on the sides, and in a circle around the inscription.
"Mr. / J. W." This slate footstone faces the headstone.

Washburn, Louisa *"LOUISA WASHBURN / Died / May 8, 1879, / Aged 72 years."* The first line is carved along an arch. This stone faces the rear of the cemetery.
"L. W." is inscribed on the footstone.

Washburn, Luther *"LUTHER WASHBURN Esq / died Jan. 21, 1856, / in his 79 th year."* Note the space between '79' and 'th'. This stone faces the rear of the cemetery.

Washburn, Lydia *"LYDIA WASHBURN, / died July 4. 1803; / aged 34 years."* is inscribed on this rear facing stone. The footstone has no inscription on it.

Washburn, Olive *"OLIVE WASHBURN / died July 30. 1847 / aged 75 years."* is inscribed on this rear facing stone. The footstone has no inscription on it.

Washburn, Phebe *"PHEBE WASHBURN. / died Aug. 26. 1844, / aged 75 years."* is inscribed on this rear facing stone. The footstone has no inscription on it.

Washburn, Prudence   *"PRUDENCE, / widow of Capt. / AMOS WASHBURN. / died Oct. 30, 1804. / aged 63 years."* is inscribed on this rear facing stone. A footstone is present, but there is no inscription on it.

Washburn, Prudence   *"PRUDENCE WASHBURN / died / Dec. 28, 1868; / in her 88 ͭʰ year."* The first line on this rear facing stone is carved along an arch. *"P. W."* is inscribed on the footstone.

Washburn, William F.   *"Sacred / to the memory of / WILLIAM FREDRICK, / son of Luther & / Hannah Washburn; / he died / Jan. 14, 1829, / in his 16 year."* There is an urn and willow carved at the top of this rear facing, slate stone. A curved design is carved on the shoulders and surrounds the inscription.

Westgate, Alfred F.   See Gertrude F. Westgate Monument entry. *"DAD"* is inscribed on this flat 1 inch high footstone. It is located in front of the monument, on the right.

Westgate, Arthur F.   See Elisha Westgate Monument entry.

Westgate, Baby   *"BABY / 1933"* is inscribed on this flat 6 inch square, 1 inch high marker. A low cement wall surrounds this stone and the Russell Westgate Monument. The threshold to this walled area has *"1934"* in white letters nailed into the cement.

Westgate, Baby   *"BABY"* is inscribed on this flat, ground level stone. It is located in front of the Charles H. Westgate Monument, on the right.

Westgate, Beatrice E.   See Nelson Westgate Monument entry.

Westgate, Bert   See Jeannette Westgate Monument entry.

Westgate, Bertha A.   See Young / Westgate Monument entry. *"BERTHA A."* is inscribed on this flat, ground level stone. It is located in front of the monument, on the right.

Westgate, Catherine A.   See James W. Westgate Monument entry.

Westgate, Charles H. Monument   *"WESTGATE"* is inscribed on the front of this monument. There are floral carvings in the top corners. *"CHARLES H. WESTGATE / 1869 – 1939 / MARY L. WESTGATE / 1893 – 1957"* is inscribed on the back, with *"MAY THEY REST IN PEACE"* inscribed at the bottom of the monument. A Flint Monument Works metal tag is present. A low cement wall surrounds this monument and the stones of Amelia Burnham, Baby, and the Gilbert Westgate Monument.

Westgate, Dorothy   See Russell Westgate Monument entry.

Westgate, Elisha   See Elisha Westgate Monument entry.

Westgate, Elisha B.   *"E. B. WESTGATE / CO. F. / 29 MASS. INF."* The inscription is carved in relief within a recessed shield shaped area. A veteran's marker and flag are present. There are no dates on this stone. *Massachusetts Civil War Soldiers and Sailors, 1861-1865,* Vol. III, p. 309, lists Elisha B. Westgate, 31, from Freetown enlisting with this unit in November, 1861. Lakeville Vital Records list his death on January 7, 1906, at 75 years, 4 months, and 20 days old.

Westgate, Elisha F. Monument   *"W* (monogram) */ WESTGATE / ELISHA F. WESTGATE / FEB. 20, 1867 – NOV. 3, 1950 / ELIZABETH M. HIS WIFE / FEB. 22, 1869 – MAY 17, 1945 / HAROLD L. WESTGATE / 1899 – 1977"* The monogram is carved in shallow relief. There are floral designs in the upper corners of this rear facing stone.   A cement border with *"1945"* inscribed on it surrounds this monument and its footstones. An A. F. Richmond metal tag is present.
"FATHER" is inscribed on this flat, 0-2 inch high footstone. It is located directly behind the monument, on the right. There are three upright 7-12 inch high stone markers in front of the monument. These stones may have been inscribed on the top surface at one time, but nothing is legible now.

Westgate, Elisha Monument   *"W* (monogram) */ ELISHA WESTGATE / 1835 – 1918. / His Wife / EMILY WESTGATE / 1849 – 1922. / Their Son / ARTHUR F. / 1879 – 1914."* *"WESTGATE"* is carved in relief on the base. Floral designs are carved on either side of the monogram, and down the sides. A *"GAR 8 423"* marker and flag are present. *Massachusetts Civil War Soldiers and Sailors, 1861-1865,* Vol. III, p. 309, lists Elisha as enlisting with the 29th Infantry, Co. F. in Nov. 1861. *Vital Records of the Town of Freetown, Massachusetts, 1686 through 1890* shows he was Elisha B. Westgate's brother-in-law, having married his younger sister, Emily.

Westgate, Elizabeth M.   See Elisha F. Westgate Monument entry.
"MOTHER" is inscribed on this flat, ground level footstone. It is located directly behind the monument, on the left. There is also a broken, second footstone inscribed with *"MOTHE_"* inside this bordered area.   It is located to the right of the monument.

Westgate, Emily   See Elisha Westgate Monument entry.

Westgate, Emma J.   See Reuben Westgate Monument entry.
"EMMA." is carved in relief on this flat, ground level footstone. It faces the rear of the cemetery and is located behind the monument, on the left.

Westgate, Eva L.   See William Westgate Monument entry.
"MOTHER" is inscribed on a 2 inch high, flat footstone. Leaf carvings are on the sides. It is located in front of the monument, on the left.

"EVA L. WESTGATE
1886 – 1944"

is embossed on this ground level funeral home marker. A wreath is embossed at the top. It is located to the left of the monument.

Westgate, Everett W.   See William Westgate Monument entry.

Westgate, Gertrude F. Monument   *"WESTGATE"* is inscribed at the top of this

slanted monument. *"GERTRUDE F. / AUG. 7, 1921 / JUNE 30, 1990"* is inscribed on the bottom left, and *"ALFRED F. / DEC. 3, 1919 / OCT. 19, 1991"* is inscribed on the bottom right. Hands folded in prayer are carved on the upper right side. Ivy leaves are carved around them. A low concrete wall surrounds this plot.
"MOM" is inscribed on this flat, one-inch high footstone. It is located in front of the monument, on the left.

Westgate, Gilbert H. *"WESTGATE / LOVING SON / GILBERT H. / 1922 – 1998"* A porcelain portrait is located at the center top of this monument, above the inscription. Floral carvings are in the upper corners. The low cement wall which surrounds this monument includes the stones of Amelia Burnham, Baby, and the Charles H. Westgate Monument.

Westgate, Harold L. See Elisha F. Westgate Monument entry.

Westgate, James W. Monument *"WESTGATE"* is inscribed at the top of this slanted monument. *"JAMES W. / 1877 – 1962"* is inscribed below this on the left, and *"CATHERINE A. / 1889 – 1970"* is inscribed on the right.

Westgate, Jeannette Stone *"Westgate / Jeannette / 1919 – 1960 / Bert / 1907 – 1970"* This crudely inscribed cement stone faces the rear of the cemetery.

Westgate, John E. See Young / Westgate Monument entry.
His obituary in *The Middleborough Gazette* 08/15/2002:6 reports his death date as Aug. 11, 2002.

Westgate, Mary L. See Charles H. Westgate Monument entry.

Westgate, Nancy R. See William J. Westgate Monument entry.

Westgate, Nelson Monument *"WESTGATE"* is carved in outline inside a black heart on the front of this monument. A porcelain portrait is attached above the inscription. *"NELSON BEATRICE"* is inscribed below the heart at the bottom. *"NELSON L. WESTGATE / 1914 – 1977 / HIS WIFE / BEATRICE E. BURNHAM / 1911 – 1995"* is inscribed on the back. A low cement wall encloses this plot. An S. Barnicoat metal tag is present. There are two flags present at this site.

Westgate, Reuben F. Monument *"W"* monogram is carved in shallow relief at the top of this monument on both the front and back. It is surrounded by vine carvings. *"REUBEN F. WESTGATE / FEB. 16, 1858 – APR. 2, 1933 / HIS WIFE EMMA J. / OCT. 26, 1860 – FEB. 2, 1913"* is inscribed on the front of this monument. *"WESTGATE"* is carved in relief on the front base. *"1881 THOMAS P. ELLIS 1955 / HIS WIFE / 1902 M. MAUDE 1958"* is inscribed on the back.

Westgate, Richard E. *"✝ / RICHARD WESTGATE / 1939 – 2000 / EGGER & ASHLEY"* is embossed on a funeral home marker. No stone is present at this time.

Westgate, Russell Monument *"WESTGATE"* is inscribed at the top of this monument. Floral designs adorn the upper corners. *"RUSSELL DOROTHY"* is inscribed at the bottom on the front. *"RUSSELL L. WESTGATE / FEB. 14, 1913 ____ / HIS WIFE / DOROTHY E. DeMORANVILLE / JULY 21, 1911 – SEP. 3, 1991"* is inscribed on the back. A Barnicoat Monuments metal tag is present. A low cement wall surrounds this stone and the *"Baby 1933"* stone. The threshold to this walled area has *"1934"* in white letters nailed into the cement.

Westgate, William F. Monument   *"WESTGATE / 1876 WILLIAM F. 1944 / 1886EVA. L. 1944"* is inscribed on the front of this monument. A geometric design is carved at the top, and ivy designs are carved on the sides. *"1902 EVERETT W. WESTGATE 1922"* is inscribed on the back.
"WILLIAM F. WESTGATE / 1876 – 1944" is embossed on a ground level funeral home marker. It is located to the far left of the monument. A wreath is embossed at the top.
"FATHER" is inscribed on this flat, ground level stone. It is located in front of the monument, on the far left. A low concrete wall surrounds this plot.

Westgate, William J. Monument   *"WESTGATE"* is inscribed on the front of this monument. Floral designs adorn the upper corners. An overgrown yew is planted on the right and is blocking part of the inscriptions. *"WILLIAM J. WESTGATE / 1874 – 1969 / WIFE – NANCY R. / 1878 – 1971"* is inscribed on the back.

Weston, Charles L.   See James Weston Monument entry.

Weston, James A. Monument   *"WESTON"* is inscribed on the front of this monument. *"1866 JAMES A. 1938 / 1900 CHARLES L. 1963 / 1891 KATHERINE J. 1969"* is inscribed on the back. A Central Monument Co. metal tag is present.

Weston, Katherine J.   See James Weston Monument entry.

Whittemore, Harriet   *"In memory of / Miss HARRIET. Dau. of / Mr. Richard Whittemore & / Mrs. Elizabeth his wife / she died / May 23, 1823 / in her 21 year"*
An urn and willow carving is at the top of this small, lichen encrusted, slate stone. *"H. W."* is inscribed on the slate footstone.

Wilbur, Edith L.   See Wilbur Monument entry.

Wilbur, Emma E.   See Wilbur Monument entry.

Wilbur, Ethel L.   See Wilbur Monument entry.

Wilbur, George E. Monument   *"WILBUR / GEORGE E.   EDITH L. / EMMA E. RALPH E. / ETHEL L.   LEROY M."* A bowl with ivy leaves are carved at the top of this monument. No dates are present and there is no room for them on this stone. A Barnicoat Monuments metal tag is present.

Wilbur, Leroy M.   See Wilbur Monument entry.

Wilbur, Ralph E.   See Wilbur Monument entry.

Williams, Isabell F.   See Marshall B. Williams Monument entry.

Williams, John H.   *"JOHN H. WILLIAMS, / DIED / MAY 12, 1855, / Æ. 53 yrs..*
& 10 Ms. /   *"Be ye therefore ready also*
                      For the son of man cometh
                      At an hour when ye think not.""
The first line is carved in relief in an arch.
"J. H. W." This footstone is located in front of the headstone.

Williams, Marshall B. Monument   *"MARSHALL B. WILLIAMS / BORN / FEB. 24. 1859 / ISABELL F. ELMES / WIFE OF / M. B. WILLIAMS / BORN MAY 3, 1860 / DIED NOV. 18, 1895."* is inscribed on the front of this tall monument. *"WILLIAMS"* is carved in relief on the base. The first line is carved along an arch. *"CYRUS O. ELMES / BORN JAN. 4. 1826. / NANCY C. WILBUR / WIFE OF / CYRUS O. ELMES / BORN MARCH 11. 1832"* is carved on the left side. The first line is carved along an arch. *"ELMES"* is carved in relief on the base below. The right side and back are not inscribed. There is an urn sculpture at the top of this monument with designs carved on it. Designs are also carved at the top and bottom of all four sides of the monument. There are no death dates for Marshall, Cyrus or Nancy, but there is room for them.

Williams, Phebe K.   *"PHEBE K. / Wife of / John H. Williams, / died Nov. 30. 1848. / Aged 40 years. / Farewell dear suffering Mother,*
All thy pains and toils are o'er;
Thou hast gained a home with Jesus,
On that peaceful happy shore."
The first line is carved in relief.
"P. K. W." This footstone is located in front of the headstone.

Wordell, Arthur E.   *"ARTHUR E. WORDELL / 1881 – 1945 / EGGER FUNERAL HOME"* is embossed on this ground level funeral home marker. A wreath is embossed at the top. No gravestone is present at this time.

Wordell, Baby Girl Monument   *"WORDELL / BABY GIRL – 1946 / SUSAN – 1947 / DEBORAH – 1951"* is inscribed on this flat, ground level stone. There is a 2½ foot tall upright metal pole next to it.
"BABY GIRL WORDELL / 1946 – 1946" is embossed on a small funeral home marker which is 3 inches above the ground. A wreath is embossed at the top. It is located behind the stone.

Wordell, Deborah M.   See Baby Girl Wordell Monument entry.
"DEBORAH MAY WORDELL / 1951 – 1951" is embossed on a small funeral home marker which is 3 inches above the ground. A wreath is embossed at the top. There are two upright metal poles on either side of this marker.

Wordell, John Monument   *"IN LOVING MEMORY OF"* is inscribed on a banner carved at the top of the monument. It is surrounded by floral carvings. Carved in relief in the center of the banner is a heart with thorns around it, and a cross. *"JOHN WORDELL / 1906 – 1945 / LOTTIE WORDELL / 1907 – 1968"* is inscribed below this in a recessed area.

Wordell, Lottie   See John Wordell Monument entry.

Wordell, Lottie E.   See LeRoy P. Crossman Monument entry.

Wordell, Raymond E.   *"RAYMOND E WORDELL SR / PFC   US ARMY / WORLD WAR II / DEC 3 1923   MAY 19 1983"* This flat, ground level stone has a circled cross carved at the top. It is beginning to be buried on the left side. A 30 inch upright metal pole is next to it. A veteran's marker and flag are present.

Wordell, Susan A.   *"SUSAN A. WORDELL / 1884 – 1965 / EGGER FUNERAL HOME"* is embossed on a funeral home marker which is flat on the ground. A wreath is embossed at the top. No gravestone is present at this time.

Wordell, Susan M.   See Baby Girl Wordell Monument entry.
"SUSAN MARIE WORDELL / 1947 – 1948" is embossed on a small funeral home marker which is 3 inches above the ground. A wreath is embossed at the top. There is a 2-foot tall upright metal pole placed in the ground next to this marker.

Young, Edith M.   See William H. Young Monument entry.
"EDITH" is inscribed on this flat, ground level stone, which faces the rear of the cemetery. It is located directly behind the monument, on the right.

Young, Grace L.   See Young / Westgate Monument entry.
"GRACE L." is inscribed on this flat, ground level stone. It is located in front of the monument, on the far right. Taunton Vital Records show Grace L. Westlake married George Edward Young in 1906.

Young, Robert L.   See William H. Young Monument entry.
"✝ / ROBERT L. YOUNG / MASSACHUSETTS / CPL   ARMY AIR FORCES / WORLD WAR II / OCT 15 1914   APRIL 14 1971" is embossed on a metal plaque which is attached to a flat, ground level stone. A veteran's marker and flag are present. It faces the rear of the cemetery, and is located behind the monument, on the left.

Young/Westgate Monument   *"YOUNG / WESTGATE"* is inscribed on the front of the monument. *"JOHN E. WESTGATE / 1908 – ____ / SISTERS / GRACE L. YOUNG / 1888 – 1971 / BERTHA A. WESTGATE / 1903 – 1979"* is inscribed on the back. There are two small stones with the word *"BABY"* roughly carved on them. These 1 inch high stones face the rear of the cemetery, and are located behind the monument, one directly behind it, and one on the right. Taunton Vital Records document a Charles Edward was born to George and Grace Young on May 14, and died May 21, 1907. Perhaps one of these is his stone.

Young, William H. Monument   *"YOUNG"* is inscribed on the front of this monument. Floral carvings adorn the upper corners. *"1887   WILLIAM H. YOUNG 1967 / 1889   EDITH M. HIS WIFE   1983 / 1914   ROBERT L.   1971"* is inscribed on the back. An Albert F. Richmond Memorials metal tag is present.

"WILLIAM" is inscribed on this flat, ground level stone, which faces the rear of the cemetery. It is located directly behind the monument, on the left.

Additional Notes:

A veteran's *"1812"* marker and flag are located between the gravestones of Hannah Staples and Joanna Thompson's marble stone. No stone is present, and it is unclear if there is actually a grave here.

Thatcher lists the following people as buried in Thompson Hill Cemetery, but no stone was found for them:
"Sampson, Emily Frances, dau. of Nathaniel & Zilpah, Mar. 20, 1832, 1 yr., 1mo. Sampson, Son & Dau., twin Children of Nathaniel & Zilpah, June 30, 1828."

Nicholas Roche and Phebe Turner table monuments.

Thompson Hill Cemetery Map Index

Alphabetical:

Bassett, Sarah M. (~1796-1830) – 101
Blackman, Lucy (~1792-1860) – 113
Braley, Serena J. (1860-1927) – 117
Briggs, Anna M. (~1824-1884) – 268
Briggs, Daniel (~1796-1849) – 267
Briggs, Julia (1798-1880) – 267
Burnham, Ada E. (1894-1979) – 320, 345
Burnham, Amelia M. (1946) – 489
Burnham, Bessie (1909) – 60
Burnham, Chester W. (1890-1954) – 319, 345
Burnham, Harry L. (1896-1978) – 449
Burnham, Mary V. (1894-1938) – 450
Burnham, William H. (1865-1943) – 61
Burr, George J. (1827-1859) – 348
Burrell, Lony (1797-1876) – 115
C., D. (no dates) – 190
C., T. (no dates) – 189
Cain, George S. (~1829-1840) – 73
Cain, Lucy (1777-1856) – 134
Cain, Samuel (1772-1857) – 133
Cain, Samuel (1801-1876) – 99
Cain, Serena (1803-1857) – 100
Canedy, Barnabas (1785) – 77
Canedy, Barnebus, Ens. (~1735-1776) – 110
Canedy, Charity (~1732-1805) – 108
Canedy, Elizabeth (~1702-1780) – 141
Canedy, Elkanah L. (1800) – 78
Canedy, Hope (~1762-1829) – 79
Canedy, Mary B. (~1818-1832) – 76
Canedy, William, Capt. (~1730-1804) – 109
Canedy, William, Esq. (~1689-1774) – 142
Caswell, Abiah (~1785-1817) – 120
Caswell, Abigail W. (1817-1888) – 370, 378
Caswell, Abraham (1791-1859) – 378, 379
Caswell, Abraham (1816-1880) – 378
Caswell, Annis (~1756-1830) – 123
Caswell, Belony W. (1855-1856) – 347
Caswell, Benj. W. (1860-1942) – 304
Caswell, David (~1742-1825) – 124
Caswell, David (~1779-1837) – 381
Caswell, David B. (1863-1894) – 119
Caswell, Edward T. (1868-1948) – 114
Caswell, Eliab (1800-1873) – 121
Caswell, Eliza (1799-1860) – 118
Caswell, Eliza C. (1796-1884) – 378
Caswell, Ella M. (1865-1943) – 304
Caswell, Grace M. (1870-1927) – 114
Caswell, Kenneth E. (1907-1977) – 85
Caswell, Kenneth M. (1898) – 45, 48
Caswell, Leavitt C. (1860-1946) – 43, 45

Caswell, Lois (~1785-1868) – 380
Caswell, Lucy (~1778-1808) – 122
Caswell, Lucy P. (1811-1872) – 52
Caswell, Mary E. (1854-1855) – 305
Caswell, Mary Jane (1828-1903) – 116
Caswell, Mary Jane (1843-1881) – 378
Caswell, Nettie P. (1864-1931) – 42, 45
Caswell, Phebe H. (1816-1848) – 378
Caswell, Phebe J. (~1821-1842) – 371
Caswell, Richard B. Jr. (1943-1971) – 87
Caswell, Richard B. Sr. (1909-1985) – 88
Caswell, S. Helen (1918-2001) – 88
Caswell, Sarah M. (1837-1915) – 41, 45
Caswell, Stetson (1823-1902) – 40
Churchill, Chloe (~1815-1877) – 83
Churchill, Libeus C. (1811-1892) – 80
Churchill, Malancy J. (1810-1886) – 81
Churchill, Sarah (~1790-1874) – 82
Cobb, Harriet (1816-1882) – 6
Cornell, Russell E., Jr. (1946-1947) – 428
Crafts, Thomas (~1759-1819) – 140
Crane, Betsey A. (1818-1846) – 312, 313
Crane, Caroline (1817-1846) – 311, 313
Crane, Ebenezer (1820-1899) – 313, 331
Crane, Gershom (1778-1848) – 313
Crane, Sally (1795-1875) – 313, 332
Crossman, LeRoy P. (1922-1983) – 480
Crossman, LeRoy R. (1944-____) – 480
Crossman, Stella P. (1925-____) – 480
Dean, Barney T. (1840-1928) – 53
Dean, Betsey (1814-1840) – 53
Dean, Drusilla (1831-1905) – 22
Dean, Henry A. (1816-1898) – 53
Dean, James A. (1830-1908) – 22
Dean, Joshua, Rev. (1788-1824) – 295
Dean, Julia (1820-1869) – 53, 54
Dean, Julia M. (1845-1846) – 389
Dean, Mary M. (1788-1843) – 295
Dean, Rhoda F. (1852-1913) – 53
DeMaranville, E. May (1893-1977) – 455, 457
DeMaranville, George M. (1870-1949) – 453, 457
DeMaranville, Mabel A. (1872-1936) – 454, 457
DeMoranville, Charles (1964) – 474
DeMoranville, Deborah F. (1852-1928) – 436
DeMoranville, Evelyn L. (1918-1970) – 475
DeMoranville, Frederick E. (1875-1970) – 508

DeMoranville, Gerald C. (1916-1964) – 475
DeMoranville, Harriet E. (1941-1985) – 479
DeMoranville, Inez L. (1917-1974) – 478
DeMoranville, James F. (1948-1988) – 477
DeMoranville, Jamie F. (1978-2003) – 476
DeMoranville, Jesse H. (1942-1993) – 479
DeMoranville, Jesse N. (1914-1965) – 478
DeMoranville, Leo F. (1923-1998) – 463,
    465
DeMoranville, Leo F. Jr. (1945-1948) – 464,
    465
DeMoranville, Myron V. (1877-1965) – 434
DeMoranville, Rose A. (1876-1962) – 508
DeMoranville, Shoman A. (1850-1882) –
    436
Dietrich, Anna M. (1873-1930) – 61, 64
Dugan, Nellie F. (1878-1916) – 500
Dushane, Adeline (1836-1914) – 432
Dushane, Chauncey E. (1873-1911) – 432
Dushane, Francis (1815-1902) – 432
Dushane, Frank E. (1872-1908) – 432
Dushane, Minnie (1879-1906) – 432
Eaton, Agusta S. (~1824-1893) – 276
Ellis, M. Maude (1902-1958) – 491
Ellis, Thomas P. (1881-1955) – 491
Elmes, Anner E. (~1766-1788) – 246
Elmes, Cyrus (~1801-1864) – 328
Elmes, Cyrus O. (1826-1903) – 431
Elmes, Phebe A. (~1843-1850) – 330
Elmes, Nancy C. (1832-1900) – 431
Elmes, Phebe (~1769-1849) – 248
Elmes, Silence (~1803-1865) – 329
Elms, Abner (~1765-1836) – 247
Forrest, John A. (1886-1948) – 457, 459
Forrest, John A. (1927-1994) – 457, 458
Forrest, Josephine (1899-1992) – 457, 460
Forrest, Louise K. (1928-____) – 457, 458
Fredette, Alfred J. (1868-1955) – 130
French, Hadon (1740-1787) – 86
Gay, Bradley L. (1866-1948) – 291
Gay, Edna R. (1894-1941) – 291
Gay, Horace F. (1900-1974) – 291
Gay, Katherine B. (1868-1948) – 291
Gay, Lewis (1890-1942) – 290, 291
Gibbs, Dennis (1810-1811) – 377
Gibbs, Elisha (~1769-1831) – 387
Goodwin, Sarah P. (1798-1827) – 157
H., F. (no dates) – 310
Hacket, John, Elder (~1689-1767) – 367
Hall, Abigail (____-1747) – 314
Haskell, George E. (no dates) – 430

Haskins, Adam J. (1993) – 471
Haskins, Albert (~1826-1837) – 390
Haskins, Amelia K. (1804-1885) – 399
Haskins, Andrew, Dea. (~1789-1855) – 398
Haskins, Apollos (1796-1865) – 400
Haskins, Austin (1830-1908) – 39
Haskins, Betsey S. (1836-1905) – 38
Haskins, Elmore P. (1849-1930) – 32
Haskins, Emily A. (1837-1850) – 391
Haskins, Hannah (~1757-1820) – 411
Haskins, Harriot (~1814-1834) – 393
Haskins, Joseph C. (1817-1904) – 37
Haskins, Joshua (~1755-1849) – 412
Haskins, Joshua, Jr. (~1784-1861) – 404
Haskins, Levi (1794-1862) – 25
Haskins, Levi H. (1834-1908) – 26
Haskins, Lydia B. (~1794-1841) – 398
Haskins, Lydia B. (1819-1887) – 31
Haskins, Martha (1830-1831) – 392
Haskins, Mary (~1803-1871) – 24
Haskins, Mary K. (1821-1860) – 386
Haskins, Mary S. (1829-1884) – 27
Haskins, Mirick (~1787-1810) – 401
Haskins, Orin E. (1845-1922) – 23
Haskins, Orville (1815-1893) – 30
Haskins, Rebecca S. (~1790-1839) – 402
Haskins, Serena (~1787-1809) – 403
Hopkins, Bertha (1868) – 307
Hopkins, Charles W. (1861-1929) – 306
Hopkins, Ella T. (1865-1951) – 306
Hopkins, Fanny (1888-1952) – 306
Hopkins, Fanny A. (1821-1879) – 325
Hopkins, Fanny Maria (1847-1922) – 323
Hopkins, Lydia A. (1849-1900) – 324
Hopkins, Lydia E. (1825-1909) – 327
Hopkins, Rosseter (1843) – 309
Hopkins, Sadie (1855-1856) – 308
Hopkins, William H. (1820-1902) – 326
Hopkins, William H. (1844-1909) – 322
Isaacsen, Kristin L. (1987) – 480
Jones, Consider (~1741-1820) – 422
Jones, Patience (~1761-1847) – 421
Jones, Paul L. (1820-1900) – 413
Jones, Sarah M. (1828-1854) – 413
King, Bathsheba (~1778-1788) – 106
King, Mary C. (1824-1866) – 33
King, Silas S. (1818-1890) – 34
Kinsley Alvin E. (~1826-1841) – 373
Kinsley, Betsey (1824-1906) – 376
Kinsley, John (1829-1899) – 375
Kinsley, Sarah (1832-1833) – 374

Kinsley, Susanna A. (1794-1875) – 385
Kinsley, Unite (1791-1833) – 384
Leonaid, E. L. (____-1911) – 506
Leonard, Anna (~1792-1863) – 281
Leonard, child (1711) – 227
Leonard, Deliverance (1723-1751) – 181
Leonard, Elisabeth (~1704-1780) – 221
Leonard, Elizabeth (~1754-1791) – 250
Leonard, Elkanah (~1676-1714) – 224
Leonard, Elkanah, Esq. (~1704-1777) – 222
Leonard, Gideon (~1757-1811) – 277
Leonard, Gideon (1789-1872) – 282
Leonard, Hannah (~1732-1796) – 219
Leonard, Hannah (~1759-1840) – 279
Leonard, Henry (1714) – 228
Leonard, Joseph (~1753-1844) – 251
Leonard, Joseph J. C. (1801-1872) – 253
Leonard, Joseph O. L. (1791-1792) – 249
Leonard, Lydia (~1804-1874) – 280
Leonard, Thomas (no dates) – 226
Leonard, Timothy M. (~1800-1854) – 278
Leonard, Zebulon (~1729-1794) – 220
Leonard, Zilpha (~1766-1827) – 252
MacAulay, Annie M. (1872-1946) – 84
Manchester, Horace A. (1842-1910) – 451
Matteson, Flora M. (1872-1966) – 456, 457
McCully, Martha (1740-1760) – 182
Meack, Timothy (1960) – 346
Merick, Roxana (1808) – 388
Miller, Joanna (~1732-1758) – 318
Miller, Rhoda (~1761-1801) – 344
Miller, Susa S. (1800-1801) – 343
Montgomery Monument (no dates) – 292
Montgomery, Anna S. (~1764-1828) – 296
Montgomery, Augustus (~1780-1782) – 272
Montgomery, Fannie (1876-1891) – 259
Montgomery, Hugh (~1756-1835) – 297
Montgomery, Hugh (1802-1883) – 264
Montgomery, Isadore L. (1852-1916) – 261
Montgomery, James (~1808-1849) – 266
Montgomery, John, Elder (~1708-1787) – 299
Montgomery, John (1799-1881) – 294
Montgomery, John F. (1843-1918) – 260
Montgomery, Mary A. (1847-1935) – 262
Montgomery, Mary Ann (1804-1886) – 293
Montgomery, Mary S. (~1718-1790) – 298
Montgomery, Nancy (1789-1881) – 265
Montgomery, Rebecca (~1760-1798) – 270
Montgomery, Samuel, Dr. (~1754-1787) – 271

Montgomery, William (~1767-1804) – 269
Montgomery, William (1804-1898) – 263
Moranville, Alice M. (1881-1947) – 89, 93
Moranville, Bernice L. (1902-1978) – 91, 93
Moranville, Dennis L. (1942-2002) – 92, 93
Moranville, Edson V. (1869-1944) – 93, 94
Moranville, Flora E. (1870-1933) – 93, 95
Moranville, Jarvis R. (1838-1908) – 132
Moranville, Lucana J. (1841-1929) – 93, 96
Moranville, Russell S. (1911-1949) – 90, 93
Morse, Rose A. (1901-1971) – 303
Morton, Alice (1863-1942) – 20
Muthow, Benno (1865-1940) – 152, 153
Muthow, Sarah (1870-1922) – 151 152
Nelson, Susan A. (1816-1860) – 382
Nelson, Susan F. (1841-1862) – 372
Nelson, William W. (~1811-1844) – 383
Paddock, Elisabeth (~1700-1761) – 445
Paddock, Joseph (~1700-1768) – 443
Paddock, Josiah (~1761-1815) – 448
Paddock, Lydia (~1731-1807) – 444
Page, Carlton A. (1853-1854) – 69
Page, Homer A. (1862) – 68
Page, Infant Dau. (1842) – 71
Page, John B. (1820-1890) – 97
Page, Susannah (1821-1866) – 98
Page, Susannah A. (1848) – 70
Page, Susannah M. (1857-1858) – 72
Perkins, Charity (1685-1759) – 223
Perry, George H. (~1844-1917) – 131
Perry, Anna A. (~1846-1916) – 131
Pickens, Archie H. (1869) – 9, 10
Pickens, Gissell (~1753-1779) – 161
Pickens, Henry C. (1938-1911) – 5, 10
Pickens, John (~1719-1798) – 160
Pickens, John (~1791-1798) – 143
Pickens, Mary (~1768-1781) – 158
Pickens, Ruth (~1726-1798) – 159
Pickens, S. Irving (~1872-1955) – 10, 11
Pickens, Sarah (1748-1765) – 162
Pickens, Sophia A. (1836-1890) – 4, 10
Pierce, Eben. S. (1850-1857) – 203, 205, 206
Pierce, James (1821-1889) – 203, 207
Pierce, James A. (1857-1878) – 203, 204
Pierce, Mary (1829-1912) – 203
Pierce, Mary E. (1856-1930) – 202, 203
Pittsley, Kenneth E. (1913-1916) – 507
Poak, James (~1712-1749) – 166
Poak, Jennet (~1681-1749) – 163
Poak, Martha (~1709-1749) – 165
Poak, Samuel (~1662-1747) – 164

Porter, Charles A. (1836-1910) – 44
Porter, Charles F. (1870) – 44
Porter, Clara O. (1860-1903) – 44
Porter, Hattie C. (1881) – 44
Porter, Mary E. (1840-1908) – 44
R., E. (no dates) – 283
R., G. (no dates) – 284
R., M. E. (no dates) – 452
R., S. (____-1756) – 188
Ramsdell, Anna (1867) – 7
Ramsdell, Hepsy A. (~1849-1867) – 1
Ramsdell, Mary M. (1830-1910) – 3
Ramsdell, Stephen C. (~1823-1873) – 2
Reed, Abraham W. (1833-1840) – 414
Reed, Charles (~1736-1810) – 424
Reed, Elisabeth (1763-1793) – 419
Reed, Irena R. (~1811-1835) – 420
Reed, Isaac N. (1835-1859) – 415
Reed, Lois (~1765-1855) – 425
Reed, Nathan (~1766-1800) – 426
Reed, Zilphia (~1741-1808) – 423
Reynolds, Ellery J. (1964-1969) – 467
Reynolds, Hannah M. (1871-1941) – 499
Ricard, Arthur H. (1942-2003) – 125
Ricard, Esther R. (1949-____) – 125
Richards, Fred E. (1901-1960) – 289, 302
Richards, Hazel A. (1913-1970) – 302
Richards, Lynn Ann (1963) – 288
Richmond, Allen (1778-1862) – 418
Richmond, Elisabeth (~1702-1782) – 169
Richmond, Jones (~1824-1833) – 416
Richmond, Joseph, Dea. (~1724-1792) – 358
Richmond, Nancy (~1786-1855) – 417
Richmond, Prudence (~1758-1789) – 357
Richmond, Rufus (~1773-1795) – 355
Richmond, Sarah (____-1761) – 187
Roche, Nicholas (~1723-1808) – 212
Rogers, Hiram (1827-1885) – 17
Rogers, Hiram F. (1860-1891) – 20, 21
Rogers, R. Grace (1882-1900) – 20
Rogers, Ruby (1889-1892) – 20
Rogers, Ruby A. (1821-1864) – 16
S., B. (no dates) – 145
Sampson, Anna (~1729-1801) – 170
Sampson, Daniel (1775-1814) – 148
Samson, Deborah (1790-1792) – 129
Samson, Deborah (~1760-1844) – 146
Samson, Deliverance (~1764-1821) – 149
Sampson, Emeline (1822-1826) – 126
Sampson, Ezra (1800-1802) – 128
Sampson, Isaac (~1762-1846) – 150

Sampson, Isaac (1794-1808) – 127
Sampson, John, Dr. (~1751-1830) – 147
Samson, Nathaniel (~1719-1778) – 144
Samson, Uriah (~1718-1790) – 171
Sears, Elkanah Capt. (~1765-1838) – 254
Sears, Mary (~1737-1771) – 225
Sears, Remember (~1776-1803) – 255
Sears, Zebedee (1735-1779) – 180
Shaw, Abraham (~1730-1808) – 214
Shaw, Abraham (~1788-1822) – 177
Shaw, Abraham, Jr. (1822-1901) – 178
Shaw, Betsey (~1771-1854) – 179
Shaw, Desire (~1708-1772) –368
Shaw, Samuel, Ensign (~1707-1768) – 369
Shaw, Sarah (~1734-1804) – 215
Shaw, Susanna (1754-1836) – 176
Shaw, Zebedee (~1772-1838) – 213
Shove, Betsey (~1793-1817) – 447
Shove, Eliza P. (1810-1884) – 446
Simmons, Methyl D. (1901-1941) – 45, 46
Simmons, Stanley C. (1896-1978) – 45, 47
Simon, Ben (~1751-1831) – 429
Smith, Elisabeth (~1701-1772) – 274
Smith, Lydia (~1704-1790) –315
Smith, Nathaniel (~1701-1782) – 273
Smith, Nathaniel, Capt. (~1696-1777) – 316
Smith, Polly (1781-1782) – 301
Smith, Polley (1786) – 300
Smith, Rachel (~1756-1772) – 275
Smith, Susanna (1695-1768) – 317
Southworth, Ebenezer (~1717-1751) – 168
Southworth, Elizabeth (~1725-1755) – 167
Staples, Edward F. (1846-1931) – 8
Staples, Hannah (~1784-1842) – 364
Staples, Paul (~1786-1853) – 363
Staples, Sarah (~1782-1865) –362
Strobridge?,____ – 111
Strobridge, B. Frank (1848-1881) – 154
Strobridge, Benjamin (~1766-1827) – 336
Strobridge, Benjamin H. (1822-1888) – 154
Strobridge, Chattie H (1858-1880) – 154
Strobridge, Ebenezer (1792-1849) – 209,
    210
Strobridge, Ebenezer (1834-1839) – 174,
    210
Strobridge, Ebenezer A. (1821-1829) – 173,
    210
Strobridge, Eddie W. (1881-1882) – 154
Strobridge, Elisabeth (~1768-1792) – 335
Strobridge, Hannah (1760-1826) – 313, 333
Strobridge, Henry (~1722-1795) – 287

Strobridge, Infant Dau. (1858) – 154, 156
Strobridge, James (~1695-1773) – 231
Strobridge, Jane (~1732-1815) – 286
Strobridge, Jane (1762) – 112
Strobridge, Jean (~1728-1759) – 185
Strobridg, Margaret (~1694-1776) – 230
Strobridge, Myra E. (1858-1864) – 154, 155
Strobridge, Nellie C. (1860-1882) – 154
Strobridge, Olive D. (1827-1907) – 154
Strobridge, Phebe M. (1825-1831) – 172, 210
Strobridge, Polly M. (1800-1827) – 210, 211
Strobredg, Robert, Lt. (~1752-1790) – 256
Strobridge, Sarah (~1728-1817) – 183
Strobridge, Susan P. (1802-1878) – 208, 210
Strobridge, Thomas (~1700-1724) – 233
Strobridge, Thomas (~1727-1749) – 232
Strobridge, Thomas (~1752-1777) – 186
Strowbridg, William (~1691-1777) – 229
Strobridge, William (~1725-1797) – 184
Strobridge, William (1762-1842) – 313, 334
Sweatt, Emma C. (1868-1869) – 49
Thompson, Joanna (1785-1837) – 351
Tatro, Andrew M. (1875-1933) – 408, 409
Tatro, Rose E. (1876-1968) – 408, 410
Tetro, Francis (~1826-1899) – 407
Thomas, Sabrina (~1805-1871) – 201
Thompson, Joanna (1785-1837) – 349, 365
Thompson, John T. (~1826-1832) – 350
Thompson, Nathaniel (1777-1856) – 366
Thompson, Phebe (~1771-1850) – 353
Thompson, Sally (~1783-1809) – 352
Thomson, Samuel (1773-1774) – 354
Thresher, Edwin C. (1874-1877) – 35, 36
Thresher, Elias C. (1830-1868) – 19
Thresher, Ellen A. (1841-1916) – 35
Thresher, George E. (1833-1906) – 13
Thresher, Israel (1802-1882) – 29
Thresher, Job P. (~1800-1878) –15
Thresher, Mary A. (1827-1912) – 12
Thresher, Mary B. (1798-1882) – 14
Thresher, Mary W. (1805-1898) – 28
Thresher, Phebe A. (1828-1896) – 18
Thresher, Stephen M. (1840-1900) – 35
Tilson, Timothy (~1707-1780) – 433
Tinkham, Caleb (~1739-1798) – 396
Tinkham, Elisha (1792-1868) – 338
Tinkham, Elisha H. (1817-1893) – 50
Tinkham, Francis M. (1819-1892) – 337
Tinkham, Hilkiah (~1751-1773) – 397
Tinkham, Jeremiah (1778-1858) – 340

Tinkham, Jeremiah E. (1823-1825) – 342
Tinkham, Mary J. (1830–1894) – 337
Tinkham, Nabby (1786-1838) – 341
Tinkham, Rhoda (~1795-1848) – 339
Townsend, Betsey (~1745-1804) – 405
Townsend, John (~1744-1835) – 406
Turner, Almira (1810-1885) – 8
Turner, Caleb Jr. (1805-1890) – 8
Turner, Caleb, Rev. (~1733 or 1735-1803) – 8, 139
Turner, Josiah R. (1816-1823) – 103
Turner, Phebe or Phoebe (~1738 or 1740-1818) – 8, 138
Turner, Philip (1805-1806) – 105
Turner, Philip (1810-1818) – 104
Turner, Polly (1820-1904) – 8
Walker, Phebe (~1724-1803) – 137
Warren, Anna (1700-1770) – 285
Washburn, Amos Esq. (~1774-1853) – 240
Washburn, Amos, Capt. (~1742-1794) – 258
Washburn, Betsy (~1763-1845) – 238
Washburn, Charles E. (~1819-1880) – 197
Washburn, Charles F. (1808-1810) – 193
Washburn, Charlotte (~1816-1854) – 200
Washburn, Christiana W. (1827-1904) – 191
Washburn, Cyrus (1805-1875) – 199
Washburn, Emily A. (1811-1815) – 194
Washburn, Francis (~1818-1892) – 196
Washburn, Hannah F. (~1785-1853) – 242
Washburn, James (1820-1897) – 192
Washburn, James Esq. (~1767-1815) – 234
Washburn, Joshua (~1779-1818) – 236
Washburn, Louisa (~1807-1879) – 198
Washburn, Luther E. (~1798-1856) – 241
Washburn, Lydia (~1769-1803) – 235
Washburn, Olive (~1772-1847) – 239
Washburn, Phebe (~1769-1844) – 237
Washburn, Prudence (~1741-1804) – 257
Washburn, Prudence (~1781-1868) – 243
Washburn, William F. (~1814-1829) – 195
Westgate, Alfred F. (1919-1991) – 473, 484
Westgate, Arthur F. (1879-1914) – 501
Westgate?, Baby (no dates) – 487
Westgate, Baby (1933) – 469
Westgate, Beatrice E. (1911-1995) – 470
Westgate, Bert (1906-1970) – 360
Westgate, Bertha A. (1903-1979) – 502, 503
Westgate, Catherine A. (1889-1970) – 505
Westgate, Charles H. (1869-1939) – 486
Westgate, Dorothy (1911-1991) – 468
Westgate, Elisha (1835-1918) – 501

Urn at the top of the
Marshall B. Williams Monument

Thompson Hill Cemetery Map Index
By Location:

1 – Ramsdell, Hepsy A. (~1849-1867)
2 – Ramsdell, Stephen C. (~1823-1873)
3 – Ramsdell, Mary M. (1830-1910)
4 – Pickens, Sophia A. (1936-1890)
5 – Pickens, Henry C. (1938-1911)
6 – Cobb, Harriet (1816-1882)
7 – Ramsdell, Anna (1867)
8 – Staples, Edward F. (1846-1931)
    Turner, Caleb, Rev. (1735-1803)
    Turner, Phoebe (1738-1818)
    Turner, Caleb Jr. (1805-1890)
    Turner, Almira (1810-1885)
    Turner, Polly (1820-1904)
9 – Pickens, Archie H. (1869)
10 – Pickens, Henry C. (1938-1911)
    Pickens, Sophia A. (1836-1890)
    Pickens, Archie H. (1869)
    Pickens, S. Irving (~1872-1955)
11 – Pickens, S. Irving (~1872-1955)
12 – Thresher, Mary A. (1827-1912)
13 – Thresher, George E. (1833-1906)
14 – Thresher, Mary B. (1798-1882)
15 – Thresher, Job P. (~1800-1878)
16 – Rogers, Ruby A. (1821-1864)
17 – Rogers, Hiram (1827-1885)
18 – Thresher, Phebe A. (1828-1896)
19 – Thresher, Elias C. (1830-1868)
20 – Morton, Alice M. (1863-1942)
    Rogers, Hiram F. (1860-1891)
    Rogers, Ruby (1889-1892)
    Rogers, R. Grace (1882-1900)
21 – Rogers, Hiram F. (1860-1891)
22 – Dean, Drusilla (1831-1905)
    Dean, James A. (1830-1908)
23 – Haskins, Orin E. (1845-1922)
24 – Haskins, Mary (~1803-1871)
25 – Haskins, Levi (1794-1862)
26 – Haskins, Levi H. (1834-1908)
27 – Haskins, Mary S. (1829-1884)
28 – Thresher, Mary W. (1805-1898)
29 – Thresher, Israel (1802-1882)
30 – Haskins, Orville (1815-1893)
31 – Haskins, Lydia B. (1819-1887)
32 – Haskins, Elmore P. (1849-1930)
33 – King, Mary C. (1824-1866)
34 – King, Silas S. (1818-1890)
35 – Thresher, Stephen M. (1840-1900)

    Thresher, Ellen A. (1841-1916)
    Thresher, Edwin C. (1874-1877)
36 – Thresher, Eddie C. (1874-1877)
37 – Haskins, Joseph C. (1817-1904)
38 – Haskins, Betsey S. (1836-1905)
39 – Haskins, Austin (1830-1908)
40 – Caswell, Stetson (1823-1902)
41 – Caswell, Sarah M. (1837-1915)
42 – Caswell, Nettie P. (1864-1931)
43 – Caswell, Leavitt C. (1860-1946)
44 – Porter, Charles A. (1836-1910)
    Porter, Mary E. (1840-1908)
    Porter, Clara O. (1860-1903)
    Porter, Charles F. (1870)
    Porter, Hattie C. (1881)
45 – Simmons, Stanley C. (1896-1978)
    Simmons, Methyl D. (1901-1941)
    Caswell, Kenneth M. (1898)
    Caswell, Nettie P. (1864-1931)
    Caswell, Leavitt C. (1860-1946)
    Caswell, Stetson (1803-1902)
    Caswell, Sarah M. (1837-1915)
46 – Simmons, Methyl D. (1901-1941)
47 – Simmons, Stanley C. (1896-1978)
48 – Caswell, Kenneth M. (1898)
49 – Sweatt, Emma C. (1868-1869)
50 – Tinkham, Elisha H. (1817-1893)
51 – Ball, Ida C. (1900-1938)
52 – Caswell, Lucy P. (1811-1872)
53 – Dean, Henry A. (1816-1898)
    Dean, Betsey (1814-1840)
    Dean, Julia (1820-1869)
    Dean, Barney T. (1840-1928)
    Dean, Rhoda F. (1852-1913)
54 – Dean, Julia (1820-1869)
55 – Ashley, Henry A. (1861-1864)
    Ashley, Infant Dau. (1866)
56 – Ashley, Asenath L. (1839 –1908)
57 – Ashley, J. C. (1837-1897)
58 – Westgate, Elisha B. (1830-1906)
59 – _____, Alton (no dates)
60 – Burnham, Bessie (1909)
61 – Burnham, William H. (1865-1943)
    Dietrich, Anna M. (1873-1930)
62 – Westgate, Elisha F. (1867-1950)
    Westgate, Elizabeth M. (1869-1945)
    Westgate, Harold L. (1899-1977)

63 – Westgate, Elizabeth M. (1869-1945)
64 – Dietrich, Anna M. (1873-1930)
65 – Westgate, Elizabeth M. (1869-1945)
66 – Westgate, Elisha F. (1867-1950)
67 – Wilbur, George E. (no dates)
    Wilbur, Edith L. (no dates)
    Wilbur, Emma E. (no dates)
    Wilbur, Ralph E. (no dates)
    Wilbur, Ethel L. (no dates)
    Wilbur, Leroy M. (no dates)
68 – Page, Homer A. (1862)
69 – Page, Carlton A. (1853-1854)
70 – Page, Susannah A. (1848)
71 – Page, Infant Dau. (1842)
72 – Page, Susannah M. (1857-1858)
73 – Cain, George S. (~1829-1840)
74 – Williams, John H. (1801-1855)
75 – Williams, Phebe K. (~1808-1848)
76 – Canedy, Mary B. (~1818-1832)
77 – Canedy, Barnabas (1785)
78 – Canedy, Elkanah L. (1800)
79 – Canedy, Hope (~1762-1829)
80 – Churchill, Libeus C. (1811-1892)
81 – Churchill, Malancy J. (1810-1886)
82 – Churchill, Sarah (~1790-1874)
83 – Churchill, Chloe (~1815-1877)
84 – MacAulay, Annie M. (1872-1946)
85 – Caswell, Kenneth E. (1907-1977)
86 – French, Hadon (1740-1787)
87 – Caswell, Richard B. Jr. (1943-1971)
88 – Caswell, Richard B. Sr. (1909-1985)
    Caswell, S. Helen (1918-2001)
89 – Moranville, Alice M. (1881-1947)
90 – Moranville, Russell S. (1911-1949)
91 – Moranville, Bernice L. (1902-1978)
92 – Moranville, Dennis L. (1942-2002)
93 – Moranville, Edson V. (1869-1944)
    Moranville, Alice M. (1881-1947)
    Moranville, Russell S. (1911-1949)
    Moranville, Bernice L. (1902-1978)
    Moranville, Dennis L. (1942-2002)
    Moranville, Lucana J. (1841-1929)
    Moranville, Flora E. (1870-1933)
94 – Moranville, Edson V. (1869-1944)
95 – Moranville, Flora E. (1870-1933)
96 – Moranville, Lucana J. (1841-1929)
97 – Page, John B. (1820-1890)
98 – Page, Susannah (1821-1866)
99 – Cain, Samuel (1801-1876)
100 – Cain, Serena (1803-1857)
101 – Bassett, Sarah M. (~1796-1830)

102 – Bassett, Lewis (~1790-1822)
103 – Turner, Josiah R. (1816-1823)
104 – Turner, Philip (1810-1818)
105 – Turner, Philip (1805-1806)
106 – King, Bathsheba (~1778-1788)
107 – Ammon (~1750-1778)
108 – Canedy, Charity (~1732-1805)
109 – Canedy, William, Capt. (~1730-1804)
110 – Canedy, Barnebus, Ens. (~1735-1776)
111 – Strobridge?,_____ (no dates)
112 – Strobridge, Jane (1762)
113 – Blackman, Lucy (~1792-1860)
114 – Caswell, Edward T. (1868-1948)
    Caswell, Grace M. (1870-1927)
115 – Burrell, Lony (1797-1876)
116 – Caswell, Mary Jane (1828-1903)
117 – Braley, Serena J. (1860-1927)
118 – Caswell, Eliza (1799-1860)
119 – Caswell, David B. (1863-1894)
120 – Caswell, Abiah (~1785-1817)
121 – Caswell, Eliab (1800-1873)
122 – Caswell, Lucy (~1778-1808)
123 – Caswell, Annis (~1756-1830)
124 – Caswell, David (~1742-1825)
125 – Ricard, Arthur H. (1942-2003)
    Ricard, Esther R. (1949-____)
126 – Sampson, Emeline (1822-1826)
127 – Sampson, Isaac (1794-1808)
128 – Sampson, Ezra (1800-1802)
129 – Samson, Deborah (1790-1792)
130 – Fredette, Alfred J. (1868-1955)
131 – Perry, George H. (~1844-1917)
    Perry, Anna A. (~1846-1916)
132 – Moranville, Jarvis R. (1838-1908)
133 – Cain, Samuel (1772-1857)
134 – Cain, Lucy (1777-1856)
135 – Bassett, Bethiah (~1763-1832)
136 – Bassett, Caleb, Dea. (~1758-1841)
137 – Walker, Phebe (~1724-1803)
138 – Turner, Phebe (~1740-1818)
139 – Turner, Caleb, Rev. (~1733-1803)
140 – Crafts, Thomas (~1759-1819)
141 – Canedy, Elizabeth (~1702-1780)
142 – Canedy, William, Esq. (~1689-1774)
143 – Pickens, John (~1791-1798)
144 – Samson, Nathaniel (~1719-1778)
145 – S., B. (no dates)
146 – Sampson, Deborah (~1760-1844)
147 – Sampson, John, Dr. (~1751-1830)
148 – Sampson, Daniel (1775-1814)
149 – Sampson, Deliverance (~1764-1821)

150 – Sampson, Isaac (~1762-1846)
151 – Muthow, Sarah (1870-1922)
152 – Muthow, Benno (1865-1940)
       Muthow, Sarah (1870-1922)
153 – Muthow, Benno (1865-1940)
154 – Strobridge, Infant Dau. (1858)
       Strobridge, Myra E. (1858-1864)
       Strobridge, Chattie H (1858-1880)
       Strobridge, B. Frank (1848-1881)
       Strobridge, Nellie C. (1860-1882)
       Strobridge, Eddie W. (1881-1882)
       Strobridge, Benjamin H. (1822-1888)
       Strobridge, Olive D. (1827-1907)
155 – Strobridge, Myra E. (1858-1864)
156 – Strobridge, Infant Dau. (1858)
157 – Goodwin, Sarah P. (1798-1827)
158 – Pickens, Mary (~1768-1781)
159 – Pickens, Ruth (~1726-1798)
160 – Pickens, John (~1719-1798)
161 – Pickens, Grissell (~1753-1779)
162 – Pickens, Sarah (1748-1765)
163 – Poak, Jennet (~1681-1749)
164 – Poak, Samuel (~1662-1747)
165 – Poak, Martha (~1709-1749)
166 – Poak, James (~1712-1749)
167 – Southworth, Elizabeth (~1725-1755)
168 – Southworth, Ebenezer (~1717-1751)
169 – Richmond, Elisabeth (~1702-1782)
170 – Sampson, Anna (~1729-1801)
171 – Samson, Uriah (~1718-1790)
172 – Strobridge, Phebe M. (1825-1831)
173 – Strobridge, Ebenezer A. (1821-1829)
174 – Strobridge, Ebenezer (1834-1839)
175 – Whittemore, Harriet (1803-1823)
176 – Shaw, Susanna (1754-1836)
177 – Shaw, Abraham (~1788-1822)
178 – Shaw, Abraham, Jr. (1822-1901)
179 – Shaw, Betsey (~1771-1854)
180 – Sears, Zebedee (1735-1779)
181 – Leonard, Deliverance (1723-1751)
182 – McCully, Martha (1740-1760)
183 – Strobridge, Sarah (~1728-1817)
184 – Strobridge, William (~1725-1797)
185 – Strobridge, Jean (~1728-1859)
186 – Strobridge, Thomas (~1752-1777)
187 – Richmond, Sarah (____-1761)
188 – R., S. (____-1756)
189 – C., T. (no dates)
190 – C., D. (no dates)
191 – Washburn, Christiana W. (1827-1904)
192 – Washburn, James (1820-1897)

193 – Washburn, Charles F. (1808-1810)
194 – Washburn, Emily A. (1811-1815)
195 – Washburn, William F. (~1814-1829)
196 – Washburn, Francis (~1818-1892)
197 – Washburn, Charles E. (~1819-1880)
198 – Washburn, Louisa (~1807-1879)
199 – Washburn, Cyrus (1805-1875)
200 – Washburn, Charlotte (~1816-1854)
201 – Thomas, Sabrina (~1805-1871)
202 – Pierce, Mary E. (1856-1930)
203 – Pierce, Eben. S. (1850-1857)
       Pierce, James A. (1857-1878)
       Pierce, James (1821-1889)
       Pierce, Mary (1829-1912)
       Pierce, Mary E. (1856-1930)
204 – Pierce, James A. (1857-1878)
205 – Pierce, Eben. S. (1850-1857)
206 – Pierce, Eben. S. (1850-1857)
207 – Pierce, James (1821-1889)
208 – Strobridge, Susan P. (1802-1878)
209 – Strobridge, Ebenezer (1792-1849)
210 – Strobridge, Ebenezer (1792-1849)
       Strobridge, Polly M. (1800-1827)
       Strobridge, Susan P. (1802-1878)
       Strobridge, Ebenezer (1834-1839)
       Strobridge, Ebenezer A. (1821-1829)
       Strobridge, Phebe M. (1825-1831)
211 – Strobridge, Polly M. (1800-1827)
212 – Roche, Nicholas (~1723-1808)
213 – Shaw, Zebedee (~1772-1838)
214 – Shaw, Abraham (~1730-1808)
215 – Shaw, Sarah (~1734-1804)
216 – Barrows, John (1743-1782)
217 – Barrows, Mary (~1741-1759)
218 – Barrows, Susannah (~1736-1749)
219 – Leonard, Hannah (~1732-1796)
220 – Leonard, Zebulon (~1729-1794)
221 – Leonard, Elisabeth (~1704-1780)
222 – Leonard, Elkanah Esq. (~1704-1777)
223 – Perkins, Charity (1685-1759)
224 – Leonard, Elkanah (~1676-1714)
225 – Sears, Mary (~1737-1771)
226 – Leonard, Thomas (no dates)
227 – Leonard, child (1711)
228 – Leonard, Henry (1714)
229 – Strowbridg, William (~1691-1777)
230 – Strobridg, Margaret (~1694-1776)
231 – Strobridge, James (~1695-1773)
232 – Strobridge, Thomas (~1727-1749)
233 – Strobridge, Thomas (~1700-1724)
234 – Washburn, James Esq. (~1767-1815)

235 – Washburn, Lydia (~1769-1803)
236 – Washburn, Joshua (~1779-1818)
237 – Washburn, Phebe (~1769-1844)
238 – Washburn, Betsy (~1763-1845)
239 – Washburn, Olive (~1772-1847)
240 – Washburn, Amos Esq.(~1774-1853)
241 – Washburn, Luther E. (~1798-1856)
242 – Washburn, Hannah F. (~1785-1853)
243 – Washburn, Prudence (~1781-1868)
244 – Barrows, Sarah (~1705-1793)
245 – Barrows, Ebenezer (1702-1792)
246 – Elmes, Anner E. (~1766-1788)
247 – Elms, Abner (~1765-1836)
248 – Elmes, Phebe (~1769-1849)
249 – Leonard, Joseph O. L. (1791-1792)
250 – Leonard, Elizabeth (~1754-1791)
251 – Leonard, Joseph (~1753-1844)
252 – Leonard, Zilpha (~1766-1827)
253 – Leonard, Joseph J. C. (1801-1872)
254 – Sears, Elkanah Capt. (~1765-1838)
255 – Sears, Remember (~1776-1803)
256 – Strobredg, Robert, Lt. (~1752-1790)
257 – Washburn, Prudence (~1741-1804)
258 – Washburn, Amos, Capt. (~1742-1794)
259 – Montgomery, Fannie (1876-1891)
260 – Montgomery, John F. (1843-1918)
261 – Montgomery, Isadore L. (1852-1916)
262 – Montgomery, Mary A. (1847-1935)
263 – Montgomery, William (1804-1898)
264 – Montgomery, Hugh (1802-1883)
265 – Montgomery, Nancy (1789-1881)
266 – Montgomery, James (~1808-1849)
267 – Briggs, Julia (1798-1880)
      Briggs, Daniel (~1796-1849)
268 – Briggs, Anna M. (~1824-1884)
269 – Montgomery, William (~1767-1804)
270 – Montgomery, Rebecca (~1760-1798)
271 – Montgomery, Samuel, Dr. (~1754-
      1787)
272 – Montgomery, Augustus (~1780-1782)
273 – Smith, Nathaniel (~1701-1782)
274 – Smith, Elisabeth (~1701-1772)
275 – Smith, Rachel (~1756-1772)
276 – Eaton, Agusta S. (~1824-1893)
277 – Leonard, Gideon (~1757-1811)
278 – Leonard, Timothy M. (~1800-1854)
279 – Leonard, Hannah (~1759-1840)
280 – Leonard, Lydia (~1804-1874)
281 – Leonard, Anna (~1792-1863)
282 – Leonard, Gideon (1789-1872)
283 – R., E. (no dates)

284 – R., G. (no dates)
285 – Warren, Anna (1700-1770)
286 – Strobridge, Jane (~1732-1815)
287 – Strobridge, Henry (~1722-1795)
288 – Richards, Lynn Ann (1963)
289 – Richards, Fred E. (1901-1960)
290 – Gay, Lewis (1890-1942)
291 – Gay, Bradley L. (1866-1948)
      Gay, Katherine B. (1868-1948)
      Gay, Edna R. (1894-1941)
      Gay, Lewis (1890-1942)
      Gay, Horace F. (1900-1974)
292 – Montgomery Monument
293 – Montgomery, Mary Ann (1804-1886)
294 – Montgomery, John (1799-1881)
295 – Dean, Mary M. (1788-1843)
      Dean, Joshua, Rev. (1788-1824)
296 – Montgomery, Anna S. (~1764-1828)
297 – Montgomery, Hugh (~1756-1835)
298 – Montgomery, Mary S. (~1718-1790)
299 – Montgomery, John, Elder (~1708-
      1787)
300 – Smith, Polley (1786)
301 – Smith, Polly (1781-1782)
302 – Richards, Fred E. (1901-1960)
      Richards, Hazel A. (1913-1970)
303 – Morse, Rose A. (1901-1971)
304 – Caswell, Ella M. (1865-1943)
      Caswell, Benj. W. (1860-1942)
305 – Caswell, Mary E. (1854-1855)
306 – Hopkins, Charles W. (1861-1929)
      Hopkins, Ella T. (1865-1951)
      Hopkins, Fanny (1888-1952)
307 – Hopkins, Bertha (1868)
308 – Hopkins, Sadie (1855-1856)
309 – Hopkins, Rosseter (1843)
310 – H., F. (no dates)
311 – Crane, Caroline (1817-1846)
312 – Crane, Betsey A. (1818-1846)
313 – Crane, Gershom (1778-1848)
      Crane, Sally (1795-1875)
      Crane, Caroline (1817-1846)
      Crane, Betsey A.(1818-1846)
      Crane, Ebenezer (1820-1899)
      Strobridge, William (1762-1842)
      Strobridge, Hannah (1760-1826)
314 – Hall Abigail (____-1747)
315 – Smith, Lydia (~1704-1790)
316 – Smith, Nathaniel, Capt. (~1696-1777)
317 – Smith, Susanna (1695-1768)
318 – Miller, Joanna (~1732-1758)

319 – Burnham, Chester W. (1890-1954)
320 – Burnham, Ada E. (1894-1979)
321 – ____, Lois (no dates)
322 – Hopkins, William H. (1844-1909)
323 – Hopkins, Fanny Maria (1847-1922)
324 – Hopkins, Lydia A. (1849-1900)
325 – Hopkins, Fanny A. (1821-1879)
326 – Hopkins, William H. (1820-1902)
327 – Hopkins, Lydia E.(1825-1909)
328 – Elmes, Cyrus (~1801-1864)
329 – Elmes, Silence (~1803-1865)
330 – Elmes, Phebe A. (~1843-1850)
331 – Crane, Ebenezer (1820-1899)
332 – Crane, Sally (1795-1875)
333 – Strobridge, Hannah (1760-1826)
334 – Strobridge, William (1762-1842)
335 – Strobridge, Elisabeth (~1768-1792)
336 – Strobridge, Benjamin (~1766-1827)
337 – Tinkham, Mary J. (1830–1894)
       Tinkham, Francis M. (1819-1892)
338 – Tinkham, Elisha (1792-1868)
339 – Tinkham, Rhoda (~1795-1848)
340 – Tinkham, Jeremiah (1778-1858)
341 – Tinkham, Nabby (1786-1838)
342 – Tinkham, Jeremiah E. (1823-1825)
343 – Miller, Susa S. (1800-1801)
344 – Miller, Rhoda (~1761-1801)
345 – Burnham, Chester W. (1890-1954)
       Burnham, Ada E. (1894-1979)
346 – Meack, Timothy (1960)
347 – Caswell, Belony W. (1855-1856)
348 – Burr, George J. (1827-1859)
349 – Thompson, Joanna (1785-1837)
350 – Thompson, John T. (~1826-1832)
351 – Thompson, Joanna (1785-1837)
352 – Thompson, Sally (~1783-1809)
353 – Thompson, Phebe (~1771-1850)
354 – Thomson, Samuel (1773-1774)
355 – Richmond, Rufus (~1773-1795)
356 – B., C. (no dates)
357 – Richmond, Prudence (~1758-1789)
358 – Richmond, Joseph, Dea. (~1724-
       1792)
359 – Weston, James A. (1866-1938)
       Weston, Charles L. (1900-1963)
       Weston, Katherine J. (1891-1969)
360 – Westgate, Jeannette (1917-1960)
       Westgate, Bert (1907-1970)
361 – Westgate, Richard E. (1939-2000)
362 – Staples, Sarah (~1782-1865)
363 – Staples, Paul (~1786-1853)

364 – Staples, Hannah (~1784-1842)
365 – Thompson, Joanna (1785-1837)
366 – Thompson, Nathaniel (1777-1856)
367 – Hacket, John, Elder (~1689-1767)
368 – Shaw, Desire (~1708-1772)
369 – Shaw, Samuel, Ensign (~1707-1768)
370 – Caswell, Abigail W. (1817-1888)
371 – Caswell, Phebe J. (~1821-1842)
372 – Nelson, Susan F. (1841-1862)
373 – Kinsley Alvin E. (~1826-1841)
374 – Kinsley, Sarah (1832-1833)
375 – Kinsley, John (1829-1899)
376 – Kinsley, Betsey (1824-1906)
377 – Gibbs, Dennis (1810-1811)
378 – Caswell, Abraham (1816-1880)
       Caswell, Phebe H. (1816-1848)
       Caswell, Abigail W. (1817-1888)
       Caswell, Abraham (1791-1859)
       Caswell, Eliza C. (1796-1884)
       Caswell, Mary Jane (1843-1881)
379 – Caswell, Abraham (1791-1859)
380 – Caswell, Lois (~1785-1868)
381 – Caswell, David (~1779-1837)
382 – Nelson, Susan A. (1816-1860)
383 – Nelson, William W. (~1811-1844)
384 – Kinsley, Unite (1791-1833)
385 – Kinsley, Susanna A. (1794-1875)
386 – Kinsley, Mary (1821-1860)
387 – Gibbs, Elisha (~1769-1831)
388 – Merick, Roxana (1808)
389 – Dean, Julia M. (1845-1846)
390 – Haskins, Albert (~1826-1837)
391 – Haskins, Emily A. (1837-1850)
392 – Haskins, Martha (1830-1831)
393 – Haskins, Harriot (~1814-1834)
394 – Barrows, Esther (~1766-1809)
395 – Barrows, George (~1752-1826)
396 – Tinkham, Caleb (~1739-1798)
397 – Tinkham, Hilkiah (~1751-1773)
398 – Haskins, Andrew, Dea. (~1789-1855)
       Haskins, Lydia B. (~1794-1841)
399 – Haskins, Amelia K. (1804-1885)
400 – Haskins, Apollos (1796-1865)
401 – Haskins, Mirick (~1787-1810)
402 – Haskins, Rebecca S. (~1790-1839)
403 – Haskins, Serena (~1787-1809)
404 – Haskins, Joshua (~1784-1861)
405 – Townsend, Betsey (~1745-1804)
406 – Townsend, John (~1744-1835)
407 – Tetro, Francis (~1826-1899)
408 – Tatro, Andrew M. (1875-1933)

Tatro, Rose E. (1876-1968)
409 – Tatro, Andrew M. (1875-1933)
410 – Tatro, Rose E. (1876-1968)
411 – Haskins, Hannah (~1757-1820)
412 – Haskins, Joshua (~1755-1849)
413 – Jones, Paul L. (1820-1900)
Jones, Sarah M. (1828-1854)
414 – Reed, Abraham W. (1833-1840)
415 – Reed, Isaac N. (1835-1859)
416 – Richmond, Jones (~1824-1833)
417 – Richmond, Nancy (~1786-1855)
418 – Richmond, Allen (1778-1862)
419 – Reed, Elisabeth (1763-1793)
420 – Reed, Irena R. (~1811-1835)
421 – Jones, Patience (~1761-1847)
422 – Jones, Consider (~1741-1820)
423 – Reed, Zilphia (~1741-1808)
424 – Reed, Charles (~1736-1810)
425 – Reed, Lois (~1765-1855)
426 – Reed, Nathan (~1766-1800)
427 – ____, Son (no dates)
428 – Cornell, Russell E., Jr. (1946-1947)
429 – Simon, Ben (~1751-1831)
430 – Haskell, George E. (no dates)
431 – Williams, Marshall B. (1859-____)
Williams, Isabell F. (1860-1895)
Elmes, Cyrus O. (1826-1903)
Elmes, Nancy C. (1832-1900)
432 – Dushane, Francis (1815-1902)
Dushane, Adeline (1836-1914)
Dushane, Frank E. (1872-1908)
Dushane, Chauncey E. (1873-1911)
Dushane, Minnie (1879-1906)
433 – Tilson, Timothy (~1707-1780)
434 – Demoranville, Myron V. (1877-1965)
435 – Wordell, Susan A. (1884-1965)
436 – DeMoranville, Shoman A. (1850-1882)
DeMoranville, Deborah F. (1852-1928)
437 – Wordell, Arthur E. (1881-1945)
438 – Wordell, Raymond E. (1923-1983)
439 – Wordell, Baby girl (1946)
Wordell, Susan M. (1947-1948)
Wordell, Deborah M. (1951)
440 – Wordell, Baby girl (1946) – 431
441 – Wordell, Susan M. (1947-1948)
442 – Wordell, Deborah M. (1951)
443 – Paddock, Joseph (~1700-1768)
444 – Paddock, Lydia (~1731-1807)
445 – Paddock, Elisabeth (~1700-1761)

446 – Shove, Eliza P. (1810-1884)
447 – Shove, Betsey (~1793-1817)
448 – Paddock, Josiah (~1761-1815)
449 – Burnham, Harry L. (1896-1978)
450 – Burnham, Mary V. (1894-1938)
451 – Manchester, Horace A. (1842-1910)
452 – R., M. E. (no dates)
453 – DeMaranville, George M. (1870-1949)
454 – DeMaranville, Mabel A. (1872-1936)
455 – DeMaranville, E. May (1893-1977)
456 – Matteson, Flora M. (1872-1966)
457 – DeMaranville, George M. (1870-1949)
DeMaranville, Mabel A. (1872-1936)
DeMaranville, E. May (1893-1977)
Matteson, Flora M. (1872-1966)
Forrest, John A. (1886-1948)
Forrest, Josephine (1899-1992)
Andrews, E. Frank (1924-1984)
Andrews, Mildred (1925-1994)
Forrest, John A. (1927-1994)
Forrest, Louise K. (1928-____)
458 – Forrest, John A. (1927-1994)
Forrest, Louise K. (1928-____)
459 – Forrest, John A. (1886-1948)
460 – Forrest, Josephine (1899-1992)
461 – Andrews, Mildred (1925-1994)
462 – Andrews, E. Frank (1924-1984)
463 – DeMoranville, Leo F. (1923-1998)
464 – DeMoranville, Leo F. Jr. (1945-1948)
465 – DeMoranville, Leo F. (1923-1998)
DeMoranville, Leo F. Jr. (1945-1948)
466 – Wordell, John (1906-1945)
Wordell, Lottie (1907-1968)
467 – Reynolds, Ellery J. (1964-1969)
468 – Westgate, Russell (1913-____)
Westgate, Dorothy (1911-1991)
469 – Westgate, Baby (1933)
470 – Westgate, Nelson (1914-1977)
Westgate, Beatrice E. (1911-1995)
471 – Haskins, Adam J. (1993)
472 – Westgate, Gertrude F. (1921-1990)
473 – Westgate, Alfred F. (1919-1991)
474 – DeMoranville, Charles E. (1964)
475 – DeMoranville, Gerald C. (1916-1964)
DeMoranville, Evelyn L. (1918-1970)
476 - DeMoranville, Jamie F. (1978-2003)
477 – DeMoranville, James F. (1948-1988)
478 – DeMoranville, Inez L. (1917-1974)
DeMoranville, Jesse N. (1914-1965)

479 – DeMoranville, Jesse H. (1942-1993)
DeMoranville, Harriet E. (1941-1985)
480 – Crossman, LeRoy P. (1922-1983)
Crossman, Stella P. (1925-____)
Crossman, LeRoy R. (1944-____)
Isaacsen, Kristin L. (1987)
Wordell, Lottie E. (1968)
481 – Westgate, William J. (1874-1969)
Westgate, Nancy R. (1878-1971)
482 – Westgate, William F. (1876-1944)
483 – Westgate, Eva L. (1886-1944)
484 – Westgate, Gertrude F. (1921-1990)
Westgate, Alfred F. (1919-1991)
485 – Westgate, William F. (1876-1944)
Westgate, Eva L. (1886-1944)
Westgate, Everett W. (1902-1922)
486 – Westgate, Charles H. (1869-1939)
Westgate, Mary L.(1893-1957)
487 – Westgate, Baby (no dates)
488 – Westgate, Gilbert H. (1922-1998)
489 – Burnham, Amelia M. (1946-1946)
490 – Westgate, Emma (1860-1913)
491 – Westgate, Reuben F. (1858-1933)
Westgate, Emma J. (1860-1913)
Ellis, Thomas P. (1881-1955)
Ellis, M. Maude (1902-1958)
492 – Young, Robert L. (1914-1971)
493 – Young, William H. (1887-1967)

Young, Edith M. (1889-1983)
Young, Robert L. (1914-1971)
494 – Young, William H. (1887-1967)
495 – Young, Edith M. (1889-1983)
496 – Allen, Clara M. (1888-1968)
497 – Allen, John G. (1886-1972)
498 – Allen, John G. (1886-1972)
Allen, Clara M. (1888-1968)
499 – Reynolds, Hannah M. (1871-1941)
500 – Dugan, Nellie F. (1878-1916)
501 – Westgate, Elisha (1835-1918)
Westgate, Emily (1849-1922)
Westgate, Arthur F. (1879-1914)
502 – Westgate, Bertha A. (1903-1979)
503 – Westgate, John E. (1908-2002)
Young, Grace L. (1888-1971)
Westgate, Bertha A. (1903-1979)
504 – Young, Grace L. (1888-1971)
505 – Westgate, James W. (1877-1962)
Westgate, Catherine A. (1889-1970)
506 – Leonaid, E. L. (____-1911)
507 – Pittsley, Kenneth E. (1913-1916)
508 – DeMoranville, Frederick E. (1875-1970)
DeMoranville, Rose A. (1876-1962)
509 – Young/Westgate?, Baby (no dates)
510 – Young/Westgate?, Baby (no dates)

The Montgomery Plot

Thompson Hill Cemetery Map Overview

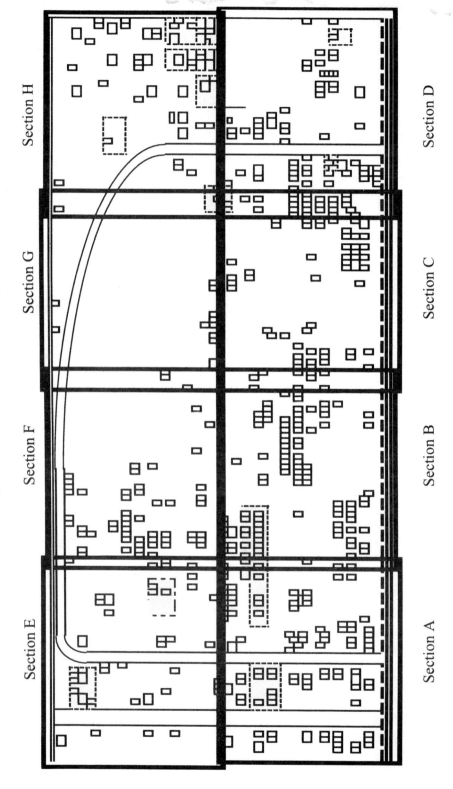

Section H

Section G

Section F

Section E

Section D

Section C

Section B

Section A

Thompson Hill Cemetery Map   Section A

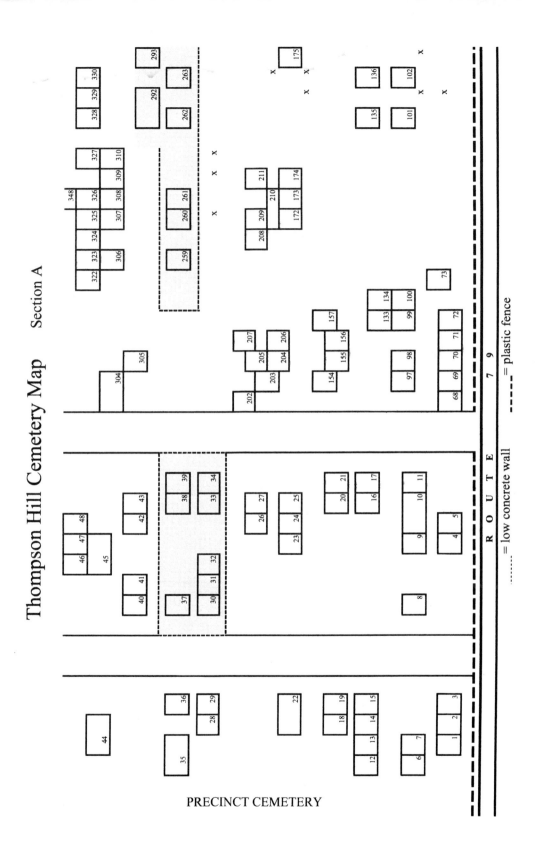

PRECINCT CEMETERY

-------- = low concrete wall

- - - - - = plastic fence

Thompson Hill Cemetery Map   Section B

R O U T E   7   9

.... = low concrete wall

‑‑‑‑‑ = plastic fence

Thompson Hill Cemetery Map   Section C

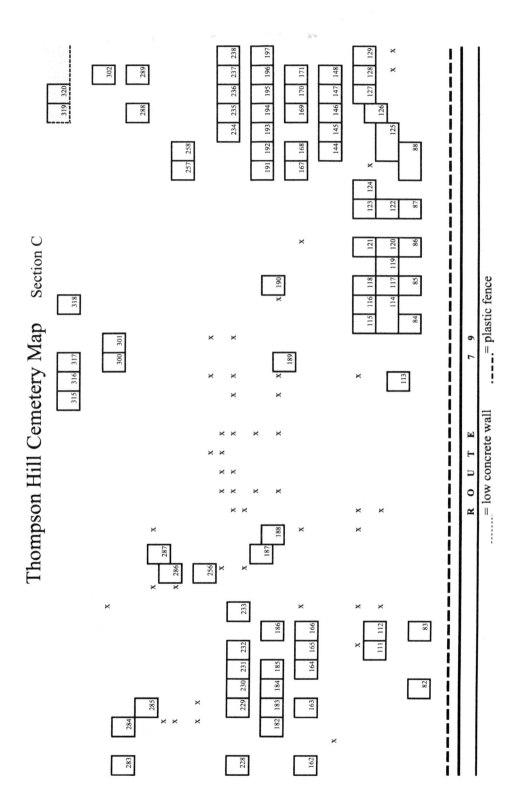

Thompson Hill Cemetery Map   Section D

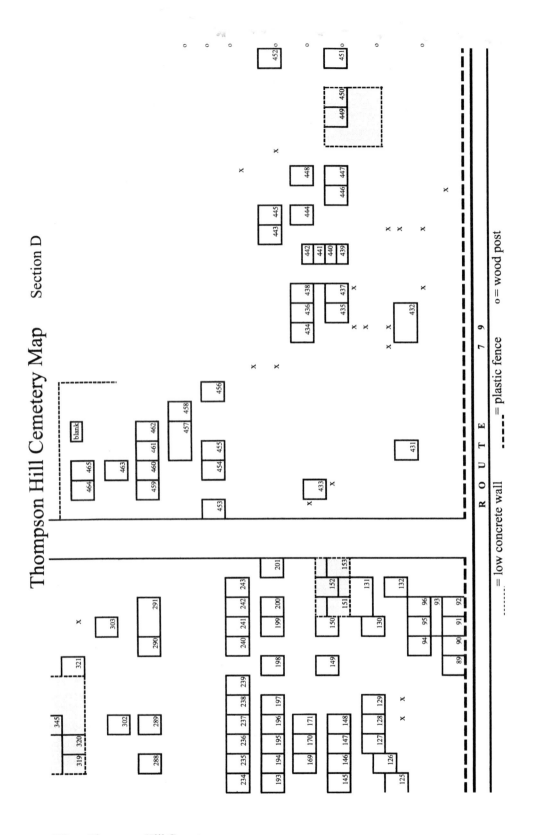

ROUTE 79

------ = plastic fence   o = wood post

········· = low concrete wall

Thompson Hill Cemetery Map   Section E

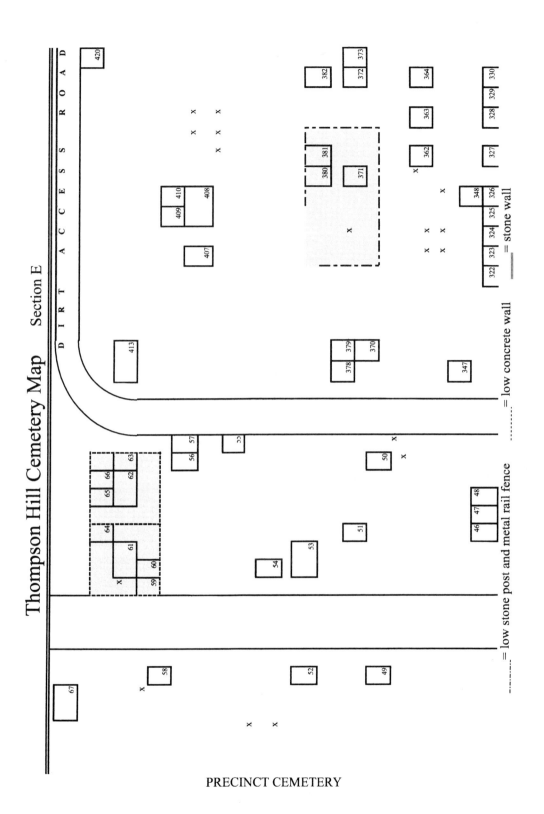

= stone wall

= low concrete wall

= low stone post and metal rail fence

PRECINCT CEMETERY

Thompson Hill Cemetery Map   Section F

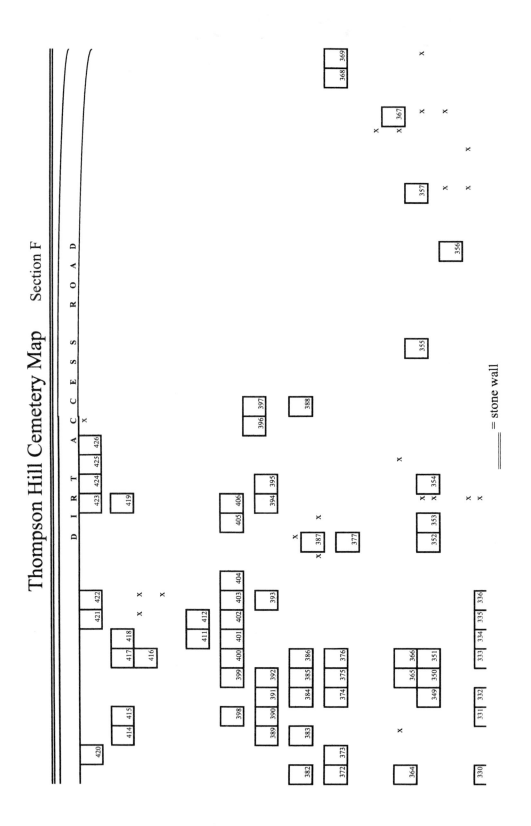

= stone wall

Thompson Hill Cemetery Map   Section G

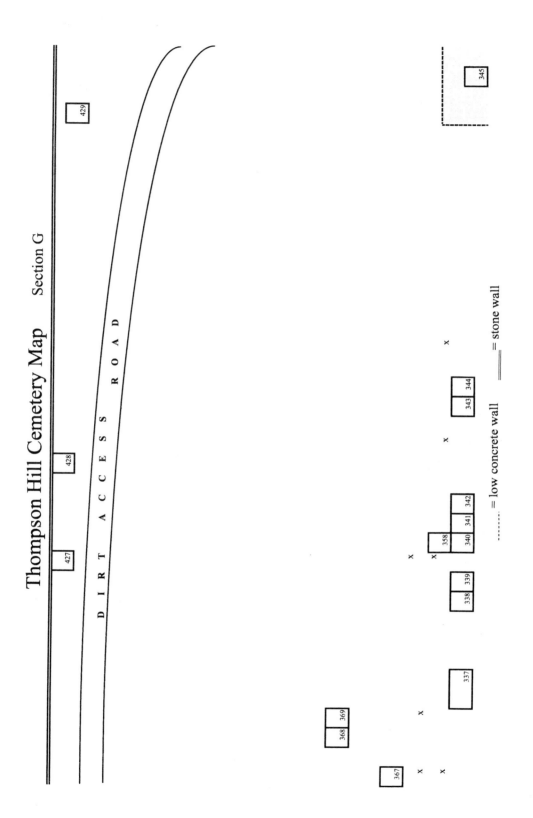

DIRT ACCESS ROAD

429

428

427

345

343 | 344

341 | 342

358
340

339
338

x

x

x

x

337

368 | 369

367

x

x

x

.... = low concrete wall   ═══ = stone wall

Thompson Hill Cemetery Map   Section H

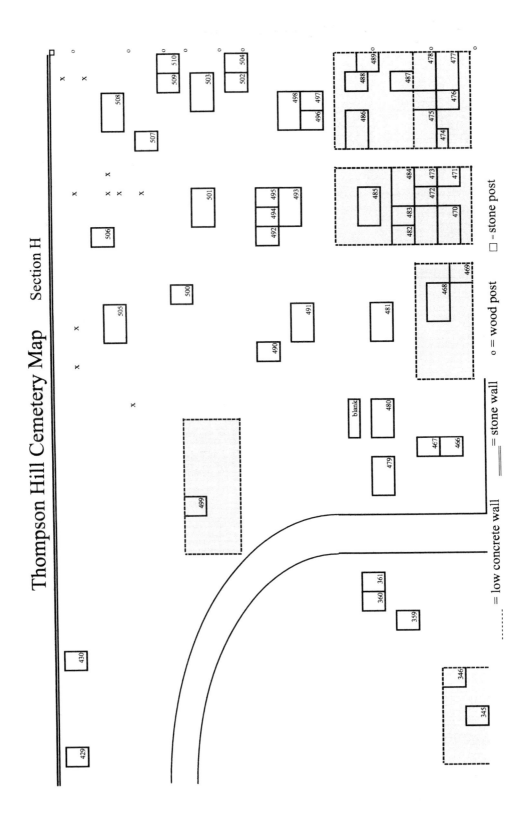

□ = stone post

o = wood post

═══ = stone wall

------- = low concrete wall

Chapter 31
Ward Cemetery

Ward Cemetery is accessed from the driveway for 45 Crooked Lane. When the driveway turns to the right, a dirt road continues straight and leads to the cemetery at the top of the hill. This cemetery is bordered by stone posts, with bolts in the stone facing out. No rails are present. The sign is in good repair. Another area on the left side of the cemetery is bordered with a stone post and metal rail fence. Sunken areas indicate that there are graves here, however no gravestones are present. Several empty bases are lying outside of the cemetery, on the left. Four areas within the cemetery are partitioned off with low stone post and metal rail fences. Gravestones face west, and date from 1790 to 1967. The Lakeville Assessor's Office lists this cemetery as town owned, 18,730 square feet in size. Thatcher calls this the "Cemetery on a Hill, back of Elbridge Cushmans." Vigers states it has been known as the "Cushman Cemetery" and the "Peirce Hill Cemetery, the land being taken from the farm of Captain Job Peirce." Mansfield states it was also referred to as the "Hill Burying Ground." Inscriptions were recorded May 12, 15, and 16, 2000.

Ametuc   *"AMETUC / A 70 Y / D 1817"* is inscribed on this upright fieldstone. Thatcher lists his information as: "A70Y Ametuc, 1807 (Tucker mother-in-law of Job Parish)."
"1817" is inscribed on this upright fieldstone.

Anderson, Pontius   *"PONTIUS ANDERSON / BORN AUG. 18. 1885. / DIED NOV. 24, 1887."* Lakeville Vital Records indicate that he was born in West Farmington N. Y., the son of Adolphus and Nellie Anderson.

Bassett, Charles H.   *"CHARLES H. BASSETT / 1842 – 1907"* is inscribed on this flat, 1 inch high stone. *Massachusetts Civil War Soldiers and Sailors, 1861-1865,* Vol. VII, p. 583 shows that he enlisted in the Navy in 1862.

Bassett, Helen P.   *"HELEN P. BASSETT / 1883 – 1885"* is inscribed on this flat,

3-6 inch high stone.

Bassett, Julia E. *"JULIA E. BASSETT / 1846 – 1930"* is inscribed on this flat, 0-3 inch high stone.

Bassett, Marcus N. *"MARCUS N. BASSETT / 1890 – 1937"* is inscribed on this flat, 1-3 inch high stone.

Bassett, Margaret S. *"MARGARET S. BASSETT / JAN 4, 1876 / MARCH 29, 1951 / WIFE OF RALPH M."* There are floral carvings in the upper corners of this flat, 0-1 inch high stone.

Bassett, Mary *"MARY BASSETT / 1879 – 1952"* is inscribed on this slanted stone.

Bassett, Mary C. See Ralph Bassett Monument entry.

Bassett, Nathaniel S. *"NATHANIEL S. BASSETT / 1879 – 1946"* is inscribed on this slanted stone.

Bassett, Ralph M. Monument *"RALPH MORTON BASSETT / 1877 – 1956 / HIS WIFE / MARY CORBETT BASSETT / 1883 – ____ "* There are floral designs carved in the upper corners of this stone. Leaning against the back of this gravestone is a small slate footstone inscribed with *"Peter Hoar – Esq."*

Bowen, Everett A. Monument *"BOWEN"* is inscribed on the front of this monument. Floral designs are carved in the upper corners. *"EVERETT A. BOWEN / 1869 – 1964 / HIS WIFE / JENNIE S. / 1870 – 1953 / ASLEEP IN JESUS"* is inscribed on the back. Jennie was the granddaughter of Ephraim Ward. A low stone post and metal rail fence surrounds this Ward family plot on three sides.

Bowen, Jennie S. See Everett Bowen Monument entry.

Brown, Edward Stone *"EDWARD BROWN / 1824 – 1899 / LUCY S. HIS WIFE / 1830 – 1901"* The first line is carved along an arch. This stone is loose on its base.

Brown, Lucy S. See Edward Brown Stone entry.

Caswell, Alanson L. *"ALANSON L. / son of / Henry & Amanda / Caswell, / died May 8, 1844 / Æ 2 years & 3 mo's /*
A pleasant plant, a lovely flower
Cut down and withered in an hour."
"A. L. C." is inscribed on the footstone. Both the gravestone and footstone are leaning against the front of the gravestone for Lusanna Tucker Peirce.

Clark, Martha *"MARTHA, / wife of / EZRA CLARK. / Born Sept. 28, 1786, / Died May / 28, 1851."* *"D. A. BURT, TAUNTON."* is inscribed on the bottom center of the stone.
"M. C." is inscribed on the footstone.

Coombs, Clarence A. Monument *"CLARENCE A. COOMBS / 1839 – 1910 / JULIA F. / HIS WIFE / 1844 – 1914."* This is a double arched stone, with the writing extending from one side to the other. Oak leaves are carved under the left arch, and ivy leaves are carved under the right arch.

Coombs, Cora S. *"CORA"* is carved in relief on the front of this monument. *"CORA S. / WIFE OF / HORACE L. COOMBS, / JULY 7, 1866, / JAN. 27, 1891."* is inscribed on the back. The first line is carved in relief. Ivy is carved at the top of both the front and back of this monument.

Coombs, Horace L. *"HORACE L. COOMBS / APR. 27, 1865 / FEB. 12, 1942"* is inscribed on this flat, ground level stone.

Coombs, Julia F. See Clarence Coombs Monument entry.

Cushman, Anne L. *"ANNE L. CUSHMAN / 1825 – 1902"* The first line is carved along an arch. This stone is located inside the Ward family plot.

Cushman, Mary *"MARY CUSHMAN / Born Apr. 22, 1810, / Died Dec. 24, 1882."* The first line is carved in relief along an arch. This gravestone is broken off at its base, and is lying face up, in front of it. This stone is located inside the Ward family plot.

Dunham, Lucinda *"SACRED / To the memory of / LUCINDA, / wife of Warren Dunham, / who died / Jan. 13, 1848, / aged 42 Yrs. /*

> *Though in the paths of death I tread,*
> *With gloomy horrors overspread;*
> *My steadfast heart shall fear no ill,*
> *For thou O Lord art with me still."*

"L. D." is inscribed on the footstone.

Dunham, Warren *"SACRED / to the memory of / WARREN / DUNHAM, / who died / Aug 17, 1838, in / his 36 year /*

> *Hold me O Jesus, in thine arms,*
> *And ____ me with immortal charms*
> *'Till I awake in realms above*
> *Forever to enjoy thy love."*

This poem is very weathered and hard to read.
"W. D." is inscribed on the footstone.

Emery, Dexter E. *"DEXTER E. / Son of John D. P. & / Susan H. Emery. / died Aug. 23, 1862 / Aged 8 yrs. 2 m. / & 14 d's. /*

> *This little plant of life and love,*
> *Just lent us for a day;*
> *Came like a blessing from above,*
> *Passed like a dream away."*

Emery, Susan H. *"MOTHER"* is inscribed on the top curved surface of this gravestone. *"Susan H. Emery."* is inscribed on the front and *"At rest"* is inscribed on the back. Canton Vital Records list her death on April 12, 1865, at 38 years, 9 months, and 16 days old. Taunton Vital Records document that her husband, John D. P. Emery, died in Taunton in 1909, and was buried in Gloucester.

Fletcher, Ella B. *"ELLA BROWN / WIFE OF / F. P. FLETCHER. / 1862 – 1904"* is inscribed on the front of this stone. A sculptured carving of flowers is above this. A curved roof tops the stone, and scroll carvings are on the sides. *"AND I HEARD*

A VOICE FROM HEAVEN SAYING UNTO ME WRITE, BLESSED / ARE THE DEAD WHICH DIE IN THE LORD FROM HENCEFORTH: YEA, SAITH / THE SPIRIT, THAT THEY MAY REST FROM THEIR LABOURS: AND THEIR / WORKS DO FOLLOW THEM. / REV 14-13." is inscribed on the front base of this gravestone. Lakeville Vital Records list her as Lydia E. Fletcher (nee Brown), wife of Francis P. Fletcher.

Hinds, John   *"In memory of / Mr. JOHN HINDS / who died / Dec. 1, 1811 / aged 26*
/ years. /   *How lov'd, how valu'd once, avails thee not,*
                              To whom related or [by] *whom begot:*
                              A heap of dust alone remains of thee,
                              'Tis all thou art, and all the proud shall be."

An urn and willow are carved in relief at the top of this stone. Columns are carved on the sides.
"Mr. / J. H. / 1811." is inscribed on the footstone.

Hoar, Mercy
          "MERCY,
          WIFE OF
          PETER HOAR.
          BORN
          APRIL 24, 1762.
          DIED
          MAY 20, 1847."

This reddish brown replacement stone is rectangular is shape. Thatcher lists her first name as Mary, "wife of Peter, Esq."

Hoar, Peter, Esq.   *"Departed this life / March 12, 1815 / PETER HOAR Esq. /*
aged 60 years. /   *Blessed are the dead which die in the Lord*
                          from henceforth ' yea' saith the Spirit, that
                          they may rest from their labours, and their
                          works do follow them."

An urn is carved in relief at the top of this slate stone. Branches are carved on either side. Horizontal lines are carved around the inscribed area, and fan carvings are in the corners. There is a *"SAR 1775"* marker and a flag present.
"Peter / Hoar - Esq." is inscribed on this slate footstone underneath a carving of a branch. It is located leaning against the back of the Ralph M. Bassett Monument.

Holmes, Betsey W. Monument   *"BETSEY WARD HOLMES / 1813 – 1844 / LUCY HER DAUGHTER / 1844 – 1844."* Thatcher lists, "Holmes, Betsey W. daughter of Ephraim and Priscilla Ward, died Sept. 4th 1844, age 31 years." Her original stone was not found. This monument is located within the Ward family plot.

Holmes, Lucy   See Betsey Holmes Monument entry.
"LUCY HO.../ daugh___..." This is inscribed on the only piece of this gravestone found. The first line is carved in relief. A broken flower bud is carved in relief at

the top. It is lying flat on the ground next to a stone post at the front of the cemetery. This partial stone probably belongs to the original stone for Lucy Holmes, infant daughter of Betsey Ward Holmes. Thatcher lists, "Holmes, Lucy dau. of Betsey W. Aug. 4, 1844, age 3 mos."
"L. H." This footstone is lying on the ground on the right side of the cemetery, next to a stone post.

Howard, Seth, Capt. *"CAPT. SETH HOWARD, / died in Middleborro, / July 30, 1852; / aged 73 y'rs, / and 23 d'ys."* Note the spelling of *Middleborro*.
"S. H." is inscribed on the footstone.

Howland, Lydia *"LYDIA, / widow of / Timothy Howland. / died June 1, 1853: / in her 70 th / year."*
"L. H." is inscribed on the footstone.

Leach, Abiel *"Abiel son of Mr / Ephraim Leach & / Mrs. Susan his wife / died July 16. 1813 / aged 1 year 3 m. / 14 d."* A willow is carved above the inscriptions on this small, slate stone. The last line is buried underground. Remnants of a low stone post and metal rail fence surround this Leach and Southworth plot.
"A. L." This slate footstone was found leaning against the Ward Obelisk.

Leach, Abigail *"ABIGAIL HARLOW, / Wife of / EDWIN J. LEACH, / Born Aug, 11, 1809. / Died / Feb. 10. 1858. /*
> *Oh well for thee! So safe, so sure*
> *Untill eternity:*
> *Jesus defends thy sleep.*
> *Jesus sure watch will keep:*
> *How sweet, how soft thy rest shall be."*

This stone is separated from its base. It is broken in two along the last line of the poem, and is lying face up. The top part is located behind the base, with the small bottom portion located on top of the base. Note the spelling of *Untill* in the poem. Remnants of a low stone post and metal rail fence surround this Edwin J. Leach plot.

Leach, Almira R. *"ALMIRA RYARSON, / Dau. of / Ephraim O. & / Mary A. Leach: / Died ___ _6, 1852, / aged 3 ...0 Ms. / ... ys. /*
> *God saw the flower so beautiful,*
> *And pluck'd the precious gem,*
> *And placed it in His coronet,*
> *To grace His diadem."*

This stone has crumbled around the death date and age. Taunton Vital Records list her birth on December 13, 1848. Her death notice in *The Middleboro Gazette* 11/04/1852:3 lists her death date as October 26, 1852. Remnants of a low stone post and metal rail fence surround this Ephraim O. Leach plot.

Leach, Celia *"CELIA RICHMOND / wife of / ISAAC W. LEACH / Mar. 19, 1829. / Sept. 13, 1911. / Well we know thy living faith / Had the power to conquer death."* The first line is carved in relief. This stone is separated from its base, and is lying face up on the ground behind it. It shared the same base with the gravestone of Isaac Leach, her husband. Remnants of a low stone post and metal rail fence surround this Leach and Southworth plot.

Leach, Clarinda B. *"CLARINDA BARROWS / Wife of / EDWIN J. LEACH. / Born Nov. 18, 1820. / Died / Nov. 29, 1905. / At Rest."* Lakeville Vital Records show she was his second wife. This stone is separated from its base and is lying face up on top of it. There is a break between the 4th and 5th line that has been successfully repaired. Remnants of a low stone post and metal rail fence surround this Edwin J. Leach plot.

Leach, Edwin J. *"EDWIN J. / Son of / Ephraim O. & Mary A. / LEACH, / Died April 29, 1872. / Aged / 26 years, 6 months. / Blessed are the pure in heart, / For they shall see God."* *"BURT & KING, Taunton."* is inscribed at the bottom center of this stone. Remnants of a low stone post and metal rail fence surround this Ephraim O. Leach plot.

Leach, Edwin J. *"EDWIN J. LEACH, / Born / May 11, 1808. / Died / Sept. 1, 1889. At rest."* This stone is broken between the last two lines, and both pieces are lying face up on the ground, behind the base. A small corner is also broken off on the bottom left. Remnants of a low stone post and metal rail fence surround his plot.

Leach, Ephraim, Dea. *"DEA. / EPHRAIM LEACH / died / June 4, 1864; / Aged 82 yrs. 4 m's. / The memory of the Just is blessed."* The second line is carved in relief. Remnants of a low stone post and metal rail fence surround this Leach and Southworth plot.
"E. L." is inscribed on the footstone.

Leach, Ephraim O. Monument *"LEACH"* is carved in relief on top slanted surface of this large monument. *"EPHRAIM O. LEACH / DEC. 4, 1816 – OCT. 18, 1885 / MARY A. LEACH / NOV. 17, 1822 – OCT. 25, 1909"* is inscribed on the front. Remnants of a low stone post and metal rail fence surround this plot.

Leach, Harry *"HARRY / Son of I. W. & / C. R. Leach, / died Oct 4, 1865, / Aged 4 m's, 3 d's. / Not lost, but gone before."* The first line is carved in relief. Remnants of a low stone post and metal rail fence surround this Leach and Southworth plot.
"H. L." is inscribed on the footstone.

Leach, Infant Daughter *"INFANT. / Daughter of / EDWIN J. & ABIGAIL H. / LEACH. / Died Oct. 31, / 1833."* Remnants of a low stone post and metal rail fence surround this Edwin J. Leach plot.

Leach, Isaac *"ISAAC W. LEACH. / Dec. 13, 1829, / May 8, 1891. / Thy Memory shall ever be / A guiding Star to Heaven."* The first line is carved in relief along an arch. This stone is separated from its base, and is lying face up on the ground behind it. It originally shared the same base with the gravestone of Celia, his wife. Remnants of a low stone post and metal rail fence surround this Leach and Southworth plot.

Leach, Mary A. See Ephraim O. Leach Monument entry.

Leach, Nathaniel S. *"Nathaniel S. / son of / Mr. Ephraim Leach / & Mrs. Susan his / wife died Oct. 19. / 1813 aged 3 years / 3 m. 12 d."* A willow tree is carved above the inscription on this small, slate stone. The last line is buried underground. Remnants of a low stone post and metal rail fence surround this Leach and

Southworth plot.

"N. S. L." This small, slate footstone is located in the position of the headstone for Virtue Southworth. It was missing at a later visit.

Leach, Nathaniel S.   *"NATHANIEL S. / son of / Mr. Ephraim & / Mrs. Susan Leach / died Jan. 11. 1824 / aged 2 years / 7 m. 11 d."* An urn and willow carving is at the top of this slate stone. Curved designs are carved down the sides. Remnants of a low stone post and metal rail fence surround this Leach and Southworth plot. *"N. S. L."* is inscribed on this slate footstone. It is located leaning against Virtue Southworth's headstone.

Leach, Simeon R.   *"LEACH"* is carved in relief on the top slanted surface of this large, monument. *"SIMEON R. LEACH / JULY 6, 1860 – JUNE 3, 1912 / SAY NOT GOOD NIGHT BUT IN SOME / BRIGHTER CLIME BID US GOOD MORNING."* is inscribed on the front. Remnants of a low stone post and metal rail fence surround this Ephraim O. Leach plot.

Leach, Susan   *"SUSAN, / wife of / Dea. Ephraim Leach, / died Nov. 4, 1864; / Aged 78 yrs. 9 d's. / Thou art gone, but not forgotten."* The first line is carved in relief along an arch. Remnants of a low stone post and metal rail fence surround this Leach and Southworth plot.
"S. L." is inscribed on the footstone.

Leach, Susan J.   *"SUSAN J. / dau. of Edwin J. / & Abigail H. Leach / died / Oct. 2, 1836. / Aged 1 mo. & 14 dᵉ. /*

> *This lovely bud so fresh so fair,*
> *Called home by early doom;*
> *Just came to show how fair a flower,*
> *In Paradise could bloom."*

Remnants of a low stone post and metal rail fence surround this Edwin J. Leach plot.

Leonard, Charity   *"In memory of / Mrs. Charity Leonard / widᵒ. of / Dea. George Leonard / who died Febrʸ 12. 1805 / in her 76 year. /*

> *lain*
> *No more my fiends shall I comp*
> *For Jesus makes up ev'ry pain"*

A rising sun is carved on top of this slate stone. The carver ran out of room on the first line of the poem and carved *lain* is above the *comp* in the word complain.
"Mrs. / C. Leonard" Pieces of slate are missing on the shoulders of this footstone.

Leonard, George, Dea.   *"In memory of / Dea. George Leonard / who died Janʸ. 22, 1801 / in his 78 year. / In sacred order rang'd along;*

> *Saints new releas'd by death,*
> *Join the bold seraphs warbling breath*
> *And aid th' immortal song"*

A rising sun is carved on top of this slate stone. It had been broken off at ground level, just below the inscription. The top portion was placed in the ground in front of the bottom section, thus burying the last three lines of the poem. A flag is present at the gravesite.
"Dea. / G. Leonard" is inscribed on the slate footstone.

Macomber, Almira   *"ALMIRA MACOMBER / Died Oct. 3, 1848; / aged 43 Yrs. /* *"Blessed are the dead that die in the / LORD.""*
"A. M." is inscribed on the footstone. The inscription is buried underground.

Macomber, Bathsheba   *"BATHSHEBA, / wife of / Nathaniel Macomber, / died Dec. 5, 1818, aged / 69 years."* The first line is carved in shadow on this slate stone. *"B. M."* is inscribed on this slate footstone.

Macomber, Bathsheba   *"BATHSHEBA, / daughter of Nathaniel & / Bathsheba Macomber, / died Dec. 12, 1820, / Aged 35 / years."* The first line is carved in shadow on this slate stone.
"B. M." This slate footstone is leaning against the headstone.

Macomber, Daniel   *"DANIEL MACOMBER, / Died / Feb. 27, 1861. / Aged / 91 years."*
"D. M." is inscribed on the footstone.

Macomber, Fidelia   *"FIDELIA, / daughter of / Daniel & Abigal / Macomber, / died March 29, 1842, / in her 19th year."*
"F. M." is inscribed on the footstone. The inscription is buried underground.

Macomber, Nathaniel   *"In / Memory of / Mr. NATHANIEL MACOMBER / who died / July 7, 1814 / in his 72. / year. /*
> *My flesh must slumber in the ground.*
> *'Till the last trumpets joyful sound*
> *Then burst the bands with sweet surprise*
> *And in my Savior's image rise."*

An urn and willow carving is at the top of this slate stone. Part of the urn carving is recessed. Small designs are carved along the border. All but the first line of the poem is underground.
"Mr. / N. M." This slate footstone was found leaning against the Ward Obelisk.

Macomber, Sarah   *"Miss, Sarah / Daughter of Mr. / Nathaniel and Mrs. / Bathsheba Macom- / ber died September / 14 [th] 1808 aged 25 Yea- / rs 6 months & / 8 days."* This slate stone has a narrow urn carved at the top. A branch is carved on either side. Small line designs encircle the carving, and the inscription, and also are carved along the border. The last two lines are underground. Thatcher lists her death date as September 4th, and does not include the number of days in her age.

Morgan, Helen R.   See Joseph Morgan Monument entry.

Morgan, Joseph F. Monument   *"JOSEPH F. MORGAN / 1863 – 1948 / HELEN R. HIS WIFE / 1867 – 1928"*

Morgan, Kenneth F.   *"KENNETH F. MORGAN / MARCH 22. 1890 / APRIL 30. 1920 / MIZPAH"* There is a simple floral design carved above the inscription.

Morgan, Lena G.   *"LENA G. MORGAN / WIFE OF KENNETH / OCT. 23, 1892 / OCT. 9, 1967 / MIZPAH"* A frame in front of her gravestone supports climbing roses.

Mother   *"Mother"* is inscribed on the top curved surface of this stone. No other inscriptions are present.

Nason, Ida J. *"IDA J. NASON, / Born / Dec. 8, 1854. / Died / May 5, 1859. /*
A flower lent, not given,
To bud on Earth
And bloom in Heaven."
The first line is inscribed along an arch.

Nason, Sarah W. Monument

"SARAH W. NASON /
1827 – 1896"

is inscribed on the convex
front surface of this
monument. On the right and
left sides of the monument, at
the top, a floral design is
carved.

Omy, Elizabeth *"ELIZABETH OMY, / born / Feb. 2, 1755. / died / June 7, 1837. /*
Æ 82 years. / For more than 30 years / a resident in the family of / Ephraim Ward."
The first line is carved along an arch. This stone is located within the Ward family
plot.

Pierce, Abiah *"Mrs. Abiah Pierce / wife of / Mr. Ephriam Pierce / & dau'. of /*
De.ⁿ George Leonard / & Mrs. Charity his wife died / Oct.ʳ 27 1800 in her 35 year /
As in a glass here all may see / their best estate is vanity" A peeking rising sun is
carved at the top of this slate stone. A flag is present. Thatcher lists her death day
as February 27th.
"Mrs / Abiah Pierce" is inscribed on this slate footstone.

Peirce, Benajah *"In Memory / of / BENAJAH PEIRCE, / Who died / May 5, 1844,*
/ Aged / 73 years. / He hoped in God." This stone is broken between the fifth and
sixth lines, but has been successfully repaired.

Peirce, Charity *"In memory of / CHARITY, / Wife of / BENAJAH PEIRCE, / who*
died Dec. 2, 1831, / Æ. 63 Years. / Blessed are the peace makers: for / they shall be
called the children of God." *"Warren F. R."* is inscribed in the lower right corner
of this stone. The second line is carved in relief.

Peirce, Elisabeth *"Memento Mori. / H / In Memory of M.ʳˢ / Elisabeth Peirce wife*
of / Cap.ᵗ Job Peirce who died / June yᵉ 9 .ᵗʰ Æ, 1790 in yᵉ 47 .ᵗʰ / Year of her Age. /
Afflictions ___ Pain I ___
Physicians then ___
Till God did please to give ___
And free me from this life of Pain
Come hither Mortals cast your Eye
Then ___ your way prepare to Die:
Gon___ ell that you must Die

Prepare for Death before it's nigh..
C.T.S."

The significance of the *H* in the second line is unknown. A winged angel with a deeply carved nose is carved in relief between the first and second line. Scalloped designs are carved around the inscription and the carving. The poem was very hard to read due to weathering and lichen growth.

"Mrs. / Elisabeth Peirce." is inscribed on the slate footstone, which is leaning against the back of her headstone.

Peirce, Elnathan   *"In memory of Elnathan / son of Capt. Job Peirce & / Mrs. Betsy his wife, who / died Octo^r, 5, 1797. aged 15 / Years. 11 months 16 days. /*
> *This pleasant youth whose dust is laid*
> *In the dreary mansions of the dead*
> *Shall, rise and leave its native ground*
> *As the last trumpet solomn sound."*

A head with long wings is carved at the top of this slate stone. The top part of the tympanum is broken off and set in place on the stone. The area around his age in days is beginning to exfoliate. Notice the spelling of *solomn*. Thatcher lists his age as only 15 years, 11 months.

Peirce, Experience   *"EXPERIENCE PEIRCE, / died July 13, 1845, / in the 73rd year / of her age. / "Blessed are the pure in heart for they / shall see God.""*
"E. P." is inscribed on the footstone.

Peirce, Infant   *"INFANT / Son of / Gen. Ebenezer W. Peirce, / & Irene Isabel, his wife. / Died May 29, 1851."* *"D. A. BURT."* is inscribed at the bottom right of this stone. This stone is leaning against a tree to the left of Capt. Job Peirce Jr.'s stone.

Peirce, Job, Capt.   *"In memory of / Capt. JOB PEIRCE / who died / July 22, 1819 / aged 82 / years."* There is an urn and willow carving at the top of this slate stone. Small designs are carved along border. A *"SAR 1775"* marker and flag are present. *"Capt. / J. P. / 1819."* is inscribed on this slate footstone.

Peirce, Job, Jr., Capt.   *"Here lies the Remains of / Capt. JOB PEIRCE Junr / who Died Septr 22^d, 1805. / In the 38th Year of his / Age. /*
> *His Death was as* calm *and* resigned *as his*
> *Life was* pure *and* virtuous.
> *When Death that foe to human happiness has*
> *entombed in his dark and dreary mansions a*
> *Form in whose society we once derived the most*
> *endearing tenderness and refined felicity, how*
> *blessed is every earthly enjoyment, and every*
> *hope of promised joys. The world itself appears*
> *a dreary void and all creation seems to mourn*
> *our loss."*

The last line is buried underground. An urn with two large handles is carved at the top of this textured stone. Note the change in lettering for the words *calm, resigned, pure and virtuous.*

Peirce, Louissa   *"In memory of Louissa / dau^{tr}. of Mr. Samuel & . / Mrs. Hannah*

Peirce she / died Feb.^{ry.} 22.^d 1807 / Aged 3 years / 7 months." A rising sun is carved at the top of this slate stone. The last line is buried underground.
"L P" is carved on the slate footstone.

Peirce, Lusanna

"In memory of
LUSANNA TUCKER .
daughter of
Capt. Job and
Mrs. Abigail E. Peirce.
who died Sept. 24, 1836.
aged 7 years & 11 mo.
Vain world how transient is its joy,
Its pleasures soon will end in pain;
But when I'm gone there's no alloy;
Who would not die this bliss to gain!
Then cease t' indulge th' falling tear,
I now with Jesus ever dwell
If you my praises did but hear
You'd surely say that all is well."

There is a sculpted carving of an urn and willow at the top of this stone. Thatcher lists her first name as Joanna.

Peirce, Mary A. *"In memory of Mary / Allen Dau^{t.r} of Mr. Samuel / ___ Hannah Peirce / ...^{br} 7th / ...9 Aged 15. / months."* This slate stone is lying face up on the ground. It is broken into several pieces below the third line. The footstone was broken off near the ground, and is missing. No inscription was found on the intact piece. Thatcher lists her death date as October 7, 1809, age 15 months.

Pierce, Mercy *"MERCY PIERCE, / Died / Nov. 14, 1858, / Aged / 34 years."* This stone is broken off below the inscription and is lying face down on the ground. *"M. P."* is inscribed on the footstone.

Peirce, William R. *"__ memory of Capt. / ___am R. Peirce / ... _ied in the Island of / ...holomews May 15 / ...30 years. & 26 Day_ /...nd from a ...."* A winged head is carved at the top of this slate stone. This partial stone is leaning against the back of the gravestone of Mrs. Elisabeth Peirce. *"...t's heart. / ... HOVAHs hand. / ...'ry murmuring thought depart"* is inscribed on a second piece of slate which is located to the left of Capt. Job Peirce, Jr.'s gravestone. Thatcher lists, "Peirce, William R., died in the Island of Bartholomew, May 14th, 1794, age 30 years." *Middleborough, Massachusetts Vital Records,* Vol. 1, p. 265 lists his birth date as April 19th, 1764, and on p. 267 lists, "William Rounseville Peirce, son of Capt. Job and Mrs. Elisabeth his wife, departed this life, in the West Indies, May 15, 1794, in the 31st year of his age."

Porter, George *"GEORGE PORTER / 1849 – 1939"* There is a crown carved above the inscription on this gravestone.

Porter, Kate *"KATE PORTER / WIFE OF / GEORGE PORTER / DIED JULY 24,*

1915 / AGED 75 YRS. 9 MOS." There is a crown carved above the inscription on this gravestone.

Richmond, Edward K.   *"EDWARD K. / RICHMOND / Died Jan 6. 1854 / Aged 32 years. /*
                When shall we three meet again.
                Fading, fading, all are fading,
                No substantial thing is here:
                Loved ones leave us, we are passing,
                Passing to another sphere."
The first two lines are carved in relief. In his death year, the *4* is inscribed within a recessed square. This stone had been broken through *RIC* in the second line and the death year in the third line. These breaks have been successfully repaired. *"E. K. R."* is inscribed on the footstone.

Richmond, Edward W.   *"EDWARD WARREN / son of Edward K. & / Lucinda S. Richmond / died April 7, / 1850, / aged 2 Yrs. 28 Das."*
"E. W. R." This footstone is lying next to the gravestone of Miss Sarah Macomber.

Sampson, Thomas   *"Th^e re is Hope / In memory of / Mr. Thomas Sampson / who died / Oct. 15 1813 / in his 50 year."* A right hand pointing up is carved in the top center of this slate stone. A sun with rays is carved in the upper right and left corners, and small scalloped designs are carved along the edges of this rectangular stone.
"Mr. / T. Sampson" is inscribed on this slate footstone.

Samson, Thomas   *"Momento mortis / In Memory of / Mr. THOMAS SAMSON. / who died Sep^t. 9, 1792. Aged / 57. Years 7. Months & 14. Days. /*
                Adieu my friends and kindred dear,
                For silent dust conceals me here,
                And when the mighty trump shall sound,
                To call the nations from the ground
                I'll then reanimate my clay,
                And wing my way,
                To join the great celestial Day."
A winged angel is carved at the top of this slate stone. The last two lines of the poem are underground. Thatcher spells his last name as Sampson.

Sanford, Betsey T.   *"BETSEY T. / WIFE OF / WM. T. SANFORD, / BORN JULY 26, 1842. / DIED JAN. 24, 1897."*

Sanford, Charlotte A.   *"CHARLOTTE A. / SANFORD / APRIL 25, 1862 / MAY 15, 1932"* Simple floral designs are carved above the inscription.

Sanford, William T.   *"WILLIAM T. SANFORD / BORN MAY 15, 1841, / DIED OCT. 26, 1912."*

Shaw, Abby   See Francis Shaw Monument entry.

Shaw, Francis S. Monument   *"FRANCIS S. SHAW. / DIED MAY 29, 1885, AGED 60 YRS. 11 MOS. / ABBY S. HIS WIFE. / DIED FEB. 14, 1894 AGED 64 YRS. 2 MOS."* Oak leaves are carved in the upper left corner, and ivy leaves are carved in the upper right corner. *"SHAW"* is carved in relief on the base of this large monument.

Shaw, Frank C. *"FRANK CLINTON / Son of Francis S. & / Abby S. Shaw, / Died / Oct. 2, 1856, / Æ. 1 y'r. & 3 m's. /*

> *Farewell dear Child tis hard to part.*
> *From thee our lovely one;*
> *But God who gave thee him we trust*
> *And let his will be done."*

Shaw, Herbert F. *"HERBERT FRANCIS. / son of Francis S. & / Abby S. Shaw, / Died / July 14, 1851; / aged 1 yr. & 4 ms. /*

> *Lovely babe, thy days are o'er,*
> *And thou art gone to rest,*
> *Thy home shall be forever more,*
> *In thy Redeemer's breast."*

The poem is hard to read on this small, textured stone.

Shaw, Horace E. *"HORACE ELMER, / son of Francis S. & / Abby S. Shaw, / Died / July 10, 1851; / aged 3 months. /*

> *Sleep on thou happy infant sleep,*
> *We would not break thy rest;*
> *Though o'er thee tears of love we weep,*
> *We know that thou art blest."*

The last line of this poem is buried underground.

Shaw, Infant daughter *"INFANT. / dau. of Francis S & / Abby S. Shaw."*

Shaw, Infant son *"Infant Son of / Francis S. & / Abby S. Shaw."*

Shaw, Mary A. *"MARY ABBY. / dau. of Francis S. / & Abby S. Shaw, / died Nov. 30, 1861; / Aged 2 yrs, 3 m's /*

> *That little form has passed away*
> *This world is not her home;*
> *Her Father called she could not stay*
> *He took her for his own."*

Shearman, David, Capt. *"In / Memory of / CAPT. DAVID SHEARMAN / who died / Dec.ʳ 27, 1828, / in the 41 year / of his age. /*

> *And must this body die?*
> *This mortal frame decay?*
> *And must these active limbs of mine*
> *Lie mould'ring in the clay?"*

The third line is carved in relief. There is a carving of an urn above the inscriptions. The inscribed area above the poem is circled by leaf-like carvings.
"D. S. / 1828." is inscribed on the footstone.

Smith, Elijah *"In memory of / ELIJAH SMITH, / who died / April 25, 1839, in / his 80 year."* An urn and willow carving is at the top of this rectangular slate stone. Small rectangular designs are carved along the sides of the inscription.

Smith, Janet   *"Janet daughter of Mr. / Southworth and / Mrs. Hannah Smith / died December 23ʳᵈ 1809 aged 5 / days."* There is an urn and willow carving on the top of this slate stone. Thatcher lists her death day as Dec. 25ᵗʰ.

Smith, Mary   *"In memory of / MARY, / wife of Elijah Smith; / who died / Aug. 10, 1846, in / her 87 year."* There is an urn and willow carving at the top of this rectangular, slate stone. Small rectangular designs are carved along the sides of the stone adjacent to the inscription.

Smith, Rebecca   *"In memory of / REBECCA, / dau. of Elijah & Mary / Smith; / who died / March 22, 1826, in / her 42 year."* An urn and willow are carved at the top of this rectangular, slate stone. Small rectangular designs are carved along the sides of the stone adjacent to the inscription. Thatcher lists her death month as May.

Southworth, Abial W.   *"ABIAL W. SOUTHWORTH / Born / Nov. 18, 1798. / Died / April 8, 1868. / A kind Husband and Father."* Middleborough, Massachusetts Vital Records Vol. 1, p. 277, lists him as the son of Capt. Seth and Hope Southworth.

Southworth, Albert A. Stone   *"Here Rests"* is inscribed across the top of this small stone, which is carved to look like two gravestones. *"ALBERT / ASHLAND, / died Jan. 3, 1848. / Æ. 1 Mo. & 8 Ds."* is inscribed on the left side, and *"GEORGE / OTIS, / died July 24, 1848 / Æ. 8 Mos."* is inscribed on the right side. *"Children of / Otis & Lucy W. Southworth."* is inscribed across the bottom of the stone. Remnants of a low stone post and metal rail fence surround this Leach and Southworth plot. See Otis Southworth Monument entry also.

Southworth, Annie J. Monument   *"SOUTHWORTH"* is carved in relief diagonally across the front of the monument. A cross and a crown are carved in relief at the center top, and ivy leaves are carved in relief on either side. *"ANNIE J. / OCT. 18, 1859 – NOV. 18, 1875 / ELLA F. / OCT. 7, 1861 – DEC. 7, 1875 / HATTIE N. / JULY 10, 1865 – JAN. 19. 1889 / Daughters of / Albert & Mercy T. Southworth."* is inscribed on the back.

Southworth, Betsey   *"Betsey / Daughter of / M^r. Gideon & / Mrs Mary Sout / - hworth died June / 8 th 1794 aged 7 / Years 8 months / & 4 days"* There was an urn carved on the tympanum, but most of it has exfoliated. Small rectangular designs are carved around the edges of the stone and in a circle around the carving and the inscription. This slate stone is leaning against the stone of Miss Hannah Southworth.

Southworth, Catherine P.   *"In Memory of / Catherine P. wife of / Leonard / Southworth. / who died June 8, 1828. / aged 33."* An urn is carved at the top of this small stone. Thatcher lists her middle initial as R.
"C. P. S." is inscribed on the footstone.

Southworth, Charles T.   *"Charles T. / Southworth / died / Sept. 2, 185_. / aged 32 years."* The first two lines are carved in outline. There is a crack running through the *185_* in the fourth line, and the *years* in the last line. Lakeville Vital Records list that he was the son of William and Phebe Southworth, and that he died on September 3, 1853. A *"GAR 8 481"* marker, and a flag are present. Remnants of a low stone post and metal rail fence surround this Leach and Southworth plot.

Southworth, Ella F.   See Annie J. Southworth Monument entry.

Southworth, Ellen A.   See Otis Southworth Monument entry.
*"ELLEN AUGUSTA, / daughter of Otis & / Lucy W. Southworth. / died
March 26, 1850, / aged 7 Yrs. & / 3 Mos. /*

> *Shed not for her the bitter tear*
> *Give not your heart to vain regret*
> *Tis but the Casket that lies here*
> *The Gem that filled it sparkles yet."*

Remnants of a low stone post and metal rail fence surround this Leach and Southworth plot.

Southworth, Emma L.   *"EMMA LIZZIE. / Daughter of / Albert & Mercy / SOUTHWORTH. / Born June 27, 1852. / Died / May 19, 1858."* *"D. A. Burt."* is inscribed at the bottom of this stone, on the right.

Southworth, Enoch   *"ENOCH / SOUTHWORTH, / Born April 13, 1804; / Died April 18, 1871."*
"E. S." is inscribed on the footstone.

Southworth, George O.   See Otis Southworth Monument entry.
See also Albert Southworth Stone entry.

Southworth, Gideon   *"In memory of / GIDEON SOUTHWORTH, / who died / Jan 13, 1827, / in his 77 year."* An urn and willow are carved at the top of this slate stone. Small curved designs are carved down the sides. A diagonal crack on the right side extends to the word *year* in the last line.

"G. S." This footstone is leaning against the stone for Miss Hannah Southworth.

Southworth, Hannah *"Miss Hannah / Daughter of Mr. / Gideon & Mrs. Ma-/ ry. Southworth di- / ed. Sept*. *1*ˢᵗ *1808 aged / 18 Years 3 months / & 18 days"* The last line is buried underground. A bottle like urn is carved at the top of this slate stone. A branch is carved on either side. There are many diagonal cracks on its face. Small rectangular designs are carved along the border of the stone. They also encircle the carving and the inscription. The gravestone for Betsey Southworth is leaning against this stone. Thatcher lists her age in months as 5. *Middleborough, Massachusetts Vital Records*, Vol. 2, p. 14 lists his age in months as 3.

"Mr Peter / H. S," is inscribed on this slate footstone. Semicircular designs are carved at the top and down the sides. *H. S.* is carved more deeply than *Mr Peter.* The stone has probably been recycled.

Southworth, Hannah *"In memory of / HANNAH, / wife of Nathaniel / Southworth; / who died / Nov. 8, 1845, in / her 85 year."* An urn and willow carving is at the top of this slate stone.
"H. S." is inscribed on the slate footstone.

Southworth, Hattie N. See Annie J. Southworth Monument entry.

Southworth, Hopy *"HOPY, / Wife of / SETH SOUTHWORTH, / Died / Sept. 25, 1865. / Aged / 86 years, 5 months, / 24 days."*

Southworth, Jerusha L. *"JERUSHA L. / Dau. of / Albert & Mercy T. / Southworth, / Died / May 19, 1851; / aged 1 yr. & 4 ms. /*
   Sh'll never more to us return
   Oh! may we follow her to heaven."

Southworth, Job H. *"In / Memory of / Job H. Son of / Leonard & / Catherine / Southworth, / who died May 15, / 1832. / Aged 6."* is inscribed on this small stone. Thatcher lists his age as 6 months.
"J. H. S." is inscribed on the footstone.

Southworth, Leonard *"LEONARD SOUTHWORTH, / Born / April 28, 1795, / Died / March 4, 1857."* The first line is carved along an arch in shadow on this textured stone. A flag is present.
"L. S." is inscribed on the footstone.

Southworth, Lewis H. *"LEWIS HARTLEY, / Son of / Albert & Mercy / SOUTHWORTH, / Born May 1, 1855. / Died / May 21, 1858."* *"BURT."* is inscribed in the lower right corner.

Southworth, Lois T. *"SACRED / To the memory of / LOIS T. / wife of / Enoch Southworth / who died Nov. 5, 1840. / aged 34 Yrs."* *"Hathaway, Taunton."* is inscribed in the lower left corner of the stone. The third line is carved in shadow. This gravestone is lying face up on the ground. Thatcher lists her death year as 1846.
"L. T. S." is inscribed on the footstone.

Southworth, Lucinda *"In memory of / LUCINDA, / wife of / Thomas Southworth / who died / March 5, 1832, / in the 52 year / of her age. /*

> *Hark hear the trumpet's solemn sound*
> *Proclaim the mournful theme:*
> *Go tell the nations I have found,*
> *That death is not a dream."*

The last two lines are buried underground.
"L. S." is inscribed on the footstone.

Southworth, Lucy W. See Otis Southworth Monument entry.
Lakeville Vital Records list her as the daughter of Ephraim and Susan Leach.

Southworth, Mary *"In memory of / Mrs. Mary, wife of / Mr. Gideon Southworth / she died Nov. 30, 1795 / in her 41. year."* There is an urn and simple willow carved on the top of this slate stone.
"____ Southworth" The left shoulder of this slate footstone has broken off. It is also beginning to exfoliate.

Southworth, Mary *"MARY / Wife of / ABIAL W. SOUTHWORTH, / Born / July 4, 1801. / Died / Jan. 26, 1891."*

Southworth, Nathaniel *"In memory of Nathan_ / iel son of Mr. Nathaniel / Southworth & Mrs. / Hannah his wife / who died April 18th 1799 / in his 8 year."* A winged angel is carved at the top of this slate stone. The last line is buried underground.
"N Southworth" is inscribed on this slate footstone. It is leaning against Virtue Southworth's headstone.

Southworth, Nathaniel *"In memory of / Mr. NATHANIEL SOUTHWORTH / who died / Jan. 23, 1819 / in his 60. / year."* An urn and willow are carved at the top of this slate stone. Curved designs are carved above the inscription, and down the sides.
"Mr / N. S. / 1819." is inscribed on the slate footstone.

Southworth, Otis Monument *"SOUTHWORTH"* is carved in relief on the top slanted surface of this monument. *"OTIS SOUTHWORTH / 1814 – 1905 / LUCY W. LEACH / HIS WIFE / 1818 – 1863"* is inscribed on the front. *"Ellen A. / 1842 – 1850 / George O. Albert A. / 1847 – 1848"* is inscribed on the back. Remnants of a low stone post and metal rail fence surround this Leach and Southworth plot.

Southworth, Phebe *"PHEBE, / wife of / WILLIAM SOUTHWORTH: / died / March 23, 1855, in / her 76 year."* The first line is carved in outline. Remnants of a low stone post and metal rail fence surround this Leach and Southworth plot.

Southworth, Polly *"M^{ss} Polly / Daughter of M^r. / Gideon & M^{rs} Ma- / -ry. Southworth died / May 21st 1798 aged 15 / Years 7 months & / 9 days"* A tall urn and branch are carved on the top of this slate stone. Designs are carved along the edges the stone. They also encircle the inscription and the carving. A large crack extends from the bottom of the carving to the bottom of the inscription. The tympanum area is beginning to exfoliate.

Southworth, Seth, Capt. *"CAPT. / SETH SOUTHWORTH, / Died / Nov. 30, 1862; / Aged 89 yrs. 6 mo, / & 24 d's."* The second line is carved along an arch.

Southworth, Thomas *"THOMAS SOUTHWORTH, / Died / June 19 1867: / Aged 91 yrs."* The first line is carved along an arch.
"T. S." is inscribed on the footstone.

Southworth, Virtue *"VIRTUE. / wife of / Leonard Southworth, / died Oct. 23, 1863; / Aged 66 years."* This stone is leaning against the back of a large tree. Two slate footstones are leaning against this stone. *"N Southworth"* and *"N.S.L."* are the inscriptions on these stones. An *"I.O.O.L.M.U. / Olympia Lodge 9648 / FLT / Middleboro"* marker is present next to Virtue's stone.
"V. S." is inscribed on this footstone. It is located two rows behind the tree, to the right of Catherine Southworth's footstone.

Southworth, William *"WILLIAM SOUTHWORTH. / Died / Nov. 28, 1861. / Aged / 83 years, 2 months / 8 days."* This stone is broken off below the inscriptions, and is leaning against the bottom section, which is still in the ground. Remnants of a low stone post and metal rail fence surround this Leach and Southworth plot.

Staples, Job M. *"JOB M. STAPLES / 1844 – 1922"* is inscribed on this 5 inch high flat stone. *Massachusetts Civil War Soldiers and Sailors, 1861-1865,* Vol. VI, p. 206, shows that he enlisted in 1861 at age 17. He served with the 1st Calvary, Co. K, and the 4th Calvary, Co. K.

Staples, Julia E. See Nathaniel G. Staples Monument entry.
Her obituary in *The Middleborough Gazette* 08/08/1957:11 reports her death on August 5, 1957, at 96 years old.

Staples, Lydia *"MOTHER / LYDIA STAPLES, / his wife / Died Dec. 26, 1863, / Æt. 82 y'rs, 2 mo's / Sleep on and take thy rest."* The first line is carved along an arch. The lower front corners of this stone had been broken, and were successfully repaired. *Middleborough, Massachusetts Vital Records,* Vol. 2, p. 173, records her marriage to Mr. William Jenne (sic) of New Bedford in 1805. *Vital Records of the Town of Freetown, Massachusetts 1686 Through 1890* lists her as the widow of Mr. Jenny (sic) when she married Capt. Nathaniel Staples in 1816. Lakeville Vital Records indicate that she was the daughter of Henry and Salome (Hinds) Peirce.

Staples, Nathaniel *"FATHER / NATHANIEL STAPLES / Died / July 17, 1862, / Æt. 83 y'rs. 6 mo's. / Fond hearts cherish his many / virtues."* The first line is carved along an arch.

Staples, Nathaniel G. Monument *"NATHANIEL G. STAPLES / 1851 – 1930 /*

JULIA EUDORA HIS WIFE / 1861 _____ " There are floral carvings at the top of this monument. The death year is not filled in for Julia.

Starrett, Elizabeth A. *"ELIZABETH A. / STARRETT / 1847 – 1932"*

Starrett, Elsie A. See Ralph Starrett Monument entry.

Starrett, Ralph G. Monument *"RALPH G. STARRETT / 1885 – 1922 / HIS WIFE / ELSIE A. MORGAN / 1886 – 1959"*

Stetson, Jennie E.

> *"JENNIE E. STETSON
> 1859."*

The inscriptions are carved in relief. The first line is carved along an arch. This stone had been broken below the inscription, and successfully repaired. Lakeville Vital Records state Jennie was the daughter of Peleg & Priscilla Stetson. She died on July 27, 1859, at the age of 21 years, 10 months, and 9 days. She was the granddaughter of Ephraim Ward. A low stone post and metal rail fence surround this Ward family plot.

Stetson, Martha S. *"MARTHA S. / daughter of / Peleg H. & Priscilla W. / STETSON, / born Jan. 4, 1848, / died Aug. 9, 1849 / Aged 1 year 7 m's / & 5 d's."* The first line is carved in relief. There is a carving of a broken rosebud above the inscriptions. She was the granddaughter of Ephraim Ward. A low stone post and metal rail fence surround this Ward family plot.

Stetson, Peleg H. *"CAPT. / PELEG H. STETSON / died / Jan. 23, 1865; Aged 65 years."* The second line on this textured stone is carved in relief along an arch. The lower part of this stone has numerous cracks in it radiating from the center bottom. The age was very hard to read. Lakeville Vital Records indicate that he was born in New Bedford, the son of Charles and Jane Stetson. He was a "master mariner" and died at the age of 66 years 6 months, and 10 days. His father-in-law was Ephraim Ward. A low stone post and metal rail fence surrounds this Ward family plot.

Stetson, Priscilla W. *"PRISCILLA W. / Wife of / Capt. / Peleg. H. Stetson, / died Oct. 17, 1871; / Aged 63 years."* The first line is carved in relief along an arch. This stone had been broken diagonally below the inscription, and successfully repaired. Lakeville Vital Records show she was the daughter of Ephraim and Priscilla Ward. A low stone post and metal rail fence surround this Ward family plot.

Stetson, Sprague S. Monument *"SPRAGUE S. STETSON / FEBY. 12, 1841 - JANY. 12, 1899 / THALIA W. STETSON / MAY 2, 1841 – DECR. 15, 1905"* *"STETSON"* is carved in relief on the base of monument. Lakeville Vital Records show he was the son on Peleg and Priscilla, the grandson of Ephraim Ward. A low stone post and metal rail fence surround this Ward family plot.

Stetson, Thalia W.   See Sprague Stetson Monument entry.

Tillson, Hannah   *"In / memory of / Mrs. HANNAH / wife of / Cap. Silvanus Tillson / who died . Nov 30, 1821 / in her 66 year."*   An urn and willow are carved at the top of this gravestone. The first line is carved on a raised pedestal for the urn. The rest of inscription is carved on a raised circle. This stone is weathered. *"H. T."* is inscribed on the footstone. The letters are half buried.

Tillson, Silvanus   *"In memory of / CAPT. SILVANUS TILLSON, / who died / April 21, 1822; / in his 64 year"*   There is no carving on the tympanum. A flag is present. *"S. T."* is inscribed on the footstone.

Tinkham, Josiah F.   *"JOSIAH F. TINKHAM. / Sept. 10, 1835. / March 12, 1892. / There is sweet rest in Heaven."*   The first line is carved in relief along an arch. Remnants of a low stone post and metal rail fence surround this Leach and Southworth plot.

Tinkham, Susan J.   *"SUSAN J. TINKHAM. / Wife of / Josiah F. Tinkham. / Sept. 30, 1839. / Feb. 8, 1919. / I have Kept the Faith."*   The first line is carved in relief along an arch. *Middleborough Marriage Records* online through the Digital Library show she was the daughter of Otis and Lucy Southworth. Remnants of a low stone post and metal rail fence surround this Leach and Southworth plot.

Ward Obelisk   *"WARD"* is carved in relief about 6 feet from the ground level on this tall obelisk. No other inscriptions are present. A low stone post and metal rail fence surround the Ward plot.

Ward, Caroline L.   *"CAROLINE L. LEONARD / Born / May 28, 1817. / Married / Geo. Ward, Oct. 20, 1840, / Married / Rev. James W. Ward, / Dec. 8 1862. / Died Jan. 30, 1895."*   The first line is carved in relief along an arch. A six-inch crack extends from the center bottom of the stone. A low stone post and metal rail fence surround this Ward family plot.

Ward, Ephraim, Gen.   *"ERECTED / in memory of / GEN. EPHRAIM WARD / who died / April 10, 1856, / Aged 78 years."*   The third line is carved in relief. A veteran's *"1812"* marker, *"GAR 8 374"* marker and a flag are present. A low stone post and metal rail fence surround this Ward family plot.

Ward, George   *"GEORGE WARD. / died / Aug. 29, 1856, / Aged 42 years."*   The first line is carved in deep relief on this roofed stone. There are two cracks radiating from the bottom of the stone up into the inscribed area. A low stone post and metal rail fence surround this Ward family plot.

Ward, Mary   *"In memory of / MARY WARD, / Daughter of / Ephraim & Priscilla / WARD, / Born Mar. 9. 1818. / Died Sept. 18. 1841, / Aged 23 years."*   The second line is carved in relief. Thatcher lists her as birth month as November. A low stone post and metal rail fence surround this Ward family plot.

Ward, Priscilla   *"Erected / In Memory of / PRISCILLA WARD / Consort of / Gen.*

Ephraim Ward, / died Nov. 13, 1826: / in the 46 year / of her age. /
"Calm on the bosom of thy GOD,
Fair spirit rest thee now!
E'en while with ours thy footsteps trod,
His seal was on thy brow.
Dust, to its narrow home beneath!
Soul, to its place on high!
They that have seen thy look in death,
No more may fear to die."
J. Tribell. Plymouth."

The third line is carved in relief. An urn is carved in relief at the top of the stone. Flower and leaves are carved outside the encircled inscription. A low stone post and metal rail fence surround this Ward family plot.

Additional Notes:

Although no gravestones were found for the following people, Thatcher lists them as buried in Ward Cemetery also.

"**Adams: Benjamin,** a pedler, (no stone – JH. Nelson)" *Middleborough, Massachusetts Vital Records,* Vol. 2, p. 27, list, "Benjamin Adams, a Pedlar, was taken sick and died at Hiram Nelson's, Aug. 27th, 1830." It does not state his age or where he was buried.

"**Caswell: Seth**, (no stone) J. H. Nelson" *Middleborough, Massachusetts Vital Records,* Vol. 1, p. 174, lists, "Seth Caswell, son of Joshua Caswell by Zilpha his wife was born April 21st 1767." Although there is no record of his death in the Middleborough Vital Records books or Lakeville Vital Records, the Vital Records index cards at the Middleborough Town Clerk's Office list Seth Caswell's death date as June 1, 1841, at 72 years old. No burial location listed.

"**Caswell: Ira**, (no stone) J. H. Nelson" *Middleborough, Massachusetts Vital Records,* Vol. 1, p. 285, lists, "Ira Caswell, son of Seth Caswell, was born Dec. 23, 1790." There is no record of his death in the Middleborough Vital Records books or Lakeville Vital Records.

Although no gravestones were found, the cemetery cards at the Lakeville Town Hall also include:

"**Jenney, Edwin** b. Oct. 30, 1804: d. Dec. 3, 1885" Lakeville Vital Records show that he was born in Fairhaven, the son of Charles Jenny (sic). He was 80 years old when he died. He is listed as buried in Taunton.

"**Jenney, James Garfield** b. July 4, 1884; d. July 22, 1884" Lakeville Vital Records indicate that he was the son of James and Julia Jenny (sic) who died July 18, 1884, at 14 days old. He is listed as buried in Lakeville, no cemetery noted.

"**Jenney, Mary Olive Davis**, wife of James Allen Jenney, b. Oct. 26, 1831 Geneva, NY, d. Nov. 26, 1876" Lakeville Vital Records indicate that she is the daughter of Daniel and Mary Davis. Her age is listed as 45 years and 2 months. She is listed as buried in Lakeville, no cemetery noted.

"**Jenney, Sarah Besmare**, wife of Edwin, b. Feb. 7, 1808, d. Dec. 3, 1889" Lakeville Vital Records indicate that she was born in Fairhaven and was the daughter of Lydia Bismore. She died at 81 years, 10 months, and 1 day. She is listed as being buried in Lakeville, no cemetery noted.

Gen. Ephraim Ward's *"1812"* marker

Ward Cemetery Map Index

Alphabetical:

Leach, Edwin J. (1845-1872) – 29
Leach, Edwin J. (1808-1889) – 6
Leach, Ephraim, Dea. (1782-1864) – 74
Leach, Ephraim O. (1816-1885) – 14
Leach, Harry (1865) – 51
Leach, Infant Daughter (1833) – 3
Leach, Isaac (1829-1891) – 50
Leach, Mary A. (1822-1909) – 14
Leach, Nathaniel S. (1810-1813) – 28, 97
Leach, Nathaniel S. (1821-1824) – 13, 98
Leach, Simeon R. (1860-1912) – 31
Leach, Susan (1786-1864) – 75
Leach, Susan J. (1836) – 4
Leonard, Charity (~1730-1805) – 71
Leonard, George, Dea. (~1724-1801) – 70
Macomber, Almira (~1805-1848) – 58
Macomber, Bathsheba (~1749-1818) – 140
Macomber, Bathsheba (~1785-1820) – 143
Macomber, Daniel (~1770-1861) – 34
Macomber, Fidelia (~1824-1842) – 57
Macomber, Nathaniel (~1743-1814) – 46,
    139
Macomber, Sarah (1783-1808) – 144
Morgan, Helen R. (1867-1928) – 39
Morgan, Joseph F. (1863-1948) – 39
Morgan, Kenneth F. (1890-1920) – 11
Morgan, Lena G. (1892-1967) – 12
Mother (no dates) – 65
Nason, Ida J. (1854-1859) – 145
Nason, Sarah W. (1827-1896) – 146
Omy, Elizabeth (1755-1837) – 25
Pierce, Abiah (~1766-1800) – 91
Peirce, Benajah (~1771-1844) – 89
Peirce, Charity (~1768-1831) – 90
Peirce, Elizabeth (~1744-1790) – 113
Peirce, Elnathan (1781-1797) – 133
Peirce, Experience (~1773-1845) – 56
Peirce, Infant (1851) – 135
Peirce, Job, Capt. (~1737-1819) – 112
Peirce, Job, Jr., Capt. (~1768-1805) – 134
Peirce, Louissa (1803-1807) – 117
Peirce, Lusanna (1828-1836) – 132
Peirce, Mary A. (1808-1809) – 116
Pierce, Mercy (~1824-1858) – 118
Peirce, William R. (1764-1794) – 113
Porter, George (1849-1939) – 129
Porter, Kate (1839-1915) – 130
Richmond, Edward K. (~1822-1854) – 126
Richmond, Edward W. (1848-1850) – 125
Sampson, Thomas (~1764-1813) – 137
Samson, Thomas (1735-1792) – 136

Sanford, Betsey T. (1842-1897) – 109
Sanford, Charlotte A. (1862-1932) – 110
Sanford, William T. (1841-1912) – 108
Shaw, Abby (1829-1894) – 35
Shaw, Francis S. (1824-1885) – 35
Shaw, Frank C. (1855-1856) – 59
Shaw, Herbert F. (1850-1851) – 63
Shaw, Horace E. (1851) – 62
Shaw, Infant Son (no dates) – 60
Shaw, Infant Daughter (no dates) – 61
Shaw, Mary A. (1859-1861) – 64
Shearman, David, Capt. (~1788-1828) – 32
Smith, Elijah (~1760-1839) – 122
Smith, Janet (1809) – 138
Smith, Mary (~1760-1846) – 123
Smith, Rebecca (~1785-1826) – 124
Southworth, Abial W. (1798-1868) – 15
Southworth, Albert (1847-1848) – 77, 99
Southworth, Annie J. (1859-1875) – 9
Southworth, Betsey (1786-1794) – 120
Southworth, Catherine (~1795-1828) – 27
Southworth, Charles F. (~1821-1853) – 76
Southworth, Ella F. (1861-1875) – 9
Southworth, Ellen (1842-1850) – 77, 100
Southworth, Emma L. (1852-1858) – 80
Southworth, Enoch (1804-1871) – 106
Southworth, George (1847-1848) – 77, 99
Southworth, Gideon (~1751-1827) – 92
Southworth, Hannah (1790-1808) – 120
Southworth, Hannah (~1761-1845) – 95
Southworth, Hattie N. (1865-1889) – 9
Southworth, Hopy (1779-1865) – 18
Southworth, Jerusha L. (1850-1851) – 79
Southworth, Job H. (~1826-1832) – 49
Southworth, Leonard (1795-1857) – 26
Southworth, Lewis H. (1855-1858) – 78
Southworth, Lois T. (~1806-1840) – 105
Southworth, Lucinda (~1781-1832) – 102
Southworth, Lucy W (1818-1863) – 77
Southworth, Mary (~1755-1795) – 93
Southworth, Mary (1801-1891) – 16
Southworth, Nathaniel (~1791-1799) – 13,
    121
Southworth, Nathaniel (~1760-1819) – 94
Southworth, Otis (1814-1905) – 77
Southworth, Phebe (~1780-1855) – 53
Southworth, Polly (1782-1798) – 119
Southworth, Seth, Capt. (1773-1862) – 17
Southworth, Thomas (~1776-1867) – 101
Southworth, Virtue (~1797-1863) – 13, 28
Southworth, William (1778-1861) – 52

Staples, Job M. (1844-1922) – 69
Staples, Julia E (1861-1957) – 66
Staples, Lydia (1781-1863) – 68
Staples, Nathaniel (1779-1862) – 67
Staples, Nathaniel G. (1851-1930) – 66
Starrett, Elizabeth A. (1847-1932) – 40
Starrett, Elsie A. (1886-1959) – 38
Starrett, Ralph G. (1885-1922) – 38
Stetson, Jennie E. (1837-1859) – 44
Stetson, Martha S. (1848-1849) – 45
Stetson, Peleg H., Capt. (~1800-1865) – 42
Stetson, Priscilla W. (~1808-1871) – 43

Stetson, Sprague S. (1841-1899) – 2
Stetson, Thalia W. (1841-1905) – 2
Tillson, Hannah (~1756-1821) – 73
Tillson, Silvanus (~1759-1822) – 72
Tinkham, Josiah F. (1835-1892) – 54
Tinkham, Susan J. (1839-1919) – 55
Ward, Caroline L. (1817-1895) – 20
Ward, Ephraim, Gen. (~1778-1856) – 23
Ward, George (~1814-1856) – 19
Ward, Mary (1818-1841) – 22
Ward, Priscilla (~1781-1826) – 24
Ward Obelisk (no dates) – 46

By Location:

1 – Bowen, Everett A. (1869-1964)
　　Bowen, Jennie S. (1870-1953)
2 – Stetson, Sprague S. (1841-1899)
　　Stetson, Thalia W. (1841-1905)
3 – Leach, Infant Daughter (1833)
4 – Leach, Susan J. (1836)
5 – Leach, Abigail (1809-1858)
6 – Leach, Edwin J. (1808-1889)
7 – Leach, Clarinda B. (1820-1905)
8 – Holmes, Lucy (1844)
9 – Southworth, Annie J. (1859-1875)
　　Southworth, Ella F. (1861-1875)
　　Southworth, Hattie N. (1865-1889)
10 – Coombs, Clarence A. (1839-1910)
　　Coombs, Julia F. (1844-1914)
11 – Morgan, Kenneth F. (1890-1920)
12 – Morgan, Lena G. (1892-1967)
13 – Southworth, Virtue (~1797-1863)
　　Leach, Nathaniel S. (1821-1824)
　　Southworth, Nathaniel (~1791-1799)
14 – Leach, Ephraim O. (1816-1885)
　　Leach, Mary A. (1822-1909)
15 – Southworth, Abial W. (1798-1868)
16 – Southworth, Mary (1801-1891)
17 – Southworth, Seth, Capt. (1773-1862)
18 – Southworth, Hopy (1779-1865)
19 – Ward, George (~1814-1856)
20 – Ward, Caroline L. (1817-1895)
21 – Holmes, Betsey W. (1813-1844)
　　Holmes, Lucy (1844)
22 – Ward, Mary (1818-1841)
23 – Ward, Ephraim, Gen. (~1778-1856)
24 – Ward, Priscilla (~1781-1826)
25 – Omy, Elizabeth (1755-1837)
26 – Southworth, Leonard (1795-1857)
27 – Southworth, Catherine (~1795-1828)

28 – Leach, Nathaniel S. (1810-1813)
　　Southworth, Virtue (~1797-1863)
29 – Leach, Edwin J. (1845-1872)
30 – Leach, Almira R. (1849-1852)
31 – Leach, Simeon R. (1860-1912)
32 – Shearman, David (~1788-1828)
33 – Howland, Lydia (~1784-1853)
34 – Macomber, Daniel (~1770-1861)
35 – Shaw, Francis S. (1824-1885)
　　Shaw, Abby (1829-1894)
36 – Coombs, Horace L. (1865-1942)
37 – Coombs, Cora S. (1866-1891)
38 – Starrett, Ralph G. (1885-1922)
　　Starrett, Elsie A. (1886-1959)
39 – Morgan, Joseph F. (1863-1948)
　　Morgan, Helen R. (1867-1928)
40 – Starrett, Elizabeth A. (1847-1932)
41 – Howard, Seth, Capt. (1779-1852)
42 – Stetson, Peleg H., Capt. (~1800-1865)
43 – Stetson, Priscilla W. (~1808-1871)
44 – Stetson, Jennie E. (1837-1859)
45 – Stetson, Martha S. (1848-1849)
46 – Ward Obelisk (no dates)
　　Macomber, Nathaniel (~1743-1814)
47 – Cushman, Anne L. (1825-1902)
48 – Cushman, Mary (1810-1882)
49 – Southworth, Job H. (~1826-1832)
50 – Leach, Isaac (1829-1891)
　　Leach, Celia (1829-1911)
51 – Leach, Harry (1865)
52 – Southworth, William (1778-1861)
53 – Southworth, Phebe (~1780-1855)
54 – Tinkham, Josiah F. (1835-1892)
55 – Tinkham, Susan J. (1839-1919)
56 – Peirce, Experience (~1773-1845)
57 – Macomber, Fidelia (~1824-1842)

58 – Macomber, Almira (~1805-1848)
59 – Shaw, Frank C. (1855-1856)
60 – Shaw, Infant Son (no dates)
61 – Shaw, Infant Daughter (no dates)
62 – Shaw, Horace E. (1851)
63 – Shaw, Herbert F. (1850-1851)
64 – Shaw, Mary A. (1859-1861)
65 – Mother (no dates)
66 – Staples, Nathaniel G. (1851-1930)
 Staples, Julia E (1861-1957)
67 – Staples, Nathaniel (1779-1862)
68 – Staples, Lydia (1781-1863)
69 – Staples, Job M. (1844-1922)
70 – Leonard, George, Dea. (~1724-1801)
71 – Leonard, Charity (~1730-1805)
72 – Tillson, Silvanus (~1759-1822)
73 – Tillson, Hannah (~1756-1821)
74 – Leach, Ephraim, Dea. (1782-1864)
75 – Leach, Susan (1786-1864)
76 – Southworth, Charles F. (~1821-1853)
77 – Southworth, Otis (1814-1905)
 Southworth, Lucy W (1818-1863)
 Southworth, Ellen A. (1842-1850)
 Southworth, George (1847-1848)
 Southworth, Albert A. (1847-1848)
78 – Southworth, Lewis H. (1855-1858)
79 – Southworth, Jerusha L. (1850-1851)
80 – Southworth, Emma L. (1852-1858)
81 – Bassett, Mary (1879-1952)
82 – Bassett, Nathaniel S. (1879-1946)
83 – Bassett, Marcus N. (1890-1937)
84 – Bassett, Charles H. (1842-1907)
85 – Bassett, Julia E. (1846-1930)
86 – Bassett, Helen P. (1883-1885)
87 – Bassett, Ralph Morton (1877-1956)
 Bassett, Mary Corbett (1883-____)
88 – Bassett, Margaret S. (1876-1951)
89 – Peirce, Benajah (~1771-1844)
90 – Peirce, Charity (~1768-1831)
91 – Pierce, Abiah (~1766-1800)
92 – Southworth, Gideon (~1751-1827)
93 – Southworth, Mary (~1755-1795)
94 – Southworth, Nathaniel (~1760-1819)
95 – Southworth, Hannah (~1761-1845)
96 – Leach, Abiel (1812-1813)
97 – Leach, Nathaniel S. (1810-1813)
98 – Leach, Nathaniel S. (1821-1824)
99 – Southworth, Albert A. (1847-1848)
 Southworth, George (1847-1848)
100 – Southworth, Ellen A. (1842-1850)
101 – Southworth, Thomas (~1776-1867)

102 – Southworth, Lucinda (~1781-1832)
103 – Dunham, Warren (~1803-1838)
104 – Dunham, Lucinda (~1806-1848)
105 – Southworth, Lois T. (~1806-1840)
106 – Southworth, Enoch (1804-1871)
107 – Clark, Martha (1786-1851)
108 – Sanford, William T. (1841-1912)
109 – Sanford, Betsey T. (1842-1897)
110 – Sanford, Charlotte A. (1862-1932)
111 – Holmes, Lucy (1844)
112 – Peirce, Job, Capt. (~1737-1819)
113 – Peirce, Elizabeth (~1744-1790)
 Peirce, William R. (1764-1794)
114 – Hoar, Mercy (1762-1847)
115 – Hoar, Peter, Esq. (~1755-1815)
116 – Peirce, Mary A. (1808-1809)
117 – Peirce, Louissa (1803-1807)
118 – Pierce, Mercy (~1824-1858)
119 – Southworth, Polly (1782-1798)
120 – Southworth, Hannah (1790-1808)
 Southworth, Betsey (1786-1794)
121 – Southworth, Nathaniel (~1791-1799)
122 – Smith, Elijah (~1760-1839)
123 – Smith, Mary (~1760-1846)
124 – Smith, Rebecca (~1785-1826)
125 – Richmond, Edward W. (1848-1850)
126 – Richmond, Edward K. (~1822-1854)
127 – Brown, Edward (1824-1899)
 Brown, Lucy S. (1830-1901)
128 – Fletcher, Ella B. (1862-1904)
129 – Porter, George (1849-1939)
130 – Porter, Kate (1839-1915)
131 – Anderson, Pontius (1885-1887)
132 – Caswell, Alanson L. (1842-1844)
 Peirce, Lusanna T. (1828-1836)
133 – Peirce, Elanthan (1781-1797)
134 – Peirce, Job, Jr., Capt. (~1768-1805)
135 – Peirce, Infant (1851)
136 – Hinds, John (~1785-1811)
 Samson, Thomas (1735-1792)
137 – Sampson, Thomas (~1764-1813)
138 – Smith, Janet (1809)
139 – Macomber, Nathaniel (~1743-1814)
140 – Macomber, Bathsheba (~1749-1818)
141 – Emery, Dexter E. (1854-1862)
142 – Emery, Susan H. (1826-1865)
143 – Macomber, Bathsheba (~1785-1820)
144 – Macomber, Sarah (1783-1808)
145 – Nason, Ida J. (1854-1859)
146 – Nason, Sarah W. (1827-1896)
147 – Ametuc (~1747-1817)

Ward Cemetery Map

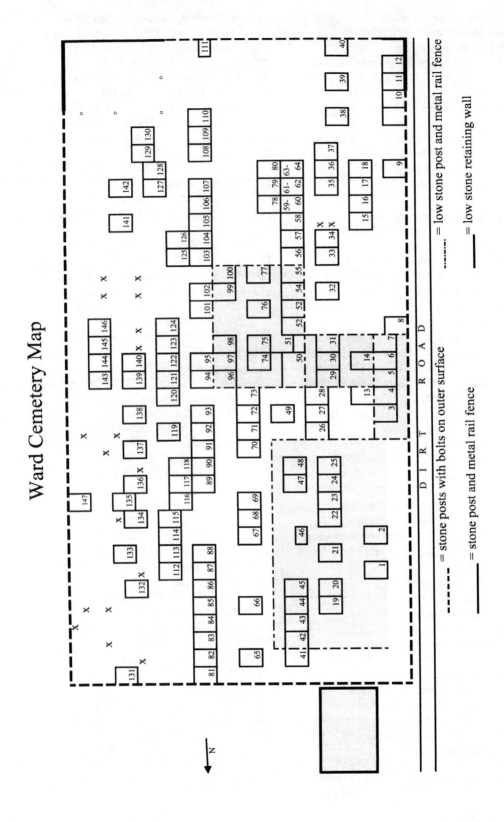

= low stone post and metal rail fence
.... = stone posts with bolts on outer surface
——— = stone post and metal rail fence
= low stone retaining wall

DIRT ROAD

N

Appendix A
Unconfirmed Cemeteries

Charles M. Thatcher documented the following additional cemeteries in the Town of Lakeville:

Cemetery behind Elisha Cudworth's house   "Cemetery on Hill back of Elisha Cudworths house: Indians & colored people, nothing but rough Markers." The Elisha Cudworth house is located at 416 Bedford Street. This was confirmed with the current property owner. Permission was not obtained to search for these graves.

Ichabod Leonard Grave   "Grave at edge of Cedar Swamp about ¼ mile back of Canedy school house by stone wall. Leonard: Ichabod, died of smallpox in 1840" The location of the school was found on an 1853 map to be on County Road, approximately opposite Mullein Hill Church, and its former presence was confirmed with the current property owner. Permission was not obtained to search for the grave.

Staples Cemetery   "Staples Cemetery Nearly a dozen graves way down in the field, nearly opposite Mr. James P. Peirce's house on Myricks road from Canedy's Corner Marked only with stub stones." The James P. Peirce house is located at 22 Pierce Avenue The current property owner confirmed this and stated that the stones were removed unknowingly decades ago when the field was cleared for planting by his father. Permission was not obtained to search the area.

Cranberry Pond Graves   "Graves on edge of Cranberry Pond Betty's Neck Felix: 2 women." Local residents were contacted and reported that they had not seen any graves around this area. No attempt was made to "walk the pond" as it is surrounded by swampland.

Massey Grave   "Grave on Island at Mouth of River: Massey: Colored woman, died 1828."

Gladys Vigers mentions in her book, *The History of Lakeville,* the following Indian burying grounds:

Bedford Street Indian Graves   "...Indian burying ground between Assawompsett Lake and Bedford Street, back of the old George Spooner place. It is located on a small hill or mound. The only markers are field stones. It is said that these Indian graves were opened over thirty years ago (1921)." The George Spooner house is believed to be located at 421 Bedford Street.

Lang Street Indian Graves   "... Indians were buried in the woods off Lang Street..." Five graves are rumored to be across the street from Lang Cemetery behind a stone wall. No markers were visualized from Lang Street at this location.

Taunton Street Indian Graves   Indians were buried "... off Taunton Street in

North Lakeville, but there is no proof of this." No further information was available for these graves.

Rhode Island Road Indian Graves   This ancient Indian burial site was behind the house at 194 Rhode Island Road. The current owner stated it was excavated in the 1950s.

Additional Notes:

Haskins #2 and Haskins #3   In the *1969 Lakeville Town Report,* p. 80-81, the Cemetery Commission lists two Haskins Cemeteries in the southwestern part of town. Haskins #2 is listed "off Mill Street on Old Howland Road," and Haskins #3 is listed "off Mill Street, ½ mile off road in back of Old Dan's house." According to Lois Atwood, former Cemetery Commissioner from 1964 to 1967, these two cemeteries are one and the same. In the *1973 Lakeville Town Report,* the Cemetery Commission reports that Haskins #2 Cemetery (no mention of a Haskins #3 in this report) was found to be in Freetown. In December of 2004 all that remains of this cemetery are two empty bases and half of the stone post and metal rails. It is located just over the town line in the backyard of 14 Joaquin Avenue, Freetown.

Tack Factory Cemetery   This cemetery is mentioned in notes contained in the Cemetery Commission's files in the Lakeville Town Hall. The cemetery is actually located on Taunton Street in Middleborough, just over the town line.

Appendix B
Other Memorials
Various Locations

Only memorials constructed of gravestone like materials (metal plaques on boulders or inscribed stones) are included in this section.

Alvilhiera, Frank B., Sr.   *"ALVILHIERA ISLAND / IN MEMORY OF / FRANK B. ALVILHIERA, SR. / DEDICATED / MAY 24 1992"* is inscribed on this stone, which is located on the traffic island at the corner of Highland Road and Bedford Street.

DesRoche, William J.   *"This Scoreboard Is Dedicated To / The Memory Of / William J. DesRoche / 1953 – 1998 / A Dedicated Husband, Father, Coach / and Friend. / April 26, 1998"* is embossed on a plaque which is attached to a boulder. It is located near the scoreboard at John Paun Park on Vaughan Street.

Gamache, Alexander R.   *"ALEXANDER R. GAMACHE / MEMORIAL PLAYGROUND / MAY 1993 / TO / NOV 1994"* is embossed on this metal plaque which is attached to a boulder near the entrance to the playground at The Former Ted Williams Camp, 28 Precinct Street. A profile of a child's head is embossed to the right of the last three lines.

Hitchcock, William F.   *"✝ IN MEMORY OF / WILLIAM F. HITCHCOCK / 1945 – 1969 / JESUS SAID: / "MY SHEEP HEAR MY VOICE, AND I KNOW THEM, / AND THEY FOLLOW ME, AND I GIVE THEM ETERNAL / LIFE, AND THEY SHALL NEVER PERISH, AND NO ONE / SHALL SNATCH THEM OUT OF MY HAND." / JOHN 10: 27-28 / MR. HITCHCOCK BELIEVED IN THE POWER OF PRAYER / TO ALMIGHTY GOD THROUGH JESUS CHRIST AND / DESIRED TO HAVE OTHERS TURN IN THIS DIRECTION."* is embossed on this metal plaque which is attached to a boulder. It is located on the left side of the entrance to Assawompset Elementary School, 232 Main Street.
"IN MEMORY OF WILLIAM F. HITCHCOCK, TEACHER / AND FRIEND AT ASSAWOMPSET SCHOOL, / 1967 – 1968, WHO WAS KILLED IN VIETNAM, / APRIL 1969, WHILE SERVING HIS COUNTRY. / HIS FRIENDSHIP, COURAGE,

LOVE AND / UNDERSTANDING OF MANKIND WILL HOLD / A SPECIAL PLACE IN OUR MEMORY. / HIS INSPIRATION TO THE CHILDREN OF LAKEVILLE / AND THE REFLECTION OF HIS SPIRIT WILL LIGHT OUR LIVES." This second plaque was attached to a square stone, located on the ground in front of the above boulder.

Johnson, Robert F.   *"In Memory of Chief Fire Engineer / Robert F. Johnson / In Recognition / Of His Service to the Town / Lakeville Fire Assoc."* is embossed on a metal plaque which is attached to a white boulder. It is located at the northeast corner of Route 79 and Johnson Road. In 2006, the landscaping at this location was in the process of being redone. The plaque will be replaced when the landscaping is completed.

The Unborn

"LIFE
GOD'S GREATEST GIFT
IN MEMORY OF THE
INNOCENT VICTIMS OF
ABORTION
MIDDLEBORO LAKEVILLE
KNIGHTS OF COLUMBUS 223
JUNE 1999"

is inscribed on this black monument. At the top of this stone there is carved a sleeping infant in the palm of a hand. A Knights of Columbus emblem is inscribed between the fifth and sixth lines. A Knights of Columbus marker and a flag are present. This monument is located on the front lawn of Sts. Martha and Mary Church, 354 Bedford Street.

Veteran's Memorial   *"DEDICATED TO THE HEROIC / VALOR AND PATRIOTIC SPIRIT / OF THE   MEN AND WOMEN OF / THE TOWN OF LAKEVILLE WHO / SERVED IN THE ARMED FORCES / OF THE UNITED STATES OF / AMERICA IN ALL OF ITS WARS. / MAY THE GOOD LORD / KEEP HIS HAND IN YOURS."* is inscribed on this metal plaque which is attached to a white boulder. The Lakeville Town Seal is embossed at the top. It is located under the flagpole in front of the Lakeville Town Hall and Fire Station at 346 Bedford Street. Two veteran's markers and flags are present.

World War I Memorial   *"ERECTED BY / THE RED WHITE AND BLUE CLUB / IN COMMEMORATION OF THE / LAKEVILLE BOYS WHO SERVED / IN THE WORLD WAR"* is embossed on a metal plaque which is attached to a boulder. This boulder is located at the intersection of Routes 18 and 105, on the east side of the front lawn of the old Lakeville Library.

World War I Memorial   *"LAKEVILLE HONOR ROLL / IN HONOR OF THE MEN WHO RESPONDED TO / THEIR COUNTRY'S CALL IN THE GREAT WORLD WAR / 1917-1919 /*

ARMY	ARMY
DAVID P. ASHLEY	ARTHUR C. METCALF
RALPH W. BAKER CANADIAN	WILLIAM H. MILLER
FREDERICK A. BARTON	FRANK E. MINOTT
ISAAC S. BARTON	JOSEPH A. MOQUIN
COMMI BEECH	RICHARD H. MORANVILLE
CLIFFORD C. BERNIER	+ JOHN MURDOCK
WILLIAM L. BERNIER	⊹ WILLIAM MURDOCK JR.
RICHARD C. BOWEN	GEORGE R. PERKINS
NATHAN D. BROWN	JESSE C. PERKINS
GEORGE E. BURNHAM	HAROLD P. REED
WILLIAM H. CAMPBELL	WILSON D. SPOONER
+ GEORGE D. CARR	CHARLES I. WAMBOLT
JUSTIN H. CASWELL	WILLIAM J. WAMBOLT
EVERETT E. CHARRON	CLARENCE C. WHITE
ROY S. CHASE	GEORGE M. WHITNEY
FRED F. CLAFLIN JR.	ARCHIE I WILBUR
MAX A COHEN	NAVY
JOHN COOLRIDGE	LUCIUS J. N. ALLEY
AUGUSTUS S. DEMORANVILLE	OTIS E. ALLEY
GORDON E. DEMORANVILLE	PATRICK ARMSTRONG
LEON R. DEMORANVILLE	EVERETT L. CASWELL
* DICKRAN DIRAN	J. MYRON DEMARANVILLE
CLARENCE M. GURNEY	GEORGE F. FROST
FRANK P. HAMEL	J. WILLIAM GRANTHAM
MICHAEL P. HARRINGTON	ARTHUR S. HALL
LESTER W. HASKINS	CLARENCE A. HOLMES
JOSEPH F. LAVALLEY	WALTER W. METCALF
CHARLES MACLELLAN	BLAKE S. NORRIS
KENNETH MAKER	ELWIN H. NORRIS
BERTRAM A. MANTON	LESTER PFISTER
LESLIE C. MARANVILLE	CARL F. PILLSBURY
FREDERICK L. MATTHEWS	

* KILLED IN ACTION   *+ WOUNDED IN SERVICE"*

This large metal plaque is attached to a large boulder which is in front of the United Church of Christ at the southwest corner of Bedford and Precinct Streets in Dickran Diran Square. There are two veteran's markers and flags here.

Appendix C
Location of Cemeteries
by Assessor's Plot Number and GPS Coordinates
GPS readings were taken from the center of the cemetery

Cemetery	Plot Number	Latitude	Longitude
Booth #1	033-004-018	N 41 48 457	W 070 57.999
Booth #2	034-002-016A	N 41 48.334	W 070 57.895
Canedy	014-006-007	N 41 48.881	W 070 58.466
Clark	066-003-007	N 41 48.608	W 070 55.157
Douglas	032-005-001A	N 41 49.412	W 070 57.602
Hafford	033-004-025	N 41 48.359	W 070 57.848
Haskell	067-002-001	N 41 47.978	W 070 54.877
Haskins	025-001-002	N 41 52.286	W 070 57.562
Horr	066-003-007	N 41 48.624	W 070 55.167
Howland	012-002-028	N 41 47.699	W 070 59.566
Indian Shore	065-004-032	N 41 49.395	W 070 54.913
Keith	014-004-011	N 41 48.788	W 070 59.030
Lang	006-003-012	N 41 49.799	W 071 00.267
Malbone	003-002-001	N 41 48.976	W 071 01.723
McCully	032-002-005	N 41 49.080	W 070 58.138
Mullein Hill	015-005-008	N 41 49.031	W 070 58.339
Pickens #1	030-001-004	N 41 50.454	W 070 57.486
Pickens #2	016-004-004	N 41 49.904	W 070 58.220
Pierce	004-002-002	N 41 49.190	W 071 01.850
Pond	056-006-003A	N 41 50.004	W 070 56.249
Precinct	026-001-003	N 41 51.791	W 070 58.135
Race Course	015-005-003A	N 41 49.069	W 070 58.705
Reynolds	034-003-006	N 41 47.935	W 070 57.516
Richmond	021-003-011	N 41 53.260	W 070 58.467
Robbins	015-004-003	N 41 49.040	W 070 58.801
Royal Wampanoag	067-001-001	N 41 47.726	W 070 54.762
Sampson	030-005-002	N 41 50.842	W 070 56.984
Smallpox	015-003-020	N 41 49.043	W 070 59.213
Strobridge	016-005-006	N 41 49.946	W 070 59.075
Thompson Hill	026-001-004	N 41 51.824	W 070 58.085
Ward	058-003-038	N 41 51.569	W 070 56.476

Unconfirmed Cemeteries
GPS readings were taken from the street in front of the property

Graves	Plot Number	Latitude	Longitude
Ichabod Leonard Grave	014-004-001-03	N 41 48.543	W 070 58.522
Graves behind E. Cudworth's	055-005-006	N 41 49.341	W 070 55.621
Staples Cemetery	014-004-016	N 41 48.795	W 070 59.543
Lang Street Indian Graves	006-002-005	N 41 49.774	W 070 00.267
Rhode Island Indian Graves	018-003-002	N 41 51.665	W 070 58.284
Bedford Street Indian Graves	065-004-020	N 41 49.279	W 070 55.583

Appendix D
Monument Company Addresses
Taken from the metal tags present on the base of monuments

S. Barnicoat or
Barnicoat Monuments
Route 28
Middleboro, MA

Central Monument Co.
938 Center St.
Middleboro, Mass.

Flint Monument Works
Algerine St.
Berkley, Mass.
Telephone VAndyke 2-3991

Hancock Monument Co.
970 Ashley Blvd.
New Bedford

R. L. Linton
110 Carver
No. Carver, Mass

Maver Memorials
79 North Pearl St.
Brockton, Massachusetts

Memorial Granite Co. Inc.
159 Hancock St
Quincy, Mass.

Charles G. Morse Granite Co.
218 Willard St.
Quincy, Mass.

Quincy Memorial Co.
218 Willard St.
Quincy, Mass.

REX Memorials
(no address listed on tag)

Albert F. Richmond, or
A. F. Richmond Memorials
Taunton, MA
Tel. 824-8951

A. Souza & Sons
Taunton, MA
822-9167

Taunton Monument Co.
George A Saxon, Jr.
123 Broadway, Taunton, Mass. or
Taunton Monuments Co.
Taunton, MA 02780
823-8256 or
Taunton Monument Co.
440 East Britannia St.
Taunton, MA

James E. Tootell Monument Co.
196 Robeson St.
New Bedford, Mass. or
Tootell Monument Works
1007 Rockdale Ave.
New Bedford, Mass.

Albert F. Richmond Memorials metal tag

Appendix E
Signed Gravestones

Sculptor	Name	Died	Cemetery	Page
B. Adams	Haskel, Thomas	1795	Haskell	27
Bryant & Co.	McCully, Ezra	1870	McCully	94
Burt	Southworth, Lewis	1859	Ward	430
Burt, Taunton	Haskins, Hannah	1874	Haskins	32
	Hinds, John C.	1877	Mullein Hill	112
	Winslow, Lydia	1838	Pierce	138
	Dunham, William	1863	Richmond	242
	Richmond, Deborah	1857	Richmond	247
	Haskins, Apollos	1865	Thompson Hill	348
Burt & Co.	Nickerson, Frances	1878	Strobridge	318
	Nickerson, Joanna	1885	Strobridge	318
Burt & King, Taunton	Coombs, Simeon	1871	Haskins	31
	Leach, Edwin J.	1872	Ward	420
D. A. Burt	Peirce, Infant	1851	Ward	424
	Southworth, Emma	1858	Ward	429
	Reed, Isaac	1859	Thompson Hill	366
D. A. Burt, Taunton	Pierce, Hope	1857	Pierce	135
	Peirce, Simeon	1859	Pierce	138
	Caswell, Eliza	1860	Thompson Hill	338
	Caswell, Mary E.	1855	Thompson Hill	339
	Pierce, Eben S.	1857	Thompson Hill	364
	Clark, Martha	1851	Ward	416
H. Cobb, F. R.	Clark, Samuel	1850	Keith	62
F. Cooley	Sherman, Sarah	1822	Lang	77
M. Gallagher	Townsend, Daniel	1835	Pond	184
J. H.	Haskell, Thomas A.	1816	Pond	157
F. Hanson	Dean, Henry	1898	Thompson Hill	342
Harrington	Howland, Seth	1872	Howland	53
	Sampson, Betsey	1886	Mullein Hill	115
	Sampson, Uriah	1880	Mullein Hill	115
	Barker, Emma	1896	Strobridge	315
C. Harrington	Crane, Gershom	1848	Thompson Hill	341

Sculptor	Name	Died	Cemetery	Page
C. Harrington, Warren	McGee, Ann	1879	Strobridge	318
C. Harrington, Warren, R. I.	McCully, Stephen	1898	McCully	96
	Carver, James	1890	Strobridge	316
O. Harrington	Bishop, Dexter, Jr.	1873	Mullein Hill	107
Hathaway	Reed, Levi	1877	Haskins	35
	Tinkham, Caleb, Jr.	1840	Strobridge	322
Hathaway, Taunton	Pierce, Luther	1822	Pierce	136
	Richmond, William	1849	Richmond	248
	Stevens, Olive	1854	Strobridge	320
	Tinkham, Rhoda	1848	Thompson Hill	382
	Southworth, Lois	1840	Ward	431
W. H. Jackson & Co., Taunton	McGee, Andrew	1871	Strobridge	317
	Montgomery, Fannie	1891	Thompson Hill	357
	Tinkham, Elisha H.	1893	Thompson Hill	382
Kavanagh Bros Boston	Shaw, John	1919	McCully	98
B. Leonard, Bridger.	Bassett, Sarah	1830	Thompson Hill	332
B. Leonard, Sc. Bridger.	Crafts, Thomas	1819	Thompson Hill	340
C. T. S.	Peirce, Elisabeth	1790	Ward	423
J. B. Sullivan, Taunton	Pierce, Apollos	1865	Pierce	134
	Tinkham, Mary	1896	Strobridge	322
J. B. Sullivan Son	Montgomery, John	1918	Thompson Hill	358
G. Thompson	Haskins, Joshua	1849	Thompson Hill	349
	Sampson, Deliverance	1821	Thompson Hill	369
	Sampson, Isaac	1846	Thompson Hill	370
Geo. Thompson	Shepard, Priscilla	1831	McCully	99
	Pickens, Louisa	1830	Pickens #1	126
	Pickens, Silas	1847	Pickens #1	127
	Cole, Abigail	1830	Pond	150
	Canedy, Hope	1829	Thompson Hill	336
	Townsend, John	1835	Thompson Hill	383
George Thompson, Middleborough	Nelson, Hannah	1822	Pond	167
George Thompson (no signature, swirl only)	Winslow, Tisdale	1827	Lang	78
	Clark, Xenophon	1829	Pond	149
	Cole, Nancy	1828	Pond	151

Sculptor	Name	Died	Cemetery	Page
George Thompson	Haskell, Thomas A.	1816	Pond	157
(no signature,	Nelson, Anna	1828	Pond	165
swirl only, con't.)	Williams, Elijah	1818	Pond	187
	Caswell, Abiah	1817	Thompson Hill	337
	Caswell, Lucy	1808	Thompson Hill	339
	Turner, Philip	1818	Thompson Hill	384
	Washburn, James	1815	Thompson Hill	385
	Washburn, Joshua	1818	Thompson Hill	385
(Ce)phas Tomson, (S)cu.	Strobredg, Robert	1790	Thompson Hill	378
J. Tribell	Ward, Priscilla	1826	Ward	434
Warren	Bassett, Mary	1841	Strobridge	316
Warren, Taunton	Clark, Noah	1841	Clark	11
Warren, Fall River	Dunham, Erastus	1840	Richmond	242
Warren, F. R.	Peirce, Charity	1831	Ward	423
E. Warren, F. R.	Baker, Simeon D.	1846	Howland	45
	Pierce, Edmund	1845	Lang	70

George Thompson swirl and signature on
Louisa Picken's gravestone

Bibliography

Amon, William. Personal Interview. 9/14/06 and 9/21/2006.

Atwood, Lois. Telephone Interview. 12/13/2004.

Avila, Stephen. Personal Interview. 4/14/2000.

Barber, Roan. Telephone Interview. 10/12/2006.

Barnicoat, Jackie. Telephone Interview. 8/28/2006, 10/19/2006.

Thompson, Dick "The Baseball Biography Project: Jim Cudworth." 2002-2003. The Society for American Baseball Research. <http://bioproj.sabr.org>.

Benes, Peter. *The Masks of Orthodoxy: Folk Gravestone Carving in Plymouth County, Massachusetts, 1689-1805.* Amherst: University of Massachusetts Press, 1977.

_____. Ed. *Puritan Gravestone Art II.* Boston MA: Boston University, 1978.

Carmack, Sharon D. *Your Guide to Cemetery Research.* Cincinnati, Ohio: Betterway Books, 2002.

Crosby, Gerel. Telephone Interview. 9/26/2005.

Darling, Robert. Telephone Interview. 10/23/2005.

Decas, George C. *Col. Peter H. Peirce (1788-1861): A Plymouth County Life.* 1st ed. Middleborough, MA: Middleborough Historical Association, Inc., 2001.

Dickenson, Lawrence. Personal Interview. 12/11/2004.

Early Vital Records of Bristol County, Massachusetts to about 1850. CD-ROM, 2nd ed. Wheat Ridge, CO: Search & Research Publishing Corporation, 2002.

Forbes, Harriette Merrifield. *Gravestones of Early New England, and the Men Who Made Them. 1653-1800.* [1927]. Reprint. Princeton: Pyne Press, 1973.

Gabel, Laurel K. Association for Gravestone Studies. "Gravestones." E-mail to the author. 1/25/2007.

Genealogical Records: Massachusetts Town, Probate, and Vital Records, 1600s-1900s. Family Archives CD #502. Broderbund, 1999.

Gillon, Edmund Vincent. *Early New England Gravestone Rubbings.* New York: Dover Publications, 1966.

Gravestone Symbols. Calloway Co. Cemeteries. 2001. Calloway County, Missouri Journal. <http://www.rootsweb.com/~mocallaw/Cemetery/StoneSymbols.html>.

Guild, Mary S. *Strobridge, Morrison or Morison, Strawbridge.* Lowell, MA, 1891.

Haggar, Reginald G. *A Dictionary of Art Terms.* New York: Hawthorn Books, 1962.

Haskins, Denise. Personal Interview. 12/11/2004.

Hawes, Benjamin. Personal Interview. 9/26/2006.

Headstones and Markers. US Department of Veteran's Affairs, <http://www.cem.va.gov/cem/hm_hm.asp>.

Heritage Books archives. Massachusetts cemetery records. Vol. 1, CD-ROM, Bowie, MD: Heritage Books, 2000.

Heritage Quest Online. ProQuest Information and Learning Co. 1999-2006. accessed through New England Historical and Genealogical Society <http://www.newenglandancestors.org/>.

Hoard, David. Telephone Interview. 10/12/2006.

Horne, Ron. Association for Gravestone Studies. "Recent gravestones, photographs." E-mail to the author. 11/4/2005.

Hurney, Beverly E. *St. Mary's Cemetery, Newton, Massachusetts: Epitaphs.* Boston, MA: New England Historic Genealogical Society, 2000.

Jacobs, G. Walker. *Stranger Stop and Cast an Eye; A Guide to Gravestones and Gravestone Rubbing.* 3rd ed. Brattleboro, VT: S. Greene Press, 1973.

Lakeville Assessor's Office. 239 Main Street. Lakeville, MA 02347.

Lakeville Town Reports. 1934-2005. Lakeville Town Hall. 346 Bedford Street. Lakeville, MA 02347.

Lakeville Vital Records. Lakeville Town Hall. 346 Bedford Street. Lakeville, MA 02347.

Latham, Williams. *Epitaphs in old Bridgewater, Massachusetts.* Bowie, MD: Heritage Books, 1986.

Leonard, Ken. Telephone Interview. 4/27/2003.

List of Names in the Town of Middleborough of Persons Assessed a pole Tax in 1935. Middleborough, Massachusetts. 1935.

Ludwig, Allan I. *Graven Images: New England Stonecarving and its Symbols, 1650-1815.* 3rd ed. Hanover, NH: Published by University Press of New England for Wesleyan University Press, 1999.

Mansfield, Chris. "Veteran's in Lakeville Cemeteries." Lakeville, MA. Eagle Scout Project. 1985.

Markson, William. Telephone Interview. 4/27/2003.

Massachusetts Vital Records to 1850. 2004. Online database: *NewEnglandAncestors.org*, New England Historical and Genealogical Society, Boston, MA. <http://www.newenglandancestors.org/>.

Massachusetts Vital Records, 1841–1910. From original records held by the Massachusetts Archives. 2004. Online database: *NewEnglandAncestors.org*, New England Historical and Genealogical Society, Boston, MA. <http://www.newenglandancestors.org/>.

Merrick, Barbara L. and Alicia C. Williams. *Middleborough, Massachusetts Vital Records*. 2 vols. Boston, MA: Massachusetts Society of Mayflower Descendants, 1986.

Middleborough Gazette Index, The. Online database. "The Digital Library." through the Middleborough Public Library. <http://www.midlib.org/dlib/main.htm>.

Middleborough Vital Records. Middleborough Town Clerk's Office. 20 Centre Street. Middleborough, MA 02346.

Military Records: Massachusetts Civil War Soldiers & Sailors, 1861-1865. Family Tree Maker's Family Archives CD# 134. Novato, CA: Broderbund, 2000.

Military Records: Revolutionary War Soldiers and Sailors, 1775-1782. CD #147 Family Tree Maker. Novato, CA: Broderbund, 1997.

Nelson, W. Ripley. *The Nelson family of Plymouth, Middleboro, and Lakeville, Massachusetts; a genealogical and biographical record and family history story*. Nantucket, MA: self published, 1963.

Obituaries. *The Middleborough Gazette*. Middleborough, Massachusetts. 1852-2003. Various issues.

Ranahan, Robert. Personal Interview. 1/4/2000.

Reynolds, Barbara. Telephone Interview. 8/21/2006.

Reynolds, Brian. Personal Interview. 7/31/2006. Telephone Interview. 9/22/2006.

Reynolds, Sheldon. Telephone Interview. 8/21/2006.

Rochester Vital Records. Rochester Town Clerk's Office. 1 Constitution Way. Rochester, MA 02770.

Social Security Death Index, MyFamily.com, Inc. 1998-2006. RootsWeb.com. <http://ssdi.genealogy.rootsweb.com/>.

Spaulding, John. Association for Gravestone Studies. "Gravestone carvings." E-mail to the author. 11/2/2006 and 11/11/2006.

St. George, Kevin. Personal Interview. 7/28/2000.

Tashjian, Dickran, Ann Tashjian. *Memorials for Children of Change; the Art of Early New England Stonecarving*. Middletown, CT: Wesleyan University Press, 1974.

Taunton Vital Records. Taunton City Clerk's Office. 15 Summer Street. Taunton, MA 02780.

Terry, Gail E. *Berkley, Massachusetts Cemetery Inscriptions*. Bowie, MD: Heritage Books, 1997.

Thatcher, Charles M. "Thatcher papers." Original handwritten transcriptions of gravestone through 1850. Available in the Genealogy Room at the Middleborough Public Library, 102 North Main Street, Middleborough, MA 02346.

Thomas, Helen Gurney. comp. *Vital Records of the Town of Freetown, Massachusetts, 1686 Through 1890.* Bowie, MD: Heritage Books, 1988.

Town of Middleboro Vital Records Index: 1649 – 1945. 3/16/05. Online database. "The Digital Library." through the Middleborough Public Library. <http://www.midlib.org/dlib/main.htm>.

Vigers, Gladys. *History of the Town of Lakeville Massachusetts.* Lakeville, MA. self published, 1952.

Vital records of Taunton, Massachusetts, to the year 1850. 3 vols. Boston, MA: The New England historic genealogical society at the charge of the Eddy town-record fund. 1928-29.

Weston, Thomas. *History of the Town of Middleboro, Massachusetts.* Boston: Houghton, Mifflin, 1906.

Index

When the surname is used only as a first or middle name, the page number is in italics.